CCH® Study MATE™

Your Personal Online Ta...7!

MW00967002

If you find taxes difficult, you're not alone! Now you have CCH® Study MATE™, a personal online "tutor." With Study MATE you can plug into online learning any time of day or night. Study MATE walks you through the most important concepts covered in your textbook using individual learning sessions designed to make learning as easy as possible.

Study MATE is easy to use, and since you've bought our book, you have free access to our Fundamental Tax Topics Library for a full year! Study MATE courses are designed with web learning in mind, so you can navigate your way through them independently. They are relatively short, but each course covers a substantial amount of material—including the top concepts covered in your textbook. These are student-centered courses with presentations that are different than those found in the text, so they give you another voice—another opportunity for concepts to sink in.

CCH® Study MATE™
Mentor for Accounting and Tax Education

Home | Log In | Register

HOME >

Technical Support
866 798-5897 • support@learning.net

Welcome to Study MATE.

Study MATE provides a new and exciting way to expand your knowledge of taxes, auditing, and accounting. The courses provide examples, observations, and study questions to help you further develop your knowledge in these areas. Think of Study MATE as your own personal study partner.

Already enrolled?
Member Login

User Name:
Password:

Forget Password? | Login

New Users:

If you have an *access code* (provided with your CCH textbook)...
1. Whether you are a professor or student, register for an account by clicking on the appropriate sign up box.
2. Click on a library title or course name to enroll in a library and use your access code as payment.
3. Complete the courses in the library.

If you want to *purchase* a topic or entire library...
1. Whether you are a professor, student, or practitioner, register for an account by clicking on the appropriate sign up box.
2. Click on a library title to view the courses available, and then click on a library title or course name to enroll and pay by credit card.
3. Complete the courses you purchased.

» **Students** Sign up here if you are a student
» **Professors** Sign up here if you are a professor

» **Students** Sign up here if you are a student
» **Professors** Sign up here if you are a professor
» **Practitioners** Other members may sign up here.

How Many Courses Do I Take?

Your instructor may want you to access all the courses in the fundamental series, you may be asked to take selective courses on certain topics, or your instructor may leave it up to you to use Study MATE as you choose.

So, How Do I Get In?

Getting started is easy.

1 Go to www.cchstudymate.com and follow the instructions for new users with an access code to sign up for a free account. Fill in the information on the registration page including a user ID and password of your choice.

2 Once you have registered, click on the Fundamental Tax Topics library title to view the list of courses. Click to enroll in the entire Fundamental Tax Topics library. At the payment screen, use your access code as payment. Now you are ready to start your first course.

3 Click on the course title to begin. Use your access code now and begin using Study MATE today!

ACCESS CODE:

CCH:001_1U3KT

Technical Support: 866-798-5897 • support@learning.net

Over for course features ▶ ▶ ▶

Access CCH Study MATE at www.cchstudymate.com

For your records, print your User ID and Password below:

User ID: _____

Password: _____

CCH INCORPORATED • 4025 West Peterson Ave. • Chicago, IL 60646-6085

Features of each course:

CCH® StudyMATE™

Learning Objectives

This course has been designed to explain what the federal income tax is and how it is computed. After completing this course, you should be able to:

- Understand what the federal income tax is and distinguish it from other types of federal taxes.
- Distinguish between the regular income tax and the alternative minimum tax.
- Understand how Congress derived its authority to impose the federal income tax.
- Understand the objectives of the federal income tax.
- Understand what steps have to be taken to compute a taxpayer's federal income tax liability.
- Understand what "adjusted gross income" is and to which taxpayers it applies.
- Distinguish between deductions that can be subtracted from gross income and deductions that can be subtracted from adjusted gross income.

Print This Page

Notebook

Ask an Expert

Course PDF

Learning Objectives
A list of what you will learn in the course.

Introduction
A brief introduction to the course.

Discussions and Illustrations of the Concepts
Each course is designed to cover only the most important concepts. Your teacher may expect you to understand more than the concepts covered in Study MATE, but here you will see the core concepts.

Paced Learning
After some concepts are presented, the "Test Your Knowledge" feature helps you think back on what you've just read so you retain it.

Introduction

This course is one of a series of courses to federal taxation. Each course takes one divides it into key concepts, and concisely

To help you understand a particular aspect course includes special learning aids:

- Examples—clarify what you have
- Observations—give you greater i discussed.
- Tests of Knowledge—help you r learned.

At the end of each course, there are quest completing this quiz, you can demonstrate

Objectives of the Federal Income Tax

Although the primary purpose of the federal income tax is to raise revenue, it also serves economic, social, and political objectives. Much of its complexity is due to its multiple objectives, which often are competing.

Economic Objectives

The federal income tax has been used to stimulate the economy in general, aid particular industries, and encourage certain types of investments. For example:

- Tax rates ha
- Tax rates on investment i
- Interest on s investment i
- Depreciatio property.
- Percentage

Example
Nonrefundable credits: The credit for child care and dependent care expenses, the credit for the elderly and those with a disability, the credit for adoption expenses, the Hope Scholarship and Lifetime Learning credits, and the general business credit.

Observation: Nonrefundable credits are allowed before refundable credits.

Helpful Tools
On the right side of your screen, you will see clickable features such as additional reading materials, a tax term glossary, a special PDF print feature that allows you to print the entire course for offline reading and more.

CCH® StudyMATE™

Gross Income

Adjusted Gross Income

Deductions from Gross Income

Deductions from Adjusted Gross Income

Test Your Knowledge

Tax Credits

Test Your Knowledge

1. In 2004, Lea Tenenbaum and her husband, Jay, have an adjusted gross income of $188,700 and the following itemized deductions: $8,500 for medical expenses (after applying the 7.5% limitation), $6,000 for real property taxes, and $4,000 for charitable contributions. What amount of those itemized deductions may Lea and Jay deduct?

- a. $18,500
- b. $17,120
- c. $8,620

Check Answers

Examples and Observations
Presented to illustrate ideas and principles using colors and graphics to make your experience more memorable.

Testing—One, Two, Three

At the end of each course, a 15-question quiz is presented. The quiz questions are not easily answered—they really test whether you understand the concepts! You can take the quiz up to three times if you like and after successfully completing the quiz, you can print a certificate for your records and e-mail the certificate to your instructor to show you've successfully completed the course.

Get started! ▶ ▶ ▶

A WoltersKluwer Company

Essentials of
FEDERAL
Income Taxation
For Individuals and Business

2006 EDITION

Herbert C. Sieg, MAS, CPA
Emeritus, Illinois State University

Linda M. Johnson, Ph.D., CPA
Georgia State University

.CCH
a Wolters Kluwer business

Editorial Staff

Editor: Lawrence M. Norris, M. S.

ISBN 0-8080-1382-3

©2005, **CCH** INCORPORATED
4025 W. Peterson Ave.
Chicago, IL 60646-6085
1 800 248 3248
http://tax.cchgroup.com

This book was previously published by Prentice-Hall, Inc.

List of acronyms used:

AAA—Accumulated Adjustments Account
ACRS—Accelerated Cost Recovery System
ACV—Amortized Carrying Value
ADS—Alternate Depreciation System
AEP—Accumulated Earnings and Profits
AET—Accumulated Earnings Tax
AFR—Applicable Federal Rate
AGI—Adjusted Gross Income
AMT—Alternative Minimum Tax
AMTI—Alternative Minimum Tax Income
APR—Annual Percentage Rate
CD—Certificate of Deposit
CEP—Current Earnings and Profits
CPA— Certified Public Accountant
CPI—Consumer Price Index
CTC—Child Tax Credit
DB—Declining Balance
DISC—Domestic International Sales Corporation
DRD—Dividend Received Deduction
DRIP—Dividend Reinvestment Plan
E&P—Earnings and Profits
EIC—Earned Income Credit
EFT—Electronic Funds Transfer
EIN—Employer Identification Number
FEMA—Federal Emergency Management
  Agency
FICA—Federal Insurance Contributions Act
FMV—Fair Market Value
FUTA—Federal Unemployment Tax Act
HDHP—High-Deductible Health Plan
HI—Health Insurance
HMO—Health Maintenance Organization
HOH—Head of Household
HSA—Health Savings Account
IRA—Individual Retirement Arrangement
IRS—Internal Revenue Service
LLC—Limited Liability Company
LLP—Limited Liability Partnership
MACRS—Modified Accelerated Cost Recovery
  System
MD—Market Discount
MFJ—Married Filing Jointly
MFS—Married Filing Separately
NOL—Net Operating Loss
OASDI—Old Age, Survivors, and Disability
  Insurance
OID—Original Issue Discount
PHC—Personal Holding Company
PSC—Personal Service Corporation
SBA—Small Business Administration
SEP—Simplified Employee Pension
SIMPLE—Savings Incentive Match Plan for
  Employees
SSN—Social Security Number
TI—Taxable Income
TIN—Taxpayer Identification Number

Contents

Tax Forms

Preface

WHY STUDY FEDERAL INCOME TAXATION?

Essentials of Federal Income Taxation for Individuals and Business, 2006 Edition, covers the taxation of individuals for the 2005 tax year. It provides complete coverage in an easy-to-read and easy-to-understand form for your first course in taxation. This practical text helps you understand tax laws and improve the reporting quality of your tax returns. The coverage does not assume that you have had an introductory accounting course. If you are interested in learning how to prepare tax returns, including your own, studying this text and mastering its content will help you solve actual tax problems and succeed in business. At press time, the 2006 Edition contains the latest information and tax forms available for the 2005 tax year. It also contains the latest information for the 2006 tax planning process.

FULL OF OUTSTANDING FEATURES

Many outstanding features make the new 2006 Edition the main reference for completing 2005 federal income tax returns. Before you start reading *Essentials of Federal Income Taxation for Individuals and Business, 2006 Edition,* you are encouraged to spend a little time looking over the next few pages. The 2006 Edition benefits from the helpful comments and suggestions contributed by instructors and students who have taught and learned federal income taxation from previous editions.

BUSINESS ENTITY OPTION

While this text focuses on the income taxation of individuals, it is also makes available an optional course of study that examines the taxation of income earned by corporations and partnerships, as well as sole proprietorships. This option is included in response to the growing number of instructors who believe that an introductory tax course should compare and contrast the tax challenges facing the different forms of business organizations.

Those who choose to place more attention on the taxation of business entities are encouraged to study the chapters in the following sequence: 1, 2, 14, 3, 4, 5, 6, 7, 8, 9, 10, 11, 12, and 13. Chapters 1 and 2 cover the basic tax structure for individuals. Chapter 14 introduces the students to the taxation of income earned by corporations and partnerships. All subsequent chapters (3–13) include at least one special business entity problem. These problems require students to relate material covered in the chapter to the different forms of business.

The business entity problems are located near the end of each chapter's "Questions and Problems." Their solutions generally require information from Chapter 14. Consequently, students will be reviewing Chapter 14 on a regular basis throughout the course. The business entity problems are indicated by the icon.

OTHER SPECIAL FEATURES

- Highlighted tax tips, observations, and facts designed to enrich the learning experience are included in every chapter. These highlights are indicated by the icon.

- Homework problems suitable for completion using 1040 software are indicated by the icon.

- The new tax rules from the Katrina Emergency Tax Relief Act of 2005 (signed into law by the President on September 23, 2005) have been incorporated into the chapters and are indicated by the icon.

- Information for filled-in tax forms is included.

Feature: Each filled-in tax form is supported by information given by the taxpayer.

Benefit: This concise presentation makes it easier for you to relate tax data to the form. The format presents required information supplied by the taxpayer and entered by the taxpayer or tax preparer. You can then follow along and see how this information is used to complete the form.

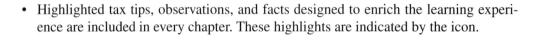

Reporting Rental Activities on Schedule E   **9-9**

(line 21) cannot exceed rental income (line 3). For taxpayers who answer "No" to this question, the vacation home rules do not apply and there is no limit on the total expenses. However, the expenses may be limited under either the *at-risk* or *passive loss* rules (discussed later in the chapter).

Information for Figure 9-1: Filled-In Schedule E

During 2005, Kurt F. and Heather M. Reding received rents of **$38,168** from an eight-unit apartment complex. The Redings paid $375,000 for the apartment building in 1996, which includes $100,000 for the land. They depreciate the building using MACRS (straight-line over 27.5 years). Expenses related to the building include **$250** advertising, **$2,500** cleaning and maintenance, **$1,227** insurance, **$300** legal fees, **$14,329** mortgage interest, **$3,262** supplies, **$4,290** real estate taxes, and **$1,800** utilities.

The Redings also own a condominium in Naples, Florida, that they used for 30 days in 2005. The Redings rented the condo for 90 days and received fair rentals totaling **$12,000**. None of the tenants were members of the Redings' family. The Redings paid $220,000 for the condo in 1995 and depreciate it using MACRS (straight-line over 27.5 years). The expenses related to the condo include $9,200 home mortgage interest, $3,400 real estate taxes, $1,000 utilities, $300 insurance, and $100 cleaning and maintenance.

Other Information

1A: Description: 8-unit apartment building, 505 West Street, Verona, WI

1B: Description: Condominium, 1500 Vanderbelt Beach Road, Naples, FL

2A: **No.** Personal use did not exceed the greater of 14 days or 10% of the days rented at fair rental.

2B: **Yes.** The Redings's 30 days of personal use exceeds the greater of (1) 14 days or (2) 9 days (10% of the 90 days rented at fair rental). Therefore, total rental expenses cannot exceed rental income.

7B: Cleaning and maintenance, **$75.00** (90 rental days/120 total days used × $100)

9B: Insurance, **$225.00** (90/120 × $300)

12B: Mortgage interest, **$6,900.00** (90/120 × $9,200)

16B: Taxes, **$2,550.00** (90/120 × $3,400)

17B: Utilities, **$750.00** (90/120 × $1,000)

20A: Depreciation expense, **$10,000.00** ($275,000/27.5)

20B: Depreciation expense, **$1,500.00** ($220,000/27.5 × 90/120 = $6,000; however, total rental expenses cannot exceed rental income of $12,000. Expenses other than depreciation total $10,500 [line 19B]; therefore depreciation is limited to $1,500).

FIGURE 9-1 Filled-In Schedule E, Page 1

SCHEDULE E (Form 1040)	Supplemental Income and Loss (From rental real estate, royalties, partnerships, S corporations, estates, trusts, REMICs, etc.)	OMB No. 1545-0074
Department of the Treasury Internal Revenue Service (99)	▶ Attach to Form 1040 or Form 1041. ▶ See Instructions for Schedule E (Form 1040).	**2005** Attachment Sequence No. **13**

Name(s) shown on return Kurt F. and Heather M. Reding   Your social security number 885 : 46 : 5566

Part I **Income or Loss From Rental Real Estate and Royalties** Note. If you are in the business of renting personal property, use Schedule C or C-EZ (see page E-3). Report farm rental income or loss from **Form 4835** on page 2, line 40.

1 List the type and location of each rental real estate property:

A 8-unit apartment building, 505 West Street, Verona, WI

B Condominim 1500 Vanderbelt Beach Road, Naples, FL

C

2 For each rental real estate property listed on line 1, did you or your family use it during the tax year for personal purposes for more than the greater of: • 14 days or • 10% of the total days rented at fair rental value? (See page E-3.)

	Yes	No
A		X
B	X	
C		

		Properties			Totals (Add columns A, B, and C.)
Income:		A	B	C	
3 Rents received	3	38,168 00	12,000 00		3 50,168 00
4 Royalties received	4				4
Expenses:					
5 Advertising	5	250 00			
6 Auto and travel (see page E-4)	6				
7 Cleaning and maintenance	7	2,500 00	75 00		
8 Commissions	8				
9 Insurance	9	1,227 00	225 00		
10 Legal and other professional fees	10	300 00			
11 Management fees	11				
12 Mortgage interest paid to banks, etc. (see page E-4)	12	14,329 00	6,900 00		12 21,229 00
13 Other interest	13				
14 Repairs	14				
15 Supplies	15	3,262 00			
16 Taxes	16	4,290 00	2,550 00		
17 Utilities	17	1,800 00	750 00		
18 Other (list) ▶	18				
19 Add lines 5 through 18	19	27,958 00	10,500 00		19 38,458 00
20 Depreciation expense or depletion (see page E-4)	20	10,00 00	1,500 00		20 11,500 00
21 Total expenses. Add lines 19 and 20	21	37,958 00	12,000 00		
22 Income or (loss) from rental real estate or royalty properties. Subtract line 21 from line 3 (rents) or line 4 (royalties). If the result is a (loss), see page E-4 to find out if you must file **Form 6198**	22	210 00	0		
23 Deductible rental real estate loss. **Caution.** Your rental real estate loss on line 22 may be limited. See page E-4 to find out if you must file **Form 8582**. Real estate professionals must complete line 43 on page 2	23 (	)(	)(	)	
24 **Income.** Add positive amounts shown on line 22. **Do not** include any losses					24 210 00
25 **Losses.** Add royalty losses from line 22 and rental real estate losses from line 23. Enter total losses here					25 ( )
26 **Total rental real estate and royalty income or (loss).** Combine lines 24 and 25. Enter the result here. If Parts II, III, IV, and line 40 on page 2 do not apply to you, also enter this amount on Form 1040, line 17. Otherwise, include this amount in the total on line 41 on page 2					26 210 00

For Paperwork Reduction Act Notice, see Form 1040 instructions.   Cat. No. 11344L   Schedule E (Form 1040) 2005

- Comprehensive problems are included in most chapters.

  Feature: A tax return problem has been included in most chapters.

  Benefit: This learning application integrates and summarizes the concepts covered in the chapter. Completing the comprehensive problems will help you see how the concepts from the chapter are reported on Form 1040.

COMPREHENSIVE PROBLEM

17. On January 2, 1995, Janis R. Jetson (SSN 344-46-5768), a cash basis taxpayer, purchased a two-unit apartment building at 1626 Flat Street, Detroit, Michigan 48270-8224. The costs of the land and building were $10,000 and $41,250, respectively. Jetson depreciates the building using the straight-line method over 27.5 years. Both apartments are the same size, with one on the ground floor and the other upstairs. Jetson has lived in the upstairs apartment since she acquired the building. The tenant in the ground-floor apartment at the time the building was purchased has continued to rent from Jetson. The tenant pays $350 a month in rent. On June 30 the tenant moved. The apartment was vacant until August 1, even though Jetson advertised and attempted to rent it. On August 1, a new tenant moved in, paying rent of $400 per month. Rent is due on the first day of the month. Information on the apartment follows:

Revenue

Rent from the first tenant (6 months @ $350)	$2,100
Rent from the second tenant (5 months @ $400)	2,000
Total revenue	$4,100

Expenses

Entire house:	
Real estate taxes	$1,700
Janitor and yard work	160
Electricity and water	440
Repairs	300
Heat (gas)	800
Interest on mortgage	1,100
Insurance	376
Expenses other than depreciation	$4,876
Ground-floor apartment:	
Advertising	100
Painting and papering	420
Repairs	70
	$ 590
Upstairs apartment:	
Repairs	$ 90
Cleaning and maintenance	480
	$ 570

In addition to the rental property, Jetson works as an administrative assistant and earned $17,600 in wages. From this amount, $1,080 of federal income tax was withheld. Jetson also earned $147 in interest from Bank of America. Jetson is single and has no dependents. She does not want to contribute $3 to the presidential campaign fund.

Prepare Form 1040 and Schedule E, Supplemental Income and Loss, reproduced on pages 9-29 to 9-31.

- Three major cumulative problems are included.

  Feature: Cumulative Problem 1 covers Chapters 1–4; Cumulative Problem 2 covers Chapters 1–6; and Cumulative Problem 3 covers Chapters 1–12.

  Benefit: These learning applications integrate and summarize concepts of several chapters to test your understanding and help you prepare for and pass your exams.

CUMULATIVE PROBLEM (CHAPTERS 1–6)

Frank A. (SSN 811-26-3717) and Sandra K. (SSN 820-47-9231) Anderson (ages 38 and 36, respectively) reside at 2121 Century Avenue, Middleton, CA 92657, with their three children whom they fully support: Martha A. (age 9), Charles R. (age 11), and Carol T. (age 14). The children's social security numbers are Martha 998-21-5246, Charles 998-21-5247, and Carol 998-21-1827.

The Andersons file a joint return, and neither elects to have money go to the presidential election campaign fund. Frank is employed by Maintaineers, Inc., as a customer representative, and Sandra is employed by Mission Instruments as a computer operator. Details of their salaries and withholdings, are as follows:

	Gross Wages	State Income Tax Withheld	Federal Income Tax Withheld	Social Security Tax Withheld	Medicare Insurance Tax Withheld
Frank	$52,500	$3,623	$2,100	$3,255	$761
Sandra	24,000	1,656	980	1,488	348

In addition to his salary, Frank received a business travel expense reimbursement of $6,600 from Maintaineers, Inc., which was not included on his Form W-2. By agreement with his employer, none of the allowance was for meals and entertainment expenses. Frank must make an adequate accounting of his expenses to his employer and, as required, return any excess reimbursements. His daily business journal disclosed that from January 2 (the date of purchase) through December 31, he drove his own automobile 29,151 miles, of which 18,387 were business related. Frank's average roundtrip commuting distance is six miles, and his commuting miles total 1,440 for the year. Since Frank dislikes keeping records, he uses the standard mileage rate to determine his automobile tax deduction. His substantiated paid business expenses are as follows:

Travel expenses	$2,168*
Parking fees	210
Meals and entertainment	560
Miscellaneous expenses	91

*Excludes meals, entertainment, and auto expenses

Sandra belongs to a car pool and drives to work every fourth week. In addition, her car is used on vacations.

In August, Sandra received $400 of interest when she cashed in a CD from State Bank. The Middleton Farmers Bank credited $300 of interest to the Andersons' joint savings account during the year. The Andersons itemized deductions in 2004 and overpaid their state income tax by $142, all of which provided a tax benefit. They received a refund of this amount in March, 2004. Since they both work outside the home, they are unable to be there when their children return from school. This year the Andersons paid a neighbor, Gloria Dryden (SSN 992-31-4270), $4,100 to care for their children in her home after school hours and during the summer vacation period while they were at work. Gloria Dryden's address is 2132 Century Avenue, Middleton, CA 92657.

During January, Sandra received unemployment compensation of $200, covering two weeks between jobs. Sandra's former husband paid her $2,400 of alimony on the basis of a written alimony agreement, which did not expire upon her marriage to Frank. Neither Frank nor Sandra is covered by a qualified pension plan at work. Frank contributed $3,000 to his traditional IRA account. Sandra contributed $2,000 to her traditional IRA account. Both contributions took place before April 15, 2006.

- Tax questions and problems requiring use of the IRS Internet Web site are included in each chapter.

  Feature: The answers to these questions and problems are found in the information contained in IRS forms and/or publications.

  Benefit: You will learn how to find answers to tax questions from IRS publications available on the internet. You will also learn how to find needed tax forms, fill them out while on the internet, and print out copies of the completed forms. These learning applications provide you the opportunity to obtain knowledge about tax law using information outside of the textbook. Step-by-step instructions on how to access the relevant IRS forms/publications are provided to guide you through the process.

- The new tax rules from the Katrina Emergency Tax Relief Act of 2005 are included in the 2006 Edition.

  Feature: New tax rules passed by Congress and signed into law by the President on September 23, 2005 contain many provisions designed to provide tax relief to persons living in and around the various areas that were greatly affected by Hurricane Katrina. A couple provisions give tax relief to taxpayers who have provided assistance to persons affected by the hurricane. The new tax laws that affect topics covered in the 2006 Edition have been incorporated into the chapters.

  Benefit: These rules affect the preparation of 2005 tax returns, and many rules will also affect 2006 tax returns. By including these tax rules in the 2006 Edition, you are up to date with all of the rules needed to complete a 2005 individual tax return.

6-34   *CHAPTER 6   Other Itemized Deductions*

15. Internet Problem: Researching Publication 463.

The Alpha-Beta Company rents a twelve-seat luxury skybox at a football stadium for the entire season. The season consists of eight home games. Alpha-Beta uses the sky-box exclusively for entertaining clients. The cost of renting the skybox for the season is $20,000. In contrast, nonluxury box seats sell for $50 for each game.

How much can Alpha-Beta deduct for its luxury skybox?

Go to the IRS Web site. Locate Publication 463, and find an answer to the above question involving luxury skyboxes. Print out a copy of the page where you found your answer. Underline or highlight the pertinent information.

See Appendix A for instructions on use of the IRS Web site.

16. Business Entity Problem: This problem is designed for those using the "business entity" approach. The solution may require information from Chapter 14.

For each statement, check true or false.	True	False
a. Self-employed taxpayers use Form 2106 to report their deductible travel expenses.	____	____
b. A self-employed taxpayer may claim the federal per diem for meals instead of deducting the actual meal costs	____	____.
c. Employers that reimburse their employees using an "accountable reimbursement plan" are able to deduct the entire cost of meal reimbursements paid to their employees.	____	____
d. The owner of a corporation may claim the federal per diem for meals instead of deducting the actual meal costs.	____	____
e. When a self-employed taxpayer incurs deductible education expenses, the expenses are deductible as a miscellaneous itemized deduction subject to the 2% test.	____	____
f. When a taxpayer owns an S corporation that breeds and races horses, the pass-through losses from the corporation may be treated as hobby losses if the corporation has never shown a profit in its ten years of operation.	____	____

5-18   *CHAPTER 5   Personal Itemized Deductions*

limit occurs if the taxpayer reports the donation of the appreciated capital gain property at the taxpayer's basis. Then the limitation increases to 50% of AGI. When taxpayers contribute capital gain property, instead of cash, to certain private foundations not operating for the benefit of the public at large, they limit the contribution to 20% of AGI.

These limitations sometimes reduce or eliminate a taxpayer's net contribution. Taxpayers carry forward the unused contributions for up to five years. When carried forward, the contribution limits of 50%, 30%, and 20% apply to the specific contributions. For example, an unused contribution with a 30% limitation in 20x1 retains the same 30% limitation when carried to 20x2. If the taxpayer does not itemize, charitable contributions generated in that year are not carried forward.

EXAMPLE 16

The Neals donated land worth $80,000 to their church for a building site. The land was acquired as an investment 15 years ago for $20,000. The amount deductible for appreciated capital gain property in the current year is limited to $43,125 (30% of AGI). The Neals' total contribution of appreciated property is $80,350 (IBM stock, $350 + land, $80,000). Thus, the Neals deduct $43,125 currently, and the remaining $37,225 carries forward for up to five years. Note that the total charitable contribution deduction of $46,975 ($3,725 + $125 + $43,125) does not exceed 50% of AGI, $71,875.

The Katrina Emergency Tax Relief Act of 2005 contains a provision that allows individual to increase the limit for "qualified contributions" to 100% of the taxpayer AGI (up from the normal 50% AGI limit). A **qualified contribution** is any cash contribution paid between August 28, 2005 and December 31, 2005 to a qualified public charity. It is important to note that the 100% AGI limit applies to all cash contributions (including contributions other than for hurricane relief) made to qualified public charities during this time period. Therefore, a taxpayer whose AGI is $100,000 and who prior to August 28, 2005 had given $20,000 to a qualified public charity would normally be allowed to give another $30,000 to a qualified public during 2005 before being subject to AGI limitation. Under this new rule, this taxpayer could give up to $80,000 ($100,000-$20,000) to public charties between August 28,2005 and December 31,2005 and be allowed to deduct the entire $100,000 in 2005.

CASUALTY AND THEFT LOSSES, SCHEDULE A (LINE 19)

On personal use property, taxpayers measure each casualty loss as the lower of two amounts: (1) the difference between the FMV before and after the casualty or (2) the basis of the property. Taxpayers must reduce the lower of these two numbers by both of the following:

1. Insurance and other proceeds received
2. $100 per event (not per item)

Taxpayers then total the net loss from each casualty event occurring during the year. From this total they subtract 10% of AGI. Only the remaining amount is deductible.

These provisions make losses from personal casualties hard to deduct. Personal casualty deductions rarely take place without a major uninsured disaster. Lesser casualties generally result in losses below the 10% of AGI threshold and result in no tax benefits. Taxpayers

**Helpful information included in the
2006 Edition!!**

- Highlights of 2005 and 2006 tax changes are listed and described in the Preface.

    Feature: A summary of 2005 and 2006 tax law changes and IRS interpretations appears on pages x–xii.
    Benefit: This summary brings you up to date quickly with major tax law changes since the last edition.

- Frequently used tax facts are given.

    Feature: Frequently used tax facts appear on the inside front cover.
    Benefit: This helpful page provides a quick and easy reference source for frequently used tax facts.

- Numerous examples are provided.

    Feature: Every chapter includes numerous easy-to-follow examples.
    Benefit: These examples illustrate the application of tax laws and relate tax laws to true-life situations.

- Information on how to access IRS forms and publications from the IRS Web site is given.

    Feature: Information on how to obtain forms and publications from the IRS through the internet appears in Appendix A after the Tax Tables and EIC Tables.
    Benefit: This information will help you access the most up-to-date forms, instructions to forms, and IRS publications referenced in the text.

Other Successful Features of *Essentials of Federal Income Taxation for Individuals and Business, 2006 Edition*

- Comprehensive coverage of self-employed taxpayers (Chapter 7)
- Index of tax forms, schedules, and worksheets following the table of contents
- Detailed outline at beginning of each chapter
- Line numbers set off in parentheses to show location of tax facts on forms
- Tax tips throughout book for tax planning and tax reduction
- Teaching suggestions in Instructor's Manual to help with class preparation
- Problems at end of chapters designated for tax software solution
- Assignments that provide actual application and check understanding
- Acronym list on copyright page that provides actual words
- Computerized version of test bank with true-false, multiple-choice, matching, fill-in-the-blank and essay questions
- Printed version of test bank in Instructor's Manual also includes fill-in-the-form questions

Highlights of 2005 and 2006 Tax Changes

Inside Front Cover

- 2005 Tax Rate Schedules
- 2005 and 2006 Standard Deduction amounts
- 2005 and 2006 Personal and Dependency Exemption amounts
- 2005 and 2006 FICA Tax Rates and Base amounts
- 2005 Standard Mileage Rates

Chapter 1

- The personal and dependency exemption for 2005 increased to $3,200.
- Starting in 2005, the rules for dependency exemptions have been revised. A new provision for "qualifying children" has been added. The definition of "qualifying children" is also used to identify children for purposes of determining head of household status. In addition, it is used in determining the child and dependent care credit, the child tax credit, and the earned income credit.
- Inflation adjustments increased the basic standard deduction amounts for taxpayers in 2005. The additional standard deduction also increased for both unmarried taxpayers ($1,200 to $1,250) and married taxpayers ($950 to $1,000).
- The new filing requirements for 2005 are listed as well as the new thresholds for the exemption phase-down.
- An additional $500 exemption is allowed in 2005 or 2006 to certain taxpayers providing rent-free housing to a "displaced Katrina individual."

Chapter 2

- The phase-out for education credits starts at $87,000 (up from $85,000 in 2004) for marrieds filing jointly. It increases to $43,000 for single taxpayers.
- Disqualified income for purposes of the earned income credit has increased to $2,700 (up from $2,650 in 2004).
- In 2005 the child tax credit is refundable up to 15% of earned income in excess of $11,000 (up from $10,750 in 2004).
- In 2005, the adoption credit is $10,630 (up from $10,390 in 2004). The phase-out starts at $159,450 (up from $155,860 in 2004).
- To compute the earned income credit and the refundable portion of the child tax credit, "qualified Katrina individuals" may elect to use 2004 earned income if it is higher than 2005 earned income.

Chapter 3

- Taxpayers taking a "qualified Hurricane Katrina distribution" from their IRAs may spread the taxable portion of the distribution over three years.

Chapter 4

- The new phase-out ranges for deductible contributions to an IRA for participants in an employer-sponsored retirement plan are listed.
- In 2005, employees may exclude $200 per month for parking provided by the employer (up from $195 in 2004). They may also exclude $105 for employer paid qualified transportation (up from $100 in 2004).
- In 2005 taxpayers can exclude from gross income up to $10,630 of child adoption expenses paid or reimbursed by the employer (up from $10,390 in 2004).
- Taxpayers can deduct $2,000 of the cost of qualified clean-fuel vehicles placed in service in 2005. The deduction is for AGI.
- The mileage rate for moving expenses increased to 15 cents per mile (up from 14 cents in 2004). The rate is 22 cents for mileage after August 31.
- A new above–the–deduction equal to 3% of "net income" from domestically produced products is available in 2005. The deduction cannot exceed 50% of the W-2 wages paid during the year.

- The IRS will not assess the 10% penalty on the first $100,000 of "qualified Hurricane Katrina distributions."

Chapter 5

- The phase-out threshold for itemized deductions increased from $142,700 to $145,950 ($71,350 to $72,975 for marrieds filing separately).
- The mileage rate for medical transportation increased to 15 cents per mile (up from 14 cents in 2004). The rate is 22 cents for mileage after August 31.
- A special mileage deduction is available to taxpayers who use their automobile in 2005 for charitable purposes related to Hurricane Katrina.
- The Katrina Emergency Tax Relief Act of 2005 allows individuals to deduct "qualified charitable contributions" up to 100% of their AGI in 2005.
- Casualty losses arising from Hurricane Katrina are not subject to the $100 deductible or the 10% AGI limit.
- In 2005, "qualified contributions" are not used when calculating the "80% limit" for itemized deductions.

Chapter 6

- The new low per diem rate for travel is $127 (includes $36 for meals) and the high per diem rate is $199 (includes $46 for meals).

Chapter 7

- The standard mileage rate increased to 40.5 cents per mile for business miles driven between January 1, 2005 and August 31, 2005. From September 1, 2005 to December 31, 2005, the standard mileage rate increased further to 48.5 cents per mile. These amounts are up from 37.5 cents in 2004.
- In 2005, the 15.3% self-employment tax rate applies to the first $90,000 of net earnings from self-employment. The 2.9% tax rate applies to net earnings from self-employment in excess of $90,000.
- The annual limit for contributions to 401(k) retirement plans increased to $14,000 (up from $13,000 in 2004). The annual limit will continue to increase $1,000 each year until it reaches $15,000. Employees age 50 and older can contribute an additional $4,000 in 2005.
- The annual limit for contributions to a SIMPLE retirement plan increased to $10,000 for 2005 (up from $9,000 in 2004). Workers age 50 and older can contribute an additional $2,000 in 2005.

Chapter 8

- The additional first-year bonus depreciation that Congress enacted after the events of September 11, 2001, expired at the end of 2004 and was not renewed.
- The dollar limit for purposes of the immediate expensing of Section 179 property increased to $105,000 in 2005 (up from $102,000 in 2004). The phase-out of this amount begins when more than $420,000 of Section 179 property is placed in service during 2005 (up from $410,000 in 2004).
- Depreciation limits continue to apply to passenger automobiles, SUVs, trucks and vans weighing 6,000 pounds or less.

- Cost recovery deduction limits for automobiles are as follows. Slightly higher limits apply to trucks, SUVs, and vans weighing less than 6,000 pounds.

	2001	2002	2003	2004	2005
1st year*	$3,060	$7,660	$7,660/$10,710	$10,610	$2,960
2nd year	4,900	4,900	4,900	4,800	4,700
3rd year	2,950	2,950	2,950	2,850	2,850
4th year	1,775	1,775	1,775	1,675	1,675

  * The $10,710/$10,610 limit applied to new automobiles purchased after May 5, 2003 when the 50% bonus was used. The $7,660 limit applied to new automobiles purchased after September 10, 2001 when the 30% bonus was used. From 2001–2003, the limit was $3,060 for automobiles placed in service before September 11, 2001; any used automobile; and any automobile used 50% or less for business. For 2004, the limit for used automobiles and automobiles used 50% or less for business was $2,960.

- SUVs placed in service after October 22, 2004 that weigh between 6,000 and 14,000 pounds are subject to a $25,000 first year limit for Section 179 expense. SUVs weighing more than 14,000 pounds remain exempt from the luxury automobile limits. The tax law still allows taxpayers to take MACRS on any cost of the SUV not expensed under Section 179.

Chapter 10

- Taxpayers with business or investment property located in the Hurricane Katrina disaster area may have an additional 3 years to replace their property and avoid being taxed on any realized gains.

Chapter 11

- For assets sold in 2005, the tax rate on net capital gain (the amount remaining as net long-term capital gain when the netting process is complete) is 15% for taxpayers in the 25% and higher tax brackets. For taxpayers in the 10% and 15% tax brackets, the tax rate on net capital gain is 5%. However, the higher 28% maximum rate still applies to the gain on the sale of collectibles and on the gain from the sale of Section 1202 stock. Unrecaptured Section 1250 gain (from the sale of certain realty) is still taxed at a maximum 25% rate.

Chapter 12

- The AMT exemption for couples filing a joint return remains at $58,000 for 2005. The exemption for couples who file separately stays at $29,000. For unmarried taxpayers, the 2005 AMT exemption remains at $40,250.
- The work opportunity credit is scheduled to expire after 2005. However, Congress is expected to extend it, as it has done several times in the past. Congress expanded the list of eligible workers to include Hurricane Katrina employees. The rules for who qualifies as a Hurricane Katrina employee are discussed in the chapter.
- The welfare-to-work credit is scheduled to expire after 2005. However, Congress is expected to extend it, as it has done several times in the past.
- A new Employer Retention Credit was added as part of the Katrina Emergency Tax Relief Act of 2005. Details of this new General Business Credit are discussed in the chapter.

Chapter 13

- In 2005, large depositors of payroll taxes, withheld income taxes, and corporate income taxes must use the electronic funds transfer system (EFTS) to make their deposits. For 2005, large depositors are those who had deposits in excess of $200,000 in 2003. For 2006, businesses with more than $200,000 of deposits in 2004 must use the EFTS to make their deposits.

- For 2005, employers withhold 6.2% of their employees' wages, up to wages of $90,000 for each employee (up from $87,900 in 2004), for social security taxes. They also withhold 1.45% of employees' wages for Medicare taxes (no limit).

- Household employees (maids, babysitters, nannies, etc.) are subject to FICA withholding if they are paid $1,400 or more during 2005 (same as 2004).

- Employers are not required to pay FUTA taxes for domestic workers (nannies, housekeepers, gardeners, etc.) who earn less than $1,500 every quarter in both the current and previous calendar years (up from $1,000 per quarter in 2004).

- Employers whose FUTA tax liability for any quarter does not exceed $500 can carryover their liability to the next quarter (up from $100 in 2004).

- When taxpayers make estimated payments for 2006, the safe harbor equals 100% of 2005 tax liability. However, for taxpayers with 2005 AGI in excess of $150,000, the safe harbor percentage increases to 110% of 2005 tax liability.

- Employers are no longer required to send in to the IRS Forms W-4 for employees claiming more than 10 exemptions.

Chapter 14

- S corporations may now have 100 shareholders (up from 75 in 2004). However, family members may elect to be treated as one shareholder. Family members include ancestors and descendants, as well as spouses and former spouses of these individuals.

SPECIAL NOTE REGARDING FINAL TAX FORMS AND SCHEDULES FOR THE 2005 TAX YEAR

Normally, the IRS would have released the final version of the 2005 tax forms and schedules by the time this book went to press. However, in late September, Congress passed the Katrina Emergency Tax Relief Act of 2005. Numerous provisions in this Act required the IRS to incorporate the tax law changes into the 2005 tax forms and schedules. This caused a delay in the release to the final version of many forms and schedules for the 2005 tax year.

This textbook contains the most recent version of each tax form and schedule available at the time the book went to press – including the use of draft forms when the final version was not yet available. Final versions of any tax form or schedule can be obtained from the IRS website using the instructions on the inside back cover of this textbook. If you are using final forms and schedules to complete homework problems, please note that line number references used in this book reflect the line numbers on the forms and schedules used and illustrated throughout the textbook. Although the final version of a tax form often is identical to the draft version, slight differences between the draft and final versions of any tax form are possible, and changes to the line numbers may occur.

ACKNOWLEDGMENTS

We express our appreciation to the many instructors and students who have contributed suggestions to make this textbook more interesting, understandable, and practical to those who study federal income taxation. As a result of their very helpful recommendations, the 2006 Edition will better satisfy the learning needs of students and the teaching needs of instructors.

H.C.S.
L.M.J.

1

Overview of the Tax Structure

CHAPTER CONTENTS

■■ CHAPTER OVERVIEW

The Sixteenth Amendment to the Constitution empowers Congress to levy and collect income taxes. After its ratification, Congress enacted the Revenue Act of 1913. For individual taxpayers, the Act taxed income at a 1% rate. Unmarried taxpayers got an exemption of $3,000; married taxpayers got another $1,000 exemption. At $20,000, the Act imposed an additional 1% surtax. This surtax gradually increased to 6% for income above $500,000.

The government continues to use a progressive tax rate structure. As income rises, the tax rate increases. In 2005, tax rates range from 10% to 35%. The current rate schedules appear on the inside front cover of this book.

Our current tax system, like the original one, requires taxpayers to determine their taxes. It also requires each taxpayer to file a tax return and pay any tax due the government by certain deadlines. Taxpayers who fail to meet these requirements face possible fines, penalties, and imprisonment. In addition, the Internal Revenue Service (IRS) charges interest on unpaid taxes. To meet their responsibilities, many taxpayers seek professional help. Tax professionals prepare about half of filed tax returns.

Although many taxpayers use paid professionals, every taxpayer should have a basic understanding of the tax laws. This understanding will help them prepare their return or identify facts needed by a preparer. It also will help the taxpayer review a prepared return before filing it. Understanding the tax laws can help in recognizing potential problems before financial events take place. Through proper planning, the taxpayer can reduce the tax bite. The first part of this chapter provides an overview of our current tax system. The latter part presents tax planning principles.

Since 1913, the Internal Revenue Code has grown to well over 2,000 pages in length.

RESPONSIBILITIES OF TAXPAYERS

1. Prepare appropriate tax forms and schedules.
2. Determine correct tax liability.
3. Pay tax due on time.

4. File return on time with proper IRS Regional Service Center and keep evidence of on-time mailing.

5. Maintain records and documents to support tax return data.

6. Try to minimize tax return errors.

INCOME TAX OBJECTIVES

Basically, the federal income tax system raises money to cover part of the government's annual operating costs. However, to understand better certain tax rules, people must realize that Congress also uses tax laws to achieve various economic, political, and social goals. These include price stability, redistribution of the country's wealth, and encouragement of economic growth and full employment. For example, if the goal is to increase employment, Congress can lower taxes, and that will give taxpayers more money to spend. This, in turn, creates more demand for products and services. The result is a need for an increased number of workers to make the products and provide the services.

BASIC TAX FORMULA

Our federal income tax applies directly to individual taxpayers, regular corporations, estates, and trusts. Indirectly, it applies to flow-through entities (partnerships and S corporations). The owner of a flow-through entity usually pays taxes on his or her share of the entity's taxable income. On an overall basis, the same reporting formula applies to all taxpayer groups, although different groups may use different rates and follow different reporting requirements. Also, individual taxpayers must use an expanded formula. Each group, however, must compute taxable income.

After computing taxable income, the taxpayer applies the proper tax rate to determine tax liability. The taxpayer reduces this liability by certain credits and increases it by certain additions. The result represents the amount due to or from the government.

TAXABLE INCOME FORMULA

Income from all sources
– Exempt income
─────────────────────
= Gross income
– Deductions
─────────────────────
= Taxable income

INDIVIDUAL TAXPAYERS

The Internal Revenue Code (Code) divides individual taxpayers into five groups according to filing status. Later, this chapter presents more facts about members of each of these tax filing groups.

1. Single
2. Head of household (HOH)
3. Married filing a joint return
4. Married filing a separate return
5. Surviving spouse (a qualifying widow or widower with a dependent child)

These taxpayers use the Basic Tax Formula for Individuals to compute refunds or taxes due.

BASIC TAX FORMULA FOR INDIVIDUALS

	Income from all sources
−	Exempt income
=	Gross income
−	Deductions for AGI (adjusted gross income)
=	AGI
−	Deductions from AGI
	Itemized or standard deduction
	Exemptions (personal and dependency)
=	Taxable income
×	Tax rate
=	Tax liability before:
+	Additions to tax
−	Credits to tax
=	Final tax due (refund)

Frequently, tax returns include questions about taxpayers' financial activities for audits and statistical reporting. The IRS also collects facts about taxpayers from other sources (employers, banks, etc.) to test the accuracy of tax return items.

Later, this chapter presents more facts about the members of each tax filing group. It also provides facts on the filing requirements for each group. Following are the tax returns most individual taxpayers use for annual IRS reporting and the locations of related materials in the book:

1. Form 1040EZ, Income Tax Return for Single and Joint Filers With No Dependents (Chapter 2)
2. Form 1040A, U.S. Individual Income Tax Return (Chapters 2 and 4)
3. Form 1040, U.S. Individual Income Tax Return (Chapters 2 through 12)

DEDUCTIONS AND CREDITS

In the basic tax formula, note that deductions reduce income and credits reduce the tax liability. Thus, a $100 *tax credit* reduces the tax liability by $100. A $100 *deduction,* however, reduces the tax liability by only a fractional amount. This reduction equals the taxpayer's highest tax rate multiplied by the deduction. Thus, a taxpayer in the 15% tax bracket saves only $15 with a $100 deduction (15% × $100).

GROSS INCOME

The taxpayer must be able to determine his or her gross income. The Internal Revenue Code's (Code) definition of gross income includes all wealth that flows to a taxpayer from whatever source derived. It also exempts some income from taxation. The Code lists the following different gross income sources (and implies that others exist):

1. Compensation for services, including fees, commissions, fringe benefits, and similar items
2. Gross income from business
3. Property transaction gains
4. Interest
5. Rents
6. Royalties
7. Dividends
8. Alimony and separate maintenance payments
9. Annuities
10. Income from life insurance proceeds and endowment contracts
11. Pensions
12. Income from forgiven debt
13. Share of distributive partnership income
14. Income in respect of a decedent
15. Income from an interest in an estate or trust

To determine gross income, taxpayers generally examine their various sources of income and sort out taxable income from exempt income. Regardless of the form or name of an income item, proper authority must exist to exclude the item from gross income. Taxpayers may find such authority in the tax statutes, the Internal Revenue Code (IRC), Treasury Regulations, IRS rulings, or case law. From gross income, taxpayers subtract authorized deductions to arrive at taxable income (Chapters 3 and 4).

Importance of Gross Income

Gross income is an important income figure. An error can result in an incorrect assessment of the need to file a tax return. Failure to file a proper return on time can result in tax penalties. Dependency exemptions may be allowed or denied depending on a person's gross income. Also, when a taxpayer accidentally understates gross income by more than 25%, the law extends the time the IRS has to conduct an audit.

DEDUCTIONS AVAILABLE TO INDIVIDUAL TAXPAYERS

Individual taxpayers have two broad groups of deductions. They subtract one group from gross income to arrive at adjusted gross income (AGI). They subtract the other group from AGI to arrive at taxable income. Some tax professionals call them *for* or *from* deductions. Others call them *above-* or *below-the-line* deductions. Taxpayers subtract **above-the-line** deductions from gross income to arrive at AGI. They subtract **below-the-line** deductions from AGI to arrive at taxable income.

Below-the-line deductions fall into two categories. One category includes the greater of a taxpayer's itemized deductions or standard deduction. The other category includes exemptions (personal and dependency). The Code limits the amount of exemptions and itemized deductions that a taxpayer may claim. AGI generally serves as a basis for determining these limitations. Corporations, partnerships, estates, and trusts do not compute AGI.

Deductions for AGI

The Internal Revenue Code defines an individual's AGI as gross income less certain deductions. Some of the major deductions include:

1. Trade and business deductions for business owners
2. Limited losses from property transactions
3. Deductions related to rent and royalty income
4. Certain contributions to retirement plans of self-employed individuals
5. Certain contributions to traditional Individual Retirement Accounts
6. Penalties for early withdrawals from time savings accounts or deposits
7. Alimony
8. Qualified moving expenses
9. One-half of self-employment tax
10. Health insurance premiums paid by self-employed persons
11. Individual contributions to a health savings account
12. Interest paid on student loans
13. Qualified higher education expenses
14. Teachers' classroom expenses
15. Certain business expenses of reservists, performing artists, and fee basis government officials
16. Domestic production activities deduction

Deductions from AGI

After computing AGI, the taxpayer reduces it with either itemized deductions or a standard deduction. The taxpayer also reduces the AGI by personal and dependency exemptions. The next few sections present the standard deduction and exemptions. Itemized deductions fall into seven groups (Chapters 5 and 6):

1. Medical
2. Taxes
3. Interest
4. Charitable contributions
5. Casualty and theft losses
6. Job expenses and some miscellaneous deductions
7. Other miscellaneous deductions

STANDARD DEDUCTION

The standard deduction consists of two factors: the basic standard deduction and the additional standard deduction. Both factors are subject to inflation adjustments each year. Taxpayers normally use the standard deduction when it exceeds their total itemized deductions.

However, some use the standard deduction to avoid keeping detailed records. Taxpayers filing Form 1040EZ or Form 1040A have no choice; they must use the standard deduction. In addition, when spouses file separate returns, both spouses must either itemize deductions or take the standard deduction. Actually, if one spouse itemizes, the other spouse may claim a standard deduction of "zero."

Although taxpayers may deduct certain personal expenses as itemized deductions, about 70% of them choose instead the standard deduction. For most taxpayers this constitutes one of the two major deductions on the tax return. The other is the exemption amount. Generally, an employed person who does not pay alimony or make payments to a qualified retirement program has little, if anything, else to deduct. Consequently, computing taxable income is fairly easy for most Americans. They simply add up their incomes from various sources, usually evidenced by the paying organizations on Form W-2 or Form 1099. From this total they deduct the standard deduction and the exemption amounts to arrive at taxable income.

Basic Standard Deduction

There are four basic standard deduction amounts. Filing status usually determines which amount applies. Although most taxpayers are eligible to take the basic standard deduction, some are not. One who is a dependent of another taxpayer generally does not use these figures, as will be explained later (Standard Deduction for Dependents).

BASIC STANDARD DEDUCTION FOR 2005

Taxpayer Status	Amount
Married filing jointly, or surviving spouse	$10,000
Head of household	7,300
Single	5,000
Married filing separately	5,000

Additional Standard Deduction

In addition to the basic standard deduction, blind and elderly taxpayers claim extra deductions. Taxpayers become elderly when they reach age 65. This additional deduction is available only for the taxpayer and spouse. A taxpayer cannot claim an additional standard deduction for a dependent who is elderly or blind. Also, the additional standard deduction increases only the basic standard deduction; it never increases the taxpayer's itemized deductions. There are two additional amounts available. Marital status determines which one is used.

ADDITIONAL STANDARD DEDUCTION FOR 2005

Married and surviving spouse	$1,000
Single and head of household	1,250

Each incidence of age and blindness carries with it an additional deduction. In the case of married taxpayers, each spouse is eligible for both deductions. Thus, if both spouses are age 65, the total additional standard deduction is $2,000 (2 × $1,000). If both spouses are age

65 and one is blind, the extra deduction is $3,000 (3 × $1,000). For a single person, age 65 and blind, the extra deduction is $2,500 (2 × $1,250).

For a taxpayer to get an additional standard deduction, his or her status as elderly or blind must exist at the end of the tax year (or at death). For tax purposes, the taxpayer ages the day before his or her calendar birthday. Thus, a taxpayer who turns 65 on January 1 becomes 65 on December 31 of the preceding year.

To receive the blindness deduction, a taxpayer attaches a supporting statement to the return. A taxpayer may claim the deduction by failing a visual ability or field of vision test. For the visual ability test, sight in either eye cannot exceed 20/200 with a corrective lens; the field of vision cannot exceed 20 degrees.

The taxpayer supports a blindness claim with a certified statement from an eye doctor (ophthalmologist or optometrist). The statement verifies that the taxpayer is totally blind or fails either the visual ability or field of vision test. If the blindness is irreversible, the taxpayer simply refers to this statement on future returns.

Standard Deduction for Dependents

A person (e.g., child) who qualifies as a dependent of another taxpayer (e.g., parent) computes the basic standard deduction as the greater of two amounts: (1) $800 or (2) earned income plus $250. The deduction cannot exceed the basic standard deduction for the dependent's filing class. However, any additional standard deduction for which the dependent qualifies increases the basic standard deduction otherwise allowable.

When married taxpayers are claimed as dependents and file separate returns, the following provisions govern. If one or both spouses are dependents of other taxpayers, and both spouses use the standard deduction, the basic standard deduction is limited to the greater of (1) $800, or (2) earned income plus $250. However, if one spouse itemizes deductions, the standard deduction for the other spouse is zero.

A dependent usually completes a worksheet similar to Figure 1-1, which helps in computing the standard deduction.

Information for Figure 1-1: Filled-In Standard Deduction Worksheet for Dependents

This figure presents a filled-in Standard Deduction Worksheet for 16-year-old Gloria Moore. Gloria's parents claim her as a dependent. Gloria has perfect vision. She earned $1,400 at a weekend office job. Her standard deduction equals $1,650, the larger of (1) $800 or (2) her earned income plus $250. This amount does not exceed the basic standard deduction for a single individual ($5,000).

FIGURE 1-1:   Filled-In Standard Deduction Worksheet for Dependents

1.	Enter your earned income (defined below) plus $250.	1.	1,650
2.	Minimum amount.	2.	800
3.	Enter the larger of line 1 or line 2.	3.	1,650
4.	Enter $5,000 if single ($5,000 if married filing separately; $10,000 if married filing jointly, or qualifying widow(er); $7,300 if head of household).	4.	5,000
5.	Standard deduction:		
	a. Enter the smaller of line 3 or line 4. If under 65 and not blind, this is the standard deduction. Otherwise go to line 5b.	5a.	1,650

   b. If 65 or older or blind, multiply $1,250 ($1,000 if married filing
       jointly or separately, or qualifying widow[er]) by the number
       of incidences of age and blindness.   5b.   0

   c. Add lines 5a and 5b to determine standard deduction.   5c. 1,650

Earned income includes salaries, tips, professional fees, and other compensation received for personal services performed. It also includes taxable scholarships and net profit from self-employment activities.

EXEMPTIONS

Exemptions, like the standard deduction, reduce AGI. For 2005, this reduction is $3,200 for each qualified exemption. Generally, the taxpayer may claim an exemption for one's self, spouse, and each person who qualifies as a dependent. Exemptions provide many taxpayers with their biggest tax deductions. For example, a married taxpayer with two dependent children reduces AGI by $12,800 (4 × $3,200). This far exceeds the couple's standard deduction of $10,000.

A taxpayer who changes his or her tax year must file a fractional year (short year) return. The taxpayer must also prorate the exemption *amount*.

Phase-Down of Exemptions

When AGI reaches a certain level, the taxpayer phases down (reduces) the dollar amount of the exemptions. For every $2,500 ($1,250 for marrieds filing separately) of AGI (or fraction thereof) over a base amount, the exemption deduction goes down by 2 percentage points. When the number of $2,500 ($1,250) increments exceeds 49, the phase-down ends, and the taxpayer receives no exemption deduction.

BASE AMOUNTS—EXEMPTION PHASE-DOWN

Filing Status	Start When AGI Over	Stop When AGI Over
Married filing jointly	$218,950	$341,450
Surviving spouse	218,950	341,450
Head of household	182,450	304,950
Single	145,950	268,450
Married filing separately	109,475	170,725

Information for Figure 1-2: Filled-In Personal Exemption Worksheet

This figure shows the phase-down worksheet for Jack and Laura Johnson. The Johnsons use the worksheet to compute their deduction for four exemptions. They file jointly and have $222,950 of AGI.

FIGURE 1-2: Filled-In Personal Exemption Worksheet

Is the amount of AGI more than the amount shown on line 3 below for your filing status?

NO. Stop. Multiply $3,200 by the total number of exemptions claimed. This is your exemption deduction.

YES. Complete the worksheet below to figure your deduction for exemptions.

1.	Multiply $3,200 by the total number of exemptions claimed.	1. 12,800
2.	Enter the amount of AGI.	2. 222,950
3.	Enter the amount shown below for your filing status: a. Married filing separately, enter $109,475. b. Single, enter $145,950. c. Head of household, enter $182,450. d. Married filing jointly, or qualifying widow(er), enter $218,950.	3. 218,950
4.	Subtract line 3 from line 2. If zero or less, stop here; the amount from line 1 above is the exemption deduction.	4. 4,000
	Note: If line 4 is more than $122,500 (more than $61,250 if married filing separately), stop here; you cannot take a deduction for exemptions.	
5.	Divide line 4 by $2,500 ($1,250 if married, filing separately). If the result is not a whole number, round it up to the next higher whole number (for example, round 0.0004 to 1).	5. 2
6.	Multiply line 5 by 2% (.02) and enter the result as a decimal amount.	6. .04
7.	Multiply line 1 by line 6.	7. 512
8.	Deduction for exemptions. Subtract line 7 from line 1 to determine exemption deduction.	8. 12,288

Personal Exemptions

Normally, a taxpayer deducts a personal exemption for him or herself. However, a person (e.g., child) who qualifies as the dependent of another taxpayer (e.g., parent) cannot take a personal exemption. This rule applies even if the other taxpayer does not actually claim an exemption for the qualifying dependent.

The death of a taxpayer does not affect the amount of the personal exemption. A decedent's final return carries the full exemption; no proration or reduction is necessary.

Exemptions for Spouse

Spouses are covered by special rules. They are not "dependents." A taxpayer may claim an exemption for the spouse (spousal exemption) on a joint return. When filing separately, a taxpayer may claim a spousal exemption only if the spouse

1. Has no gross income, and
2. Does not qualify as a dependent of another taxpayer.

A spousal exemption is available for a spouse when spouses are separated by a temporary (pending) divorce decree. However, if the spouse obtains a final decree of divorce or separate maintenance by year end, the taxpayer may not claim a spousal exemption.

The taxpayer takes a full exemption for a spouse who dies during the year. If the taxpayer remarries during that year, the Code denies a spousal exemption for the deceased.

Exemptions for Dependents

The taxpayer also claims an exemption for each person who qualifies as a "dependent." While minor children and elderly parents generally make up the taxpayer's list of dependents, others may qualify. Dependents fall into one of three groups: 1) qualifying relatives, 2) qualifying nonrelatives, or 3) qualifying children. Several requirements must be met if the taxpayer is to claim a dependency exemption for a person in one of these groups. If a person fails to meet any requirement, no dependency exemption may be taken for that individual.

An additional $500 exemption is allowed during 2005 and 2006 to taxpayers who provide rent-free housing to a "Hurricane Katrina displaced individual" for at least 60 consecutive days. **Hurricane Katrina displaced individuals** are persons whose principal place of abode on August 28, 2005 was in the Hurricane Katrina disaster area (as specified by the federal government) and (1) whose homes were located in the core disaster area (as specified by the federal government) and who were displaced from their homes, or (2) whose homes were located outside the core disaster area and who were displaced from their homes because their homes were damaged or because they were evacuated from their homes. Only one $500 additional exemption is allowed for each qualified displaced person. The exemption is taken in the year in which the 60 consecutive day period ends. Taxpayers can deduct up to $2,000 in total additional exemptions over the 2005 and 2006 tax years (the equivalent for providing housing to four qualified displaced persons). For example, a taxpayer who provides rent-free housing to a family of five from October 1, 2005 until May 1, 2006, would take an additional $2,000 exemption on their 2005 tax return (the 60 consecutive day period ends on November 30, 2005). To claim an additional exemption, taxpayers would be required to provide on their tax returns the SSN of the displaced person(s) for whom they are taking the additional exemption.

DEPENDENCY EXEMPTION REQUIREMENTS

The following sections examine the dependency requirements for each group of dependents. A dependent must meet all requirements listed for the applicable group. The taxpayer may claim an exemption for a qualified dependent, even if the dependent files a tax return. That dependent, however, cannot claim a personal exemption on his or her own return.

The taxpayer may also claim a full exemption for a dependent who either was born or died during the year. An exemption cannot be claimed for a stillborn child.

QUALIFYING RELATIVES

A qualifying relative is anyone who meets the following five tests but does not meet the definition of a "qualifying child" (defined later in the chapter).

1. Relationship test
2. Citizenship test
3. Support test

4. Gross income test
5. Joint return test

Relationship Test

For income tax purposes, the Internal Revenue Code specifies the individuals who qualify as a taxpayer's relatives. A relative does not have to live in the taxpayer's household to qualify as a dependent.

RELATIVES OF A TAXPAYER

- Brother, sister, stepbrother, or stepsister
- Descendant of the taxpayer, including a legally adopted child
- Father-in-law, mother-in-law, son-in-law, daughter-in-law, brother-in-law, or sister-in-law
- Nephew or niece (but only if related by blood, not by marriage)
- Parent, grandparent, or other direct ancestor (but not a foster parent, foster grandparent, foster grandchild, etc.)
- Stepchild of the taxpayer, but not the stepchild's descendants
- Stepparent
- Uncle or aunt (but only if related by blood, not by marriage)

At the time of a couple's marriage, the law sets up permanent legal relationships with the in-laws. These relationships continue after divorce or death. Thus, a husband may claim an exemption for his mother-in-law after his wife's death. The mother-in-law, a permanent relative, does not have to live with her son-in-law. Although a spouse qualifies as a potential exemption, the spouse's aunts, uncles, nephews, and nieces are not relatives of the taxpayer. On a joint return, however, relatives of either spouse may qualify as dependents.

Citizenship Test

A dependent usually must be a citizen of the United States. However, a resident of the United States, Canada, or Mexico for part of the tax year can also qualify as a dependent. A foreign-born relative living in another country normally will not qualify.

Support Test

For a calendar year, a taxpayer claiming a dependency exemption usually must provide more than 50% of the dependent's total support. On a joint return, the support payments from either spouse qualify. Support comprises the taxpayer's payments for a variety of items, including food, clothing, education, medical and dental care, entertainment, transportation, and lodging.

When a taxpayer furnishes a dependent's lodging, the IRS treats its fair rental value as support. Fair rental value means the rent a taxpayer could expect to receive from a stranger for the same lodging. Fair rental value covers the use of one room or a proportionate share of a house.

Capital items such as automobiles and furniture qualify as support if given to (or purchased for) a dependent. Also, support includes wedding costs paid for a dependent.

Support does not include scholarships received at educational institutions. For example, a relative receives a $4,500 college scholarship in a year in which the taxpayer provides $3,800 for the relative's support. If no other sources of support exist, the taxpayer meets the support requirements to claim a dependency exemption. Here, the law treats the taxpayer as providing 100% of the relative's support.

Usually the status and source of support funds make no difference. Social security income, school payments under the GI bill, and welfare payments qualify if the dependent uses them to buy support items. However, the definition of support excludes amounts a state pays for training and educating a handicapped or mentally ill child. In addition, payments for life insurance and funeral expenses are not support expenditures.

To determine if a taxpayer provides over 50% of a dependent's support, the taxpayer calculates the dependent's total support, which consists of three amounts:

1. Fair rental value of lodging
2. Proper share of expenses incurred or paid directly to or for the dependent
3. Share of household expenses (such as food but not lodging) unrelated to specific household members

EXAMPLE 1

Martha Friedman's elderly parents have lived with Friedman for the entire year. They share the home with Friedman, her husband, and their dependent child. Friedman's parents do not pay any rent. The fair rental value of the lodging the parents use equals $3,800 ($1,900 for each parent). Friedman's father receives nontaxable social security income of $3,250, which he spends equally on support items for himself and for his wife. Dental expenses for Friedman's mother total $2,200. Friedman pays $700 of these expenses, and Friedman's brother pays $1,500. Friedman's parents eat their meals with Friedman's family. The cost of all meals consumed in the home equals $4,670. Each parent's share comes to $934 (1/5 of $4,670). The separate and combined support for Friedman's parents for the year are as follows:

	Mother	**Father**	**Total**
Lodging (fair rental value provided by Friedman)	$1,900	$1,900	3,800
Direct expenses:			
Social security spent by parents	1,625	1,625	3,250
Dental expense paid by Friedman	700	0	700
Dental expense paid by Friedman's brother	1,500	0	1,500
Share of food provided by Friedman	934	934	1,868
Total	$6,659	$4,459	$11,118

Friedman provided support of $3,534 ($1,900 + $700 + $934) to her mother and $2,834 ($1,900 + $934) to her father. Because this constitutes over 50% of the support for each parent, she qualifies to claim an exemption for each of them.

Multiple Support Agreement

Sometimes, a group of people (e.g., children) provide for a dependent's (e.g., parent) support, and no individual provides over 50% of the support. A special rule allows one member of the group to claim the dependency exemption. The group member claiming the dependency exemption may change from year to year. To qualify for the exemption, the group member must pass the following tests:

1. Provide more than 10% of the dependent's support
2. Provide, with the other group members, more than 50% of the dependent's support
3. Meet the other dependency tests

In addition, the group must agree as to the member receiving the exemption. It is not uncommon to rotate the dependency exemption among members from year to year. Once the group reaches this agreement,

1. Group members who do not claim the exemption need to complete and deliver to the claiming member a signed statement waiving their right to claim the exemption. The statement must include: a) applicable year, b) name of person supported, and c) name, address, and social security number of person waiving the exemption.
2. The claiming member must retain this statement to support the claimed exemption. It is not filed with the tax return.
3. The claiming member completes and files Form 2120, Multiple Support Declaration, with the tax return. This form lists those eligible persons waiving their right to claim the dependent in question as an exemption.

EXAMPLE 2

Elaine lives with Logan for the entire year. Logan, Marty, Nancy, Michael, and Linda provide 100% of Elaine's support. Relationship to Elaine, support amounts, and percentages are as follows:

	Amounts	%
Logan (Elaine's son)	$ 1,000	10
Marty (Elaine's son-in-law)	2,500	25
Nancy (Elaine's stepdaughter)	2,500	25
Michael (Elaine's brother)	2,500	25
Linda (Elaine's friend)	1,500	15
Total	$10,000	100%

Qualifying group members include Marty, Nancy, and Michael. Logan and Linda do not qualify as group members. Logan does not provide more than 10% of Elaine's support. Linda fails the relative requirement. For Linda to qualify, Elaine must live with Linda the entire year. Marty, Nancy, and Michael pass the relationship requirement. Thus, Elaine does not have to live with them. Marty, Nancy, and Michael must decide which of them will receive the dependency exemption.

Information for Figure 1-3: Filled-In Form 2120

Using Form 2120, Helen B. Jones, acknowledges that she will claim the dependency exemption for Joseph R. Brown, her father. She lists her brother, Robert A. Brown, as an eligible person who is waiving his right to claim the father as a dependent.

FIGURE 1-3: Filled-In Form 2120

Form **2120** (Rev. December 2005) Department of the Treasury Internal Revenue Service	**Multiple Support Declaration** ▶ Attach to Form 1040 or Form 1040A.	OMB No. 1545-0071 Attachment Sequence No. **114**

Name(s) shown on return	Your social security number
Helen B. Jones	134 : 62 : 8736

During the calendar year ....2005.................., the eligible persons listed below each paid over 10% of the support of:

Joseph R. Brown

Name of your qualifying relative

I have a signed statement from each eligible person waiving his or her right to claim this person as a dependent for any tax year that began in the above calendar year.

Robert A. Brown	132 : 48 : 9866
Eligible person's name	Social security number
321 Valley Road, Cincinnati, OH 45209-2402	
Address (number, street, apt. no., city, state, and ZIP code)	

Eligible person's name	Social security number
Address (number, street, apt. no., city, state, and ZIP code)	

Eligible person's name	Social security number
Address (number, street, apt. no., city, state, and ZIP code)	

Eligible person's name	Social security number
Address (number, street, apt. no., city, state, and ZIP code)	

Gross Income Test

For 2005, a dependent's gross income usually must be less than the $3,200 personal exemption amount. Gross income includes gross receipts from rental property before expense deductions are taken. To compute the gross income of a business, subtract cost of goods sold from net sales and add miscellaneous income. The definition of gross income excludes a dependent's tax-exempt municipal bond interest, many social security benefits, and all Medicare benefits.

Joint Return Test

To qualify as the dependent of another taxpayer, a married dependent cannot file a joint return. However, an exception applies when the IRS treats a married couple's joint return as strictly a refund claim. Generally, a joint return is a refund claim when it meets the following conditions:

1. Neither spouse is required to file a tax return.
2. A separate return filed by either spouse would not create a tax liability.
3. The only reason for filing a return is to get a refund of all federal taxes withheld.

EXAMPLE 3

Amy Adams provides 75% of her parent's support. Her father earns $3,100 at a part-time job. Her mother receives $4,000 of interest from tax-exempt bonds. To get a refund of withheld income taxes, the father and mother file a joint return. Because their combined gross income is only $3,100, the law does not require them to file a tax return. In addition, the father would have a zero tax liability on a separate return. Consequently, Adams can claim both the mother and father as dependents.

QUALIFYING NONRELATIVES

An unrelated person may qualify as the taxpayer's dependent. To qualify, a nonrelative must meet the following dependency tests that apply to relatives.

1. Citizenship test
2. Support test
3. Gross income test
4. Joint return test

In addition, an unrelated person must live with the taxpayer the entire year. However, if the relationship between the person and the taxpayer is violation of local law, no dependency exemption is allowed.

The death or birth of these people will shorten the "entire-year" requirement to that period during which they were alive. Another exception exists for temporary absences, such as school attendance, vacations, and indefinite nursing home and hospital stays.

EXAMPLE 4

For the past two years, Nancy Sharp lived with her younger cousin Mary Blunt. In January, Sharp moved to a nursing home. The doctor informed Blunt that Sharp will stay in the nursing home indefinitely. For tax purposes, Sharp still lives with Blunt. Thus, if the other dependency tests are met, Blunt can claim an exemption for Sharp.

QUALIFYING CHILDREN

Qualifying children must meet all of the conditions listed below.

1. **Relationship.** Qualifying children fall into one of these categories:
   a. Taxpayer's natural children, step-children, adopted children, eligible foster children, or descendants of any of these children. An eligible foster child is a child placed with the taxpayer by an authorized agency or by a court order.
   b. Taxpayer's brothers and sisters, half-brothers and half-sisters, step-brothers and step-sisters, or descendants of any such relatives.
2. **Age.** Children must be under the age of 19, or under the age of 24 and full-time students. The age test does not apply to children who are permanently and totally disabled. Students need to meet the educational institution's full-time enrollment standard and attend classes during some part of each of five calendar moths of the year. The institution must have a full-time faculty and course offerings and a regular body of attending students. The child does not have to attend school at the end of the year. Though a child graduates, a taxpayer may claim an exemption if the other dependency requirements are met. A child who was a full-time day job and attends night school cannot qualify as a full-time student. Enrollment in correspondence or employment training courses will not qualify a person as a full-time student.
3. **Principal Residence.** Children must have the same principal residence as the taxpayer for more than half of the year. Temporary absences, such as those due to illness, education, business, or vacations, are disregarded.
4. **Support.** Children must not provide over half of their own support.

5. **Joint Return**. As with relatives, children may not file a joint return in situations where a tax return is required.

6. **Citizenship**. The children must be citizens of the United States, or residents of Canada or Mexico. However, an exception exists for foreign born children adopted by U.S. citizens living abroad. Such children qualify as dependents if they live with the taxpayer the entire year.

Special Note. Qualifying children are not subject to the "gross income test" and the "over half support test" that apply to qualifying relatives. Also, children who are not "qualifying children" because of not meeting one of the requirements, may still qualify as dependents under the "qualifying relative" rules.

Dependency Exemption for Child of Divorced or Separated Parents

Another situation arises when the parents of the children are divorced or separated. One of the parents can claim an exemption for their child if together they have custody of the child more than 50% of the year. The law gives the exemption to the parent with the longer actual custody (**custodial parent**). However, the custodial parent may give the exemption to the noncustodial parent. Here, the custodial parent completes Form 8332 (Figure 1-4) and delivers it to the noncustodial parent. In place of Form 8332, the custodial parent may deliver a signed and dated release statement to the noncustodial parent. The release document must state that the custodial parent (signing parent) will not claim the exemption. The release may cover either one or several years. For each year affected, the noncustodial parent must attach the release statement to Form 1040 of Form 1040A.

In situations where multiple taxpayers qualify to claim a child (e.g., the father, mother, grandfather, and grandmother), the custodial parent receives the exemption. If this solution does not resolve the problem (e.g., separate returns where both parents live together the entire year in the grandparents' home), the exemption goes to the parent with the highest AGI. If the parents do not claim the child, the child is deemed the dependent of the qualified taxpayer (e.g., the grandmother) with the highest AGI.

The "qualifying child" requirements are new for 2005. Taxpayers also use these rules to determine their eligibility for:

1. Head of household status
2. Earned income credit
3. Child tax credit
4. Child and dependent care credit

Information for Figure 1-4: Filled-In Form 8332

Using Form 8332, Anthony B. Black, the custodial parent, agrees not to claim an exemption for Janet A. Black, his daughter. The exemption belongs to Joyce C. Redding (mother), who files her tax return and Form 8332 with the IRS.

The parent who has custody of the child prepares Form 8332. That form contains two parts. The top part covers the current year, and the bottom part covers future years.

FIGURE 1-4:   Filled-In Form 8332

Form **8332** (Rev. December 2003) Department of the Treasury Internal Revenue Service	**Release of Claim to Exemption for Child of Divorced or Separated Parents** ▶ **Attach** to noncustodial parent's return **each year** exemption is claimed.	OMB No. 1545-0915

Name of noncustodial parent claiming exemption
Joyce C. Redding

Noncustodial parent's social security number (SSN) ▶ 693 : 24 : 6802

Attachment Sequence No. **115**

Part I   Release of Claim to Exemption for Current Year

I agree not to claim an exemption for Janet A. Black
Name(s) of child (or children)

for the tax year 20 05 .

Anthony B. Black
Signature of custodial parent releasing claim to exemption

280 : 64 : 2396
Custodial parent's SSN

2-5-06
Date

Note: *If you choose not to claim an exemption for this child (or children) for future tax years, also complete Part II.*

Part II   Release of Claim to Exemption for Future Years (If completed, see **Noncustodial parent** below.)

I agree not to claim an exemption for
Name(s) of child (or children)

for the tax year(s)
(Specify. See instructions.)

Signature of custodial parent releasing claim to exemption

Custodial parent's SSN

Date

TAX BASE FORMULA—ANOTHER VIEW

Figure 1-5 provides another view of the tax base formula. It should enhance the meaning of new tax terms and concepts.

FIGURE 1-5:   Computation of 2005 Taxable Income

Income from all sources:		
Rent from apartment, $2,400; Salary, $16,200; Dividends on common stock, $720; Interest on savings, $80; Municipal bond interest, $30		$19,430
Gross income exclusions:		
Municipal bond interest, $30		(30)
Gross income inclusions:		
Rent from apartment, $2,400; Salary, $16,200; Dividends on common stock, $720; Interest on savings, $80		$19,400
Deductions for AGI:		
Expenses of apartment (rental property)		(1,400)
AGI		$18,000
Deductions from AGI:		
Standard deduction (single person)	$5,000	
Exemptions (one personal exemption)	3,200	(8,200)
Taxable Income:		
AGI, $18,000; less deductions from AGI ($8,200)		$ 9,800

FILING STATUS

As previously stated, any taxpayer who files a return falls into one of five filing status groups. In some cases, filing status determines which tax return the taxpayer must file. The filing status also determines the standard deduction amount used in computing taxable income and the tax rate schedule or table used in calculating the tax liability.

Married taxpayers generally have two filing options: married filing jointly with their spouse or married filing separately. The filing statuses available to unmarried taxpayers include surviving spouse, head of household, and single. Both married filing jointly and surviving spouse share the most favorable tax rates, followed by head of household and then single. The least favorable of the tax rates apply to taxpayers who file married filing separately. Whenever possible, taxpayers would like to qualify for the most favorable tax rate possible for their marital status.

Married Filing a Joint Return

For tax purposes, a taxpayer's marital status is determined on the last day of the tax year. Thus, a taxpayer who is married on the last day of the tax year may file a joint return with his or her spouse. Likewise, a taxpayer who receives a legal divorce or separation before the end of the year may not file a joint return. However, when the divorce or separation has not been finalized at year-end, the couple may file a joint return.

A husband and wife can file a joint return even if only one has income. If both have income, they need to use the same tax year to file jointly. A husband and wife must both sign a jointly filed tax return. Usually, each spouse is liable for the entire tax liability. Thus, the law may enforce the collection of any tax liability against either spouse. This liability continues after a divorce.

When an asset is jointly owned, it can be seized to settle the debt of either owner.

Year of Death

Marital status is also determined at the date of death in the event that one spouse dies. The tax law generally requires a final income tax return for a decedent. The due date for this final return is the same date that would apply if the deceased were still living.

The final return and any other return(s) still due would be filed by the executor, administrator, legal representative, or survivor. A widow(er) may file a joint return with the decedent. When the widow(er) files a joint return, two personal exemptions are allowed in the year of death.

Special reporting rules apply if the spouse dies in 2005 or dies in 2006 before the 2005 return is filed. The survivor should enter the word *deceased,* the name of the deceased spouse, and the date of death across the top of the return. In the signature space, the survivor should enter *filing as surviving spouse.* When someone other than the widow(er) is the personal representative of the deceased, that person's signature should appear in the deceased's signature line with the words *personal representative.*

If a widowed person remarries before the end of the year, the widow(er) may file a joint return with the new spouse. A remarried widow(er) cannot file a joint return with the deceased spouse even if the survivor's new spouse files separately.

Technical assistance should be obtained when affairs of a decedent are complex. Assistance is especially helpful when the problems relate to the determination of income and expenses properly reported on the taxpayer's final return. These items must be separated from those properly recognized after the date of death and are not included on the final return. For example, a cash-basis taxpayer includes in income only those amounts actually or constructively received as of the date of death. Income received after death is attributable to the beneficiary of the decedent's property.

Married Filing a Separate Return

When a husband and a wife have separate incomes, they may save money by filing separate returns. Taxpayers should compute their tax liabilities using both the joint and separate return statuses to see which one yields the least tax liability.

On rare occasion, a taxpayer may list a spouse as an exemption on a separate return. For the taxpayer to do so, the spouse cannot have any gross income or qualify as a dependent of another taxpayer. Also, the spouse cannot file a separate return. The taxpayer reports the full name and social security number of the spouse on the return.

Several factors may work against filing separate returns. Several tax credits, like the child and dependent care credit or the earned income credit, are not available to taxpayers who file married filing separately. If spouses live together at any time in the tax year and file separately, neither may claim an elderly or disabled person credit.

Filing Separate Returns in Community Property States

The laws of the state of the taxpayer's residence control whether property is considered community property or separate property. Classification of expenses as community or separate usually follows the classification of the income that caused their creation. If a taxpayer and spouse live in the same community property state and itemize deductions, they usually divide equally expenses paid from joint funds.

Election to File Joint or Separate Return

An election to file a joint or separate return for one year does not carry over to future years. Each year stands alone. After a couple files a joint return, they cannot change to separate returns after the due date of the tax return. However, spouses who file separately may change to a joint return even after the due date passes. This change must be made within three years of the due date of the tax return.

Surviving Spouse (Qualifying Widow[er] with Dependent Child)

For two tax years following the year of a spouse's death, special status as a "surviving spouse" may apply. A taxpayer with this status uses the "married filing jointly" tax rates to compute the tax liability. This taxpayer also uses the married filing jointly basic and additional standard deduction amounts. For phasing down exemptions, surviving spouse status uses the "married filing jointly" threshold. It is important to note that even though surviving spouses use the joint return tax rates and other amounts they do not file "joint returns." Surviving spouse status is not available to a spouse who remarries.

The Code classifies a **surviving spouse** as a qualifying widow(er) with a dependent son or daughter. Frequently, taxpayers confuse the special surviving spouse status with the common definition of surviving spouse (the spouse whose life continues after the other spouse dies). A surviving spouse under the common definition may or may not qualify for the special status. To qualify for the surviving spouse status for tax purposes, a widow(er) must:

1. Qualify to file a joint return with the deceased spouse in the year of death,
2. Furnish over 50% of the household maintenance costs where the widow(er) and a dependent son or daughter child live for the entire year. This dependent may be the taxpayer's qualifying foster, adopted, natural, or stepchild, and
3. Not remarry before the end of the year.

Temporary absences from the household do not affect the filing status of a surviving spouse. Thus, a son or daughter who attends a boarding school and returns home for vacation periods remains a member of the surviving spouse's household. Hospital stays receive the same treatment.

Tax filers with special surviving spouse status cannot use Form 1040EZ. They instead use Form 1040A or Form 1040.

Head of Household (HOH)

Tax rates for taxpayers filing as HOH are higher than for those who file married filing jointly. However, HOH rates fall below those for single persons. Head of household status usually applies to unmarried taxpayers.

To qualify for HOH status, the taxpayer must furnish over half the cost of maintaining a household for a "qualifying child" (see definition presented earlier) or a dependent relative. Generally these people must live with the taxpayer for more than half of the year.

1. A "qualifying child" who is married must meet the dependency tests for a relative (see dependency tests for relatives presented earlier).

2. Other children who do not meet the definition of a "qualifying child" (e.g., a child age 25) must also meet the dependency tests for a relative.

3. When a dependent child is needed to obtain HOH status, custodial parents do not lose this status when they waive their right to claim the child's dependency exemption.

4. Relatives who qualify as a dependent of the taxpayer include: parent, grandparent, brother, sister, brother-in-law, stepsister, mother-in-law, aunt, nephew, and the like.

5. A dependent parent need not live with the taxpayer. However, the taxpayer must provide over 50% of the parent's household costs for the year.

6. HOH status is not available if the dependency exemption is obtained through a multiple support agreement.

Maintaining a household means that the taxpayer pays more than 50% of the household costs for the year, which usually cover payments for the mutual benefit of household occupants. These costs include payments for food, telephone, water, fuel, electricity, and repairs. Household maintenance costs do not include the value of services supplied by the taxpayer or household members.

Abandoned Spouses (Married Persons Who Live Apart)

Married persons not living with their spouses during the last six months of the year may qualify as abandoned spouses. For tax purposes, abandoned spouses are treated as not married and thus can qualify for head of household (HOH) filing status. To qualify for abandoned spouse treatment, the taxpayer and spouse need to meet the following tests.

1. The taxpayer does not file a joint return.

2. For more than six months of the year, the taxpayer lives with a son or daughter who is a natural, step-, adopted, or qualifying foster child.

3. The taxpayer pays more than 50% of the home's maintenance cost for the tax year.

4. At least one child qualifies as a dependent of the taxpayer. This requirement does not apply if the taxpayer meets the requirements to claim the exemption but, by written agreement, gives it to the noncustodial parent.

5. The taxpayer's spouse did not live with the taxpayer at any time during the last six months of the tax year.

Single Taxpayer

An unmarried person who does not qualify to file as surviving spouse or as head of household must file as a single taxpayer. A person separated by a final divorce decree or separate maintenance agreement files as a single taxpayer unless head of household filing status applies. Likewise, a widow(er) files as a single taxpayer unless the requirements to file as a surviving spouse or as head of household are met.

FILING REQUIREMENTS FOR INDIVIDUALS

Under our self-reporting tax system, a taxpayer who meets certain conditions must file a tax return. Current filing requirements depend primarily on

1. Net earnings from self-employment, or
2. Gross income and filing status.

The filing requirements apply to all minors and adults, single and married, U.S. citizens and resident aliens. These requirements can apply to nonresident aliens married to U.S. citizens. In addition, the filing requirements apply to resident aliens who subject their worldwide incomes to U.S. taxes by filing joint returns. Nonresident aliens who earn income in the U.S. must file income tax returns.

Self-Employment Income Test

A self-employed person files a tax return when net earnings from the self-employment is at least $400. Note that net earnings, not gross income, determines when a self-employed person files a return.

Gross Income Test

When gross income reaches a specified level, a person must file a tax return. Basically, gross income includes a person's total income from all sources. It does not include a taxpayer's return of capital and income specifically exempt from taxation by proper authority (Chapters 3 and 4).

Generally, for non-self-employed individuals, the gross income filing requirements represent a combination of the exemption amount and the standard deduction available for the taxpayer and spouse. Filing requirements normally include the additional standard deduction available for attaining age 65. Usually, the requirements do not take blindness into consideration. Nor do they consider dependency exemptions. Thus, for marrieds filing jointly, where one spouse is 65 and the other is blind, the filing requirement is $17,400. This represents a combination of the exemption amount, $6,400 (2 × $3,200); the basic standard deduction, $10,000; and the additional standard deduction for age 65, $1,000. Blindness is not a factor.

However, to determine whether a dependent must file, note that the additional standard deductions for both age and blindness increase the filing requirement threshold. For example, the filing requirement for a blind, 65-year-old, single dependent with no earned income is $3,300. This amount includes the basic standard deduction ($800) and the extra standard deductions for both age ($1,250) and blindness ($1,250). Because the personal exemption for a dependent is zero, it does not increase the filing requirement. Figure 1-6 illustrates the filing requirements for individuals.

FIGURE 1-6: Who Must File a 2005 Return

U.S. citizens and resident aliens must file 2005 tax returns if their gross income amounts equal or exceed the following:

1.	Single	$ 8,200
	65 or over	9,450
2.	Married filing jointly	16,400
	One 65 or over	17,400
	Both 65 or over	18,400
3.	Married filing separately	3,200
4.	Head of household	10,500
	65 or over	11,750
5.	Surviving spouse	13,200
	65 or over	14,200

A **single dependent** with "unearned income" (investment income) files when gross income exceeds the larger of (1) $800 or (2) earned income (up to $4,750) plus $250. Any "additional standard deductions" for age and blindness that apply increase the filing requirement. When there is no unearned income, a taxpayer files when gross income exceeds $5,000 plus any additional standard deductions.

A **married dependent** (of another taxpayer) files when earned income exceeds $5,000. When unearned income is present, a taxpayer files when gross income exceeds the greater of (1) $800 or (2) earned income (up to $4,750) plus $250. In both situations, the filing requirement threshold rises for the additional standard deductions for both age and blindness. A married dependent whose spouse files separately and itemizes deductions must file when gross income is $5 or more.

The following persons must file regardless of gross income:

1. A person with $400 of net earnings from self-employment,
2. A person receiving advanced earned income credit payments from his or her employer, and
3. A person receiving tips from which social security tax was not withheld.

EXAMPLE 5

John Jones works part time as a waiter at a local restaurant. Jones receives tips from customers that he does not report to his employer for income tax withholding purposes. Because Jones owes social security and Medicare taxes on these tips, he files a return and pays the tax.

TAX YEAR

Although most individuals use the calendar year for tax reporting, a few use a fiscal year. Some corporations and partnerships use a fiscal year. A **fiscal year** consists of any twelve-month period that ends on the last day of a calendar month other than December. Unless otherwise stated, this book assumes that all taxpayers use the calendar year.

Tax returns for individuals are due on or before the fifteenth day of the fourth month following the close of the tax year. For calendar year taxpayers, this is normally April 15 of the following year (corporate returns are due one month earlier). An exception occurs when the due date falls on Saturday, Sunday, or a legal holiday. In these situations, the filing date becomes the next business day. A taxpayer files a timely return when the return is postmarked on or before the due date and it is properly addressed with the correct amount of postage.

TAXPAYER RESPONSIBILITIES

Under our self-reporting tax system, the law requires taxpayers to compute their tax liabilities, file proper returns on time, and pay the taxes when due. Taxpayers who do not meet these responsibilities face possible fines, penalties, and imprisonment. In addition, the IRS charges them interest on unpaid taxes. The IRS wants taxpayers to file their returns with the proper regional service centers.

Packaged filing materials sent to taxpayers at return time usually contain special mailing envelopes. The IRS encourages the use of these envelopes for mailing of completed returns. If the envelopes bear special codes, their use may speed return processing and reduce related costs. Taxpayers who expect to receive refunds should use the mailing envelopes when they are marked with special codes.

Taxpayers should develop and maintain organized tax record systems. In addition, they should carefully review their returns and correct any preparation errors before mailing their returns to the IRS.

Maintain Records

The taxpayer needs to keep adequate records to support all return items. The retention period usually ends six years after a return's due date (or filing date if later). However, the taxpayer should keep records showing the cost of property (home) longer. A photocopy of the return and tax calculations should also be retained. Last year's return and calculations can serve as a checklist for next year's return.

RECORD KEEPING—HOW LONG?

Keep records for general tax items for seven years.

- The normal closing date for a tax year occurs three years after the later of the return's due date or the filing date. If a taxpayer files a return for the year 20x0 before its due date (April 15, 20x1), tax year 20x0 closes with April 15, 20x4.

- The closing date for inadvertent omission of more than 25% of gross income reported on a return occurs six years after the later of the return's due date or the filing date. If a taxpayer files a return for the year 20x0 before its due date (April 15, 20x1), and the inadvertent omission rule for gross income applies, tax year 20x0 closes with April 15, 20x7.

- Keep general tax records for seven years after the year for which tax return is filed as support for IRS audit queries.

Keep records on *all* property for as long as it is owned plus seven years.

• Investment in depreciable property decreases yearly until property is fully depreciated. Property disposals may take place after property is fully depreciated. Taxpayers must report gain (and sometimes loss) on disposal of *all* property items. Keep *all* property records for the later of the last open tax year or the year of property disposal, plus seven years, as support for IRS audit queries.

Minimize Errors

Honesty and care in preparing returns will help reduce the chances of controversy. Taxpayers should follow these suggestions:

1. Get appropriate forms, schedules, and instructions. The IRS normally mails packages of forms, schedules, and instructions to last year's tax filers. A taxpayer who does not receive these items should get the materials from the local IRS office, the proper IRS regional service center, or from the IRS web page. The instructions contain tollfree telephone ordering numbers.
2. Study the instructions and assemble data before preparing the return.
3. Enter data on a tax organizer (if available).
4. Review the IRS identification label for correct facts. Supply all data. Check all calculations. Look for minor omissions due to carelessness or hasty processing.

STATUTORY LIMIT FOR ASSESSING ADDITIONAL TAXES

Normal Limit
Three years after the later of the return's due date or the filing date

Income Omissions
Six years after the later of the return's due date or the filing date for taxpayer's inadvertent omission of more than 25% of gross income reported on return

Fraudulent Return
Tax year never closes

PROPERTY DISPOSALS

Earlier, this chapter stated that gross income includes gains from dealings in property. It also stated that losses from the sale or exchange of certain property can qualify as deductions for AGI. The following overview shows how these transactions mesh with previously presented concepts and with the tax calculation process.

Uses of Property

Taxpayers hold property for personal-use, for investment (income-producing), and for business purposes. The Code taxes most gains from property disposals. However, some disposals fall under the nontaxable sale or exchange rules (Chapter 10).

A taxpayer who disposes of personal-use property (e.g., automobile, personal residence, snowblower) at a loss cannot deduct it. An exception exists for property destroyed by a casualty or taken by theft (Chapter 5). A sale of business or investment property at a loss generally creates a tax deduction for the seller. If the property is sold to a related party, however, the taxpayer cannot deduct the loss.

Capital Assets

Most property items owned by individuals fall under the broad grouping known as capital assets. Basically, the Code defines capital assets as all property except

1. Property held for resale (inventory),
2. Real and depreciable property used in a trade or business,
3. Accounts receivable acquired in normal business operations, and
4. Artistic works created by the taxpayer.

Thus, with few exceptions, capital assets include all assets not identified on the preceding list.

Rate of Tax on Capital Gains

Ordinary income (e.g., salary and wages) may be taxed at 10%, 15%, 25%, 28%, 33%, or 35% depending on the level of income. However, on sales of capital assets, a maximum tax rate of 15% (5% for people in the 10% or 15% tax bracket) may apply. Generally, people must hold capital assets over 12 months to receive the special 15% (5%) tax rate. The sale of capital assets held for 12 months or less produces short-term capital gain or loss. Short-term gains do not receive the lower, more favorable tax rates. Usually, the holding period for property starts the day after a taxpayer gets it. Thus, the purchase date belongs to the seller.

To receive the more favorable tax rates, capital gains must exceed capital losses. If losses exceed gains, an individual taxpayer can deduct up to $3,000 as a deduction "for AGI." Any remaining loss is deductible in future years. Computing the net capital gain or loss may require an involved computation. Chapter 11 provides in-depth coverage of capital gains and losses.

EXAMPLE 6

Mary Martin sold stock held for investment. The result was a $500 short-term capital loss. She also had a $2,000 gain from the sale of stock held for 24 months. Thus, she had a net gain of $1,500. A maximum rate of 15% applies to this gain because the stock was held for over 12 months.

EXAMPLE 7

Frank Wanto sells stock that results in a short-term capital loss of $6,000. He also sells stock held for 16 months at a gain of $2,000. The net result is a loss of $4,000. He deducts $3,000 as a deduction for AGI and the other $1,000 is available as a deduction next year.

REDUCING THE TAX BITE

A taxpayer has the right to use all legal means to avoid or postpone a tax. Through proper tax planning, the taxpayer may reduce the tax bite. As a basic goal, taxpayers should try to reduce current and future taxes. In addition, it is generally a good idea to defer taxes to future years if possible. Although personal aims can alter these goals, taxpayers should follow acceptable, proven principles when setting up tax plans.

TAX PLANNING PRINCIPLES

1. Acquire working knowledge of tax laws.
2. Plan transactions in advance to reduce taxes.
3. Maximize unrealized income.
4. Keep good records.

Acquire Working Knowledge of Tax Laws

The tax laws contain an overwhelming number of provisions covering a multitude of personal, business, and investment situations. The average taxpayer should not expect to develop even a general familiarity with all aspects of these laws. However, the "game of life" necessarily involves taxation, and it is difficult to play the game without a working knowledge of the basic rules. Taxpayers should focus on those laws that impact their particular personal and business environments. Developing a working knowledge of these rules is most beneficial in reducing current and future taxes. It will improve tax problem recognition skills. It will also lead to improved record keeping and reduced time for tax return preparation. For taxpayers who use computer tax software, knowledge of the tax laws will provide some assurance that the software produces proper results.

Although taxpayers may use tax advisers to prepare their returns, knowledge of the tax laws can save money. If a taxpayer uses an adviser, knowledge of the tax laws should help reduce the adviser's fee or keep it low. Most advisers base their fees on a return's complexity and the preparation time. For a knowledgeable taxpayer, the adviser will not have to charge for explaining simple transactions. Although advisers can prepare tax plans, they charge fees for their time. If the taxpayer wastes the adviser's time with general conversation, the taxpayer should expect a bill for this time. To the tax adviser, time is money.

Plan Transactions in Advance to Reduce Taxes

Generally, the way the law taxes a completed event or transaction is fairly clear. Consequently, it is important for taxpayers to plan their transactions in advance. Once an action is taken, the tax consequences are usually locked in. Proper planning of the action, however, can produce desirable tax results.

To facilitate planning, taxpayers should become familiar with methods that will

1. Accelerate or postpone the recognition of revenue.
2. Accelerate or postpone the recognition of expenses.

Taxpayers also need to be aware of those available deductions and tax credits that will benefit their particular situations.

A taxpayer whose itemized deductions approximate his or her standard deduction amount can use the bunching process, which results in a slowdown or a speedup of itemized deduction payments. By using the bunching process, the taxpayer influences the year in which an itemized deduction falls. Taxpayers who use this process itemize their deductions in one year and take the standard deduction in the next. Most taxpayers who use bunching find charitable contributions, medical expenses, property taxes, and state income taxes easiest to control.

Usually, taxpayers do not bunch their personal and dependency exemptions. However, taxpayers with dependents under the multiple support rules can use the bunching process. Also, couples might arrange their marriage dates and the dates they have children (December or January) to reduce the tax bite. By controlling the amount they pay to support other taxpayers, they can control the numbers of claimable dependency exemptions. Finally, to some degree, taxpayers can control their tax credits. Usually, they should claim their credits as early as possible.

Although tax planning is advantageous for everyone, the law restricts the advantages for the average employed person. Because the great majority of such people use the standard deduction, tax planning has its limits. Most tax benefits, unfortunately, favor business owners. People who have their own businesses stand to gain the most through tax planning. Those who are not business owners lose out. However, current trends show an increasing number of people starting their own businesses. Consequently, a greater number of taxpayers will benefit from comprehensive tax planning.

For business owners, greater deduction possibilities exist. They can convert many itemized deductions and nondeductible items into deductions from gross income. Knowledge of these situations is highly beneficial.

Timing the recognition of revenues and expenses is more easily done in a business setting. For example, taxpayers in service businesses who use the cash method of accounting can control end-of-year income. They might increase income by accelerating service billings or postpone it by delaying them. Other taxpayers who use the cash method of accounting (most persons) can control end-of-year gains and losses by advancing or delaying the closing dates in property transactions. Taxpayers who control transaction timing can adjust their income and deductions to take full advantage of the tax laws.

As indicated previously, taxpayers can reduce their taxes by careful planning. Some tax plans cover a short-term period, while others cover a long-term period. A short-term plan tries to reduce taxes over the next few years; a long-term plan tries to reduce them over a longer time span. Long-term plans usually involve complex techniques beyond the scope of this book. They include selecting retirement plans and developing estate, gift, and trust strategies. A taxpayer with stable income, deductions, exemptions, and credits usually uses a one-to-three-year tax plan. When uncertainty exists, the taxpayer should consider liberal, conservative, and middle-of-the-road assumptions. In all cases, the plan should be updated annually.

Maximize Unrealized Income

Some taxpayers want more after-tax dollars so they can spend it on consumable items. Others prefer to accumulate wealth. For those who want to accumulate wealth, the principle of maximizing unrealized income is important. Taxpayers can generally accumulate more wealth by investing in assets that produce income that is not currently taxable. Such income can then compound without being taxed each year.

Keep Good Records

To do a good job of tax planning, a taxpayer needs a good record-keeping system, which allows easy access to the nature, purposes, and amounts of old transactions. The underlying files should contain invoices, canceled notes or checks, payment receipts, property titles, and copies of old tax returns. An orderly indexing system helps the taxpayer find stored documents. Finally, a good record-keeping system helps prevent a taxpayer from overlooking deductions at tax return time.

WATCH FOR TAX OPPORTUNITIES

As taxpayers learn more about the tax laws, they can spot planning opportunities more quickly. Remember the basic goal: reduce current and future taxes. As you study the book, keep this goal in mind and watch for tax-reducing suggestions.

QUESTIONS AND PROBLEMS

1. **Tax Laws.**

   a. Which amendment to the Constitution gave Congress the power to levy and collect income taxes? What was the origination date of our current income tax system?

   b. List several objectives of our income tax system.

   c. Most individual taxpayers use the calendar year for reporting their taxable income. However, a few use the fiscal year. What is a fiscal year?

   d. Is the basic tax calculation formula the same for most taxpayers? What is the difference between the basic formula and the expanded calculation formula for individuals?

   e. The Internal Revenue Code lists a number of different gross income sources. When a taxpayer receives something that is not one of the listed items, is it exempt from tax? Explain your answer.

2. **Tax Laws.** Susan Klammer engages a local tax professional to prepare her tax return each year. She sees no reason to learn more about the tax laws. At tax return time every year, all she wants to know is the fastest route to her tax preparer's office. After she files her return each year, she just wants to forget the whole thing. Explain why it would be to Klammer's advantage to know about the tax laws.

3. **Itemized Deductions.** Itemized deductions fall into one of seven groups. Two of the groups are (1) job expenses and most other miscellaneous itemized deductions and (2) other miscellaneous deductions. What are the other five groups?

4. **Standard or Itemized Deductions.**

   a. Clarence Archer is eligible to claim itemized deductions. Explain how itemized deductions relate to the determination of taxable income.

   b. Who qualifies for the additional standard deduction? What additional amount is available?

5. **Standard Deduction.** What standard deduction is available to the following taxpayers?

   a. Bryce, age 20, is a full-time student and a dependent of his parents. Bryce has interest income of $320 and wages from a part-time job of $3,800.

   b. If Bryce, in Part a., had $5,200 of wages, what would be his standard deduction?

   c. Heather, age 66, is married and files a separate return. Her husband also uses the standard deduction on his return.

d. Juliet, age 19, is blind and a dependent of her parents. Her only income is $5,200 of interest.

[handwritten calculations:]
5200   5450   5000
280   800   1250
5450   5450 $6250
          5000

6. **Exemptions.** Henry and Margaret were married on December 28. Henry, age 22 and a full-time student, had no gross income during the year. He lived with his parents and was supported by them prior to his marriage. Margaret's gross salary for the year was $35,000.

a. Under what circumstances is Margaret entitled to claim an exemption for Henry?

[handwritten:] He is not her dependent if they file joint return.

b. Under what circumstances are Henry's parents entitled to claim an exemption for him?

[handwritten:] He had no gross income & he qualifies as their dependent — if file seperately.

7. **Exemptions.** How many exemptions can be claimed on a joint income tax return by an employed taxpayer who is married and has two unmarried children? One child, a daughter age 17, has no income. The other child, a son age 22, is a part-time college student. The son earned $3,400 during the year. The taxpayer provides over half of each child's support. The taxpayer's spouse is not employed.

[handwritten margin note:] 2nd child → age 22 → school status PT → earning more than deduction

[handwritten:] 4

8. **Exemptions.** Kevin Kirby, age 67 and blind, is married to Susan Kirby, age 56 with good vision. They have a divorced daughter, age 37, who, along with her 18-year-old son, is living with them. The Kirbys provided more than half the support of their daughter and her son. The daughter has earned wages of $4,800, and her son, who is a part-time college student, has earned wages of $3,600. How many exemptions can the Kirbys claim on their 2005 tax return? Explain.

[handwritten:] 6 — Kevin, Susan, divorced daughter & grandson
Kevin over age 65 & blind
Provided +50% of support for daughter & grandson, who are both qualified dependents

9. **Exemptions.** Vera and Billy Cohen were divorced during the year. Vera was awarded custody of the children, George, age 6, and Jean, age 9. There was no agreement about who would receive the dependency exemptions for the children. All support for the children is provided by Billy.

a. Who is to receive the dependency exemptions?

Vera

b. Might the other parent receive the exemptions under certain conditions? Explain.

Yes if a form 8332, Release of Claim to Exemption for Child of Divorced or Seperated Parents is signed by Vera.

10. **Exemptions.**

a. If Shirley Brown has a child born at 10 P.M. on December 31 of the taxable year, can she claim a full exemption for this child for the year without proration?

Yes

b. If a qualifying dependent of a taxpayer dies on January 4 of the taxable year, may the taxpayer claim a full exemption for the dependent for the year without proration?

No

c. If Mark Freeze's divorce decree is finalized before the end of the taxable year, can he claim a full exemption for his spouse for the part of the year during which he was married? Explain. *No, he must file for his martial status at year end.*

11. **Exemptions.**

a. What is the amount of each exemption in 2005?

b. How does adjusted gross income affect the amount allowed for exemptions?

12. **Dependents.** Indicate by inserting an *X* in the proper column which of the following persons may qualify as dependents. Assume the listed person is not a member of the taxpayer's household.

Dependent		Yes	No
a.	Taxpayer's cousin		X
b.	Taxpayer's father	X	
c.	Taxpayer's foster mother		X
d.	Taxpayer's dependent friend	X	
e.	Taxpayer's spouse's brother	X	
f.	Taxpayer's foster grandparent		X
g.	Taxpayer's half brother	X	
h.	Taxpayer's nephew by blood	X	
i.	Taxpayer's spouse —not concerned dependent	X	
j.	Taxpayer's uncle (on deceased spouse's side)		X
k.	Taxpayer's daughter's husband	X	
l.	Taxpayer's grandfather	X	
m.	Taxpayer's mother-in-law (taxpayer's spouse deceased)	X	

13. **Filing Status.** Using the following data, indicate each taxpayer's proper filing status for the current year.

a. Unmarried; divorced last year; no dependents ___single___

b. Married; spouse has been properly claimed as a dependent on another taxpayer's return ___married filing seperately___

c. Married on December 31, no dependents ___married filing jointly___

d. Widower; spouse died last year; has a dependent 6-year-old child; has not remarried ___Surviving spouse___

e. Married; separated from spouse by a separate maintenance decree; has no dependents ___Married filing seperately___ *single*

f. Married; maintains a household for more than six months of the year for self and an adopted 4-year-old child who qualifies as a dependent; spouse left home on February 15 of current year and has not been seen since ___HOH___

g. Unmarried; maintains a principal residence for entire year for self and an 8-year-old grandchild who is a dependent of the taxpayer ___HOH___

h. Married; has $15,000 of gross income; spouse has filed a separate return ___MFS___

i. Widower; spouse died January 16 last year; has not remarried; has a parent who lives alone; maintained parent's home for the entire year; parent qualifies as a dependent ___Surviving spouse___ *HOH (parents)*

14. **Filing Status.** If Graciela Autry provides 52% of the household costs for her widowed mother during the year and claims her as a dependent, can she file a return as a HOH if her mother lives alone? Explain the reason behind your answer.

15. **Tax Years.** The date a tax year closes is an important date from a taxpayer's point of view because it stops the Internal Revenue Service from assessing a tax deficiency on a closed tax year. It is an important date from the government's point of view because it stops a taxpayer from making a refund claim on a closed tax year.

   a. If a taxpayer files her tax return for 2005 on April 1, 2006, when does her 2005 tax year close under the normal closing rule? In your answer, provide a specific closing date and time.

   b. If a taxpayer inadvertently omits too much gross income from his or her income tax return, the normal closing of a tax year is extended by three years. What percentage of the taxpayer's gross income must be omitted from his or her income tax return in order for the closing year to be extended? As part of your answer, indicate exactly how this percentage is applied.

   c. Joe Blystone, age 20 and single, graduated from college last year. He has not been able to find a full-time job. For the current year, Blystone had gross income from a part-time job of $5,000. He had no other income sources. Although he used some of his earned income for support items, the majority of his support came from his parents. Blystone is not required to file a return for the current year. Should he file a return? Why or why not?

16. **Filing Requirements.**

   a. Andy Fryer, age 15, is claimed as a dependent on his parents' tax return. He earned $392 from his paper route and other after-school jobs. Fryer deposited most of his earnings in a savings account at the local bank. The bank notified him that his interest income was $400. Must Fryer file an income tax return for 2005? Provide a full explanation for your answer, including how his threshold (beginning or minimum amount) filing requirement is calculated.

b. Marla Tierney, age 25, is claimed as a dependent on her parents' tax return. She is one of several full-time students at Milton College who received a $5,000 tax-free academic scholarship. Also, her bank informed her that she has interest income of $125. Tierney also earned $525 from her work as a self-employed, independent living consultant. Her expenses in connection with this work were $75. Must Tierney file an income tax return for 2005? Provide a full explanation for your answer, including how her threshold filing requirement is calculated.

17. Capital Assets.

a. In the tax laws, a capital asset is defined in terms of what it is not. What broad groups of assets are not capital assets?

b. Explain the general holding period rules for capital assets, and indicate the time an asset must be held to receive a maximum tax rate of 15% (5%).

18. Capital Gains.

a. Jerry Long sold some stock certificates held for investment during the year. Describe how the following sales would be treated.

Stock	Purchase Date	Sale Date	Cost	Selling Price	
ABC	1-5-05	11-5-05	$10,000	$ 8,000	− 2000
XYZ	8-9-00	9-8-05	6,000	10,500	+4500

net gain +2500

tax @ LTCG rate of 15%

b. If the selling price of the stock Long sold on 11-5-05 were $5,000 (instead of $8,000), how would this affect his tax return?

(Could deduct $3000 from AGI)

net loss $(5000)

19. **Tax Planning.**

    a. Define the concept of tax planning and distinguish between short-term and long-term tax planning.

    b. What is the primary reason for tax planning?

    c. Identify three tax-planning principles that will help a taxpayer achieve a tax-planning objective.

    d. Under what circumstances should a taxpayer plan to control the timing of payments that are deductible as itemized deductions?

20. **Internet Problem: Downloading and Completing Form 2120.**

    Go to the IRS Web site, download Form 2120, and complete the form manually using the following information:

    Helen Baker (SSN 123-45-6789) has acknowledged in writing that Jim Moon (SSN 987-65-4321), her brother, will take the dependency exemption in 2005 for Mary C. Moon, their mother.

    Jim's address: 420 Dogwood Lane, Marlborough, NH 03455.

    Helen's address: 5283 West Main Street, Keene, NH 03431.

    See Appendix A for instructions on use of the IRS Web site.

2

Tax Determination, Payments, and Reporting Procedures

CHAPTER CONTENTS

■■ CHAPTER OVERVIEW

*C*hapter 1 presented the tax structure and the process for determining taxable income. Chapter 2 shows how individual taxpayers compute the amount of their tax liability. It reviews the role of tax payments and personal tax credits in determining the final amount due to or from the government. The chapter illustrates Form W-2, Form 1040EZ, Form 1040A, and Form 4868, Application for Automatic Extension of Time to File U.S. Individual Tax Return.

INDIVIDUAL INCOME TAX RATES

The Code dictates the tax rates for individual taxpayers. It currently specifies the use of a progressive rate structure—the higher the income, the higher the marginal tax rate that applies. The rates currently in use are 10%, 15%, 25%, 28%, 33%, and 35%. The IRS presents these rates to taxpayers as **Tax Rate Schedules** and a **Tax Table.** Understanding their structure helps in understanding the tax calculation process.

To determine their tax, taxpayers need to know their taxable income and filing status. Taxpayers with $100,000 or more of taxable income must use the Tax Rate Schedules. Those with less than $100,000 must use the Tax Table. All Form 1040EZ and Form 1040A filers must find their tax on the Tax Table. They cannot use the Tax Rate Schedules. The Tax Rate Schedules are found on the inside front cover of this book. The Tax Tables are in the back of the book.

TAXPAYER FILING STATUS BY RANK—LOWEST TO HIGHEST TAX FOR THE SAME AMOUNT OF INCOME

1. Married filing jointly [also, qualifying widow(er)]
2. Head of household
3. Single
4. Married filing separately

Tax Rate Schedules

Four Tax Rate Schedules apply, one for each filing status. The rate schedules are more challenging to use than the Tax Table. Taxpayers using a rate schedule must actually compute their tax. The Tax Table requires no tax calculations.

People using the Tax Rate Schedule to compute their tax follow these steps:

1. Choose the correct rate schedule (based on filing status).
2. Locate the proper income bracket and note the tax applicable to the lowest income in that bracket.
3. Subtract the lowest income in that bracket from taxable income.
4. Multiply this difference by the listed tax rate.
5. Add this result to the tax in Step 2 to arrive at the tax on taxable income.

Example 1 illustrates an application of the Tax Rate Schedules.

EXAMPLE 1

Four taxpayers each have $100,000 of taxable income. The following list shows their filing status and income tax for 2005 as determined from the Tax Rate Schedules.

Filing Status	Tax
Married filing jointly	$18,330
Head of household	20,498
Single	22,507
Married filing separately	23,296

The following schedule illustrates the tax calculation for marrieds filing jointly.

	Computations	Tax
Taxable income (TI)	$100,000	
Less	− 59,400*	$ 8,180
TI taxed at 25% rate	$ 40,600	
Multiply by rate	× 25%	10,150
Tax on TI of $100,000		$18,330

*Note that the 10% rate and the 15% rate combined produce a tax of $8,180 on $59,400 of TI. Also note that the 25% rate applies only to the next $40,600 of TI. It produces a tax of $10,150 ($40,600 × 25%). Then note that the total tax on $100,000 of TI equals the sum of the taxes for each income level, rounded to the nearest dollar.

TAX TABLE CANNOT BE USED BY

1. A person filing for a short period (less than 12 months) because of a change in accounting period
2. A person claiming the foreign earned income exclusion
3. A person filing Form 1040 with taxable income of $100,000 or more
4. An estate or trust

Tax Table

With few exceptions, the law requires that taxpayers with less than $100,000 of taxable income use the Tax Table to determine their tax. Consequently, the great majority of people use the Tax Table. It is easier to use than the Tax Rate Schedules. Taxpayers simply locate their tax on a table listing taxes according to taxable income and filing status.

The Tax Table for Form 1040 filers contains separate columns for each filing status. A surviving spouse (qualifying widow[er] with dependent child) uses the column for married taxpayers filing jointly. This book excludes the tables that go with Form 1040EZ and Form 1040A since they contain minimal differences. Thus, Form 1040EZ and Form 1040A filers can use the Tax Table in this book to find their tax.

If line 43 (taxable income) is—		And you are—			
At least	But less than	Single	Married filing jointly *	Married filing separately	Head of a household
			Your tax is—		
23,000					
23,000	23,050	3,089	2,724	3,089	2,931
23,050	23,100	3,096	2,731	3,096	2,939
23,100	23,150	3,104	2,739	3,104	2,946
23,150	23,200	3,111	2,746	3,111	2,954
23,200	23,250	3,119	2,754	3,119	2,961
23,250	23,300	3,126	2,761	3,126	2,969
23,300	23,350	3,134	2,769	3,134	2,976
23,350	23,400	3,141	2,776	3,141	2,984

To determine the Tax Table amounts, the IRS computes the tax at the midpoint of each bracket using the Tax Rate Schedules. For a single taxpayer with $23,000 of taxable income, the Tax Table shows a tax of $3,089. The table shows this amount on the line that includes taxable income of $23,000. Since the taxpayer is single, the proper tax appears at the intersection of the income line and the "single" column.

INDEXING

Congress legislated inflation adjustments for the standard deduction, additional standard deduction, personal and dependency exemptions, tax rate schedules, and the Tax Table. It also legislated inflation adjustments for phase-down formula starting points. These require taxpayers to reduce their personal and dependency exemptions and some itemized deductions using phase-down formulas. Annually, the IRS adjusts these items using Consumer Price Index data. The base period ends with August 31 of each prior year.

PAYING THE TAX LIABILITY

When it comes to paying the tax liability, taxpayers generally pay their taxes through the tax withholding system imposed on their employer, or they make estimated payments. Other factors that can reduce the tax liability include tax credits, prior year overpayments, excess social security taxes withheld, and payments mailed with the tax return. Taxpayers subtract these items from their tax liability to determine the net amount due to or from the government.

Self-employed persons usually make estimated tax payments to the government. Most employees make their tax payments through the payroll tax withholding system. Sometimes, self-employed persons also work as employees. They often cover the tax on their self-employment income through the withholding system by having their employers withhold additional taxes. Chapter 13 presents estimated tax payments and the payroll tax withholding system.

Estimated Tax Payments

Throughout the year, self-employed persons and wage earners pay income, social security, and Medicare taxes. Since a tax withholding system does not exist for self-employed persons, they estimate their taxes for the year. Usually, they make quarterly payments to the IRS to cover these estimates.

Federal Taxes Withheld

The law requires employers to withhold income, social security, and Medicare taxes from the pay of employees. However, the Code exempts some wage classes from income tax withholding and other wage classes from all tax withholding. Exempt employees might arrange for voluntary income tax withholding through their employer.

To help employers determine correct tax withholdings, the IRS publishes tax withholding tables. Employers use these tables in conjunction with personal data provided by the employee on Form W-4, Employee's Withholding Allowance Certificate (Chapter 13). By cross referencing the information on the two documents, the employer determines the proper amount of tax withholding.

Employers deposit withheld taxes with an authorized depository. Deposit frequency usually depends on the amount withheld for a specific base pay period. Employers file withholding and deposit reports with the government throughout the year and after the year ends.

Before February 1 of each year, employers inform employees of their previous year's earnings and tax withholdings. They use Form W-2, Wage and Tax Statement, to communicate this data to employees. When preparing their tax returns, employees enter their income tax withholdings on Form 1040, page 2, in the "Payments" section.

Credits against the Tax

Tax credits reduce the tax liability dollar for dollar. Some are refundable, but most are nonrefundable. **Refundable credits** offset the taxpayer's tax liability, but they also entitle the taxpayer to a payment from the government when the amount of the credits exceeds the liability. **Nonrefundable credits,** in contrast, can only offset the taxpayer's tax liability. When such credits exceed the tax liability, taxpayers receive no payments for the excess.

TAX CREDITS FOR FORM 1040A

Nonrefundable

1. Child and dependent care credit
2. Elderly or disabled credit
3. Adoption credit
4. Child tax credit
5. Education credits
6. Retirement savings contributions credit

Refundable

1. Earned income credit (EIC)
2. Additional child tax credit
3. Federal tax witholdings and payments

Form 1040 filers can claim these and other business credits (Chapter 12).

Excess Social Security Tax

In addition to withholding income taxes, employers also withhold FICA taxes as provided by the FICA Act. FICA taxes consist of two elements: (1) social security or OASDI taxes (old age, survivors, and disability insurance) and (2) Medicare or HI (hospital insurance) taxes. Taxpayers can determine their maximum OASDI tax for 2005 ($5,580) by multiplying $90,000 by 6.20%. They can determine their HI tax by multiplying their total wages, tips, and other compensation by 1.45%. No upper wage limit exists for the Medicare tax.

Sometimes employees have too much in OASDI taxes withheld from their wages. Too much withholding can occur when a person works for two or more employers. Here, each employer withholds OASDI taxes on the first $90,000 of wages and HI taxes on all wages. When a taxpayer's Forms W-2, Wage and Tax Statement, show excess OASDI withholdings via multiple employers, they treat the excess as a tax payment which may result in a refund.

Form 1040A filers add excess OASDI withholdings to their withheld federal income taxes and report the combined total on their return. To the left of the reporting line, they write "excess OASDI" and the correct amount. Form 1040 filers also show excess OASDI withholdings on their return but on a separate line, "Excess social security and tier 1 RRTA tax withheld." Taxpayers cannot use Form 1040EZ to recover excess OASDI withholding. When one employer withholds too much in OASDI taxes, the taxpayer should ask that employer for a refund. Taxpayers cannot recover excess withholding by one employer using their tax returns.

On a joint return, a taxpayer and spouse determine their withheld OASDI taxes separately. Then, each determines if too much withholding took place by subtracting the tax from the proper maximum.

EXAMPLE 2

The Forms W-2 for Elaine and Morton Levy contain OASDI information shown below. Because Elaine works for only one employer, her withheld OASDI tax is limited to $5,580. Morton can claim a credit for excess OASDI withholdings of $620 ($6,200.00 – $5,580.00).

Employer	Total Social Security Wages Paid in 2005	OASDI Tax Withheld
Elaine Levy:		
Melville Dye Co.	$100,000	$5,580.00
Morton Levy:		
Step Mfg. Co.	$60,000	$3,720.00
United Corp.	40,000	2,480.00
	$100,000	$6,200.00

FORM W-2, WAGE AND TAX STATEMENT

Employers use Form W-2, Wage and Tax Statement, to report to the employee and the government the amount of the employee's earnings and taxes withheld. Form W-2 must be sent to the employee before February 1, and to the government before March 1.

Information for Figure 2-1: Filled-In Form W-2

Figure 2-1 shows a filled-in Form W-2 for Elaine Levy who works for Melville Dye Co.

Other Information

- Levy's 2005 wages, **$100,000.00**
- Federal income tax withheld, **$19,250.00**
- Social security tax withheld, **$5,580.00**
- Medicare taxes withheld, **$1,450.00**
- **WI** (Wisconsin)
- State income tax withheld, **$3,000.00**

FIGURE 2-1 Filled-In Form W-2

a Control number							

Control number · 22222 · Void ☐ · For Official Use Only ►
OMB No. 1545-0008

b Employer identification number (EIN)
88-6045185

1 Wages, tips, other compensation
100000.00

2 Federal income tax withheld
19250.00

c Employer's name, address, and ZIP code
Melville Dye Co.
2722 Grandview Blvd.
Green bay, WI 54307

3 Social security wages
90000.00

4 Social security tax withheld
5580.00

5 Medicare wages and tips
100000.00

6 Medicare tax withheld
1450.00

7 Social security tips

8 Allocated tips

d Employee's social security number
259-42-8041

9 Advance EIC payment

10 Dependent care benefits

e Employee's first name and initial
Elaine A.

Last name
Levy

11 Nonqualified plans

12a See instructions for box 12

104 Bayside Drive
Green Bat, WI 54307

13 Statutory employee ☐ Retirement plan ☐ Third-party sick pay ☐

12b

14 Other

12c

12d

f Employee's address and ZIP code

15 State Employer's state ID number
WI

16 State wages, tips, etc.
100000.00

17 State income tax
3000.00

18 Local wages, tips, etc.

19 Local income tax

20 Locality name

Form **W-2** **Wage and Tax Statement**   **2005**   Department of the Treasury—Internal Revenue Service

Copy A For Social Security Administration — Send this entire page with Form W-3 to the Social Security Administration; photocopies are **not** acceptable.
Cat. No. 10134D

For Privacy Act and Paperwork Reduction Act Notice, see back of Copy D.

Do Not Cut, Fold, or Staple Forms on This Page — Do Not Cut, Fold, or Staple Forms on This Page

PERSONAL TAX CREDITS

Some tax credits are personal in nature, whereas others relate to business activities. This chapter covers personal tax credits. Chapter 12 covers the business tax credits.

Congress created several personal tax credits for individual taxpayers in an attempt to encourage specific desired behaviors and to provide tax relief to certain deserving taxpayer groups.

Child and Dependent Care Credit

A nonrefundable child and dependent care credit is available to taxpayers who pay someone to care for a qualifying person while they work. The credit equals a percentage of the **qualifying expenses** incurred for the care of one or more qualified persons. The percentage used in computing the credit ranges from 20% to 35%, depending on the taxpayer's AGI. Taxpayers with AGI up to $15,000 compute their credit by multiplying their qualifying expenses by 35%. For each $2,000 step of AGI over $15,000, this percentage decreases by 1% until it reaches 20% for taxpayers with AGI in excess of $43,000. Figure 2-2 shows the percentages that apply for each level of AGI.

FIGURE 2-2   Child and Dependent Care Credit

Amount of AGI	Applicable Percentage	Amount of AGI	Applicable Percentage
Up to $15,000	35%	$29,001–31,000	27%
$15,001–17,000	34%	31,001–33;000	26%
17,001–19,000	33%	33,001–35,000	25%
19,001–21,000	32%	35,001–37,000	24%
21,001–23,000	31%	37,001–39,000	23%
23,001–25,000	30%	39,001–41,000	22%
25,001–27,000	29%	41,001–43,000	21%
27,001–29,000	28%	43,001 and over	20%

Qualified Person

To claim the child and dependent care credit, one of the following persons must live with the taxpayer for more than half of the year:

1. A "qualifying child" (Chapter 1) under age 13 whom the taxpayer may claim as a dependent
2. A dependent physically or mentally unable to provide self-care
3. A spouse physically or mentally unable to provide self-care

The taxpayer is not required to provide over half the cost of maintaining the household. In addition for divorced or separated couples, only the custodial parent can claim the child as a qualified person. Even when the custodial parent allows the noncustodial parent to claim the dependency exemption (by signing Form 8332; Chapter 1), the noncustodial parent cannot claim the child as a qualified person. When both parents share custody of a child, the parent having custody for the longer period during the year can claim the child as a qualified person.

Qualified Expenses

For purposes of the child and dependent care credit, **qualified expenses** are the amounts taxpayers spend for child and dependent care so that they can work, look for work, or go to school. The costs can include payments for household services such as cooking and housekeeping. However, the main function for the cost must be to provide protection and care for a qualifying person.

The qualified expenses can be for services provided in the taxpayer's home or for out-of-home care. Payments to a relative qualify for the credit unless the taxpayer can claim the relative as a dependent. However, payments to the taxpayer's child under age 19 or the taxpayer's spouse never count as qualified costs.

EXAMPLE 3

While Jerry Herron works, he pays his 22-year-old daughter, Frances, to watch his 4-year-old son, Adam. Herron claims Adam, but not Frances, as a dependent. Payments to Frances for Adam's care are qualified expenses. Had Frances been 18 years old or younger, or had Herron been able to claim Frances as a dependent, the payments would not have been qualified expenses.

Qualified expenses must be reduced by reimbursements the taxpayer receives from an employer's dependent care plan (Chapter 4) when the reimbursements are excluded from the taxpayer's gross income. Reimbursements that are included in the taxpayer's gross income do not affect the child and dependent care credit calculation.

EXAMPLE 4

During the year, Al and Lisa Sherman paid a child care provider $6,000 to look after their sons (ages 4 and 6) while they worked. Al was reimbursed $2,500 from his employer's dependent care plan. The $2,500 was not included in Al's gross income. The Shermans' qualified expenses equal $3,500 ($6,000 – $2,500).

Limitations on Qualifying Expenses

The Code initially limits the amount of qualified expenses to (1) $3,000 for one qualifying person and (2) $6,000 for two or more qualifying persons. These dollar amounts are also reduced by nontaxable reimbursements that the taxpayer receives from an employer's dependent care plan. The Code further limits these amounts to the taxpayer's earned income. If the taxpayer is married, the maximum qualifying costs are limited to the earned income of the lower-income spouse. Thus, the **maximum qualifying expenses** are the lesser of (1) the taxpayer's qualified expenses reduced by nontaxable reimbursements from a dependent care plan, (2) the dollar limits ($3,000/$6,000) reduced by the nontaxable reimbursements, or (3) the taxpayer's earned income.

EXAMPLE 5

Marlin Jones paid $2,100 in qualified expenses for the care of his 7-year-old son. Jones's earned income equals $15,500. Jones's maximum qualifying expenses are $2,100 [the lesser of (1) qualified expenses of $2,100, (2) $3,000 limit for one qualifying person, or (3) earned income of $15,500].

EXAMPLE 6

Assume the same facts as in Example 5, except that Jones's employer has a dependent care plan, from which Jones received $1,500 during the year. The $1,500 reimbursement was excluded from Jones's gross income. Jones's maximum qualifying expenses are $600 [the lesser of (1) $600 of qualified expenses ($2,100 – $1,500), (2) $1,500 limit for one qualifying person ($3,000 – $1,500), or (3) earned income of $15,500].

Usually a taxpayer's spouse must be gainfully employed to qualify for the child and dependent care credit. However, a special rule applies to spouses who either are disabled or are full-time students. This rule assumes the spouse has some earned income for purposes of the earned income limitation. The amount deemed earned is $250 per month when the taxpayer has one qualifying person and $500 when the taxpayer has two or more qualifying persons. The amount is "deemed" earned only for those months that the spouse is a full-time student or incapable of self-care.

EXAMPLE 7

Paul and Kim Foxx have two children, ages 3 and 5. During the year Paul worked full time. Kim did not work, but she attended college full time 10 months out of the year. The Foxxes paid $6,600 in qualified child care expenses. Since the Foxxes' child care expenses of $6,600 exceed the $6,000 limit for two or more qualifying persons, the Foxxes' qualified expenses are initially limited to $6,000. Even though Kim does not work, she is "deemed" to be employed for 10 months of the year with earnings of $5,000 ($500 × 10 months). Since Kim's "deemed" earnings of $5,000 are less than $6,000, the Foxxes' maximum qualifying expenses for purposes of computing the child and dependent care credit are $5,000.

Giving a full-time student spouse who does not work "deemed" earned income of $250/$500 a month allows the couple to claim the child care credit. Without this special rule, the lesser of qualified expenses, the dollar limits, and earned income would be zero in situations where the full-time student spouse did not work. However, these "deemed" earnings are not income to the spouse and are not included in the calculation of the couples' taxable income.

To compute the child and dependent care credit, taxpayers multiply their maximum qualifying expenses by the applicable percentage (from Figure 2-2).

EXAMPLE 8

Assume that in Example 5 Jones's AGI is $29,500. Taxpayers with AGI between $29,001 and $31,000 multiply their maximum qualifying expenses by 27% (Figure 2-2). Thus, Jones's nonrefundable child and dependent care credit would equal $567 ($2,100 × 27%).

Claiming the Credit

To claim the child and dependent care credit, married taxpayers must file a joint return. An exception exists for abandoned spouses (Chapter 1). Taxpayers filing Form 1040 claim this credit on Form 2441, Child and Dependent Care Expenses. Taxpayers filing Form 1040A claim the credit on Schedule 2 (Form 1040A), Child and Dependent Care Expenses. Because Schedule 2 (Form 1040A) and Form 2441 are similar, only Form 2441 is illustrated in Figure 2-3.

Information for Figure 2-3: Filled-In Form 2441

Patricia E. and Clyde R. Smith live and work in Chicago. Patricia works full time during 2005 and earns $30,000. Clyde works part time during the year and earns $10,500. The Smiths have no other sources of income and have no deductions for AGI. The Smiths' 6-year-old twins live with them and qualify as their dependents. For the year, the Smiths paid Lucy Burke $6,200 to care for their children after school until the Smiths got home from work.

Other Information

2(c): Qualified expenses paid during the year for the person listed in column (a), **$3,100.00** (one-half of $6,200) This amount is listed for both Michael and Mary.

  7: AGI, **$40,500.00** ($30,000 + $10,500)

  8: Decimal amount from table, **.22** (based on AGI of $40,500)

 10: Form 1040, line 46, minus Form 1040, line 47, **$2,049.00.**

FIGURE 2-3   Filled-In Form 2441, Page 1

Form **2441**	**Child and Dependent Care Expenses**	OMB No. 1545-0068

Department of the Treasury
Internal Revenue Service   (99)

▶ Attach to Form 1040.

▶ See separate instructions.

2005

Attachment
Sequence No. **21**

Name(s) shown on Form 1040

Patricia E. and Clyde R. Smith

Your social security number

376 78 7371

Before you begin: You need to understand the following terms. See **Definitions** on page 1 of the instructions.

● **Dependent Care Benefits**   ● **Qualifying Person(s)**   ● **Qualified Expenses**

Part I   **Persons or Organizations Who Provided the Care—**You **must** complete this part.
(If you need more space, use the bottom of page 2.)

1	**(a)** Care provider's name	**(b)** Address (number, street, apt. no., city, state, and ZIP code)	**(c)** Identifying number (SSN or EIN)	**(d)** Amount paid (see instructions)
	Lucy Burke	1606 N. Elm Street Chicago, IL 60631-1314	677-33-6605	6,200 00

Did you receive **dependent care benefits?**

No ──── Complete only Part II below.

Yes ──── Complete Part III on the back next.

Caution. If the care was provided in your home, you may owe employment taxes. See the instructions for Form 1040, line 62.

Part II   **Credit for Child and Dependent Care Expenses**

2   Information about your **qualifying person(s).** If you have more than two qualifying persons, see the instructions.

(a) Qualifying person's name First Last	**(b)** Qualifying person's social security number	**(c)** Qualified expenses you incurred and paid in 2005 for the person listed in column (a)
Michael Smith	559 47 8493	3,100 00
Mary Smith	559 47 8403	3,100 00

3	Add the amounts in column (c) of line 2. **Do not** enter more than $3,000 for one qualifying person or $6,000 for two or more persons. If you completed Part III, enter the amount from line 32	3	6,000 00
4	Enter your **earned income.** See instructions	4	30,000 00
5	If married filing jointly, enter your spouse's earned income (if your spouse was a student or was disabled, see the instructions); **all others,** enter the amount from line 4 . . .	5	10,500 00
6	Enter the **smallest** of line 3, 4, or 5	6	6,000 00
7	Enter the amount from Form 1040, line 38 . . . . **7**	40,500 00	
8	Enter on line 8 the decimal amount shown below that applies to the amount on line 7		

If line 7 is:			If line 7 is:		
Over	But not over	Decimal amount is	Over	But not over	Decimal amount is
$0	15,000	.35	$29,000	31,000	.27
15,000	17,000	.34	31,000	33,000	.26
17,000	19,000	.33	33,000	35,000	.25
19,000	21,000	.32	35,000	37,000	.24
21,000	23,000	.31	37,000	39,000	.23
23,000	25,000	.30	39,000	41,000	.22
25,000	27,000	.29	41,000	43,000	.21
27,000	29,000	.28	43,000	No limit	.20

8   ✕ .22

9	Multiply line 6 by the decimal amount on line 8. If you paid 2004 expenses in 2005, see the instructions	9	1,320 00
10	Enter the amount from Form 1040, line 46, minus any amount on Form 1040, line 47 . .	10	2,029 00
11	**Credit for child and dependent care expenses.** Enter the **smaller** of line 9 or line 10 here and on Form 1040, line 48	11	1,320 00

For Paperwork Reduction Act Notice, see page 4 of the instructions.   Cat. No. 11862M   Form **2441** (2005)

Child Tax Credit (CTC)

In 2005, taxpayers may be able to claim a $1,000 tax credit for each "qualifying child" (Chapter 1). However, the child must be under the age of 17 as of the end of the tax year and claimed as a dependent on the taxpayer's tax return. For divorced or separated parents, the CTC is available only to the parent that claims the child as a dependent. Also, no age limit applies to children who are permanently and totally disabled.

The full CTC is available to unmarried taxpayers whose AGI does not exceed $75,000. For married couples, the full CTC is available as long as AGI does not exceed $110,000 if they file a joint return; $55,000 if they file separate returns. The taxpayer loses $50 of the credit for each $1,000 (or portion thereof) that AGI exceeds these thresholds. For purposes of the CTC, AGI is computed by adding back excluded foreign income (Chapter 4).

EXAMPLE 9

In 2005, Tom and Carol Normand file a joint tax return. They claim their two children, ages 8 and 9, as dependents. The Normands' 2005 AGI is $116,400. Because AGI exceeds $110,000, the Normands are not entitled to the full $2,000 CTC ($1,000 × 2). Their $1,650 CTC is determined as follows.

Initial CTC ($1,000 × 2 qualifying children)		$2,000
AGI	$116,400	
AGI threshold for MFJ	(110,000)	
Excess AGI	6,400	
	÷ $1,000	
	6.4	
Number of $1,000 intervals, including portions thereof	7	
	× $50	(350)
Total CTC for 2005		$1,650

EXAMPLE 10

In 2005, John Myers files as head of household and claims his 10-year-old son as a dependent. Myers's 2005 AGI is $77,430. He computes the $850 CTC as follows.

Initial CTC ($1,000 × 1 qualifying child)		$1,000
AGI	$77,430	
AGI threshold for unmarried taxpayers	(75,000)	
Excess AGI	2,430	
	÷ $1,000	
	2.43	
Number of $1,000 intervals, including portions thereof	3	
	× $50	(150)
Total CTC for 2005		$850

The phase out of the CTC is $50 per $1,000 of excess AGI (or portion thereof). Thus, the amount of AGI which causes the CTC to be completely phased out depends not only on the taxpayer's filing status, but also on the number of qualifying children.

While the CTC is generally nonrefundable, it may be a refundable credit for certain taxpayers. However, before computing the refundable portion of the CTC, taxpayers first compute the amount of the CTC that is nonrefundable. They do this by subtracting from their total tax liability all nonrefundable personal credits, other than the CTC, the adoption credit, the retirement savings contributions credit, and the foreign tax credit. The lesser of the remaining tax liability or the taxpayer's CTC represents the nonrefundable portion of the credit. Taxpayers report their nonrefundable CTC on Form 1040 (line 52) or Form 1040A (line 33).

EXAMPLE 11

In 2005, Kate and Matthew Stewart file a joint return, claiming their three children (all under age 17) as dependents. The Stewarts' AGI for 2005 is $55,970 and their total tax liability is $3,766. They are only entitled to one tax credit—the CTC. Since the Stewarts' AGI is less than $110,000, they do not lose any of their $3,000 CTC ($1,000 × 3 children) due to AGI limitations. Therefore, the Stewarts report the entire $3,000 CTC as a nonrefundable credit on Form 1040 (line 52).

Calculation of Refundable Child Tax Credit

The amount of the taxpayer's CTC that cannot be taken as a nonrefundable credit is refundable up to the 15% of the taxpayer's earned income in excess of $11,000. Taxpayers compute the refundable portion of the CTC on Form 8812, Additional Child Tax Credit, and report this amount on Form 1040 (line 68) or Form 1040A (line 42).

EXAMPLE 12

In 2005, Joel and Ruth Floyd file a joint return, claiming their two children, ages 8 and 10, as dependents. The Floyds' 2005 AGI is $41,700, which includes Joel and Ruth's wages of $40,200. The Floyds' tax liability before credits is $2,109, and they are entitled to a $1,260 child and dependent care credit. After subtracting this credit from their tax liability, the Floyds' remaining tax liability is $849 ($2,109 – $1,260). Since their AGI is less than $110,000, the $2,000 CTC ($1,000 × 2) is not reduced due to excess AGI. Therefore, they report $849 as their nonrefundable CTC on Form 1040 (line 52). They then complete Form 8812, Additional Child Tax Credit, to determine the refundable portion of their CTC.

Because of the rest of the CTC of $1,151 ($2,000 – $849) does not exceed 15% of the Floyds' earned income in excess $11,000 (15% × ($40,200 – $11,000) = $4,380), the Floyds report a $1,151 refundable CTC on Form 1040 (line 68).

A provision in the Katrina Emergency Tax Relief Act of 2005 allows "qualified individuals" whose 2005 earned income is less than their 2004 earned income to elect to use the higher amount (i.e., 2004 earned income) for purposes of computing the refundable portion of the CTC. By using a higher earned income amount, these taxpayers are less likely to be limited on the amount of their refundable CTC. **Qualified individuals** are persons whose principal place of abode on August 25, 2005 was located in the core disaster area (as specified by the federal government). They also include persons whose principal place of abode on August 25, 2005 was located in the Hurricane Katrina disaster area (as specified by the federal government), but outside the core disaster area, and who were displaced from their homes because of the hurricane.

Information for Figure 2-4: Filled-In Form 8812

Figure 2-4 shows a completed Form 8812, Additional Child Tax Credit, for the Floyds in Example 12.

Other Information

1: CTC to be claimed ($1,000 × 2 children), **$2,000**
2: Nonrefundable CTC, **$849**
4: Taxable earned income, **$40,200**
5: Taxable earned income in excess of $11,000, **$29,200**

For most taxpayers, the refundable credit does not exceed 15% of the taxpayer's earned income in excess of $11,000. However, in situations where the refundable credit is limited, a special rule for calculating the refundable CTC exists for taxpayers with three or more qualifying children. This special rule is complex and beyond the scope of this textbook. Those interested in learning more about the calculation of the refundable CTC for taxpayers in this special situation should refer to Publication 972.

Higher Education Credits

Two nonrefundable education credits are available for taxpayers who pay tuition and fees during the year on behalf of eligible students. The first credit is the HOPE scholarship credit. The second credit is the lifetime learning credit. Taxpayers cannot claim both credits for the same student. However, they can claim both credits in the same year, but for different students. These credits are not available once a taxpayer's AGI exceeds a certain level, and married persons filing separately are not eligible for these credits.

HOPE Scholarship Credit

The HOPE scholarship credit provides for a maximum $1,500 tax credit for *each* eligible student. *Eligible students* for purposes of the HOPE tax credit are students enrolled in their first two years of post-secondary education. The student must also be enrolled at least half-time during one semester or quarter during the year. To qualify for the HOPE credit, the tuition normally must be paid in the same year as the year in which the semester or quarter begins. However, tuition paid in one year for a course that starts within three months of the next year, qualifies for the credit in the year it is paid. Thus, tuition paid in 2005 for classes that begin before April 1, 2006, counts towards the 2005 education credit.

To compute the amount of HOPE credit, taxpayers add 100% of the first $1,000 of tuition and fees to 50% of the lesser of $1,000 or the tuition and fees in excess of $1,000. The maximum HOPE tax credit is $1,500 [(100% × $1,000) + (50% × $1,000)].

EXAMPLE 13

On December 22, 2004, Brad Waltham pays $800 of his son's tuition for the Spring 2005 semester. The son is a freshman during the Spring semester. On August 15, 2005, Waltham pays $840 for his son's Fall 2005 tuition. Waltham's HOPE credit for 2005 equals $840. The $800 paid in 2004 qualified for the HOPE credit in 2004.

FIGURE 2-4 Filled-In Form 8812

Form **8812**

Department of the Treasury
Internal Revenue Service (99)

Additional Child Tax Credit

1040
1040A
8812

Complete and attach to Form 1040 or Form 1040A.

OMB No. 1545-1620

20**05**

Attachment
Sequence No. **47**

Name(s) shown on return
Joel and Ruth Floyd

Your social security number
861 22 9418

Part I — All Filers

1	Enter the amount from line 1 of your Child Tax Credit Worksheet on page 38 of the Form 1040 instructions or page 37 of the Form 1040A instructions. If you used Pub. 972, enter the amount from line 8 of the worksheet on page 4 of the publication	**1**	2,000 00
2	Enter the amount from Form 1040, line 52, or Form 1040A, line 33	**2**	849 00
3	Subtract line 2 from line 1. If zero, **stop**; you cannot take this credit	**3**	1,151 00

4a Earned income (see instructions on back) **4a** 40,200 00

b Nontaxable combat pay from Form(s) W-2, box 12, with code Q. If married filing jointly, include your spouse's amounts with yours. . . . **4b**

5 Is the amount on line 4a more than $11,000?

☐ **No.** Leave line 5 blank and enter -0- on line 6.

☒ **Yes.** Subtract $11,000 from the amount on line 4a. Enter the result . **5** 29,200 00

6 Multiply the amount on line 5 by 15% (.15) and enter the result **6** 4,380 00

Next. Do you have three or more qualifying children?

☒ **No.** If line 6 is zero, **stop**; you cannot take this credit. Otherwise, skip Part II and enter the **smaller** of line 3 or line 6 on line 13.

☐ **Yes.** If line 6 is equal to or more than line 3, skip Part II and enter the amount from line 3 on line 13. Otherwise, go to line 7.

Part II — Certain Filers Who Have Three or More Qualifying Children

7	Withheld social security and Medicare taxes from Form(s) W-2, boxes 4 and 6. If married filing jointly, include your spouse's amounts with yours. If you worked for a railroad, see instructions on back	**7**	
8	**1040 filers:** Enter the total of the amounts from Form 1040, lines 27 and 59, plus any uncollected social security and Medicare or tier 1 RRTA taxes included on line 63.	**8**	
	1040A filers: Enter -0-.		
9	Add lines 7 and 8	**9**	
10	**1040 filers:** Enter the total of the amounts from Form 1040, lines 66a and 67.		
	1040A filers: Enter the total of the amount from Form 1040A, line 41a, plus any excess social security and tier 1 RRTA taxes withheld that you entered to the left of line 43 (see instructions on back).	**10**	
11	Subtract line 10 from line 9. If zero or less, enter -0-	**11**	
12	Enter the **larger** of line 6 or line 11	**12**	
	Next, enter the **smaller** of line 3 or line 12 on line 13.		

Part III — Additional Child Tax Credit

13	**This is your additional child tax credit**	**13**	1,151 00

1040
1040A ◄

Enter this amount on Form 1040, line 68, or Form 1040A, line 42.

For Paperwork Reduction Act Notice, see back of form.   Cat. No. 10644E   Form **8812** (2005)

[Watermark: Draft as of 04/29/2005]

Lifetime Learning Credit

The lifetime learning credit provides for a maximum $2,000 tax credit *per year*. This differs from the HOPE credit where the maximum credit is $1,500 *per eligible student*. Other differences between the two credits are as follows.

1. A student need not attend at least half-time to qualify for the lifetime learning credit.
2. Tuition paid for education that extends beyond the first two years of college qualifies for the lifetime learning credit.

To compute the lifetime learning credit, taxpayers multiply 20% by the lesser of (i) $10,000 or (ii) qualified tuition costs for the year. As with the HOPE tax credit, tuition paid in 2005 for classes beginning before April 1, 2006, qualify for the lifetime learning credit in 2005.

EXAMPLE 14

On August 10, 2005, Becky Brown pays $3,000 to cover her tuition for the Fall 2005 semester. Brown is a graduate student in the nursing program at State University. Brown's lifetime learning credit for 2005 equals $600 ($3,000 × 20%).

EXAMPLE 15

On December 16, 2005, Joe and Ann Johnson pay $3,000 for their daughter's and $4,000 for their son's Spring 2006 tuition. The spring semester begins January 16, 2006. Both children are seniors in college. The Johnson's lifetime learning credit for 2005 equals $1,400 [(lesser of $10,000 or $7,000) × 20%]. The maximum lifetime learning credit is $2,000 *per taxpayer* each year.

The eligibility requirements for the HOPE tax credit are more stringent than for those for the lifetime learning credit. However; the maximum credit for the HOPE tax credit is $1,500 for each eligible student. The maximum credit for the lifetime learning credit is $2,000 per tax return.

Phase Out of Education Credits

Once both education credits have been computed, unmarried taxpayers with AGI in excess of $43,000 must reduce the amount of the credit. Married couples who file a joint return must reduce the credit if AGI exceeds $87,000. The amount of reduction in the tax credit for unmarried taxpayers equals:

$$\text{Sum of the HOPE and lifetime learning tax credits} \times \frac{[\text{AGI} - \$43,000]}{\$10,000}$$

For married taxpayers filing a joint return, the reduction equals:

$$\text{Sum of the HOPE and lifetime learning tax credits} \times \frac{[\text{AGI} - \$87,000]}{\$20,000}$$

| EXAMPLE 16 |

Steve and Judy Stein's AGI for 2005 is $89,000. The Steins are eligible to claim education credits of $2,300 in 2005 ($1,500 for the HOPE credit and $800 for the lifetime learning credit). Because the Steins' AGI exceeds $87,000, their 2005 education credit is $2,070.

Initial education tax credits		$2,300
AGI	$89,000	
Less AGI threshold	(87,000)	
Excess AGI	$2,000	
	÷ $20,000	
	10%	
	× $2,300	(230)
2005 Education Tax Credit		$2,070

Information for Figure 2-5: Filled-In Form 8863

Figure 2-5 shows a completed Form 8863, Education Credits (HOPE and Lifetime Learning Credits), for the Steins in Example 16.

Other Information

    1(c): Qualified expenses, up to $2,000, **$2,000.00**

    3(c): Qualified expenses, **$4,000.00**

      9: AGI, **$89,000.00**

    14: Tax from 1040 (line 46), **$9,886.00**

Earned Income Credit

The earned income credit (EIC) is a special tax credit that provides some tax relief to lower-paid workers. This refundable credit really works like a "negative income tax." Taxpayers showing a small amount of AGI may actually receive a government subsidy by claiming the EIC. Taxpayers receive this money when the EIC exceeds their tax liability.

Congress also designed this credit to encourage people to become contributing, working members of society. Within limits, as a person's earned income (wages) goes up, the amount of this credit increases. This, supposedly, encourages people to seek employment.

Taxpayers Qualifying for Credit

To qualify for the EIC, taxpayers must either

1. Be over age 24, but not over 64, as of the end of the tax year and not be claimed as a dependent by another person, or
2. Have a "qualifying child."

Under the "qualifying children" rules (Chapter 1), children must not provide over half of their own support. This restriction does not apply for purposes of the EIC. Tests the child must meet are the relationship test, residency test, age test, and the citizenship test used in defining "qualifying children." Also, the taxpayer's return must provide the child's name, age, and SSN.

While unmarried children do not have to be dependents, married children must qualify as dependents of the taxpayer. However, the custodial parent receives the EIC when the dependency exemption for a married child has been released to the noncustodial parent.

FIGURE 2-5 Filled-in Form 8863

Form **8863**	**Education Credits**	OMB No. 1545-1618
Department of the Treasury Internal Revenue Service (99)	**(Hope and Lifetime Learning Credits)** ▶ See instructions. ▶ Attach to Form 1040 or Form 1040A.	**20 05** Attachment Sequence No. **50**

Name(s) shown on return	Your social security number
Steven A. and Judith M. Stein	839 ⋮ 74 ⋮ 2570

Caution: *You cannot take both an education credit and the tuition and fees deduction (Form 1040, line 34, or Form 1040A, line 19) for the same student in the same year.*

Part I   Hope Credit. Caution: *You cannot take the Hope credit for more than 2 tax years for the same student.*

1	**(a)** Student's name (as shown on page 1 of your tax return) First name / Last name	**(b)** Student's social security number (as shown on page 1 of your tax return)	**(c)** Qualified expenses (see instructions). **Do not** enter more than $2,000 for each student.	**(d)** Enter the **smaller** of the amount in column (c) or $1,000	**(e)** Add column (c) and column (d)	**(f)** Enter one-half of the amount in column (e)
	Mary Stein	691 ⋮ 14 ⋮ 8330	2,000 00	1,000 00	3,000 00	1,500 00

2	Tentative Hope credit. Add the amounts on line 1, column (f). If you are taking the lifetime learning credit for another student, go to Part II; otherwise, go to Part III ▶	2	1,500 00

Part II   Lifetime Learning Credit

3	**Caution:** *You cannot take the Hope credit and the lifetime learning credit for the same student in the same year.*	**(a)** Student's name (as shown on page 1 of your tax return) First name / Last name	**(b)** Student's social security number (as shown on page 1 of your tax return)	**(c)** Qualified expenses (see instructions)
		Stanley Stein	642 ⋮ 83 ⋮ 1922	4,000 00

4	Add the amounts on line 3, column (c), and enter the total	4	4,000 00
5	Enter the **smaller** of line 4 or $10,000	5	4,000 00
6	Tentative lifetime learning credit. Multiply line 5 by 20% (.20) and go to Part III ▶	6	800 00

Part III   Allowable Education Credits

7	Tentative education credits. Add lines 2 and 6		7	2,300 00
8	Enter: $107,000 if married filing jointly; $53,000 if single, head of household, or qualifying widow(er)	8	107,000 00	
9	Enter the amount from Form 1040, line 38*, or Form 1040A, line 22	9	89,000 00	
10	Subtract line 9 from line 8. If zero or less, **stop;** you cannot take any education credits	10	18,000 00	
11	Enter: $20,000 if married filing jointly; $10,000 if single, head of household, or qualifying widow(er)	11	20,000 00	
12	If line 10 is equal to or more than line 11, enter the amount from line 7 on line 13 and go to line 14. If line 10 is less than line 11, divide line 10 by line 11. Enter the result as a decimal (rounded to at least three places)	12	× .90	
13	Multiply line 7 by line 12 ▶	13	2,070 00	
14	Enter the amount from Form 1040, line 46, or Form 1040A, line 28	14	9,886 00	
15	Enter the total, if any, of your credits from Form 1040, lines 47 through 49, or Form 1040A, lines 29 and 30	15	0 00	
16	Subtract line 15 from line 14. If zero or less, **stop;** you cannot take any education credits ▶	16	9,886 00	
17	**Education credits.** Enter the **smaller** of line 13 or line 16 here and on Form 1040, line 50, or Form 1040A, line 31 ▶	17	2,070 00	

* If you are filing Form 2555, 2555-EZ, or 4563, or you are excluding income from Puerto Rico, see Pub. 970 for the amount to enter.

For Paperwork Reduction Act Notice, see page 3.	Cat. No. 25379M	Form **8863** (2005)

Married couples must file a joint return to claim the EIC. However, if the parents are divorced or separated and the child is a qualifying child for both parents, the parent with the highest AGI gets to claim the EIC. In other situations where the child may be a qualifying child for more than one taxpayer, the credit goes to the child's parent. If neither person is the child's parent, then the taxpayer with the highest AGI gets the EIC for the child.

EXAMPLE 17

Jake, age 26, and his son, age 5, live with Jake's father Frank for the whole year. Jake's AGI is $15,000, and Frank's AGI is $20,000. The son is a qualifying child to both Jake and Frank. Since Jake is the parent, he claims the EIC.

Taxpayers with disqualified income in excess of $2,700 cannot take the EIC. Disqualified income generally includes dividends, interest (including tax-exempt interest), net rental income, and net capital gain.

Credit Rates and Dollars

Generally, as taxable earned income increases, the EIC increases. However, the credit is phased out when income exceeds a certain level. This phase-down is based on the higher of earned income or AGI. Taxpayers use the Earned Income Credit Worksheet to compute their credit. The worksheet helps the taxpayer compute the proper EIC using the IRS credit tables (found after the tax tables at the back of the textbook). Taxpayers retain this worksheet for their records. However, those with qualifying children must also complete and file Schedule EIC.

For purposes of the EIC, earned income does not include nontaxable employee compensation such as: salary deferrals under retirement plans, salary reductions under cafeteria plans, dependent care and adoptions benefits, and educational assistance benefits.

A provision in the Katrina Emergency Tax Relief Act of 2005 allows "qualified individuals" whose 2005 earned income is less than their 2004 earned income to elect to use the higher amount when computing their EIC. **Qualified individuals** are persons whose principal place of abode on August 25, 2005 was located in the core disaster area (as specified by the federal government). They also include persons whose principal place of abode on August 25, 2005 was located in the Hurricane Katrina disaster area (as specified by the federal government), but outside the core disaster area, and who were displaced from their homes because of the hurricane. Qualified persons should elect to use the higher earned income amount in situations where using the higher amount provides them with a higher EIC in 2005.

Advance Payment of EIC

Employees with a qualifying child may have the right to an advance payment of the EIC. Taxpayers without a qualifying child cannot receive an advance payment of EIC. Eligible employees wanting to receive advance EIC payments must file with their employer Form W-5, Earned Income Credit Advance Payment Certificate. Employees who do not want to receive advance EIC payments can claim the credit when they file their returns and do not file a Form W-5.

Taxpayers who receive an advance EIC payment must file Form 1040 or 1040A. They must file a return even if they do not meet the general tax return filing requirements. The employer reports the amount of advance EIC payments to employees and to the IRS on Form W-2, Wages and Tax Statement (box 9). When advance credit payments exceed a taxpayer's allowable EIC, the taxpayer must return the excess to the government.

Information for Figure 2-6: Filled-In Schedule EIC

James Williams earned $9,665 in wages in 2005. His employer did not withhold income taxes. James filed a Form W-5, Earned Income Credit Advance Payment Certificate, and received $630 in EIC advance payments. Sarah Williams earned $6,100 in wages. Her employer withheld $384 for federal income taxes. The Williamses also earned $1,150 of interest on their joint savings account.

The Williamses file a joint tax return and claim dependency exemptions for their three children. Figure 2-6 shows the Williamses' filled-in Schedule EIC. They claim a $4,283 EIC on Form 1040 (line 66a) and attach Schedule EIC (Form 1040A or 1040) to their tax return. The Williamses report their $630 advance EIC payment on Form 1040 (line 61).

Information for Filled-In Schedule EIC Worksheet

Other Information

1: Wages from Form 1040, line 7, **$15,765** ($9,665 + $6,100)
3: AGI (Form 1040, line 38), **$16,915**

FIGURE 2-6   Filled-In Schedule EIC Worksheet

1. Enter your earned income.   1. 15,765

2. Look up the EIC on the amount on line 1 above in the EIC Table. Enter the credit here.   2. 4,400

3. Enter your AGI.   3. 16,915

4. Are the amounts on lines 1 and 3 the same?
    Yes. Skip line 5; enter the amount from line 2 on line 6
    No. Go to line 5.

5. If you have:

    a. No qualifying children, is the amount on line 3 less than $6,550 ($8,550 if married filed jointly)?

    b. 1 or more qualifying children, is the amount on line 3 less than $14,400 ($16,400 if married filed jointly)?

        Yes. Leave line 5 blank; enter the amount from line 2 on line 6

        No. Look up the EIC on the amount on line 3 above in the EIC Table. Enter the credit here.   5. 4,283

    Enter the smaller of line 2 or line 5 on line 6.

6. **This is your earned income credit.**   6. 4,283

Adoption Credit

nonrefundable credit

Taxpayers can take a tax credit for qualified adoption expenses. The tax credit is taken in the year the expenses are paid only if the adoption becomes final in that year. Otherwise, the credit is allowed in the year it becomes final. The credit is limited to the first $10,630 of

FIGURE 2-6   Filled-In Schedule EIC

| SCHEDULE EIC
(Form 1040A or 1040)

Department of the Treasury
Internal Revenue Service | **Earned Income Credit**
Qualifying Child Information
*Complete and attach to Form 1040A or 1040
only if you have a qualifying child.* | 1040A
1040
EIC | OMB No. 1545-0074

2005

Attachment
Sequence No. **43** |

Name(s) shown on return	Your social security number
James R. and Sarah O. Williams	282 56 9320

Before you begin: See the instructions for Form 1040A, lines 41a and 41b, or Form 1040, lines 66a and 66b, to make sure that **(a)** you can take the EIC and **(b)** you have a qualifying child.

⚠ **CAUTION**

- If you take the EIC even though you are not eligible, you may not be allowed to take the credit for up to 10 years. See back of schedule for details.
- It will take us longer to process your return and issue your refund if you do not fill in all lines that apply for each qualifying child.
- Be sure the child's name on line 1 and social security number (SSN) on line 2 agree with the child's social security card. Otherwise, at the time we process your return, we may reduce or disallow your EIC. If the name or SSN on the child's social security card is not correct, call the Social Security Administration at 1-800-772-1213.

Qualifying Child Information	Child 1	Child 2
1 Child's name If you have more than two qualifying children, you only have to list two to get the maximum credit.	First name / Last name Martha A. Williams	First name / Last name Karl B. Williams
2 Child's SSN The child must have an SSN as defined on page 42 of the Form 1040A instructions or page 44 of the Form 1040 instructions unless the child was born and died in 2005. If your child was born and died in 2005 and did not have an SSN, enter "Died" on this line and attach a copy of the child's birth certificate.	826 34 3710	850 21 5263
3 Child's year of birth	Year 1 9 9 1 *If born after 1986, skip lines 4a and 4b; go to line 5.*	Year 1 9 9 4 *If born after 1986, skip lines 4a and 4b; go to line 5.*
4 If the child was born before 1987— **a** Was the child under age 24 at the end of 2005 and a student?	☐ **Yes.** *Go to line 5.* ☐ **No.** *Continue*	☐ **Yes.** *Go to line 5.* ☐ **No.** *Continue*
b Was the child permanently and totally disabled during any part of 2005?	☐ **Yes.** *Continue* ☐ **No.** *The child is not a qualifying child.*	☐ **Yes.** *Continue* ☐ **No.** *The child is not a qualifying child.*
5 Child's relationship to you (for example, son, daughter, grandchild, niece, nephew, foster child, etc.)	daughter	son
6 Number of months child lived with you in the United States during 2005 • If the child lived with you for more than half of 2005 but less than 7 months, enter "7." • If the child was born or died in 2005 and your home was the child's home for the entire time he or she was alive during 2005, enter "12."	12 months *Do not enter more than 12 months.*	12 months *Do not enter more than 12 months.*

TIP You may also be able to take the additional child tax credit if your child **(a)** was under age 17 at the end of 2005, **and** **(b)** is a U.S. citizen or resident alien. For more details, see the instructions for line 42 of Form 1040A or line 68 of Form 1040.

| For Paperwork Reduction Act Notice, see Form 1040A or 1040 instructions. | Cat. No. 13339M | Schedule EIC (Form 1040A or 1040) 2005 |

qualified adoption expenses. The credit is further limited for taxpayers with AGI in excess of $159,450. Taxpayers with AGI in excess of $159,450 reduce their credit by

(the lesser of the $10,630 or adoption expenses) ×
(AGI in excess of $159,450 ÷ $40,000)

EXAMPLE 18

In 2004, Lester and Amy Holden paid $12,000 in qualified adoption expenses. The adoption is finalized in 2005. The Holdens' AGI for both 2004 and 2005 is $169,450. Since the adoption was not finalized in 2004, the Holdens will take a $7,972 adoption credit in 2005.

Initial credit, lesser of $10,630 or $12,000 of qualified adoption expenses	$10,630
Less phase-out of credit [$10,630 × (($169,450 − $159,450) ÷ $40,000)]	(2,658)
Adoption credit	$7,972

Qualified adoption expenses include the expenses directly related to the legal adoption of a child who is under the age of 18 at the time of the adoption or is physically and mentally incapable of self-care. Such costs include adoption fees (provided they are reasonable and necessary), court costs, and attorney's fees. Both the qualified adoption expenses and the $10,630 limit must be reduced by nontaxable reimbursements that the taxpayer receives from an employer's adoption assistance plan.

EXAMPLE 19

Assume the same facts as in Example 18, except that the Holdens receive $2,000 from an employer adoption assistance plan. The Holdens' credit would be $6,472.

Initial credit, lesser of ($10,630 − $2,000) or ($12,000 − $2,000)	$8,630
Less phase-out of credit [$8,630 × (($169,450 − $159,450) ÷ $40,000)]	(2,158)
Adoption credit	$6,472

 The full $10,630 credit is allowed for the adoption of a special needs child regardless of the amount actually paid for qualified adoption expenses.

Form to Use

Taxpayers claiming the adoption credit complete Form 8839, Qualified Adoption Expenses. The adoption credit is nonrefundable. However, any portion of the credit not allowed because the taxpayer does not have enough tax liability can be carried over for five years. Taxpayers claiming the adoption credit enter the amount of the credit on Form 1040 (line 53) or Form 1040A (line 34).

Retirement Savings Contributions Credit

Certain taxpayers may take a nonrefundable tax credit for contributions (including amounts withheld from their paychecks) to retirement savings plans. The credit is in addition to any deduction or exclusion relating to the retirement plan contribution. The credit applies to traditional and Roth IRAs and other qualified retirement plans such as 401(k) plans, 403(b) annuities, 457 plans, SIMPLE and SEP plans.

The amount of the credit is based on filing status and AGI. The credit is determined by multiplying the contribution (not to exceed $2,000 per person) by a percentage taken from the following table which is based on AGI levels. The contribution eligible for the credit must be reduced by any distributions received from qualified retirement plans.

Joint Return		Head of Household		All Other Cases		Applicable%
Over	Not Over	Over	Not Over	Over	Not Over	
$ 0	$30,000	$ 0	$22,500	$ 0	$15,000	50%
30,000	32,500	22,500	24,375	15,000	16,250	20
32,500	50,000	24,375	37,500	16,250	25,000	10
50,000	—	37,500	—	25,000	—	0

Joint filers with AGI in excess of $50,000 receive no credit. For heads of households the amount is $37,500, and for all others it is $25,000. No credit is available for dependents and full-time students. Additionally, taxpayers must be at least 18 years old to qualify for the credit.

EXAMPLE 20

Dave Ogg reports $31,000 of AGI on his joint return. During the year Ogg contributed $2,000 to his Roth IRA. Ogg reports a tax credit of $400 ($2,000 × 20%) for his Roth IRA contribution on Form 1040 (line 51) or Form 1040A (line 32).

Foreign Tax Credit

The foreign tax credit applies to both individuals and corporations. This credit reduces the U.S. income tax by the taxes paid to foreign countries. The credit results in more equitable tax treatment, because it prevents foreign income from being taxed twice, once by the foreign country and again by the United States. As an alternative, individuals can use foreign taxes paid as an itemized deduction. When taxpayers use foreign taxes as a credit, the credit cannot exceed the U.S. income tax that applies to the foreign income. Form 1116, Foreign Tax Credit, is available from the IRS and should be used to compute the amount of foreign tax credit.

Elderly or Disabled Credit

Taxpayers age 65 or older, and taxpayers under 65 who retire with a permanent and total disability, may receive a special nonrefundable credit. Primarily, this credit benefits elderly, low-income taxpayers who receive little or no social security income. When both spouses are 65 or older, the maximum credit available under this provision is $1,125. It decreases as AGI and social security payments increase.

Form 1040A filers use Schedule 3 (Form 1040A) to compute their credit for the elderly or the disabled. Form 1040 filers use Schedule R to determine their credit. The credit is not available to Form 1040EZ taxpayers.

FORM 1040EZ *simplest form*

Preparers of Form 1040EZ, Income Tax Return for Single and Joint Filers with No Dependents, will find it easy to use. It is a one-page form that is fairly simple to complete. Taxpayers using this form may report only several types of income: wages, salaries, tips, taxable scholarships/fellowships, unemployment compensation, interest totaling $1,500 or less, and Alaska Permanent Fund dividends. They have only two possible deductions: the standard deduction and allowable exemptions. Taxpayers who are dependents, however, receive no exemption, and their standard deduction may require an adjustment.

Also available on Form 1040EZ is the earned income credit (EIC). Taxpayers who do not have a "qualifying child" in their household may use Form 1040EZ to claim the EIC. The presence of a "qualifying child" requires Form 1040A or Form 1040 (see Earned Income Credit). Other tax credits also require use of these forms.

FORM 1040EZ TESTS—USERS MUST

1. Be single or joint filers, under age 65 and not blind
2. Claim the standard deduction
3. Make no claim for a dependency exemption
4. Have gross income only from wages, salaries, tips, taxable scholarship or fellowship grants, interest, unemployment compensation, qualified state tuition program earnings, and Alaska Permanent Fund dividends
5. Have taxable interest income of $1,500 or less
6. Have taxable income of less than $100,000
7. Have no dividend income
8. Earn less than $20 in monthly tips from one employer that are omitted from Form W-2
9. Not receive any advance earned income credit (EIC) payments

---

Taxpayer Identification

On all tax returns, taxpayers must clearly identify themselves. They must place their name, address, and social security number at the top of the form. Those receiving a preaddressed taxpayer identification label should examine the label carefully, correct errors in ink, and paste the corrected label in the space provided. When unclear data appears on this label, taxpayers should not use it. They should insert their own identification data at the top of the return.

Presidential Election Campaign Fund

Taxpayers can instruct the IRS whether or not to transfer $3 of their tax payments to the presidential election campaign fund. They simply place an *X* in the proper box located under the name and address data. This optional instruction does not affect the amount of tax.

Reporting Taxable Income

Form 1040EZ tax filers use lines 1 through 4 to report and summarize their income. These filers then subtract out their standard deduction and any exemptions that may apply (line 5). The remainder is taxable income.

All taxpayers receive a standard deduction. However, persons who are dependents may not claim an exemption for themselves. **Nondependents** deduct $8,200 ($5,000 + $3,200) if single and $16,400 ($10,000 + $3,200 + $3,200) if married. **Dependents** use a worksheet to determine their standard deduction, which is the higher of, 1) $800 or 2) earned income plus $250. It cannot exceed $5,000 if single or $10,000 if married.

Figuring the Tax, Refund, or Amount Due

After figuring taxable income, 1040EZ taxpayers list all their tax payments. An item that acts as a tax payment is the earned income credit (EIC) (line 8a). Taxpayers then use taxable income (line 6) to determine their tax from the Tax Tables. They enter it on the form (line 10) and subtract the total payments (line 9) to compute the refund (line 11a) or the amount owed (line 12).

Taxpayers receiving a refund may choose to receive it in the form of a check or a direct deposit. They may also apply the refund to next year's tax liability. Direct deposit refunds are faster, more secure, and more convenient for the taxpayer than refunds by check. They are also less expensive for the government to issue. To receive a direct deposit refund, taxpayers must include two numbers in the spaces provided on the tax return: 1) bank's routing number, and 2) taxpayer's account number. This information is found on the taxpayer's check, but one should verify these figures with the financial institution to make sure the correct numbers are used.

All tax filers must attach Copy B of Form W-2 to their tax return. If an amount is owed, the taxpayer should also enclose a check for the balance due.

Taxpayers may incur a penalty for not paying enough tax during the year. People in this situation who file Form 1040EZ let the IRS compute the penalty and send a bill. If they choose to compute the penalty themselves, they cannot use Form 1040EZ. Instead, they must use either Form 1040A or Form 1040.

DO NOT MAKE A PAYMENT TO *IRS*

Due to the loss of some taxpayer payments (checks or money orders being altered or stolen), make all payments to the *United States Treasury*. Never leave a payee line blank. Also, include the following taxpayer data and form identification on each payment:

1. Name

2. Address

3. Social security number (SSN)

4. Daytime phone number

5. Year and form name (2005 Form 1040EZ, 2005 Form 1040A, or 2005 Form 1040)

Signature and Certification

Taxpayers sign Form 1040EZ at the bottom of page one. They also enter their occupation and the current date. Taxpayers should normally file their return no later than April 15, the due date for calendar year filers. If this date falls on Saturday, Sunday, or a legal holiday, the law extends the filing date to the end of the next business day.

After attaching Copy B of Form W-2 to the return, the return is ready for mailing. Taxpayers should keep evidence of their timely mailing by sending the return by certified or registered mail. With either of these methods, the postal clerk gives the taxpayer a dated mailing receipt that the taxpayer stores with copies of the completed return.

Information for Figure 2-7: Filled-In Form 1040EZ

Amelia Z. Sanchez works as a sales clerk. In addition to her wages, Sanchez received interest earned on her savings account. Sanchez has no other sources of income. Also, no other taxpayer can claim her as a dependent. Figure 2-7 shows Sanchez's Form 1040EZ.

Other Information

- Total wages, salaries, and tips, **$22,920.00** (source: Form W-2)
- Taxable interest income, **$395.00** (source: Form 1099-INT)
- Federal income tax withheld, **$2,002.00** (source: Form W-2)

FORM 1040A

Form 1040A, U.S. Individual Income Tax Return, a two-page return, is more challenging than Form 1040EZ but much less complex than Form 1040. It accommodates more types of income than Form 1040EZ, permits additional deductions, and allows for all personal tax credits.

Page one lists the taxpayer's various incomes. It also allows four deductions to arrive at adjusted gross income. Page two provides for the standard deduction and allowable exemptions to produce taxable income. After identifying the amount of the tax, the form allows for tax reductions: tax credits, withheld taxes, and other payments. The taxpayer then computes the refund or the amount due. Finally, taxpayers report any estimated tax penalty and add it to the amount due.

Form 1040A has four supporting schedules. Taxpayers use Schedule 1 to report their taxable interest and dividend income, Schedule 2 to compute their child and dependent care credit, and Schedule 3 to compute their elderly or disabled credit. They may also use Schedule EIC (Form 1040A or 1040). The next paragraph contains a brief discussion of Form 1040A. Chapter 4 contains the main presentation on this form.

Who May Use Form 1040A

Only taxpayers with taxable incomes of less than $100,000 can use Form 1040A. The income of Form 1040A filers can include only wages, salaries, interest, dividends, tips, annuities, pensions, social security benefits, distributions from individual retirement arrangements (IRAs), unemployment compensation, taxable scholarships and fellowships, Alaska Permanent Fund dividends, and certain capital gain distributions. (Chapters 3 and 4). Form 1040A permits only four deductions for AGI: educator expenses, qualifying IRA contributions, certain interest on student loans, and a tuition and fees deduction. Also, this form allows taxpayers to reduce AGI only by the standard deduction and allowable exemptions.

FIGURE 2-7 Filled-In Form 1040EZ

Form **1040EZ**	Department of the Treasury—Internal Revenue Service **Income Tax Return for Single and Joint Filers With No Dependents** (99) **2005**				OMB No. 1545-0675

Label

(See page 11.)
Use the IRS label.
Otherwise,
please print
or type.

Presidential Election Campaign (page 11) ▶

L A B E L H E R E	Your first name and initial Amelia Z.	Last name Sanchez		Your social security number 295:24:1408
	If a joint return, spouse's first name and initial	Last name		Spouse's social security number
	Home address (number and street). If you have a P.O. box, see page 11. 8290 Edgewater Drive		Apt. no.	▲ You **must** enter your SSN(s) above. ▲
	City, town or post office, state, and ZIP code. If you have a foreign address, see page 11. Chula Vista, CA 91911			Checking a box below will not change your tax or refund.

Check here if you, or your spouse if a joint return, want $3 to go to this fund? . . . ▶ [X] **You**   ☐ **Spouse**

Income

Attach Form(s) W-2 here.
Enclose, but do not attach, any payment.

1	Wages, salaries, and tips. This should be shown in box 1 of your Form(s) W-2. Attach your Form(s) W-2.	1	22,920	00
2	Taxable interest. If the total is over $1,500, you cannot use Form 1040EZ.	2	395	00
3	Unemployment compensation and Alaska Permanent Fund dividends (see page 13).	3		
4	Add lines 1, 2, and 3. This is your **adjusted gross income.**	4	23,315	00
5	If someone can claim you (or your spouse if a joint return) as a dependent, check the applicable box(es) below and enter the amount from the worksheet on back. ☐ **You** ☐ **Spouse** If someone cannot claim you (or your spouse if a joint return), enter $8,200 if **single;** $16,400 if **married filing jointly.**	5	8,200	00
6	Subtract line 5 from line 4. If line 5 is larger than line 4, enter -0-. This is your **taxable income.** ▶	6	15,115	00

Payments and tax

7	Federal income tax withheld from box 2 of your Form(s) W-2.	7	2,002	00
8a	Earned income credit (EIC).	8a		
b	Nontaxable combat pay election. 8b			
9	Add lines 7 and 8a. These are your **total payments.** ▶	9	2,002	00
10	**Tax.** Use the amount on **line 6 above** to find your tax in the tax table on pages 24–32 of the booklet. Then, enter the tax from the table on this line.	10	1,904	00

Refund

Have it directly deposited! See page 18 and fill in 11b, 11c, and 11d.

11a	If line 9 is larger than line 10, subtract line 10 from line 9. This is your **refund.** ▶	11a	98	00
▶ **b**	Routing number	▶ **c** Type: ☐ Checking ☐ Savings		
▶ **d**	Account number			

Amount you owe

12	If line 10 is larger than line 9, subtract line 9 from line 10. This is the **amount you owe.** For details on how to pay, see page 19. ▶	12	

Third party designee

Do you want to allow another person to discuss this return with the IRS (see page 19)? ☐ **Yes.** Complete the following. ☐**No**

Designee's name ▶	Phone no. ▶ ( )	Personal identification number (PIN) ▶

Sign here

Joint return?
See page 11.
Keep a copy
for your records.

Under penalties of perjury, I declare that I have examined this return, and to the best of my knowledge and belief, it is true, correct, and accurately lists all amounts and sources of income I received during the tax year. Declaration of preparer (other than the taxpayer) is based on all information of which the preparer has any knowledge.

Your signature *Amelia Z. Sanchez*	Date 4/5/06	Your occupation Sales Clerk	Daytime phone number ( )
Spouse's signature. If a joint return, **both** must sign.	Date	Spouse's occupation	

Paid preparer's use only

Preparer's signature ▶		Date	Check if self-employed ☐	Preparer's SSN or PTIN
Firm's name (or yours if self-employed), address, and ZIP code	▶		EIN	
			Phone no. ( )	

For Disclosure, Privacy Act, and Paperwork Reduction Act Notice, see page 23.   Cat. No. 11329W   Form **1040EZ** (2005)

Information for Figure 2-8: Filled-In Form 1040A

Sarah and James Wilson's filled-in Form 1040A is shown in Figure 2-8. The Wilsons have three dependent children, two of whom are under age 17.

Other Information

- Wages, **$31,765** ($19,665 + $12,100) (source: Form W-2)
- Taxable interest, **$150** (source: Form 1099-INT)
- Child tax credit to be claimed, **$2,000** (two qualified children × $1,000.00). Reported as follows: child tax credit (line 33): **$593** (source: Form 8812) additional child tax credit (line 42): **$1,407** (source: Form 8812).
- Tax withheld, **$0** (source: Form W-2)
- Earned income credit, **$1,124** (source: Schedule EIC Worksheet)

Since the Wilsons have no tax liability, they cannot give money to the presidential election campaign.

FORM 1040

Form 1040, U.S. Individual Income Tax Return, is the most common tax return. Form 1040, a two-page return, has a similar format to Form 1040A. Page one focuses on the computation of AGI, and page two provides for the computation of the refund or amount owed. Form 1040 may involve numerous supporting schedules.

Taxpayers must use Form 1040 when they do not qualify to use either Form 1040EZ or Form 1040A. They may also elect Form 1040 over one of these other forms to save taxes (more deductions and credits are available). This form is the taxpayer's most comprehensive reporting device. It provides for all types of income, deductions, credits, and other taxes that might be owed. Basically Form 1040 has no limits on the amounts and the items that can be reported. Chapter 4 illustrates Form 1040.

Form 1040PC

Another version of Form 1040 is Form 1040PC. As the ownership of personal computers increases, more and more people prepare their tax return using approved computer software. The IRS can process this return (Form 1040PC) faster and more accurately than the regular Form 1040.

ELECTRONIC FILING

The IRS encourages electronic filing of tax returns. The IRS Restructuring and Reform Act of 1998 requires the IRS to have 80% of all tax returns filed electronically by 2007. Half of the 2004 tax returns were filed electronically.

IRS HOME PAGE

The IRS provides much useful information through its Internet home page (http://www.irs .gov). This is a good source of forms, publications, and other material that may be downloaded. (See the inside back cover and Appendix A.)

FIGURE 2-8 Filled-In Form 1040A, Page 1

Form **1040A**

Department of the Treasury—Internal Revenue Service

U.S. Individual Income Tax Return (99) **2005** — IRS Use Only—Do not write or staple in this space.

OMB No. 1545-0085

Label (See page 18.)

Your first name and initial: Sarah R. — Last name: Wilson

Your social security number: 282 56 9320

If a joint return, spouse's first name and initial: James E. — Last name: Wilson

Spouse's social security number: 271 04 7926

Use the IRS label. Otherwise, please print or type.

Home address (number and street). If you have a P.O. box, see page 18.
1624 West Third Street — Apt. no.

You **must** enter your SSN(s) above.

City, town or post office, state, and ZIP code. If you have a foreign address, see page 18.
Muskegon, MU 49441

Checking a box below will not change your tax or refund.

Presidential Election Campaign ▶ Check here if you, or your spouse if filing jointly, want $3 to go to this fund (see page 18) ▶ ☐ You ☐ Spouse

Filing status Check only one box.

1 ☐ Single
2 ☒ Married filing jointly (even if only one had income)
3 ☐ Married filing separately. Enter spouse's SSN above and full name here. ▶
4 ☐ Head of household (with qualifying person). (See page 19.) If the qualifying person is a child but not your dependent, enter this child's name here. ▶
5 ☐ Qualifying widow(er) with dependent child (see page 19)

Exemptions

6a ☒ **Yourself.** If someone can claim you as a dependent, **do not** check box 6a.
b ☒ **Spouse**

Boxes checked on 6a and 6b: 2

c **Dependents:**

(1) First name — Last name	(2) Dependent's social security number	(3) Dependent's relationship to you	(4) ✓ if qualifying child for child tax credit (see page 21)
Martha A. Wilson	826 45 3710	daughter	☐
Karl B. Wilson	850 21 5263	son	☒
Susan K. Wilson	860 40 5721	daughter	☒
			☐
			☐
			☐

No. of children on 6c who:
• lived with you: 3
• did not live with you due to divorce or separation (see page 21):
Dependents on 6c not entered above:

If more than six dependents, see page 20.

d Total number of exemptions claimed.

Add numbers on lines above ▶ 5

Income

Attach Form(s) W-2 here. Also attach Form(s) 1099-R if tax was withheld.

If you did not get a W-2, see page 22.

Enclose, but do not attach, any payment.

7 Wages, salaries, tips, etc. Attach Form(s) W-2. — 7 — 31,765 00
8a Taxable interest. Attach Schedule 1 if required. — 8a — 150 00
b Tax-exempt interest. **Do not** include on line 8a. — 8b
9a Ordinary dividends. Attach Schedule 1 if required. — 9a
b Qualified dividends (see page 23). — 9b
10 Capital gain distributions (see page 23). — 10
11a IRA distributions. — 11a — 11b Taxable amount (see page 23). — 11b
12a Pensions and annuities. — 12a — 12b Taxable amount (see page 24). — 12b
13 Unemployment compensation and Alaska Permanent Fund dividends. — 13
14a Social security benefits. — 14a — 14b Taxable amount (see page 26). — 14b
15 Add lines 7 through 14b (far right column). This is your **total income.** ▶ 15 — 31,915 00

Adjusted gross income

16 Educator expenses (see page 26). — 16
17 IRA deduction (see page 26). — 17
18 Student loan interest deduction (see page 29). — 18
19 Tuition and fees deduction (see page 29). — 19
20 Add lines 16 through 19. These are your **total adjustments.** — 20
21 Subtract line 20 from line 15. This is your **adjusted gross income.** ▶ 21 — 31,915 00

For Disclosure, Privacy Act, and Paperwork Reduction Act Notice, see page 57. — Cat. No. 11327A — Form **1040A** (2005)

FIGURE 2-8 Filled-In Form 1040A, Page 2

Form 1040A (2005)					Page **2**
Tax, credits, and payments	**22**	Enter the amount from line 21 (adjusted gross income).		22	31,915 00
	23a	Check if: ☐ **You** were born before January 2, 1941, ☐ Blind ☐ **Spouse** was born before January 2, 1941, ☐ Blind } **Total boxes checked ▶** 23a			
Standard Deduction for—	**b**	If you are married filing separately and your spouse itemizes deductions, see page 30 and check here ▶ 23b ☐			
• People who checked any box on line 23a or 23b **or** who can be claimed as a dependent, see page 31.	**24**	Enter your **standard deduction** (see left margin).		24	10,000 00
	25	Subtract line 24 from line 22. If line 24 is more than line 22, enter -0-.		25	21,915 00
	26	If line 22 is $109,475 or less, multiply $3,200 by the total number of exemptions claimed on line 6d. If line 22 is over $109,475, see the worksheet on page 32.		26	16,000 00
	27	Subtract line 26 from line 25. If line 26 is more than line 25, enter -0-. This is your **taxable income.** ▶		27	5,915 00
• All others: Single or Married filing separately, $5,000	**28**	**Tax,** including any alternative minimum tax (see page 31).		28	593 00
	29	Credit for child and dependent care expenses. Attach Schedule 2.	29		
	30	Credit for the elderly or the disabled. Attach Schedule 3.	30		
Married filing jointly or Qualifying widow(er), $10,000	**31**	Education credits. Attach Form 8863.	31		
	32	Retirement savings contributions credit. Attach Form 8880.	32		
Head of household, $7,300	**33**	Child tax credit (see page 36). Attach Form 8901 if required.	33	593 00	
	34	Adoption credit. Attach Form 8839.	34		
	35	Add lines 29 through 34. These are your **total credits.**		35	593 00
	36	Subtract line 35 from line 28. If line 35 is more than line 28, enter -0-.		36	0
	37	Advance earned income credit payments from Form(s) W-2.		37	
	38	Add lines 36 and 37. This is your **total tax.** ▶		38	0
	39	Federal income tax withheld from Forms W-2 and 1099.	39	0	
	40	2005 estimated tax payments and amount applied from 2004 return.	40		
If you have a qualifying child, attach Schedule EIC.	**41a**	**Earned income credit (EIC).**	41a	1,124 00	
	b	Nontaxable combat pay election. 41b			
	42	Additional child tax credit. Attach Form 8812.	42	1,407 00	
	43	Add lines 39, 40, 41a, and 42. These are your **total payments.** ▶		43	2,531 00
Refund	**44**	If line 43 is more than line 38, subtract line 38 from line 43. This is the amount you **overpaid.**		44	2,531 00
Direct deposit? See page 50 and fill in 45b, 45c, and 45d.	**45a**	Amount of line 44 you want **refunded to you.** ▶		45a	2,531 00
	▶ **b**	Routing number	**▶ c** Type: ☐ Checking ☐ Savings		
	▶ **d**	Account number			
	46	Amount of line 44 you want **applied to your 2006 estimated tax.**	46		
Amount you owe	**47**	**Amount you owe.** Subtract line 43 from line 38. For details on how to pay, see page 51. ▶		47	
	48	Estimated tax penalty (see page 51).	48		
Third party designee	Do you want to allow another person to discuss this return with the IRS (see page 52)? ☐ **Yes.** Complete the following. ☐ **No**				
	Designee's name ▶	Phone no. ▶ ( )	Personal identification number (PIN) ▶		
Sign here Joint return? See page 18. Keep a copy for your records.	Under penalties of perjury, I declare that I have examined this return and accompanying schedules and statements, and to the best of my knowledge and belief, they are true, correct, and accurately list all amounts and sources of income I received during the tax year. Declaration of preparer (other than the taxpayer) is based on all information of which the preparer has any knowledge.				
	Your signature *Sarah R. Wilson*	Date 2-26-06	Your occupation Cook	Daytime phone number ( )	
	Spouse's signature. If a joint return, **both** must sign. *James E. Wilsion*	Date 2-26-06	Spouse's occupation Janitor		
Paid preparer's use only	Preparer's signature ▶	Date	Check if self-employed ☐	Preparer's SSN or PTIN	
	Firm's name (or yours if self-employed), address, and ZIP code ▶		EIN Phone no. ( )		
	✿ *Printed on recycled paper*			Form **1040A** (2005)	

EXTENSIONS OF TIME TO FILE *Automatic 6 mth extension*

Individuals and other tax entities may obtain an extension of time to file their tax returns. The extension provides taxpayers with more time to file their tax returns but *does not* provide more time for them to pay their taxes. Taxpayers must still pay their taxes in a timely manner (usually paid in full by original due date for the return) even when they obtain an extension of time to file their returns.

Entity	Form Number for Extension	Extension of Time
Individual (Form 1040, Form 1040A, or Form 1040EZ)		
Automatic	Form 4868	Four months
Second extension	Form 2688	Up to two more months
Partnership (Form 1065)		
Automatic	Form 8736	Three months
Second extension	Form 8800	Up to three more months
S Corporation (Form 1120S)		
Automatic	Form 7004	Six months
C Corporation (Form 1120 or Form 1120A)		
Automatic	Form 7004	Six months

Information for Figure 2-9: Filled-In Form 4868

Figure 2-9 shows a filled-in Form 4868, Application for Automatic Extension of Time to File U.S. Individual Income Tax Return, for Carla Kramer. She expects her total tax liability to be $4,580, and she has had $4,400 withheld from her wages. Kramer sends a check for $180 payable to the United States Treasury with the extension.

FIGURE 2-9　Filled-In Form 4868

Form **4868** Department of the Treasury Internal Revenue Service	**Application for Automatic Extension of Time To File U.S. Individual Income Tax Return** For calendar year 2005, or other tax year beginning , 2005, ending , 200 .	OMB No. 1545-0188 20**05**
	Caution: Incorrect or missing information may cause a delay in processing.	

Part I　　　Identification	**Part II**　　　Individual Income Tax
1 Your name(s) (see instructions) Carla A. Kramer	**4** Estimate of total tax liability for 2005 . $ 4,580.00
Address (see instructions) 6820 W. 59th Street	**5** Total 2005 payments 4,400.00
City, town, or post office　|　State　|　ZIP code Memphis　|　TN　|　38105-1960	**6 Balance due.** Subtract line 5 from line 4 (see instructions) 180.00
2 Your social security number　|　**3** Spouse's social security number 652 19 9990	**7** Amount you are paying (see instructions) . ▶ 180.00
	8 Check here if you are "out of the country" and a U.S. citizen or resident . . . . ▶ ☐
For Privacy Act and Paperwork Reduction Act Notice, see page 4.	Cat. No. 13141W　　Form **4868** (2005)

2

QUESTIONS AND PROBLEMS

1. **Using the Tax Rate Schedules.** The IRS publishes Tax Rate Schedules and a Tax Table. When must taxpayers use the Rate Schedules instead of the Tax Table to compute their income tax liability?

2. **Comparison of Tax Table and Rate Schedule.** Mark Long, a single person, files his tax return as a HOH. He has taxable income of $40,100.

    a. Enter Long's tax liability from the Tax Table in the space provided.

    $5529

    b. Compute Long's tax liability using the Tax Rate Schedule that applies. Is there a difference in the two tax figures? Why?

    40,100   5447.50 × 25% =
    39800

    Tax table is based on $50.00 increments ($40,125), used addt'l $25 of income.

    40100
    39800
    _____
    300
    × 25%
    _____
    75.00

    5447.50
    _____
    75.00
    _____
    $5522.50

3. **Tax Computation.** Barbara Landerson, age 25 and single, is employed at a monthly salary of $2,050. She claims one exemption. Her employer withheld $2,214 from her wages for income taxes for 12 months of work. Compute the amount of Landerson's income tax due to or from the IRS. $184.50/mth income taxes

    AGI 2050 × 12 = 24600
    Standard deduction = -5000
    _____
    19600
    less: Pers'nal exemption - 3200
    _____
    16400

    Amt withheld   2214
    less: Income tax table 2099
    _____
    $115 refund due

4. **Tax Computations.** Compute the taxable income and income tax liability (before refunds and credits) for each of the following taxpayers who claims a standard deduction:

Item	A	B	C	D	E
AGI*	$39,600	$14,642	$11,700	$17,736	$39,980
Exemptions	2 – 6,400	1 – 3,200	2 – 6,400	3 – 9,600	4 12,800 ✓
Filing status	Surviving – 10,000 spouse	Single – 5,000	Married filing separately – 5,000	HOH – 7,300	Married filing jointly 10,000 ✓
Other	—	Over 65 – 1,250	—	—	One spouse blind 1,000 ✓
Taxable income	$ 22,200	$ 5,192	$ 300	$ 836	$ 16,180
Income tax	$ 2,754	$ 518	$ 31	$ 84	$ 1,696

*Salaries

5. **The Value of Tax Credits.** What is the difference between a tax credit and a tax deduction? If a taxpayer with a marginal tax rate of 15% has a $1,000 deduction, how much tax will she save? How much tax will she save with a $1,000 tax credit?

6. **Child and Dependent Care Credit.** Bud and Katie Milner file a joint return. During 2005, they paid $11,000 to their nanny to look after their 3 children, ages 2, 9, and 11. Bud and Katie both work and earned $24,000 and $31,000, respectively. The wages are the Milners' only source of income, and they have no deductions for AGI.

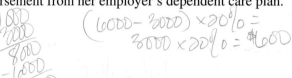

a. Compute the Milners' child and dependent care credit.

$6000 \times 20\% = \$1200$

b. Compute the Milners' child and dependent care credit assuming Katie received a $3,000 reimbursement from her employer's dependent care plan.

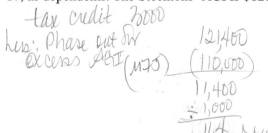

$(6000 - 3000) \times 20\% =$
$3000 \times 20\% = \$600$

7. **Child Tax Credit.** For each of the following taxpayers, compute the 2005 child tax credit.

a. Jay and Marie Stockton file a joint return and claim their three children, all under age 17, as dependents. The Stocktons' AGI is $121,400.

tax credit 3000
less: Phase out for excess AGI (1175)

121,400
(110,000)
11,400
÷ 1,000
11.4 rounded up 12
×50
600

3000
(600)
$2400

b. Tom Stevenson files as head of household. He claims his twin sons, age 4, as dependents. Stevenson's AGI is $80,340.

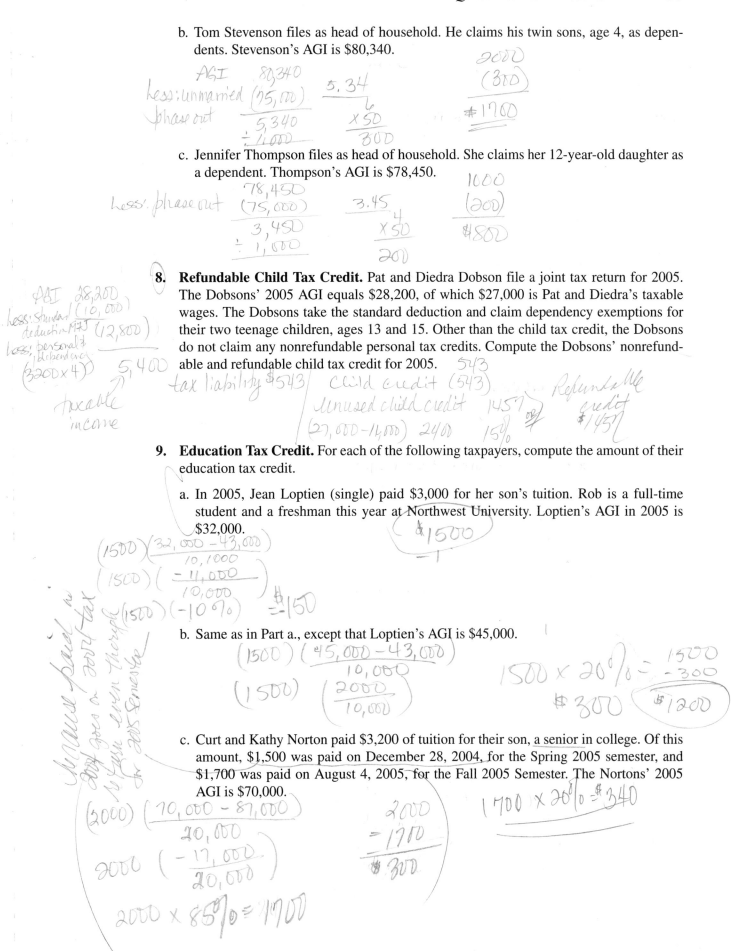

c. Jennifer Thompson files as head of household. She claims her 12-year-old daughter as a dependent. Thompson's AGI is $78,450.

8. **Refundable Child Tax Credit.** Pat and Diedra Dobson file a joint tax return for 2005. The Dobsons' 2005 AGI equals $28,200, of which $27,000 is Pat and Diedra's taxable wages. The Dobsons take the standard deduction and claim dependency exemptions for their two teenage children, ages 13 and 15. Other than the child tax credit, the Dobsons do not claim any nonrefundable personal tax credits. Compute the Dobsons' nonrefundable and refundable child tax credit for 2005.

9. **Education Tax Credit.** For each of the following taxpayers, compute the amount of their education tax credit.

a. In 2005, Jean Loptien (single) paid $3,000 for her son's tuition. Rob is a full-time student and a freshman this year at Northwest University. Loptien's AGI in 2005 is $32,000.

b. Same as in Part a., except that Loptien's AGI is $45,000.

c. Curt and Kathy Norton paid $3,200 of tuition for their son, a senior in college. Of this amount, $1,500 was paid on December 28, 2004, for the Spring 2005 semester, and $1,700 was paid on August 4, 2005, for the Fall 2005 Semester. The Nortons' 2005 AGI is $70,000.

d. In 2005, Paul and Karen Mitchell pay $2,000 for their daughter's tuition for the Spring and Fall 2005 semesters. Their daughter is a full-time graduate student. The Mitchells also paid $3,500 for their son's tuition for the Spring and Fall semesters. In Fall 2005, their son began his sophomore year of college. The Mitchells' AGI is $44,200.

HOPE (1000 + (50% × 1000) = 1500
lifetime (2000 × 20%) + 400
$1900

e. Same as in Part d., except that the Mitchells' AGI is $91,200.

1900 (87000 - 91,200)   1900 × 21% = 399   1900
20000   - 399
1900 (4200) $1501
20000

10. **Earned income credit.** For each of the following cases, compute the taxpayer's earned income credit.

a. Pat and Ron Barnett file a joint return, claiming their two sons, ages 3 and 5, as dependents. The Barnetts' AGI is $14,400, which consists entirely of Ron's wages.

14,400
4388
14,400

$4400

b. Joseph Williams is a 25-year-old graduate student. During 2005 his income consists of $5,000 of wages, and $80 in interest from a savings account. Williams files as single and claims no dependents.

5000
384
5080

$384

c. Suzanne and Vernon Zimmerman file a joint return, claiming their 6-year-old daughter as a dependent. The Zimmermans' AGI consists of Vernon's $16,375 in wages, and $400 in dividend income.

16375
2662
16775

$2597

d. Sarah Sprinter files as head of household, claiming her 2-year-old son as a dependent. Sprinter's AGI consists of $14,000 in wages and $3,300 in interest income.

14000
2662
17300

$2190

Disqualifying income exceeds $2700 not eligible for EIC.

11. Adoption Credit. John and Mary Hoppe paid $14,000 in qualified adoption expenses of a healthy child for an adoption that was finalized in 2005. The Hoppes' AGI for 2005 is $177,060. In addition, the Hoppes received $3,000 from an employer adoption assistance plan. What is the Hoppes' adoption credit?

7630 − [(7630)×((177,060 − 159,450) ÷ 40,000)]

−3357

$4273

(17610 ÷ 40,000)

(7630)(.4490) = 3357

12. Retirement Savings Contributions Credit. Tom Wherry's joint tax return shows $45,000 of AGI. During the year, Wherry contributed $1,500 to his Roth IRA and $1,500 to his wife's Roth IRA. What credit is available for these contributions?

10%   (3000 × 10%) = 300

13. 1040EZ Requirements. The taxpayers described in Parts a. through g. want to file Form 1040EZ. For each taxpayer, state whether he or she can file Form 1040EZ. If a taxpayer cannot file Form 1040EZ, state the reason(s) for your answer.

a. A single taxpayer has tax-exempt interest income of $1,400 and taxable income of $99,900 from wages.

b. A married taxpayer filing a separate return has taxable income of $47,290, including interest income of $100.

c. A single taxpayer has taxable income of $35,683, including $1,700 of interest income. The taxpayer also has $200 of tax-exempt interest.

d. A HOH taxpayer has taxable income of $30,400, including interest income of $250. The taxpayer has two dependents.

e. A single taxpayer has taxable income of $47,800, including dividend income of $300.

f. A single taxpayer has taxable income of $31,654, including tip income of $4,500 included as wages on Form W-2 and interest income of $75.

g. A married taxpayer filing jointly has taxable income of $47,290, including interest income of $100. Both the taxpayer and spouse are elderly and blind. They cannot claim another person as a dependency exemption.

14. **Form 1040EZ.** Jeanne M. Searson (SSN 369-48-5783), a 27-year-old unmarried clerk, lives at 4502 Lakeside Drive, Echo, CA 92040-1234. Her Forms W-2, Wage and Tax Statements, contain the following information:

	Gross Wages	Income Tax Withheld	FICA Wages	FICA Taxes Withheld
Interlake Co.	$ 5,240	$169	$ 5,240	$400.86
Data-Mate Co.				
(present employer)	6,280	206	6,280	480.42
Totals	$11,520	$375	$11,520	$881.28

In addition to her wages, Searson received $25 in interest on her passbook account at the Echo Savings and Loan Bank. She wants $3 of her tax money to go to the presidential election campaign fund. Using the Form 1040EZ provided, prepare her tax return for 2005. She signs the return on February 6, 2006.

15. **Tax Planning.** Marilyn Doming and Charles Smith, unmarried individuals, are both 29 years of age. For 2005 Doming and Smith will earn wages of $60,000 and $35,000 respectively, their only source of income. They are thinking about getting married in either December or January. Before setting a wedding date, they want to know how much they will save in federal income taxes if they get married in December and file a joint return. They ask you to compare their combined federal income taxes as single individuals with their taxes as a married couple filing jointly. Neither taxpayer has any dependents. Also, no other taxpayer can claim Doming or Smith as a dependent. Regardless of their marital status, they will claim the standard deduction(s).

(Use for Problem 14.)

Form **1040EZ**	Department of the Treasury— Internal Revenue Service **Income Tax Return for Single and Joint Filers With No Dependents** (99) **2005**		OMB No. 1545-0675

Label
(See page 11.)
Use the IRS label.
Otherwise, please print or type.

L A B E L   H E R E

Your first name and initial	Last name	Your social security number
Jeanne M	Searson	369 98 5783
If a joint return, spouse's first name and initial	Last name	Spouse's social security number

Home address (number and street). If you have a P.O. box, see page 11. — Apt. no.
4502 Lakeside Drive

City, town or post office, state, and ZIP code. If you have a foreign address, see page 11.
Echo, CA 92040-1234

▲ You **must** enter your SSN(s) above. ▲

Presidential Election Campaign (page 11) ▶

Checking a box below will not change your tax or refund.

Check here if you, or your spouse if a joint return, want $3 to go to this fund? . . . ▶ ☒ **You**   ☐ **Spouse**

Income

Attach Form(s) W-2 here.

Enclose, but do not attach, any payment.

1	Wages, salaries, and tips. This should be shown in box 1 of your Form(s) W-2. Attach your Form(s) W-2.	1	11 520
2	Taxable interest. If the total is over $1,500, you cannot use Form 1040EZ.	2	25
3	Unemployment compensation and Alaska Permanent Fund dividends (see page 13).	3	
4	Add lines 1, 2, and 3. This is your **adjusted gross income.**	4	11 545
5	If someone can claim you (or your spouse if a joint return) as a dependent, check the applicable box(es) below and enter the amount from the worksheet on back. ☐ **You** ☐ **Spouse** If someone cannot claim you (or your spouse if a joint return), enter $8,200 if **single**; $16,400 if **married filing jointly.**	5	8200
6	Subtract line 5 from line 4. If line 5 is larger than line 4, enter -0-. This is your **taxable income.** ▶	6	3 345

Payments and tax

7	Federal income tax withheld from box 2 of your Form(s) W-2.	7	375
8a	Earned income credit (EIC).	8a	17
b	Nontaxable combat pay election. 8b		
9	Add lines 7 and 8a. These are your **total payments.** ▶	9	392
10	**Tax.** Use the amount on **line 6** above to find your tax in the tax table on pages 24–32 of the booklet. Then, enter the tax from the table on this line.	10	333

Refund

Have it directly deposited! See page 18 and fill in 11b, 11c, and 11d.

11a	If line 9 is larger than line 10, subtract line 10 from line 9. This is your **refund.** ▶	11a	59

▶ b Routing number ☐☐☐☐☐☐☐☐☐   ▶ c Type: ☐ Checking ☐ Savings

▶ d Account number ☐☐☐☐☐☐☐☐☐☐☐☐☐☐☐☐☐

Amount you owe

12	If line 10 is larger than line 9, subtract line 9 from line 10. This is the **amount you owe.** For details on how to pay, see page 19. ▶	12	

Third party designee

Do you want to allow another person to discuss this return with the IRS (see page 19)? ☐ **Yes.** Complete the following. ☐ **No**

Designee's name ▶ ____   Phone no. ▶ ( )   Personal identification number (PIN) ☐☐☐☐☐

Sign here

Joint return? See page 11. Keep a copy for your records.

Under penalties of perjury, I declare that I have examined this return, and to the best of my knowledge and belief, it is true, correct, and accurately lists all amounts and sources of income I received during the tax year. Declaration of preparer (other than the taxpayer) is based on all information of which the preparer has any knowledge.

Your signature	Date	Your occupation	Daytime phone number
Jeanne Searson	2/6/06	Clerk	( )
Spouse's signature. If a joint return, **both** must sign.	Date	Spouse's occupation	

Paid preparer's use only

Preparer's signature ▶	Date	Check if self-employed ☐	Preparer's SSN or PTIN
Firm's name (or yours if self-employed), address, and ZIP code ▶		EIN	
		Phone no. ( )	

For Disclosure, Privacy Act, and Paperwork Reduction Act Notice, see page 23.   Cat. No. 11329W   Form **1040EZ** (2005)

16. Form 1040EZ. Cele P. (SSN 248-40-8455) and Marvin K. (SSN 248-40-7834) Goldman, ages 36 and 38, received interest income of $390 on their savings account at the Portage Bank in 2005. Cele and Marvin are both employed by Portage Hardware, 13 W. Main Street, Portage, MO 49067. Cele is a cashier at the hardware store, and Marvin is a sales representative. Their home address is 248 Maple Street in Portage. Cele and Marvin had no other sources of income. Since they have no itemized deductions, they claim the standard deduction. Neither Cele nor Marvin is blind, disabled, or a dependent. They decide to take advantage of the opportunity for joint filers to use Form 1040EZ. Both want $3 to go to the presidential election campaign fund. Using the following Form W-2 data, prepare the Goldmans' Form 1040EZ for 2005. They sign and file their Form 1040EZ on January 20, 2006.

	Gross Wages	Income Tax Withheld	OASDI Wages	OASDI Tax Withheld	Medicare Wages	Medicare Tax Withheld	State Income Tax Withheld
Cele	$13,400	$ 957	$13,400	$ 830	$13,400	$194	$ 402
Marvin	21,900	1,228	21,900	1,358	21,900	318	657
Totals	$35,300	$2,185	$35,300	$2,188	$35,300	$512	$1,059

17. Form 1040A. John J. (SSN 291-27-4631) and Mary A. (SSN 293-41-7032) Jackson, ages 66 and 65 respectively, have good vision. John is a retired electrician. Mary is a homemaker. The Jacksons live at 4622 Beaver Lake Road, Blooming Grove, MN 55164. They have no dependents. They decide to file a joint return on Form 1040A. From their traditional IRAs, they received $3,517, all of which is taxable. John received a pension of $20,000 from the Huellett Company, of which $16,800 is taxable. The Jacksons also receive $3,100 in nontaxable social security benefits. From time to time their five children, who are all farmers, help them with gifts of food. Prepare the Jacksons' Form 1040A tax return. The Jacksons sign and file their return on February 7, 2006.

18. Internet Problem: Filling out Form 4868.

Cheryl Bier chooses to obtain an extension of time to file her tax return. Bier expects her total tax liability to be $16,500. She had $15,800 withheld from her wages. Bier (SSN 678-59-1234) lives at 829 North Broadway, Garden Grove, CA 92842.

Go to the IRS Web site and locate Form 4868. Using the computer, fill in the form for Bier and print out a completed copy.

See Appendix A for instructions on use of the IRS Web site.

(Use for Problem 16.)

Form **1040EZ**	Department of the Treasury—Internal Revenue Service **Income Tax Return for Single and Joint Filers With No Dependents** (99)	**2005**	OMB No. 1545-0675

Label

(See page 11.)

Use the IRS label. Otherwise, please print or type.

L A B E L H E R E

Your first name and initial | Last name

Your social security number

If a joint return, spouse's first name and initial | Last name

Spouse's social security number

Home address (number and street). If you have a P.O. box, see page 11. | Apt. no.

▲ **You must enter your SSN(s) above.** ▲

City, town or post office, state, and ZIP code. If you have a foreign address, see page 11.

Checking a box below will not change your tax or refund.

Presidential Election Campaign (page 11) ▶

Check here if you, or your spouse if a joint return, want $3 to go to this fund? . . . ▶ ☐ **You**   ☐ **Spouse**

Income

Attach Form(s) W-2 here. Enclose, but do not attach, any payment.

1   Wages, salaries, and tips. This should be shown in box 1 of your Form(s) W-2. Attach your Form(s) W-2.   **1**

2   Taxable interest. If the total is over $1,500, you cannot use Form 1040EZ.   **2**

3   Unemployment compensation and Alaska Permanent Fund dividends (see page 13).   **3**

4   Add lines 1, 2, and 3. This is your **adjusted gross income.**   **4**

5   If someone can claim you (or your spouse if a joint return) as a dependent, check the applicable box(es) below and enter the amount from the worksheet on back.

☐ **You**   ☐ **Spouse**

If someone cannot claim you (or your spouse if a joint return), enter $8,200 if **single**; $16,400 if **married filing jointly.**   **5**

6   Subtract line 5 from line 4. If line 5 is larger than line 4, enter -0-. This is your **taxable income.**   ▶ **6**

Payments and tax

7   Federal income tax withheld from box 2 of your Form(s) W-2.   **7**

8a   **Earned income credit (EIC).**   **8a**

  b   Nontaxable combat pay election.   **8b**

9   Add lines 7 and 8a. These are your **total payments.**   ▶ **9**

10   **Tax.** Use the amount on **line 6 above** to find your tax in the tax table on pages 24–32 of the booklet. Then, enter the tax from the table on this line.   **10**

Refund

Have it directly deposited! See page 18 and fill in 11b, 11c, and 11d.

11a   If line 9 is larger than line 10, subtract line 10 from line 9. This is your **refund.**   ▶ **11a**

▶ b   Routing number   ▶ c   Type: ☐ Checking ☐ Savings

▶ d   Account number

Amount you owe

12   If line 10 is larger than line 9, subtract line 9 from line 10. This is the **amount you owe.** For details on how to pay, see page 19.   ▶ **12**

Third party designee

Do you want to allow another person to discuss this return with the IRS (see page 19)? ☐ **Yes.** Complete the following. ☐**No**

Designee's name ▶ | Phone no. ▶ ( ) | Personal identification number (PIN) ▶

Sign here

Joint return? See page 11. Keep a copy for your records.

Under penalties of perjury, I declare that I have examined this return, and to the best of my knowledge and belief, it is true, correct, and accurately lists all amounts and sources of income I received during the tax year. Declaration of preparer (other than the taxpayer) is based on all information of which the preparer has any knowledge.

Your signature | Date | Your occupation | Daytime phone number ( )

Spouse's signature. If a joint return, **both** must sign. | Date | Spouse's occupation

Paid preparer's use only

Preparer's signature ▶ | Date | Check if self-employed ☐ | Preparer's SSN or PTIN

Firm's name (or yours if self-employed), address, and ZIP code ▶ | EIN | Phone no. ( )

For Disclosure, Privacy Act, and Paperwork Reduction Act Notice, see page 23.   Cat. No. 11329W   Form **1040EZ** (2005)

(Use for Problem 17.)

Form **1040A**	Department of the Treasury—Internal Revenue Service			
	U.S. Individual Income Tax Return (99) **2005**		IRS Use Only—Do not write or staple in this space.	

Label (See page 18.)

Use the IRS label. Otherwise, please print or type.

Presidential Election Campaign

	Your first name and initial	Last name	Your social security number
L A B E L	Jackson	John	29127 4631
H E R E	If a joint return, spouse's first name and initial	Last name	Spouse's social security number
	Jackson	Mary	293 41 7032

Home address (number and street). If you have a P.O. box, see page 18. | Apt. no.
4622 Beaver Lake Rd.

You must enter your SSN(s) above. ▲

City, town or post office, state, and ZIP code. If you have a foreign address, see page 18.
Bloomington, MN

Checking a box below will not change your tax or refund.

► Check here if you, or your spouse if filing jointly, want $3 to go to this fund (see page 18) ► ☐ You ☐ Spouse

Filing status
Check only one box.

1 ☐ Single
2 ☒ Married filing jointly (even if only one had income)
3 ☐ Married filing separately. Enter spouse's SSN above and full name here. ►
4 ☐ Head of household (with qualifying person). (See page 19.) If the qualifying person is a child but not your dependent, enter this child's name here. ►
5 ☐ Qualifying widow(er) with dependent child (see page 19)

Exemptions

If more than six dependents, see page 20.

6a ☒ **Yourself.** If someone can claim you as a dependent, **do not** check box 6a.
b ☒ **Spouse**

Boxes checked on 6a and 6b — 2

c Dependents:		(2) Dependent's social security number	(3) Dependent's relationship to you	(4) ✓ if qualifying child for child tax credit (see page 21)
(1) First name	Last name			
				☐
				☐
				☐
				☐
				☐
				☐

No. of children on 6c who:
• lived with you
• did not live with you due to divorce or separation (see page 21)

Dependents on 6c not entered above

d Total number of exemptions claimed.

Add numbers on lines above ► 2

Income

Attach Form(s) W-2 here. Also attach Form(s) 1099-R if tax was withheld.

If you did not get a W-2, see page 22.

Enclose, but do not attach, any payment.

7	Wages, salaries, tips, etc. Attach Form(s) W-2.	7	
8a	**Taxable** interest. Attach Schedule 1 if required.	8a	
b	**Tax-exempt** interest. **Do not** include on line 8a.	8b	
9a	Ordinary dividends. Attach Schedule 1 if required.	9a	
b	Qualified dividends (see page 23).	9b	
10	Capital gain distributions (see page 23).	10	
11a	IRA distributions. 11a 3517	**11b** Taxable amount (see page 23). 11b	3517
12a	Pensions and annuities. 12a 20,000	**12b** Taxable amount (see page 24). 12b	16800
13	Unemployment compensation and Alaska Permanent Fund dividends.	13	
14a	Social security benefits. 14a 3100	**14b** Taxable amount (see page 26). 14b	0
15	Add lines 7 through 14b (far right column). This is your **total income.** ►	15	20317

Adjusted gross income

16	Educator expenses (see page 26).	16		
17	IRA deduction (see page 26).	17		
18	Student loan interest deduction (see page 29).	18		
19	Tuition and fees deduction (see page 29).	19		
20	Add lines 16 through 19. These are your **total adjustments.**	20		
21	Subtract line 20 from line 15. This is your **adjusted gross income.** ►	21	20317	

For Disclosure, Privacy Act, and Paperwork Reduction Act Notice, see page 57. Cat. No. 11327A Form **1040A** (2005)

(Use for Problem 17.)

Form 1040A (2005)			Page **2**

Tax, credits, and payments	22	Enter the amount from line 21 (adjusted gross income).	22	*2031 7*
Standard Deduction for— • People who checked any box on line 23a or 23b **or** who can be claimed as a dependent, see page 31. • All others: Single or Married filing separately, $5,000 Married filing jointly or Qualifying widow(er), $10,000 Head of household, $7,300	23a	Check if: ☒ **You** were born before January 2, 1941, ☐ Blind ☐ **Spouse** was born before January 2, 1941, ☐ Blind } **Total boxes checked ▶** 23a		*2*
	b	If you are married filing separately and your spouse itemizes deductions, see page 30 and check here ▶ 23b	☐	
	24	Enter your **standard deduction** (see left margin).	24	*12000*
	25	Subtract line 24 from line 22. If line 24 is more than line 22, enter -0-.	25	*8317*
	26	If line 22 is $109,475 or less, multiply $3,200 by the total number of exemptions claimed on line 6d. If line 22 is over $109,475, see the worksheet on page 32.	26	*6400*
	27	Subtract line 26 from line 25. If line 26 is more than line 25, enter -0-. This is your **taxable income.** ▶	27	*1917*
	28	**Tax,** including any alternative minimum tax (see page 31).	28	*191*
	29	Credit for child and dependent care expenses. Attach Schedule 2.	29	
	30	Credit for the elderly or the disabled. Attach Schedule 3.	30	
	31	Education credits. Attach Form 8863.	31	
	32	Retirement savings contributions credit. Attach Form 8880.	32	
	33	Child tax credit (see page 36). Attach Form 8901 if required.	33	
	34	Adoption credit. Attach Form 8839.	34	
	35	Add lines 29 through 34. These are your **total credits.**	35	*0*
	36	Subtract line 35 from line 28. If line 35 is more than line 28, enter -0-.	36	*191*
	37	Advance earned income credit payments from Form(s) W-2.	37	
	38	Add lines 36 and 37. This is your **total tax.** ▶	38	*191*
	39	Federal income tax withheld from Forms W-2 and 1099.	39	
If you have a qualifying child, attach Schedule EIC.	40	2005 estimated tax payments and amount applied from 2004 return.	40	
	41a	**Earned income credit (EIC).**	41a	
	b	Nontaxable combat pay election. 41b		
	42	Additional child tax credit. Attach Form 8812.	42	
	43	Add lines 39, 40, 41a, and 42. These are your **total payments.** ▶	43	*0*
Refund Direct deposit? See page 50 and fill in 45b, 45c, and 45d.	44	If line 43 is more than line 38, subtract line 38 from line 43. This is the amount you **overpaid.**	44	
	45a	Amount of line 44 you want **refunded to you.** ▶	45a	
	▶ b	Routing number [ ] ▶ c Type: ☐ Checking ☐ Savings		
	▶ d	Account number [ ]		
	46	Amount of line 44 you want **applied to your 2006 estimated tax.**	46	
Amount you owe	47	**Amount you owe.** Subtract line 43 from line 38. For details on how to pay, see page 51. ▶	47	*191*
	48	Estimated tax penalty (see page 51).	48	

Third party designee	Do you want to allow another person to discuss this return with the IRS (see page 52)? ☐ **Yes.** Complete the following. ☐ **No**
	Designee's name ▶ Phone no. ▶ ( ) Personal identification number (PIN) [ ]

Sign here Joint return? See page 18. Keep a copy for your records.	Under penalties of perjury, I declare that I have examined this return and accompanying schedules and statements, and to the best of my knowledge and belief, they are true, correct, and accurately list all amounts and sources of income I received during the tax year. Declaration of preparer (other than the taxpayer) is based on all information of which the preparer has any knowledge.

Your signature	Date	Your occupation	Daytime phone number ( )
Spouse's signature. If a joint return, **both** must sign.	Date	Spouse's occupation	

Paid preparer's use only	Preparer's signature ▶	Date	Check if self-employed ☐	Preparer's SSN or PTIN
	Firm's name (or yours if self-employed), address, and ZIP code ▶		EIN	
			Phone no. ( )	

♻ *Printed on recycled paper*   Form **1040A** (2005)

3

Gross Income Inclusions

CHAPTER CONTENTS

■■ CHAPTER OVERVIEW

*C*hapters 1 and 2 presented an overview of the basic tax and reporting structure. They illustrated several tax forms, schedules, and worksheets, including the two simplest tax returns, Form 1040EZ and Form 1040A. Remaining chapters will focus on particular segments of the basic tax liability formula, starting with gross income.

Gross income helps determine whether a taxpayer must file a tax return or whether a person qualifies as a dependent. Strangely, however, none of the tax forms includes a line for reporting gross income; it does not appear on any of the tax returns. This chapter identifies many income items that taxpayers must include in gross income. Chapter 4 examines income sources the tax law excludes from gross income.

GENERAL GUIDELINES

Gross income is all income from every source, except those sources specifically excluded by law. Thus, taxpayers face two problems:

1. Recognizing potential income items
2. Identifying those income items specifically excluded by law

This situation raises the question, "What is income?" Unfortunately, the Internal Revenue Code does not define income, but it is generally considered an increase in wealth (assets minus liabilities). However, a taxpayer generally reports income only in the year it is realized (earned) as determined by the taxpayer's accounting method (cash or accrual). Cash basis taxpayers report income in the year money, property, or services are actually or constructively received in an income producing event. **Constructive receipt** takes place when assets are credited or made available to the taxpayer without restriction (e.g., interest on a bank deposit credited to the taxpayer's account.) Taxpayers report property and services received at their fair market value (FMV). Accrual basis taxpayers report income when they make the sale or perform the services, regardless of when they collect the cash. However, the law frequently taxes prepaid income of accrual basis taxpayers in the year of receipt.

Sometimes, taxpayers sell property under installment plans. Certain qualified installment sales allow a taxpayer to spread the income from such a sale over the period of collection (Chapter 11). Although appreciation in property values may cause an increase in wealth, the law does not recognize mere appreciation of assets as income. A taxpayer must convert the property into cash or other property before realizing a gain.

Exceptions

Cash basis taxpayers usually recognize income when they collect it. However, when taxpayers purchase bonds at a discount, the law sometimes requires that they recognize the discount as income before collecting it at maturity (see Example 6). The law normally allows accrual basis taxpayers to defer recognition of "service income" until the service is performed. When these taxpayers receive advance payments for services extending into future years, income earned on current services is recognized in the current tax year. Any remaining income to be earned in future years must all be recognized in the next tax year. In addition, all taxpayers must recognize prepaid rent and prepaid interest as income in the year of receipt; these items may not be deferred.

EXAMPLE 1

On November 5, 20x1, Jennifer Merry purchases a one-year warranty contract on her new TV set from Ajax appliance store, an accrual basis taxpayer. Ajax may prorate the income over the one-year contract period. If, however, Merry purchases a two-year warranty, Ajax recognizes 2/24 of the income in 20x1 and 22/24 of the income in 20x2.

PROFIT OR LOSS FROM BUSINESS OR PROFESSION

The Code taxes a person's income from a business or profession. Also, it usually allows a taxpayer to deduct losses from such activities. Taxpayers report their business or professional profits or losses on Form 1040. They report supporting details on Schedule C (Chapter 7). For a taxpayer involved with passive income activities, loss limitations can apply. A passive activity is one in which a taxpayer does not spend a regular, continuous, and substantial amount of time (Chapter 9).

COMPENSATION

Employees may report bonuses, commissions, salaries, tips, and wages on Form 1040EZ, Form 1040A, or Form 1040. Students who receive taxable scholarships may also report them on any of these forms. To use Form 1040EZ or Form 1040A, a taxpayer must have taxable income under $100,000. Also, when total compensation from more than one employer exceeds $90,000, the taxpayer cannot use Form 1040EZ. Independent contractors who receive fees for their services report them on Schedule C.

Fees, Bonuses, Commissions, Salaries, and Wages

Compensation is something received for services rendered, and most compensation is taxable under the Code regardless of the form it takes. When a person receives compensation in the form of property, the Code taxes its fair market value (FMV). For example, a taxpayer who receives an honorarium for making a speech includes its FMV in gross income. Also included in gross income are so-called gifts received for helping other taxpayers. Thus, barter and swap arrangements create taxable compensation.

FAIR MARKET VALUE (FMV)

FMV is the price that a willing buyer wants to pay and a willing seller wants to accept. FMV assumes that neither buyer nor seller must buy or sell. FMV also assumes that buyer and seller have reasonable knowledge of all necessary facts. Finally, in the absence of an actual sale or exchange, FMV can be determined by expert appraisal or other supporting evidence.

Compensation includes fees charged by accountants, doctors, lawyers, and engineers for professional services. It also includes fees for baby-sitting, grass cutting, snow shoveling, and newspaper delivery. Unless an exception applies, any taxpayer providing services for another taxpayer and receiving something of value in return receives taxable compensation. Taxpayers include as compensation amounts withheld from their pay for social security, Medicare, and income taxes. Compensation also includes amounts withheld for life insurance premiums, health insurance premiums, union dues, work clothes, and so on. Unless specifically exempt by statute, U.S. Constitution, or IRS de minimis rule, compensation includes all employee fringe benefits. Although some exceptions exist, compensation includes military service pay.

Tips

The Code taxes tips as other compensation. The IRS requires taxpayers who receive tips to follow special reporting rules.

Reporting to Employer

The IRS expects employees to file tip reports with their employers by the tenth of the month following the month in which they receive tips. An employer may require more frequent reporting. Employees who receive tips in December 20x1 and report the tips to their employers in January 20x2 include the tips in 20x2 gross income. When employees fail to turn in tip reports they include their tips in gross income in the year of receipt.

Tips of Less than $20.00

An employee who receives less than $20.00 in monthly tips while working for one employer need not tell the employer about the tips. In addition, the employee does not have to pay social security or Medicare taxes on these tips. However, the employee must report the tips as compensation on either Form 1040EZ, Form 1040A, or Form 1040.

Tips of $20.00 or More

An employee who receives $20.00 or more in monthly tips while working for one employer must report them to the employer. The IRS provides Form 4070, Employee's Report of Tips to Employer, for this purpose. Employees do not have to use Form 4070, but they must supply the same data in an acceptable format.

Taxpayers who have monthly tips of $20.00 or more, but do not report them to their employers, add the unreported tips to their other wages on Form 1040. Then they compute related social security and Medicare taxes on Form 4137, Social Security and Medicare Tax on Unreported Tip Income, and enter the total on Form 1040. In addition, they fill in Schedule U (Form 1040), U.S. Schedule of Unreported Tip Income. Taxpayers attach the form and schedule to their tax returns. The social security office uses Schedule U to determine the employee's retirement benefits. Employees reporting all their tips to their employers do not use Form 4137.

Employees who do not report tips to their employers when required to do so may be assessed penalties equal to 50% of the related social security and Medicare taxes.

Information for Figure 3-1: Filled-In Form 4070

Susan K. Maples works Friday and Saturday evenings as a waitress. Most of Maples's customers enter her tips on their credit charge slips. However, some leave cash tips. At the end of the evening, the restaurant bookkeeper informs Maples of her total charges in tips and pays her cash for these tips. Maples pays out some money to the head chef and one of the bus persons. At month's end, Maples prepares Form 4070 and gives it to her employer. Figure 3-1 shows Maples's Form 4070.

FIGURE 3-1 Filled In Form 4070

Form **4070** (Rev. June 1999) Department of the Treasury Internal Revenue Service	**Employee's Report of Tips to Employer** ► For Paperwork Reduction Act Notice, see back of form.	OMB No. 1545-0065
Employee's name and address Susan K. Maples 2132 Marshall Street Tampa, FL 33603		Social security number 810 ⋮ 26 ⋮ 3192
Employer's name and address (include establishment name, if different) Firesides Restaurant 22 South Shore Drive Tampa, FL 33614		**1** Cash tips received 304.00
		2 Credit card tips received 790.00
		3 Tips paid out 245.00
Month or shorter period in which tips were received from May 1 , 2005 , to May 31 , 2005		**4** Net tips (lines **1 + 2 - 3**) 849.00
Signature *Susan K. Maples*		Date June 2, 2005

Information for Figure 3-2: Filled-In Form 4137

Robert R. Cooper works part time as a waiter. Cooper lost his record of tips for November 1. In February, he found his tally sheet for November 1 and discovered that he understated his reported tips for the previous November by $45.

Cooper fills in Form 4137 and Schedule U. He attaches a statement explaining why he did not report the $45 to his employer. On his tax return, he adds the $45 to his other "Wages, salaries, tips, etc." on Form 1040. He also enters $3.44 on Form 1040 for social security and Medicare taxes. Figure 3-2 shows Cooper's filled-in Form 4137 and Schedule U.

Allocating Tips to Employees

The government generally assumes that food and beverage servers make at least 8% of gross sales in tips. Consequently, when employees of certain large restaurants and cocktail lounges report less than this amount to their employers, the employers must report the difference as additional income on the employees' Form W-2. These "allocated tips" appear on Form W-2 (box 8) as a separate item. Employers do not report them with wages and reported tips. When determining gross sales, employers exclude carry-out sales, state and local taxes, and sales with service fees of 10% or more.

FIGURE 3-2 Filled-In Form 4137 and Schedule U

Form **4137**	**Social Security and Medicare Tax on Unreported Tip Income** ▶ See instructions on back. ▶ Attach to Form 1040.	OMB No. 1545-0059 **20**05
Department of the Treasury Internal Revenue Service (99)		Attachment Sequence No. **24**

Name of person who received tips (as shown on Form 1040). If married, complete a separate Form 4137 for each spouse with unreported tips.	Social security number
Robert R. Cooper	394 99 1132

Name(s) of employer(s) to whom you were required to, but did not, report your tips:

Pig & Poke Restaurant

1	Total cash and charge tips you **received** in 2005 (see instructions)	1	5,045 00
2	Total cash and charge tips you **reported** to your employer in 2005	2	5,000 00
3	Subtract line 2 from line 1. This amount is income you **must** include in the total on Form 1040, line 7	3	45 00
4	Cash and charge tips you received but did not report to your employer because the total was less than $20 in a calendar month (see instructions)	4	
5	Unreported tips subject to Medicare tax. Subtract line 4 from line 3. Enter here and on line 2 of Schedule U below	5	45 00
6	Maximum amount of wages (including tips) subject to social security tax 6	90,000 00	
7	Total social security wages and social security tips (total of boxes 3 and 7 on Form(s) W-2) or railroad retirement (tier 1) compensation 7	16,200 00	
8	Subtract line 7 from line 6. If line 7 is more than line 6, enter -0- here and on line 9 and go to line 11	8	73,800 00
9	Unreported tips subject to social security tax. Enter the **smaller** of line 5 or line 8 here and on line 1 of Schedule U below. If you received tips as a federal, state, or local government employee, see instructions.	9	45 00
10	Multiply line 9 by .062	10	2 79
11	Multiply line 5 by .0145	11	65
12	Add lines 10 and 11. Enter the result here and on Form 1040, line 59 ▶	12	3 44

For Paperwork Reduction Act Notice, see instructions on back. Form **4137** (2005)

Do Not Detach

SCHEDULE U (Form 1040) Department of the Treasury Internal Revenue Service	**U.S. Schedule of Unreported Tip Income** For crediting to your social security record	**20**05

Note: *The amounts you report below are for your social security record. This record is used to figure any benefits, based on your earnings, payable to you and your dependents or your survivors. Fill in each item accurately and completely.*

Print or type name of person who received tip income (as shown on Form 1040)		Social security number
Robert R. Cooper		349 99 1132

Address (number, street, and apt. no., or P.O. box if mail is not delivered to your home)	Occupation
748 Grand Road	Waiter

City, town or post office, state, and ZIP code
Denison, OH 44621

1 Unreported tips subject to social security tax. Enter the amount from line 9 (Form 4137) above ▶	1	45 00
2 Unreported tips subject to Medicare tax. Enter the amount from line 5 (Form 4137) above ▶	2	45 00

Please do not write in this space

DLN—

Cat. No. 12626C   Schedule U (Form 1040) 2005

Sometimes an IRS district director will approve a threshold percentage below 8%. However, a director cannot approve a percentage below 2%. When a percentage below 8% applies, employers allocate tips using this percentage.

When customers of a business tip less than 8%, the employer or a majority of employees should petition the IRS for an allocation rate less than 8%.

Only employees who get tips directly from customers receive allocated tips. Also, only employees reporting tips below the threshold percentage participate in the allocation. Cooks and service bartenders do not receive allocated tips.

To ensure that employees report and employers allocate properly, the IRS requires affected business owners or managers to keep supporting records. It also requires them to report annually gross sales and employee tips to the IRS. To report, businesses use Form 8027, Employer's Annual Information Return of Tip Income and Allocated Tips.

The allocation and reporting requirement usually applies to a business employing more than ten persons on a typical business day. Only businesses that serve food or beverages on the premises and have regular tipping customers file Form 8027. Cafeterias, fast-food outlets, and businesses outside the U.S. do not file Form 8027. Also, businesses that add service charges of 10% or more to 95% of their food or beverage bills do not file Form 8027.

Employers do not withhold income, social security, or Medicare taxes from allocated tips. Thus, employees receiving allocated tips must file Form 4137 with Form 1040 and pay related taxes.

Sometimes, a business asks customers using its dining or banquet rooms to pay a service fee instead of tipping. Later, the business apportions and pays this fee to employees. Employees receiving a share of this fee do not include it on their Form 4070 tip reports. Their employer reports the tips as wages on the employees' Form W-2, Wage and Tax Statement. As reported wages, they are subject to withholding and employment taxes at the employer level.

DIVORCE AND SEPARATION AGREEMENTS

When a married couple gets a divorce or becomes legally separated, three money issues arise:

1. Division of property acquired during the marriage (property settlement)
2. Spousal support (alimony)
3. Support of the children (child support)

Property Settlement

Property settlement includes noncash transfer of property to a former spouse. Neither party has income or deductions on such a settlement. The transferee's investment (basis) in the property received is the same as that of the transferor. The same rules apply to property settlements involving cash payments.

Alimony

Although property settlements (cash and noncash) are neither taxable nor deductible, spousal support payments are both. Thus, a person receiving alimony or separate maintenance reports it as "Alimony received" on Form 1040. The payer deducts that amount for AGI and reports the recipient's social security number (SSN). The IRS charges the taxpayer $50 for failure to report the recipient's SSN. Taxpayers cannot use Form 1040EZ or Form 1040A to report either receipt or payment of alimony.

Taxpayers who receive payments for child support exclude them from gross income. On the other side, taxpayers who make child support payments may not deduct them.

To qualify as alimony under the post-1984 rules, payments to a divorced or separated spouse must meet several conditions:

alimony is deductible by person who pays & taxable income by the person who receives it

1. Only cash payments qualify.
2. Child support payments do not qualify.
3. Only payments under a legal divorce decree or a separate maintenance or divorce instrument qualify.
4. The governing decree or instrument must not label payments as something other than alimony.
5. The payer must not be required to make payments after the recipient's death.
6. The parties to divorce or separation may not live in the same household at payment time.

Usually, the Code does not classify payments between legally separated or divorced taxpayers as alimony when they live together. Even when taxpayers separate themselves within a household, the rule still applies. However, there is an exception when a taxpayer moves out within a month after a payment date. Here, the Code treats the payment as alimony.

A different set of rules applies to divorces and separations occurring before 1985. These rules may be found in IRS Publication 504.

Alimony Recapture

Special rules apply when alimony payments in the second or third year decrease by more than $15,000 from the payments made in the previous year. Because property settlement generally takes place soon after the divorce or separation agreement, these rules act as a safeguard against taxpayers disguising property settlements as alimony. When the change in payments exceeds the statutory limits, the law requires a "recapture" of the excessive alimony payments. The payer must include the excessive payments in gross income, and the payee may deduct them for AGI. These recapture rules apply only in the third year. In that year, the taxpayer computes excessive payments for both year one and year two and includes them on the tax return accordingly. These rules generally keep taxpayers from using alimony as a method of converting property settlements into deductible alimony payments.

> Because the alimony recapture rules do not apply after the third postseparation year, the payor of alimony could arrange for payments declining by more than $15,000 to start after the third postseparation year. This will avoid the recapture rules. Also, the recapture rules do not affect level payments and payments increasing during the three-year period.

Child Support

not taxable nor deductible

The Code excludes child support payments from income. The exclusion applies to payments clearly labeled as child support as well as those that can be implied as child support. For example, if payments to a former spouse decline when the child reaches age 18, the law treats the reduction amount as child support. For a divorce or separation before 1985, child support must be clearly labeled in the agreement. Otherwise, the payments receive alimony treatment. When the total alimony and child support payments are less than the required amount, payments will first apply toward child support.

DIVIDEND INCOME

Corporations frequently distribute cash, property, stock, rights to purchase stock, use of services, and other accommodations to shareholders. Annually, they report the value of these distributions to shareholders on information return Form 1099-DIV, Dividends and Distributions.

Ordinary Dividends

The Code taxes distributions from a corporation's earnings and profits as ordinary dividends. Both cash and accrual basis shareholders include dividends in gross income in the year received. When a corporation makes an ordinary property distribution, shareholders increase gross income by the property's market value at distribution date. Unless a corporation identifies a distribution for special tax treatment, the Code taxes it as an ordinary dividend.

Most ordinary dividends received by individuals are taxed at a rate of 15%. A 5% rate applies to taxpayers in the 15% and 10% tax brackets. These are the same rates that apply to long-term capital gains. Some dividends are ineligible for these reduced rates. Examples of nonqualifying dividends include those paid by credit unions, mutual insurance companies, farmer's cooperatives, and mutual savings banks. These items are really interest.

EXAMPLE 2

James Arbogast, single, has taxable income of $49,000, including qualified dividends of $5,000. This level of income places Arbogast in the 25% tax bracket and qualifies him for the 15% tax rate on dividends. Thus, he determines his tax on $44,000 ($49,000 – $5,000) from the Tax Table—$7,671. To this amount he adds his tax on the dividends—$750 ($5,000 × 15%). His total tax is $8,421 ($7,671 + $750).

Nominee Dividends

Sometimes, taxpayers receive ordinary dividends as nominees (intermediaries who forward the payment to the actual owners) for other taxpayers. Thus, parents can receive dividends for their children. If the paying corporation shows the nominee's TIN (taxpayer identification number) on information return Form 1099-DIV, the nominee usually prepares another Form 1099-DIV. Then, the nominee sends the original of the newly prepared Form 1099-DIV to the IRS, keeps a copy, and gives a copy to the actual shareholder.

Dividend Reinvestment Plans (DRIPs)

Some corporations offer shareholders dividend reinvestment plans. In such a plan, a trustee receives the dividends and usually purchases additional stock in the paying corporation for participating shareholders. Thus, the shareholders never actually receive the dividends. However, they include them in gross income as ordinary dividends.

Return-of-Capital Distributions

Sometimes, corporations with no earnings and profits distribute cash or property to its shareholders. The Code treats these distributions as return-of-capital distributions. Consequently, a shareholder reduces his or her investment (basis) in the stock until it reaches zero. Once the stock's basis reaches zero, the Code taxes any additional distribution as a capital gain. The gain may receive long-term or short-term treatment, depending on how long the taxpayer has owned the stock.

Distributions of Mutual Funds

Mutual funds make five types of distributions: (1) ordinary dividends, (2) return-of-capital distributions, (3) capital gain distributions, (4) exempt interest dividends, and (5) foreign investment dividends. Preceding sections covered ordinary dividends and return-of-capital distributions. The following sections cover the remaining types of distributions.

Capital Gain Distribution

A capital gain distribution from a mutual fund represents its net long-term capital gain for the year. Distributing companies report such distributions to shareholders on Form 1099-DIV. Shareholders report them as long-term capital gains on Schedule D, Capital Gains and Losses, rather than as dividends on Schedule B, Interest and Ordinary Dividends. Some mutual funds keep the long-term capital gains and pay capital gains tax. They pass the tax on to shareholders, who claim it as a tax payment on Form 1040. The shareholder increases his or her basis in the mutual fund shares by the long-term capital gains net of tax. Mutual funds pay a 35% tax rate on undistributed capital gains. Mutual funds report the gain and related tax to shareholders on Form 2439, Notice to Shareholder of Undistributed Long-Term Capital Gains. Shareholders attach this form to their tax returns.

EXAMPLE 3

At the end of the year, Medical Investors (MI), a mutual fund, had 5,650,200 shares of issued and outstanding stock. For the year, it elected to retain net long-term capital gains of $833,726 and pay the related tax of $291,804 ($833,726 × 35%). On Form 2439, MI told its shareholders to include $0.1475569 per share in gross income as undistributed net long-term capital gains. It also told them to claim a credit of $0.0516448 per share for the amount of tax it paid on the gains.

During the year, Margaret Smith owned 2,000 shares of MI. She reports the undistributed "long-term capital gain from Form 2439" of $295.11 (2,000 × $0.1475569) on Schedule D, Capital Gains and Losses. Then, she claims a credit of $103.29 (2,000 × $0.0516448) under "Other payments" on Form 1040 for her share of the taxes paid by MI.

Exempt Interest Dividends

Under certain conditions, the Code does not tax an exempt interest dividend from a mutual fund. For tax-free treatment, the fund must hold 50% or more of its investments in tax-exempt municipal bonds at the end of each calendar quarter. Also, it must pay out 90% or more of this interest to shareholders annually.

Foreign Investment Dividends

Some mutual funds invest in foreign corporations. Dividends from these companies are subject to foreign income taxation. When a fund receives dividends from a foreign corporation, it will pay income tax to the foreign country. The fund may forward some or all of the dividends to the shareholders who must then pay U.S. income taxes on the distribution. Annually, the mutual fund will inform shareholders about their shares of income taxes paid to the

[handwritten margin note: # 300 Single 600 married Do not need to complete form 1116.]

foreign country on the dividends which were distributed to them. The shareholders deduct these taxes as itemized deductions or claim them as foreign tax credits on Form 1116, Foreign Tax Credit (Individual, Estate, or Trust).

Reporting Dividend Income

Taxpayers cannot use Form 1040EZ to report corporate dividends. However, they may report exempt bond interest from mutual funds on Form 1040EZ with identifying letters TEI (tax-exempt interest). A taxpayer enters the letters *TEI* and the interest amount in the blank space following the request for "Taxable interest."

Taxpayers may use Form 1040A to report ordinary dividends, nominee dividends, and tax-exempt mutual fund bond interest. They can also use it to report capital gain distributions. The IRS wants taxpayers to report all dividends received. Any dividends not taxed to the taxpayer (e.g., nominee dividends and return of capital distributions) are then shown as a deduction from the reported dividends. This technique is shown in Figure 3-3, which illustrates the use of Schedule 1 (Form 1040A) to report dividends. Schedule B (Form 1040) is not illustrated because it is basically identical to Schedule 1. Dividends totaling over $1,500 requires the filing of either Schedule 1 or Schedule B. Taxpayers report capital gain distributions directly on Schedule D, Capital Gains and Losses. Also, when taxpayers are required to use Schedule D, the tax on dividends is computed on that schedule. When Schedule D is not required, taxpayers compute their tax on dividends using a special worksheet.

Information for Figure 3-3:
Filled-In Schedule 1 (Form 1040A), Part II

Jackie C. Hirsch uses Schedule 1 (Form 1040A), Part II to report the ordinary dividends she receives. Hirsch receives dividends from Blue Publishing Company and Native Son Corporation as a nominee for her 10-year-old son. Hirsch owns stock in Bay Weaving Company and Pike Moving Company. Thus, these dividends belong to her.

FIGURE 3-3   Filled-In Schedule 1 (Form 1040A), Part II

Part II	Note. If you received a Form 1099-DIV or substitute statement from a brokerage firm, enter the firm's name and the ordinary dividends shown on that form.		
Ordinary dividends	**5** List name of payer.		Amount
	Blue Publishing Company	5	210 00
(See back of schedule and the instructions for Form 1040A, line 9a.)	Native Son Corporation		75 00
	Nominee Distribution		285 00
	Bay Weaving Company		530 00
	Pike Moving Company		1,340 00
	Total		2,155 00
	Less: Nominee Distribution		(285 00)
	6 Add the amounts on line 5. Enter the total here and on Form 1040A, line 9a.	6	1,870 00

For Paperwork Reduction Act Notice, see Form 1040A instructions.   Cat. No. 12075R   Schedule 1 (Form 1040A) 2005

FARM INCOME OR LOSS

Taxpayers report net income (or loss) from farming on Form 1040. They report the details of income and expenses on Schedule F. Special income and expense rules apply to farming because of the unique activities associated with growing crops, raising animals, and maintaining land and other resources. IRS Publication 225 provides information on farming activities.

GAINS AND LOSSES

When a taxpayer sells or exchanges property, a gain or loss results. As a general rule, taxpayers report on their tax returns all gains, but they report losses only from sales or exchanges of investment or business property. Chapter 10 explains how gains and losses are computed.

A taxpayer reports individual gains and losses from the sale or exchange of business property on Form 4797, Sale of Business Property. The sum of these gains and losses appears on Form 1040. Taxpayers report gains from sales or exchanges of personal-use property and both gains and losses from investment property on Schedule D, Capital Gains and Losses. The total gain or loss from these sales eventually appears on Form 1040. Chapter 11 describes Form 4797 and Schedule D in detail.

INTEREST INCOME

Gross income includes interest on bank deposits, notes, mortgages (including seller-financed mortgages), corporate bonds, and debts of the United States. Gross income also includes interest on income tax refunds. Unless an exception applies, a taxpayer includes all interest in gross income in the year he or she receives it or has a right to receive it **(constructive receipt).** Usually, interest income includes all payments for the use of money. In some cases, the IRS requires taxpayers to impute interest income on low interest or no interest loans.

Interest as Dividends

Some organizations pay interest but call it something else. Also, the IRS classifies as interest some dividend distributions. These distributions include earnings on deposits and share accounts in (1) cooperative banks, (2) credit unions, (3) domestic building and loan associations, (4) savings and loan associations, and (5) mutual savings banks. Taxpayers who own money market and savings certificates report income from these investments as interest. Taxpayers who receive distributions of exempt (tax-free) interest from mutual funds report them as interest on Schedule B (Form 1040). However, they then deduct them from the total, thereby excluding them from gross income.

Savings Accounts and Certificates

Gross income includes interest from banks, savings bonds, and seller-financed mortgages. When a financial institution credits a depositor's account with interest, the depositor includes the interest in gross income under the constructive receipt rule. The inclusion does not depend on presentation of a passbook to the institution for an interest entry.

Gross income includes interest on savings certificates. For interest deferred more than one year, the Code requires taxpayers to recognize the accrued interest as income under the original issue discount (OID) rules. (See OID, later in the chapter.)

Merchandise Premiums

Some financial institutions (banks, savings and loan associations, and credit unions) offer merchandise incentives to attract deposits. Such merchandise represents prepaid interest. The Code taxes the FMV of this property as interest when a taxpayer receives it.

Interest on Insurance Dividends

Interest subject to income tax

The Code taxes the interest on dividends left with an insurance carrier when the carrier adds the interest to a taxpayer's account. When the taxpayer can withdraw the interest only on the policy's anniversary date, the Code taxes it then. However, the Code excludes from gross income interest on National Service Life Insurance dividends on deposit with the Veterans Administration. Also, the Code classifies dividends on unmatured mutual life insurance as a return of premiums (insurance rebate), and excludes them from gross income.

U.S. Savings Bonds

Can opt to pay taxes each yr as you go w/out cashing in bonds

Usually, taxpayers report interest on discounted Series E and EE United States Savings Bonds when they redeem them. An investor purchases these bonds at a fraction of their maturity value and redeems them at full price at maturity. The difference between a bond's cost and its redemption price equals interest income. However, the taxpayer can choose to report the increase in redemption value each year as income. Taxpayers choosing this reporting method must include any prior redemption value increases in gross income in the election year. Then, they include annual redemption value increases in gross income each year thereafter. This election applies to all Series E or EE bonds that a taxpayer owns at the time of election and those acquired later. An automatic reversal procedure is available.

A taxpayer obtains Series EE U.S. Savings Bonds in one of two ways: through a payroll deduction plan or by an order placed through a participating financial institution. Series E bonds issued before December 1965 mature 40 years after the issue date. Series E bonds issued after November 1965, and Series EE bonds, mature 30 years after the issue date. Once a bond reaches final maturity, it no longer pays interest.

U.S. Treasury Bills, Notes, and Bonds

The U.S. Treasury issues its Treasury bills at a discount. The difference between the issue price and the face value at maturity represents interest. Taxpayers include this interest in gross income when they receive it at maturity. Taxpayers may purchase Treasury notes and bonds in coupon or registered form. Usually, these instruments pay interest every six months. Taxpayers include this interest in gross income when they receive it or have a right to receive it.

An important tax-planning feature comes with the purchase of U.S. Treasury bills, notes, and bonds: owners of these instruments do not pay state and local income taxes on related interest.

Accrued Interest

When a taxpayer purchases a bond between interest dates, the interest up to the purchase date belongs to the seller. The bond buyer pays this interest to the seller at the time of purchase and deducts it from the first interest payment he or she receives. The buyer then includes all future interest on the bond in gross income.

Original Issue Discount (OID) Bonds

Most taxpayers include interest on bonds in gross income when they receive it. However, when a corporation issues bonds at a discount (issues them for less than their stated maturity value), another situation arises. Because bondholders receive the full maturity value at redemption time, they must recognize the discount (maturity value minus issue price) as income. But, does the taxpayer recognize it all at redemption time, or should a portion of it be recognized each year over the life of the bond? Basically, the answer depends on the size of the discount and the life of the bond issue. Also, does the taxpayer treat the income as ordinary interest or as capital gain?

The taxpayer must first determine the original issue discount (OID). The Code defines original issue discount as the difference between a bond's face value (maturity or principal value) and its issue price.

EXAMPLE 4

A corporation issues a 20-year, $100,000 zero-coupon bond (no coupons attached) for $12,861. Here, the OID equals $87,139 ($100,000 − $12,861).

For some situations, the Code treats the OID as a zero amount. This zero treatment applies to de minimis discounts (small amounts). The Code defines **de minimis discount** as less than one-fourth of 1% (0.0025) of the maturity redemption price times the number of complete years to maturity. When the de minimis rule applies, the holder includes the discount in income when the bond is sold or redeemed. If the bond is a capital asset in the holder's hands, the Code treats the income as a capital gain.

EXAMPLE 5

A corporation issues a 10-year, $100,000 bond for $98,000. Also, assume that the issuer makes no payments until the bond matures. Although the real OID equals $2,000, the Code treats it as a zero amount. Use of the de minimis discount formula shows that the $2,000 discount falls below the OID threshold of $2,500 [(.0025 × $100,000 face value of bond) × 10 full years to maturity]. In this situation, the discount is not recognized as income over the life of the bond. It is recognized as capital gain at the time of sale or redemption.

When the discount exceeds the de minimis amount, the taxpayer recognizes the OID as income over the debt instrument's life by including a portion in gross income each year. For OID instruments issued after April 3, 1993, taxpayers use the effective interest rate method to determine the interest earned. In making this computation, a taxpayer multiplies investment (basis) in the bond by a constant interest rate—the rate necessary to produce the desired yield. The interest must be compounded semiannually. The taxpayer reports the difference between the resulting product and the bond's stated interest as ordinary income. This amount reduces the remaining OID and increases the taxpayer's basis in the bonds. Note that this is an exception to the cash basis method of accounting because the bondholder must recognize income long before receiving the cash.

EXAMPLE 6

On October 1, 20x1, a corporation issues a 30-year, $1,000,000 zero-coupon bond for $12,170. The annual yield to maturity equals 15.25% compounded semiannually. The bond's original issue discount equals $987,830 ($1,000,000 − $12,170). Earned interest for 20x1 and 20x2 follows:

Interest Income for 20x1:
October 1, 20x1 through December 31, 20x1
([15.25% × $12,170] × 3/12) $ 463.98

Interest Income for 20x2:
January 1, 20x2 through March 31, 20x2 ([15.25% × $12,170] × 3/12) $ 463.98
April 1, 20x2 through September 30, 20x2
([15.25% × ($12,170 + $927.96)] × 6/12)   998.72
October 1, 20x2 through December 31, 20x2
([15.25% × ($12,170 + $927.96 + $998.72)] × 3/12)   537.44
                                 $2,000.14

Over the thirty years, the zero-coupon bond purchaser writes off the discount and recognizes interest income of $987,830. At the end of the thirty years, the face and carrying values of the bond equal $1,000,000 ($12,170 + $987,830).

Issuers of OID instruments compute the amount of discount to be included in income. They report this amount to the IRS and bondowners with Form 1099-OID, Statement for Recipients of Original Issue Discount. This reporting requirement applies when the calendar year OID equals $10 or more and the debt instrument's term exceeds one year. For original purchasers of OID debt instruments, the write-off amounts on Form 1099-OID represent interest income. They report these amounts on their tax returns with other interest income.

For OID instruments issued before April 4, 1993, different write-off rules apply. Also, original issue discount rules do not apply to U.S. Savings Bonds and short-term debt instruments with maturity dates of one year or less from their issue dates.

Market Discount (MD) Bonds

A market discount arises when an investor purchases a bond from a bondholder (rather than the issuing company) for less than its amortized carrying value. **Amortized carrying value (ACV)** equals a bond's issue price plus earlier OID write-offs (see OID). Taxpayers purchasing a bond with a market discount may elect to include a share of the MD each year as interest income or wait until the bond is sold and recognize it as interest income at that time. The MD must be recognized as ordinary interest income either at the time of sale (redemption) or annually over the life of the bond.

Some bondholders must deal with both OID and MD. Note that an investor must accrue the OID income over the life of the bond using the effective interest rate method. Bondholders with MD who elect to amortize the interest may choose either the effective rate method or the straight-line method of accruing interest.

Bond Premiums on Taxable Bonds

Taxpayers who purchase taxable bonds at a premium (an amount in excess of face value) can choose to offset interest income by a portion of the bond's premium. They decrease the basis of the bond by the premium written off. Taxpayers may also choose not to write off bond premiums and report more interest income each year; thus, they have higher bases at sale or redemption. A higher basis translates into less gain or more loss to recognize at disposition. This choice applies to all bonds a taxpayer owns, not just a specific issue.

Imputed Interest

For a loan made without a stated interest rate or at a low stated rate, the IRS may impute interest. This means the lender must recognize interest income equal to the imputed interest, and the borrower has an implied interest payment to the lender. To impute the interest, the IRS uses the AFR (applicable federal rate). The interest rates the federal government pays to borrow new money determine the AFRs, which apply to a variety of debt instruments.

Published Applicable Federal Rates

Each month the IRS publishes AFRs for short-term, mid-term, and long-term securities. They include monthly, quarterly, semiannual, and annual compounding rates. Taxpayers use the short-term rates for demand loans and loans maturing in three years or less. They use the mid-term rates for debts with four- to nine-year maturities and long-term rates for debts maturing in more than nine years.

EXAMPLES OF IMPUTED INTEREST SITUATIONS

Below-market interest rate loans:

1. Gift loans (parents to children)

2. Loans between a corporation and a shareholder

3. Compensation-related loans between employer and employee

4. Tax-avoidance loans

GIFT LOANS

Loans to family members (gift loans) fall under the imputed interest rules. Unless an exception applies, the IRS imputes interest on a gift loan where the interest is less than the AFR rate. The lender includes the interest in gross income. Under certain conditions, the borrower may deduct the interest payment (Chapter 5). In addition, as the lender does not actually have possession of this interest income, the regulations assume that the lender gives the borrower funds each year equal to the imputed interest. Depending on the amount of the gift funds, the lender may have to a file a gift tax return.

GIFT LOAN EXCEPTIONS AND LIMITATIONS

1. No interest is imputed on loans of $10,000 or less between individuals, unless loan proceeds are used to purchase income-producing property.
2. No interest is imputed on a loan of $100,000 or less between individuals if the borrower's net investment income for the year does not exceed $1,000.
3. Imputed interest cannot exceed the borrower's net investment income for the year on a loan of $100,000 or less between individuals.
4. Limitations on imputed interest do not apply if tax avoidance is the reason for a loan.

EXAMPLE 7

John and Sandra Grady, a young couple with two children, want to save money to buy a house. However, every time they get a good start on a down payment, a financial emergency occurs. Sandra's parents remember the difficult time they had getting funds for a down payment. They offer to lend John and Sandra $10,000 without interest, provided John and Sandra sign a ten-year note for the funds. John and Sandra agree to these terms and sign the note. If John and Sandra use the loan proceeds to make a house down payment, and not to buy income- producing property, the IRS will not impute interest.

EXAMPLE 8

Marilyn and Bob Lange, a young couple, want to save money for a house down payment. Bob's parents offer to lend them $10,000 on an interest-free loan. Marilyn and Bob plan to invest the funds and save the earnings for their down payment. If Marilyn and Bob buy income-producing property (e.g., stocks or bonds) with the loan proceeds, the IRS might impute interest, depending on their total net investment income. If their net investment income for the year does not exceed $1,000, the IRS will not impute interest. If it exceeds $1,000, the IRS will impute interest. However, the imputed interest cannot exceed the couple's net investment income.

Employee and Shareholder Loans

Another exception applies to employee loans and corporation-shareholder loans. No imputed interest will apply to loans of $10,000 or less. However, the exception does not apply to loans for tax avoidance purposes. Here, the IRS requires taxpayers to impute interest.

Reporting Interest Income

Taxpayers may report taxable interest income on Form 1040EZ, Form 1040A, or Form 1040. The IRS also wants to see the amount of tax-exempt interest on these forms.

Normally, a taxpayer receiving interest income of $10 or more receives a Form 1099-INT from the payer. This form identifies taxable interest and any state or federal tax withholding that might have taken place. Copies go to the payee and the IRS. Payees do not file this form with their returns, but they should keep copies with their tax records.

Information for Figure 3-4: Filled-In Form 1099-INT

Figure 3-4 illustrates a filled-in Form 1099-INT for Katrina Hansen who earned $195.28 in interest on her savings account.

FIGURE 3-4   Filled-In Form 1099-INT

9292	☐ VOID	☐ CORRECTED		
PAYER'S name, street address, city, state, ZIP code, and telephone no. Champaign Savings and Loan 1501 North Main Street La Salle, IL 61301	Payer's RTN (optional)	OMB No. 1545-0112 **20**05 Form **1099-INT**	**Interest Income**	
PAYER'S Federal identification number 77-5054162	RECIPIENT'S identification number 272-96-5023	1 Interest income not included in box 3 $ 195.28		Copy A For **Internal Revenue Service Center** File with Form 1096.
RECIPIENT'S name Katrina Hansen		2 Early withdrawal penalty $	3 Interest on U.S. Savings Bonds and Treas. obligations $	For Privacy Act and Paperwork Reduction Act Notice, see the
Street address (including apt. no.) 410 E. Locust Street		4 Federal income tax withheld $	5 Investment expenses $	2005 General Instructions for
City, state, and ZIP code LaSalle, IL 61301		6 Foreign tax paid	7 Foreign country or U.S. possession	Forms 1099, 1098, 5498, and W-2G.
Account number (see instructions)	2nd TIN not. ☐	$		

Form **1099-INT**   Cat. No. 14410K   Department of the Treasury - Internal Revenue Service

Do Not Cut or Separate Forms on This Page   —   Do Not Cut or Separate Forms on This Page

Form 1040EZ

Form 1040EZ filers can only report taxable interest income of $1,500 or less. For tax-exempt interest income, no dollar reporting limit exists. A Form 1040EZ filer reports tax-exempt interest income in the blank space after the "Taxable interest" request. The taxpayer enters first the letters *TEI,* then the amount of tax-exempt interest income. However, taxpayers who exclude Educational Savings Bond interest from gross income cannot use Form 1040EZ (Chapter 4).

A taxpayer who withdraws certificate of deposit funds before the certificate's due date usually pays a penalty. This penalty may be deducted on Form 1040 as an "Adjustment to Income." The penalty cannot be deducted on Form 1040EZ or Form 1040A.

Form 1040A

With a few exceptions, taxpayers may use Form 1040A to report all taxable interest income. One exception involves OID interest. A taxpayer cannot use Form 1040A to report OID interest over or under the amount shown on his or her Form 1099-OID. Another exception covers purchased accrued interest. A taxpayer cannot report on Form 1040A interest accrued on security transfers between interest dates. Finally, a taxpayer cannot use Form 1040A when choosing to offset interest income with a bond premium write-off. These special cases require the use of Form 1040.

A Form 1040A filer with taxable interest income of $1,500 or less reports it on the "Taxable interest" line and does not prepare a separate reporting schedule. If the filer has taxable interest income of more than $1,500, he or she completes Schedule 1, Part I. Figure 3-5 shows the filled-in Schedule 1 interest income section for a Form 1040A filer. On this schedule, interest amounts from different payers are listed separately. The listing should include all tax-exempt interest. It also should include interest the taxpayer received as a nominee and Educational Savings Bond interest excluded from gross income.

The taxpayer adds these amounts together and enters the total of all interest received. He or she then lists again tax-exempt and nominee interest, determines a subtotal for these items, and deducts it from the total of all interest received. Note that Form 1040A does not have special lines for the total and subtotals. Next to the subtotal for tax-exempt interest, the recipient writes *Tax-Exempt Interest.* Next to the subtotal for nominee interest, the taxpayer writes *Nominee Distribution.* The taxpayer also enters the total tax-exempt interest income on the face of Form 1040A.

Schedule 1 handles excludable Educational Savings Bond interest on a separate line. This interest comes from Form 8815, Exclusion of Interest From Series EE and I U.S. Savings Bonds Issued After 1989 (Chapter 4). The amount reduces the listed interest income to get taxable interest. The taxpayer transfers this final amount to the "Taxable interest" line on Form 1040A.

Form 1040

Unless specific exemptions apply, taxpayers include all interest income in gross income. There are no restrictions on the amount or type of interest income that a person may report on Form 1040. When taxable interest income exceeds $1,500, the taxpayer lists each interest item separately on Schedule B, Part I. Schedule B is not illustrated because it is very similar to Form 1040A, Schedule 1.

Information for Figure 3-5:
Filled-In Schedule 1 (Form 1040A), Part I

Ruth Baker uses Schedule 1 (Form 1040A), Part I to report her interest income. Baker receives interest from Erie Lake Distributing Company and Buckeye Lake Brewing Company as a nominee for her 7-year-old daughter. The remaining interest belongs to Baker who has tax-exempt interest of $60 from city of Madison bonds.

FIGURE 3-5 Filled-In Schedule 1 (Form 1040A), Part I

Schedule 1 (Form 1040A)	Department of the Treasury—Internal Revenue Service **Interest and Ordinary Dividends for Form 1040A Filers** (99) **2005**			OMB No. 1545-0085
Name(s) shown on Form 1040A Ruth O. Baker				Your social security number 727 ¦ 69 ¦ 3205

Part I **Interest** (See back of schedule and the instructions for Form 1040A, line 8a.)	**Note.** If you received a Form 1099-INT, Form 1099-OID, or substitute statement from a brokerage firm, enter the firm's name and the total interest shown on that form.			
	1 List name of payer. If any interest is from a seller-financed mortgage and the buyer used the property as a personal residence, see back of schedule and list this interest first. Also, show that buyer's social security number and address.			Amount
	Erie Lake Distributing Company	1		700 | 00
	Buckeye Lake Brewing Company			250 | 00
	Nominee Distribution			950 | 00
	City of Madison Bond Interest			60 | 00
	Franklin Lake Winery, Inc.			1,175 | 00
	Nym Lake Distilled Water Company			580 | 00
	Second Federal National Bank			700 | 00
	Total Interest			3,465 | 00
	Less: Nominee Distribution 950			
	Tax-exempt Interest 60			(1,010 | 00)
	2 Add the amounts on line 1.		2	2,455 | 00
	3 Excludable interest on series EE and I U.S. savings bonds issued after 1989. Attach Form 8815.		3	
	4 Subtract line 3 from line 2. Enter the result here and on Form 1040A, line 8a.		4	2,455 | 00

CHILDREN WITH UNEARNED INCOME (KIDDIE TAX)

Children under age 14 with unearned income may find that the law taxes some of this income at their parents' highest tax rates. Unearned income is basically investment income from sources such as dividends, interest, capital gains, rents, royalties, and annuities. This provision reduces the potential tax savings arising when parents transfer investments to their children, who normally pay taxes at lower rates.

The parent's highest (marginal) tax rate applies only to the child's net unearned income. The child's tax rate (from the Tax Tables) determines the tax on the remaining income.

Net Unearned Income (NUI) is

Total unearned income
Less: $800
Less: The greater of

> (1) $800 of the standard deduction or
> (2) Itemized deductions directly related
>   to the production of the unearned income

Equals: Net Unearned Income

Computation of the child's total tax for the year requires the following steps:

> NUI × parent's highest tax rate
Plus: Remaining taxable income × child's tax rate

Equals: Child's total tax

The kiddie tax applies only to a child under age 14 who has unearned income of more than $1,600 and at least one living parent or step-parent. Taxpayers use Form 8615 to calculate the tax. Figure 3-6 illustrates the use of this form.

Information for Figure 3-6: Filled-In Form 8615

Helen Wong, age 12, receives $2,000 of interest from her investments. Helen has no other income and no itemized deductions. Consequently, her taxable income is $1,200 ($2,000 − standard deduction of $800). Helen has no brothers or sisters. Her parents file a joint return. They have taxable income of $70,200 before including Helen's investment income. Helen's final tax of **$181** is computed using the following information.

Other Information

 9: Tax on parents' taxable income of $70,200 plus Helen's net unearned income of
    $400 ($2,000 – $1,600), **$10,986**
10: Tax on parents' taxable income of $70,200, **$10,886**
15: Tax on Helen's remaining taxable income of $800 ($1,200 – $400), **$81**
17: Tax on Helen's taxable income of $1,200, **$121**

FIGURE 3-6 Filled-In Form 8615

Form **8615**

Department of the Treasury
Internal Revenue Service (99)

Tax for Children Under Age 14
With Investment Income of More Than $1,600
▶ Attach only to the child's Form 1040, Form 1040A, or Form 1040NR.
▶ See separate instructions.

OMB No. 1545-0998

20**05**

Attachment
Sequence No. **33**

Child's name shown on return
Helen I. Wong

Child's social security number
344 72 0156

Before you begin: If the child, the parent, or any of the parent's other children under age 14 must use the Schedule D Tax Worksheet or has income from farming or fishing, see **Pub. 929,** Tax Rules for Children and Dependents. It explains how to figure the child's tax using the **Schedule D Tax Worksheet** or **Schedule J** (Form 1040).

A Parent's name (first, initial, and last). **Caution:** *See instructions before completing.*	**B** Parent's social security number
Kenneth A. Wong	324 51 9234

C Parent's filing status (check one):

☐ Single ☒ Married filing jointly ☐ Married filing separately ☐ Head of household ☐ Qualifying widow(er)

Part I	Child's Net Investment Income

(handwritten note in margin: anything over $1600 is taxed at parent's rate)

1	Enter the child's investment income (see instructions)	**1**	2,000 00
2	If the child **did not** itemize deductions on **Schedule A** (Form 1040 or Form 1040NR), enter $1,600. Otherwise, see instructions	**2**	1,600 00
3	Subtract line 2 from line 1. If zero or less, **stop;** do not complete the rest of this form but **do** attach it to the child's return	**3**	400 00
4	Enter the child's **taxable income** from Form 1040, line 43; Form 1040A, line 27; or Form 1040NR, line 40	**4**	1,200 00
5	Enter the **smaller** of line 3 or line 4. If zero, **stop;** do not complete the rest of this form but **do** attach it to the child's return	**5**	400 00

Part II	Tentative Tax Based on the Tax Rate of the Parent

6	Enter the parent's **taxable income** from Form 1040, line 43; Form 1040A, line 27; Form 1040EZ, line 6; Form 1040NR, line 40; or Form 1040NR-EZ, line 14. If zero or less, enter -0-	**6**	70,200 00
7	Enter the total, if any, from Forms 8615, line 5, of **all other** children of the parent named above. **Do not** include the amount from line 5 above	**7**	0
8	Add lines 5, 6, and 7 (see instructions)	**8**	70,600 00
9	Enter the tax on the amount on line 8 based on the **parent's** filing status above (see instructions). If the Qualified Dividends and Capital Gain Tax Worksheet, Schedule D Tax Worksheet, or Schedule J (Form 1040) is used to figure the tax, check here ▶ ☐	**9**	10,986 00
10	Enter the parent's tax from Form 1040, line 44; Form 1040A, line 28, minus any alternative minimum tax; Form 1040EZ, line 10; Form 1040NR, line 41; or Form 1040NR-EZ, line 15. **Do not** include any tax from **Form 4972** or **8814.** If the Qualified Dividends and Capital Gain Tax Worksheet, Schedule D Tax Worksheet, or Schedule J (Form 1040) was used to figure the tax, check here ▶ ☐	**10**	10,886 00
11	Subtract line 10 from line 9 and enter the result. If line 7 is blank, also enter this amount on line 13 and go to **Part III**	**11**	100 00
12a	Add lines 5 and 7	**12a** 400 00	
b	Divide line 5 by line 12a. Enter the result as a decimal (rounded to at least three places)	**12b**	×1.00
13	Multiply line 11 by line 12b	**13**	100 00

Part III	Child's Tax—If lines 4 and 5 above are the same, enter -0- on line 15 and go to line 16.

14	Subtract line 5 from line 4	**14** 800 00	
15	Enter the tax on the amount on line 14 based on the **child's** filing status (see instructions). If the Qualified Dividends and Capital Gain Tax Worksheet, Schedule D Tax Worksheet, or Schedule J (Form 1040) is used to figure the tax, check here ▶ ☐	**15**	81 00
16	Add lines 13 and 15	**16**	181 00
17	Enter the tax on the amount on line 4 based on the **child's** filing status (see instructions). If the Qualified Dividends and Capital Gain Tax Worksheet, Schedule D Tax Worksheet, or Schedule J (Form 1040) is used to figure the tax, check here ▶ ☐	**17**	121 00
18	Enter the **larger** of line 16 or line 17 here and on the **child's** Form 1040, line 44; Form 1040A, line 28; or Form 1040NR, line 41	**18**	181 00

For Paperwork Reduction Act Notice, see the instructions.   Cat. No. 64113U   Form **8615** (2005)

Printed on recycled paper

(watermark: Draft as of 06/07/2005)

Child's Income on Parent's Return

Under certain conditions, parents can choose to report their child's income on their Form 1040. For this reporting, parents cannot use Form 1040EZ or Form 1040A.

When parents choose this reporting route, the child does not have to file a return. For the family to make the choice, the child's income must consist only of interest and dividends over $800 and under $8,000. Also, the child cannot have income taxes withheld or pay estimated income taxes. This election is available only if the child is under age 14. Parents use Form 8814, Parents' Election to Report Child's Interest and Dividends, to compute the tax due on the child's interest and dividends.

> Taxpayers can minimize the family's tax liability by making gifts of income-producing property to lower-bracket family members. Children can receive $800 of income each year without paying taxes. The next $800 is taxed at the child's lower tax rate. Shifting more than $1,600 of income to a child produces no benefit. The excess is taxed at the parents' rate.

TRADITIONAL IRA DISTRIBUTIONS

Many taxpayers are able to deduct their contributions to traditional IRAs (individual retirement arrangements). Thus, these contributions escape taxation. As a result, any funds in their IRA have never been taxed. So, all distributions from an IRA are generally taxed. However, some taxpayers make nondeductible contributions to their IRAs. This means they have paid taxes on the money they put into the fund. Thus, when they receive distributions from the fund, they should be allowed to receive the amount of their contributions without paying taxes on them a second time. Distributions from Roth IRAs are treated differently (see Chapter 4).

Taxpayers may use Form 1040A or Form 1040 to report distributions from IRAs. This reporting includes regular distributions, early distributions, rollovers, and any other money or property from IRAs. Form 1040EZ cannot be used for this reporting. Taxpayers who owe additional taxes for early IRA distributions must use Form 1040. They can use Form 1040A only when they do not owe additional taxes. The Code does not tax a rollover (conversion) from one IRA directly to another IRA.

The law requires a taxpayer to report the total IRA distribution as well as the portion that is taxable. IRA rules provide a recovery formula for determining the nontaxable portion of an IRA distribution. The taxpayer also reports rollovers directly from one IRA to another IRA and rollovers from a qualified employer's pension plan directly to an IRA. They do not, however, include these amounts in gross income.

NONTAXABLE IRA DISTRIBUTION FORMULA

$$\frac{\text{Total nondeductible contributions}}{\text{Total value of IRA (including contributions and earnings)}} \times \text{Distribution} = \text{Nontaxable distribution}$$

Taxpayers who take a "qualified Hurricane Katrina distribution" from their IRAs spread the taxable portion of the distribution over three tax years. Starting in the year they receive the distribution, they will include in gross income one-third of the taxable portion of the distribution. They also have the option to elect to include the entire taxable amount in gross income in the year they receive the distribution. A **qualified Hurricane Katrina distribution** is any distribution made after August 24, 2005 and before January 1, 2007 by an individual whose principal place of abode on August 28, 2005 was located in the Hurricane Katrina disaster area (as specified by the federal government) and who sustained an economic loss as a result of the hurricane.

PENSIONS AND ANNUITIES

Recipients of pension and annuity payments report them on Form 1040A or Form 1040. Taxpayers also may use these forms to report payments from profit-sharing plans, employee retirement plans, employee savings plans, and salary reduction plans. Pension and annuity recipients cannot use Form 1040EZ.

A recipient of a pension or an annuity generally gets a series of cash payments for his or her remaining life or for a fixed period. These payments usually consist of two elements: (1) return of previously taxed investment and (2) income. The taxpayer may exclude from income the portion of any annuity proceeds that represents the recovery of the taxpayer's previously taxed investment. Excess proceeds are included in gross income.

To determine the **excludable portion of annuity proceeds,** the taxpayer applies an exclusion ratio against the amount received:

$$\frac{\text{Taxpayer's previously taxed investment in contract}}{\text{Total expected return on contract}} \times \text{Amount received} = \text{Excludable proceeds}$$

When computing the total expected return, life expectancy tables (annuity tables) provide the estimated period over which the annuity contract will pay its annual benefits. The exclusion ratio, once determined, does not change. The taxpayer uses it each year until his or her investment is fully recovered. Thereafter, all receipts are subject to tax. Please note, if the taxpayer has never paid tax on the money invested, all proceeds are taxed.

EXAMPLE 9

Sally Smith purchased a life annuity for $72,000. It pays equal annual installments of $8,000 beginning January 1, 2005. Using life expectancy tables, Smith determines she has 12 remaining years of life at the annuity's start date. The following calculations show how Smith determines the taxable portion of each payment:

Investment in contract	$72,000
Expected return ($8,000 × 12 years)	$96,000
Income exclusion percentage ($72,000 ÷ 96,000)	75%
Amount received during a year	$ 8,000
Recovery exclusion ($8,000 × 75%)	(6,000)
Taxable portion	$ 2,000

For the first 12 years, Smith excludes $6,000 ($8,000 × 75%) from each annuity payment. Her taxable annual annuity income for each of these years equals $2,000. Each year after the 12th year, Smith includes all $8,000 in gross income.

A different procedure applies to those receiving money from a "qualified retirement plan" that has a starting date after November 18, 1996.

$$\frac{\text{Taxpayer's previously taxed investment in contract}}{\text{Number of anticipated monthly payments}} = \text{Amount excluded}$$

The number of anticipated monthly payments is determined from the following table:

Age of Annuitant on Annuity Starting Date	Number of Anticipated Monthly Payments
55 and under	360
56–60	310
61–65	260
66–70	210
71 and over	160

When the payments are not made on a monthly basis, the number of payments requires adjustment. For example, if the payments are quarterly, the taxpayer divides the number of payments by four. If the number of payments is fixed, the number of payments becomes the denominator.

These procedures apply only to qualified pension plans where some or all of the taxpayer's contributions have already been taxed. It does not apply to IRAs. If no taxes have been paid on any of the contributions into the plan, all proceeds are taxed.

Regarding pensions and annuities starting after 1986, when the annuitant dies before recovering his or her total investment, the unrecovered investment qualifies as an itemized deduction on the final tax return.

Special tax rules apply to payments received under an annuity contract before its official start date. This book does not cover those rules. Those interested in learning more about these rules should refer to IRS Publication 575.

EXAMPLE 10

Jason Smart, Age 65, retired from his job where he was a participant in a qualified retirement plan. On July 1, 20x1, he received his first monthly retirement check for $2,000. Over his years of employment, Smart contributed $162,500 to his retirement plan.

If Smart received no deduction or deferral for his contributions, he may exclude $625 ($162,500/260 payments) of each monthly payment from taxation. In 20x1, he will receive $12,000 ($2,000 × 6) and may exclude $3,750 ($625 × 6) from taxation. The remaining $8,250 ($12,000 – $3,750) is taxed. If Smart lives long enough to collect more than 260 payments, all subsequent payments will be fully taxed. If none of Smart's contributions were previously taxed, all payments received would be income.

RENTS AND ROYALTIES

Taxpayers usually report rent or royalty income on Form 1040 as "Rental real estate, royalties, etc." However, business-related rent or royalty income is reported as "Business income or (loss)." Taxpayers cannot use Form 1040EZ or Form 1040A to report rent or royalty income. "Gross income" includes the gross rent or royalty income a taxpayer receives. The tax law then treats ordinary, necessary, and reasonable rental expenses as deductions for AGI. When allowable deductions exceed related income, limits on the deductions may apply.

UNEMPLOYMENT COMPENSATION (INSURANCE)

Under federal or state law, workers unemployed for short periods receive unemployment compensation. Recipients of this compensation report it on Form 1040A or Form 1040 as "Unemployment compensation." Payers of $10 or more of this compensation report it annually to the IRS and the taxpayers on Form 1099-G, Statement for Recipients of Certain Government Payments.

STATE AND LOCAL INCOME TAX REFUNDS

A taxpayer who gets a refund of state and local taxes deducted in a prior year may have gross income. The "tax benefit rule" (below) shows how such a refund can create gross income. The taxable amount is reported on Form 1040. The taxpayer cannot use Form 1040EZ or Form 1040A to report the refund. Refunds of federal income taxes do not produce gross income.

SOCIAL SECURITY BENEFITS

Most retirees receive their social security benefits tax free. However, some retirees pay taxes on a portion of their monthly social security benefits. Tax law limits the amount subject to tax to either 50% or 85% of the benefits, depending on the taxpayer's level of income. For higher-income taxpayers, a larger portion of social security payments is subject to tax. Taxpayers report both gross and taxable social security benefits on either Form 1040A or Form 1040. Instructions to these forms contain similar worksheets for calculating taxable benefits. Example 11 illustrates the formula for determining taxable social security benefits.

EXAMPLE 11

Jim Smith, a married taxpayer filing jointly, has adjusted gross income (AGI) of $75,000 before $13,500 of social security (OASDI) and $5,000 of tax-exempt interest.

1. AGI before social security	$75,000
2. Add 50% of social security income	6,750
3. Total	$81,750
4. Add tax-exempt income	5,000
5. Revised AGI	$86,750

6. Less base amount ($0, $25,000, or $32,000)*	(32,000)
7. Net	$54,750
8. Multiplied by	× 50%
9. Base for comparison	$27,375
10. Taxable OASDI = the smaller of line 9 or line 2	$ 6,750

*$32,000, married filing jointly; $0, married filing separately and living with spouse part of year; $25,000, all others

If the amount on line 5 does not exceed $44,000 for a married taxpayer filing jointly (zero for a married taxpayer filing separately who lived with spouse part of year; $34,000 for other filers), the amount on line 10 equals the taxable amount of OASDI benefits.

If the amount on line 5 exceeds $44,000, zero, or $34,000, respectively, additional computations are needed as follows.

11. If married filing jointly, enter the smaller of $6,000 (zero for a married taxpayer filing separately who lived with spouse part of year; $4,500 for other taxpayers) or the amount on line 10	$6,000
12. For a married taxpayer filing jointly, subtract $44,000 (zero for a married taxpayer filing separately who lived with spouse part of year; $34,000 for other taxpayers) from the amount on line 5, and multiply the difference by 85%	36,338
13. Add lines 11 and 12	$42,338
14. 85% of social security	$11,475
15. Taxable OASDI = the smaller of line 13 or line 14	$11,475

TAX BENEFIT RULE

Under the tax benefit rule, taxpayers may have reportable income when they get back (recover) amounts deducted in a prior year. For a recovery to be taxable, taxable income for the prior deduction year must equal or exceed zero, and the taxpayer must have itemized deductions. A taxpayer uses three factors to determine the taxable amount: (1) itemized deduction amount for the prior year, (2) standard deduction amount for that year, and (3) amount recovered.

After determining these amounts, the taxpayer computes his or her excess itemized deductions. Excess itemized deductions equal the deducted itemized deductions for the prior year less the standard deduction for that year. Then, the taxpayer compares the recovery amount with the excess itemized deductions for the prior year and takes the lower of the two.

EXAMPLE 12

In 2004 Foster Green, age 46 and single, deducted $4,260 on his federal income tax return for Michigan income taxes. Green has excellent vision. In 2005, Green received a state income tax refund of $700. For 2004, Green deducted $8,863 in itemized deductions.

The 2004 standard deduction for a single taxpayer like Green equaled $4,850. For 2004 Green's excess itemized deductions equaled $4,013 ($8,863 − $4,850). Also, Green's 2005 recovery amount ($700) fell below his 2004 excess itemized deductions ($4,013). Thus, he includes the smaller of his recovery amount ($700) or excess itemized deductions ($4,013) in gross income. Green's gross income from the recovery equals $700.

EXAMPLE 13

In 2004 Karen Black, age 35 and single, deducted $3,260 on her federal income tax return for local real estate taxes. As a result of a billing error in the county assessor's office, Black overpaid her 2004 real estate taxes. In 2005, she received a real estate tax refund of $700. Including the $3,260 of real estate taxes that she paid in 2004, her total deducted itemized deductions for that year equaled $5,200. The standard deduction for a single taxpayer like Black equaled $4,850 in 2004. To determine her gross income from the tax refund, she first determines her excess itemized deductions for 2004. Here, Black has excess itemized deductions of $350 ($5,200 − $4,850). Because her recovery amount ($700) exceeded her excess itemized deductions ($350), she includes $350 in gross income.

ILLEGAL INCOME

Income from illegal activities is included in gross income. Taxpayers may deduct the ordinary and necessary business expenses (rents, wages, utilities, etc.) required to produce this income. However, illegal payments (bribes to police and judges) are not deductible. In the case of illegal drug trafficking, the cost of goods sold reduces gross receipts to yield gross income, but no other expenses are deductible.

OTHER INCOME

Income from various other sources is also included in gross income. These sources include awards and prizes, reimbursements for health expenses deducted in a prior year, and hobby income.

Gross income includes gambling winnings. Taxpayers may claim itemized deductions for gambling losses up to the amounts of their winnings. Persons in the trade or business of gambling deduct losses for AGI.

Gross income includes amounts taxpayers receive from sales contests, raffles, and radio and television contest programs. It also includes the value of door prizes and prizes and awards from employers. A limited exclusion ($400) exists for employees receive for length of service and safety achievement. These awards must be in the form of personal property (not cash). Unless de minimis rules apply (hams and turkeys for special holidays), gross income includes all other awards or prizes from employers. Taxpayers include property prizes and awards in gross income at their FMV. Gross income can include awards in recognition of past religious, charitable, scientific, educational, artistic, literary, or civic accomplishments. Such awards include Pulitzer and Nobel Prizes. An exception applies if the recipient of such an award immediately assigns it to a qualified governmental unit or tax-exempt charity.

Name _____

Section _____ Date _____

QUESTIONS AND PROBLEMS

1. **Compensation.** Mark Wellaby, M.D., practices medicine in Farmersville. During the current year he received the following items in payment for his services: cash of $48,000; farm produce worth $1,000; common stock with a total par value of $500; and a $500, 90-day noninterest-bearing note dated December 1. The stock at the time of receipt had a fair market value of $1,000. At December 31, the fair market value of the stock had dropped to $900. When Dr. Wellaby received the note, he immediately discounted it at the bank and received $485. Compute Dr. Wellaby's gross income.

2. **Tips.** The following questions involve tip income. Answer each question by inserting an X in the proper column.

	True	False
a. Employees receiving less than $20 in monthly tips while working for one employer need not report them to the employer.	_____	_____
b. Employees receiving less than $20 in monthly tips do not have to pay social security and Medicare taxes on their tips.	_____	_____
c. Employees receiving less than $20 in monthly tips do not have to pay income taxes on their tips.	_____	_____
d. The IRS normally assumes that food and beverage servers make at least 10% of gross sales in tips.	_____	_____
e. When tips reported to employers are less than the IRS's assumed tipping rate, some employers must report the difference as additional income on the employee's Form W-2.	_____	_____
f. "Allocated tips" are subject to withholding for income, social security, and Medicare taxes.	_____	_____

3. **Alimony.** For a divorce or legal separation after 1984, alimony payments are deductible by the payer and includable in the payee's gross income. However, to be considered alimony, the payments must meet six conditions. What are these conditions?

4. **Alimony.** Under the terms of a divorce agreement, Gary is to pay $200 per month as child support to Judy who has custody of their 12-year-old child. Judy is also to receive $1,200 per month for 12 years, but this payment will reduce to $1,000 per month when the child reaches age 18. Gary is also to transfer stock to Judy. The stock cost $20,000 and has a market value of $50,000. In the first year under the agreement, Judy receives the stock and eight months of cash payments. How will these transfers affect Judy's gross income?

5. **Tax on Dividends.** Tiffany and Randy Crowder file a joint return. They have taxable income of $79,000, including qualified dividends of $3,000. Compute their tax liability.

6. **Dividend Distributions.**

   a. Name five types of distributions that a taxpayer might receive from a mutual fund.

   b. For Form 1040A filers with more than $1,500 of gross dividends, what kinds of dividend distributions can be reported on Schedule 1?

7. **Mutual Fund Distributions.** Susan Rhiner owns shares of stock in a mutual investment fund. In January 2006, the fund sent her a distribution notice showing that she received the following distributions from the fund in 2005.

Regular cash dividend	$526
Capital gains distributed	150
Capital gains undistributed	370

   Rhiner verifies the reported data from her records. The mutual fund also sent her a Form 2439 showing that her share of the income tax paid by the fund in 2005 on its undistributed capital gains was $129.50. Rhiner has no other investments. She paid $10,100 for her mutual fund shares on January 16, 2005.

   a. What amount of the distribution of the mutual fund is reported on Rhiner's Form 1040, and how is it reported?

b. Assume that Rhiner sells the mutual fund shares in January 2006 for $10,200, and compute the amount of gain or loss on the sale.

8. **Accrued Interest on Bonds.** On September 30, 2005, Ramona Zwick purchased a $40,000 par value bond of the DPQ Corporation. She paid the seller $40,800 ($40,000 par value + $800 accrued interest). The 8% bond pays interest semiannually on December 31 and June 30. Zwick received the first semiannual interest payment of $1,600 on December 31, 2005. From the DPQ Corporation bonds, how much interest income does Zwick have in 2005? Explain.

9. **Acquiring Series EE Bonds.** Norma Demar, age 30 and single, who has never owned U.S. Savings Bonds, wants to invest $2,000 in Series EE bonds. What options does Demar have in reporting income from these bonds?

10. **Interest on Series E Bonds.** Following are the issue price, original maturity value, and selected redemption values of Series E bonds owned by Richard Grady.

| | | Redemption Value | |
| | | | |
Issue Price	*Original Maturity Value*	*End of Current Year*	*End of Subsequent Year*
$375	$ 500	$ 648.00	$ 673.20
150	200	232.56	240.72
750	1,000	1,015.60	1,051.60
75	100	79.60	82.64
150	200	156.08	162.24

In 2005, Grady elects to report the increase in redemption value each year on Series E bonds. At the election date he owned no other U.S. bonds. What is Grady's gross income from these bonds in 2005? In 2006 (assuming no redemptions or additional purchases)?

11. **Original Issue Discount.** On July 1, 2005, Gerald Johnson purchased a 25-year, zero-coupon bond with a maturity value of $1,000,000 for $52,911.96. The yield to maturity is 15.25%.

    a. What is the OID on the bond?

    b. What portion of the OID would be included in taxable interest income for 2005?

    c. What portion of the OID would be included in taxable interest income for 2006?

    d. When is a Form 1099-OID prepared? Who prepares it? To whom are copies sent? What information does it contain?

12. **Imputed Interest.**

    a. What are AFRs? How are AFRs determined?

    b. Janet Bowman's parents lend Janet and her husband $125,000 to purchase a new home. The loan is for ten years with zero interest. Must interest be imputed on the loan? Explain your answer and indicate the limitations (if any).

    c. If the loan to Janet and her husband in Part b. were $100,000, would interest have to be imputed? Explain your answer and indicate the limitations (if any).

13. **Child's Unearned Income.** Dee deCastro, age 10, received taxable interest of $4,100 during the year. She has no other income, and her total itemized deductions are $150. She has no brothers or sisters. DeCastro is a dependent of her parents, who have taxable income of $75,000. If deCastro's parents do not elect to report her income on their return, what is the amount of deCastro's income that will be taxed at her parents' tax rate?

14. **Annuity Income.** Fifteen years ago, Cal Greguska purchased an annuity contract for $92,400. The contract stated that he would receive $550 a month for life, starting on January 1, 1995. On this date, Greguska's remaining life expectancy was 20 years. For 2005, how much of the annuity payments can Greguska exclude from his gross income?

Handwritten notes:

$550 \times 12 = 6600/yr$ 1980

132,000
92,400
─────
39,600

$92,400 \div 132,000 = 70\%$

$6600 - (6600 \times 70\%)$

$6600 - 4620 = 1980$

Investment in annuity / Expected Return = % of income excluded

Amt rec'd during yr

Amt excluded $(6600 \times 70\%)$

Taxable portion

15. **Annuity Income.** On August 10, 2005, Don Wilson turned 65 and received his first retirement plan annuity check. Over the years, he had contributed $68,900 to this qualified retirement plan. Taxes were paid on $24,700 of this amount. The remaining $44,200 was contributed after the law was changed to permit pre-tax contributions to the plan. Wilson is to receive monthly annuity payments of $425 on the same day every month for the remainder of his life. On his 65th birthday, he had a life expectancy of 20 years.

Handwritten notes:

68900
44200
taxed 24700 425
            × 12
            5100

102,000 total

33100   68900 (post-tax)
        44200 (pre-tax)

a. From the annuity payments Wilson receives in 2005, what amount is part of his gross income?

Handwritten notes:

Rec'd for 5 months $2125

previously taxed investment

$24700 \div 260 = 95 = $ excludable from each payment

$2125 - (95 \times 5)$

$2125 - 475 = 1650$

b. If Wilson receives twelve annuity payments in 2006, what is his gross income from these payments?

Handwritten notes:

Gross 5100
Excludable (1140)
taxable $3960

c. If Wilson lives longer than his expected 260 payments, how much of his annual annuity receipts are part of his gross income?

Handwritten notes:

age 61-65

Once he receives all investments, he would be taxed on all payments of gross income.

$(425 \times 12 = \$5100)$

16. **Taxable Social Security Benefits.** Taxpayers A through D have reported the following social security (SS) information. Fill in blank lines e through h on the table for each taxpayer. On line h, show how to compute the amount of the taxable SS benefits included in income for each taxpayer. Assume C did not live with spouse in the tax year.

Item	A	B	C	D
a. Taxpayer status	Single	Married filing jointly	Married filing separately	Married filing jointly
b. AGI before SS benefits	$25,000	$32,300	$12,000	$24,000
c. SS benefits received	_3900_ 7,800	_4700_ 9,400	_3100_ 6,200	_5500_ 11,000
d. Tax-exempt interest	500	0	0	400
e. Revised AGI	$ _29400_	$ _37000_	$ _15100_	$ _29900_
f. Less base exemption	$ _(25000)_	$ _(32000)_	$ _(25000)_	$ _(32000)_
g. Net amount /Excess	$ _4400_	$ _5000_	$ _0_	$ _0_
h. Taxable SS benefits included in income	$ _2200_	$ _2500_	$ _0_	$ _0_

(handwritten note at left:) less of: 1/2 of net/excess OR 1/2 SS benefits rec'd

17. **Taxable Social Security Benefits.** Taxpayers E through G have reported the following social security (SS) information for the year. Assume the taxpayers married and filing separately lived together part of the tax year. Fill in the blank lines d through r on the table for each taxpayer. On line r, show how to compute the amount of taxable SS benefits included in income for each taxpayer.

	E Single	F Married filing jointly	G Married filing separately
First-Tier Formula			
a. AGI before SS	$50,000	$48,000	$5,000
b. SS benefits received	_3900_ 7,800	_6450_ 12,900	_5500_ 11,000
c. Tax-exempt interest	500	400	400
d. Revised AGI	_54400_	_54800_	_10900_
e. Less base for first-tier benefits ($0, $25,000, or $32,000)	_(25000)_	_(32000)_	_(0)_
f. Net	_29400_	_22800_	_11900_
g. One-half of line f	_14700_	_11425_	_5950_
h. One-half of SS	_3900_	_6450_	_5450_
i. Taxable first-tier benefits (lesser of line g or h)	_3900_	_6450_	_5450_
Second-Tier Formula			
j. Revised AGI (line d above)	_54400_	_54850_	_10900_
k. Less base for second-tier benefits ($0, $34,000, or $44,000)	_(34000)_	_(44000)_	_(0)_
l. Net	_20400_	_10850_	_10900_
m. Multiplied by 85%	_85%_	_83%_	_85%_
n. Product	_17340_	_9223_	_9265_
o. Add lesser of line i or w	_3900_	_6000_	_0_
p. Total	_21240_	_15223_	_9265_

	7800×85% =	12900×85% =	11000×85% =
q. SS × 85%	6630	10965 9350	
r. Taxable benefits (lesser of line p or q)	6630	10965 9265	
s. Base amount for second-tier benefits	34,000	44,000	0
t. Less base amount for first-tier benefits	−25,000	−32,000	−0
u.	9,000	12,000	0
v. Multiplied by 50%	×50%	×50%	×50%
w. Product	4,500	6,000	0

18. Tax Benefit Rule.

a. Explain the tax benefit rule as it applies to refunds of state and local income taxes.

b. Explain the tax benefit rule as it applies to refunds of federal income taxes.

c. In 2004 Lou Sharp, age 35 and single, deducted $5,325 on his federal income tax return for California income taxes. Sharp has excellent vision. In 2005, Sharp received a state income tax refund of $875. For 2004, Sharp deducted $11,154 in itemized deductions. After these deductions, Sharp's taxable income equaled $100,000. The 2004 standard deduction for a single taxpayer like Sharp equaled $4,850. For 2005, how much must Sharp include in his gross income from the California income tax refund?

19. Internet Problem: Filling out Form 4137.

Hannah Homerding (SSN 234-56-7891) works as a waitress at the Texas Steakhouse Restaurant. As she prepared her tax return for 2005, she discovered that she forgot to report tips of $1,250 to her employer for the month of June. She had properly reported the rest of her tips, $28,750, to the restaurant during the year. Homerding lives at 19 Cabintown Road, Fort Worth, TX 76101. Her Form W-2 for the year lists her total social security wages and tips at $35,750.

Go to the IRS Web site and locate Form 4137. Using the computer, fill in Form 4137 and Schedule U for Homerding and print out a completed copy.

See Appendix A for instructions on use of the IRS Web site.

20. Business Entity Problem: This problem is designed for those using the "business entity" approach. The solution may require information from Chapter 14.

Please answer the following true and false questions in the space provided.

	True	False
a. Corporations owning less than 80% of another corporation are generally taxed on at least a portion of the dividends they receive from that company.	_____	_____
b. Corporations receiving dividends from another corporation may exclude 70% of the dividends from gross income if they own 10% of the other company.	_____	_____
c. S corporations receiving a dividend from another corporation do not pay taxes on the dividend.	_____	_____
d. Partnerships receiving dividends from a corporation must include the dividends in the calculation of "ordinary income."	_____	_____
e. A shareholder receiving a property distribution from a corporation must recognize the property distribution at its market value at distribution date.	_____	_____
f. A partner receiving a property distribution from the partnership must recognize the property distribution at its market value at distribution date.	_____	_____

21. Business Entity Problem: This problem is designed for those using the "business entity" approach. The solution may require information from Chapter 14.

Jason Lang owns a corporation. At December 31, the end of the corporation's tax year, the company has Earnings and Profits of $20,000 before consideration of any distribution to the owner. On December 31, the company distributes property with a market value of $50,000 to Lang. The basis of the property is $30,000.

a. If the corporation is in the 25% tax bracket, what are the tax implications to the corporation?

b. What are the tax implications to Lang?

COMPREHENSIVE PROBLEM

22. Neale D. (SSN 394-57-7584) and Judith L. (SSN 746-38-4457) Hamilton file a joint Form 1040. The Hamiltons have no foreign accounts or trusts. During the year, they received the interest and dividends shown below.

From the following information, prepare Schedule B (Form 1040), Interest and Ordinary Dividends, for the Hamiltons using the Schedule B reproduced in this problem. Assume they received information returns from all payers.

Interest Received in Cash	*Amount*
U.S. Treasury bond — *taxable (federal only)*	$600.00
State of Michigan general obligation bond — *not subject to federal taxes*	75.00
City of Meadowood utility bond — *NOT TAXABLE*	160.00
Mortgage of Mr. and Mrs. K. J. Roe (purchased from E. Johnson) — *taxable*	732.50
Ace Manufacturing Company note — *taxable*	50.00
K. R. Smith, personal note — *taxable*	115.00
American Telephone and Telegraph debenture note — *taxable*	60.00

Dividends Received in Cash *rec'd from corporation — not subject to federal taxes unless more than tax basis in stock*	*Amount*
BXL Mutual Fund return-of-capital dividend — *NOT TAXABLE*	$450.00
Red Corporation dividend on preferred stock — *TAXABLE*	280.00
Credit union dividend (interest) — *TAXABLE*	90.00
L.M.O. Mutual Fund capital gain distribution — *NOT TAXABLE*	15.00
USX Corporation dividend on common stock — *TAXABLE*	1,341.20
Dow Chemical Company dividend on common stock reinvested in common stock through company dividend reinvestment plan — *TAXABLE* *subject to income tax*	185.00

a] taxed @ 15% Gain on Schedule D not B

Interest & Dividends = Taxable items

Qualified dividends = subject to max tax rate of 15% on federal taxes

(Use for Problem 22.)

Schedules A&B (Form 1040) 2005

Name(s) shown on Form 1040. Do not enter name and social security number if shown on other side.

OMB No. 1545-0074   Page **2**

Your social security number

Schedule B—Interest and Ordinary Dividends

Attachment Sequence No. **08**

Part I
Interest

(See page B-1 and the instructions for Form 1040, line 8a.)

Note. If you received a Form 1099-INT, Form 1099-OID, or substitute statement from a brokerage firm, list the firm's name as the payer and enter the total interest shown on that form.

1 List name of payer. If any interest is from a seller-financed mortgage and the buyer used the property as a personal residence, see page B-1 and list this interest first. Also, show that buyer's social security number and address ▶

	Amount	
U.S. Treasury Bonds	600	00
State of Michigan	75	00
City of Meadwood	160	00
Mortgage	732	50
	50	00
	115	00
AT&T	60	00
Credit Union dividend	90	00
Subtotal	1882	00
Less: Tax exempt interest	(235	00)

1

2 Add the amounts on line 1 . . . . **2** | 1647 | 50

3 Excludable interest on series EE and I U.S. savings bonds issued after 1989. Attach Form 8815 . . . . **3** | 0 |

4 Subtract line 3 from line 2. Enter the result here and on Form 1040, line 8a ▶ **4** | 1647 | 50

Note. If line 4 is over $1,500, you must complete Part III.

Part II
Ordinary Dividends

(See page B-2 and the instructions for Form 1040, line 9a.)

Note. If you received a Form 1099-DIV or substitute statement from a brokerage firm, list the firm's name as the payer and enter the ordinary dividends shown on that form.

5 List name of payer ▶

	Amount	
Return on capital BXL Mutual	450	00
Red Corporation stock	280	00
USX Corporation	1341	00
Dow Chemical Co (reinvested common)	185	00
Subtotal	2256	00
Less: Return on capital	(450	00)

5

6 Add the amounts on line 5. Enter the total here and on Form 1040, line 9a . ▶ **6** | 1805 | 00

Note. If line 6 is over $1,500, you must complete Part III.

Part III
Foreign Accounts and Trusts

(See page B-2.)

You must complete this part if you **(a)** had over $1,500 of taxable interest or ordinary dividends; or **(b)** had a foreign account; or **(c)** received a distribution from, or were a grantor of, or a transferor to, a foreign trust.

	Yes	No

7a At any time during 2005, did you have an interest in or a signature or other authority over a financial account in a foreign country, such as a bank account, securities account, or other financial account? See page B-2 for exceptions and filing requirements for Form TD F 90-22.1. . . . . . .

b If "Yes," enter the name of the foreign country ▶ . . . .

8 During 2005, did you receive a distribution from, or were you the grantor of, or transferor to, a foreign trust? If "Yes," you may have to file Form 3520. See page B-2 . . . .

For Paperwork Reduction Act Notice, see Form 1040 instructions.

Schedule B (Form 1040) 2005

♻ *Printed on recycled paper*

4

Gross Income Exclusions and Adjustments to Income

CHAPTER CONTENTS

■■ CHAPTER OVERVIEW

*C*hapter 3 treated gross income inclusions. This chapter examines gross income exclusions and adjustments to income (deductions from gross income to arrive at AGI). Figures 4-6 and 4-7 show how taxpayers report income and adjustments to income on Form 1040A and Form 1040.

GROSS INCOME EXCLUSIONS

Gross income includes all wealth that flows to a taxpayer after constitutional, statutory, and IRS de miminis exclusions are considered. This section discusses several fully or partially exempt income items (gross income exclusions).

Bequest and Inheritance

Gross income excludes the value of property a taxpayer gets by bequest, devise, or inheritance. However, it includes the future income from such property.

Gifts

A person receiving a gift excludes the value of the gift from gross income. However, the law taxes future income from the gifted property. If the transferor intends the gift to cover services received, the FMV of the property is usually income, even if no obligation to make the transfer exists.

Dividends, Tax-Exempt

The Code taxes distributions from a corporation's earnings and profits (E&P) as ordinary dividends. When a distribution exceeds the corporation's earnings and profits, the excess may qualify as a tax-free return of capital. For this treatment, the excess cannot exceed the shareholder's basis in the stock.

Nontaxable Distributions

Any distribution that represents a shareholder's return-of-capital is nontaxable. When such payments exceed a shareholder's stock basis, the Code taxes the excess as capital gain. Nontaxable distributions may also include common stock dividends and stock rights. For these distributions, taxpayers assign a portion of their investment in the stock held to the new shares or rights received (Chapter 10). A taxpayer who owns a small quantity of stock may not receive a full share of stock or stock right. Here, the corporation usually gives the shareholder cash. The Code treats the cash as an ordinary dividend to the extent of the corporation's E&P.

The Code also taxes a common stock dividend when a shareholder has an option to receive cash or property instead of the stock. Shareholders include the FMV of any stock received in gross income.

Another nontaxable distribution is the stock split (additional shares issued to existing shareholders). The number of shares received depends on the number of shares already owned. Here again, shareholders allocate the cost of their investment to all the shares owned after the split.

Mutual Insurance Company Dividends

Most mutual insurance company dividends do not qualify as true dividends for tax purposes. Dividends to a policyholder of a mutual insurance company represent a return of premiums. Until the dividends exceed paid premiums, policyholders exclude them from gross income and reduce their investments in the insurance policies.

Foreign-Earned Income Exclusion

A taxpayer may elect to exclude up to $80,000 of "earned income" from foreign countries each year. The taxpayer may also exclude housing costs that exceed 16% of the salary of a government employee at grade GS-14. To qualify for these exclusions, the taxpayer must be a bona fide resident of a foreign country for an entire year or must be physically present in a foreign country for 330 full days out of a twelve-consecutive-month period.

The taxpayer must calculate these exclusions on a daily basis. For example, if a taxpayer resides in France for the last 210 days in 20x1 and the first 300 days in 20x2, the taxpayer meets the 330-day/twelve month requirement for each year. However, the $80,000 maximum exclusion must be prorated in both years:

	Maximum Exclusion
20x1: (210/365) × $80,000 =	$46,027
20x2: (300/365) × $80,000 =	$65,753

As an alternative to the exclusion, a taxpayer may elect to include the foreign income in taxable income and take a credit for the income tax paid to foreign countries.

Fringe Benefits

Employers often provide employees with fringe benefits. The Code taxes some fringe benefits and provides partial or full exemption for others. The following presentation covers some common fringe benefits.

Cafeteria Plans

A **cafeteria plan** lets employees customize their fringe benefits. For employees to avoid taxes on employer contributions to a fringe benefit plan, the employer should prepare a written plan. It should specify that all employees get plan benefits and can choose from two or more benefits that include cash and qualifying tax-free benefits. Cafeteria plans qualifying for tax-free benefits include dependent care, group-term life insurance, health insurance, and accident insurance. In addition to cafeteria plans, taxpayers may also receive tax-free benefits from qualifying scholarships, fellowships, and tuition reductions. For graduate students to get the exemption for tuition reductions, they must perform teaching or research activities as employees of the school. Educational assistance and employer-paid adoption expenses also qualify for tax-free treatment.

> The major advantage of cafeteria plans is that employees do not pay taxes on the income used to pay for their product or service.

Dependent Care

An employee can exclude from gross income up to $5,000 of employer-provided dependent care help. The exclusion applies when the care lets the employee work. Only an employee's children and dependents (qualifying persons) can receive such care. Any help provided under the plan cannot favor officers, owners, or high-pay employees, including their dependents. Instead of making care payments to outsiders, an employer can provide care at the work site.

An annual earnings limit affects the amount of the dependent care exclusion. The exclusion cannot exceed the smaller of two amounts: (1) $5,000 or (2) the earned income of the spouse with the smaller earnings. For married persons filing separately, the dollar limit cannot exceed $2,500. When calculating the earned income limits, if the taxpayer or spouse is a full-time student or is incapacitated, the Code assumes that this person earns at least $250 a month. When two persons are receiving care, the assumed $250 a month rises to $500 a month. Please note that these "assumed earnings" are not taxable. A person who uses the exclusion must reduce his or her child and dependent care payments by the excluded amount when computing child and dependent care credit. A taxpayer who claims the exclusion must report the name, address, and social security number of the care provider on the tax return.

Educational Assistance

Under a qualifying plan, employees can exclude educational assistance from their employer. The annual exclusion cannot exceed $5,250. The assistance can cover tuition, fees, books, and supplies for both undergraduate and graduate courses. However, the exclusion does not apply when more than 5% of an employer's help goes to those who own 5% or more of the company.

Group-Term Life Insurance

Sometimes, an employer buys life insurance for employees under a group-term plan, and the employees name their beneficiaries. For each employee, the employer can purchase up to $50,000 of plan insurance without increasing the employee's gross income. However, the insurance must be purchased under a plan that does not favor officers, shareholders, or high-pay personnel. When the coverage exceeds $50,000, the employee must add to gross income the cost of the excess insurance. To determine this cost, the employer must use a government table of uniform premiums (Figure 4-1) found in the regulations. Actual cost may vary from the table amount. By age group, the table lists the monthly cost for $1,000 of insurance.

FIGURE 4-1 Uniform One-Month Premiums for $1,000 of Group-Term Life Insurance Protection

Age*	Cost for $1,000 of Protection for One-Month Period
Under 30	$ .08
30–34	.09
35–39	.11
40–44	.17
45–49	.29
50–54	.48
55–59	.75
60–64	1.17
65–69	2.10
70 and over	3.76

*Applicable bracket depends on employee's age at employer's year end.

When using the table, the employer determines the excess coverage under the plan for employees with more than $50,000 of insurance. Here, the employer subtracts $50,000 from each employee's coverage. Next, the employer divides the excess coverage by $1,000. The premium table lists the insurance rates by age. The employer determines each employee's age on the last day of the business year and finds the given monthly rate for each employee's age. Then, the employer multiplies the given monthly rate by the excess coverage stated in $1,000 units. Finally, the employer multiplies the product by the number of months of insurance coverage. Following is the cost formula:

Cost of Excess Insurance = Monthly Rate for Each $1,000 of Excess Coverage × Number of $1,000 Increments of Excess Coverage × Number of Months of Coverage

When the employee pays part of the premiums, the employer subtracts *all* of the employee's payments from the cost of the excess insurance. When the cost exceeds an employee's payments, the employee has gross income. When an employee's payments exceed the cost of the excess insurance, the employee does not have any gross income.

If an employer pays the premiums on *ordinary life insurance* (as opposed to term insurance), the employee usually has gross income when the employee receives a benefit. Thus, when the employee names the person who collects on the policy at death, the employee has gross income. The amount of gross income equals the premiums paid.

The employer includes the taxable portion of purchased life insurance as wages on the employee's Form W-2, Wage and Tax Statement. Also, the employee may find that the employer withheld FICA taxes on the taxable portion of the insurance. An employer usually includes with the Form W-2 a separate statement explaining the extra income.

EXAMPLE 1

Bow Company pays an annual premium for $90,000 of life insurance for Harry R. Socket, age 56. Bow shares the cost with Socket, who pays Bow $22.50 a month through the payroll deduction plan. With these payments, Socket gets twelve months of group-term life insurance protection. If Socket dies before the coverage period ends, his wife collects $90,000. Bow purchases the insurance under a group plan that does not favor officers, shareholders, or high-pay personnel. Figure 4-1 shows the monthly cost for $1,000 of group-term life insurance. For Socket's age, the table shows a monthly cost of $0.75. As a result of the described transactions, Socket includes $90 in gross income.

Group-term life insurance coverage	$90,000
Less Exempt coverage	(50,000)
Taxable coverage	$40,000
Cost subject to gross income inclusion	
[$40,000/$1,000 = 40; 40 × 12 × $0.75 (Figure 4-1)]	$ 360
Payments by Socket (12 × $22.50)	270
Gross income	$ 90

Key employees must include the employer's total "actual cost" of group-term life insurance in gross income when the plan discriminates in their favor. Discrimination exists when a plan favors the type and amount of their benefits. Key employees include company officers, the company's ten largest owners, and persons who own 5% of the company. Also, key employees include persons who own 1% of a company and have annual earnings that exceed $150,000. These tests apply to the current plan year and the four prior plan years.

Health and Accident Plans

Employees usually exclude from gross income employer-paid premiums for their health and accident insurance. Also, they exclude any reimbursements for medical care and payments for permanent injury or loss of bodily function under an employer-financed accident or health plan. However, when an employer's self-insured health and accident plan favors key employees, their gross income increases by any "excess reimbursements" received. These are reimbursements not available to other plan participants.

Adoption Expenses

Under a qualifying adoption assistance program, an employee can exclude up to $10,630 of child adoption expenses paid or reimbursed by the employer. However, a proportional phase-out applies when AGI reaches $159,450. The phase-out range is $159,450 to $199,450.

Noncash Compensation

The Code excludes certain noncash employee fringe benefits from gross income. Generally, these benefits cannot discriminate in favor of key employees. Exceptions exist, however (see items 1, 3, and 6 below). When benefits to key employees fail the discrimination test, the FMV of the discriminating benefits is taxable. However, benefits to the other employees still qualify for tax-free treatment. When employers report employees' wages on Form W-2, they include taxable fringe benefits. Following are some additional tax-free fringe benefits:

1. **De minimis (small-value) fringe benefits** such as the use of copy machines, stationery, and office supplies. The IRS also excludes low-value holiday gifts such as turkeys and hams from gross income under its de minimis rule. Discrimination rules do not apply to these benefits. Taxable benefits can result when a taxpayer receives the benefits frequently or the benefits have a large value.
2. **Qualifying employee discounts** such as clothing discounts, brokerage fee discounts, and lodging or meal discounts. When an employer in the trade or business gives employee discounts, employees may usually exclude them from gross income. However, the employees must work in that segment of the employer's business giving the discount (e.g., airline employees cannot receive tax-free discounts at hotels owned by the airlines.) For **services,** the discount cannot exceed 20% of an item's retail value. For **property,** the discount cannot exceed the employer's gross profit percentage for the property line. Here, the property line's average markup percentage governs. Discrimination rules apply.

    Discounts on some property items are taxable. An employee who gets discounts on the purchase of gold coins and securities includes the discounts in gross income. Any discount on the purchase of mineral-producing property is likewise included in gross income. An employee who gets a discount on the purchase of residential or commercial real estate includes that discount in gross income.
3. **Working condition fringe benefits,** meaning goods and services provided by the employer for use in the employer's business. Normally, employees deduct their job-related expenses as itemized deductions (e.g., tools, professional dues). When the employer provides these benefits, the employee does not report their value in gross income. Discrimination rules do not apply to these benefits.

4. **No-additional-cost services,** which include the use of hotel rooms, telephone service, and travel on airlines, railroads, and subways. These services qualify for tax-free treatment when they do not cause large additional costs or lost revenues to the employer. Employees who get these benefits must work in the business line that provides the benefits. When employer-provided services favor key employees, the Code taxes the key employees on the value of the discriminating benefits received.

5. **Athletic facilities,** including tennis courts, swimming pools, putting greens, and the like, on the employer's property. The value of the use of these services is tax-free when substantially all use of these facilities is attributable to employees and their families. An employee's family includes an employee's dependent children and the employee's spouse.

6. **Parking and transportation** provided by employers. These benefits may qualify for tax-free treatment. **Qualified parking** includes parking provided near the employer's business or near the place where the employee commutes to work using mass transit or carpools. Employees may exclude up to $200 per month for parking provided by the employer. **Qualified transportation** may include transit passes and transportation between the employee's home and the work place in a commuter highway vehicle. The maximum exclusion is $105 per month for this benefit. These benefits may be provided directly by the employer or they may take the form of employer reimbursements. Discrimination rules do not apply to these benefits.

Retirement Plans

Employers often fund retirement plans for employees. Later, when eligible employees receive plan benefits, they pay related taxes. If the employees also contribute to these retirement plans, they can recover their nondeductible contributions tax free.

Meals and Lodging

Some employers provide meals to their employees. The value of these meals is tax-free to the employee if the meal is served on the premises of the employer for the convenience of the employer. For example, a hospital may allow nurses to eat in the hospital cafeteria free-of-charge. This provides an incentive to the nurses to eat on the premises where their services may be required in the case of an emergency.

Lodging furnished to an employee may also be tax-free. In this case, however, the lodging must be required as a condition of employment. For example, a counselor in a university dormitory may receive tax-free room and board only if the university requires the counselor to live in the dormitory. When tax-free lodging is provided to an employee, the value of the meals and lodging furnished to the spouse and dependents is also tax-free.

Income of Minors

Legally, parents are responsible for taking care of their minor children. If a minor child cannot prepare and file an income tax return, the parents must do it for the child. The filing parent should sign the return as follows: *By (signature), parent for minor child.*

Parents can deduct reasonable wage payments to their children for business and farm work. The children include these wages in gross income and report them on their (the children's) tax returns. When a child uses the wages to purchase clothing and other support items, the parents can still deduct the wages. However, the parents cannot deduct the cost of meals and lodging furnished to their children. Usually, parents who receive payments from a working child for meals and lodging do not include them in gross income. However, when these payments exceed the child's share of household expenses, the excess is income.

Insurance, Proceeds from Life Policy

Usually, life insurance proceeds paid because of the insured's death are tax-free. However, income results when an insurance company holds the proceeds of the policy and pays out the interest. Under such an arrangement, gross income usually includes the interest when the company adds it to the beneficiary's account. A beneficiary who can withdraw the interest on a policy's anniversary date gets gross income on this date.

Interest, Tax-Exempt

Interest on the general obligation bonds of a state, a territory, or the District of Columbia is tax-exempt. The exemption also applies to political subdivisions of these units (cities, counties, and school districts). Under some conditions, interest on U.S. Savings Bonds used to finance the higher education of a taxpayer, a spouse, or dependents is also tax-exempt. Although gross income does not include tax-exempt interest, taxpayers must report such interest separately on their returns as an information item.

Sometimes, a government unit issues bonds and uses the funds for nongovernment activities. These **industrial development** or **private activity bonds** may qualify for exempt income treatment, but restrictions apply. Before buying such bonds, taxpayers should check out the official tax status of such an investment.

Educational Savings Bonds, Series EE and I

Under certain conditions, qualifying taxpayers can exclude the interest on redeemed Series EE and I U.S. Savings Bonds. The exclusion applies when a taxpayer uses the redemption proceeds for qualified educational expenses at an eligible institution. When there are proceeds left over after the educational expenses are paid, some of the interest will be taxed. Also, when the taxpayer's income rises above a certain level, the interest exclusion phases out. The registered owner must be the taxpayer or spouse. Bonds issued to a taxpayer under age 24 do not qualify for the exclusion. However, anyone can qualify to receive the bonds on the death of the registered owner. To compute the excludable interest, the taxpayer uses Form 8815, Exclusion of Interest From Series EE and I U.S. Savings Bonds Issued After 1989. This exclusion only applies to bonds purchased after 1989. A taxpayer who elects to report Series EE bond interest on a year-by-year basis will not get much of an exclusion.

Eligible institutions include public and nonprofit higher education schools, as well as postsecondary institutions. However, the definition of eligible schools does not include proprietary schools.

Qualified educational expenses include tuition and fees paid to an eligible institution for a taxpayer, a spouse, and dependents. Such expenses do not include payments for room, board, and clothing. Also, these expenses do not include payments for courses involving sports, games, or hobbies. An exception exists for courses taken under a degree- or certificate-granting program in sports. The taxpayer must reduce these qualified expenses by certain nontaxable benefits received by the student during the year. These benefits include scholarships and employer-provided educational assistance. Qualified expenses must also be reduced by expenses taken into account for the HOPE scholarship and lifetime learning credits.

Taxpayers use the following formula to determine the excludable interest before applying the phase-out rules.

EXCLUDABLE EDUCATIONAL SAVINGS BONDS INTEREST BEFORE PHASE-DOWN

$$\begin{matrix} \text{Excludable} \\ \text{Bond} \\ \text{Interest} \end{matrix} = \begin{matrix} \text{Interest} \\ \text{Portion of} \\ \text{Proceeds} \end{matrix} \times \frac{\text{Qualifying Expenses} - (\text{Nontaxable Scholarships} + \text{Expenses Used for Education Credits})}{\text{Redemption Proceeds}}$$

After using the above formula to determine the potential excludable bond interest, taxpayers must determine if the phase-out applies. First, they determine a modified AGI amount (AGI without the Educational Savings Bond interest and the foreign earned income exclusions). Second, they compare this figure with a $61,200 threshold ($91,850 for a joint return). If modified AGI exceeds the threshold, the phase-out applies, and the interest exclusion phases out proportionately over a range of $15,000 ($30,000 for joint filers).

PHASE-DOWN OF EXCLUDABLE EDUCATIONAL SAVINGS BONDS INTEREST

$$\text{Excludable Bond Interest} \times \frac{\text{Modified AGI} - \$61,200^*}{\$15,000^{**}} = \text{Reduction in Excludable Interest}$$

*$91,850 for a joint return
**$30,000 for a joint return  *$61,200 Single & HOH*

Information for Figure 4-2: Filled-In Form 8815

Figure 4-2 shows the use of Form 8815 to compute excludable Educational Savings Bond interest for Frederick and Ida Smith who file a joint return. Fred and Ida have a dependent child, Inez. She attends Kent State University as a full-time student.

On September 30 of the current year, the Smiths redeemed $10,000 of Series EE bonds. Of the cash received, $1,500 is interest and $8,500 is principal.

Other Information

- Qualified educational expenses paid in the current year by the Smiths, **$5,000**
- Nontaxable scholarship received during the year by Inez, **$1,000**
- Modified AGI, **$96,500** (AGI before educational savings bond and foreign earned income exclusions)

After reporting all $1,500 as interest, the Smiths enter the $507 on Form 1040, Schedule B, as "Excludable interest on Series EE and I U.S. Savings Bonds."

FIGURE 4-2   Filled-In Form 8815

Form **8815**	**Exclusion of Interest From Series EE and I**	OMB No. 1545-1173

Department of the Treasury
Internal Revenue Service   (99)

Exclusion of Interest From Series EE and I U.S. Savings Bonds Issued After 1989
(For Filers With Qualified Higher Education Expenses)
► Attach to Form 1040 or Form 1040A.

2005

Attachment
Sequence No. **57**

Name(s) shown on return

Frederick B. and Ida A. Smith

Your social security number

382 : 60 : 1057

1	**(a)** Name of person (you, your spouse, or your dependent) who was enrolled at or attended an eligible educational institution	**(b)** Name and address of eligible educational institution
	Inez I. Smith	Kent State University West Lake Road, Ashtabula, OH 44004

If you need more space, attach a statement.

2	Enter the total qualified higher education expenses you paid in 2005 for the person(s) listed in column (a) of line 1. See the instructions to find out which expenses qualify	**2**	5,000	00
3	Enter the total of any nontaxable educational benefits (such as nontaxable scholarship or fellowship grants) received for 2005 for the person(s) listed in column (a) of line 1 (see instructions)	**3**	1,000	00
4	Subtract line 3 from line 2. If zero or less, **stop**. You **cannot** take the exclusion	**4**	4,000	00
5	Enter the total proceeds (principal and interest) from all series EE and I U.S. savings bonds **issued after 1989** that you **cashed during 2005** (see instructions)	**5**	10,000	00
6	Enter the interest included on line 5 (see instructions)	**6**	1,500	00
7	If line 4 is equal to or more than line 5, enter "1.000." If line 4 is less than line 5, divide line 4 by line 5. Enter the result as a decimal (rounded to at least three places)	**7**	× .40	
8	Multiply line 6 by line 7	**8**	600	00

9	Enter your modified adjusted gross income (see instructions) . . . **9** 96,500 00 **Note:** *If line 9 is $76,200 or more if single or head of household, or $121,850 or more if married filing jointly or qualifying widow(er),* **stop**. *You* **cannot** *take the exclusion.*			
10	Enter: $61,200 if single or head of household; $91,850 if married filing jointly or qualifying widow(er) **10** 91,850 00			
11	Subtract line 10 from line 9. If zero or less, skip line 12, enter -0- on line 13, and go to line 14 . . . . **11** 4,650 00			
12	Divide line 11 by: $15,000 if single or head of household; $30,000 if married filing jointly or qualifying widow(er). Enter the result as a decimal (rounded to at least three places)	**12**	× .155	
13	Multiply line 8 by line 12	**13**	93	00
14	**Excludable savings bond interest.** Subtract line 13 from line 8. Enter the result here and on Schedule B (Form 1040), line 3, or Schedule 1 (Form 1040A), line 3, whichever applies . . ►	**14**	507	00

Scholarship and Fellowship Grants

A taxpayer's gross income does not include some scholarship and fellowship grants. Only degree candidates get this exclusion. The exclusion applies to tuition and course-required fees, as well as required books, supplies, and equipment. Degree candidates include undergraduate and graduate students who pursue studies to meet the requirements for academic or professional degrees. Postdoctoral fellows do not qualify as degree candidates. The exclusion does not apply to room, board, or other expenses. Graduate students who do teaching or research at their degree-granting institutions can exclude tuition waivers.

> The exclusion for scholarships does not apply to compensation for services rendered even if all candidates for the degree are required to perform the services.

Social Security Benefits

Social security includes payments to retired taxpayers and disability payments. For high-income taxpayers, gross income may include a portion of the benefits (Chapter 3). For taxpayers with income below specified levels, gross income does not include such benefits.

Compensation for Physical Injury and Sickness

A taxpayer who receives workers' compensation for a physical injury or illness omits it from gross income. Any payments received from accident and health insurance plans purchased by the taxpayer are also tax-free. However, when a taxpayer's employer purchases the insurance, only medical expense reimbursements receive tax-free treatment. When such payments exceed related medical expenses, the taxpayer includes the excess in gross income.

Generally, any compensation a person receives for physical injury or sickness is excludable from gross income. However, punitive damages received out of a physical injury case are generally taxable. All damages received for nonphysical injuries (e.g., employment discrimination, injury to reputation, and emotional distress) are taxable.

Roth IRAs

Another source of tax-free income is the Roth IRA. Initially, taxpayers make non-deductible contributions to this special savings incentive program which allows the earnings to accumulate tax-free. It also allows taxpayers to make withdrawals tax- and penalty-free if the withdrawal is made after the Roth IRA has been open for five tax years and any one of the following conditions is met.

1. The distribution is made after the taxpayer attains age 59½.
2. The distribution is made to a beneficiary as a result of the taxpayer's death.
3. The distribution is made on account of the taxpayer's disability.
4. The distribution is used to pay first-time homebuyer expenses ($10,000 lifetime limit).

When distributions do not meet at least one of the above criteria, amounts received in excess of contributions are included in gross income and taxed. A 10% early withdrawal penalty also applies to the amount taxed. Please note, however, that taxpayers can withdraw their contributions at any time and for any reason without tax or penalty. Since contributions to a Roth IRA are not deductible, there is never any tax when only contributions are taken from a Roth IRA. However, once the taxpayer has withdrawn amounts from the Roth IRA they can not be returned to the IRA to earn tax-free earnings.

EXAMPLE 2

After making contributions of $4,500 over a three-year period, Arlo Brown withdraws the $5,400 balance in his Roth IRA to buy a new car. Of this amount, $4,500 is a tax-free withdrawal of his contribution. However, Brown must pay income tax on the earnings of $900. He also pays a nondeductible early withdrawal penalty of $90 (10% × $900).

The maximum annual contribution to a Roth IRA is the lesser of $4,000 or 100% of the taxpayer's earned income). This amount phases out proportionately between the following AGI levels:

1. Unmarried: $95,000–$110,000
2. Married—Joint filers: $150,000–$160,000; Married—Separate filers: $0–$10,000

Taxpayers round their reduced contribution limit up to the nearest $10. If their reduced contribution limit is more than $0, but less than $200, they increase the limit to $200.

EXAMPLE 3

Grace Matteo is single and wants to contribute $4,000 to a Roth IRA. Her AGI is $97,160. This limits the amount Matteo may contribute to $3,430. She computes her maximum contribution as follows:

Reduction factor:

[$2,160 ($97,160 − $95,000) / $15,000 phase-out range] × $4,000 = $576

Contribution limit:

$4,000 − $576 = $3,424, rounded up to nearest $10: $3,430

Taxpayers filing jointly with over $160,000 of AGI ($110,000 for singles) do not qualify to make contributions to a Roth IRA. They may, however, make contributions to a traditional IRA. The contribution would be deductible unless one or both spouses are covered under an employer plan.

Taxpayers at least 50 years old may make an additional "catch-up" contribution to their Roth IRAs. This is an opportunity to make up for retirement contributions missed earlier in life. The extra contribution for 2005 is $500 before applying the phase-out limits.

Taxpayers may take the funds from one Roth IRA and deposit them into another Roth IRA tax-free. Some taxpayers may also convert a traditional IRA into a Roth IRA. Such a conversion produces taxable income to the extent of any earnings or deductible contributions converted into the Roth IRA. However, amounts converted to a Roth IRA are not subject to the 10% penalty on early withdrawal.

Coverdell Education Savings Accounts

Taxpayers may contribute up to $2,000 per child (beneficiary) per year to an education savings account. The contribution is nondeductible. Distributions from such a savings account are excluded from the income of the student (beneficiary) if the funds are used to pay qualified education expenses. The student must be under age 30. In addition, the exclusion is not available in a year in which either the HOPE credit or the lifetime learning credit is claimed.

Qualified expenses include the following postsecondary education expenses: tuition, fees, books, supplies, equipment, and room and board. For room and board to qualify, the student must attend school on at least a half-time basis in a program leading to a recognized educational credential. When distributions during the year exceed the qualified higher education expenses, the law treats some of the excess as a distribution of earnings and taxes it.

Contributions must be for a child of the taxpayer under the age of 18. The annual contribution limit of $2,000 is phased out proportionately between these AGI levels:

1. Unmarried: $95,000–$110,000
2. Married—Joint filers: $190,000–$220,000; Married—Separate filers: $0–$10,000

Because the maximum annual contribution to a child's education savings account is $2,000, the combined contributions from all donors (e.g., parents and grandparents) cannot exceed $2,000 per child. A 6% penalty applies to excess contributions.

When the beneficiary reaches age 30, any unused amount in the account must be distributed to the beneficiary. Any earnings included in the distribution will be added to the beneficiary's gross income and taxed. An additional 10% penalty tax on the earnings will also apply to the beneficiary. To escape from this situation, the unused amount may be rolled over into an education savings account of a sibling or child of the beneficiary tax and penalty free.

Qualified Tuition Programs *529 Plans*

Some states and private institutions of higher learning have established qualified tuition programs so that parents can prepay their children's college expenses. Parents make payments to an account on behalf of their children for payment of their future qualified higher education expenses. When the accumulated funds are used to pay these expenses, the entire distribution, including appreciation (earnings), is tax free. Qualified expenses include tuition, fees, books, supplies, and room and board.

EXAMPLE 4

Paul West paid $12,000 into a qualified state tuition program for the benefit of his daughter, Susan. The amount represented tuition of $3,000 per year for four years. During Susan's first year at college tuition had risen to $4,000. Susan's tuition is locked in at $3,000 each year, but the tuition savings of $1,000 is tax free.

If the child does not go to college, the program refunds the parent's contribution, plus interest, to the parents. The parents must include this interest in gross income.

ADJUSTMENTS TO INCOME

The IRS classifies certain deductions from gross income (to arrive at AGI) as **adjustments to income.** Other deductions from gross income appear on supporting forms and schedules (e.g., Schedule C), with the net result shown in the income section of Form 1040. A taxpayer using Form 1040EZ has no adjustments to income. A Form 1040A filer has only four adjustments to income: educator expenses, contributions to an individual retirement arrangement, payments of student loan interest, and tuition and fees for higher education. A Form 1040 filer can deduct a number of adjustments to income. Figure 4-3 lists adjustments for which there are separate lines on the form. The taxpayer can also write in more adjustments on the dotted portion of line 36 before entering the total adjustments.

FIGURE 4-3   Adjustments to Income Listed on Form 1040

1. Educator expenses
2. Certain business expenses of reservists, performing artists, and fee-basis government officials
3. IRA deduction
4. Student loan interest deduction
5. Tuition and fees deduction
6. Health savings account deduction
7. Moving expenses
8. One-half of self-employment tax
9. Self-employed health insurance deduction
10. Self-employed SEP, SIMPLE, and qualified plans
11. Penalty on early withdrawal of savings
12. Alimony paid
13. Domestic production activities deduction

WRITE-IN ADJUSTMENTS TO INCOME ON FORM 1040 (LINE 36)

1. Jury duty pay that an employee transfers to an employer for regular pay
2. Foreign housing deduction
3. Write-off of forestation or reforestation costs
4. Some supplemental unemployment benefit repayments
5. Deduction for clean-fuel vehicles

DEDUCTIONS FROM GROSS INCOME NOT LISTED SEPARATELY ON FORM 1040 (PAGE 1)

1. Trade or business deductions, Schedule C (Chapter 7)
2. Losses from property sales, Schedule D (Chapter 11)
3. Rent and royalty expenses, Schedule E (Chapter 9)
4. Expenses of life tenants and income beneficiaries, Schedule E

The following sections examine adjustments to income that are available to taxpayers.

Educator Expenses

Over $250 goes on itemized deduct on itemized deduction as misc. deduction

In 2005, an above-the-line deduction is available for primary and secondary school teachers for amounts paid for books and supplies used in the classroom. The deduction is limited to $250. Expenditures in excess of $250 are employee business expenses which may be deducted as an itemized deduction (Chapter 6).

Certain Business Expenses of Reservists, Performing Artists, and Fee-Basis Government Officials

Members of a reserve component of the Armed Forces who travel more than 100 miles away from home to perform services as a member of the reserves can deduct their travel expenses as an adjustment to income. The deduction is limited to the amount the Federal government pays its employees for travel expenses. Expenses of travel that do not take reservists more than 100 miles form home are deducted as a miscellaneous itemized deduction. Reservists initially report their travel expenses on Form 2106, Employee Business Expenses. Chapter 6 describes the use of Form 2106.

Certain performing artists may qualify to deduct their employee business expenses as an adjustment to income rather than as a miscellaneous itemized deduction. To qualify, all of the following requirements must be met.

1. Performing artist must be employed by at least two employers in the performing arts.
2. Performing artist must receive at least $200 from each of two of these employers.
3. Performing-arts business expenses must exceed 10% of gross income from the performing arts.
4. Adjusted gross income cannot exceed $16,000 before deducting these business expenses.

Taxpayers who do not meet all of the above requirements deduct their business expenses as a miscellaneous itemized deduction. The business expenses are initially reported on Form 2106. To claim a deduction for AGI, married taxpayers must file jointly unless they have lived apart at all times during the year.

State and local government officials who are paid on a fee basis may also deduct their related employee business expenses as an adjustment to income. They initially report their expenses on Form 2106.

Individual Retirement Arrangements (IRAs)

[handwritten: eligibility: — must have earned income]

To provide greater savings for retirement, working taxpayers can contribute to a traditional Individual Retirement Arrangement (IRA). Like the Roth IRA, this savings program allows the earnings to accumulate tax-free. Certain taxpayers can also deduct their IRA contributions as a deduction from gross income. For these people, the contributions and the earnings are tax-free until funds are withdrawn from the account. When withdrawn, both the earnings and the deductible contributions are taxed.

[handwritten margin note: deduction from gross income]

Eligible IRA Programs

Eligible taxpayers can make IRA contributions to retirement programs of either of the following types:

1. A domestic trust or custodial account. An employer or the employee's labor union can serve as the trustee. Also, a bank, savings and loan, credit union, insurance company, or regulated investment company can serve as the trustee. Under some conditions, another organization can qualify as the trustee. Although a trustee or custodian controls the retirement funds, the taxpayer can still direct investments.

2. An individual annuity contract issued by an insurance company.

IRA Contribution Limits

Contributions to an IRA must come from earned income. For IRA purposes, the tax law treats alimony as earned income. However, interest, dividends, and other types of investment income are not earned income.

[handwritten margin note: alimony is treated as earned income]

The maximum annual contribution to an IRA is the lesser of $4,000 or 100% of the taxpayer's earned income. The amount is $8,000 for a married couple, as long as the couple has at least $8,000 of combined earnings. Each spouse must establish a separate IRA, and the maximum annual contribution to one person's IRA cannot exceed $4,000 a year. Otherwise, the contribution may be split between the accounts as the spouses see fit. Taxpayers at least 50 years old can contribute an extra $500 to their accounts.

[handwritten margin note: Over 50 yrs old add $500 ($4500)]

A married taxpayer need not file a joint return to contribute to an IRA. However, in the year a taxpayer reaches age 70½, usually no further contributions are allowed. The deadline for making both traditional and Roth IRA contributions for the current year is April 15, of the next year.

EXAMPLE 5

Jim and Jeanette Beckman (both age 45) file a joint return. During 2005, Jim earns $50,000 at his job. Jeanette does not work. Jim and Jeanette can contribute up to $4,000 to their respective IRAs. They have until April 15, 2006 to make their contributions.

IRA contributions made between January 1 and April 15 could be considered IRA contributions for either the current or previous tax year. Generally IRA trustees will assume the contribution made in this time frame is for the current year. If the taxpayer wants the contribution to count towards the prior year, then the taxpayer needs to instruct the IRA trustee of this in writing at the time the payment is made.

Excess Contributions to an IRA

When traditional and Roth IRA contributions exceed the allowed limit, the IRS assesses a 6% excise tax on the excess. This tax is not assessed if the taxpayer withdraws the excess (plus any related earnings) before the due date of the taxpayer's tax return. Taxpayers who must pay the excise tax use Form 5329, Return For Additional Taxes Attributable to Qualifying Retirement Plans (including IRAs), Annuities, and Modified Endowment Contracts.

Limitation on IRA Deductions

Taxpayers who are not active participants in an employer-sponsored retirement plan can deduct up to $4,000 ($4,500 if at least 50 years old) for contributions made to a traditional IRA for 2005. Anyone participating in an employer-sponsored retirement plan may face an IRA deduction phase-out if "net AGI" exceeds a certain amount. However, the spouse of a participant in an employer plan can still receive a full IRA deduction as long as the couple's "net AGI" does not exceed $150,000.

For participants in an employer-sponsored retirement plan, the phase-out takes place when "net AGI" falls within these ranges:

Single (also head of household)	$50,000–$60,000
Married filing jointly	$70,000–$80,000
Married filing separately and not living with spouse any part of the year	$50,000–$60,000
Married filing separately and living with spouse part of the year	$0–$10,000
Nonparticipating spouse who files married filing joint with participating spouse	$150,000–$160,000

When "net AGI" exceeds these ranges, no deduction is allowed. However, a retirement plan participant with "net AGI" less than these amounts can deduct up to $4,000 ($4,500) in IRA contributions. The taxpayer determines **net AGI** before the IRA deduction, the interest exclusion for Series EE and I Educational Savings Bonds, the earned foreign income exclusion, and the foreign housing exclusion/deduction.

A participant in a qualified plan whose AGI is within the phase-out range must compute a reduced IRA deduction. The maximum $4,000 ($4,500) deduction is reduced proportionately for each dollar of AGI that falls within the $10,000 phase out range. As with the Roth IRA, taxpayers round their reduced contributions limit up to the nearest $10. If their reduced contributions limit is more than $0, but less than $200, they increase the limit to $200.

EXAMPLE 6

Stan Decker, age 52, is married and files a joint return with his wife, Dorothy, age 48. They both want to make the largest possible deductible contributions to their IRAs. Their net AGI is $74,000. Stan is an active participant in his employer's retirement plan. Dorothy does not have a retirement plan at work. Because the Decker's net AGI is within the phase-out range and Stan is in a retirement plan at work, Stan's maximum deductible contribution is $2,700 [$4,500 − ($4,000/$10,000 × $4,500)]. In contrast, Dorothy is not in an employer-sponsored retirement plan, and because net AGI does not exceed $150,000, she can contribute and deduct $4,000 to her traditional IRA.

EXAMPLE 7

Assume that in the above example that the Decker's net AGI was $157,000. In this case, Stan cannot deduct any contribution to his IRA because net AGI exceeds the $80,000 ceiling of the phase-out range. However, Dorothy can deduct up to $1,200 in contributions [$4,000 − ($7,000/$10,000 × $4,000)]. If she contributes $4,000, she will only be able to deduct $1,200.

Employer Plans

Employer plans include qualifying pension plans, profit-sharing plans, stock bonus plans, qualifying annuity plans, 401(k), and simplified employee pension plans. Keoghs and other retirement plans of self-employed taxpayers also count as employer plans. Finally, employers' retirement plans include tax-sheltered annuities and pension plans under Sections 403(b) and 457.

Nondeductible Contributions

While some taxpayers do not qualify to deduct their contributions to a traditional IRA, they can still make nondeductible contributions of up to $4,000 ($4,500) to their IRAs. When they withdraw amounts from these IRAs, the previously taxed (nondeductible) contributions are not taxed. For people who cannot deduct the full $4,000 ($4,500) contribution to a traditional IRA, the law encourages the use of a Roth IRA. Taxpayers can deposit the nondeductible portion of their IRA contribution into a Roth IRA instead of a traditional IRA. When amounts are withdrawn from their Roth IRA after retirement, neither the contributions nor the earnings are taxed. However, not all taxpayers qualify to contribute to a Roth IRA (see discussion earlier in the chapter.)

Taxpayers who make both deductible and nondeductible contributions to the same IRA should keep good records. They must be able to show the amount of their nondeductible contributions, which are tax-free when withdrawn. To help with this task, the IRS provides Form 8606. Taxpayers who make nondeductible IRA contributions should file Form 8606, even if they do not file a tax return.

The maximum contribution taxpayers under age 50 can make to all IRAs during the year (includes both Roth and traditional) is the lesser of $4,000 or the taxpayer's earned income. Thus, qualifying taxpayers can not contribute $4,000 to a traditional IRA and another $4,000 to a Roth IRA. Doing this will result in a 6% excise tax on the excess $4,000 contribution.

Distributions from an IRA

When taxpayers begin receiving IRA distributions, they must determine what part represents nondeductible contributions. The Code taxes the distribution of deductible contributions and earnings withdrawn as ordinary income. The part relating to nondeductible contributions is not taxed. Taxpayers use the IRA distribution formula from Chapter 3 to compute the nontaxable portion of the amounts withdrawn from a traditional IRA.

If a taxpayer receives an IRA distribution before reaching age 59½, the IRS can assess a 10% penalty on the taxable amount withdrawn. However, the IRS does not assess the penalty when the distribution is:

1. Due to death or disability,
2. Used to pay medical expenses in excess of 7.5% of AGI,
3. Used by an unemployed person to buy health insurance,
4. Used to pay qualified higher education expenses, or
5. Used to pay expenses of a qualified first-time homebuyer ($10,000 lifetime limit).

> The IRS also will not assess the 10% penalty on the first $100,000 of "qualified Hurricane Katrina distributions." A **qualified Hurricane Katrina distribution** is any distribution made after August 24, 2005 and before January 1, 2007 by an individual whose principal place of abode on August 28, 2005 was located in the Hurricane Katrina disaster area (as specified by the federal government) and who sustained an economic loss as a result of the hurricane.

A taxpayer does not have to start withdrawing IRA funds until April 1 of the calendar year after turning 70½. Thus, a taxpayer who reaches age 70½ in 20x1 does not have to start withdrawing IRA funds until April 1, 20x2. The taxpayer may choose to withdraw the entire balance or to receive periodic distributions. Failure to make a timely decision may result in penalties.

Student Loan Interest

Taxpayers may deduct $2,500 from gross income for interest paid on money borrowed to pay qualified higher education expenses of the taxpayer, spouse, or dependents. There is no deduction for interest paid on the educational debts of dependents of another taxpayer.

Acceptable education expenses include tuition, books, supplies, and room and board. These expenses must be those of a student enrolled at least half-time in a program leading to a recognized credential at a qualified institution of higher education.

Taxpayers should be aware of certain other limiting factors. First, the interest deduction is phased out ratably as AGI increases from $50,000 to $65,000 ($105,000 to $135,000 on joint returns). AGI requires certain modifications for this computation. Second, taxpayers may not use this interest deduction if the interest is deductible under another section of the Internal Revenue Code (e.g., home equity loan). In addition, married taxpayers must file jointly to claim the deduction.

Tuition and Fees Deduction

A $4,000 deduction for AGI may be taken for tuition and related expenses (but not room and board) to attend a postsecondary college or vocational education program. An expense deductible under any other provision is not deductible under this provision. Also, qualified expenses must be reduced by:

1. Distributions from a qualified tuition program (but not the portion representing a return of contributions to the plan).
2. Distributions from an education IRA.
3. Interest on U.S. Savings bonds used to pay the educational expenses.

Single taxpayers may deduct up to $4,000 when AGI does not exceed $65,000 ($130,000 for joint filers). The deduction is limited to $2,000 for single taxpayers when AGI is $65,001–$80,000 ($130,001–$160,000 for joint filers). However, if the HOPE scholarship credit or the lifetime learning credit is taken for a student, the student's expenses are not deductible. In addition, dependents and married individuals who file separately are not eligible for the deduction.

Health Savings Account Deduction

Workers with high-deductible health insurance plans may deduct their contributions to health savings accounts (HSA) to determine adjusted gross income. HSAs allow taxpayers to save money to pay for medical expenses. The maximum contribution is limited to the lesser of (1) 100% of the annual deductible for the high deductible health plan, or (2) $2,650 for individuals/$5,250 for families. Contributions in excess of the limit are subject to an excise tax. Taxpayers at least 55 years old may contribute an additional $600 to their HSAs. The deadline for current year contributions is April 15 of the following year. Contributions must stop when the taxpayer retires.

A high-deductible health plan (HDHP) is one that has at least a $1,000 deductible for individual coverage and a $2,000 deductible for family coverage. Eligible taxpayers cannot also be covered by a non-HDHP offering the same coverage.

Withdrawals used to pay medical expenses are excluded from gross income. However, withdrawals not used to pay medical expenses are included in gross income and are also subject to a 10% excise tax. Funds withdrawn after retirement for nonmedical purposes are included in gross income, but they are not subject to the 10% excise tax. Any balance in an HSA at the end of the year rolls over for future use. Thus, a healthy worker and family can accumulate a sizeable sum in this account over the years.

Moving Expenses

A taxpayer may deduct certain unreimbursed moving expenses as an adjustment to income. These expenses arise when a change in principal residence occurs as a result of a change in job location. Moving expenses include payments to move a taxpayer and the taxpayer's family and property to the new location so the taxpayer can start work. An employed or self-employed individual who does not receive reimbursement for qualified moving expenses can deduct the expenses paid as adjustments for AGI. To get the deduction, the individual must meet mileage and employment tests. Many employees receive reimbursements for their moving expenses. The Code treats reimbursements for certain qualified expenses as excludable fringe benefits. An employer reports an excludable reimbursement on Form W-2, Wage and Tax Statement (box 12), using the letter *P* to label the reimbursement as nontaxable.

Timing the Move

Usually, a taxpayer moves to a new job location near the time employment starts. However, circumstances may delay the moving of some family members. The delay may result from children's being in school or the family's waiting to sell the old residence. Moving expenses qualify for the exclusion or deduction if they are incurred within one year of the taxpayer's start-of-work date. If moving expenses are incurred later than one year after the start-of-work date, the taxpayer may still get a deduction. Here, the taxpayer must prove that something prevented an earlier move (for example, waiting for a child to graduate from high school). However, the IRS does not consider failure to sell one's previous residence an acceptable reason for delay.

Definition of Principal Residence

The moving taxpayer must live in the old and new principal residences, treating both as primary homes. Here, *home* may be a house, a condominium, or an apartment. A second residence, such as a beach house or seasonal residence, does not qualify as a principal residence. The need for a principal residence can create problems for a new college graduate starting a first job. A person starting work for the first time can deduct moving expenses as long as he or she moves from a former principal residence to a new one. Usually, a college student's residence hall living quarters do not qualify as a principal residence.

Fully Deductible Moving Expenses

Moving expenses include the reasonable costs of transportation and lodging for the taxpayer and members of the household (including expenses on the arrival day). Although only one trip is deductible, all household members need not travel together or at the same time. Moving expenses also include the costs of packing, crating, in-transit storage, and moving of household goods and personal effects. In addition, they include expenses for special handling of pets. In one case, a taxpayer deducted the cost of moving a sailboat because the boat was used regularly for recreation. However, moving expenses usually exclude the cost of moving a nurse or a personal attendant. In addition, no deduction exists for meals eaten along the way.

EXAMPLE 8

A taxpayer paid the following expenses for moving to a distant city to start work at a new job. The expenses, which totaled $4,200, included the cost of a moving van, $3,500; transportation, $550; and meals $150. The taxpayer can deduct $4,050 ($3,500 + $550). The meals represent nondeductible moving expenses.

A taxpayer using a personal automobile for moving can deduct out-of-pocket expenses like gasoline, oil, minor repairs, and so on. To deduct those expenses, the taxpayer must maintain an adequate expense record. However, a taxpayer can use the optional 15-cents-per-mile method (22 cents after August 31). Here, the taxpayer needs only to verify the mileage. If the vehicle was serviced before and after the move by independent garages that recorded the mileage figures and service dates, good verification exists. When coupled with map mileage, those records provide excellent verification. A taxpayer adds parking fees and tolls to the expenses under either method.

> For 2005, the standard mileage rate used to compute the moving expense deduction is only 15 (22) cents per mile, while the standard rate for business mileage is 40.5 cents per mile (48.5 cents after August 31). Both, however, require a business purpose.

Nondeductible Expenses

Nondeductible moving expenses include such items as mortgage prepayment penalties, costs of refitting carpets and draperies, losses arising from the disposal of property, and similar items. These nondeductible expenses also include a commission paid to sell a former residence or acquire a new one or to break a lease or get a new one. House-hunting expenses and costs of temporary quarters are also not deductible.

Mileage and Employment Tests

A taxpayer can deduct moving expenses only if he or she meets mileage and employment tests. These tests help ensure that deductible expenses cover a proper employment move, not a personal move.

Mileage Test. A taxpayer can deduct moving expenses only if the new job site is 50 or more miles farther from the former residence than was the old job site. When measuring these distances, the taxpayer uses the shortest of commonly traveled routes.

EXAMPLE 9

If the distance between a taxpayer's old residence and former place of employment was 12 miles, the location of the new place of employment must be at least 62 miles from the old residence (50 miles + 12 miles). If an old job location does not exist, the distance between the new place of work and the former residence must equal or exceed 50 miles.

Employment Test. An employee who deducts moving expenses must have full-time employment in the area of the new job site for 39 weeks during the 12 months right after the move. This test does not apply if a failure results from disability, death, discharge not due to willful misconduct, or transfer for the employer's benefit. The employee can deduct moving expenses in the year of payment even though the 39-week employment test has not been met by the tax return's due date. However, the employee must have a reasonable expectation of meeting this test in the future.

EXAMPLE 10

A taxpayer moved to a new job on September 1, 20x1, and expects to work indefinitely at the new job site. Deductible moving expenses equal $3,450. On the 20x1 tax return, the taxpayer deducts these expenses even though the employment test will not be met until 20x2.

A taxpayer may deduct moving expenses in the year of payment. However, if at a later date the taxpayer fails to meet the employment test, two choices exist. The taxpayer can include the deducted expenses in gross income of the year of failure. Alternatively, he or she can file an amended return for the deduction year and remove the deduction. Some taxpayers take the second choice to avoid problems if audited by the IRS.

Self-Employed Individuals

A self-employed person can deduct the same kinds of moving expenses as an employee if he or she meets the mileage test and a different employment test. For a self-employed individual, a longer employment test exists. During the 24-month period right after arrival at a new job site, a self-employed person must provide services on a full-time basis (as either a self-employed person or an employee) for 78 weeks. Thirty-nine of those weeks must fall within the 12-month period right after the arrival at the new job site. Like an employee, a self-employed person can take the moving expense deduction even though the 78-week employment test has not been met by the tax return's due date. A self-employed taxpayer who fails the employment test has the same choices as an employee: include the deducted amounts in gross income of the failure year, or file an amended return for the deduction year.

Reporting

Employers must give employees a detailed breakdown of their moving expense reimbursement or direct-to-supplier payments. An employer completes Form 4782 for each move an employee makes for the company. The employee does not file the form with his or her tax return. Taxpayers report their deductible moving expenses on Form 3903, which they file with their tax returns. Figure 4-4 illustrates form 4782, and Figure 4-5 shows Form 3903.

Information for Figure 4-4: Filled-In Form 4782

The Lew Company employs Lois Clarke as an accountant. Clarke's recent promotion to senior accountant in April required a move from Chicago, Illinois, to St. Louis, Missouri. After the move, Clarke filed a moving expense reimbursement request with Lew for $2,225. Under a companywide policy, Lew pays set amounts for different types of moving expenses. Figure 4-4 shows that Lew paid Clarke **$2,000** for moving expenses (**$1,900** for moving household goods and personal effects and **$100** for travel and lodging).

Information for Figure 4-5: Filled-In Form 3903

Lois Clarke (see Figure 4-4) uses Form 3903 to report deductible moving expenses.

Other Information

- Miles from old home to new workplace, **222** (source: odometer readings)
- Miles from old home to old workplace, **25** (source: odometer readings)
- Cost of moving personal effects, **$2,105** (source: receipts)
- Travel and lodging expenses, **$125** (source: receipts)
- Employer reimbursement, **$2,000** (source: Form W-2, box 12)

Clarke enters her deductible moving expenses ($230) on Form 1040 as "Moving expenses."

Self-Employment Tax

People who are self-employed pay a self-employment tax of 15.3% on the first $90,000 of net earnings from self-employment and 2.9% on earnings over that amount. They deduct one-half of this tax as an adjustment to income. Chapter 7 provides a more detailed discussion of the self-employment tax.

Self-Employed Health Insurance Deduction

A self-employed taxpayer usually takes a deduction for AGI for medical insurance (Form 1040, "Self-employed health insurance deduction"). The deduction equals the smaller of two amounts: (1) 100% of the health insurance premiums paid for the taxpayer, spouse, and dependents or (2) net profit and other earned income from the taxpayer's business with the medical insurance plan. When making this comparison, the taxpayer reduces net profit by related Keogh, SEP, and SIMPLE retirement plan contributions. The taxpayer treats any nondeductible premiums for health insurance as a medical expense (Chapter 5).

A taxpayer who qualifies to participate in an employer's health plan (or in the plan of a spouse's employer) cannot take the deduction. Here, the Code contains a monthly determination clause. Also, a self-employed taxpayer with employees cannot take the deduction when the plan favors the taxpayer.

FIGURE 4-4   Filled-In Form 4782

Form **4782** (Rev. July 1997) Department of the Treasury Internal Revenue Service	**Employee Moving Expense Information** Payments made during the calendar year ☉ ....2005.... ► **Instructions for employers are on the back.**	OMB No. 1545-0182 **Do not file. Keep for your records.**

Name of employee
Lois A. Clarke

Social security number
296 : 26 : 6254

Moving Expense Payments		**(a)** Amount paid to employee	**(b)** Amount paid to a third party for employee's benefit and value of services furnished in kind	**(c)** Total (Add columns **(a)** and **(b)**.)
1 Transportation and storage of household goods and personal effects	**1**	1,900 00		1,900 00
2 Travel and lodging payments for expenses of moving from old to new home. **Do not** include meals	**2**	100 00		100 00
3 All other payments (list type and amount). **Note:** *These amounts must be included in the employee's income and are subject to withholding* ☉ --------------------------------- --- --- --- ---	**3**			
4 Total. Add the amounts in column (c) of lines 1 through 3 . . . . ☉	**4**			2,000 00

FIGURE 4-5   Filled-In Form 3903

Form **3903** Department of the Treasury Internal Revenue Service	**Moving Expenses** ► **Attach to Form 1040.**	OMB No. 1545-0062 **2005** Attachment Sequence No. **62**

Name(s) shown on Form 1040
Lois A. Clarke

Your social security number
296 : 26 : 6254

Before you begin: √ See the **Distance Test** and **Time Test** in the instructions to find out if you can deduct your moving expenses.

√ See **Members of the Armed Forces** on the back of the form, if applicable.

1 Transportation and storage of household goods and personal effects (see instructions) . .	**1**	2,105	00
2 Travel (including lodging) from your old home to your new home (see instructions). **Do not** include the cost of meals	**2**	125	00
3 Add lines 1 and 2	**3**	2,230	00
4 Enter the total amount your employer paid you for the expenses listed on lines 1 and 2 that is **not** included in box 1 of your Form W-2 (wages). This amount should be shown in box 12 of your Form W-2 with code **P**	**4**	2,000	00
5 Is line 3 **more than** line 4?			
☐ **No.** You **cannot** deduct your moving expenses. If line 3 is less than line 4, subtract line 3 from line 4 and include the result on Form 1040, line 7.			
☒ **Yes. Moving expense deduction.** Subtract line 4 from line 3. Enter the result here and on Form 1040, line 26	**5**	230	00

Keogh, SIMPLE, and SEP Retirement Plans

Keogh, SIMPLE, and simplified employee pension (SEP) plans allow self-employed persons to make deductible contributions to retirement plans for themselves. A taxpayer deducts the contributions as an adjustment to income ("Self-employed SEP, SIMPLE, and qualified plans"). Chapter 7 describes the rules for contributing to these plans.

Penalty on Early Withdrawal of Savings

Deposits in special time certificates or savings accounts (CDs) usually get higher return rates than passbook accounts. Financial institutions guarantee the higher rates for funds that remain on deposit until maturity. Often, the governing instrument contains interest forfeiture and penalty provisions for early withdrawal. A taxpayer who withdraws funds early includes the full interest income in gross income on Form 1040 ("Taxable interest") and deducts the lost interest as an adjustment to income ("Penalty on early withdrawal of savings"). Usually, the institution paying the interest reports the lost interest on Form 1099-INT, Interest Income.

Alimony

A person who pays alimony deducts it for AGI. The recipient includes the alimony payments in gross income. When the law requires the person who pays alimony to recapture some of it as income, the recipient gets a deduction for the same amount (Chapter 3).

Domestic Production Activity Deduction

Taxpayers have available an above-the-line deduction equal to 3% of their qualified production activity income or taxable income, whichever is lower. This deduction is available to anyone who manufactures, grows, or extracts products in the United States. The amount deductible cannot exceed 50% of the W-2 wages paid during the year. Thus, to increase their W-2 wages, companies may want to hire more employees instead of independent contractors.

Qualified production activity income is basically "net income" computed on receipts from the disposition of domestically produced products. This amount is compared with the company's taxable income, and the lower of the two amounts is used in calculating the deduction. However, for individual taxpayers, adjusted gross income is substituted for taxable income.

Deduction for Clean-Fuel Vehicles

A deduction for adjusted gross income gaining in popularity is the deduction for purchasing an IRS certified clean-fuel motor vehicle. This is a write-in adjustment taxpayers claim on line 36. The deduction is $2,000 for most certificated vehicles. The deduction increases for vehicles weighing above 10,000 pounds. The taxpayer must be the original owner of the vehicle. The IRS provides a list of qualified vehicles.

REPORTING EXHIBITS

Figure 4-6 shows how taxpayers use Form 1040A to determine AGI, taxable income, the tax, and a tax refund. Figure 4-7 shows how taxpayers determine AGI using Form 1040 (page 1) and Schedule B.

Information for Figure 4-6: Filled-In Form 1040A

Karl and Jill Cook file a joint Form 1040A for 2005. They have a 7-year-old dependent daughter.

The payroll data for Karl and Jill from their Forms W-2 are as follows:

Employer	Wages	Federal Income Tax Withheld	FICA Taxes Withheld	Other Deductions	Net
Pike Corp.:					
Karl E. Cook	$26,200	$192	$2,004.30	$1,500 IRA 60 Ins.	$22,443.70
First Bank:					
Jill R. Cook	5,950	24	455.18		5,470.82
Totals	$32,150	$216	$2,459.48	$1,560	$27,914.52

Karl's employer carries a $10,000 group-term insurance policy on his life. He shares the cost of this policy with his employer through payroll deductions. The total withheld from Karl's pay for insurance premiums equals $60. Although the Cooks received net wages of $27,914.52, they must report their gross wages of $32,150 ($26,200 and $5,950).

Karl has a traditional IRA account. During the past two years he made contributions of $125 a month ($1,500 each year) by payroll deduction.

Other Information

8a: Taxable interest, **$640** from Citizens Bank (source: Form 1099-INT)
17:   IRA deduction, **$1,500** (source: computation)
29:   Credit for child care, **$389** (source: Schedule 2, Form 1040A)
32:   Retirement savings contribution credit, **$300** (source: Form 8880)
33:   Child tax credit, **$479** ($1,168 – ($389 + $300))
39:   Federal income tax withheld, **$216** (source: Form W-2)
42:   Additional child tax credit, **$521** ($1,000 – $479)

Karl uses the Tax Table to find the couple's tax on taxable income ($1,168). After deducting the child care credit ($389), the child tax credit ($479), the retirement savings contribution credit ($300), withheld taxes ($216), and the additional child tax credit ($521), the Cooks choose to receive the excess ($737) as a refund.

Because the interest income does not exceed $1,500, the Cooks do not report it on Schedule 1.

FIGURE 4-6 Filled-In Form 1040A, Page 1

Form **1040A**	Department of the Treasury—Internal Revenue Service **U.S. Individual Income Tax Return** (99) **2005**	IRS Use Only—Do not write or staple in this space.

OMB No. 1545-0085

Label (See page 18.)

Use the IRS label. Otherwise, please print or type.

Your first name and initial: Karl E. Last name: Cook

Your social security number: 269 09 9092

If a joint return, spouse's first name and initial: Jill R. Last name: Cook

Spouse's social security number: 390 16 2222

Home address (number and street). If you have a P.O. box, see page 18.: 400 South Elm Street Apt. no.

You **must** enter your SSN(s) above. ▲

City, town or post office, state, and ZIP code. If you have a foreign address, see page 18.: Chicago, IL 60631-1314

Checking a box below will not change your tax or refund.

Presidential Election Campaign ▶ Check here if you, or your spouse if filing jointly, want $3 to go to this fund (see page 18) ▶ [X] You [X] Spouse

Filing status Check only one box.

1 ☐ Single
2 [X] Married filing jointly (even if only one had income)
3 ☐ Married filing separately. Enter spouse's SSN above and full name here. ▶
4 ☐ Head of household (with qualifying person). (See page 19.) If the qualifying person is a child but not your dependent, enter this child's name here. ▶
5 ☐ Qualifying widow(er) with dependent child (see page 19)

Exemptions

6a [X] **Yourself.** If someone can claim you as a dependent, **do not** check box 6a.
b [X] **Spouse**

Boxes checked on 6a and 6b: 2

c **Dependents:**

(1) First name Last name	(2) Dependent's social security number	(3) Dependent's relationship to you	(4) ✓if qualifying child for child tax credit (see page 21)
Nan C. Wilson	624 18 1111	daughter	[X]
			☐
			☐
			☐
			☐
			☐

If more than six dependents, see page 20.

No. of children on 6c who:
• lived with you: 1
• did not live with you due to divorce or separation (see page 21)
Dependents on 6c not entered above

d Total number of exemptions claimed.

Add numbers on lines above ▶ 3

Income

Attach Form(s) W-2 here. Also attach Form(s) 1099-R if tax was withheld.

If you did not get a W-2, see page 22.

Enclose, but do not attach, any payment.

7	Wages, salaries, tips, etc. Attach Form(s) W-2.	7	32,150 00
8a	**Taxable** interest. Attach Schedule 1 if required.	8a	640 00
b	**Tax-exempt** interest. **Do not** include on line 8a. 8b		
9a	Ordinary dividends. Attach Schedule 1 if required.	9a	
b	Qualified dividends (see page 23). 9b		
10	Capital gain distributions (see page 23).	10	
11a	IRA distributions. 11a	11b Taxable amount (see page 23). 11b	
12a	Pensions and annuities. 12a	12b Taxable amount (see page 24). 12b	
13	Unemployment compensation and Alaska Permanent Fund dividends.	13	
14a	Social security benefits. 14a	14b Taxable amount (see page 26). 14b	
15	Add lines 7 through 14b (far right column). This is your **total income.** ▶	15	32,790 00

Adjusted gross income

16	Educator expenses (see page 26).	16		
17	IRA deduction (see page 26).	17	1,500 00	
18	Student loan interest deduction (see page 29).	18		
19	Tuition and fees deduction (see page 29).	19		
20	Add lines 16 through 19. These are your **total adjustments.**	20		1,500 00
21	Subtract line 20 from line 15. This is your **adjusted gross income.** ▶	21		31,290 00

For Disclosure, Privacy Act, and Paperwork Reduction Act Notice, see page 57.   Cat. No. 11327A   Form **1040A** (2005)

FIGURE 4-6 Filled-In Form 1040A, Page 2

Form 1040A (2005)			Page **2**

Tax, credits, and payments

	22	Enter the amount from line 21 (adjusted gross income).	22	31,290 00
	23a	Check if: ☐ **You** were born before January 2, 1941, ☐ Blind / ☐ **Spouse** was born before January 2, 1941, ☐ Blind / **Total boxes checked ▶** 23a		
Standard Deduction for—	b	If you are married filing separately and your spouse itemizes deductions, see page 30 and check here ▶ 23b ☐		
• People who checked any box on line 23a or 23b **or** who can be claimed as a dependent, see page 31.	24	Enter your **standard deduction** (see left margin).	24	10,000 00
	25	Subtract line 24 from line 22. If line 24 is more than line 22, enter -0-.	25	21,290 00
	26	If line 22 is $109,475 or less, multiply $3,200 by the total number of exemptions claimed on line 6d. If line 22 is over $109,475, see the worksheet on page 32.	26	9,600 00
• All others:	27	Subtract line 26 from line 25. If line 26 is more than line 25, enter -0-. This is your **taxable income**. ▶	27	11,690 00
Single or Married filing separately, $5,000	28	**Tax,** including any alternative minimum tax (see page 31).	28	1,168 00
Married filing jointly or Qualifying widow(er), $10,000	29	Credit for child and dependent care expenses. Attach Schedule 2. — 29 — 389 00		
	30	Credit for the elderly or the disabled. Attach Schedule 3. — 30		
Head of household, $7,300	31	Education credits. Attach Form 8863. — 31		
	32	Retirement savings contributions credit. Attach Form 8880. — 32 — 300 00		
	33	Child tax credit (see page 36). Attach Form 8901 if required. — 33 — 479 00		
	34	Adoption credit. Attach Form 8839. — 34		
	35	Add lines 29 through 34. These are your **total credits**.	35	1,168 00
	36	Subtract line 35 from line 28. If line 35 is more than line 28, enter -0-.	36	0
	37	Advance earned income credit payments from Form(s) W-2.	37	
	38	Add lines 36 and 37. This is your **total tax**. ▶	38	0
	39	Federal income tax withheld from Forms W-2 and 1099. — 39 — 216 00		
	40	2005 estimated tax payments and amount applied from 2004 return. — 40		
If you have a qualifying child, attach Schedule EIC.	41a	**Earned income credit (EIC).** — 41a		
	b	Nontaxable combat pay election. 41b —		
	42	Additional child tax credit. Attach Form 8812. — 42 — 521 00		
	43	Add lines 39, 40, 41a, and 42. These are your **total payments**. ▶	43	737 00
Refund	44	If line 43 is more than line 38, subtract line 38 from line 43. This is the amount you **overpaid**.	44	737 00
Direct deposit? See page 50 and fill in 45b, 45c, and 45d.	45a	Amount of line 44 you want **refunded to you**. ▶	45a	737 00
	▶ b	Routing number ☐☐☐☐☐☐☐☐☐ ▶ c Type: ☐ Checking ☐ Savings		
	▶ d	Account number ☐☐☐☐☐☐☐☐☐☐☐☐☐☐☐☐☐		
	46	Amount of line 44 you want **applied to your 2006 estimated tax**. — 46		
Amount you owe	47	**Amount you owe.** Subtract line 43 from line 38. For details on how to pay, see page 51. ▶	47	
	48	Estimated tax penalty (see page 51). — 48		

Third party designee

Do you want to allow another person to discuss this return with the IRS (see page 52)? ☐ **Yes.** Complete the following. ☐ **No**

Designee's name ▶ _____ Phone no. ▶ (_____) _____ Personal identification number (PIN) ☐☐☐☐☐

Sign here

Joint return? See page 18.
Keep a copy for your records.

Under penalties of perjury, I declare that I have examined this return and accompanying schedules and statements, and to the best of my knowledge and belief, they are true, correct, and complete. Declaration of preparer (other than the taxpayer) is based on all information of which the preparer has any knowledge.

Your signature	Date	Your occupation	Daytime phone number
Karl E. Cook	2-16-06	Clerk	(_____)
Spouse's signature. If a joint return, **both** must sign.	Date	Spouse's occupation	
Jill R. Cook	2-16-06	Teller	

Paid preparer's use only

Preparer's signature ▶	Date	Check if self-employed ☐	Preparer's SSN or PTIN
Firm's name (or yours if self-employed), address, and ZIP code ▶		EIN	
		Phone no. ( )	

✸ *Printed on recycled paper*

Form **1040A** (2005)

Information for Figure 4-7: Filled-In Form 1040, Page 1 and Schedule B, Form 1040, Page 2

Neal and Jane Cole file a joint return using Form 1040. They have no dependents.

Other Information

7:   Wages, **$45,000** ($17,600 + $27,400) (source: Form W-2)
8a: Interest, **$1,600** from **Heartland Bank** (source: Form 1099-INT)
32:   IRA deduction: **$1,380** (source: taxpayer, $880, and spouse, $500)

Because the Coles have over $1,500 in interest income, they prepare Schedule B (Form 1040), Parts I and III. They have no interest in any foreign accounts or trusts.

FIGURE 4-7 Filled-In Form 1040, Page 1

Form **1040** Department of the Treasury—Internal Revenue Service
U.S. Individual Income Tax Return **2005** (99) IRS Use Only—Do not write or staple in this space.

For the year Jan. 1–Dec. 31, 2005, or other tax year beginning , 2005, ending , 20 OMB No. 1545-0074

Label (See instructions on page 16.) **Use the IRS label.** Otherwise, please print or type.

LABEL HERE

Your first name and initial: Neal R.	Last name: Cole		**Your social security number:** 678 : 42 : 1720
If a joint return, spouse's first name and initial: Jane B.	Last name: Cole		**Spouse's social security number:** 701 : 62 : 3714
Home address (number and street). If you have a P.O. box, see page 16.: 1002 Lakeview Lane		Apt. no.	▲ You **must** enter your SSN(s) above. ▲
City, town or post office, state, and ZIP code. If you have a foreign address, see page 16.: Dallas, TX 75211-3674			Checking a box below will not change your tax or refund.

Presidential Election Campaign ▶ Check here if you, or your spouse if filing jointly, want $3 to go to this fund (see page 16) ▶ ☒ **You** ☒ **Spouse**

Filing Status

Check only one box.

1 ☐ Single
2 ☒ Married filing jointly (even if only one had income)
3 ☐ Married filing separately. Enter spouse's SSN above and full name here. ▶
4 ☐ Head of household (with qualifying person). (See page 17.) If the qualifying person is a child but not your dependent, enter this child's name here. ▶
5 ☐ Qualifying widow(er) with dependent child (see page 17)

Exemptions

6a ☒ **Yourself.** If someone can claim you as a dependent, **do not** check box 6a . . . . .
b ☒ **Spouse** . . . .

Boxes checked on 6a and 6b: 2

c **Dependents:**

(1) First name Last name	(2) Dependent's social security number	(3) Dependent's relationship to you	(4) ✓ if qualifying child for child tax credit (see page 18)
	: :		☐
	: :		☐
	: :		☐
	: :		☐

If more than four dependents, see page 18.

No. of children on 6c who:
• **lived with you** ____
• **did not live with you due to divorce or separation (see page 18)** ____
Dependents on 6c not entered above ____

d Total number of exemptions claimed . . . . **Add numbers on lines above ▶** 2

Income

Attach Form(s) W-2 here. Also attach Forms W-2G and 1099-R if tax was withheld.

If you did not get a W-2, see page 19.

Enclose, but do not attach, any payment. Also, please use **Form 1040-V.**

Line	Description			Amount
7	Wages, salaries, tips, etc. Attach Form(s) W-2		7	45,000 00
8a	**Taxable** interest. Attach Schedule B if required		8a	1,600 00
b	**Tax-exempt** interest. **Do not** include on line 8a	8b		
9a	Ordinary dividends. Attach Schedule B if required		9a	
b	Qualified dividends (see page 20)	9b		
10	Taxable refunds, credits, or offsets of state and local income taxes (see page 20)		10	
11	Alimony received		11	
12	Business income or (loss). Attach Schedule C or C-EZ		12	
13	Capital gain or (loss). Attach Schedule D if required. If not required, check here ▶ ☐		13	
14	Other gains or (losses). Attach Form 4797		14	
15a	IRA distributions 15a	b Taxable amount (see page 22)	15b	
16a	Pensions and annuities 16a	b Taxable amount (see page 22)	16b	
17	Rental real estate, royalties, partnerships, S corporations, trusts, etc. Attach Schedule E		17	
18	Farm income or (loss). Attach Schedule F		18	
19	Unemployment compensation		19	
20a	Social security benefits 20a	b Taxable amount (see page 24)	20b	
21	Other income. List type and amount (see page 24)		21	
22	Add the amounts in the far right column for lines 7 through 21. This is your **total income** ▶		22	46,600 00

Adjusted Gross Income

Line	Description				Amount
23	Educator expenses (see page 26)	23			
24	Certain business expenses of reservists, performing artists, and fee-basis government officials. Attach Form 2106 or 2106-EZ	24			
25	Health savings account deduction. Attach Form 8889	25			
26	Moving expenses. Attach Form 3903	26			
27	One-half of self-employment tax. Attach Schedule SE	27			
28	Self-employed SEP, SIMPLE, and qualified plans	28			
29	Self-employed health insurance deduction (see page XX)	29			
30	Penalty on early withdrawal of savings	30			
31a	Alimony paid b Recipient's SSN ▶ : :	31a			
32	IRA deduction (see page XX)	32	1,380 00		
33	Student loan interest deduction (see page XX)	33			
34	Tuition and fees deduction (see page XX)	34			
35	Domestic production activities deduction. Attach Form 8903	35			
36	Add lines 23 through 31a and 32 through 35			36	1,380 00
37	Subtract line 36 from line 22. This is your **adjusted gross income** ▶			37	45,220 00

For Disclosure, Privacy Act, and Paperwork Reduction Act Notice, see page 75. Cat. No. 11320B Form **1040** (2005)

FIGURE 4-7   Filled-In Parts I and III, Schedule B, Form 1040, Page 2

Schedules A&B (Form 1040) 2005 — OMB No. 1545-0074 — Page **2**

Name(s) shown on Form 1040. Do not enter name and social security number if shown on other side.
Neal R. and Jane B. Cole

Your social security number: 678 42 1720

Schedule B—Interest and Ordinary Dividends

Attachment Sequence No. **08**

Part I Interest

(See page B-1 and the instructions for Form 1040, line 8a.)

Note. If you received a Form 1099-INT, Form 1099-OID, or substitute statement from a brokerage firm, list the firm's name as the payer and enter the total interest shown on that form.

		Amount
1	List name of payer. If any interest is from a seller-financed mortgage and the buyer used the property as a personal residence, see page B-1 and list this interest first. Also, show that buyer's social security number and address ▶ Hearthland Bank	1,600 00
2	Add the amounts on line 1	1,600 00
3	Excludable interest on series EE and I U.S. savings bonds issued after 1989. Attach Form 8815	
4	Subtract line 3 from line 2. Enter the result here and on Form 1040, line 8a ▶	1,600 00

Note. If line 4 is over $1,500, you must complete Part III.

Part II Ordinary Dividends

(See page B-2 and the instructions for Form 1040, line 9a.)

Note. If you received a Form 1099-DIV or substitute statement from a brokerage firm, list the firm's name as the payer and enter the ordinary dividends shown on that form.

		Amount
5	List name of payer ▶	
6	Add the amounts on line 5. Enter the total here and on Form 1040, line 9a ▶	

Note. If line 6 is over $1,500, you must complete Part III.

Part III Foreign Accounts and Trusts

(See page B-2.)

You must complete this part if you **(a)** had over $1,500 of taxable interest or ordinary dividends; or **(b)** had a foreign account; or **(c)** received a distribution from, or were a grantor of, or a transferor to, a foreign trust.

		Yes	No
7a	At any time during 2005, did you have an interest in or a signature or other authority over a financial account in a foreign country, such as a bank account, securities account, or other financial account? See page B-2 for exceptions and filing requirements for Form TD F 90-22.1.		X
b	If "Yes," enter the name of the foreign country ▶		
8	During 2005, did you receive a distribution from, or were you the grantor of, or transferor to, a foreign trust? If "Yes," you may have to file Form 3520. See page B-2		X

For Paperwork Reduction Act Notice, see Form 1040 instructions.

Schedule B (Form 1040) 2005

Printed on recycled paper

QUESTIONS AND PROBLEMS

Name _____

Section _____ Date _____

1. **Fringe Benefits.** Certain fringe benefits may not discriminate in favor of key employees, whereas other fringe benefits may be discriminatory.

   For each category of fringe benefits given, state whether the discrimination rules apply, and give two examples of specific fringe benefits in that category.

Fringe Benefit Category	Discrimination Rules Apply (Yes or No)	Examples of Specific Benefits in Each Category
De minimis fringe benefits	_____	_____
Qualified employee discounts	_____	_____
Working condition fringe benefits	_____	_____
No-additional-cost services	_____	_____
On-premise athletic facilities	_____	_____

2. **Premiums on Group-Term Life Insurance.** The Painesville Distributing Company pays an annual premium for $90,000 of nondiscriminatory group-term life insurance coverage on its president, Fred J. Noble. Fred is 44 years of age. His wife, Melanie, is the policy's beneficiary. For this group-term life insurance, Fred pays the Painesville Distributing Company $0.80 per year for each $1,000 of coverage. His share of the insurance premium is deducted from his gross salary under the Painesville Distributing Company payroll deduction plan. What portion of the group-term life insurance cost must Mr. Noble include in his gross income?

3. **Tax-Free Bonds.** Marilyn A. Sippola is a single taxpayer who owns bonds from each of the issues listed. She does not own any stock. During the current year she received the interest amounts shown. In the space provided for each bond, state the amount of interest to be included in or excluded from gross income, and, if excluded, state why.

Bond	Issue	Date Purchase Bonds Owned	Interest Received
A	Racer Tannery	12–10–95	$ 276
B	Village of Austinburg	7–1–97	800
C	U.S. Treasury	2–1–99	600
D	Matured Series EE U.S. Savings	11–1–98	1,000
E	Kingsville School District	7–10–96	500

Bond	Interest Includable	Interest Excludable and Why
A	_____	_____
B	_____	_____
C	_____	_____
D	_____	_____
E	_____	_____

4. **Form 8815.** Michael J. Dugan (SSN 372-90-6729) receives $15,000 ($12,000 principal and $3,000 interest) from the redemption of a Series EE U.S. Savings Bond. The bond qualifies for the educational exclusion. He uses the proceeds to pay university tuition and fees totaling $8,250 for his two dependent children, Colleen R. and Patrick T. Dugan. Colleen is 21 years of age, and Patrick is 20. With the exception of temporary absences from home to attend the University of Michigan in Ann Arbor (48104) as full-time students, they live with their parents. During the year, Colleen and Patrick each receive a tax-exempt university scholarship of $2,250.

   Michael and Rachel Dugan live at 2790 Lakeview Road, Muskegon, MI 49441. Michael receives an annual salary of $81,000 and files a joint return with his wife, who has no gross income, on Form 1040. Prepare Form 8815 on the following page for the Dugans.

5. **Scholarships.** On August 1, 2005, Robert Dunnbar was granted a $5,400 scholarship for each of four academic years (nine months each year) to earn a degree from Birdhaven University. The scholarship grant includes $3,600 for tuition, fees, and books and $1,800 for room and board. Payment is one-ninth each month, starting September 10, 2005, and is made on the tenth of each month thereafter.

   a. How much of the scholarship payments can Dunnbar exclude from gross income in 2005? Why?

   b. If Dunnbar is not a degree candidate, is there any limitation to the amount of his exclusion? Explain.

6. **Roth IRA.** Kathy Craig, age 40, is single and wants to make a contribution to a Roth IRA. Her AGI is $97,500. Compute the maximum contribution that she may make to her Roth IRA. Is this amount deductible on her tax return?

$(2,500 / 15,000) \times 4,000 = 667$

Roth IRA = $3,340 · $(4,000 - 667 = 3333$ — rounded to nearest $10
contribution $3340)$

(Use for Problem 4.)

Form **8815**	**Exclusion of Interest From Series EE and I U.S. Savings Bonds Issued After 1989** (For Filers With Qualified Higher Education Expenses) ▶ Attach to Form 1040 or Form 1040A.	OMB No. 1545-1173
Department of the Treasury Internal Revenue Service (99)		**20**05 Attachment Sequence No. **57**

Name(s) shown on return	Your social security number

1	**(a)** Name of person (you, your spouse, or your dependent) who was enrolled at or attended an eligible educational institution	**(b)** Name and address of eligible educational institution

If you need more space, attach a statement.

2	Enter the total qualified higher education expenses you paid in 2005 for the person(s) listed in column (a) of line 1. See the instructions to find out which expenses qualify	**2**	8 250
3	Enter the total of any nontaxable educational benefits (such as nontaxable scholarship or fellowship grants) received for 2005 for the person(s) listed in column (a) of line 1 (see instructions)	**3**	4500
4	Subtract line 3 from line 2. If zero or less, **stop**. You **cannot** take the exclusion	**4**	3750
5	Enter the total proceeds (principal and interest) from all series EE and I U.S. savings bonds **issued after 1989** that you **cashed during 2005**	**5**	15 000
6	Enter the interest included on line 5 (see instructions)	**6**	3000
7	If line 4 is equal to or more than line 5, enter "1.000." If line 4 is less than line 5, divide line 4 by line 5. Enter the result as a decimal (rounded to at least three places)	**7**	× .25
8	Multiply line 6 by line 7	**8**	750 00

9	Enter your modified adjusted gross income (see instructions) . . .	**9**	84,000	
	Note: *If line 9 is $76,200 or more if single or head of household, or $121,850 or more if married filing jointly or qualifying widow(er),* **stop**. *You* **cannot** *take the exclusion.*			

less than $121,850 ▶

10	Enter: $61,200 if single or head of household; $91,850 if married filing jointly or qualifying widow(er)	**10**	91,850	
11	Subtract line 10 from line 9. If zero or less, skip line 12, enter -0- on line 13, and go to line 14	**11**	(7,850)	
12	Divide line 11 by $15,000 if single or head of household; $30,000 if married filing jointly or qualifying widow(er). Enter the result as a decimal (rounded to at least three places)	**12**	× .
13	Multiply line 8 by line 12	**13**	
14	**Excludable savings bond interest.** Subtract line 13 from line 8. Enter the result here and on Schedule B (Form 1040), line 3, or Schedule 1 (Form 1040A), line 3, whichever applies . . ▶	**14**	750 00

For Paperwork Reduction Act Notice, see back of form.	Cat. No. 10822S	Form **8815** (2005)

7. **IRA Contributions.** Joyce and Barry Bright are both employed and 56 years of age. In 2005 Barry has earned wages of $1,500, and Joyce has earned wages of $27,530. Joyce is an active participant in her employer-maintained qualified annuity pension plan. For 2005, the Brights plan to file a joint tax return and claim the maximum deduction for payments made to an IRA.

a. What is the latest date by which an IRA payment must be made in order for it to be claimed on the Brights' 2005 return?

April 15, 2006

b. Can the payments be claimed on Form 1040EZ? On Form 1040A?

1040A

c. What is the maximum amount Joyce and Barry can each contribute to an IRA and deduct for 2005? *$4500 each*

d. Are the earnings on the IRA payments made in 2005 subject to federal income taxes in 2005? Explain.

No, not taxed in contribution yr. deferred until withdrawan.

8. **IRA Deduction.** Fred and Diane Workingman file a joint return. Neither taxpayer is covered by a retirement plan at work. Fred's gross income from wages is $37,900. Diane's gross income from wages is $31,500. Diane also received taxable interest income of $600. Since establishing their IRAs, Diane and Fred have contributed the following amounts to them:

No pension plan = unlimited AGI for IRA contributions

Diane:	April 6, 2005	$ 750	
	July 1, 2005	750	3000
	October 3, 2005	750	
	January 4, 2006	750	
Fred:	June 16, 2005	$1,500	3000
	February 3, 2006	1,500	

Earnings from their IRAs during 2005 were $890 for Diane and $340 for Fred. Calculate the Workingmans' maximum allowable 2005 IRA deductions and their AGI.

Fred 37,900
Diane 31,500
Interest 600
70,000
IRA deductions 6,000
64,000 AGI

9. **Traditional IRA Characteristics.** For each statement, check true or false.

		True	False
a.	Contributions to a nonworking spouse's IRA must be equal to the IRA contributions of the working spouse.		X
b.	Contributions to a traditional IRA are deductible in the determination of AGI for a single employee whose only income is wages of $25,000.	X	
c.	Distributions from a traditional IRA must begin no later than April 1 of the calendar year after the IRA depositor reaches age 70½.	X	
d.	The earnings of a traditional IRA are taxed to the employee in the year earned.		X
e.	The income earned on nondeductible traditional IRA contributions is not taxable until it is withdrawn.	X	
f.	The maximum deductible amount for contributions to an IRA in 2005 is $4,000 by a married couple of which only one spouse works and earns $25,000.		X

10. **Nondeductible IRA Contributions.** Mike and Mary Sweeney, both age 42, each want to set aside $4,000 for their retirement using a retirement account. They prefer to make their contributions deductible if possible. Mike and Mary have $40,000 and $45,000 of earned income respectively. Their net AGI is $97,000. Mary is covered by an employer-maintained retirement plan. Mike has no such plan.

    a. What tax consequences do they face if they use traditional IRAs for their savings plans?

    b. Can you suggest a better plan? If so, what would it be?

    c. How would your responses change if her earned income was $95,000 and his was $80,000?

11. **Deductions for AGI.** For each statement, check true or false.

		True	False
a.	Primary school teachers have an above-the-line deduction for up to $500 for amounts paid for supplies used in the classroom.		X
b.	Secondary school teachers deduct all amounts paid for school supplies used in the classroom as an itemized deduction.		X

$250 *remaining after $250 deduction*

	True	*False*
c. Reservists who travel less than 100 miles from home to perform services as a member of the reserves deduct their travel expenses as a miscellaneous itemized deduction.	X	___
d. Qualified performing artists may deduct their business expenses from gross income to arrive at adjusted gross income.	X	___
e. To receive the tax benefits of a "performing artist," the individual's adjusted gross income cannot exceed $14,000 16,000 before deducting business expenses.	___	X
f. State and local government officials paid on a fee basis report their business expenses on Form 2106.	X	___
g. To maximize their deduction benefits, "performing artists" who are married must file jointly unless they have lived apart at all times during the year.	X	___
h. Taxpayers 55-years-old may contribute an additional $1,000 $500 to their health savings accounts.	___	X
i. Retired taxpayers may continue to make deductible contributions to a health savings account.	___	X
j. Withdrawals from a health savings account that are not used for medical expenses may be subject to a 15% 10% excise tax.	___	X

12. **Moving Expenses.** Jim Beam incurs the following moving expenses as a result of a change in job location:

Expenses of moving household goods	$ 4,500
Travel and lodging for family in moving to new residence	345
Meals en route	72
Pre-move house-hunting trips	925
Temporary living expenses in new location	700
Real estate commission on sale of old residence	12,000
Total moving expenses	$18,542

If Beam qualifies for a moving expense deduction, what amount may he deduct?

13. **Savings Situations.**

a. Explain the deduction for the penalty on early withdrawal of savings.

b. What are the tax consequences of purchasing a new truck with funds from a Roth IRA when the taxpayer is age 50?

c. What are the tax consequences of purchasing a new truck with funds from a traditional IRA when the taxpayer is age 50?

14. Self-Employed Health Insurance Deduction.

a. What is the maximum self-employed health insurance deduction that can be claimed as an adjustment to income?

b. Under what conditions would a taxpayer not be eligible for the self-employed health insurance deduction?

15. Miscellaneous Questions. For each statement, check true or false.

		True	*False*
a.	Withdrawals from a Roth IRA may be subject to a 6% early withdrawal penalty. *10%*		X
b.	Regardless of the number of children, a taxpayer may contribute only $2,000 each year to a Coverdell Education Savings Account. *$2000 per child*		X
c.	Contributions to a Coverdell Education Savings Account are deductible for AGI. *not deductible*		X
d.	Contributions to a Coverdell Education Savings Account must be for a person under age 18. *for*	X	
e.	Taxpayers may deduct $2,500 from AGI for interest paid on money borrowed to pay qualified higher education expenses.		X
f.	The student loan interest deduction is available only for the first 60 months of interest payments. *Unlimited*		X
g.	Employees may exclude up to $195 per month for parking provided by the employer, even if the parking privilege is discriminatory. *$230*		X
h.	Some states make it possible for parents to prepay their children's college tuition and lock in current tuition rates. When the child goes to college, the child pays taxes on the difference between actual tuition and the lock-in rate.		X
i.	Under a qualified tuition program (see "h" above), if the child does not go to college, a refund is made to the child who must pay taxes on the interest income included in the refund. *Parent pays*		X
j.	Some employers provide meals to their employees. For the value of the meals to be tax-free, the meals must be served on the premises of the employer for the convenience of the employer.	X	

for-before
from-after

		True	*False*
k.	College professors may claim an above-the-line deduction for purchases of books and supplies used in the classroom.		X
l.	A father with AGI of $52,000 may deduct for AGI college tuition payments of $2,500 that he made for his dependent son.	X	
m.	A dependent daughter may receive an above-the-line deduction for $2,700 of tuition she paid to go to college.		X
n.	Taxpayers may claim a $2,000 tax credit for purchasing a certified clean-fuel vehicle.		X

16. **Computation of Tax Liability.** Jim Krainer has gross income of $24,995. Sue Krainer, his wife, has gross income of $14,898. Jim and Sue are both 42 years old. Each contributed $1,000 to a traditional IRA and is entitled to claim an IRA deduction of $1,000. The Krainers will use the standard deduction to determine their tax liability. They are entitled to claim three exemptions.

   a. What will be the amount of their income tax if they file a joint return using Form 1040A?

   b. If the Krainers file separate returns and Jim claims two exemptions and Sue claims one, what will be the amount of income tax on each return and the total combined tax?

17. **Gross Income Exclusions.** Indicate, by placing an *X* in the proper column, the includable or excludable status of the following income items received relative to gross income.

Item		*Includable*	*Excludable*
a.	Dividend on life insurance policy		
b.	Dismissal pay received by employee		
c.	Dividends from employees' credit union		
d.	Embezzlement proceeds		
e.	FMV of automobile won on television giveaway program		
f.	Free parking in employer's lot		
g.	Gambling winnings (no losses)		
h.	Gold necklace found in ocean		
i.	Health resort fee paid for taxpayer by employer		
j.	Life insurance proceeds paid because of insured's death		
k.	Veterans' disability compensation		
l.	Workers' compensation		

18. **Computing Taxable Income.** Using the following information for an unmarried taxpayer with no dependents, compute taxable income. Prepare an analysis showing each item and amount under the appropriate headings of (1) income; (2) gross income exclusions; (3) gross income inclusions; (4) deductions for AGI; (5) AGI; (6) deductions from AGI, including both the standard deduction and exemptions; and (7) taxable income.

Cash Received

Interest on savings account	$ 1,728
Gift of money from parent	1,000
Rent from farmland owned	30,000
Proceeds of life insurance policy of parent	40,000
Nondegree candidate fellowship, granted 8/20/05, of $450	
per month for four months	1,800
Gross salary of $33,000 less $8,100 state and federal income taxes, $2,046	
social security taxes, and $479 health insurance program.	
Net pay received	22,375
De minimis employee fringe benefits valued at $25	0
Company provided parking costing employer $300 per month for 12 months.	0
Total cash received	$96,903

Cash Payments

Expenses of farmland rental	$ 1,750
Personal living expenditures	6,600
Total cash payments	$ 8,350

19. **Internet Problem: Filling out Form 3903.**

In April, Charles Randall (SSN 567-89-1234), who works for Evergreen Productions, received a promotion and was required to move from Cleveland, Ohio, to Kansas City, Missouri, a move of 825 miles. Randall paid the following moving expenses:

House-hunting trip expenses	$1,600
Moving van	3,300
Cost of meals enroute	85
Lodging enroute	120

Randall also drove his personal automobile 825 miles to the new residence. Evergreen Productions reimbursed Randall for only 75% of his "qualified moving expenses."

Go to the IRS Web site and locate Form 3903. Using the computer, fill in the form for Randall and print out a completed copy.

See Appendix A for instructions on use of the IRS Web site.

20. Business Entity Problem: This problem is designed for those using the "business entity" approach. The solution may require information from Chapter 14.

For each statement, check true or false.   *True*   *False*

a. Self-employed persons may deduct 50% of their self-employment tax from AGI.   _____ _____

b. Companies reimbursing their employees for house-hunting expenses and temporary quarters do not report these reimbursements as income on the employee's Form W-2.   _____ _____

c. When a company provides "free meals" as part of the employee's compensation package, the company includes the value of the meals as taxable income on the employee's Form W-2.   _____ _____

d. A company pays $250 per month to provide its CEO with a parking space. The company must include $840 on the CEO's Form W-2 as taxable income.   _____ _____

e. When a company reimburses an employee for qualified, excludable moving expenses, it must report the excludable reimbursement on the employee's Form W-2.   _____ _____

f. Self-employed persons can deduct wage payments to a minor child for working in the business, and the child does not have to include these wages in their gross income.   _____ _____

g. Employers may annually provide up to $5,250 of tax-free educational assistance to their employees to pursue a Master's Degree.   _____ _____

h. When a company provides over $50,000 of group-term life insurance to an employee, it must report the taxable portion of the premiums as wages on the employee's Form W-2.   _____ _____

i. A self-employed person who provides health insurance for himself, but not his three employees, may deduct the premium for AGI.   _____ _____

j. Taxpayers may claim a tax credit equal to 3% of their qualified production activity income or taxable income, whichever is lower.   _____ _____

k. The domestic production activities deduction cannot exceed 100% of the W-2 wages paid during the year.   _____ _____

CUMULATIVE PROBLEM (CHAPTERS 1–4)

This problem is suitable for manual preparation or computer software application.

Using the following information, prepare a tax return for Erica Hansen. Use Form 1040A with supporting Schedule 1, Schedule EIC, Form 8812, Form 8815, and Form 8863.

Erica L. Hansen (SSN 376-38-4930), age 42, is a single parent with three children. She resides at 19 Sunset Road, Normal, Illinois 61761. She chooses to support the presidential campaign fund.

Her household includes Randall L. Hansen, her 19-year-old son (SSN 369-62-3418), Tiffany A. Hansen, her 12-year-old daughter (SSN 396-30-6439), and Donna M. Hansen, her 14-year-old daughter (SSN 653-29-8177). Erica provides over half of the support of each child. Donna has no income of her own, but Randall earns $4,200 during the year delivering papers and mowing grass. All children were in the household for 12 months.

Erica works as an office manager for Universal Development Corporation. Her Form W-2 information follows:

Gross wages	$33,500
Social security tax withheld	2,077
Medicare tax withheld	486
Federal income tax withheld	300
State income tax withheld	1,005

Erica had other income consisting of the following:

Interest received:	
First Federal Savings Bank	$25
Olympic Savings—certificate of deposit cashed in	175
State of Maryland bonds	300
Dividends received:	
Dividend on life insurance policy with Country Farm	
Insurance Company	$20

Randall, a freshman, is a full-time student at Heartland College in Normal, Illinois. To help finance his education Erica cashes in some Series EE, Educational Savings Bonds. The proceeds were $6,000 of which $1,500 was interest. Qualified education expenses paid during the year were $6,000. Randall also received a tax-free scholarship of $1,000.

Erica is a participant in an employer-sponsored retirement plan. However, she wants to make the largest possible *deductible* contribution to her traditional IRA. She also wants to take advantage of the HOPE scholarship credit.

If Erica has overpaid her taxes, she prefers to receive a refund. She signs and dates her return on April 5, 2006.

Additional Information:

Form 8812: on line 1, the amount to enter is $2,000. It represents the maximum credit available for two qualifying children.

The deductible IRA contribution should be computed before filling out Form 8815. The amount on line 9 (Form 8815) starts with Erica's total income (Form 1040A, line 15). However, the interest to be included is that shown on Schedule 1, line 2. This total income figure is then decreased by the IRA deduction (Form 1040A, line 17). Also, line 3, (Form 8815) includes nontaxable scholarships as well as the amount of educational expenses taken into account to compute the HOPE scholarship credit.

The IRA deduction phaseout is based on AGI before the interest exclusion for Series EE Educational Savings Bonds and the IRA deduction.

EIC Calculation:

Compare earned income (Form 1040A, line 7) with AGI (Form 1040A, line 22). Use the larger number to look up the EIC on the EIC Table.

IRA deduction
Wages   33,500
Add'l Int.   1,700
Net AGI   35,200
Phase out   50,000
Max IRA   4,000
deduction

(Use for Cumlative Problem.)

Form **1040A**	Department of the Treasury—Internal Revenue Service **U.S. Individual Income Tax Return** (99) **2005**		IRS Use Only—Do not write or staple in this space.

Label
(See page 18.)

Use the IRS label.
Otherwise, please print or type.

Presidential Election Campaign

L A B E L H E R E	Your first name and initial *Erica*	Last name *Hansen*	OMB No. 1545-0085
	If a joint return, spouse's first name and initial	Last name	Your social security number
			Spouse's social security number
	Home address (number and street). If you have a P.O. box, see page 18. *19 Sunset Rd*	Apt. no.	▲ You **must** enter your SSN(s) above. ▲
	City, town or post office, state, and ZIP code. If you have a foreign address, see page 18. *Norman, IL 61767*		Checking a box below will not change your tax or refund.

► Check here if you, or your spouse if filing jointly, want $3 to go to this fund (see page 18) ► ☐ **You** ☐ **Spouse**

Filing status
Check only one box.

1 ☐ Single
2 ☐ Married filing jointly (even if only one had income)
3 ☐ Married filing separately. Enter spouse's SSN above and full name here. ►
4 ☒ Head of household (with qualifying person). (See page 19.) If the qualifying person is a child but not your dependent, enter this child's name here. ►
5 ☐ Qualifying widow(er) with dependent child (see page 19)

Exemptions

If more than six dependents, see page 20.

6a ☒ **Yourself.** If someone can claim you as a dependent, **do not** check box 6a.

b ☐ **Spouse**

c **Dependents:**		(2) Dependent's social security number	(3) Dependent's relationship to you	(4) ✓ if qualifying child for child tax credit (see page 21
(1) First name	Last name			
Randall	*Hansen*	*369 42 3418*	*son*	☐
Tiffany	*Hansen*	*155 29 8177*	*daughter*	☑
Donna	*Hansen*	*396 30 6478*	*daughter*	☑
				☐
				☐
				☐

Boxes checked on 6a and 6b *1*

No. of children on 6c who:
• lived with you *3*
• did not live with you due to divorce or separation (see page 21)
Dependents on 6c not entered above

d **Total number of exemptions claimed.**

Add numbers on lines above ► *4*

Income

Attach Form(s) W-2 here. Also attach Form(s) 1099-R if tax was withheld.

If you did not get a W-2, see page 22.

Enclose, but do not attach, any payment.

7	Wages, salaries, tips, etc. Attach Form(s) W-2.	7	*33,500*
8a	**Taxable** interest. Attach Schedule 1 if required.	8a	*950*
b	**Tax-exempt** interest. **Do not** include on line 8a. 8b		
9a	Ordinary dividends. Attach Schedule 1 if required.	9a	
b	Qualified dividends (see page 23). 9b		
10	Capital gain distributions (see page 23).	10	
11a	IRA distributions. 11a	11b Taxable amount (see page 23). 11b	
12a	Pensions and annuities. 12a	12b Taxable amount (see page 24). 12b	
13	Unemployment compensation and Alaska Permanent Fund dividends.	13	
14a	Social security benefits. 14a	14b Taxable amount (see page 26). 14b	
15	Add lines 7 through 14b (far right column). This is your **total income.** ►	15	

Adjusted gross income

16	Educator expenses (see page 26).	16	
17	IRA deduction (see page 26).	17	
18	Student loan interest deduction (see page 29).	18	
19	Tuition and fees deduction (see page 29).	19	
20	Add lines 16 through 19. These are your **total adjustments.**	20	
21	Subtract line 20 from line 15. This is your **adjusted gross income.** ►	21	

For Disclosure, Privacy Act, and Paperwork Reduction Act Notice, see page 57.   Cat. No. 11327A   Form **1040A** (2005)

(Use for Cumlative Problem.)

Form 1040A (2005)		Page **2**

Tax, credits, and payments	22	Enter the amount from line 21 (adjusted gross income).	22	
Standard Deduction for—	23a	Check if: ☐ **You** were born before January 2, 1941, ☐ Blind ☐ **Spouse** was born before January 2, 1941, ☐ Blind } Total boxes checked ▶ 23a		
• People who checked any box on line 23a or 23b **or** who can be claimed as a dependent, see page 31.	b	If you are married filing separately and your spouse itemizes deductions, see page 30 and check here ▶ 23b ☐		
	24	Enter your **standard deduction** (see left margin).	24	
	25	Subtract line 24 from line 22. If line 24 is more than line 22, enter -0-.	25	
	26	If line 22 is $109,475 or less, multiply $3,200 by the total number of exemptions claimed on line 6d. If line 22 is over $109,475, see the worksheet on page 32.	26	
• All others: Single or Married filing separately, $5,000	27	Subtract line 26 from line 25. If line 26 is more than line 25, enter -0-. This is your **taxable income.** ▶	27	
	28	**Tax,** including any alternative minimum tax (see page 31).	28	
	29	Credit for child and dependent care expenses. Attach Schedule 2.	29	
Married filing jointly or Qualifying widow(er), $10,000	30	Credit for the elderly or the disabled. Attach Schedule 3.	30	
	31	Education credits. Attach Form 8863.	31	
Head of household, $7,300	32	Retirement savings contributions credit. Attach Form 8880.	32	
	33	Child tax credit (see page 36). Attach Form 8901 if required.	33	
	34	Adoption credit. Attach Form 8839.	34	
	35	Add lines 29 through 34. These are your **total credits.**	35	
	36	Subtract line 35 from line 28. If line 35 is more than line 28, enter -0-.	36	
	37	Advance earned income credit payments from Form(s) W-2.	37	
	38	Add lines 36 and 37. This is your **total tax.** ▶	38	
	39	Federal income tax withheld from Forms W-2 and 1099.	39	
	40	2005 estimated tax payments and amount applied from 2004 return.	40	
If you have a qualifying child, attach Schedule EIC.	41a	**Earned income credit (EIC).**	41a	
	b	Nontaxable combat pay election. 41b		
	42	Additional child tax credit. Attach Form 8812.	42	
	43	Add lines 39, 40, 41a, and 42. These are your **total payments.** ▶	43	
Refund	44	If line 43 is more than line 38, subtract line 38 from line 43. This is the amount you **overpaid.**	44	
Direct deposit? See page 50 and fill in 45b, 45c, and 45d.	45a	Amount of line 44 you want **refunded to you.** ▶	45a	
	▶ b	Routing number ▶ c Type: ☐ Checking ☐ Savings		
	▶ d	Account number		
	46	Amount of line 44 you want **applied to your 2006 estimated tax.** 46		
Amount you owe	47	**Amount you owe.** Subtract line 43 from line 38. For details on how to pay, see page 51. ▶	47	
	48	Estimated tax penalty (see page 51). 48		

Third party designee	Do you want to allow another person to discuss this return with the IRS (see page 52)? ☐ **Yes.** Complete the following. ☐ **No**
	Designee's name ▶ Phone no. ▶ ( ) Personal identification number (PIN) ▶

Sign here	Under penalties of perjury, I declare that I have examined this return and accompanying schedules and statements, and to the best of my knowledge and belief, they are true, correct, and accurately list all amounts and sources of income I received during the tax year. Declaration of preparer (other than the taxpayer) is based on all information of which the preparer has any knowledge.
Joint return? See page 18.	Your signature Date Your occupation Daytime phone number ( )
Keep a copy for your records.	Spouse's signature. If a joint return, **both** must sign. Date Spouse's occupation

Paid preparer's use only	Preparer's signature ▶ Date Check if self-employed ☐ Preparer's SSN or PTIN
	Firm's name (or yours if self-employed), address, and ZIP code ▶ EIN Phone no. ( )

Printed on recycled paper   Form **1040A** (2005)

(Use for Cumlative Problem.)

Schedule 1 **(Form 1040A)**	Department of the Treasury—Internal Revenue Service **Interest and Ordinary Dividends** **for Form 1040A Filers** (99)	**2005** OMB No. 1545-0085

Name(s) shown on Form 1040A
Erica L. Hansen (handwritten)

Your social security number
316 38 4930 (handwritten)

Part I

Interest

(See back of schedule and the instructions for Form 1040A, line 8a.)

Note. If you received a Form 1099-INT, Form 1099-OID, or substitute statement from a brokerage firm, enter the firm's name and the total interest shown on that form.

1 List name of payer. If any interest is from a seller-financed mortgage and the buyer used the property as a personal residence, see back of schedule and list this interest first. Also, show that buyer's social security number and address.

                             Amount

1

2 Add the amounts on line 1.   **2**

3 Excludable interest on series EE and I U.S. savings bonds issued after 1989. Attach Form 8815.   **3**

4 Subtract line 3 from line 2. Enter the result here and on Form 1040A, line 8a.   **4**

Part II

Ordinary dividends

(See back of schedule and the instructions for Form 1040A, line 9a.)

Note. If you received a Form 1099-DIV or substitute statement from a brokerage firm, enter the firm's name and the ordinary dividends shown on that form.

5 List name of payer.   Amount

5

6 Add the amounts on line 5. Enter the total here and on Form 1040A, line 9a.   **6**

For Paperwork Reduction Act Notice, see Form 1040A instructions.   Cat. No. 12075R   **Schedule 1 (Form 1040A) 2004**

(Use for Cumlative Problem.)

SCHEDULE EIC
(Form 1040A or 1040)

Department of the Treasury
Internal Revenue Service

Earned Income Credit

Qualifying Child Information

Complete and attach to Form 1040A or 1040 only if you have a qualifying child.

OMB No. 1545-0074

2005

Attachment
Sequence No. **43**

Name(s) shown on return

Your social security number

Before you begin: See the instructions for Form 1040A, lines 41a and 41b, or Form 1040, lines 66a and 66b, to make sure that **(a)** you can take the EIC and **(b)** you have a qualifying child.

- If you take the EIC even though you are not eligible, you may not be allowed to take the credit for up to 10 years. See back of schedule for details.
- It will take us longer to process your return and issue your refund if you do not fill in all lines that apply for each qualifying child.
- Be sure the child's name on line 1 and social security number (SSN) on line 2 agree with the child's social security card. Otherwise, at the time we process your return, we may reduce or disallow your EIC. If the name or SSN on the child's social security card is not correct, call the Social Security Administration at 1-800-772-1213.

Qualifying Child Information	**Child 1**		**Child 2**	
	First name	Last name	First name	Last name
1 Child's name If you have more than two qualifying children, you only have to list two to get the maximum credit.				
2 Child's SSN The child must have an SSN as defined on page 42 of the Form 1040A instructions or page 44 of the Form 1040 instructions unless the child was born and died in 2005. If your child was born and died in 2005 and did not have an SSN, enter "Died" on this line and attach a copy of the child's birth certificate.				
3 Child's year of birth	Year ___ ___ ___ ___ *If born after 1986, skip lines 4a and 4b; go to line 5.*		Year ___ ___ ___ ___ *If born after 1986, skip lines 4a and 4b; go to line 5.*	
4 If the child was born before 1987— **a** Was the child under age 24 at the end of 2005 and a student?	☐ **Yes.** *Go to line 5.*	☐ **No.** *Continue*	☐ **Yes.** *Go to line 5.*	☐ **No.** *Continue*
b Was the child permanently and totally disabled during any part of 2005?	☐ **Yes.** *Continue*	☐ **No.** The child is not a qualifying child.	☐ **Yes.** *Continue*	☐ **No.** The child is not a qualifying child.
5 Child's relationship to you (for example, son, daughter, grandchild, niece, nephew, foster child, etc.)				
6 Number of months child lived with you in the United States during 2005 • If the child lived with you for more than half of 2005 but less than 7 months, enter "7." • If the child was born or died in 2005 and your home was the child's home for the entire time he or she was alive during 2005, enter "12."	_____ months *Do not enter more than 12 months.*		_____ months *Do not enter more than 12 months.*	

TIP You may also be able to take the additional child tax credit if your child **(a)** was under age 17 at the end of 2005, **and** **(b)** is a U.S. citizen or resident alien. For more details, see the instructions for line 42 of Form 1040A or line 68 of Form 1040.

For Paperwork Reduction Act Notice, see Form 1040A or 1040 instructions.

Cat. No. 13339M

Schedule EIC (Form 1040A or 1040) 2005

(Use for Cumlative Problem.)

Form **8812**	**Additional Child Tax Credit**	1040 / 1040A / 8812	OMB No. 1545-1620
Department of the Treasury Internal Revenue Service (99)	Complete and attach to Form 1040 or Form 1040A.		20**05** Attachment Sequence No. **47**

Name(s) shown on return   Your social security number

Part I   All Filers

1   Enter the amount from line 1 of your Child Tax Credit Worksheet on page 38 of the Form 1040 instructions or page 37 of the Form 1040A instructions. If you used Pub. 972, enter the amount from line 8 of the worksheet on page 4 of the publication **1**

2   Enter the amount from Form 1040, line 52, or Form 1040A, line 33 . . . . **2**

3   Subtract line 2 from line 1. If zero, **stop;** you cannot take this credit **3**

4a   Earned income (see instructions on back) **4a**

 b   Nontaxable combat pay from Form(s) W-2, box 12, with code Q. If married filing jointly, include your spouse's amounts with yours.   **4b**

5   Is the amount on line 4a more than $11,000?
☐ **No.**   Leave line 5 blank and enter -0- on line 6.
☐ **Yes.** Subtract $11,000 from the amount on line 4a. Enter the result . . . **5**

6   Multiply the amount on line 5 by 15% (.15) and enter the result **6**

Next. Do you have three or more qualifying children?
☐ **No.**   If line 6 is zero, **stop;** you cannot take this credit. Otherwise, skip Part II and enter the **smaller** of line 3 or line 6 on line 13.
☐ **Yes.** If line 6 is equal to or more than line 3, skip Part II and enter the amount from line 3 on line 13. Otherwise, go to line 7.

Part II   Certain Filers Who Have Three or More Qualifying Children

7   Withheld social security and Medicare taxes from Form(s) W-2, boxes 4 and 6. If married filing jointly, include your spouse's amounts with yours. If you worked for a railroad, see instructions on back **7**

8   **1040 filers:**   Enter the total of the amounts from Form 1040, lines 27 and 59, plus any uncollected social security and Medicare or tier 1 RRTA taxes included on line 63.
     1040A filers: Enter -0-.   **8**

9   Add lines 7 and 8 . . . .   **9**

10   **1040 filers:**   Enter the total of the amounts from Form 1040, lines 66a and 67.
     1040A filers: Enter the total of the amount from Form 1040A, line 41a, plus any excess social security and tier 1 RRTA taxes withheld that you entered to the left of line 43 (see instructions on back).   **10**

11   Subtract line 10 from line 9. If zero or less, enter -0- **11**

12   Enter the **larger** of line 6 or line 11 . . . . **12**

Next, enter the **smaller** of line 3 or line 12 on line 13.

Part III   Additional Child Tax Credit

13   **This is your additional child tax credit** **13**

1040 / 1040A ◄   *Enter this amount on Form 1040, line 68, or Form 1040A, line 42.* . . . .

For Paperwork Reduction Act Notice, see back of form.   Cat. No. 10644E   Form **8812** (2005)

(Use for Cumlative Problem.)

Form **8815**	**Exclusion of Interest From Series EE and I U.S. Savings Bonds Issued After 1989** (For Filers With Qualified Higher Education Expenses) ▶ Attach to Form 1040 or Form 1040A.	OMB No. 1545-1173 **2005**
Department of the Treasury Internal Revenue Service (99)		Attachment Sequence No. **57**

Name(s) shown on return | Your social security number

1	**(a)** Name of person (you, your spouse, or your dependent) who was enrolled at or attended an eligible educational institution	**(b)** Name and address of eligible educational institution

If you need more space, attach a statement.

2	Enter the total qualified higher education expenses you paid in 2005 for the person(s) listed in column (a) of line 1. See the instructions to find out which expenses qualify	**2**	
3	Enter the total of any nontaxable educational benefits (such as nontaxable scholarship or fellowship grants) received for 2005 for the person(s) listed in column (a) of line 1 (see instructions)	**3**	
4	Subtract line 3 from line 2. If zero or less, **stop.** You **cannot** take the exclusion	**4**	
5	Enter the total proceeds (principal and interest) from all series EE and I U.S. savings bonds **issued after 1989** that you **cashed during 2005**	**5**	
6	Enter the interest included on line 5 (see instructions)	**6**	
7	If line 4 is equal to or more than line 5, enter "1.000." If line 4 is less than line 5, divide line 4 by line 5. Enter the result as a decimal (rounded to at least three places)	**7**	× .
8	Multiply line 6 by line 7	**8**	
9	Enter your modified adjusted gross income (see instructions) . . . **Note:** *If line 9 is $76,200 or more if single or head of household, or $121,850 or more if married filing jointly or qualifying widow(er),* **stop.** *You* **cannot** *take the exclusion.*	**9**	
10	Enter: $61,200 if single or head of household; $91,850 if married filing jointly or qualifying widow(er)	**10**	
11	Subtract line 10 from line 9. If zero or less, skip line 12, enter -0- on line 13, and go to line 14	**11**	
12	Divide line 11 by: $15,000 if single or head of household; $30,000 if married filing jointly or qualifying widow(er). Enter the result as a decimal (rounded to at least three places)	**12**	× .
13	Multiply line 8 by line 12	**13**	
14	**Excludable savings bond interest.** Subtract line 13 from line 8. Enter the result here and on Schedule B (Form 1040), line 3, or Schedule 1 (Form 1040A), line 3, whichever applies . . ▶	**14**	

6,000 − 1,000 − 2,000 = 3,000

For Paperwork Reduction Act Notice, see back of form.   Cat. No. 10822S   Form **8815** (2005)

(Use for Cumlative Problem.)

Form **8863**	**Education Credits**	OMB No. 1545-1618
Department of the Treasury Internal Revenue Service (99)	**(Hope and Lifetime Learning Credits)** ► See instructions. ► Attach to Form 1040 or Form 1040A.	**2005** Attachment Sequence No. **50**

Name(s) shown on return	Your social security number

Caution: *You **cannot** take both an education credit and the tuition and fees deduction (Form 1040, line 34, or Form 1040A, line 19) for the **same student** in the same year.*

Part I **Hope Credit. Caution:** *You **cannot** take the Hope credit for more than 2 tax years for the **same student**.*

1	**(a)** Student's name (as shown on page 1 of your tax return) First name Last name	**(b)** Student's social security number (as shown on page 1 of your tax return)	**(c)** Qualified expenses (see instructions). **Do not** enter more than $2,000 for each student.	**(d)** Enter the **smaller** of the amount in column (c) or $1,000	**(e)** Add column (c) and column (d)	**(f)** Enter one-half of the amount in column (e)

2	Tentative Hope credit. Add the amounts on line 1, column (f). If you are taking the lifetime learning credit for another student, go to Part II; otherwise, go to Part III . . . . ►	**2**	

Part II **Lifetime Learning Credit**

3	**Caution:** *You **cannot** take the Hope credit and the lifetime learning credit for the **same student** in the same year.*	**(a)** Student's name (as shown on page 1 of your tax return) First name Last name	**(b)** Student's social security number (as shown on page 1 of your tax return)	**(c)** Qualified expenses (see instructions)

4	Add the amounts on line 3, column (c), and enter the total	**4**	
5	Enter the **smaller** of line 4 or $10,000	**5**	
6	Tentative lifetime learning credit. Multiply line 5 by 20% (.20) and go to Part III . . ►	**6**	

Part III **Allowable Education Credits**

7	Tentative education credits. Add lines 2 and 6		**7**	
8	Enter: $107,000 if married filing jointly; $53,000 if single, head of household, or qualifying widow(er)	**8**		
9	Enter the amount from Form 1040, line 38*, or Form 1040A, line 22	**9**		
10	Subtract line 9 from line 8. If zero or less, **stop;** you cannot take any education credits	**10**		
11	Enter: $20,000 if married filing jointly; $10,000 if single, head of household, or qualifying widow(er)	**11**		
12	If line 10 is equal to or more than line 11, enter the amount from line 7 on line 13 and go to line 14. If line 10 is less than line 11, divide line 10 by line 11. Enter the result as a decimal (rounded to at least three places)		**12**	× .
13	Multiply line 7 by line 12 . . . . ►		**13**	
14	Enter the amount from Form 1040, line 46, or Form 1040A, line 28		**14**	
15	Enter the total, if any, of your credits from Form 1040, lines 47 through 49, or Form 1040A, lines 29 and 30		**15**	
16	Subtract line 15 from line 14. If zero or less, **stop;** you cannot take any education credits . . . . ►		**16**	
17	**Education credits.** Enter the **smaller** of line 13 or line 16 here and on Form 1040, line 50, or Form 1040A, line 31 . . . . ►		**17**	

* If you are filing Form 2555, 2555-EZ, or 4563, or you are excluding income from Puerto Rico, see Pub. 970 for the amount to enter.

For Paperwork Reduction Act Notice, see page 3.	Cat. No. 25379M	Form **8863** (2005)

5

Personal Itemized Deductions

CHAPTER CONTENTS

■ ■ CHAPTER OVERVIEW

*G*enerally, the law does not allow the deduction of personal expenses on the tax return. There are exceptions, however. These exceptions are called **itemized deductions.** As an alternative to itemizing personal expenses, taxpayers may choose instead to take the standard deduction if that amount is greater.

Individuals have two basic types of expense deductions. One type reduces gross income to yield adjusted gross income (AGI). Expenses incurred in a trade or business are examples of this type of deduction. The other type of expense (itemized deductions) reduces AGI.

The most desirable deduction is one for AGI. One reason for this is that the law uses AGI as a base to limit deductions from AGI. Consider the following examples. Medical expenses are deductible only to the extent they exceed 7.5% of AGI. Employment-related expenses and investment expenses are deductible to the extent they exceed 2% of AGI. Thus, the lower the amount of AGI, the better the chance of deducting more itemized deductions. Another reason for the desirability of deductions for AGI is that 70–75% of taxpayers use the standard deduction in lieu of itemizing deductions. Consequently, these taxpayers lose the benefit of any possible itemized deductions.

As a result of these situations, taxpayers should look for ways to maximize their deductions for AGI. For example, many self-employed people are able to shift what normally would be either itemized deductions or nondeductible expenditures into deductions for AGI. Examples include home office expenses and costs of travel, transportation, entertainment, and business gifts.

This chapter and Chapter 6 present the most common itemized deductions, which appear on Form 1040, Schedule A. These two chapters define the categories and explain when and how to use the deductions. Several tax forms support the numbers that appear on Schedule A. Most of the remaining chapters deal with deductions for AGI.

This chapter describes the most common personal deductions available on Schedule A, such as medical expenses, taxes, interest, charitable contributions, and casualty or theft losses. The chapter explains the limits related to each type of deduction and describes the overall limit on itemized deductions for taxpayers with higher incomes. Chapter 6 expands the details of the miscellaneous and job-related deductions, which this chapter covers briefly.

Currently, the standard deduction exceeds most taxpayers' total itemized deductions, and the IRS annually indexes and increases its benefits. For those who do itemize, it should be noted that, generally, taxpayers may itemize deductions only for their own expenses, when paid from their own funds. Only in limited cases is it possible to take deductions for expenses of other people when paid by the taxpayer.

REPORTING ITEMIZED DEDUCTIONS (SCHEDULE A)

Generally, a taxpayer deducts the larger of either the standard deduction or the total amount of itemized deductions. However, when spouses file separately and one itemizes deductions, the other spouse must also itemize, or take a standard deduction of zero. When one spouse uses the regular standard deduction, so must the other spouse.

Taxpayers deciding to use Schedule A work through the computations and use related forms where appropriate. These include forms such as Form 4952 (Investment Interest), Form 8283 (Noncash Charitable Contributions), Form 4684 (Casualty and Theft Losses), and Form 2106 (Employee Business Expenses). After applying any necessary limits, the tax-payer reports the total of each itemized deduction on Schedule A and computes the overall total. Certain high-income individuals then face another limit on the total amount of itemized deductions that the law will allow. Any remaining deduction carries from Schedule A to Form 1040, page 2, where it reduces AGI.

ITEMIZED DEDUCTIONS REPORTED ON SCHEDULE A

(Personal expenses)

Medical and Dental Expenses (line 4)
Taxes You Paid (line 9)
Interest You Paid (line 14)
Gifts to Charity (line 18)
Casualty and Theft Losses (line 19)
Job Expenses and Most Miscellaneous Deductions (line 26)
Other Miscellaneous Deductions (line 27)
Total Itemized Deductions (line 28)

If itemized deductions exceed standard deduction (reduce tax income & tax liability)
we will use itemized deductions Schedule A

STANDARD DEDUCTIONS FOR 2005

Filing Status	Basic Amount		Elderly OR Blind		Elderly AND Blind
Single	$5,000	add	$1,250	or	$2,500
Married filing jointly, and qualifying widower	10,000	add	1,000*	or	2,000*
Married filing separately	5,000	add	1,000	or	2,000
Head of household	7,300	add	1,250	or	2,500

*Applies to each taxpayer.

FILLED-IN SCHEDULE A

Figure 5-1 shows a filled-in Schedule A for Steven T. and Laurie R. Neal. This Schedule A, prepared by the taxpayers' accountant, illustrates the reporting of the itemized deductions discussed in this chapter.

Information for Figure 5-1: Filled-In Schedule A

Steven and Laurie Neal file a joint return. They have $143,750 of AGI. Shown in Figure 5-1 is a copy of the filled-in Schedule A, which they received from their accountant. The amount of each deduction is described in the following pages.

FIGURE 5-1 Filled-In Schedule A

SCHEDULES A&B (Form 1040) Department of the Treasury Internal Revenue Service (99)	**Schedule A—Itemized Deductions** (Schedule B is on back) ► **Attach to Form 1040.** ► **See Instructions for Schedules A and B (Form 1040).**	OMB No. 1545-0074 2005 Attachment Sequence No. **07**

Name(s) shown on Form 1040 — Steven T. and Laurie R. Neal

Your social security number — 304 66 4201

Medical and Dental Expenses		**Caution.** Do not include expenses reimbursed or paid by others.		
	1	Medical and dental expenses (see page A-2)	1	12,000 00
	2	Enter amount from Form 1040, line 38	2	143,750 00
	3	Multiply line 2 by 7.5% (.075)	3	10,781 00
	4	Subtract line 3 from line 1. If line 3 is more than line 1, enter -0-	4	1,219 00
Taxes You Paid (See page A-2.)	5	State and local **(check only one box):** a ☒ Income taxes, **or** b ☐ General sales taxes (see page A-2)	5	2,050 00
	6	Real estate taxes (see page A-3)	6	1,000 00
	7	Personal property taxes	7	250 00
	8	Other taxes. List type and amount ►	8	
	9	Add lines 5 through 8	9	3,300 00
Interest You Paid (See page A-3.) **Note.** Personal interest is not deductible.	10	Home mortgage interest and points reported to you on Form 1098	10	2,500 00
	11	Home mortgage interest not reported to you on Form 1098. If paid to the person from whom you bought the home, see page A-4 and show that person's name, identifying no., and address ►	11	
	12	Points not reported to you on Form 1098. See page A-4 for special rules	12	
	13	Investment interest. Attach Form 4952 if required. (See page A-4.)	13	1,866 00
	14	Add lines 10 through 13	14	4,366 00
Gifts to Charity If you made a gift and got a benefit for it, see page A-4.	15	Gifts by cash or check. If you made any gift of $250 or more, see page A-4	15	3,725 00
	16	Other than by cash or check. If any gift of $250 or more, see page A-4. You **must** attach Form 8283 if over $500	16	43,250 00
	17	Carryover from prior year	17	
	18	Add lines 15 through 17	18	46,975 00
Casualty and Theft Losses	19	Casualty or theft loss(es). Attach Form 4684. (See page A-5.)	19	-0-
Job Expenses and Most Other Miscellaneous Deductions (See page A-5.)	20	Unreimbursed employee expenses—job travel, union dues, job education, etc. Attach Form 2106 or 2106-EZ if required. (See page A-6.) ►	20	
	21	Tax preparation fees	21	
	22	Other expenses—investment, safe deposit box, etc. List type and amount ► Investment Expense	22	3,009 00
	23	Add lines 20 through 22	23	3,009 00
	24	Enter amount from Form 1040, line 38	24	143,750 00
	25	Multiply line 24 by 2% (.02)	25	2,875 00
	26	Subtract line 25 from line 23. If line 25 is more than line 23, enter -0-	26	134 00
Other Miscellaneous Deductions	27	Other—from list on page A-6. List type and amount ►	27	-0-
Total Itemized Deductions	28	Is Form 1040, line 38, over $145,950 (over $72,975 if married filing separately)? ☒ **No.** Your deduction is not limited. Add the amounts in the far right column for lines 4 through 27. Also, enter this amount on Form 1040, line 40. ☐ **Yes.** Your deduction may be limited. See page A-6 for the amount to enter.	28	55,994 00
	29	If you elect to itemize deductions even though they are less than your standard deduction, check here ► ☐		

For Paperwork Reduction Act Notice, see Form 1040 instructions. Cat. No. 11330X Schedule A (Form 1040) 2005

MEDICAL AND DENTAL EXPENSES, SCHEDULE A (LINE 4)

(handwritten margin note:) ex/ 80,000 AGI 7.5% 6,000 anything over 8000 Med exp -6000 2000 deductible

Most taxpayers cannot take advantage of the medical and dental deduction. To be deductible, unreimbursed medical expenses must exceed 7.5% of the taxpayer's AGI. Taxpayers with health insurance coverage seldom exceed this limit. Generally, taxpayers deduct only their own expenses. However, for the medical deduction, taxpayers can deduct the costs of medical and dental care for others. Qualifying individuals typically include a spouse, children, or a parent. The IRS defines qualifying individuals for the medical deduction as those people who meet the following three standard dependency tests (see Chapter 1): (1) citizenship, (2) support, and (3) relationship. "Qualifying children" do not have to meet the, "Support test."

The other two tests, (4) gross income and (5) joint return, do not affect the medical expense deduction. For example, a taxpayer may deduct $750 spent on medicine for her father who is not a dependent because his gross income exceeds $3,200.

Two major areas of tax planning apply to medical costs:

1. When a spouse receives extensive medical care, the taxpayer should consider married filing separately. The 7.5% reduction of medical expenses applies to a lower AGI when separating income.

2. A group of family members sharing the costs of medical care for a relative can allow one member of the group to deduct the medical expenses. The selected family member deducts only those expenses he or she paid. All members of the group sign statements releasing the dependency exemption to the selected family member (see Chapter 1). The IRS permits group members to rotate the family member using the dependency exemptions.

Only about 5% of the taxpayers claim a medical expense deduction.

THREE GROUPS OF MEDICAL EXPENSES

1. Prescription drugs and insulin
2. All medical and dental insurance premiums paid by the taxpayer
3. Other medical expenses

Prescription Drugs and Insulin

Only medications and accessories purchased on the basis of written prescriptions generate deductible medical expenses. Taxpayers should keep copies of these prescriptions. Even when prescribed, the purchase of over-the-counter medications and vitamins does not qualify as a deductible medical expense. However, when prescribed for certain conditions, like kidney failure, some deductible items may include distilled water or special diets or foods. Taxpayers deduct these special foods only when they cost more than regular foods of the same types. Even then, only the additional cost becomes a deduction. Some commonly used over-the-counter nondeductible drugs include iron and calcium supplements, low-sodium foods, birth control devices, common cold remedies, headache and pain pills, allergy medications, and tablets for upset stomach.

EXAMPLE 1

For Steven Neal's cold and fever, a doctor prescribed an antibiotic, costing $28, and a common cold remedy, costing $5. Only the $28 paid for the antibiotic may be deducted.

Medical and Dental Insurance Premiums

Medical expenses include the full amounts of insurance premiums covering medical and dental care. Self-employed taxpayers can use the family's total insurance premiums to reduce gross income. However, these taxpayers may not use this "adjustment to income" for any month the taxpayer or spouse has eligibility under an employer's medical plan. To determine their adjustment, taxpayers total all their medical insurance expenses for months when they have no eligibility under an employer plan. Premiums not deductible as an "adjustment to income" are treated as a medical expense on Schedule A (line 1). Overlooked deductible insurance premiums may include contact lens coverage, Medicare premiums withheld from the monthly checks of taxpayers receiving social security income, premiums paid to supplement Medicare coverage, prepaid insurance plans, and payments to health maintenance organizations (HMOs) or other group providers. A deduction is also available for long-term care insurance premiums.

Certain types of medical insurance are nondeductible. They include the medical portion of auto insurance, premiums paid through cafeteria plans at work, life insurance, loss of earnings coverage, coverage for loss of limb or sight, premiums that guarantee a specific daily or weekly payment regardless of any hospitalization requirements, and any premiums paid by the employer.

EXAMPLE 2

The Neals paid $11,772 in insurance premiums during the year. The premiums consist of $9,972 for family medical coverage, $1,200 for life insurance, and $600 for disability. Only the $9,972 may be included in medical deductions.

Other Medical Expenses

General Items

Taxpayers can deduct only payments made directly to medical providers, such as doctors, dentists, nurses, hospitals, or clinics. Deductible payments to other providers include those made to authorized Christian Science practitioners, chiropractors, osteopaths, podiatrists, physiotherapists, psychologists, and psychoanalysts (for medical care only). Additional deductible forms of medical care include X-ray examinations or treatments, diagnostic and laboratory work, vasectomies, and any other legal medical treatments, when prescribed by licensed medical providers.

Some treatments designed to stop smoking also qualify as a medical expense deduction. Qualified treatments include:

1. Participation in a smoking-cessation program; and
2. The purchase of drugs requiring a physician's prescription to alleviate the effects of nicotine withdrawal.

Deductible cosmetic surgery includes cosmetic surgery necessary for medical reasons, such as correction of a birth defect or repair of damage from injury or disease. Taxpayers include these medical costs and other medical expenses on Schedule A (line 1). Taxpayers cannot deduct cosmetic surgery for vanity reasons.

Special Medical Expenses

Aside from the preceding items, other health-related expenses may qualify for the medical deduction, depending on the level of care needed. Nursing and convalescent care, in-home care, special schools, equipment and home remodeling, and transportation and travel costs are reasonable medical deductions.

Nursing Home Care

Depending on the condition of a nursing home resident and the types of services offered by the home, the entire amount paid to the facility may be deductible. When the main purpose of the stay relates to a medical condition, the taxpayer deducts all expenses, even the cost of food and lodging. Some conditions that qualify for 100% medical treatment include Alzheimer's disease, paralysis, alcoholism, drug recovery, and physical injury or handicap. If the main reason for living in the home relates to personal care or family convenience, the taxpayer includes on Schedule A (line 1) only the specific medical expenses. However, expenditures for qualified long-term care are deductible when such services are required by a "chronically" ill person.

School for the Handicapped

Amounts paid to send a mentally or physically handicapped spouse or disabled dependent to a special school or facility constitute medical costs. The School's main focus must be to help students compensate or overcome problems in order to function better.

Employee Physicals

Many employees involved with hazardous materials or dangerous jobs get annual physicals. When the employer requires physicals, the costs are deducted as miscellaneous employee business expenses (see Chapter 6). Employees getting physicals for personal benefit would take the deduction as a medical expense.

Transportation Expenses

Taxpayers may use either the standard mileage rate or actual expenses to compute deductible expenses they incur in traveling to receive medical care. For 2005, the standard mileage rate for medical expenses is 15 cents per mile (22 cents after August 31) plus the costs of tolls and parking. While individuals may deduct their actual expenses, the standard mileage rate is easier to use. When choosing to use the actual expense method, taxpayers may deduct only out-of-pocket expenses. Medical transportation includes no allowance for depreciation on an automobile (see Chapter 8). Taxpayers must keep a log showing the mileage and expenses, as well as receipts for all items paid. Under the special provision allowing a taxpayer to deduct the expenses of others, parents may deduct a child's expenses. For instance, parents can deduct the mileage for driving their child from Los Angeles to San Diego to consult a specialist for the child's illness.

Travel Expenses

When a patient and/or the taxpayer must travel overnight for medical treatments, a travel expense deduction is available. The Code limits lodging to $50 per night for each individual.

Capital Expenditures

Home improvements and special equipment installed in a home may be deducted if specifically prescribed by a medical provider as part of a specific treatment. Three common qualifying improvements are swimming pools, air conditioners, and elevators. When the improvement increases the value of the home in excess of the cost, no medical deduction results.

When the cost exceeds the increase in value of the home, the excess becomes a medical expense. One exception occurs when the improvements make it possible for a physically handicapped individual to live independently. Here, deductible expenses include constructing entrance and exit ramps, widening hallways and doorways for wheelchair use, installing support bars and railings, and adjusting outlets and fixtures. In this special case, the IRS treats the costs of the improvements as adding no value to the home for tax purposes.

EXAMPLE 3

Under a doctor's prescription for muscle problems, the Neals installed a spa costing $7,000. It increased the fair market value (FMV) of the house by $4,000. The medical expense amounts to $3,000.

Other Medical Expenditures

Other commonly deductible medical expenses include eyeglasses, dentures, braces, crutches, canes, wheelchairs, guide dogs, and ambulance costs. Common nondeductible medical items include health club memberships, steam baths, massages, cemetery or funeral expenses, and illegal drugs or operations.

Reimbursement

To compute the net medical deduction, (1) add all the costs of qualified medical items reportable on Schedule A, (2) subtract the funds received from insurance and other sources, and (3) enter the difference on Schedule A (line 1).

EXAMPLE 4

The Neals' medical expenses for all categories total $13,000. They received $1,000 in insurance checks. The Neals enter the $12,000 ($13,000 − $1,000) difference on Schedule A (line 1). They reduce this amount by 7.5% of AGI to compute the net medical expense deduction, $1,219 (line 4).

Two situations occur that make medical reimbursements taxable: (1) When an employer-paid insurance policy provides reimbursements greater than the medical expenses actually paid, the difference is taxable. When the employee pays the premium, the excess is not taxable. (2) The taxpayer pays all the medical bills in one year and takes the medical deduction. When the taxpayer receives the reimbursement in the following year, all or part of that reimbursement may constitute taxable income (based on the tax benefit rule described in Chapter 3). This rule requires reporting the current reimbursement in gross income when the taxpayer has deducted medical expenses in an earlier year.

TAXES PAID, SCHEDULE A (LINE 9)

The law limits those taxes that are deductible. Generally, only income taxes and property taxes qualify as itemized deductions, and these must be levied by an agency other than the federal government. Qualifying taxes must meet two conditions before a deduction is available: (1) The taxpayer must actually pay the taxes, and (2) the taxes paid must be those of the taxpayer. Paying someone else's taxes does not create a deductible expense.

About 35% of the total itemized deductions claimed by taxpayers is for taxes, making it the second largest itemized deduction.

DEDUCTIBLE TAXES

Tax Category	Description of Deductible Taxes
Income taxes/Sales taxes	State and local income taxes **or** general sales taxes
	Foreign income taxes (if not used as a tax credit)
	Employee contributions to a state unemployment fund
Real estate taxes	State and local real estate taxes
	Foreign real estate taxes
	Tenant's share of real estate taxes paid by a cooperative housing corporation
	Real estate taxes on condominium units
Personal property taxes	State and local personal property taxes

State and Local Income Taxes/General Sales Taxes, Schedule A (Line 5)

In 2005, taxpayers may choose to deduct either their state and local income taxes, or their general sales taxes.

Three primary sources of deductible state and local income taxes include (1) W-2 withholdings, (2) estimated taxes paid in the current tax year, and (3) additional tax bills paid for the current or previous years. The interest and penalties included in those bills are not treated as taxes. Refunds of prior year taxes do not reduce the taxes paid. When taxpayers deduct state income taxes in a prior year, they generally report any refunds of those taxes on Form 1040 as "Taxable refunds, etc."

As an alternative to deducting state and local income taxes, taxpayers may deduct their general sales taxes. Taxpayers who choose to do this may deduct either their actual sales taxes paid or an amount from the Optional Sales Tax Tables provided by the IRS. The tables are based on the state of residency, the number of exemptions claimed, and total available income. Total available income includes AGI plus any nontaxable income such as tax-exempt interest, workers' compensation, nontaxable social security benefits, and nontaxable receipts from IRAs and pension plans.

Married taxpayers filing separately and electing to deduct sales taxes must both use the same method to determine their sales tax deduction. If one spouse elects to use the Optional Sales Tax Tables, the other spouse must do likewise. In this situation spouses base their deduction on their total personal available incomes.

The amount found on the sales tax tables is increased by general sales taxes paid on motor vehicles, airplanes, boats, home, and homes building materials. If the sales tax rate on these items exceeds the general sales tax rate, the deduction cannot exceed the tax computed using the general sales tax rate.

Taxpayers living in localities that impose a local general sales tax may increase the amount found on the tables by the local sales taxes. IRS Publication 600 produces the Optional Sales Tax Tables. It also include a sales tax deduction worksheet to aid in determining both the state and local general sales tax deductions.

Taxpayers choosing to deduct actual sales taxes, must keep receipts to show actual sales tax expenses. This expense should not include taxes paid on trade or business purchases.

EXAMPLE 5

In 2005, the Neals paid various taxes:

State income tax withheld during 2005	$1,420
Estimated state income tax paid during 2005	400
2004 state income tax paid with 2004 return when filed in 2005	175
Additional tax assessment on 2003 state income tax paid in 2005	55
Total deduction for state income taxes in 2005	$2,050

EXAMPLE 6

Jim and Barb Brubeck claim four exemptions and show AGI of $48,750 on their tax return. Additionally, they have tax-exempt interest of $1,250. The Brubecks also purchased a car during the year, paying a state sales tax of $1,550. Their city does not impose a general sales tax. Using their total available income of $50,000 ($48,750 + $1,250) and their four exemptions, they find a sales tax deduction of $1,163 on the Optional Sales Tax Tables. To this amount they add the sales tax on the car purchased ($1,550) to compute a total sales deduction of $2,713.

Real Estate Taxes, Schedule A (Line 6)

Taxpayers deduct real property taxes on Schedule A (line 6) in the year paid. For taxpayers otherwise unable to itemize annually, the following strategy applies to the timing of the deduction for taxes. The taxpayer may pay two years' property taxes every other year. This strategy may increase the deductible tax expenses to an amount that permits itemizing at least in alternate years.

When taxpayers purchase or sell real estate, the *apportionment rule* requires that the taxes be split between the buyer and seller based on the number of days each one owned the property. This is usually done on the closing statement. Tax payments not in accord with this allocation require a basis adjustment for the buyer and a selling price adjustment for the seller. The tax deduction for each party is based strictly on the number of days the property was owned by the taxpayer.

Condominium and cooperative housing owners may deduct their shares of real estate taxes paid on their properties. When necessary, the association must identify the actual pass-through of property taxes to provide for a tax deduction. All other assessments from housing associations do not qualify as taxes. In addition, "special assessments" added to the property tax bill for local improvements like streets, sidewalks, and sewers do not qualify as deductible taxes. These special assessments are added to the basis of the property.

EXAMPLE 7

When the Neals bought a home on July 1, 2005, no mention was made of splitting the property taxes. They paid $2,000 on November 11, 2005, for property taxes assessed for the period of January 1, 2005, to December 31, 2005. They deduct only $1,000 (50% × $2,000) as property taxes and add the other $1,000 to the home's basis.

Personal Property Taxes, Schedule A (Line 7)

Three conditions apply to the deduction for state or local property taxes. Taxing agencies must do all of the following:

1. Base the tax on the value of the personal property,
2. Impose the tax on an annual basis, and
3. Impose the tax on personal property.

In states where automobile registration meets all three criteria, that portion of the registration cost based on the car's value is a personal property tax deduction. Taxpayers should not treat any additional fees included in personal property tax bills as deductible taxes.

EXAMPLE 8

In 2005, the Neals paid the DMV $300 for the annual cost to register their car. This sum includes a $50 license cost. The remainder of the fee is based on the value of the car. They deduct only the $250 as 2005 personal property tax.

NONDEDUCTIBLE TAXES

Federal income taxes
Social security and Medicare payments
Federal or state estate, gift, or inheritance taxes
State and local license fees (driver's, marriage, fishing)
Use and excise taxes (gasoline, cigarette, alcohol)
Qualified taxes paid on behalf of other taxpayers
Penalties and interest included in tax bills

INTEREST PAID, SCHEDULE A (LINE 14)

Most personal interest is not deductible. Within specified limits, however, personal residence interest, certain points, and investment interest qualify as itemized deductions. In contrast, interest on student loans may qualify as a deduction for AGI.

Overall, interest is the largest itemized deduction. About 40% of the total itemized deductions claimed by taxpayers is for interest.

Interest on Qualified Personal Residence, Schedule A (Line 10)

Qualified personal residences include the taxpayer's principal residence and one additional residence. A vacation home or a home in another city qualifies as a second residence. Houses, condominiums, cooperative housing units, and mobile homes all qualify under the definition of a residence. In some instances, boats and motor homes may also qualify as personal residences. To take the mortgage interest deduction, the taxpayer must hold title to the property.

A person who owns three or more residences can use the mortgage interest deduction on only two of them. Taxpayers must identify each year which residence to designate as the second home. When allowing others to use a vacation home or when renting it out, the taxpayer faces special rules and limitations. The residence will qualify for the home mortgage interest deduction if the taxpayer uses the home for more than the greater of (1) 14 days or (2) 10% of the total days rented.

To deduct interest, the taxpayer must actually pay the interest. The IRS does not consider interest added to a loan as paid. When the taxpayer actually pays the added interest, the taxpayer deducts the interest in the year paid. Also, a special rule applies to interest paid to a person rather than to a bank or other financial entity. The payer reports on Schedule A (line 11) the name and address of the person paid and the amount.

EXAMPLE 9

The Neals' make house payments of $300 per month. They pay a total of $3,600 for the year: $1,100 principal and $2,500 interest expense. They may deduct $2,500.

Acquisition Indebtedness

One type of qualifying home interest, **acquisition indebtedness,** includes money borrowed to buy, build, or extensively remodel a home. The property must secure the loan.

Special rules limit the deduction when refinancing the original debt. If the new loan has a balance higher than the old loan, some nondeductible interest may result. Only the amount of interest on the portion of the new debt that replaces the old debt qualifies for the acquisition indebtedness deduction. However, any portion of the additional debt used to remodel the home extensively also qualifies as acquisition debt. The excess may qualify as home equity indebtedness. Total acquisition debt cannot exceed $1,000,000 ($500,000 for married filing separately). However, no interest deduction limits exist on debt incurred before October 13, 1987. Still, a loan of this size on the main home may limit the interest deduction on a vacation or second home acquired after this date.

Home Equity Indebtedness

Within limits, taxpayers may deduct interest on any loan secured by their homes. These could include home equity loans and bill consolidation loans. Such debt, plus the acquisition debt, cannot exceed the fair market value (FMV) of the home. Total home equity debt cannot exceed $100,000 ($50,000 if married filing separately). Home equity debt allows homeowners to borrow up to $100,000 on their homes without any spending restrictions.

EXAMPLE 10

The Neals bought a home for $60,000 with a $40,000 acquisition debt on June 5, 1995. By February 10, 2005, the loan had a balance of $20,000. The Neals got a second mortgage of $20,000 and used the money to buy a car and take a trip. Since this money was not used to remodel the home, it falls under the definition of home equity debt.

On August 15, 2005, the Neals decided to add a pool and a patio, which cost $15,000. The builder finances the work. The property secures the builder's loan, along with the other loans. This loan qualifies as acquisition debt. Total interest on these house payments is $2,500 ($1,700 acquisition debt; $800 equity debt).

Points, Schedule A (Line 12)

The IRS defines **points** as payments for the use of money. Also called "loan origination fees" or "loan fees," points constitute a form of prepaid interest. One point equals 1% of the loan amount. Taxpayers may deduct qualified points as interest; however, not all loan costs qualify as deductible points. Charges for loan services provided by the lender on behalf of the borrower do not fit the definition of deductible points. The borrower must add to the cost or basis of the home any fees not qualifying as points. Only points charged for the use of money are deductible. Since the IRS considers points as prepaid interest, the general rule requires that borrowers take the deduction evenly over the life of the loan. The exception to this rule occurs upon the purchase or improvement of the principal residence. Here, the points can be fully deducted in the year of purchase. Vacation or second homes do not get this special treatment. To be deductible up-front, the points must meet four conditions:

1. Paying points on borrowed money is an established business practice in the area.
2. The amount of the payment does not exceed the amount usually charged in the area.
3. Funds to pay the points must come from the borrower's own money, not from the lender's funds.
4. Loan proceeds must be used to buy or improve a principal residence.

An early loan payoff may leave a taxpayer with unamortized points, or points not yet fully deducted. An early payoff arises from the sale of the property or the refinancing of the loan. If the property is sold, borrowers deduct the balance of unamortized points in the year of the sale. If the loan is refinanced, borrowers must deduct the balance of unamortized points over the life of the new loan. In addition, any new points paid on the refinancing of a principal residence or other property must be deducted over the life of the new loan. However, if part of the refinancing proceeds on a principal residence is used for improvements on the residence, a corresponding portion of the points may be deducted in the year paid. Some taxpayers incur mortgage debt with a lender who keeps all or part of the interest before paying out the rest of the loan. Lenders call this practice discounting. For tax purposes, borrowers treat the discount like points and deduct it over the life of the loan.

Investment Interest Expense, Schedule A (Line 13)

Investment interest includes any interest paid to buy or keep investment property. Investment interest includes interest paid on brokerage margin accounts and other loans obtained to buy stocks or to invest in partnerships. Investment property consists of stocks, bonds, vacant land, gemstones, or artwork. The IRS defines some investments as "passive" investments (see Chapter 9). The IRS does not treat interest expenses on a passive investment as investment interest. The investor uses this interest elsewhere on the tax return. For instance, interest expense on rental property (a passive investment) belongs on Schedule E, not on Schedule A.

The **investment interest limitation** limits the deduction of investment interest to the amount of the taxpayer's net investment income. Any investment interest not usable as a current deduction because of this limit may be carried over and used in future years. When carried to the next year, it acts just like that year's investment interest and faces the same limits.

Investment income includes interest, dividends, and certain royalties. It may also include the gain from the sale of investments. The law has complicated the meaning of investment income by offering taxpayers a choice. Taxpayers can choose to treat gains on the sale of investments as capital gains and take advantage of the favorable capital gain tax rate (see

Chapter 11). However, this choice eliminates the treatment of the gain as investment income. The other choice is to give up the favorable capital gain tax rate and pay the maximum income tax rate, up to 35%, on the gain. In this situation, the investor includes the capital gain as investment income. The second option may allow the taxpayer to take a higher amount of investment interest as a deduction in the current year.

For the purpose of the investment interest deduction limitation, **net investment income** is the excess of the taxpayer's investment income over the amount of investment expenses actually included in the final miscellaneous deduction on Schedule A (line 26). These expenses include safe deposit boxes, investment publications, and costs of trust managers. Taxpayers file Form 4952 to compute the net interest reportable on Schedule A (line 13).

Many investors acquire municipal bonds as an investment because the bonds earn tax-free interest. As a result, taxpayers may not deduct the interest paid on funds borrowed to buy these bonds. The IRS does not allow tax deductions on expenses related to nontaxable income.

EXAMPLE 11

Included in the Neals' AGI of $143,750 is $2,000 of investment income. They paid investment interest of $4,000 and investment-related expenses of $3,009 (miscellaneous deduction, line 22). The Neals may deduct investment interest of $1,866 computed as follows:

Investment income		$2,000
Investment expenses	$3,009	
Less 2% of AGI*	(2,875)	
Total adjustment		134
Net allowable investment interest expense (line 13)		$1,866

The Neals carry the $2,134 ($4,000 − $1,866) not deducted in 2005 forward to 2006.

*Only the investment expenses in excess of 2% of AGI are deductible on Schedule A.

GIFTS TO CHARITY, SCHEDULE A (LINE 18)

Contributions by Cash or Check, Schedule A (Line 15)

Deductible charitable contributions must be made to qualified nonprofit or charitable institutions. Payments may be made by cash, check, or credit card. Taxpayers may not deduct pledges unpaid by the end of the year. The IRS publishes a list identifying most of the accepted charitable organizations. To deduct contributions to foreign countries for disaster relief and other causes, taxpayers must make the donations to United States qualified nonprofit organizations. Other deductible donations include funds contributed to the United States government, the individual states, or local governments. Income taxes paid never qualify as charitable contributions. However, monies gifted to the government in excess of the income taxes due qualify as contributions.

Taxpayers must support each separate contribution of $250 or more by written receipts from the charity. The receipt must show the amount of money received and identify any noncash items donated to the charity. The taxpayer must have the receipts by the filing date for the tax return. If the charity gave the taxpayer any gifts or services in return for the donation, the receipt must identify these items. If the value of these goods and services is more than $75, the charity must provide a "good faith" estimate of their value. The statement from the organization must also spell out the net amount of the deduction. Taxpayers receive no deduction for the value of something received in return for their contribution.

EXAMPLE 12

The Neals paid $400 a plate for a YMCA benefit and made a cash donation of $3,000 at the banquet. The YMCA's cost for the dinner was $35 per person; the Neals could have bought the same two meals at the Bistro for $75. The charitable contribution deduction is $3,725, the difference between the FMV of the dinner and the total donations ($3,000 + $800 meals − $75 FMV). The Neals do not take the YMCA's cost into account. This deduction limit holds true even if they do not go to the banquet.

Gifts given to individuals are not deductible. Taxpayers may deduct only gifts and donations to religious or other qualified institutions. Handouts to people on the street may be generous, but they do not qualify as deductible contributions.

EXAMPLE 13

The Neals have a widowed neighbor to whom they gave $200 each month over a four-month period for groceries. The Neals' gifts to the widow do not qualify as a deductible charitable contribution.

Contributions to a College or University with the Right to Buy Athletic Tickets

A special rule applies to certain donations of charitable contributions to a college or university. When the taxpayer's donation provides the right to buy athletic tickets, 80% of the gift is considered the charitable contribution; the other 20% is the value of the right to buy the tickets. The taxpayer may not deduct as a charitable contribution the value of this right or the purchase price of the tickets paid to the school.

Charitable contributions account for about 14% of the total itemized deductions claimed by taxpayers.

Noncash Contributions, Schedule A (Line 16)

Among other items, taxpayers may deduct car expenses and donations of property. For car expenses, taxpayers may use either the standard mileage rate of 14 cents per mile or actual expenses. Limits on deductions of property contributed to a charity follow the same rules that apply to cash contributions. The type of property contributed, the recipient, and the property's use determine the amount of the deduction. Property contributions fall into two categories: (1) ordinary income property (includes short-term capital gain property) and (2) capital gain property held over 12 months. Contributions in both categories may include tangible or intangible personal property and real estate.

Generally, the deduction for noncash contributions is equal to the FMV of the property at the time of donation. This holds true when the FMV is less than the taxpayer's basis (investment) in the property. However, when the FMV is greater than the basis, the amount of the deduction depends on whether the item takes the form of (1) ordinary income property or long-term capital gain property and (2) how the charity uses the gift. When the deduction exceeds $500, the donor shows the details of the donation and the computation on Form 8283. For any noncash contribution, a letter from the qualifying organization must specify how the organization uses the property.

> The Katrina Emergency Tax Relief Act of 2005 allows taxpayers who use their automobile for charitable purposes related to Hurricane Katrina to deduct a (higher) mileage rate equal to 70% of the standard business mileage rate, rounded to the next highest cent. Thus, from August 25, 2005 until August 31, 2005, the mileage rate would be 29 cents per mile (40.5¢ × 70%, rounded up). From September 1, 2005 until December 31, 2005, the rate would be 34 cents per mile (48.5¢ × 70%, rounded up). The higher mileage rate remains in effect through 2006.

Tangible Personal Property

Tangible personal property consists of most property that a taxpayer owns except assets used for trade or business and real estate. The usual items contributed under this category include clothing, toys, furniture, appliances, and paperback books. For deduction purposes, the FMV of household goods and clothing is their thrift shop or garage sale value. "Blue books" are the common source of values for most types of vehicles. Normally, the FMV of these contributions is less than basis.

> In 2005, taxpayers who donate vehicles to charities will only be allowed to deduct what the charity obtains from selling it. The charity, under threat of penalties, must report the sales price to both the donor and the IRS.

Intangible Property

The intangible assets most commonly used by taxpayers as charitable contributions include stocks, bonds, and mutual funds. Less often, taxpayers donate limited partnership interests and commodities. The FMV of this type of property may be more or less than basis.

Ordinary Income Property

Ordinary income property is property that, if sold, would generate income taxed at the ordinary income rates. It includes such items as investments held for one year or less, manuscripts or works of art created by the taxpayer, and business inventory. When the taxpayers contribute ordinary income property, tax law limits the value of the contribution. Donors reduce the FMV by any ordinary gain the property would have generated had the taxpayer sold the asset. In most cases, this limits the deduction to the taxpayer's basis (investment) in the property.

EXAMPLE 14

Mr. Neal built a bookcase and donated it to the local public elementary school. The bookcase was appraised at $800. He spent $125 on materials. The Neals deduct only the $125 cost of materials (his basis) as this would be ordinary income property if he had sold it. They receive no deduction for the value of his time in constructing the bookcase.

Qualified Capital Gain Property

Qualified capital gain property consists of certain assets held for more than one year that, if sold, would produce capital gain (FMV > basis). This category includes stocks, bonds, and real estate. Usually, FMV at the date of the contribution determines the value of the gift. Taxpayers can meet the IRS's valuation requirement by getting written appraisals or stock market quotes to establish the value. Taxpayers who have decided to make donations to qualifying organizations have a tax incentive when the FMV of the item exceeds the taxpayer's basis. The donor does not report the increased value of the asset as income. While not paying taxes on the appreciated value of the asset, the donor benefits from the higher FMV of the contribution.

EXAMPLE 15

The Neals contributed a few shares of IBM stock to their church. They bought the stock for $200 several years ago. On the date of the donation, the stock had a FMV of $350. The Neals' noncash charitable contribution equals the FMV of $350. They do not report the $150 of appreciation as income.

Limitation. The law requires an adjustment to the FMV when the contribution consists of "tangible personal property" that is *not* used by the charity directly in its exempt functions. The fair market value of the property must be reduced by 100% of the capital gain that would have resulted if the property had been sold at fair market value on the day contributed. For instance, an art collector donates a $5,000 (FMV) painting to a hospital. Its cost to the collector was $2,000. Since the hospital cannot use the painting in its exempt function, treating patients, the collector's contribution deduction is only $2,000 [$5,000 – $3,000 (gain)]. This adjustment does not apply to "intangible property" and real estate.

Bargain Sales to Charity

Another problem arises when a taxpayer sells an item to a qualifying organization at a bargain price. A bargain sale (sale or trade for less than the FMV) of property is partly a charitable contribution and partly a sale or exchange. The contribution is equal to the difference between the FMV and the selling price. The sale or exchange portion may also result in a taxable gain to the donor. Taxpayers measure the gain as the difference between the selling price and the basis of the item.

Nondeductible Contributions

A taxpayer should verify an organization's status with the IRS before making a contribution. Many fund-raising groups try to look like qualified charitable institutions but do not qualify. Also, donations to the lobbying or political action groups of qualified organizations may not be deductible. Other contributions that would not qualify for the charitable contribution deduction include dues to clubs or lodges and tuition at private or religious schools. Raffle tickets are not deductible contributions.

Maximum Deduction Limitation

The IRS limits charitable contributions each year to 50%, 30%, or 20% of a taxpayer's AGI. The percentage limitation that applies depends on the type of contribution being made and the nature of the charity. The deduction of contributions of cash and property to most organizations may never exceed 50% of AGI. The deduction for appreciated capital gain property contributed to any qualified organization can never exceed 30% of AGI. The 30% limit also applies to donations of cash and ordinary income property to certain private nonoperating foundations. Appreciated capital gain property includes any capital asset held for more than one year that would result in capital gain if sold at its FMV. Avoidance of the 30% of AGI limit occurs if the taxpayer reports the donation of the appreciated capital gain property at the taxpayer's basis. Then the limitation increases to 50% of AGI. When taxpayers contribute capital gain property, instead of cash, to certain private foundations not operating for the benefit of the public at large, they limit the contribution to 20% of AGI.

These limitations sometimes reduce or eliminate a taxpayer's net contribution. Taxpayers carry forward the unused contributions for up to five years. When carried forward, the contribution limits of 50%, 30%, and 20% apply to the specific contributions. For example, an unused contribution with a 30% limitation in 20x1 retains the same 30% limitation when carried to 20x2. If the taxpayer does not itemize, charitable contributions generated in that year are not carried forward.

EXAMPLE 16

The Neals donated land worth $80,000 to their church for a building site. The land was acquired as an investment 15 years ago for $20,000. The amount deductible for appreciated capital gain property in the current year is limited to $43,125 (30% of AGI). The Neals' total contribution of appreciated property is $80,350 (IBM stock, $350 + land, $80,000). Thus, the Neals deduct $43,125 currently, and the remaining $37,225 carries forward for up to five years. Note that the total charitable contribution deduction of $46,975 ($3,725 + $125 + $43,125) does not exceed 50% of AGI, $71,875.

The Katrina Emergency Tax Relief Act of 2005 contains a provision that allows individuals to increase the limit for "qualified contributions" to 100% of the taxpayer's AGI (up from the normal 50% AGI limit). A **qualified contribution** is any cash contribution paid between August 28, 2005 and December 31, 2005 to a qualified public charity. It is important to note that the 100% AGI limit applies to all cash contributions (including contributions other than for hurricane relief) made to qualified public charities during this time period. Therefore, a taxpayer whose AGI is $100,000 and who prior to August 28, 2005 had given $20,000 to a qualified public charity would normally be allowed to give another $30,000 to qualified public charities during 2005 before being subject to the AGI limitation. Under this new rule, this taxpayer could give up to $80,000 ($100,000 – $20,000) to public charities between August 28, 2005 and December 31, 2005 and be allowed to deduct the entire $100,000 in 2005.

CASUALTY AND THEFT LOSSES, SCHEDULE A (LINE 19)

On personal use property, taxpayers measure each casualty loss as the lower of two amounts: (1) the difference between the FMV before and after the casualty or (2) the basis of the property. Taxpayers must reduce the lower of these two numbers by both of the following:

1. Insurance and other proceeds received
2. $100 per event (not per item)

Taxpayers then total the net loss from each casualty event occurring during the year. From this total they subtract 10% of AGI. Only the remaining amount is deductible.

These provisions make losses from personal casualties hard to deduct. Personal casualty deductions rarely take place without a major uninsured disaster. Lesser casualties generally result in losses below the 10% of AGI threshold and result in no tax benefits. Taxpayers report casualty losses on Form 4684 and bring the net losses over to Schedule A (line 19). If more than one casualty takes place during the year, the law requires a separate Form 4684 for each event.

EXAMPLE 17

Mr. Neal wrecked a personal automobile that originally cost $30,000. This was the Neals only casualty for the year. Industry guidelines show a FMV of $25,855 for the vehicle before the accident. The estimated FMV after the accident was $1,000. Mr. Neal collected $16,355 of insurance proceeds. The Neals' AGI of $143,750 reduces the casualty loss deduction to zero.

FMV before casualty loss	$25,855	
FMV after casualty loss	(1,000)	
Net casualty loss, FMV method		$24,855
Basis of the auto		$30,000
Lower of FMV method or basis		$24,855
Less insurance proceeds		(16,355)
Less $100 reduction		(100)
Less 10% of AGI		(14,375)
Net casualty loss deduction, not less than $0		$ 0

Katrina doesn't apply

Casualty losses that arose after August 24, 2005 in the Hurricane Katrina disaster area (as specified by the federal government) are not subject to the $100 floor or the 10% AGI limit. This provision was included in the Katrina Emergency Tax Relief Act of 2005 to provide those affected by the hurricane with a larger tax deduction for their losses than is normally allowed in the tax laws. In addition, as with any **Presidentially Declared Disaster Area** (an area determined by the President of the United States to warrant federal disaster assistance), affected taxpayers can elect to take the deduction on the previous year's tax return. For those affected by Hurricane Katrina, this would be their 2004 tax returns. Taxpayers who had already filed their 2004 tax returns could amend their 2004 returns and report the casualty loss deduction on the amended return. This special rule allows these affected taxpayers the opportunity to speed up their tax refunds associated with the casualty loss deduction.

Casualty Events

The IRS defines a **casualty** as a sudden, unexpected, or unusual event. Events creating casualty losses include accidents, fires, storms, earthquakes, floods, hurricanes, thefts, and other disasters. Taxpayers having insurance coverage must first report the damage and loss of property to insurance carriers. Then taxpayers should report the loss to a government authority, such as police, fire, or the Federal Emergency Management Agency (FEMA), to get a written report for the taxpayer's file. Any reimbursements must be deducted to yield the loss for tax purposes. Small Business Administration (SBA) loans and any other loans are not counted as reimbursements when computing the net casualty loss. When a taxpayer has insurance coverage but declines to report the incident in order to avoid raising insurance premiums, no deduction results for the insurance benefits given up. The IRS does not recognize any reason for not filing a claim for an insured loss.

Proof

The mere loss of an item does not create a casualty. The taxpayer must prove that a theft, accident, or disaster took place. The taxpayer must also establish the amount of the casualty loss. "Before" and "after" pictures (photographs or videocassettes) can help prove the extent of the damage. Objective appraisals of the asset both before and after the event provide evidence of the loss suffered. The IRS generally accepts the cost of repairing the asset as the amount of the loss. However, it does not always accept the cost of repairs as the value of the casualty damage. The repair could restore the property to a better condition and a higher value than it had before the loss. No deductions are allowed for items deliberately destroyed or damaged by willful neglect. Deductions are allowed only for damage to the taxpayer's own property. For instance, a driver hits and destroys the neighbor's fence. The cost of repairing the neighbor's fence would not qualify as a casualty loss on the driver's income tax return.

Year of Deduction

The general rule allows a casualty loss deduction only in the year the casualty occurs. However, a theft loss is deducted in the year the taxpayer discovers the theft. When the President of the United States designates a disaster area, the taxpayer has two options. The taxpayer may elect to deduct the loss in the year of the disaster or in the previous tax year. This special rule makes it possible for taxpayers to get disaster-based tax refunds sooner. Unless the casualty occurs in a federally declared disaster area, a taxpayer should attach complete documentation to the tax return. The documentation must include the costs of the items and the details of the events surrounding the loss. In a disaster area, records generally suffer complete destruction from fire, flood, earthquake, or storms. Because of these conditions, the IRS makes special allowances for reconstructed or alternate information. Some casualties result in gains which taxpayers must report as income. (See Chapter 10 for involuntary conversions.)

Events Not Considered Casualties

Many irritating events, although expensive and inconvenient, do not qualify as casualties. Some examples include long-term termite or moth damage, plant disease, property value reduction due to a landslide on a nearby lot, or loss of a diamond ring dropped down a drain.

Generally, taxpayers do not report in gross income reimbursements for temporary living expenses. Such reimbursements are nontaxable to the extent that they compensate a taxpayer for a temporary increase in living expenses. Reimbursements in excess of actual costs are taxable, as are reimbursements covering normal expenses. While often associated with casualties, these reimbursements do not affect the casualty loss deduction.

EXAMPLE 18

A storm damages the Neals' home. While repairing the home, the Neals live in another house which costs $3,500 per month. The Neals' normal living expenses before the storm amounted to $2,500 per month, which they continue to pay. The insurance company reimburses them at the rate of $4,000 per month. The Neals include $500 per month in gross income for the reimbursement they receive in excess of the storm-related expenses.

Business and Investment Casualty Losses

The computation of casualty and theft losses from business and investment property requires these changes:

1. The $100 deductible does not apply.
2. These losses are not reduced by 10% of AGI.

Also, if the property is totally destroyed (or stolen), the loss is measured as the basis of the asset. The decline in FMV is not a factor.

When business property produces a net casualty loss, the loss is a deduction "for AGI." If the loss stems from investment property (e.g., paintings, gems, antiques), the loss is deductible from AGI as a miscellaneous itemized deduction subject to the 2% AGI limitation. (See Chapter 11 for additional coverage.)

LIMITATIONS ON ITEMIZED DEDUCTIONS

The government uses an overall limit on itemized deductions, along with other provisions of the law, to collect more taxes from higher-income taxpayers. For 2005 the Code reduces certain itemized deductions by 3% of the difference between AGI and $145,950 ($72,975 married filing separately). The reduction cannot exceed 80% of the deductions subject to the limitation. Itemized deductions subject to these limits include all taxes, mortgage interest and points, charitable contributions, and most miscellaneous deductions (except gambling losses). The following deductions are not subject to reduction: medical expenses; investment interest; and casualty, theft, or gambling losses.

EXAMPLE 19

In 2005 Art McBurney and his wife file a joint tax return, showing an AGI of $183,950. The McBurneys' itemized deductions include: $14,000 of medical expenses, $12,300 of taxes, $12,500 of mortgage interest, $2,800 of investment interest, $26,200 of charitable contributions, $9,500 of casualty losses, and $6,800 of miscellaneous deductions. Their total itemized deductions are as follows:

Medical expenses [$14,000 − (7.5% × $183,950)]	$ 204
Taxes	12,300
Interest expense ($12,500 mortgage + $2,800 investment)	15,300
Charitable contributions	26,200
Casualty losses [$9,500 − $100 − (10% × $183,950)]	0
Miscellaneous deductions [$6,800 − (2% × $183,950)]	3,121
Deductible expenses before overall limitation	$57,125

Itemized deductions subject to limitation are as follows:

Taxes	$12,300
Mortgage interest	15,300
Charitable contributions	26,200
Miscellaneous deductions	3,121
Total	$56,921

Reduce otherwise allowable itemized deductions by the lesser of $45,537 (80% × $56,921) OR $1,140 [3% × ($183,950 − $145,950)]	(1,140)
Total itemized deductions in 2005	$55,985

Normally, itemized deductions used in calculating the 80% limit include all charitable contributions the taxpayer makes during the year. A provision in the Katrina Emergency Tax Relief Act of 2005 allows taxpayers to leave out from the calculation of the 80% limit all "qualified contributions." A **qualified contribution** is any cash contribution paid between August 28, 2005 and December 31, 2005 to a qualified public charity. It is important to note that this new tax law allows all cash contributions (including contributions other than for hurricane relief) made to qualified public charities during this time period to be left out of the 80% limit calculation. This special provision ensures that none of the qualified contributions are limited because the taxpayer's AGI exceeds $145,950 ($72,975 for married filing separately). Thus, 100% of the qualified contributions are allowed as an itemized deduction.

Fewer than 5% of the taxpayers are subject to the 3% limitation on itemized deductions.

QUESTIONS AND PROBLEMS

1. **Medical Expense Deduction.** Roger Brown and his wife Jenny maintain a home in which they live with their invalid daughter, Brenda, age 24. AGI on the Brown's joint return is $24,000. Payments for medical and dental expenses during the year follow.

	Brenda	The Browns
R. J. Stone, M.D. (not paid by insurance)	$260	$ 250
G. O. Wright, M.D. (not paid by insurance)	220	200
Hearing aid		525
Premium on hospital insurance		240
Eyeglasses		130
Toothpaste	20	35
Prescription drugs (not paid by insurance)	275	125
Total	$775	$1,505

2225

Using the listed information, compute the Brown's Schedule A, Medical and Dental Expenses.

7.5% = $1800   *2225*
425

2. **Medical Expense Deduction.** Mei Ling, a single taxpayer, has paid the expenses listed during the year. Her AGI is $17,900.   *$1,342.50*

a. In the space after each item, indicate whether or not the item is deductible as a medical expense. If the item is deductible, also enter the amount (without regard to the 7.5% of AGI limitation). Assume that these amounts have already been reduced by insurance reimbursement, when applicable.

Item	Deductible?	Deductible Amount
1. Premium on health insurance, $386	yes	386
2. Premium on life insurance, $275	no	
3. Premium on automobile accident insurance, $610	no	
4. Acne cream, $30	no	
5. Prescription medication, $300	yes	300
6. Over-the-counter vitamins, $60	no	
7. Cosmetics, $150	no	
8. Dr. Wall, dentist, $120	yes	120
9. Dues to health spa, $325	no	
10. X-ray examination, $60	yes	60
11. City Hospital, room and services, $375	yes	375
12. Eyeglasses, $125	yes	125
13. Cemetery plot, $600	no	
14. Medical miles—1,000 (use standard rate of 15¢)	yes	150

Item	Deductible?	Deductible Amount
15. Illegal drugs, $135	no	
16. Vacation recommended by doctor to improve general health, $875	no	
17. Dr. Root, minor surgery, $350	yes	350
18. Used wheelchair, $275	yes	275
19. Dr. Spencer for false teeth, $480, and fittings, $100	yes	580

b. Using the listed information, compute Ling's Schedule A (Medical and Dental Expenses).

3871

3. **Medical Reimbursements.** A taxpayer receives reimbursement for a medical expense of $455 in the current year. What is the proper tax treatment of the $455 if

a. The reimbursed expense was paid in the current year?

b. The reimbursed expense was paid in the prior year when itemized deductions were not used to reduce the income tax liability?

c. Some of the reimbursed expense was paid in a prior year when the medical expense was used, with other itemized deductions, to reduce the income tax liability? (Total medical expenses deducted were $840 in that year.)

d. The reimbursed expense was paid in a prior year when the medical expense was used, with other itemized deductions, to reduce the income tax liability? (Total medical expenses deducted were $350.)

e. The total reimbursement includes $75 in excess of the taxpayer's current year's medical expenses? (The premium on the policy was paid by the taxpayer.)

f. The total reimbursement includes $75 in excess of the taxpayer's current year's medical expenses? (The employer paid the total cost of the medical insurance plan, and the cost of the medical premiums were not included in the taxpayer's gross income.)

4. **Physical Exams.** If an employee pays for a periodic medical checkup required by an employer, can the amount paid be deducted, and if so, is there any limitation? Explain.

5. **Tax Deduction.** Maurice and June Prior, Milwaukee, Wisconsin, file a joint income tax return. They claim one dependent child, Jeff, on the return for 2005. AGI is $24,650. The Priors elect to itemize deductions. Using the following information, compute their Schedule A (Taxes You Paid).

   a. State income tax withheld by employer in 2005 was $1,697.

   b. Quarterly estimated payments of state income tax for 2004 and 2005 were as follows:

April 15, 2004	$100	April 13, 2005	$120
June 15, 2004	100	June 15, 2005	120
September 15, 2004	100	September 15, 2005	120
January 10, 2005	100	January 12, 2006	120

   c. Payments on real estate tax levies on personal residence were as follows:

July 31, 2004	$450
January 30, 2005	450
July 30, 2005	450
January 29, 2006	500

   d. Personal property tax on the value of a boat, paid on January 23, 2005, was $96. The tax bill had been received on December 28, 2004.

   e. Other taxes paid in 2005 include $1,511 for social security tax, $800 for special assessments against the real estate for a new sidewalk, and $32 federal excise tax on telephone bills.

   f. Additional federal income tax paid as a result of an IRS audit was $1,200.

6. Sales Tax Deduction. For each statement, check true or false.

	True	False
a. On separate returns, one spouse may deduct actual sales tax expense, and the other spouse may use the Optional Sales Tax Tables.	—	—
b. The Optional Sales Tax Tables are based on AGI.	—	—
c. Amounts found on the Optional Sales Tax Tables may be increased by the general sales tax on auto purchases.	—	—
d. Amounts found on the Optional Sales Tax Tables may be increased by the local general sales tax.	—	—
e. Taxpayers deducting their actual sales taxes must keep receipts to verify their sales tax deductions.	—	—
f. Taxpayers deducting actual sales taxes may include sales taxes paid on business items.	—	—
g. Taxpayers in states with both a general sales tax and an income tax may deduct both taxes on their tax return.	—	—

7. Property Tax Allocation. On March 14, 2004, Rudy Valquez sold a ten-acre piece of property to Eric Volkan for $40,000. In the closing of the transaction, nothing was specified about the payment of property taxes for the year 2004. Volkan paid the entire 2004 property tax bill on January 31, 2005, in the amount of $800. Based on this data, answer the following:

a. How much of the paid property taxes can Volkan deduct on his tax return?

(292/365 days × 800)

$640   *or*

b. In which year may Volkan take the property tax deduction on Schedule A for the amount of taxes determined in Part a.? Explain.

no taxes pd in 2004, so not deductible — only in 2005.

c. What is the amount of paid property taxes, if any, that Volkan may not take as an itemized deduction. Explain how, if at all, Volkan and Valquez should account for this portion of the taxes.

– Eric cannot deduct $160 ($800-$640) of taxes pd.
– add'l cost of land
– Eric would pay $40,160 / Rudy would sell for $40,160

d. What could Valquez and Volkan have done to avoid the described complications in handling the deductibility of property taxes?

Attorney to allocate all cost of sale.

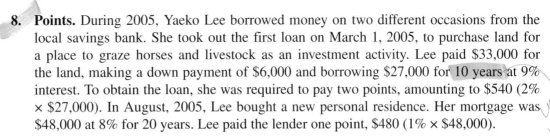

(handwritten margin notes)
→ 1st loan for investment purpose must be amortized over life of loan $4.50/mth

8. **Points.** During 2005, Yaeko Lee borrowed money on two different occasions from the local savings bank. She took out the first loan on March 1, 2005, to purchase land for a place to graze horses and livestock as an investment activity. Lee paid $33,000 for the land, making a down payment of $6,000 and borrowing $27,000 for 10 years at 9% interest. To obtain the loan, she was required to pay two points, amounting to $540 (2% × $27,000). In August, 2005, Lee bought a new personal residence. Her mortgage was $48,000 at 8% for 20 years. Lee paid the lender one point, $480 (1% × $48,000).

a. Determine the amount of points Lee may use as a 2005 interest deduction in connection with the two loans.

(handwritten) $540 ÷ 120 = $4.50

(handwritten) 525 = 480 + 45

(handwritten, boxed) Pts not from principal residence must be amortized.

(handwritten) amortize

b. What is the tax treatment of any amount paid as points (if any), to the extent not deducted in 2005?

(handwritten) Remaining $495 (540-45) deductible at the rate of $4.50/mth for remaining 9 yr 2 mths of loan as investment interest expense.

9. **Capital Expenditures on Purchase of Residence.** Gloria S. and John A. Peters obtained a loan from County Savings Bank to purchase a new residence. The loan was for $56,550, secured by the residence on the July 2, 2005, purchase date. The loan settlement statement contained the following information:

For each item a. through j., indicate in the first blank the appropriate income tax treatment of each payment made, using the following designations. Enter the applicable amount in the second blank.

A. Add to cost of residence

B. Deduct from gross income to arrive at AGI

C. Deduct from AGI (itemized deductions, Schedule A)

D. Personal, not deductible

E. Other

Description	Cost	Tax Treatment	$ Amount
Purchase price of residence	$62,500		
a. Deposit with purchase offer, 5-28-05	(2,500)	A	2500
Balance due at closing	60,000		
b. Down payment in cash	(10,000)	A	10,000
c. Purchase price, financed	50,000	A	50,000
d. Premium on homeowner's insurance policy (fire, casualty, liability, etc.) assumed from prior owner covering 7/2/05–12/31/07	480	D	480

Description	Cost	Tax Treatment	$ Amount
e. Estimated real estate taxes for 2005 from prior owner (to be levied at end of year by city) of $1,950 for 1/1/05–6/30/05	($ 975)	E	975
f. Tank of heating oil left in house	245	D	245
g. Legal fees, title, recording, and closing costs	375	A	375
h. Appraisal fee to obtain loan	215	A	215
i. Points on mortgage 2% of loan	1,000	C	1,000
j. Check from lender payable to the Peterses and Remodeling, Inc., for the remodeling of the kitchen	3,360	A	3,360

10. Interest Deduction. George and Mary Greenfield had an AGI of $98,500 in 2005 (includes $620 of investment income). They incurred the following interest expenses during the year:

Credit card interest	$ 79 — ND
Automobile loan interest (older car)	337 — ND
Mortgage interest on personal residence	13,500 — D
Investment interest expense on broker's margin account to carry corporate stocks	543 — D
Investment interest expense on broker's margin account to carry tax-exempt bonds	381 — ND
Mortgage interest on vacation home	3,080 — D
Points paid on vacation home refinancing (2% × $48,000)	960 — D

The original cost of the Greenfields' personal residence was $160,000. It now has a FMV of $166,000. There have been no capital improvements. The balance of the mortgage was $140,000 on January 1, 2005, and $139,000 on December 31, 2005. The vacation home was originally purchased in 1989 for $56,400 cash. On May 1, 2005, the Greenfields took out a ten-year mortgage of $48,000 on the vacation home. They used the proceeds to buy a new car and consolidate other loans. On December 31, 2005, the mortgage balance was $47,000.

a. Based on the preceding information, determine how much mortgage interest the Greenfields may deduct in 2005.

b. Using the preceding information, compute the Greenfields' Schedule A (Interest You Paid).

11. **Interest Deduction.** Indicate the correct treatment for each listed item by placing an *X* in the most appropriate column.

Description	*Deductible*	*Nondeductible*
a. Al took out a $20,000 home equity loan to buy an airplane. Al paid interest of $1,750.	X	
b. Betty paid $300 in credit card interest, including $30 in late fees.		X
c. Charles borrowed $50,000 to buy City of Cucamonga bonds. The interest he paid was $3,000. His net investment interest income was $2,500.		X
d. David constructed a new home for $175,000. After it was built, David borrowed $157,500 against the property to pay off the construction loan. The interest on the new mortgage was $8,500.	X	
e. Eddie paid $80 in interest on a state tax deficiency.		X
f. Fred borrowed $125 from his friend, Thomas, to buy this semester's textbooks. Fred paid 20% interest, $25.		X
g. Gabe borrowed $60,000 from a brokerage margin account to buy common stock of ASF, Inc. Gabe paid $4,000 interest for this loan. ASF, Inc. paid him $5,000 in dividends.	X	

12. **Charitable Contribution—Property.**

a. Can a contribution of a book, an antique, a wild animal, used furniture, or a work of art currently on loan to a museum be deducted? If so, how is such a contribution reported?

b. If qualified contributions exceed the amount that can be deducted in the current year, is the excess deduction lost? Explain.

13. **Charitable Contribution—Appreciated Property.** An individual with an AGI of $49,000 transfers common stock with a market value of $15,000 to an educational institution to be used for scholarships. The stock's basis is $3,575; it was purchased six years ago. What amount may be claimed as an itemized deduction resulting from this contribution?

14. **Charitable Contribution—Appreciated Property.** A taxpayer contributed an appreciated security with a FMV of $9,500 to the City General Hospital in 2005. The security has been held for five months and had a basis of $4,200. The taxpayer had an AGI of $32,000 for 2005. What is the taxpayer's charitable contribution deduction?

15. **Charitable Contribution Deduction.** John Dilly, a single man, has an AGI of $60,000. He makes the following contributions:

Item	FMV	Cost
Check to Temple Beth El		$4,000
Used clothing to Children's Hospital	$100	380
Cash to University of Fullerton		1,200
Check to Mayor Fred's election campaign		300
Used camping equipment to the Boy Scouts of America	300	1,200
Cash to homeless father for his children's clothing		100

Using the listed information, compute Dilly's Schedule A (Gifts to Charity).

16. **Charitable Contribution—Benefit Event.** A professional football team plays a game for the benefit of the Heart Association each year. The admission charge is $32 per ticket, the usual admission price for a professional football game. One-half of the purchase price goes directly to the Heart Association. Denise Clark purchases four tickets at a total cost of $128. Clark itemizes deductions.

a. How much can Clark deduct per ticket as a charitable contribution on her income tax return? Explain.

b. How would your answer to Part a. differ if Clark had no intention of going to the football game and in fact did not go, leaving the tickets unused? Explain.

c. Would your answer be different if $32 were paid for each ticket, while the usual admission charge were $20 per ticket? Explain.

17. **Charitable Contribution Deduction.** Place an *X* in the proper column to indicate whether each of the following gifts or other expenditures is deductible as a contribution, deductible but not as a contribution, or not deductible.

Item	Deductible Contribution	Deductible Noncontribution	Not Deductible
a. Cash to American Red Cross	X		
b. Pledge to church			X
c. Auto expense of church employee		X	
d. Cash to Girl Scouts of America	X		
e. Inherited land to American Legion	X		
f. Cash to political party			X
g. Cash to Library Association	X		
h. Clothing to Salvation Army	X		
i. Common stock to St. Mary's	X		
j. Cash to Brigham Young University	X		
k. U.S. Bond to Mayo Clinic	X		
l. Reading at Braille Institute (ten hours @ $5.75, minimum wage in state)			X
m. Auto expense for volunteer work with Cancer Society	X		

18. **Casualty Loss.** On May 10, 2005, Roy and Jane Wilde's home was damaged by a severe storm. The home had been purchased in 1980 for $73,000, excluding the cost of the land. The building's FMV just before the storm was $97,000, and its FMV after the storm was estimated at $79,000. The Wildes collected $15,000 in insurance proceeds, and their 2005 AGI is $22,000. This was their only casualty loss during the year.

a. Determine the amount that the Wildes can report as a casualty loss on Schedule A if they itemize their deductions for 2005.

b. The Wildes lived in a motel while their home was being repaired. The cost of living at the motel was $2,000 each month. Their normal living expenses are $900 per month, but only $500 of these expenses continued during the repair period. They were reimbursed at the rate of $1,900 per month for the three months they lived in the motel. How much of the reimbursement, if any, must they include in gross income?

19. Casualty Loss Deduction. Kevin and Jane Steel file a joint return each year. During 2005 their house was burglarized, and the following items were taken. Their AGI for 2005 is $20,000.

Item	Cost	FMV before Theft
Television set	$ 595	$ 375
Microwave oven	575	400
VCR	850	700
Jewelry	2,200	2,500

The Steels collected $500 from the insurance company. Prepare a worksheet showing the amount of the net casualty loss.

20. Itemized Deductions. Can each of the following payments be deducted from AGI (as an itemized deduction on Schedule A), assuming the amount is within any limitation applicable? Check "Yes" or "No" in the appropriate column. If deductible, indicate the number of the line on Schedule A where the amount would appear.

Item	Yes	No	Line Number
a. Payment to a convalescent home for a person physically incapable of self-care:			
(1) Meals	✓	—	I
(2) Lodging	✓	—	I
(3) Nursing care	✓	—	I
b. Interest paid on a note to purchase and carry municipal bonds	—	✓	—
c. Supplementary medical insurance premiums under Medicare	✓	—	I
d. Interest on a credit card	—	✓	—
e. Interest on a gambling debt	—	✓	—
f. Real estate taxes passed on to tenants in the form of a rent increase	—	✓	—
g. Interest paid on delinquent income tax	—	✓	—
h. Interest paid on a loan to purchase bonds of the City of Wilmington	—	✓	—
i. Finance charges paid on revolving credit	—	✓	—
j. Interest paid on a life insurance policy loan (The loan was used to buy a new convertible car.)	—	✓	—

21. **Internet Problem: Researching Instructions to Form 4684.** If a taxpayer experiences a loss from a deposit in a credit union that became financially insolvent, what options are available for recognizing this loss on the tax return?

    Go to the IRS Web site. Locate the Instructions for Form 4684 and find the solution to the above question.

    See Appendix A for instructions on use of the IRS Web site.

22. **Business Entity Problem: This problem is designed for those using the "business entity" approach. The solution may require information from Chapter 14.**

    A corporation has taxable income before consideration of charitable contributions of $350,000.

    a. If the corporation donates $50,000 to a recognized charity, what are the tax implications to the company?

    b. By what date must the corporation make its donation?

    c. If the above company is an S corporation, what are the tax implications of the charitable contribution to the company?

    d. If the above company was a partnership, what are the tax implications of the charitable contribution to the company?

23. **Business Entity Problem: This problem is designed for those using the "business entity" approach. The solution may require information from Chapter 14.**

    The Blasto Company, a proprietorship, lost its entire office building in a fire. The adjusted basis of the building was $800,000. Insurance proceeds were only $740,000. The company's taxable income before consideration of any casualty loss was $2,350,000. What amount, if any, may the company deduct as a casualty loss?

COMPREHENSIVE PROBLEM

24. John Saad (SSN 432-61-7809) and his wife Mary file a joint return. Their 2005 AGI is $162,000, including dividends and interest income of $5,000. The Saads assembled the following list of expenses:

Medical expenses	$14,300
Jacuzzi for John's aching back	2,500
Real estate taxes	4,400
Assessment for street repairs	1,200
State and local income taxes	4,800
Federal income tax	22,300
Sales taxes	785
Mortgage interest	5,200
Credit card interest	945
Investment interest	3,700
Charitable contributions (cash)	6,400
Uninsured damage to auto from accident	3,300

a. Prepare a worksheet showing the items the Saads may deduct on their Schedule A.

b. Prepare the Schedule A on the following page.

(Use for Problem 24.)

SCHEDULES A&B (Form 1040)	Schedule A—Itemized Deductions	OMB No. 1545-0074

SCHEDULES A&B
(Form 1040)

Department of the Treasury
Internal Revenue Service (99)

Schedule A—Itemized Deductions

(Schedule B is on back)

► **Attach to Form 1040.** ► **See Instructions for Schedules A and B (Form 1040).**

OMB No. 1545-0074

20**05**

Attachment
Sequence No. **07**

Name(s) shown on Form 1040

Your social security number

Medical and Dental Expenses		**Caution.** Do not include expenses reimbursed or paid by others.	
	1	Medical and dental expenses (see page A-2) . . .	**1**
	2	Enter amount from Form 1040, line 38 [**2**]	
	3	Multiply line 2 by 7.5% (.075)	**3**
	4	Subtract line 3 from line 1. If line 3 is more than line 1, enter -0-	**4**
Taxes You Paid (See page A-2.)	5	State and local **(check only one box):** a ☐ Income taxes, **or** b ☐ General sales taxes (see page A-2)	**5**
	6	Real estate taxes (see page A-3)	**6**
	7	Personal property taxes	**7**
	8	Other taxes. List type and amount ►	**8**
	9	Add lines 5 through 8	**9**
Interest You Paid (See page A-3.) **Note.** Personal interest is not deductible.	10	Home mortgage interest and points reported to you on Form 1098	**10**
	11	Home mortgage interest not reported to you on Form 1098. If paid to the person from whom you bought the home, see page A-4 and show that person's name, identifying no., and address ►	**11**
	12	Points not reported to you on Form 1098. See page A-4 for special rules	**12**
	13	Investment interest. Attach Form 4952 if required. (See page A-4.)	**13**
	14	Add lines 10 through 13	**14**
Gifts to Charity If you made a gift and got a benefit for it, see page A-4.	15	Gifts by cash or check. If you made any gift of $250 or more, see page A-4	**15**
	16	Other than by cash or check. If any gift of $250 or more, see page A-4. You **must** attach Form 8283 if over $500	**16**
	17	Carryover from prior year	**17**
	18	Add lines 15 through 17	**18**
Casualty and Theft Losses	19	Casualty or theft loss(es). Attach Form 4684. (See page A-5.)	**19**
Job Expenses and Most Other Miscellaneous Deductions (See page A-5.)	20	Unreimbursed employee expenses—job travel, union dues, job education, etc. Attach Form 2106 or 2106-EZ if required. (See page A-6.) ►	**20**
	21	Tax preparation fees	**21**
	22	Other expenses—investment, safe deposit box, etc. List type and amount ►	**22**
	23	Add lines 20 through 22	**23**
	24	Enter amount from Form 1040, line 38 [**24**]	
	25	Multiply line 24 by 2% (.02)	**25**
	26	Subtract line 25 from line 23. If line 25 is more than line 23, enter -0-	**26**
Other Miscellaneous Deductions	27	Other—from list on page A-6. List type and amount ►	**27**
Total Itemized Deductions	28	Is Form 1040, line 38, over $145,950 (over $72,975 if married filing separately)? ☐ **No.** Your deduction is not limited. Add the amounts in the far right column for lines 4 through 27. Also, enter this amount on Form 1040, line 40. ► ☐ **Yes.** Your deduction may be limited. See page A-6 for the amount to enter.	**28**
	29	If you elect to itemize deductions even though they are less than your standard deduction, check here ► ☐	

For Paperwork Reduction Act Notice, see Form 1040 instructions.   Cat. No. 11330X   **Schedule A (Form 1040) 2005**

6

Other Itemized Deductions

CHAPTER CONTENTS

■■ CHAPTER OVERVIEW

*C*hapter 5 examined itemized deductions that are somewhat personal in nature: medical expenses, taxes, interest, charitable contributions, and casualty and theft losses. This chapter focuses on the remaining itemized deductions: job-related expenses and miscellaneous deductions. It illustrates the flow of data from Form 2106, Employee Business Expenses, to Schedule A and then to Form 1040.

JOB EXPENSES AND MOST OTHER MISCELLANEOUS DEDUCTIONS

Schedule A allows for two types of miscellaneous deductions. One type is subject to a 2% floor; the other is not. This causes confusion. "Job Expenses and Most Other Miscellaneous Deductions" provides for job-related expenses of employees and any qualifying itemized deductions not reported elsewhere. Taxpayers must reduce the total of these miscellaneous expenses by 2% of the AGI before taking a deduction. Taxpayers report the net amount of these expenses on Schedule A (line 26).

While limiting most miscellaneous deductions to this 2% floor, the IRS allows some deductions in full: "Other Miscellaneous Deductions" (line 27). This book covers these specified deductions later in the chapter.

While most employees report the total amount of their job-related expenses on Schedule A, they use Form 2106 to compute their total expenses. A notable exception is the "statutory employee."

Statutory employees include full-time employees in the following occupations: outside salesperson, life insurance sales agent, certain agent-driver/commission-driver, and home-based piece-goods worker with income reported on a W-2. The tax law treats statutory employees as self-employed taxpayers. They deduct all work-related expenses on Schedule C. However, self-employment taxes do not apply since the employer and the employee must pay the FICA taxes through the tax withholding system. The employer alerts the IRS of this situation by checking the "Statutory Employee" box on the W-2. If the employer neglects to mark this box, the special treatment still applies when the taxpayer qualifies in all other respects.

EMPLOYEE BUSINESS EXPENSES, FORM 2106

Employees incurring job-related expenses may or may not receive reimbursements from their employers. However, they may deduct any unreimbursed expenses from AGI as miscellaneous itemized deductions by completing Form 2106. Treatment of reimbursed expenses depends on whether the reimbursement comes from an "accountable" or "nonaccountable" reimbursement plan.

Accountable Reimbursement Plans

Employees receiving reimbursements under an accountable plan do not report such payments as income. Employers do not include them on Form W-2. On the expense side, employees do not deduct reimbursed expenses on their tax returns. An exception arises when the expenses exceed the reimbursements received. Here, the taxpayer must show all expenses and reimbursements on Form 2106 in order to deduct the excess on Schedule A (Form 1040).

Accountable reimbursement plans must provide for each of the following requirements:

1. Employees must account for (substantiate) their expenses to the employer.
2. Employees must return any reimbursement in excess of the substantiated expenses covered under the arrangement.

Employee business expense records must include six elements:

1. Amount
2. Date
3. Place
4. Business purpose
5. Business relationship
6. Identity of individuals

When deducting business gifts, the employee must include a description of the item. To satisfy the requirement for written evidence, employees must keep a variety of records. The IRS will accept date books, diaries, logs, and trip sheets to verify travel and mileage. In order to support expenses, the employee must keep receipts and paid bills, canceled checks, expense reports, or detailed bookkeeping records. Generally, the IRS does not require documentary evidence for expenditures of less than $75. However, all payments for lodging require receipts. If the taxpayer loses any records, the IRS may accept written statements made by witnesses.

Nonaccountable Reimbursement Plans

If an employer reimbursement program does not require employees to substantiate their expenses or allows them to keep excess reimbursements, the arrangement is not an accountable plan. Under these plans, employers report reimbursements as wages on Form W-2, and employees include them as gross income on their tax return. Employees then deduct all expenses using Form 2106 and Schedule A. Even though these plans are "nonaccountable," taxpayers must still substantiate their expense claims.

Reimbursements under a nonaccountable plan are subject to income and FICA taxes. After taxes, the remaining reimbursement is less than the expense. In addition, some or all of the expense may be disallowed as a result of the 2% AGI rule. Accountable plans avoid taxation of the reimbursement and the 2% AGI limitation.

UNREIMBURSED EMPLOYEE BUSINESS EXPENSES REPORTED ON FORM 2106

- Vehicle(s) used for business
- Parking fees, tolls, and local transportation
- Travel while away from home, including lodging, airfare, car rental, etc.
- Other business expenses not included elsewhere on Form 2106
- Meals and entertainment

Vehicle Expenses

Under most circumstances, the taxpayer can choose to use either the standard mileage rate or actual expenses when using a vehicle for business purposes. Under both methods, the taxpayer reports three types of information on vehicle usage:

- Date the vehicle was first used for work
- Total miles driven during the year
- Total work-related miles driven

Taxpayers provide this information for each vehicle driven for business. The IRS also requires employees to respond to four specific questions on Form 2106:

1. Is another vehicle available for use?
2. Does the employer provide for personal use of the vehicle?
3. Does the taxpayer have evidence to support the deduction?
4. Is the evidence written?

Responding "No" to the third or fourth question may trigger an audit. If there is an audit, lack of evidence can result in the loss of the deductions.

Employee Transportation

Employees may deduct the cost of getting from one job location to another in the course of their employment. Normally, commuting costs, including parking at work and mileage to and from work, do not qualify as deductible work-related expenses. However, when a taxpayer has two jobs, the cost of getting from one job to the other is deductible. When taxpayers go home before going to the second job, they base their deduction on the distance between jobs. To claim a vehicle deduction, taxpayers must keep detailed records of their business mileage.

Standard Mileage Rate

In 2005 the standard mileage rate is 40.5 cents per mile (48.5 cents after August 31) for each business mile driven. The taxpayer must prove the business miles driven for all vehicles by using a detailed log book, an appointment book, or other similar record. When an employer reimburses an employee for all business miles at a rate in excess of 40.5 (48.5) cents per mile, the employee must report the difference in gross income. To take advantage of the standard mileage rate, the taxpayer cannot have used an accelerated depreciation method (ACRS, MACRS) or section 179 depreciation in prior years. (See Chapter 8 for depreciation.) People using the standard rate may also deduct parking and toll fees.

The standard mileage method requires taxpayers to reduce the adjusted basis of the vehicle using the following recovery rates for the total business miles driven each year. Taxpayers use the rate that applies to each year of business use.

Year	Rate Per Mile
2005	17.0 cents
2003–2004	16.0 cents
2001–2002	15.0 cents
2000	14.0 cents

Therefore, taxpayers compute the depreciation built into the standard mileage rates to adjust the vehicle's basis before a sale or exchange. The adjusted basis of the vehicle affects the gain or loss when sold or exchanged.

EXAMPLE 1

Win Yoshi, an employee, used a personal vehicle for work. During 2005, Yoshi drove 7,200 miles. This includes 1,800 miles for work, all of which occurred before September 1. Yoshi deducts $729 (1,800 × $.405) as vehicle expenses.

Actual Expenses

When the actual expenses exceed the standard rate, taxpayers can choose to use the actual costs of operating the vehicle(s). As always, taxpayers must maintain proper records and documents. To compute the deductible vehicle expenses, first determine the total expenses. Then multiply the total expenses by the percentage of business use to arrive at the total deductible vehicle expense.

Taxpayers compute depreciation using the regular depreciation methods. These methods include MACRS, which allows employees to take more depreciation in the earlier years of the vehicle's life. The "luxury automobile" rules restrict the total annual depreciation on vehicles. The listed property rules require using straight-line depreciation when the business use of the vehicle does not exceed 50%. The depreciation deduction is limited to the business use percentage times the listed property limits. (See Chapter 8.)

ITEMS INCLUDED IN DEDUCTIBLE VEHICLE EXPENSES

- Depreciation
- Lease and rental payments
- Gasoline, oil, and lubrications
- Insurance, license, and auto club fees
- Maintenance, repairs, and parts
- Personal property taxes
- Garage rent

Leasing

When leasing vehicles, employees may elect to use the standard mileage rate, or they may elect to deduct the entire business portion of the monthly lease payments, including the personal property tax and sales tax portions of the payment. When using the actual expense method, employees enter these amounts and any car rental costs incurred during repairs of the taxpayer's business vehicle on Form 2106 as "Vehicle rentals" (line 24a). The IRS, however, limits the benefit of deducting all business lease payments. It requires taxpayers to report an additional amount in gross income that effectively reduces the lease expense reported on Form 2106. This additional lease income brings the expense deduction for leasing an automobile closer to the automobile expenses allowed to vehicle owners. The IRS publishes the specific tables for this "lease income" in Publication 463 (see Chapter 8).

Parking Fees, Tolls, and Transportation That Do Not Involve Overnight Travel

In addition to vehicle expenses, employees can claim deductible parking and other transportation expenses regardless of whether the standard rate or the actual expense method of reporting is used. Employees using transportation in the course of business or work can deduct the costs of local transportation expenses. Deductible transportation expenses include the costs of parking (away from work), tolls, cab fares, buses, trains, airfares, and shuttles.

EXAMPLE 2

George Hoven spent $35 for work-related parking fees and tolls. Hoven deducts this amount on Form 2106.

Travel Expenses

Employee travel expenses include amounts paid or charged when an employee is temporarily away from home overnight for work-related reasons. "Temporary" absences from home are those not exceeding one year. Generally, travel expenses are not deductible when the absence exceeds one year. The IRS defines "home" as an employee's workplace, regardless of where the family lives. Travel expenses include all transportation costs, plus lodging and the incidental costs incurred while away from home. Employees can deduct meals purchased while traveling (subject to the same 50% limitation as other meals and entertainment). A spouse's travel expenses are deducted only when the spouse actually works during the bulk of the trip. The spouse must also work for the same employer. For instance, when an employee goes to a trade show and the spouse comes along to work in the booth, both employees deduct their total travel expenses.

EXAMPLE 3

Kathy Knott's travel expenses included airfare $120, hotel $75, car rental $35, meals $150, and a bathing suit $25. Knott's total travel expenses amount to $230 ($120 + $75 + $35). Knott deducts the $150 cost of meals with other meals and entertainment, which are only 50% deductible. The bathing suit does not qualify as a travel expense.

Per Diem Option

Instead of keeping receipts for all travel expenses, the employee can use the IRS's per diem rates for travel. Taxpayers automatically substantiate the amount of their expenses when using this approach. However, they must still provide the other five record-keeping elements.

When the employer's per diem allowance is less than or equal to the allowable federal rate, the employee has no income to report. The allowance will not appear on Form W-2. This is true even if the employee's actual expenses are less than the allowance received. The excess is not taxable, and the employee does not have to return the excess. However, when the employer's per diem allowance exceeds the federal rate, the employer reports the excess as compensation to the employee on Form W-2.

When the reimbursement is less than or equal to the federal rate and the actual expenses do not exceed the reimbursement, employees do not report the reimbursement or the expenses on their tax returns. If the actual expenses exceed the reimbursement, employees may deduct the excess on Schedule A (Form 1040) by filling out Form 2106, reporting all expenses and reimbursements. In this situation, employees must be able to prove the amounts of their expenses.

Employees who do not receive reimbursements may claim the federal per diem for meals as the amount of their meal expenses instead of deducting their actual meal costs. Unfortunately, the standard lodging allowance cannot be used for this purpose. Only the actual cost of lodging is deductible. Use of the per diem meal allowance as a measure of the meal expense also applies to self-employed individuals. However, taxpayers related to the employer may not use the per diem approach as substantiation of their expenses. They must be able to prove the amounts of all their expenses. Related parties include employers and close family employees and companies in which the employee owns more than a 10% interest. Interestingly, self-employed individuals may use the per diem system, but if they incorporate their business, they become related parties (own over 10% interest) and cannot use this method to substantiate expenses.

The IRS allows employers to reimburse employees' travel using a **per diem** (flat amount per day) that covers the costs of meals, lodging, and incidentals. (A separate rate applies to vehicle costs.) Upon selection of the per diem method, the employee must use it for all travel throughout the year. While numerous per diem rates are available, the IRS has established a simplified High-Low method using two rates, one for large, high-cost cities or counties and another for other locations. The high per diem of $199 includes $46 for meals. The low per diem of $127 includes $36 for meals. Since the per diem rates include the value of meals, taxpayers using Form 2106 must split the daily rate between line 3, travel, and line 5, meals and entertainment. Only one-half of the meal allowance is deductible.

Business and Pleasure

Employees who combine business and pleasure on the same trip face limits on the deduction. There are different limits for trips within the United States and foreign travel. When traveling in the United States on a trip primarily for business (more than 50% work-related activity), employees deduct 100% of the travel expenses to and from the destination. At destination they deduct only the work-related expenses (lodging, meals, and local transportation for work days only). On 50% or less work-related trips, employees deduct only the work-related expenses. They do not deduct any airfare or other traveling costs expended to get to and from their destination.

> When counting business and personal days, weekends and holidays count as business days if a business day precedes and follows the weekend or holiday If this condition is not met, the weekend, or holiday, counts as personal time.

On trips involving travel outside the United States, the employee must separate the business and personal portions of the trip. The employee divides the business and personal costs based on the time devoted to each activity. For instance, trips composed of 40% personal activities permit the employee to deduct only 60% of the total travel expenses. However, if the trip is primarily personal, no travel expenses to and from destination are deductible. Any of the following three conditions eliminates the need to allocate travel expenses to and from destination: (1) The employee has no control over arranging the trip and there is no element of vacation. (2) The employee travels away from home for less than eight days. (3) The personal portion of the trip is less than 25%. Business days include days devoted to travel when the travel days immediately precede or follow a business day.

EXAMPLE 4

Edward Santiago attends a trade show in Paris that begins on Tuesday and ends on Friday, with no meetings on Wednesday or Thursday. Santiago travels to the trade show on Monday and returns home on Saturday. The trip lasts less than eight days. Therefore, the trip qualifies as a deductible business trip, and all qualified travel expenses to and from destination are deductible.

Special rules apply for travel outside of North America. The IRS defines North America as the United States and its possessions, the Trust Territories, Canada, and Mexico. For an employee to deduct expenses for traveling to conventions outside the North American area, the meeting must meet the following two qualifications:

1. The convention must be directly related to the employee's job.
2. It must be as reasonable to hold the meeting outside North America as within.

Meals and Entertainment Expenses

Taxpayers may deduct 50% of all qualified meals and entertainment expenses. Two categories of meals and entertainment exist: (1) while doing business with clients and associates and (2) while traveling. In the first instance, only costs defined as either **directly related to** or **associated with** business qualify as deductions. **Directly related to** means that the meal or entertainment takes place during a business discussion. **Associated with** means that the event takes place immediately before or after a business meeting.

Taxpayers can deduct the costs of qualified meals and entertainment. However, the IRS does not permit deductions for extravagant costs. For meals to be deductible, the IRS requires the taxpayer's presence at the event. Paying for a professional dinner meeting and not attending it does not qualify the expense for a deduction. This rule does not apply to other forms of entertainment (e.g., tickets to the theater or sporting events). Here, the taxpayer does not need to be present. When taking a deduction, only the business portion of meals and entertainment is deductible.

EXAMPLE 5

Janet Johanssen spent $250 on meals and entertainment while away from home overnight on a business trip. Of that, Johanssen spent $100 on family members' meals. Johanssen deducts $150 ($250 − $100) as the business meal and entertainment expense. After applying the 50% limitation, Johanssen shows a net deduction for meals of $75 on Form 2106.

Employees often receive supper money when required to work overtime. Supper money is not reimbursement or gross income. However, when paid as a disguised form of compensation, the supper money becomes taxable.

The IRS does not allow a deduction for the practice of taking turns paying for meals or entertainment. Also, the Internal Revenue Code does not permit deductions for dues paid to various clubs and societies. The entities whose dues are not deductible include business, social, athletic, luncheon, and sporting clubs, as well as airline and hotel clubs. However, taxpayers may deduct some of the country club usage as a valid meal or entertainment expense. In addition, dues paid to professional, civic, and public service organizations (e.g., Lions, Kiwanis, Rotary) are deductible.

EXAMPLE 6

Ralph Platt gathers together receipts for employee business expenses. The totals consist of $150 meals and entertainment, $522 vehicle expenses, $35 transportation costs, and $230 travel, with no employer reimbursements. The employee business deduction on Form 2106 consists of the following amounts:

Total meals and entertainment	$150	
Less 50% limitation	(75)	
Deductible meals and entertainment		$ 75
Travel		230
Transportation		35
Vehicle expenses		522
Total employee business expenses		$862

Other Business Expenses Not Included Elsewhere on Form 2106

The other business expense category offers a variety of tax reduction opportunities. Designed primarily for the salesperson, Form 2106 also provides room for employees to deduct work-related expenses having nothing to do with sales.

Union Dues

Employees can pay deductible union dues and initiation fees either directly or through payroll deductions. If the payroll deduction includes specific retirement or savings plan contributions paid to the union by the employee, they are not included in the deductible union dues.

Licenses and Insurance

Taxpayers deduct malpractice, errors and omissions, and other professional insurance as other business expenses. Licenses include nursing licenses, hair stylist licenses, health department certifications, and any other professional licenses.

Uniforms and Safety Equipment

Employees deduct costs of special protective clothing and devices required for safety purposes as other business deductions. Hard hats, gloves, goggles, back supports, and steel-toed shoes not provided by the employer all qualify. Employees may also deduct the costs of uniforms specifically designed for the job or industry when the employer requires clothing not suitable for everyday wear. Garments suitable for general wear or street wear do not qualify as uniforms. Thus, no deduction results.

Employee Physical

Some employers require personnel to take annual physicals at the employees' own expense. The employee deducts the cost as a miscellaneous business expense, not as a medical expense.

Equipment, Telephones, and Computers

For an employee to deduct the cost of capital equipment, the employer must have a written policy requiring the items as standard job tools. All other employees of the same company doing the same or similar work must have the same equipment requirements. Employees must depreciate capital equipment with a useful life in excess of one year. Employees do not deduct the costs of capital assets directly on Form 2106. They use Form 4562 (Depreciation and Amortization) to report the costs of employees' telephone, computer, or other equipment.

EXAMPLE 7

Joseph Amir buys a home computer for the convenience of working at home at night. Amir prefers not to stay late at the office. Amir may not deduct depreciation on the computer. The IRS considers the purchase of the computer as simply for the employee's convenience.

Other equipment falling in this category includes cellular telephones, complete toolkits, videotape equipment, fax machines, and answering machines. After determining the depreciation deduction on Form 4562, the taxpayer carries the total allowable depreciation to Form 2106 as an other business expense.

Supplies

Employees may deduct office supplies, copying, organizers and other low-cost business supplies. This category also includes watches, calculators, and briefcases, depending on the job requirements. Each industry has its own version of supplies. For instance, construction workers include disposable masks and small tools.

Education

An employee's education must meet one of two conditions in order to qualify as an employee business expense:

1. The employer, the law, or professional standards must require the education or courses.
2. The education or courses must maintain or improve the employee's present skills for the employee's present job.

Generally, taxpayers must be employed or self-employed to claim a deduction for education expenses. Two conditions bar the deduction. First, the employee uses the courses to meet the minimum requirements of a present job. Second, the courses lead to a degree that qualifies the employee for a new trade or business. The IRS closely monitors the education deductions to determine if either of these two disqualifying conditions exists.

EXAMPLE 8

Brian Seth, a junior accountant with an A.A. in accounting, works for a CPA firm as a tax preparer. Seth attended Grover State College to work toward a B.A. in accounting. Seth performed the same job before and after receiving the B.A. degree. Seth may not deduct the education expenses because the degree qualifies him for another line of work.

Expenses eligible for the education deduction include tuition, books, supplies, lab fees, transportation costs, and costs of travel to seminars. Instructors and students may not deduct expenses incurred for travel as a form of education (e.g., a trip to France to study the culture).

Unless the taxpayer is self-employed or an employee, education expenses are nondeductible personal expenses. People who use a "temporary leave of absence" to pursue their education on a full-time basis are treated as maintaining their employee or business status. This holds true even if they take another job after completing their courses.

Job or Employment Search

Many taxpayers spend a great deal of time and money job hunting. Job seekers may deduct the costs of looking for a position or work in a comparable career or in the same line of employment. Neither first-time job seekers nor someone returning to the work force after a long absence can deduct the costs of the search. The job search deduction includes the cost of career counseling when used to find employment in the same trade or business. Even if the search is unsuccessful, qualified job search expenses fulfill the requirements for the miscellaneous deduction. Deductible costs include mileage, resumes, travel, postage, office supplies, printing, employment agency fees, telephones, and job counseling.

Office in Home

Under very limited circumstances, some employees qualify to take a deduction for working at home. The employee must use a specific portion of the residence exclusively and on a regular basis for work. The employee must maintain an office area as either the principal place of work or the place where the employee regularly meets with clients. In addition, the employee must work at home for the convenience of the employer. According to the IRS, for "the convenience of the employer" does not mean when appropriate or helpful. The office-in-home deduction would apply if an employee worked for a company that did not have an office in the employee's town but needed a representative in that area. (See Chapter 7 for more on this topic.)

EXAMPLE 9

Kimberly Kim teaches school 25 hours a week at Public School 51. Kim spends another 35 hours a week in the office at home grading tests, writing assignments, and developing lesson plans. While her work at home is essential and time-consuming, Kim cannot deduct the cost of the office at home. Working at home is simply more convenient for her.

People using their home office to carry out investment activities do not qualify for a home office deduction.

Information for Figure 6-1: Filled-In Form 2106

Art McBurney is a district manager for the Drake Corporation. McBurney took a five-day business trip for his employer in November. The Drake Corporation operates an accountable reimbursement plan. However, it does not reimburse all expenses. It reimbursed McBurney only for his direct expense incurred in meeting with a client (**$95**) and for air travel (**$210**). McBurney was expected to pay his own meals (**$140**) and lodging (**$250**) and other transportation (taxi) expenses (**$12**), totaling $402. In addition to this trip, McBurney drove his personal automobile on business a total of **23,840** miles of the **34,060** miles driven. Of the 23,840 business miles, 18,000 miles were driven before September 1. His commuting miles were **2,500,** and he started using his car for business on **January 2, 2004.** Employer reimbursement of **$9,655** (at 40.5 cents per mile) had been received for mileage. Reimbursements from his employer of **$9,960** ($9,655 + $95 + $210) were not included on McBurney's Form W-2. Parking fees and tolls paid for business totaled **$445.**

McBurney elects to claim the standard mileage deduction rather than the actual vehicle expenses. Since the reimbursement was paid under an accountable arrangement, only McBurney's excess employee expenses are deductible as a miscellaneous itemized deduction subject to the 2%-of-AGI rule.

MISCELLANEOUS DEDUCTIONS REPORTED ON SCHEDULE A (LINES 21 AND 22)

Schedule A also provides a place to deduct a variety of other allowable expenses. These expenses are added to employee business expenses. The taxpayer then reduces total miscellaneous deductions (line 23) by 2% of AGI. The three primary categories of other nonbusiness expense include the following:

1. Expenses paid to generate or collect income
2. Costs to manage, conserve, or operate income-producing property
3. Amounts spent to determine, contest, pay, or claim a refund of any tax

Taxpayers can deduct only expenses relating to the income they generate or the property they own. Also, taxpayers deduct the expenses related to producing interest, dividend, and other investment income. When added to other allowable expenses, small totals in each miscellaneous expense category might produce enough of a deduction to overcome the 2% limitation.

In recent years, many areas of the United States have experienced an assortment of disasters. As a result, many taxpayers have learned about documentation rules relating to casualty losses. Ensuring the deductibility of losses requires objective verification of the assets' costs. Taxpayers incur appraisal and other evaluation expenses. They deduct these expenses as miscellaneous expenses on Schedule A, not as a part of the casualty loss.

Taxpayers often employ competent tax professionals to respond to IRS, state, or local tax agency inquiries or to represent them in audits. Tax professionals also deal with refund claims and contested tax bills. Often they will also give advice on the tax aspects of a divorce, a property sale, or a financial plan. Taxpayers combine all costs associated with tax representation and tax advice under other miscellaneous deductions. Other deductible tax preparation fees include the costs of electronic filing, certified postage for tax return mailing, and tax software. The cost of refund anticipation loans is not deductible.

EXAMPLE 10

Leroy Lerner buys Quicken for $50 for personal bookkeeping. Though paying a tax professional to prepare the tax return, Lerner buys Turbo Tax for $50 to do tax projections during the year. Lerner also subscribes to *Money Magazine,* the *Wall Street Journal,* and *Value Line* for a total of $400. The deductible investment expenses total $500, before the 2% limitation.

FIGURE 6-1   Filled-In form 2106, Page 1

Form **2106**	**Employee Business Expenses**	OMB No. 1545-0139
Department of the Treasury Internal Revenue Service (99)	▶ See separate instructions. ▶ Attach to Form 1040.	20**05** Attachment Sequence No. **54**

Your name	Occupation in which you incurred expenses	Social security number
Art McBurney		727 22 7134

Part I   Employee Business Expenses and Reimbursements

Step 1   Enter Your Expenses

		Column A Other Than Meals and Entertainment	Column B Meals and Entertainment
1	Vehicle expense from line 22 or line 29. (Rural mail carriers: See instructions.) **1**	10,122 00	
2	Parking fees, tolls, and transportation, including train, bus, etc., that **did not** involve overnight travel or commuting to and from work . . **2**	445 00	
3	Travel expense while away from home overnight, including lodging, airplane, car rental, etc. **Do not** include meals and entertainment. **3**	472 00	
4	Business expenses not included on lines 1 through 3. **Do not** include meals and entertainment. **4**	95 00	
5	Meals and entertainment expenses (see instructions) **5**		140 00
6	**Total expenses.** In Column A, add lines 1 through 4 and enter the result. In Column B, enter the amount from line 5 . . . . . . **6**	11,134 00	140 00

Note: *If you were not reimbursed for any expenses in Step 1, skip line 7 and enter the amount from line 6 on line 8.*

Step 2   Enter Reimbursements Received From Your Employer for Expenses Listed in Step 1

7	Enter reimbursements received from your employer that were **not** reported to you in box 1 of Form W-2. Include any reimbursements reported under code "L" in box 12 of your Form W-2 (see instructions) **7**	9,960 00	

Step 3   Figure Expenses To Deduct on Schedule A (Form 1040)

8	Subtract line 7 from line 6. If zero or less, enter -0-. However, if line 7 is greater than line 6 in Column A, report the excess as income on Form 1040, line 7 . . . . **8**	1,174 00	140 00
	Note: *If* **both** *columns of line 8 are zero, you cannot deduct employee business expenses. Stop here and attach Form 2106 to your return.*		
9	In Column A, enter the amount from line 8. In Column B, multiply line 8 by 50% (.50). (Employees subject to Department of Transportation (DOT) hours of service limits: Multiply meal expenses incurred while away from home on business by 70% (.70) instead of 50%. For details, see instructions.) **9**	1,174 00	70 00
10	Add the amounts on line 9 of both columns and enter the total here. **Also, enter the total on Schedule A (Form 1040), line 20.** (Reservists, qualified performing artists, fee-basis state or local government officials, and individuals with disabilities: See the instructions for special rules on where to enter the total.) . . . . ▶ **10**		1,244 00

For Paperwork Reduction Act Notice, see instructions.	Cat. No. 11700N	Form **2106** (2005)

FIGURE 6-1 Filled-In form 2106, Page 2

Form 2106 (2005)		Page **2**

Part II Vehicle Expenses

Section A—General Information (You must complete this section if you are claiming vehicle expenses.)

			(a) Vehicle 1	**(b)** Vehicle 2
11	Enter the date the vehicle was placed in service	11	01 /02/ 04	/ /
12	Total miles the vehicle was driven during 2005	12	34,060 miles	miles
13	Business miles included on line 12	13	23,840 miles	miles
14	Percent of business use. Divide line 13 by line 12	14	70 %	%
15	Average daily roundtrip commuting distance.	15	10 miles	miles
16	Commuting miles included on line 12	16	2,500 miles	miles
17	Other miles. Add lines 13 and 16 and subtract the total from line 12 .	17	7,720 miles	miles
18	Do you (or your spouse) have another vehicle available for personal use?		☒ Yes ☐ No
19	Was your vehicle available for personal use during off-duty hours?		☒ Yes ☐ No
20	Do you have evidence to support your deduction?		☒ Yes ☐ No
21	If "Yes," is the evidence written?		☒ Yes ☐ No

Section B—Standard Mileage Rate (See the instructions for Part II to find out whether to complete this section or Section C.)

22	Multiply line 13 by 40.5¢ (.405)	22	10,122 00*

Section C—Actual Expenses

			(a) Vehicle 1		**(b)** Vehicle 2	
23	Gasoline, oil, repairs, vehicle insurance, etc. . .	23				
24a	Vehicle rentals	24a				
b	Inclusion amount (see instructions) .	24b				
c	Subtract line 24b from line 24a .	24c				
25	Value of employer-provided vehicle (applies only if 100% of annual lease value was included on Form W-2—see instructions)	25				
26	Add lines 23, 24c, and 25 . .	26				
27	Multiply line 26 by the percentage on line 14 . . .	27				
28	Depreciation (see instructions) .	28				
29	Add lines 27 and 28. Enter total here and on line 1	29				

Section D—Depreciation of Vehicles (Use this section only if you owned the vehicle and are completing Section C for the vehicle.)

			(a) Vehicle 1		**(b)** Vehicle 2	
30	Enter cost or other basis (see instructions)	30				
31	Enter section 179 deduction (see instructions)	31				
32	Multiply line 30 by line 14 (see instructions if you claimed the section 179 deduction or special allowance)	32				
33	Enter depreciation method and percentage (see instructions) .	33				
34	Multiply line 32 by the percentage on line 33 (see instructions) . .	34				
35	Add lines 31 and 34	35				
36	Enter the applicable limit explained in the line 36 instructions . . .	36				
37	Multiply line 36 by the percentage on line 14 . . .	37				
38	Enter the **smaller** of line 35 or line 37. If you skipped lines 36 and 37, enter the amount from line 35. Also enter this amount on line 28 above .	38				

✿ *Printed on recycled paper*   Form **2106** (2005)

* 18,000 miles	×	$.405	=	$ 7,290
5,840 miles	×	$.485	=	2,832
Total deduction				$10,122

Hobby Losses

One area of activity producing a miscellaneous deduction is hobbies. When an activity has elements of both personal pleasure and profit, the question often arises as to whether the taxpayer had a profit motive. The presence of a profit motive affects the amount of expenses taxpayers deduct as well as where on the return they deduct them. Taxpayers who enter into an activity expecting to make a profit can deduct all expenses from the activity as a deduction for AGI. In contrast, expenses from an activity in which the taxpayer did not have a profit motive (a hobby) can be deducted as a miscellaneous itemized deduction (subject to the 2% rule) to the extent of income from the activity.

Of the expenses related to the hobby activity, taxpayers would deduct expenses like home mortgage interest, property taxes, and casualty losses, even if the hobby activity did not exist. Other expenses, like supplies, utilities, insurance, and depreciation, are deductible only because of tax laws that allow taxpayers to deduct them against hobby income. The hobby loss rules limit the taxpayer's deduction for these otherwise nondeductible expenses to the gross income from the hobby activity minus the expenses deductible elsewhere on the return. Any disallowed expenses are lost and cannot be carried over to future years.

EXAMPLE 11

Rob Gray paints pictures as a hobby. Gray does his painting in a separate studio located in his home. During the year, Gray sold some paintings for $2,300. His expenses totaled $3,025 and consisted of $400 for real estate taxes on the studio, $1,125 for utilities, and $1,500 for painting supplies.

Gross income		$2,300
Less expenses deductible whether or not the activity is a hobby (real estate taxes)		(400)
Maximum "other expenses" allowed		$1,900
"Other expenses" related to the hobby:		
Utilities	$1,125	
Painting supplies	1,500	
Total "other expenses"	$2,625	
Deductible "other expenses"		(1,900)
Net hobby income or loss		$ 0

Gray reports the gross income from the hobby ($2,300) as "Other Income" on Form 1040. On Schedule A, Gray deducts the $400 of real estate taxes and the remaining $1,900 of "Other Expenses" as a miscellaneous itemized deduction. Gray adds the $1,900 to other miscellaneous deductions, subject to the 2% AGI rule, and reduces the total by 2% of AGI. Gray cannot deduct the $725 of painting supplies and utilities that exceed $1,900 ($2,625 − $1,900 = $725).

EXAMPLE 12

Assume the same facts as in Example 11 except that Gray's activity has a profit motive. In this case, Gray reports $2,300 as income and deducts the entire $3,025 of expenses on Schedule C. Gray carries the net loss of $725 to Form 1040, page 1 (line 12) to offset other income items.

Unlike hobby losses, losses from a profit activity can be used to offset other income. The drawback of having an activity treated as a hobby should help explain why taxpayers make every effort to treat an activity as a business. The fact that a taxpayer enjoys an activity does not prevent it from being profitable. The burden of proving whether an activity is engaged in for profit generally rests with the taxpayer. However, the burden of proof shifts to the IRS for an activity that shows a profit in any three of five consecutive years (two of seven for activities involving horses). When this happens, it is assumed that a profit motive exists, and the IRS must prove that the activity is a hobby.

Taxpayers involved in an activity for less than three years may elect to postpone any challenge from the IRS until after completion of the first five years. This gives taxpayers the opportunity to show a profit in three of those years and shift the burden of proof to the IRS. However, filing such an election may alert the IRS to a possible hobby activity. Factors the IRS considers in deciding whether an activity is a business or a hobby include the following:

1. The taxpayer's expertise in the area
2. Whether the taxpayer keeps separate books and records for the activity
3. Whether the activity showed profits in some years and losses in others
4. The amount of occasional profits the taxpayer earned from the activity
5. The relative amount of pleasure the taxpayer derives from the activity
6. The extent to which the taxpayer depends on the activity for financial support
7. The time and effort the taxpayer devotes to the activity
8. The taxpayer's past success with other activities
9. The taxpayer's expectation that the property used in the activity will rise in value

When taxpayers use the standard deduction, all hobby loss deductions are lost. Thus, all of the gross income from the hobby is taxed.

ILLUSTRATIONS OF OTHER EXPENSES (LINE 22)

- Safe deposit box
- Investment advice
- Subscriptions to financial newspapers, financial newsletters, mutual fund reports, financial magazines, etc.
- Investment fees
- Investment seminars and conventions
- Financial planners
- Clerical help, office expenses, and postage
- Collection fees
- Legal, accounting, and related software
- Bank/trustee costs for investment or retirement plans
- Limited depreciation on computer used for investment
- Appraisal fees for casualty loss or charitable contributions
- Repayment of excess social security received
- Trustee's commission to administer a revocable trust

OTHER MISCELLANEOUS DEDUCTIONS, SCHEDULE A (LINE 27)

Taxpayers report the following expenses as "Other Miscellaneous Deductions" (line 27). The law exempts these deductions from the 2% limitation:

- Gambling losses to the extent of gambling income
- Impairment-related work expenses
- Federal estate taxes on income in respect of a decedent
- Repayment under claim of right doctrine
- Certain unrecovered investments in pension plans

Gambling Losses

The use of the gambling loss deduction increases as more states allow various forms of gaming. Taxpayers report gross gambling winnings on Form 1040, page 1, as "Other income." Taxpayers then deduct their gambling losses up to the amount of their reported winnings as an itemized deduction. The taxpayer does not subtract the losses from the winnings before reporting the winnings as income. Taxpayers lose the gambling deduction if they do not itemize deductions.

EXAMPLE 13

In several trips to Boardwalk, Phillip Newman lost $8,000 playing blackjack and poker. However, on the state lottery, Newman won $4,500. Newman reports the $4,500 lottery winnings as "Other Income" on Form 1040. Of the gambling losses, Newman reports only $4,500 on Schedule A (line 27). Newman cannot report the other $3,500 of gambling losses anywhere. (The standard deduction for married filing jointly is $10,000 for 2005. The Newman family cannot take advantage of any deduction for the gambling loss unless their total itemized deductions exceed $10,000.)

Impairment-Related Work Expenses

The IRS defines an impairment as a physical or mental disability that limits a taxpayer's employment or other activity. Impairments include those limiting vision, hearing, or movement. When impaired taxpayers purchase special tools or devices to make it possible to work, they deduct the costs directly on Schedule A (line 27). Taxpayers need not use Form 4562 to depreciate the special purchases. Deductible expenses include modifications to computers, special listening devices, and reading devices like the Xerox Reading Edge.

Nondeductible Expenses

Over the years, some taxpayers have become accustomed to taking deductions for certain expenses that are not deductible. A list of a few of these nondeductible expenses follows:

- Adoption costs (may qualify for a tax credit)
- Funeral costs, including the lot
- Election campaigning
- Political contributions
- Personal bank fees

- Parking tickets and fines
- Hobby losses in excess of income
- Personal rent, insurance, repairs, and telephone
- Illegal bribes and kickbacks
- Life insurance premiums
- Personal disability insurance
- Losses from sale of the taxpayer's home, car, or furniture
- Costs of meals while working late

Information for Figure 6-2: Filled-In Schedule A (Form 1040)

Gary and Nancy Redlin have **$91,517** of AGI. They use the following substantiated information to determine their itemized deductions on Schedule A.

- Medical and dental expenses paid
  (not compensated by insurance) **$7,466**
- Income and property taxes:
  - State of Wisconsin income taxes **1,730**
  - Real estate taxes paid on residence **2,858**
  - Personal property taxes **96**
- Interest on home mortgage **1,426**
- Charitable contributions:
  - Gifts by cash or check **1,287**
  - Noncash clothing and furniture to Thrift Shop $160
  - Use of personal automobile for church business
    (150 miles × 14 cents per mile, standard rate) 21
  - Other than by cash or check $181 **181**
  - Carryover from prior year **200**
- Casualty and theft losses:
  - Property damage sustained as the result
    of an automobile collision:
  - FMV of loss (less than cost basis) $5,734
  - Less insurance proceeds (2,000)
  - Balance $3,734
  - Less (100)
  - Balance $3,634
  - Less 10% of $91,517 (9,152)
  - Deductible casualty loss $ 0 **0**
- Miscellaneous itemized deductions:
  - Unreimbursed employee expenses (reported
    on Form 2106) **1,850**
  - 2004 income tax preparation fee **400**
  - Safe deposit box rent $ 50
  - Subscriptions to investment periodicals 273
  - Other expenses ($50 + $273) $ 323 **323**

FIGURE 6-2 Filled-In Schedule A (Form 1040)

SCHEDULES A&B	**Schedule A—Itemized Deductions**	OMB No. 1545-0074
(Form 1040)	(Schedule B is on back)	2005
Department of the Treasury Internal Revenue Service (99) Form 1040	▶ **Attach to Form 1040.** ▶ **See Instructions for Schedules A and B (Form 1040).**	Attachment Sequence No. 07

Name(s) shown on Form 1040: Gary B. and Nancy L. Redlin
Your social security number: 272 11 8345

Medical and Dental Expenses		**Caution.** Do not include expenses reimbursed or paid by others.			
	1	Medical and dental expenses (see page A-2)	1	7,466 00	
	2	Enter amount from Form 1040, line 38	2	91,517 00	
	3	Multiply line 2 by 7.5% (.075)	3	6,864 00	
	4	Subtract line 3 from line 1. If line 3 is more than line 1, enter -0-	4		602 00
Taxes You Paid (See page A-2.)	5	State and local (**check only one box**): a ☒ Income taxes, **or** b ☐ General sales taxes (see page A-2)	5	1,730 00	
	6	Real estate taxes (see page A-3)	6	2,858 00	
	7	Personal property taxes	7	96 00	
	8	Other taxes. List type and amount ▶	8	0	
	9	Add lines 5 through 8	9		4,684 00
Interest You Paid (See page A-3.)	10	Home mortgage interest and points reported to you on Form 1098	10	1,426 00	
	11	Home mortgage interest not reported to you on Form 1098. If paid to the person from whom you bought the home, see page A-4 and show that person's name, identifying no., and address ▶	11		
Note. Personal interest is not deductible.	12	Points not reported to you on Form 1098. See page A-4 for special rules	12		
	13	Investment interest. Attach Form 4952 if required. (See page A-4.)	13		
	14	Add lines 10 through 13	14		1,426 00
Gifts to Charity If you made a gift and got a benefit for it, see page A-4.	15	Gifts by cash or check. If you made any gift of $250 or more, see page A-4	15	1,287 00	
	16	Other than by cash or check. If any gift of $250 or more, see page A-4. You **must** attach Form 8283 if over $500	16	181 00	
	17	Carryover from prior year	17	200 00	
	18	Add lines 15 through 17	18		1,668 00
Casualty and Theft Losses	19	Casualty or theft loss(es). Attach Form 4684. (See page A-5.)	19		0
Job Expenses and Most Other Miscellaneous Deductions (See page A-5.)	20	Unreimbursed employee expenses—job travel, union dues, job education, etc. Attach Form 2106 or 2106-EZ if required. (See page A-6.) ▶	20	1,850 00	
	21	Tax preparation fees	21	400 00	
	22	Other expenses—investment, safe deposit box, etc. List type and amount ▶ Safe Deposit 50 Periodicals 273	22	323 00	
	23	Add lines 20 through 22	23	2,573 00	
	24	Enter amount from Form 1040, line 38	24	91,517 00	
	25	Multiply line 24 by 2% (.02)	25	1,830 00	
	26	Subtract line 25 from line 23. If line 25 is more than line 23, enter -0-	26		743 00
Other Miscellaneous Deductions	27	Other—from list on page A-6. List type and amount ▶	27		
Total Itemized Deductions	28	Is Form 1040, line 38, over $145,950 (over $72,975 if married filing separately)? ☒ **No.** Your deduction is not limited. Add the amounts in the far right column for lines 4 through 27. Also, enter this amount on Form 1040, line 40. ▶ ☐ **Yes.** Your deduction may be limited. See page A-6 for the amount to enter.	28		9,123 00
	29	If you elect to itemize deductions even though they are less than your standard deduction, check here ▶ ☐			

For Paperwork Reduction Act Notice, see Form 1040 instructions. Cat. No. 11330X **Schedule A (Form 1040) 2005**

[handwritten note in left margin: Remaining half of post-tax retirement contribution taken by wife after husband's death]

[watermark: Draft as of 06/06/2005]

FORM 1040 ILLUSTRATED

Taxpayers who choose to itemize deductions must use Form 1040. They determine AGI on page 1 of this two-page form. On page 2, they compute their refund or tax due using the following basic format:

	AGI
−	Itemized or standard deduction
−	Exemptions
=	Taxable income
×	Taxable income rate (or Tax Table)
=	Tax liability before:
+	Additions to tax
−	Credit to tax (including tax payments)
=	Final tax due (refund)

 ## Information for Figure 6-3: Filled-In Form 1040, Pages 1 and 2

Gary and Nancy Redlin elect to itemize deductions and file a joint return using the following amounts.

Neither is a participant in an employer's pension program.

Other Information

- Wages, **$87,000** (Gary, $55,000; Nancy, $32,000) (source: Form W-2)
- Taxable interest, **$1,913** (source: Form 1099-INT)
- Taxable refund, **$342** (source: 2004 state income tax return)
- Short-term capital gain, **$250** (source: Schedule D)
- Net rent from apartments, **$5,212** (source: Schedule E)
- Door prize, **$800** (source: Form 1099-MISC)
- IRA deduction, **$4,000** (personal decision)
- Itemized deductions, **$9,123** (source: Schedule A)
- Child care credit, **$1,200** (source: Form 2441)
- Child tax credit, **$2,000** (2 children × $1,000)
- Federal income tax withheld, **$7,200** (Gary, $5,200; Nancy, $2,000) (source: Form W-2)

FIGURE 6-3 Filled-In Form 1040, Page 1

Form 1040 Department of the Treasury—Internal Revenue Service
U.S. Individual Income Tax Return **2005** (99) IRS Use Only—Do not write or staple in this space.

For the year Jan. 1–Dec. 31, 2005, or other tax year beginning , 2005, ending , 20 OMB No. 1545-0074

Label (See instructions on page 16.) **Use the IRS label.** Otherwise, please print or type.

Your first name and initial: Gary R.   Last name: Redlin   Your social security number: 272 11 8245

If a joint return, spouse's first name and initial: Nancy L.   Last name: Redlin   Spouse's social security number: 369 41 3822

Home address (number and street). If you have a P.O. box, see page 16.: 1438 East Second Street   Apt. no.

▲ You **must** enter your SSN(s) above. ▲

City, town or post office, state, and ZIP code. If you have a foreign address, see page 16.: Verona, WI 53593-9088

Checking a box below will not change your tax or refund.

Presidential Election Campaign ▶ Check here if you, or your spouse if filing jointly, want $3 to go to this fund (see page 16) ▶ ☒ You ☒ Spouse

Filing Status
Check only one box.

1. ☐ Single
2. ☒ Married filing jointly (even if only one had income)
3. ☐ Married filing separately. Enter spouse's SSN above and full name here. ▶
4. ☐ Head of household (with qualifying person). (See page 17.) If the qualifying person is a child but not your dependent, enter this child's name here. ▶
5. ☐ Qualifying widow(er) with dependent child (see page 17)

Exemptions

6a ☒ **Yourself.** If someone can claim you as a dependent, **do not** check box 6a
b ☒ **Spouse**

Boxes checked on 6a and 6b: **2**
No. of children on 6c who:
• lived with you **3**
• did not live with you due to divorce or separation (see page 18)

If more than four dependents, see page 18.

c **Dependents:**

(1) First name Last name	(2) Dependent's social security number	(3) Dependent's relationship to you	(4)✓ if qualifying child for child tax credit (see page 18)
Mary R. Relin	453 26 8190	daughter	☒
Douglas J. Redlin	453 26 8189	son	☒
Mildred A. Redlin	168 29 4501	mother	☐
			☐

Dependents on 6c not entered above

Add numbers on lines above ▶ **5**

d Total number of exemptions claimed

Income

Attach Form(s) W-2 here. Also attach Forms W-2G and 1099-R if tax was withheld.

If you did not get a W-2, see page 19.

Enclose, but do not attach, any payment. Also, please use **Form 1040-V.**

7	Wages, salaries, tips, etc. Attach Form(s) W-2	7	87,000 00
8a	**Taxable** interest. Attach Schedule B if required	8a	1,913 00
b	Tax-exempt interest. **Do not** include on line 8a 8b		
9a	Ordinary dividends. Attach Schedule B if required	9a	
b	Qualified dividends (see page 20) 9b		
10	Taxable refunds, credits, or offsets of state and local income taxes (see page 20)	10	342 00
11	Alimony received	11	
12	Business income or (loss). Attach Schedule C or C-EZ	12	
13	Capital gain or (loss). Attach Schedule D if required. If not required, check here ▶ ☐	13	250 00
14	Other gains or (losses). Attach Form 4797	14	
15a	IRA distributions 15a b Taxable amount (see page 22)	15b	
16a	Pensions and annuities 16a b Taxable amount (see page 22)	16b	
17	Rental real estate, royalties, partnerships, S corporations, trusts, etc. Attach Schedule E	17	5,212 00
18	Farm income or (loss). Attach Schedule F	18	
19	Unemployment compensation	19	
20a	Social security benefits 20a b Taxable amount (see page 24)	20b	
21	Other income. List type and amount (see page 24) Door Prize	21	800 00
22	Add the amounts in the far right column for lines 7 through 21. This is your **total income** ▶	22	95,517 00

Adjusted Gross Income

23	Educator expenses (see page 26)	23		
24	Certain business expenses of reservists, performing artists, and fee-basis government officials. Attach Form 2106 or 2106-EZ	24		
25	Health savings account deduction. Attach Form 8889	25		
26	Moving expenses. Attach Form 3903	26		
27	One-half of self-employment tax. Attach Schedule SE	27		
28	Self-employed SEP, SIMPLE, and qualified plans	28		
29	Self-employed health insurance deduction (see page XX)	29		
30	Penalty on early withdrawal of savings	30		
31a	Alimony paid b Recipient's SSN ▶	31a		
32	IRA deduction (see page XX)	32	4,000 00	
33	Student loan interest deduction (see page XX)	33		
34	Tuition and fees deduction (see page XX)	34		
35	Domestic production activities deduction. Attach Form 8903	35		
36	Add lines 23 through 31a and 32 through 35	36		4,000 00
37	Subtract line 36 from line 22. This is your **adjusted gross income** ▶	37		91,517 00

For Disclosure, Privacy Act, and Paperwork Reduction Act Notice, see page 75.   Cat. No. 11320B   Form **1040** (2005)

FIGURE 6-3 Filled-In Form 1040, Page 2

Form 1040 (2005)				Page **2**

Tax and Credits

38	Amount from line 37 (adjusted gross income)		38	91,517 00
39a	Check if: ☐ **You** were born before January 2, 1941, ☐ Blind. ☐ **Spouse** was born before January 2, 1941, ☐ Blind. **Total boxes** checked ▶ 39a			
b	If your spouse itemizes on a separate return or you were a dual-status alien, see page 31 and check here ▶ 39b ☐			

Standard Deduction for—

• People who checked any box on line 39a or 39b or who can be claimed as a dependent, see page 31.

• All others:

Single or Married filing separately, $5,000

Married filing jointly or Qualifying widow(er), $10,000

Head of household, $7,300

40	**Itemized deductions** (from Schedule A) **or** your **standard deduction** (see left margin)		40	10,000 00
41	Subtract line 40 from line 38		41	81,517 00
42	If line 38 is $109,475 or less, multiply $3,200 by the total number of exemptions claimed on line 6d. If line 38 is over $109,475, see the worksheet on page 33		42	16,000 00
43	**Taxable income.** Subtract line 42 from line 41. If line 42 is more than line 41, enter -0-		43	65,517 00
44	**Tax** (see page 33). Check if any tax is from: **a** ☐ Form(s) 8814 **b** ☐ Form 4972		44	9,711 00
45	**Alternative minimum tax** (see page 35). Attach Form 6251		45	
46	Add lines 44 and 45 ▶		46	9,711 00
47	Foreign tax credit. Attach Form 1116 if required	47		
48	Credit for child and dependent care expenses. Attach Form 2441	48	1,200 00	
49	Credit for the elderly or the disabled. Attach Schedule R	49		
50	Education credits. Attach Form 8863	50		
51	Retirement savings contributions credit. Attach Form 8880	51		
52	Child tax credit (see page 37). Attach Form 8901 if required	52	2,000 00	
53	Adoption credit. Attach Form 8839	53		
54	Credits from: **a** ☐ Form 8396 **b** ☐ Form 8859	54		
55	Other credits. Check applicable box(es): **a** ☐ Form 3800 **b** ☐ Form 8801 **c** ☐ Specify	55		
56	Add lines 47 through 55. These are your **total credits**		56	3,200 00
57	Subtract line 56 from line 46. If line 56 is more than line 46, enter -0- ▶		57	6,511 00

Other Taxes

58	Self-employment tax. Attach Schedule SE		58	
59	Social security and Medicare tax on tip income not reported to employer. Attach Form 4137		59	
60	Additional tax on IRAs, other qualified retirement plans, etc. Attach Form 5329 if required		60	
61	Advance earned income credit payments from Form(s) W-2		61	
62	Household employment taxes. Attach Schedule H		62	
63	Add lines 57 through 62. This is your **total tax** ▶		63	6,511 00

Payments

If you have a qualifying child, attach Schedule EIC.

64	Federal income tax withheld from Forms W-2 and 1099	64	7,200 00	
65	2005 estimated tax payments and amount applied from 2004 return	65		
66a	**Earned income credit (EIC)**	66a		
b	Nontaxable combat pay election ▶	66b		
67	Excess social security and tier 1 RRTA tax withheld (see page 54)	67		
68	Additional child tax credit. Attach Form 8812	68		
69	Amount paid with request for extension to file (see page 54)	69		
70	Payments from: **a** ☐ Form 2439 **b** ☐ Form 4136 **c** ☐ Form 8885	70		
71	Add lines 64, 65, 66a, and 67 through 70. These are your **total payments** ▶		71	7,200 00

Refund

Direct deposit? See page 54 and fill in 73b, 73c, and 73d.

72	If line 71 is more than line 63, subtract line 63 from line 71. This is the amount you **overpaid**		72	689 00
73a	Amount of line 72 you want **refunded to you** ▶		73a	689 00
▶ b	Routing number	▶ c Type: ☐ Checking ☐ Savings		
▶ d	Account number			
74	Amount of line 72 you want **applied to your 2006 estimated tax** ▶	74		

Amount You Owe

75	**Amount you owe.** Subtract line 71 from line 63. For details on how to pay, see page 55 ▶		75	
76	Estimated tax penalty (see page 55)	76		

Third Party Designee

Do you want to allow another person to discuss this return with the IRS (see page 56)? ☐ **Yes.** Complete the following. ☐ **No**

Designee's name ▶	Phone no. ▶ ( )	Personal identification number (PIN) ▶

Sign Here

Joint return? See page 17.
Keep a copy for your records.

Under penalties of perjury, I declare that I have examined this return and accompanying schedules and statements, and to the best of my knowledge and belief, they are true, correct, and complete. Declaration of preparer (other than taxpayer) is based on all information of which preparer has any knowledge.

Your signature	Date	Your occupation	Daytime phone number
Gary R. Redlin	4/12/06	Hrdwre Mgr	( )
Spouse's signature. If a joint return, **both** must sign. *Nancy L. Redlin*	4/12/06	Spouse's occupation Nurse	

Paid Preparer's Use Only

Preparer's signature ▶	Date	Check if self-employed ☐	Preparer's SSN or PTIN
Firm's name (or yours if self-employed), address, and ZIP code ▶		EIN	
		Phone no. ( )	

Form **1040** (2005)

✿ *Printed on recycled paper*

QUESTIONS AND PROBLEMS

1. **Miscellaneous Deductions.** Identify the following as (A) deductible for AGI as an adjustment to income, (B) deductible from AGI as an itemized deduction, or (C) not deductible. Ignore the AGI limitations that are used to determine the deductibility of certain types of expenses.

Item		Answer
a.	State inheritance taxes	C
b.	Commuting costs	C
c.	Rent on safe deposit box (used to store securities)	B
d.	CPA examination testing fee	C
e.	IRS penalty for late filing	C
f.	Fee to accountant to prepare the personal property tax return on rental property	A
g.	Loss on bookstore operations (Schedule C is used)	A
h.	Auto registration for business vehicle (above the line)	A / B
i.	Purchase of uniforms suitable for street wear	C
j.	Insurance on personal residence	C
k.	Union dues paid by a steelworker	B
l.	Unreimbursed employee business travel expense	B
m.	Mortgage interest on apartment building	A
n.	Storm damage to trees in front yard of home, after casualty loss limitations	B
o.	Loss on sale of personal automobile	C
p.	Repairs to friend's car for damage caused when taxpayer's car hit friend's car	C
q.	Loss on sale of stock (from Schedule D)	A
r.	Interest on loan to pay for vacation	C
s.	Unreimbursed salesperson's entertainment expenses	B
t.	Depreciation on apartment building	A
u.	Charitable contributions to a university	B
v.	Proprietor's cost for continuing education seminar	A
w.	Storm damage to farmer's rental property (Sch F)	A

2. **Transportation Expense.** Ricardo Montella works two jobs each day, Monday through Friday. He works eight hours at his first job and three hours at his second job. He drives the following miles each day:

Home to first job	20 miles
First job to second job	12 miles
Second job to home	30 miles

If Montella follows this routine for 250 days during the year, how many miles qualify for the mileage deduction?

3. **Travel Expense.** Joshua Jones went on a business trip lasting ten days. He spent six days on business (includes travel time). He spent four days playing golf. He incurred the following unreimbursed expenses:

Lodging	$1,250
Meals	500
Entertainment of clients	130
Airfare	1,500

a. If the trip was within the United States, how much can Jones deduct?

b. If the trip was outside the United States, how much can Jones deduct?

4. **Employee Business Expenses.** Wendy Rogers, a single taxpayer, is a plumber employed by a company in the city where she lives. She attends the monthly dinner meeting of the local union. During the year, she paid $120 of meeting expenses and drove 240 miles (20 miles each month) to attend the meetings. Rogers paid union dues of $110 and a plumbing license fee of $35.

a. Compute Rogers's itemized deductions for the work-related expenses.

b. Explain how to use the employee business expenses as itemized deductions.

5. **Employee Business Expenses.** Betty McGregor, a single woman, teaches the third grade at Laurel Elementary School. In the past few years, the public school budget has been very tight, making funds for classes supplies quite scarce. McGregor, a conscientious teacher, often buys paper, pencils, drawing materials, and other supplies for use by the students

in her classes. McGregor has receipts for all her purchases and a letter from the principal acknowledging their use in school. The school cannot reimburse her for these purchases.

a. Do McGregor's expenses meet the requirements of the employee business expense deduction? Explain why or why not.

b. Would these expenses qualify as charitable contributions? Explain why or why not.

c. On the basis of your answers to Parts a. and b., describe how McGregor should report the expenses for school materials on her income tax return.

6. **Education Expenses.** For each situation described in Parts a. through d., state whether the expenses paid qualify as deductible educational expenses. If the expenses qualify as deductions, state whether the expenses are deductible for (adjustments to income) or from AGI (itemized deductions).

a. Accounting courses taken by an accountant, who works for a CPA firm to meet the state's continuing professional education (CPE) requirement. (Total CPE expenses were $525.) *Yes, adjustment to income / deductible from AGI deductible educational expense*

b. Tuition and books totalling $3,500 for a CPA enrolled in law school. *no — different job & career*

c. Tuition and books totalling $2,700 for a high school teacher enrolled in graduate school to meet the state law requirements in order to renew her teaching certificate. *yes, itemized deduction (2% rule of AGI)*

d. A company executive's expenditure of $8,000 on tuition, books, and transportation to attend an executive program to improve his business management, employee relations, and marketing skills. *yes, itemized deduction (2% rule of AGI)*

7. Hobby Criteria.

     a. What are the criteria for determining whether an activity is a legitimate business or a hobby?

     b. If a doctor operates on the side a farm that is used to graze cattle, will the showing of a Schedule F profit automatically exempt the doctor from the possibility that the IRS will consider the activity a hobby? Explain.

[Handwritten margin notes:]

Allocated expenses of house:
Property taxes 3600
Electricity 2400
Heat 2900
TOTAL 8900
Business usage 12%
Painting activity 1068
Interest on loan 140
Supplies 1750
2958
Revenue 2300
Total exp. (2958)
Net loss (658)

8. Hobby Losses.

Russell Long is retired from his regular work and now spends his time painting landscapes in a studio set up in his home. The studio occupies 12% of the living space in his home. During 2005 Long sold some of his paintings for the first time. Long is not certain whether he is required to file a tax return and, if so, whether he will be required to pay any taxes on his painting as a business. The revenue from sales of paintings in 2005 was $2,300. Long's expenses were as follows: property taxes on his home, $3,600; interest on a loan for painting supplies, $140; painting supplies, $1,750; electricity for the home, $2,400; and heat for the home, $2,900.

     a. How much can Long deduct of the above expenses if his painting activity is treated as a business? Show calculations.

[Handwritten:] Could deduct the loss on assumption that the painting activity is a business & expects to report a profit in 3 of the 1st 5 yrs.

     b. How much can Long deduct of the above expenses if his painting activity is treated as a hobby? Show calculations.

[Handwritten:] Revenues 2300
Total expenses (2300) ($2958 but limited to hobby income).
① (12% x 3600) $432 is deductible as property tax.
② $1,868 remainder deductible only to the extent that misc itemized deduction exceed 2% of AGI

     c. Explain what Long might do in the way of tax planning to further support a claim that his painting is a business activity.

[Handwritten:] Put paintings in gallery or on display to make effort to earn profit over years.

9. **Gambling Losses.** During the year, Mark Downing won $1,400 from football bets. He lost $750 from basketball wagering. Downing also lost $1,150 at the track.

a. How do these gambling activities affect Downing's gross income and his deductible expenses?

[handwritten: gain football bets – $1,400 / loss basketball wagers – $750 / loss track – $1,150]

[handwritten: $1,400 gain & $1,400 losses – include in gross income. not subject to 2% limitation.]

b. Where would the appropriate income and expenses be entered on Downing's income tax returns?

[handwritten: $1,400 → "Other Income" on form 1040 / $1,400 → losses on Sch. A as misc. deduction not subject to 2% AGI limitations]

10. **Tax Planning.**

a. Under what circumstances should a taxpayer plan to control the timing of payments that are deductible as itemized deductions?

b. Identify some specific ways in which the current tax law allows for tax planning with regard to itemized deductions.

11. **Form 2106.** Nancy Lopez (SSN 234–56–7891) works for Professional Services, Inc. (PSI). During the year, she incurs the following employment-related expenses:

Travel expenses (not including meals, entertainment, and auto expenses)	$3,750
Parking	180
Toll charges	30
Meals (while away overnight)	1,500
Entertainment of clients	426
Miscellaneous	135

[handwritten: 180, 30 → 210]
[handwritten: 1,500, 426 → 1926]

Lopez's employer provides a business expense allowance of $750 per month *[handwritten: (included on W2)]* to cover all expenses. Lopez does not account to PSI for her expenses, but she keeps detailed records of her business expenses and mileage. During the year she drove 25,200 miles, and 17,136 of these miles were business related (5,700 miles after August 31). The 17,136 miles do not include Lopez's ten-mile round-trip commuting distance when she is not traveling. Her total commuting miles for the year are 2,200. Lopez uses the standard mileage rate to determine the tax deduction for the use of her automobile, which she acquired on November 10, 2004. Using this data, prepare Form 2106 for Nancy Lopez.

(Use for Problem 11.)

Form **2106**	**Employee Business Expenses**	OMB No. 1545-0139

Form **2106**

Department of the Treasury
Internal Revenue Service (99)

▶ See separate instructions.

▶ Attach to Form 1040.

20**05**

Attachment
Sequence No. **54**

Your name	Occupation in which you incurred expenses	Social security number

Part I   **Employee Business Expenses and Reimbursements**

Step 1   **Enter Your Expenses**

			Column A Other Than Meals and Entertainment	**Column B** Meals and Entertainment
1	Vehicle expense from line 22 or line 29. (Rural mail carriers: See instructions.)	1	7396	
2	Parking fees, tolls, and transportation, including train, bus, etc., that **did not** involve overnight travel or commuting to and from work	2	210	
3	Travel expense while away from home overnight, including lodging, airplane, car rental, etc. **Do not** include meals and entertainment	3	(3750)	
4	Business expenses not included on lines 1 through 3. **Do not** include meals and entertainment	4	135	
5	Meals and entertainment expenses (see instructions)	5		1926
6	**Total expenses.** In Column A, add lines 1 through 4 and enter the result. In Column B, enter the amount from line 5	6	11491	1926

Note: *If you were not reimbursed for any expenses in Step 1, skip line 7 and enter the amount from line 6 on line 8.*

Step 2   **Enter Reimbursements Received From Your Employer for Expenses Listed in Step 1**

7	Enter reimbursements received from your employer that were **not** reported to you in box 1 of Form W-2. Include any reimbursements reported under code "L" in box 12 of your Form W-2 (see instructions)	7	0	0

Step 3   **Figure Expenses To Deduct on Schedule A (Form 1040)**

8	Subtract line 7 from line 6. If zero or less, enter -0-. However, if line 7 is greater than line 6 in Column A, report the excess as income on Form 1040, line 7	8	11491	1926

Note: *If **both** columns of line 8 are zero, you cannot deduct employee business expenses. Stop here and attach Form 2106 to your return.*

9	In Column A, enter the amount from line 8. In Column B, multiply line 8 by 50% (.50). (Employees subject to Department of Transportation (DOT) hours of service limits: Multiply meal expenses incurred while away from home on business by 70% (.70) instead of 50%. For details, see instructions.)	9	11491	963

10	Add the amounts on line 9 of both columns and enter the total here. **Also, enter the total on Schedule A (Form 1040), line 20.** (Reservists, qualified performing artists, fee-basis state or local government officials, and individuals with disabilities: See the instructions for special rules on where to enter the total.) ▶	10		12454

For Paperwork Reduction Act Notice, see instructions.   Cat. No. 11700N   Form **2106** (2005)

(Use for Problem 11.)

Form 2106 (2005)   Page **2**

Part II   Vehicle Expenses

Section A—General Information (You must complete this section if you are claiming vehicle expenses.)

			(a) Vehicle 1	(b) Vehicle 2
11	Enter the date the vehicle was placed in service	11	11 / 10 / 04	/ /
12	Total miles the vehicle was driven during 2005	12	25,200 miles	miles
13	Business miles included on line 12	13	17,136 miles	miles
14	Percent of business use. Divide line 13 by line 12	14	68 %	%
15	Average daily roundtrip commuting distance	15	10 miles	miles
16	Commuting miles included on line 12	16	2,200 miles	miles
17	Other miles. Add lines 13 and 16 and subtract the total from line 12	17	5,864 miles	miles

		Yes	No
18	Do you (or your spouse) have another vehicle available for personal use?	☐ Yes	☒ No
19	Was your vehicle available for personal use during off-duty hours?	☒ Yes	☐ No
20	Do you have evidence to support your deduction?	☒ Yes	☐ No
21	If "Yes," is the evidence written?	☒ Yes	☐ No

Section B—Standard Mileage Rate (See the instructions for Part II to find out whether to complete this section or Section C.)

22	Multiply line 13 by 40.5¢ (.405)	22	7396 00	*

Section C—Actual Expenses

			(a) Vehicle 1	(b) Vehicle 2
23	Gasoline, oil, repairs, vehicle insurance, etc.	23		
24a	Vehicle rentals	24a		
b	Inclusion amount (see instructions)	24b		
c	Subtract line 24b from line 24a	24c		
25	Value of employer-provided vehicle (applies only if 100% of annual lease value was included on Form W-2—see instructions)	25		
26	Add lines 23, 24c, and 25	26		
27	Multiply line 26 by the percentage on line 14	27		
28	Depreciation (see instructions)	28		
29	Add lines 27 and 28. Enter total here and on line 1	29		

Section D—Depreciation of Vehicles (Use this section only if you owned the vehicle and are completing Section C for the vehicle.)

			(a) Vehicle 1	(b) Vehicle 2
30	Enter cost or other basis (see instructions)	30		
31	Enter section 179 deduction (see instructions)	31		
32	Multiply line 30 by line 14 (see instructions if you claimed the section 179 deduction or special allowance)	32		
33	Enter depreciation method and percentage (see instructions)	33		
34	Multiply line 32 by the percentage on line 33 (see instructions)	34		
35	Add lines 31 and 34	35		
36	Enter the applicable limit explained in the line 36 instructions	36		
37	Multiply line 36 by the percentage on line 14	37		
38	Enter the **smaller** of line 35 or line 37. If you skipped lines 36 and 37, enter the amount from line 35. Also enter this amount on line 28 above	38		

♻ *Printed on recycled paper*   Form **2106** (2005)

* January–August mileage @ $.405
September–December mileage @ $.485

11436 × .405 = 4631.58
5700 × .485 = 2764.50
$ 7396.08

12. **Miscellaneous Deductions.** Mr. and Mrs. Virgil Pierre had an AGI of $47,400. They incurred the following expenses:

Mr. Pierre:

Employee business expenses:

Employee mileage deduction	$569
Meals while away from home overnight	90
Hotels	185
Miscellaneous travel expenses	18
Total travel expenses	$862

Travel expenses reimbursed by employer (including all meals) under a qualified plan	(486)
Net travel expenses paid out of pocket	$376

Other business expenses:

Subscriptions to professional journals	$115
Unreimbursed meals and entertainment	256

Other expenses:

Tax return preparation fee	175
Gambling losses (gambling winnings of $65)	120

Mrs. Pierre:

Safe deposit box rent (stock stored)	$ 45
Investment publications	120
Nurse's uniform cost and upkeep	340
Professional liability insurance	85

Using the preceding information, fill in the following lines, which summarize Schedule A (Job Expenses and Most Other Miscellaneous Deductions):

Job Expenses and Most Other Miscellaneous Deductions:

1. Unreimbursed employee expenses   _____
2. Tax preparation fees   _____
3. Other expenses subject to the 2% rule   _____
4. Total expenses   _____
5. Less 2% of AGI   _____
6. Deductible expenses   _____

Other Miscellaneous Deductions:

7. Miscellaneous expenses not subject to the 2% rule   _____

13. **Schedule A.** Charlie P. (SSN 367-83-9403) and Maggie S. (SSN 361-73-4098) Church file a joint income tax return with an AGI of $74,105. They reside in Evanston, IL. Mr. Church, a chemist, worked for Drake Corporation for the first six months of the year. He was employed by Potter Company for the last six months of the year. Mrs. Church worked part-time as a nurse at City Hospital.

The Churchs's expenses follow. They have canceled checks or receipts for each item.

Mortgage interest on home	$4,200 yes
Contributions to church (with receipts)	900 yes
Hunting license	90 no
Marriage license	16 no
Cash to street person begging for money	50 no
Contribution to American Red Cross (with receipts)	30 yes
Paid to United Way (no canceled check or receipt)	310 no
Property tax on residence	2,450 yes
R. K. Snell, physician (unreimbursed by insurance)	980 yes
E. I. Newman, dentist (unreimbursed by insurance)	290 yes
G. R. Gross, veterinarian (unreimbursed by insurance)	125 no
Medical insurance premiums	556 yes
Safe deposit box rental (storing securities)	22 yes
Paid to Evanston Drug for over-the-counter medications	160 no
State income taxes withheld	2,890 yes

1270
556
1826

Complete the Schedule A on page 6-32 for Charlie and Maggie Church.

14. **Schedule A.** Roberto (SSN 123-45-6789) and Lena Gomez, both engineers, file a joint return reporting AGI of $155,000, including $150,000 in wages and $5,000 in dividend income. Their Schedule A shows the following itemized deductions:

Medical expenses	$12,000
State income taxes	2,500
Property taxes	2,000
Mortgage interest	3,000
Investment interest	2,000
Charitable contributions (with receipts)	4,000

a. Prepare a worksheet determining the net deductions for each category. Take into account any limitations that Schedule A requires to arrive at the net allowable itemized deductions. Using your worksheet, prepare the Gomez's Schedule A on page 6-33.

b. Assuming they are entitled to three exemptions, determine the Gomez's taxable income.

c. Assuming a marginal tax rate of 28%, determine the effect, if any, of the itemized deduction limitation on the net income tax liability.

(Use for Problem 13.)

SCHEDULES A&B
(Form 1040)

Department of the Treasury
Internal Revenue Service (99)

Name(s) shown on Form 1040

Schedule A—Itemized Deductions

(Schedule B is on back)

▶ **Attach to Form 1040.** ▶ **See Instructions for Schedules A and B (Form 1040).**

OMB No. 1545-0074

2005

Attachment
Sequence No. **07**

Your social security number

Medical and Dental Expenses		Caution. Do not include expenses reimbursed or paid by others.				
	1	Medical and dental expenses (see page A-2)	1	1826		
	2	Enter amount from Form 1040, line 38	**2**	74,105		
	3	Multiply line 2 by 7.5% (.075).	3	5558		
	4	Subtract line 3 from line 1. If line 3 is more than line 1, enter -0-			4	0
Taxes You Paid (See page A-2.)	5	State and local (**check only one box**): a ☐ Income taxes, **or** b ☐ General sales taxes (see page A-2)	5	2890		
	6	Real estate taxes (see page A-3)	6	2450		
	7	Personal property taxes	7			
	8	Other taxes. List type and amount ▶	8			
	9	Add lines 5 through 8			9	5340
Interest You Paid (See page A-3.)	10	Home mortgage interest and points reported to you on Form 1098	10	4200		
	11	Home mortgage interest not reported to you on Form 1098. If paid to the person from whom you bought the home, see page A-4 and show that person's name, identifying no., and address ▶	11			
Note. Personal interest is not deductible.	12	Points not reported to you on Form 1098. See page A-4 for special rules	12			
	13	Investment interest. Attach Form 4952 if required. (See page A-4.)	13			
	14	Add lines 10 through 13			14	4200
Gifts to Charity If you made a gift and got a benefit for it, see page A-4.	15	Gifts by cash or check. If you made any gift of $250 or more, see page A-4	15	930		
	16	Other than by cash or check. If any gift of $250 or more, see page A-4. You **must** attach Form 8283 if over $500	16			
	17	Carryover from prior year	17			
	18	Add lines 15 through 17			18	930
Casualty and Theft Losses	19	Casualty or theft loss(es). Attach Form 4684. (See page A-5.)			19	
Job Expenses and Most Other Miscellaneous Deductions (See page A-5.)	20	Unreimbursed employee expenses—job travel, union dues, job education, etc. Attach Form 2106 or 2106-EZ if required. (See page A-6.) ▶	20			
	21	Tax preparation fees	21			
	22	Other expenses—investment, safe deposit box, etc. List type and amount ▶	22	22		
	23	Add lines 20 through 22	23	22		
	24	Enter amount from Form 1040, line 38	**24**	74,105		
	25	Multiply line 24 by 2% (.02)	25	1482		
	26	Subtract line 25 from line 23. If line 25 is more than line 23, enter -0-			26	0
Other Miscellaneous Deductions	27	Other—from list on page A-6. List type and amount ▶			27	0
Total Itemized Deductions	28	Is Form 1040, line 38, over $145,950 (over $72,975 if married filing separately)? ☐ **No.** Your deduction is not limited. Add the amounts in the far right column for lines 4 through 27. Also, enter this amount on Form 1040, line 40. ☐ **Yes.** Your deduction may be limited. See page A-6 for the amount to enter.	▶		28	10470
	29	If you elect to itemize deductions even though they are less than your standard deduction, check here ▶ ☐				

For Paperwork Reduction Act Notice, see Form 1040 instructions.   Cat. No. 11330X   **Schedule A (Form 1040) 2005**

(Use for Problem 14.)

SCHEDULES A&B	Schedule A—Itemized Deductions	OMB No. 1545-0074

SCHEDULES A&B
(Form 1040)
Department of the Treasury
Internal Revenue Service (99)

Schedule A—Itemized Deductions
(Schedule B is on back)
► Attach to Form 1040.   ► See Instructions for Schedules A and B (Form 1040).

OMB No. 1545-0074
2005
Attachment
Sequence No. **07**

Name(s) shown on Form 1040 | Your social security number

Medical and Dental Expenses

Caution. Do not include expenses reimbursed or paid by others.
1 Medical and dental expenses (see page A-2) . . . | 1
2 Enter amount from Form 1040, line 38 |_2_|
3 Multiply line 2 by 7.5% (.075) . . . . . | 3
4 Subtract line 3 from line 1. If line 3 is more than line 1, enter -0- . . . . . . | 4

Taxes You Paid
(See page A-2.)

5 State and local **(check only one box):**
  a ☐ Income taxes, **or**
  b ☐ General sales taxes (see page A-2) } . . | 5
6 Real estate taxes (see page A-3) . . . . . | 6
7 Personal property taxes . . . . | 7
8 Other taxes. List type and amount ► _____ | 8
9 Add lines 5 through 8 . . . . | 9

Interest You Paid
(See page A-3.)

Note.
Personal interest is not deductible.

10 Home mortgage interest and points reported to you on Form 1098 | 10
11 Home mortgage interest not reported to you on Form 1098. If paid to the person from whom you bought the home, see page A-4 and show that person's name, identifying no., and address ► _____ | 11
12 Points not reported to you on Form 1098. See page A-4 for special rules . . . . | 12
13 Investment interest. Attach Form 4952 if required. (See page A-4.) . . . . | 13
14 Add lines 10 through 13 . . . . | 14

Gifts to Charity
If you made a gift and got a benefit for it, see page A-4.

15 Gifts by cash or check. If you made any gift of $250 or more, see page A-4 . . . . | 15
16 Other than by cash or check. If any gift of $250 or more, see page A-4. You **must** attach Form 8283 if over $500 | 16
17 Carryover from prior year . . . . | 17
18 Add lines 15 through 17 . . . . | 18

Casualty and Theft Losses

19 Casualty or theft loss(es). Attach Form 4684. (See page A-5.) . . . . . . | 19

Job Expenses and Most Other Miscellaneous Deductions
(See page A-5.)

20 Unreimbursed employee expenses—job travel, union dues, job education, etc. Attach Form 2106 or 2106-EZ if required. (See page A-6.) ► _____ | 20
21 Tax preparation fees . . . | 21
22 Other expenses—investment, safe deposit box, etc. List type and amount ► _____ | 22
23 Add lines 20 through 22 . . . . . | 23
24 Enter amount from Form 1040, line 38 |_24_|
25 Multiply line 24 by 2% (.02) . . . . . . | 25
26 Subtract line 25 from line 23. If line 25 is more than line 23, enter -0- . . . . . | 26

Other Miscellaneous Deductions

27 Other—from list on page A-6. List type and amount ► _____ | 27

Total Itemized Deductions

28 Is Form 1040, line 38, over $145,950 (over $72,975 if married filing separately)?
  ☐ **No.** Your deduction is not limited. Add the amounts in the far right column for lines 4 through 27. Also, enter this amount on Form 1040, line 40. } ► | 28
  ☐ **Yes.** Your deduction may be limited. See page A-6 for the amount to enter.
29 If you elect to itemize deductions even though they are less than your standard deduction, check here ► ☐

For Paperwork Reduction Act Notice, see Form 1040 instructions.   Cat. No. 11330X   **Schedule A (Form 1040) 2005**

15. Internet Problem: Researching Publication 463.

The Alpha-Beta Company rents a twelve-seat luxury skybox at a football stadium for the entire season. The season consists of eight home games. Alpha-Beta uses the skybox exclusively for entertaining clients. The cost of renting the skybox for the season is $20,000. In contrast, nonluxury box seats sell for $50 for each game.

How much can Alpha-Beta deduct for its luxury skybox?

Go to the IRS Web site. Locate Publication 463, and find an answer to the above question involving luxury skyboxes. Print out a copy of the page where you found your answer. Underline or highlight the pertinent information.

See Appendix A for instructions on use of the IRS Web site.

16. Business Entity Problem: This problem is designed for those using the "business entity" approach. The solution may require information from Chapter 14.

For each statement, check true or false.

	True	False
a. Self-employed taxpayers use Form 2106 to report their deductible travel expenses.	_____	_____
b. A self-employed taxpayer may claim the federal per diem for meals instead of deducting the actual meal costs.	_____	_____ .
c. Employers that reimburse their employees using an "accountable reimbursement plan" are able to deduct the entire cost of meal reimbursements paid to their employees.	_____	_____
d. The owner of a corporation may claim the federal per diem for meals instead of deducting the actual meal costs.	_____	_____
e. When a self-employed taxpayer incurs deductible education expenses, the expenses are deductible as a miscellaneous itemized deduction subject to the 2% rule.	_____	_____
f. When a taxpayer owns an S corporation that breeds and races horses, the pass-through losses from the corporation may be treated as hobby losses if the corporation has never shown a profit in its ten years of operation.	_____	_____

CUMULATIVE PROBLEM (CHAPTERS 1–6)

Frank A. (SSN 811-26-3717) and Sandra K. (SSN 820-47-9231) Anderson (ages 38 and 36, respectively) reside at 2121 Century Avenue, Middleton, CA 92657, with their three children whom they fully support: Martha A. (age 9), Charles R. (age 11), and Carol T. (age 14). The children's social security numbers are Martha 998-21-5246, Charles 998-21-5247, and Carol 998-21-1827.

The Andersons file a joint return, and neither elects to have money go to the presidential election campaign fund. Frank is employed by Maintaineers, Inc., as a customer representative, and Sandra is employed by Mission Instruments as a computer operator. Details of their salaries and withholdings, are as follows:

	Gross Wages	State Income Tax Withheld	Federal Income Tax Withheld	Social Security Tax Withheld	Medicare Insurance Tax Withheld
Frank	$52,500	$3,623	$2,100	$3,255	$761
Sandra	24,000	1,656	980	1,488	348

In addition to his salary, Frank received a business travel expense reimbursement of $6,600 from Maintaineers, Inc., which was <u>not included on his Form W-2</u>. By agreement with his employer, none of the allowance was for meals and entertainment expenses. Frank must make an adequate accounting of his expenses to his employer and, as required, return any excess reimbursements. His daily business journal disclosed that from January 2 (the date of purchase) through December 31, he drove his own automobile 29,151 miles, of which 17,202 were business related. Of the 17,202 business miles, 6,000 miles were driven after August 31. Frank's average roundtrip commuting distance is six miles, and his commuting miles total 1,440 for the year. Since Frank dislikes keeping records, he uses the standard mileage rate to determine his automobile tax deduction. His substantiated paid business expenses are as follows:

Travel expenses	$2,168*
Parking fees	210
Meals and entertainment	560
Miscellaneous expenses	91

*Excludes meals, entertainment, and auto expenses

Sandra belongs to a car pool and drives to work every fourth week. In addition, her car is used on vacations.

In August, Sandra received $400 of interest when she cashed in a CD from State Bank. The Middleton Farmers Bank credited $300 of interest to the Andersons' joint savings account during the year. The Andersons itemized deductions in 2004 and overpaid their state income tax by $142, all of which provided a tax benefit. They received a refund of this amount in March, 2005. Since they both work outside the home, they are unable to be there when their children return from school. This year the Andersons paid a neighbor, Gloria Dryden (SSN 992-31-4270), $4,100 to care for their children in her home after school hours and during the summer vacation period while they were at work. Gloria Dryden's address is 2132 Century Avenue, Middleton, CA 92657.

During January, Sandra received unemployment compensation of $200, covering two weeks between jobs. Sandra's former husband paid her $2,400 of alimony on the basis of a written alimony agreement, which did not expire upon her marriage to Frank. Neither Frank nor Sandra is covered by a qualified pension plan at work. Frank contributed $3,000 to his traditional IRA account. Sandra contributed $2,000 to her traditional IRA account. Both contributions took place before April 15, 2006.

Cancelled checks, receipts, and paid bills support the following expenditures:

Orlo T. Miller, M.D. (not covered by insurance)	$ 818 yes
Qualified Stop Smoking program for Sandra	175 yes
Alex B. Kramer, D.V.M. (treatment of Fritz, the Andersons' dog)	168 no
Life insurance on Frank with Sandra as beneficiary	1,200 no
Kathryn R. Smith, dentist (not covered by insurance)	459 yes
Weight loss program for Frank (cosmetic purposes)	180 no
Martin R. Anderson, optometrist (not covered by insurance)	50 yes
Maternity clothes for Sandra	450 no
Eyeglasses for Martha (not covered by insurance)	175 yes
Driver's license renewal for Sandra	32 no
Fishing license for Frank	12 no
Interest on personal loan for vacation	275 no
Interest on home mortgage secured at purchase date	1,272 yes
Real estate taxes	2,851 yes
Trash pickup fees	120 no
Home repairs and improvements	620 no
Homeowner's insurance	500 no
General sales taxes	572 no
State gasoline taxes	98 no
Contribution to First Unity Church of California	1,200 yes
Value of Frank's time volunteered to Girl Scouts	300 no
Political contributions	50 no
Bingo and lottery tickets	260 no
Rental for safe deposit box to store investment items	27 yes
Meals bought by Frank while working late	275 no
Legal fees paid on personal injury case	875 no

In addition, the Andersons paid $280 yes to Homer P. Gill (SSN 726-20-3334) of 5732 Monona Drive, Madison, CA 92657, to prepare their 2004 tax return.

Carol earned $360 no from baby-sitting on weekends. Her parents also paid $500 for summer computer camp for her to get ready for the fall semester.

When Frank's father died on Christmas day, Frank immediately inherited the father's savings account (on which he also had signed, as an emergency measure). The account contained $20,000. — not taxable

Part of Frank's compensation package included group-term life insurance equal to three-fourths of his annual salary. The cost to the company for the premium was $240.

Sandra's best friend, Nancy, had moved to Sweden. Nancy's daughter, Inga, came to stay with the Andersons for the school year. Inga had a part-time job after school and earned $3,500 to use for spending money and touring. The Andersons provided all of her support.

Required: Assume you are Homer P. Gill. Prepare the Andersons' joint income tax return using Form 1040, Schedule A, Form 2106, and Form 2441. All parties sign and date the income tax return on April 1, 2006.

(Use for Cumlative Problem.)

Form **1040** Department of the Treasury—Internal Revenue Service **2005** (99) IRS Use Only—Do not write or staple in this space.
U.S. Individual Income Tax Return

		OMB No. 1545-0074

For the year Jan. 1–Dec. 31, 2005, or other tax year beginning _____ , 2005, ending _____ , 20 _____

Label (See instructions on page 16.)

Use the IRS label. Otherwise, please print or type.

L A B E L   H E R E

Your first name and initial | Last name | Your social security number

If a joint return, spouse's first name and initial | Last name | Spouse's social security number

Home address (number and street). If you have a P.O. box, see page 16. | Apt. no. |

▲ You **must** enter your SSN(s) above. ▲

City, town or post office, state, and ZIP code. If you have a foreign address, see page 16.

Checking a box below will not change your tax or refund.

Presidential Election Campaign ▶ Check here if you, or your spouse if filing jointly, want $3 to go to this fund (see page 16) ▶ ☐ **You** ☐ **Spouse**

Filing Status

Check only one box.

1 ☐ Single
2 ☐ Married filing jointly (even if only one had income)
3 ☐ Married filing separately. Enter spouse's SSN above and full name here. ▶
4 ☐ Head of household (with qualifying person). (See page 17.) If the qualifying person is a child but not your dependent, enter this child's name here. ▶
5 ☐ Qualifying widow(er) with dependent child (see page 17)

Exemptions

6a ☐ **Yourself.** If someone can claim you as a dependent, **do not** check box 6a
b ☐ **Spouse**

c **Dependents:**

(1) First name Last name	(2) Dependent's social security number	(3) Dependent's relationship to you	(4) ✔ if qualifying child for child tax credit (see page 18)
			☐
			☐
			☐
			☐

If more than four dependents, see page 18.

d Total number of exemptions claimed

Boxes checked on 6a and 6b _____
No. of children on 6c who:
• lived with you _____
• did not live with you due to divorce or separation (see page 18) _____
Dependents on 6c not entered above _____
Add numbers on lines above ▶ ☐

Income

Attach Form(s) W-2 here. Also attach Forms W-2G and 1099-R if tax was withheld.

7 Wages, salaries, tips, etc. Attach Form(s) W-2 | 7 |
8a **Taxable** interest. Attach Schedule B if required | 8a |
b **Tax-exempt** interest. **Do not** include on line 8a | 8b | |
9a Ordinary dividends. Attach Schedule B if required | 9a |
b Qualified dividends (see page 20) | 9b | |
10 Taxable refunds, credits, or offsets of state and local income taxes (see page 20) | 10 |
11 Alimony received | 11 |
12 Business income or (loss). Attach Schedule C or C-EZ | 12 |
13 Capital gain or (loss). Attach Schedule D if required. If not required, check here ▶ ☐ | 13 |

If you did not get a W-2, see page 19.

14 Other gains or (losses). Attach Form 4797 | 14 |
15a IRA distributions | 15a | b Taxable amount (see page 22) | 15b |
16a Pensions and annuities | 16a | b Taxable amount (see page 22) | 16b |
17 Rental real estate, royalties, partnerships, S corporations, trusts, etc. Attach Schedule E | 17 |
18 Farm income or (loss). Attach Schedule F | 18 |

Enclose, but do not attach, any payment. Also, please use **Form 1040-V.**

19 Unemployment compensation | 19 |
20a Social security benefits | 20a | b Taxable amount (see page 24) | 20b |
21 Other income. List type and amount (see page 24) | 21 |
22 Add the amounts in the far right column for lines 7 through 21. This is your **total income** ▶ | 22 |

Adjusted Gross Income

23 Educator expenses (see page 26) | 23 |
24 Certain business expenses of reservists, performing artists, and fee-basis government officials. Attach Form 2106 or 2106-EZ | 24 |
25 Health savings account deduction. Attach Form 8889 | 25 |
26 Moving expenses. Attach Form 3903 | 26 |
27 One-half of self-employment tax. Attach Schedule SE | 27 |
28 Self-employed SEP, SIMPLE, and qualified plans | 28 |
29 Self-employed health insurance deduction (see page XX) | 29 |
30 Penalty on early withdrawal of savings | 30 |
31a Alimony paid b Recipient's SSN ▶ | 31a |
32 IRA deduction (see page XX) | 32 |
33 Student loan interest deduction (see page XX) | 33 |
34 Tuition and fees deduction (see page XX) | 34 |
35 Domestic production activities deduction. Attach Form 8903 | 35 |
36 Add lines 23 through 31a and 32 through 35 | 36 |
37 Subtract line 36 from line 22. This is your **adjusted gross income** ▶ | 37 |

For Disclosure, Privacy Act, and Paperwork Reduction Act Notice, see page 75. | Cat. No. 11320B | Form **1040** (2005)

(Use for Cumulative Problem.)

Form 1040 (2005)				Page **2**

Tax and Credits

38	Amount from line 37 (adjusted gross income)	**38**
39a	Check if: ☐ **You** were born before January 2, 1941, ☐ Blind. ☐ **Spouse** was born before January 2, 1941, ☐ Blind. } Total boxes checked ▶ 39a	
b	If your spouse itemizes on a separate return or you were a dual-status alien, see page 31 and check here ▶ 39b ☐	

Standard Deduction for—

• People who checked any box on line 39a or 39b **or** who can be claimed as a dependent, see page 31.

• All others:

Single or Married filing separately, $5,000

Married filing jointly or Qualifying widow(er), $10,000

Head of household, $7,300

40	**Itemized deductions** (from Schedule A) **or** your **standard deduction** (see left margin) . .	**40**
41	Subtract line 40 from line 38	**41**
42	If line 38 is $109,475 or less, multiply $3,200 by the total number of exemptions claimed on line 6d. If line 38 is over $109,475, see the worksheet on page 33	**42**
43	**Taxable income.** Subtract line 42 from line 41. If line 42 is more than line 41, enter -0-	**43**
44	**Tax** (see page 33). Check if any tax is from: **a** ☐ Form(s) 8814 **b** ☐ Form 4972 . .	**44**
45	**Alternative minimum tax** (see page 35). Attach Form 6251	**45**
46	Add lines 44 and 45 . . . . ▶	**46**
47	Foreign tax credit. Attach Form 1116 if required	**47**
48	Credit for child and dependent care expenses. Attach Form 2441	**48**
49	Credit for the elderly or the disabled. Attach Schedule R	**49**
50	Education credits. Attach Form 8863	**50**
51	Retirement savings contributions credit. Attach Form 8880	**51**
52	Child tax credit (see page 37). Attach Form 8901 if required	**52**
53	Adoption credit. Attach Form 8839	**53**
54	Credits from: **a** ☐ Form 8396 **b** ☐ Form 8859	**54**
55	Other credits. Check applicable box(es): **a** ☐ Form 3800 **b** ☐ Form 8801 **c** ☐ Specify _____	**55**
56	Add lines 47 through 55. These are your **total credits**	**56**
57	Subtract line 56 from line 46. If line 56 is more than line 46, enter -0- . . . . . . ▶	**57**

Other Taxes

58	Self-employment tax. Attach Schedule SE	**58**
59	Social security and Medicare tax on tip income not reported to employer. Attach Form 4137 . .	**59**
60	Additional tax on IRAs, other qualified retirement plans, etc. Attach Form 5329 if required	**60**
61	Advance earned income credit payments from Form(s) W-2	**61**
62	Household employment taxes. Attach Schedule H	**62**
63	Add lines 57 through 62. This is your **total tax** . . . . ▶	**63**

Payments

If you have a qualifying child, attach Schedule EIC.

64	Federal income tax withheld from Forms W-2 and 1099 . .	**64**
65	2005 estimated tax payments and amount applied from 2004 return	**65**
66a	**Earned income credit (EIC)**	**66a**
b	Nontaxable combat pay election ▶	**66b**
67	Excess social security and tier 1 RRTA tax withheld (see page 54)	**67**
68	Additional child tax credit. Attach Form 8812	**68**
69	Amount paid with request for extension to file (see page 54)	**69**
70	Payments from: **a** ☐ Form 2439 **b** ☐ Form 4136 **c** ☐ Form 8885	**70**
71	Add lines 64, 65, 66a, and 67 through 70. These are your **total payments** . . . . ▶	**71**

Refund

Direct deposit? See page 54 and fill in 73b, 73c, and 73d.

72	If line 71 is more than line 63, subtract line 63 from line 71. This is the amount you **overpaid** . . ▶	**72**
73a	Amount of line 72 you want **refunded to you** . . . . ▶	**73a**
b	Routing number ☐☐☐☐☐☐☐☐☐ ▶ **c** Type: ☐ Checking ☐ Savings	
d	Account number ☐☐☐☐☐☐☐☐☐☐☐☐☐☐☐☐☐	
74	Amount of line 72 you want **applied to your 2006 estimated tax** ▶	**74**

Amount You Owe

75	**Amount you owe.** Subtract line 71 from line 63. For details on how to pay, see page 55 ▶	**75**
76	Estimated tax penalty (see page 55)	**76**

Third Party Designee

Do you want to allow another person to discuss this return with the IRS (see page 56)? ☐ **Yes.** Complete the following. ☐ **No**

Designee's name ▶	Phone no. ▶ ( )	Personal identification number (PIN) ▶ ☐☐☐☐☐

Sign Here

Joint return? See page 17.

Keep a copy for your records.

Under penalties of perjury, I declare that I have examined this return and accompanying schedules and statements, and to the best of my knowledge and belief, they are true, correct, and complete. Declaration of preparer (other than taxpayer) is based on all information of which preparer has any knowledge.

Your signature	Date	Your occupation	Daytime phone number ( )
Spouse's signature. If a joint return, **both** must sign.	Date	Spouse's occupation	

Paid Preparer's Use Only

Preparer's signature ▶	Date	Check if self-employed ☐	Preparer's SSN or PTIN
Firm's name (or yours if self-employed), address, and ZIP code ▶		EIN	
		Phone no. ( )	

Form **1040** (2005)

♻ *Printed on recycled paper*

(Use for Cumlative Problem.)

SCHEDULES A&B	**Schedule A—Itemized Deductions**	OMB No. 1545-0074	
(Form 1040)	(Schedule B is on back)	20**05**	
Department of the Treasury Internal Revenue Service (99)	▶ **Attach to Form 1040.** ▶ **See Instructions for Schedules A and B (Form 1040).**	Attachment Sequence No. **07**	
Name(s) shown on Form 1040		Your social security number	

Medical and Dental Expenses	**Caution.** Do not include expenses reimbursed or paid by others.		
	1	Medical and dental expenses (see page A-2) . . .	**1**
	2	Enter amount from Form 1040, line 38 ⌊ **2** ⌋	
	3	Multiply line 2 by 7.5% (.075).	**3**
	4	Subtract line 3 from line 1. If line 3 is more than line 1, enter -0-	**4**

Taxes You Paid
 	
(See
page A-2.)
	5	State and local **(check only one box):**
		  a ☐ Income taxes, **or**
		  b ☐ General sales taxes (see page A-2)
			5

	6	Real estate taxes (see page A-3)	**6**
	7	Personal property taxes	**7**
	8	Other taxes. List type and amount ▶	**8**
	9	Add lines 5 through 8	**9**
Interest You Paid (See page A-3.) **Note.** Personal interest is not deductible.	10	Home mortgage interest and points reported to you on Form 1098	**10**
	11	Home mortgage interest not reported to you on Form 1098. If paid to the person from whom you bought the home, see page A-4 and show that person's name, identifying no., and address ▶	**11**
	12	Points not reported to you on Form 1098. See page A-4 for special rules	**12**
	13	Investment interest. Attach Form 4952 if required. (See page A-4.)	**13**
	14	Add lines 10 through 13	**14**
Gifts to Charity If you made a gift and got a benefit for it, see page A-4.	15	Gifts by cash or check. If you made any gift of $250 or more, see page A-4	**15**
	16	Other than by cash or check. If any gift of $250 or more, see page A-4. You **must** attach Form 8283 if over $500	**16**
	17	Carryover from prior year	**17**
	18	Add lines 15 through 17	**18**
Casualty and Theft Losses	19	Casualty or theft loss(es). Attach Form 4684. (See page A-5.)	**19**
Job Expenses and Most Other Miscellaneous Deductions (See page A-5.)	20	Unreimbursed employee expenses—job travel, union dues, job education, etc. Attach Form 2106 or 2106-EZ if required. (See page A-6.) ▶	**20**
	21	Tax preparation fees	**21**
	22	Other expenses—investment, safe deposit box, etc. List type and amount ▶	**22**
	23	Add lines 20 through 22	**23**
	24	Enter amount from Form 1040, line 38 ⌊ **24** ⌋	
	25	Multiply line 24 by 2% (.02)	**25**
	26	Subtract line 25 from line 23. If line 25 is more than line 23, enter -0-	**26**
Other Miscellaneous Deductions	27	Other—from list on page A-6. List type and amount ▶	**27**

Total Itemized Deductions	28	Is Form 1040, line 38, over $145,950 (over $72,975 if married filing separately)?
		  ☐ **No.** Your deduction is not limited. Add the amounts in the far right column for lines 4 through 27. Also, enter this amount on Form 1040, line 40. ▶
		  ☐ **Yes.** Your deduction may be limited. See page A-6 for the amount to enter.
			28

	29	If you elect to itemize deductions even though they are less than your standard deduction, check here ▶ ☐	

For Paperwork Reduction Act Notice, see Form 1040 instructions.	Cat. No. 11330X	**Schedule A (Form 1040) 2005**

(Use for Cumlative Problem.)

Form **2106**	**Employee Business Expenses**	OMB No. 1545-0139

Department of the Treasury
Internal Revenue Service (99)

▶ See separate instructions.

▶ Attach to Form 1040.

2005

Attachment Sequence No. **54**

Your name | Occupation in which you incurred expenses | Social security number

Part I **Employee Business Expenses and Reimbursements**

		Column A Other Than Meals and Entertainment		Column B Meals and Entertainment	
Step 1	**Enter Your Expenses**				
1	Vehicle expense from line 22 or line 29. (Rural mail carriers: See instructions.)	1			
2	Parking fees, tolls, and transportation, including train, bus, etc., that **did not** involve overnight travel or commuting to and from work . .	2			
3	Travel expense while away from home overnight, including lodging, airplane, car rental, etc. **Do not** include meals and entertainment.	3			
4	Business expenses not included on lines 1 through 3. **Do not** include meals and entertainment.	4			
5	Meals and entertainment expenses (see instructions)	5			
6	**Total expenses.** In Column A, add lines 1 through 4 and enter the result. In Column B, enter the amount from line 5	6			

Note: *If you were not reimbursed for any expenses in Step 1, skip line 7 and enter the amount from line 6 on line 8.*

Step 2 **Enter Reimbursements Received From Your Employer for Expenses Listed in Step 1**

7	Enter reimbursements received from your employer that were **not** reported to you in box 1 of Form W-2. Include any reimbursements reported under code "L" in box 12 of your Form W-2 (see instructions)	7			

Step 3 **Figure Expenses To Deduct on Schedule A (Form 1040)**

8	Subtract line 7 from line 6. If zero or less, enter -0-. However, if line 7 is greater than line 6 in Column A, report the excess as income on Form 1040, line 7	8			
	Note: *If **both** columns of line 8 are zero, you cannot deduct employee business expenses. Stop here and attach Form 2106 to your return.*				
9	In Column A, enter the amount from line 8. In Column B, multiply line 8 by 50% (.50). (Employees subject to Department of Transportation (DOT) hours of service limits: Multiply meal expenses incurred while away from home on business by 70% (.70) instead of 50%. For details, see instructions.)	9			
10	Add the amounts on line 9 of both columns and enter the total here. **Also, enter the total on Schedule A (Form 1040), line 20.** (Reservists, qualified performing artists, fee-basis state or local government officials, and individuals with disabilities: See the instructions for special rules on where to enter the total.) . . . . ▶	10			

For Paperwork Reduction Act Notice, see instructions.   Cat. No. 11700N   Form **2106** (2005)

(Use for Cumlative Problem.)

Form 2106 (2005)   Page **2**

Part II   Vehicle Expenses

Section A—General Information (You must complete this section if you are claiming vehicle expenses.)

			(a) Vehicle 1	(b) Vehicle 2
11	Enter the date the vehicle was placed in service	11	/ /	/ /
12	Total miles the vehicle was driven during 2005	12	miles	miles
13	Business miles included on line 12	13	miles	miles
14	Percent of business use. Divide line 13 by line 12	14	%	%
15	Average daily roundtrip commuting distance	15	miles	miles
16	Commuting miles included on line 12	16	miles	miles
17	Other miles. Add lines 13 and 16 and subtract the total from line 12	17	miles	miles
18	Do you (or your spouse) have another vehicle available for personal use?		☐ Yes ☐ No	
19	Was your vehicle available for personal use during off-duty hours?		☐ Yes ☐ No	
20	Do you have evidence to support your deduction?		☐ Yes ☐ No	
21	If "Yes," is the evidence written?		☐ Yes ☐ No	

Section B—Standard Mileage Rate (See the instructions for Part II to find out whether to complete this section or Section C.)

22	Multiply line 13 by 40.5¢ (.405)	22	*

Section C—Actual Expenses

			(a) Vehicle 1	(b) Vehicle 2
23	Gasoline, oil, repairs, vehicle insurance, etc.	23		
24a	Vehicle rentals	24a		
b	Inclusion amount (see instructions)	24b		
c	Subtract line 24b from line 24a	24c		
25	Value of employer-provided vehicle (applies only if 100% of annual lease value was included on Form W-2—see instructions)	25		
26	Add lines 23, 24c, and 25	26		
27	Multiply line 26 by the percentage on line 14	27		
28	Depreciation (see instructions)	28		
29	Add lines 27 and 28. Enter total here and on line 1	29		

Section D—Depreciation of Vehicles (Use this section only if you owned the vehicle and are completing Section C for the vehicle.)

			(a) Vehicle 1	(b) Vehicle 2
30	Enter cost or other basis (see instructions)	30		
31	Enter section 179 deduction (see instructions)	31		
32	Multiply line 30 by line 14 (see instructions if you claimed the section 179 deduction or special allowance)	32		
33	Enter depreciation method and percentage (see instructions)	33		
34	Multiply line 32 by the percentage on line 33 (see instructions)	34		
35	Add lines 31 and 34	35		
36	Enter the applicable limit explained in the line 36 instructions	36		
37	Multiply line 36 by the percentage on line 14	37		
38	Enter the **smaller** of line 35 or line 37. If you skipped lines 36 and 37, enter the amount from line 35. Also enter this amount on line 28 above	38		

✿ Printed on recycled paper   Form **2106** (2005)

* January–August mileage @ $.405
September–December mileage @ $.485

(Use for Cumlative Problem.)

Form **2441** Department of the Treasury Internal Revenue Service (99)	**Child and Dependent Care Expenses** ▶ Attach to Form 1040. ▶ See separate instructions.	OMB No. 1545-0068 **2005** Attachment Sequence No. **21**

Name(s) shown on Form 1040 | Your social security number

Before you begin: You need to understand the following terms. See **Definitions** on page 1 of the instructions.

● **Dependent Care Benefits**   ● **Qualifying Person(s)**   ● **Qualified Expenses**

Part I **Persons or Organizations Who Provided the Care—You must complete this part.**
(If you need more space, use the bottom of page 2.)

1	**(a)** Care provider's name	**(b)** Address (number, street, apt. no., city, state, and ZIP code)	**(c)** Identifying number (SSN or EIN)	**(d)** Amount paid (see instructions)

Did you receive **dependent care benefits?**

No ──────▶ Complete only Part II below.

Yes ──────▶ Complete Part III on the back next.

Caution. If the care was provided in your home, you may owe employment taxes. See the instructions for Form 1040, line 62.

Part II **Credit for Child and Dependent Care Expenses**

2   Information about your **qualifying person(s).** If you have more than two qualifying persons, see the instructions.

(a) Qualifying person's name		**(b)** Qualifying person's social security number	**(c) Qualified expenses** you incurred and paid in 2005 for the person listed in column (a)
First	Last		

3	Add the amounts in column (c) of line 2. **Do not** enter more than $3,000 for one qualifying person or $6,000 for two or more persons. If you completed Part III, enter the amount from line 32	3	
4	Enter your **earned income.** See instructions	4	
5	If married filing jointly, enter your spouse's earned income (if your spouse was a student or was disabled, see the instructions); **all others,** enter the amount from line 4 . . .	5	
6	Enter the **smallest** of line 3, 4, or 5	6	
7	Enter the amount from Form 1040, line 38	7		

8   Enter on line 8 the decimal amount shown below that applies to the amount on line 7

If line 7 is:			If line 7 is:		
Over	**But not over**	**Decimal amount is**	**Over**	**But not over**	**Decimal amount is**
$0	15,000	.35	$29,000	31,000	.27
15,000	17,000	.34	31,000	33,000	.26
17,000	19,000	.33	33,000	35,000	.25
19,000	21,000	.32	35,000	37,000	.24
21,000	23,000	.31	37,000	39,000	.23
23,000	25,000	.30	39,000	41,000	.22
25,000	27,000	.29	41,000	43,000	.21
27,000	29,000	.28	43,000	No limit	.20

8 | ✕ .

9	Multiply line 6 by the decimal amount on line 8. If you paid 2004 expenses in 2005, see the instructions	9	
10	Enter the amount from Form 1040, line 46, minus any amount on Form 1040, line 47 .	10	
11	**Credit for child and dependent care expenses.** Enter the **smaller** of line 9 or line 10 here and on Form 1040, line 48	11	

For Paperwork Reduction Act Notice, see page 4 of the instructions.   Cat. No. 11862M   Form **2441** (2005)

7

Self-Employment

CHAPTER CONTENTS

■■ CHAPTER OVERVIEW

*C*hapters 1 through 6 presented the basic structure for reporting income and deductions. This chapter focuses on the tax reporting for self-employed taxpayers and shows how they compute their self-employment net income and self-employment taxes. This chapter also covers retirement plans available to self-employed taxpayers.

Sole proprietors report income and expenses on Schedule C (Form 1040), Profit or Loss From Business. They then compute the self-employment tax on their profits on Schedule SE (Form 1040), Self-Employment Tax.

To understand the reporting process for self-employed taxpayers, it is important to realize that tax and financial accounting rules may differ. Thus, net income shown on Schedule C may not be the same as the net income reflected on the "books" of the business. For example, self-employed taxpayers who sell business property do not report the gain or loss on Schedule C. Instead, they report it on Form 4797, Sales of Business Property. However, for financial accounting purposes, they include the gain or loss in computing "book" net income. With the exception of the section on plans for self-employed taxpayers, the discussion in this chapter is limited to income and expense items reported on Schedule C.

ACCOUNTING METHODS

All businesses must keep records to support the calculation of taxable income. Most taxpayers use either the cash or accrual method of accounting, but other methods may apply. Some taxpayers use one method for tax purposes and another for their financial statements. However, for tax purposes, taxpayers must consistently use a method that clearly reflects income. In addition, taxpayers using the cash method to report income must use it to deduct expenses. Likewise, those who deduct expenses using the accrual method must use the accrual method to report income.

Taxpayers may use the accrual method to compute business income and the cash method for nonbusiness items. Also, those with more than one business may use different accounting methods for each separate and distinct business. Most businesses with gross receipts in excess of $5 million must use the accrual method.

Cash Method

Under the cash method, taxpayers report income when they actually or constructively receive it. Taxpayers constructively receive income when it is credited to their accounts or made available to them without restrictions. Taxpayers who receive income other than cash report as income the fair market value (FMV) of the property or services received.

EXAMPLE 1

On December 31, 20x1, Ben Carson receives a check for $200 in payment of fees earned. Carson constructively receives the $200 in 20x1, even if the check cannot be cashed until January 2, 20x2. Thus, Carson reports the $200 as income in 20x1.

EXAMPLE 2

On December 30, 20x1, Jane Dillow receives a check for $500 as payment for services rendered. The customer informs Dillow that the check will bounce if cashed before January 2, 20x2. Because the funds are not available until 20x2 Dillow has not constructively received the $500 in 20x1. Dillow reports the $500 as income in 20x2.

EXAMPLE 3

Scott Edwards receives ten shares of stock in exchange for services rendered. The market value of a share of stock is $28. Edwards reports income of $280 ($28 × 10 shares).

Under the cash method, taxpayers deduct expenses when they pay the cash, but only if the expenses relate to the current or a previous tax year. Taxpayers usually deduct prepaid amounts in the year the prepaid item is used in their businesses. Thus, cash basis taxpayers who pay cash for inventory cannot deduct it as cost of goods sold until they use it in their businesses. Likewise, cash basis taxpayers who prepay rent, insurance, etc., must wait until it is used in their businesses before deducting it.

EXAMPLE 4

On September 23, 20x1, Laura Fuller pays $36,000 for two years' insurance coverage that begins on October 1, 20x1. Although Fuller is a cash basis taxpayer, she cannot deduct the $36,000 payment in 20x1. Instead she deducts $4,500 ($36,000/24 × 3) in 20x1. Fuller will deduct $18,000 ($36,000/24 × 12) in 20x2 and the rest ($36,000/24 × 9 = $13,500) in 20x3.

Businesses that sell services rather than merchandise often use the cash method of accounting. For example, lawyers who use the cash method will keep logs of fees charged to clients but record the fees as income only when they receive the cash. Likewise, they record expenses for rent, supplies, and other items when they pay the cash.

Accrual Method

Under the accrual method, income includes amounts earned or accrued but not received; expenses include liabilities incurred but not paid. The accrual method acts on the right to receive the revenue rather than the actual receipt of cash. It acts on the use of the asset or service rather than the actual cash payment.

EXAMPLE 5

On January 3, 20x2, an employer pays salaries that employees earned for the week ended December 31, 20x1. Under the accrual method, the employer reports the salaries as an expense in 20x1. Under the cash method, the employer reports the expense in 20x2.

Taxpayers account for prepaid expenses the same way under both the cash and accrual methods. That is, they deduct only the amounts properly allocable to a given year and carry forward the rest to the next year. In Example 4, the amount deducted each year would be the same had Fuller used the accrual method of accounting.

The tax law generally requires taxpayers using the accrual method to recognize prepaid income in the year they receive it. However, when the taxpayer sells goods or performs services that extend beyond the current tax year, most prepaid income can be spread over the current year and the next tax year. Also, some accrual-method taxpayers do not have to accrue service revenue that experience indicates will not be collectible. These taxpayers include those who perform qualified services (like health, law, consulting) and those whose businesses had average annual gross receipts of $5 million or less for the last 3 years.

EXAMPLE 6

James Clark is in the business of selling and repairing televisions. In conjunction with his business, on April 1, 2005, Clark receives $1,200 from one of his customers for a 2-year warranty contract. Clark can report $450 ($1,200 × 9/24) on his 2005 tax return and the rest ($1,200 × 15/24 = $750) on his 2006 tax return. Clark must report the entire $1,200 on his 2005 and 2006 tax returns, even though some of the services extend into 2007.

The exception for postponing prepaid income does not extend to prepaid rent, prepaid insurance, or prepaid interest. Taxpayers who receive these types of prepaid items report the full amounts in income in the year they receive it.

EXAMPLE 7

On July 1, 2005, Julie Reeves collected $6,000 from a tenant for 12 months' rent. Reeves must report the entire $6,000 as income in 2005.

REPORTING PROFIT OR LOSS BY INDIVIDUALS, PARTNERSHIPS, AND CORPORATIONS

Partnerships and corporations are entities separate from their owners and must file separate returns. A self-employed taxpayer who owns a business reports net profit or (loss) on Form 1040. Schedule C (Form 1040), Profit or Loss From Business, summarizes the revenues and expenses of sole proprietors. Schedule F (Form 1040), Profit or Loss From Farming, summarizes the revenues and expenses of farmers.

Only self-employment income and related expenses are reported on Schedule C. Income that is not self-employment income is not reported on Schedule C. Instead, it is reported on some other form or schedule. For example, fees earned from an occasional lecture are not self-employment income. These fees are reported as Other Income on Form 1040, page 1.

EXAMPLES OF SELF-EMPLOYMENT INCOME

[handwritten: $90,000 × 15.3% or less]

- Consulting fees
- Director's fees
- Earnings of a registered nurse or licensed practicing nurse employed directly by the patient
- Fees charged by a child-care provider, unless services are provided in the parent's home
- Earnings of a newspaper vendor over age 17

- Fees earned by a clergy member or a Christian Science practitioner
- General partner's distributive share of partnership income and loss
- Guaranteed payments to a limited partner
- Fees earned by a professional executor
- Commissions earned by a real estate agent
- Royalties received by an author

[handwritten: Not subject to self-employment tax]

EXAMPLES OF INCOME OTHER THAN SELF-EMPLOYMENT

- Dividends, unless a dealer in securities
- Earnings of a corporate employee, even if a 100% shareholder of the corporation
- Fees earned from an occasional lecture
- Gains and losses on the sale of property
- Interest

- Real estate rentals, unless a real estate dealer
- Payment to a registered nurse or licensed nurse hired by an agency, doctor, or hospital
- Wages and tips received for services performed as an employee
- Wages of a newspaper carrier under age 18

To be deductible, expenses from a business must be *ordinary and necessary* for its operation. Also, the expenses must be *reasonable* in amount. An expense is ordinary if it is customary or usual in the taxpayer's line of business. An expense is necessary if it helps the taxpayer's business. As a general rule, revenue need not exceed expenses in any given year. However, in the case of a hobby activity, a taxpayer cannot deduct expenses in excess of revenues. (Hobby losses were covered in Chapter 6.) For the most part, the same rules for reporting revenues and expenses apply to all businesses. For example, all self-employed taxpayers must elect an accounting method regardless of whether they operate a farm or a professional practice.

DEDUCTIBLE BUSINESS EXPENSES

- Accounting and bookkeeping fees
- Advertising
- Bad debts
- Bank service charges
- Commissions and fees
- Contract labor costs
- Cost of goods sold
- Depletion and depreciation
- Education
- Employee achievement awards
- Employee benefit programs
- Employees' pension and profit-sharing plans
- Employment agency fees
- Gifts

- Insurance, license fees, and taxes
- Interest on business loans
- Legal and professional services
- Maintenance and repairs
- Meals and entertainment
- Office supplies and expense
- Rent
- Salaries and wages
- Professional dues and subscriptions
- Tax planning and tax preparation fees
- Telephone and utilities
- Transportation, including car and truck expenses
- Travel away from home

REPORTING NET PROFIT (OR LOSS) BY SOLE PROPRIETORSHIPS

Any net profit derived from a business or a profession operated as a sole proprietorship is taxable. A net loss is deducted in arriving at Adjusted Gross Income. In computing the amount of net profit (or loss), sole proprietors deduct from business income the cost of goods sold and all ordinary, necessary, and reasonable business expenses. The costs of capital expenditures, such as trucks, office machinery, and buildings, are deducted over several years through annual depreciation deductions (covered in Chapter 8).

Sole proprietorships report net profit on either Schedule C-EZ, Net Profit From Business, or Schedule C, Profit or Loss From Business. Since Schedule C-EZ has limited usage, this chapter focuses on Schedule C.

REQUIREMENTS FOR USING SCHEDULE C-EZ

- Cash method of accounting is used
- Only one business operated as a sole proprietor
- No employees during the year
- No inventory at any time during the year
- Business expenses of $5,000 or less
- No net loss from the business
- No unallowed prior year passive activity loss from the business
- No deduction for business use of the home
- Not required to file Form 4562, Depreciation and Amortization, for the business

STRUCTURE OF SCHEDULE C

Schedule C, Profit or Loss From Business, is a two-page schedule that reports the net profit or (loss) from a business operated as a sole proprietorship. A sole proprietor must pay self-employment tax on Schedule C profits. When a married couple files a joint return and each spouse owns a business, each spouse must file a Schedule C. If only one spouse owns a business, only the proprietor's name appears on Schedule C. If a proprietor owns more than one business, a separate Schedule C must be filed for each business.

Schedule C (Figure 7-1) supports the amount shown on Form 1040, page 1 (line 12). Page 1 (Schedule C) focuses on the calculation of net profit (or loss). It also requests general information about the business. Page 2 provides the supporting data for cost of goods sold and other expenses shown on page 1.

Information for Figure 7-1: Filled-In Schedule C (Form 1040)

Figure 7-1 illustrates Schedule C for George L. Monroe, owner of George L. Monroe, Consulting. The principal business code for consulting is 541600 (found in instructions to Schedule C). Monroe uses the cash method and materially participates in the operation of his consulting business. Because Monroe is required to withhold and pay payroll taxes on behalf of his employees, he applied for and received from the IRS an Employer ID number. Monroe reports this number on Schedule C (line D).

ITEM-BY-ITEM REPORTING ON SCHEDULE C

This section comments on each line item shown on Schedule C. The amounts reported relate to Monroe's filled-in Schedule C from Figure 7-1.

Schedule C, Part I: Income

Gross Receipts or Sales, $156,921 (Line 1)

Monroe operates a consulting practice (line A) and uses the cash method of accounting to report income and expenses (line F). Thus, Monroe's gross sales include amounts actually or constructively received during the year.

Returns and Allowances, $0 (Line 2)

Taxpayers subtract returns and allowances from gross receipts or sales to arrive at net receipts or sales (line 3). Since Monroe operates a service business, he had no returns or allowances. Thus, net receipts or sales of $156,921 equals gross receipts or sales.

Cost of Goods Sold, $0 (Line 4)

Taxpayers deduct the cost of goods sold from net receipts or sales to arrive at gross profit (line 5). Taxpayers calculate cost of goods sold on Schedule C, Part III (covered later in the chapter). Since Monroe's business does not involve selling products, he does not complete Part III. Monroe's gross profit of $156,921 equals net receipts or sales.

Gross Income, $156,921 (Line 7)

Gross income equals other income (line 6) plus gross profit (line 5). Other income includes federal and state gasoline fuel tax credits or refunds. It also includes interest income earned by the business.

FIGURE 7-1 Filled-In Schedule C, Form 1040, Page 1

SCHEDULE C (Form 1040) Department of the Treasury Internal Revenue Service	**Profit or Loss From Business** (Sole Proprietorship) ▶ Partnerships, joint ventures, etc., must file Form 1065 or 1065-B. ▶ Attach to Form 1040 or 1041. ▶ See Instructions for Schedule C (Form 1040).	OMB No. 1545-0074 **2005** Attachment Sequence No. **09**

Name of proprietor	Social security number (SSN)
George L. Monroe	139 24 6880

A Principal business or profession, including product or service (see page C-2 of the instructions) Management Consultant	**B** Enter code from pages C-7, 8, & 9 ▶ 5 4 1 6 0 0

C Business name. If no separate business name, leave blank. George L. Monroe, Consulting	**D** Employer ID number (EIN), if any 3 9 6 4 2 0 7 9 7

E Business address (including suite or room no.) ▶ 1712 Market Street
City, town or post office, state, and ZIP code   Cincinnati, OH 45227-3193

F Accounting method: **(1)** ☒ Cash   **(2)** ☐ Accrual   **(3)** ☐ Other (specify) ▶ _____

G Did you "materially participate" in the operation of this business during 2005? If "No," see page C-3 for limit on losses   ☒ Yes ☐ No

H If you started or acquired this business during 2005, check here . . . . ▶ ☐

Part I   Income

1	Gross receipts or sales. **Caution.** If this income was reported to you on Form W-2 and the "Statutory employee" box on that form was checked, see page C-3 and check here ▶ ☐	**1**	156,921 00
2	Returns and allowances	**2**	
3	Subtract line 2 from line 1	**3**	156,921 00
4	Cost of goods sold (from line 42 on page 2)	**4**	
5	**Gross profit.** Subtract line 4 from line 3	**5**	156,921 00
6	Other income, including Federal and state gasoline or fuel tax credit or refund (see page C-3)	**6**	
7	**Gross income.** Add lines 5 and 6 ▶	**7**	156,921 00

Part II   Expenses. Enter expenses for business use of your home **only** on line 30.

8	Advertising	**8**	492 00	18	Office expense	**18**	1,640 00
9	Car and truck expenses (see page C-3)	**9**	2,940 00	19	Pension and profit-sharing plans	**19**	
				20	Rent or lease (see page C-5):		
10	Commissions and fees	**10**			**a** Vehicles, machinery, and equipment	**20a**	1,200 00
11	Contract labor (see page C-4)	**11**			**b** Other business property	**20b**	
12	Depletion	**12**		21	Repairs and maintenance	**21**	1,389 00
13	Depreciation and section 179 expense deduction (not included in Part III) (see page C-4)	**13**	1,619 00	22	Supplies (not included in Part III)	**22**	1,642 00
				23	Taxes and licenses	**23**	7,210 00
				24	Travel, meals, and entertainment:		
					a Travel	**24a**	842 00
14	Employee benefit programs (other than on line 19)	**14**			**b** Deductible meals and entertainment (see page C-5)	**24b**	215 00
15	Insurance (other than health)	**15**	742 00	25	Utilities	**25**	3,600 00
16	Interest:			26	Wages (less employment credits)	**26**	40,616 00
	a Mortgage (paid to banks, etc.)	**16a**		27	Other expenses (from line 48 on page 2)	**27**	780 00
	b Other	**16b**					
17	Legal and professional services	**17**	310 00				

28	**Total expenses** before expenses for business use of home. Add lines 8 through 27 in columns . ▶	**28**	65,237 00
29	Tentative profit (loss). Subtract line 28 from line 7	**29**	91,684 00
30	Expenses for business use of your home. Attach **Form 8829**	**30**	1,084 00
31	Net profit or (loss). Subtract line 30 from line 29. • If a profit, enter on **Form 1040, line 12,** and **also** on **Schedule SE, line 2** (statutory employees, see page C-6). Estates and trusts, enter on Form 1041, line 3. • If a loss, you **must** go to line 32.	**31**	90,600 00
32	If you have a loss, check the box that describes your investment in this activity (see page C-6). • If you checked 32a, enter the loss on **Form 1040, line 12,** and **also** on **Schedule SE, line 2** (statutory employees, see page C-6). Estates and trusts, enter on Form 1041, line 3. • If you checked 32b, you **must** attach **Form 6198.** Your loss may be limited.	**32a** ☐ All investment is at risk. **32b** ☐ Some investment is not at risk.	

For Paperwork Reduction Act Notice, see Form 1040 instructions.   Cat. No. 11334P   Schedule C (Form 1040) 2005

FIGURE 7-1 Filled-In Schedule C, Form 1040, Page 2

Schedule C (Form 1040) 2005   Page **2**

Part III **Cost of Goods Sold** (see page C-6)

33 Method(s) used to value closing inventory: **a** ☐ Cost   **b** ☐ Lower of cost or market   **c** ☐ Other (attach explanation)

34 Was there any change in determining quantities, costs, or valuations between opening and closing inventory? If "Yes," attach explanation . . . . ☐ **Yes**   ☐ **No**

35 Inventory at beginning of year. If different from last year's closing inventory, attach explanation . . | 35 |

36 Purchases less cost of items withdrawn for personal use . . . . . . | 36 |

37 Cost of labor. Do not include any amounts paid to yourself . . . . . | 37 |

38 Materials and supplies . . . . | 38 |

39 Other costs . . . . | 39 |

40 Add lines 35 through 39 . . . . | 40 |

41 Inventory at end of year . . . . | 41 |

42 **Cost of goods sold.** Subtract line 41 from line 40. Enter the result here and on page 1, line 4 . . | 42 |

Part IV **Information on Your Vehicle.** Complete this part **only** if you are claiming car or truck expenses on line 9 and are not required to file Form 4562 for this business. See the instructions for line 13 on page C-4 to find out if you must file Form 4562.

43 When did you place your vehicle in service for business purposes? (month, day, year) ▶ ..../......./.......

44 Of the total number of miles you drove your vehicle during 2005, enter the number of miles you used your vehicle for:

a Business .... **b** Commuting (see instructions) .... **c** Other ....

45 Do you (or your spouse) have another vehicle available for personal use?. . . . . ☐ **Yes** ☐ **No**

46 Was your vehicle available for personal use during off-duty hours? . . . . ☐ **Yes** ☐ **No**

47a Do you have evidence to support your deduction? . . . . ☐ **Yes** ☐ **No**

  b If "Yes," is the evidence written? . . . . ☐ **Yes** ☐ **No**

Part V **Other Expenses.** List below business expenses not included on lines 8–26 or line 30.

Education expenses	780	00
48 Total other expenses. Enter here and on page 1, line 27 . . . . **48**	780	00

Printed on recycled paper   **Schedule C (Form 1040) 2005**

Schedule C, Part II: Expenses

Sole proprietors generally can deduct all ordinary, necessary, and reasonable expenses of operating a business. Schedule C, Part II lists 19 separate expenses that sole proprietors can deduct.

Advertising, $492 (Line 8)

Taxpayers generally can deduct advertising expenses related to their businesses. They cannot, however, deduct advertising for purposes of influencing legislation.

Car and Truck Expenses, $2,940 (Line 9)

Chapter 6 covered the deduction of transportation costs for employees. Employees use either the actual method or the standard mileage method (40.5 cents per mile from 1/1/05–8/31/05 and 48.5 cents per mile from 9/1/05–12/31/05), plus business parking and tolls to compute their deductible transportation costs. Employees provide support for their deduction on Form 2106. Self-employed taxpayers compute their transportation deduction using the same two methods. However, self-employed taxpayers support their transportation deduction on Schedule C, page 2, Part IV (or on Form 4562, Depreciation and Amortization, page 2). Monroe uses the standard mileage method in 2005. Monroe drove a total of 6,398 miles from 1/1/05–8/31/05 and 720 miles from 9/1/05–12/31/05. His car and truck expense deduction equals $2,940 [(6,398 × $.405) + (720 × $.485)]. Because Monroe completes Form 4562 to support his depreciation deduction, he does not complete Schedule C, Part IV.

DEDUCTIBLE CAR AND TRUCK EXPENSES

- Garage rent, parking, and tolls
- Gasoline, oil, and lubrication
- Insurance, licenses, and auto club dues
- Lease payments
- Maintenance and repairs
- Property taxes
- Tires and batteries
- Washing and polishing

EXAMPLE 8

In 2005, Terry Madden drove 6,000 business miles and 20,000 total miles. All business miles were driven before September 1. In 2004, Madden used the actual method to deduct expenses related to the business use of his car. Madden's 2005 expenses for the car include the following:

Business parking and tolls	$ 100
Depreciation	3,000
Gas	1,000
Insurance	450
License tags	50
Oil change	20
Total	$4,620

Under the actual method, Madden deducts $1,456 [($4,520 × 6,000/20,000) + $100 business parking and tolls] in 2005. Since Madden used the actual method in 2004, the IRS requires its use in 2005. Had Madden been able to use the standard mileage method, the deduction would have been $2,530 [(6,000 × $.405) + $100].

Commissions and Fees, $0 (Line 10)

Taxpayers can deduct commissions and fees paid for business purposes.

Contract Labor, $0 (Line 11)

Taxpayers deduct amounts paid for contract labor on Schedule C (line 11). They do not include on this line any wages paid to employees. Wages paid to employees are reported on Schedule C (line 26).

Depletion, $0 (Line 12)

Taxpayers who own and operate a business with a natural resource, such as an oil well, mineral deposit, or gold mine, may claim a depletion deduction. **Depletion** is the process that allows taxpayers to deduct the cost of natural resources as units from the resource are sold (under the accrual method) or sold and payment is received (under the cash method). The two methods for computing the depletion deduction are the cost method and the percentage depletion method. Each year the taxpayer may use whichever method produces the greatest deduction.

The *cost method* allows taxpayers to deduct the costs of natural resources as the resource units are recovered and sold. The cost of the natural resource is divided by the number of units expected to be recovered. This provides depletion per unit. This per unit cost is multiplied by the number of units sold during the year.

Under the *percentage depletion method*, taxpayers multiply a set percentage by the "gross income" generated by the resource during the year. The government specifies the percentages used, which range from 5% for sand and gravel to 22% for lead, zinc, tin, and sulfur. A 15% rate applies to copper, gold, silver, iron, oil, and gas. The percentage depletion method has a distinct advantage over cost depletion in that the taxpayer can continue to take the percentage depletion deduction even after the entire cost invested in the natural resource has been fully recovered through annual depletion deductions.

Depreciation and Section 179 Expense Deduction, $1,619 (Line 13)

Monroe completes and attaches Form 4562, Depreciation and Amortization, to support the depreciation and section 179 expense deduction. Also on Form 4562, Monroe will provide information to support his car and truck expenses reported on Schedule C. Depreciation expense is the focus of Chapter 8.

Employee Benefit Programs, $0 (Line 14)

Employers generally can deduct the costs of benefits they provide for their employees. For example, employers can deduct life insurance premiums paid for policies on employees' lives, but only for policies that do not list the employer as the beneficiary. Employers also can deduct the cost of medical insurance paid for employees. Other examples include adoption expenses, child care, parking, transportation, and recreational facilities.

Insurance, $742 (Line 15)

Taxpayers can deduct insurance premiums on business property, including real estate, furniture, machinery, and equipment. Employers deduct premiums paid for medical and life insurance for employees as employee benefits (line 14). As mentioned earlier in the chapter, cash method taxpayers cannot deduct advance payments for premiums on policies that cover more than one tax year. They can deduct only the portions that apply during the year.

Interest, $0 (Lines 16a and 16b)

loans or credit card interest (included)

Business interest includes interest on mortgages (line 16a) and other business loans (line 16b). If the taxpayer borrows money and uses the loan proceeds partly for nonbusiness purposes, then only the interest related to the business-use portion of the borrowed funds can be deducted.

EXAMPLE 9

Jay Jackson borrows funds secured by business property. Jackson uses one-half of the funds to buy a car for personal use and uses the rest in his business. Jackson deducts one-half of the interest on Schedule C. The personal interest cannot be deducted.

Legal and Professional Services, $310 (Line 17)

Taxpayers can deduct legal and professional fees, including the portion of tax preparation fees that relate to preparation of Schedule C. They cannot deduct legal fees incurred to acquire business property. Instead, these amounts are added to the amount the taxpayer pays for the property.

Office Expense, $1,640 (Line 18)

Office expense includes postage, stationery, and other general expenses of operating a business office.

Pension and Profit-Sharing Plans, $0 (Line 19)

amt contributed for employees

Sole proprietors deduct on Schedule C amounts they contribute to their employees' qualified pension and profit-sharing plans. Under a qualified plan, the employer must offer the plan to all eligible full-time employees. Two common qualified plans are defined contribution and defined benefit plans.

A **defined benefit plan** focuses on the annual benefits at retirement. Employers must contribute annually to the plan so that the promised benefits will be available at retirement. The benefit formula used in computing the annual contribution considers employees' compensation levels and years of service. This calculation usually requires professional assistance.

In contrast, a **defined contribution plan** focuses on annual contributions. The amount contributed is usually a percentage of the employee's compensation. Unlike a defined benefit plan, this type of plan promises no predetermined benefits. Instead, annual contributions are made to individual employee accounts and employees receive whatever benefits the accumulated contributions (plus any earnings) provide.

A **simplified employee pension (SEP) plan** is a defined contribution plan employers can establish for their employees. In 2005, the maximum contribution an employer can make to an employee's SEP is the lesser of $42,000 or 25% of the employee's compensation. For SEP plans established after 1986, only employers (not employees) can make contributions to an employee's SEP plan.

SEP not taxed until taken

An alternative to a SEP is a 401(k) plan. The main advantage to a 401(k) plan over a SEP is that employees can make pre-tax contributions to their 401(k) plans and reduce their taxable salaries. In 2005, employees can contribute up to $14,000 to a 401(k) plan. Employees age 50 and older can contribute up to $18,000 in 2005. Employers may match employees' contributions, but are not required to do so. The most common match for employers is 50% of the employee's contributions, up to 6% of the employee's wages. Employers deduct only their matching contributions on Schedule C (line 19).

Employers that have 100 or fewer employees who earned $5,000 or more in the prior year can adopt a **savings incentive match plan for employees (SIMPLE).** Employers can set up SIMPLE plans using either IRAs or 401(k)s. Employees who earned at least $5,000 in any two prior years and expect to earn at least $5,000 in the current year would be allowed to contribute up to $10,000 of their salaries to the plan for 2005. (Employees age 50 and older can contribute up to $12,000 for 2005.) Employers generally are required to make matching contributions up to 3% of the employee's compensation. Only the employer's contribution is deductible on Schedule C.

> Calculating the annual contribution to a defined benefit plan often requires professional assistance from an actuary. The additional administrative costs may keep employers from setting up defined benefit plans. SEP, SIMPLE and 401(k) plans are much easier and less costly to administer. SIMPLE plans offer the advantage of allowing employees the option of whether they want to participate in the plan. However, employer matching is required for all employees who elect to participate. Employer matching is elective for 401(k) plans.

Rent or Lease, $1,200 (Line 20a) and $0 (Line 20b)

Rent or lease expense is the amount paid for the use of property not owned by the taxpayer. However, if the taxpayer will receive title to the property at the end of the lease, then the amount paid is not rent expense, but instead is added to the taxpayer's cost in the property.

Taxpayers generally can deduct rent on property used in their trade or business. Taxpayers who pay rent in advance only deduct the amount that applies to the tax year to which they made the rent payment. They deduct the rest in the year or years to which the rent applies.

EXAMPLE 10

Katie Norton leases property for three years beginning June 1, 20x1. On June 1, 20x1, Norton pays $12,000 for 12 months' rent, but can deduct only $7,000 in 20x1 ($12,000/12 × 7) using either the cash or the accrual method. On June 1, 20x2, she pays $12,000 for another 12 months' rent. In 20x2, Norton will deduct the remaining $5,000 paid in 20x1, and $7,000 of the $12,000 paid on June 1, 20x2.

Taxpayers who lease a car deduct the costs related to the business-use portion of the lease. Taxpayers must spread any advance lease payments over the entire lease period. Payments made to buy a car are not deductible as rent, even if they are described as lease payments. Chapter 8 describes the rules for leased cars in greater detail.

Repairs and Maintenance, $1,389 (Line 21)

Taxpayers can deduct the costs of keeping business property in its normal operating condition. Deductible costs include labor, supplies, and other related types of expenses. Repair expenses must be distinguished from capital expenditures. Taxpayers capitalize any costs that either add to the value or usefulness of the property or significantly extend its useful life. Repairs and maintenance allocable to the cost of goods sold should be deducted on Schedule C under Part III in calculating cost of goods sold, and not in Part II.

Supplies, $1,642 (Line 22)

Taxpayers can deduct the cost of supplies that they normally use within one year. The cost of supplies not expected to be used within one year are deducted in the year the supplies are used.

Taxes and Licenses, $7,210 (Line 23)

Sole proprietors can deduct property taxes paid on business property. They also can deduct their share of social security and Medicare taxes paid for employees plus amounts paid for state and federal unemployment taxes. Deductible licenses include business licenses required by state and local governments for operating a trade or business.

Travel, $842 (Line 24a), Deductible Meals and Entertainment, $215 (Line 24b)

Chapter 6 presented the deduction for employees' travel, meals, and entertainment. For the most part, the same rules govern the amount sole proprietors can deduct. Amounts owners pay for business-related travel, meals and entertainment on behalf of themselves or their employees are deductible on Schedule C. When an owner reimburses an employee, the treatment depends on whether an "accountable" or "nonaccountable" plan is in place. An accountable plan requires the employee to, (1) adequately report the expenses to the employer, and (2) return any excess reimbursements to the employer. Owners with an accountable plan deduct the reimbursements under "Travel, meals, and entertainment," but can deduct only 50% of the meals and entertainment.

DEDUCTIBLE TRAVEL EXPENSES

- Air, rail, and bus transportation, including transportation to and from the airport and the hotel, from one customer to another, or from one place of business to another
- Baggage charges
- Dry cleaning and laundry
- Lodging
- Meals and entertainment (subject to limitations)
- Car expenses, including car rental
- Telephone and fax costs
- Tips related to travel

As described in Chapter 6, some employers use the "per diem" approach to reimburse employees for the costs of meals and lodging. Employers deduct the reimbursement under "Travel, meals, and entertainment," but deduct only 50% of the per diem meal allowance. The rules regarding the use of per diems in lieu of actual expenses for meals and entertainment also apply to sole proprietors. However, the per diem for lodging can only be used for purposes of reimbursing employees. When the owner of the business is away from home overnight on business, the owner must deduct the actual costs for lodging.

 The federal per diem rate varies from city to city. These rates can be found in IRS publication 1542.

When a nonaccountable plan exists (one that does not meet both criteria for an accountable plan), the reimbursement is treated as "Wages" and is deductible as such on Schedule C. Employees are taxed on these additional wages and can deduct their expenses (but only 50% of meals and entertainment) as miscellaneous deductions subject to the 2% rule.

EXAMPLE 11

Gene Keys is self-employed. He reimbursed his employees $10,000 for travel expenses and $2,000 for meals and entertainment under an accountable plan. Keys deducts $10,000 as travel on Schedule C (line 24a) and $1,000 (50% × $2,000) as deductible meals and entertainment (line 24b).

EXAMPLE 12

Assume the same facts as in Example 11 except that Keys has a nonaccountable plan. Keys deducts all $12,000 as wages on Schedule C (line 26). The employees are taxed on the $12,000, and can deduct $11,000 (only 50% of meals and entertainment) as miscellaneous deductions subject to the 2% rule.

Utilities, $3,600 (Line 25)

Utilities include the costs for heat, light, power, and telephone. Taxpayers can deduct the costs for utilities to the extent the costs are not incurred for personal use. They can deduct the cost of operating a cellular phone, but only for the time it is used for conducting business. Taxpayers deduct utilities for an office located in their home on Form 8829, Business Use of the Home (covered later in the chapter).

Wages, $40,616 (Line 26)

Employers deduct amounts paid as wages to employees. They also deduct amounts paid to them as bonuses, vacation pay, taxable employee achievement awards, and reimbursements under nonaccountable plans. The amount reported on Schedule C *excludes any wages included* in cost of goods sold. It also does not include any withdrawals the proprietor makes from the business.

Other Expenses, $780 (Line 27)

Other expenses are amounts not deductible elsewhere on Schedule C. Sole proprietors deducting other expenses list the type and amount of each expense on Schedule C, page 2, Part V. Four common other expenses sole proprietors incur are education expenses, business gifts, dues and subscriptions, and bad debts.

Self-employed taxpayers can deduct on Schedule C professional dues and subscriptions related to their line of business. They also can deduct the ordinary and necessary costs incurred to educate and train employees in operating the business. Deductible education expenses include tuition, books, transportation, meals (subject to the 50% rule), and lodging. In addition, sole proprietors can deduct amounts spent on their own education as long as it does not (1) prepare them to meet the minimum education requirements of their present profession or (2) qualify them for a new trade or business. Assuming neither of these situations apply, to deduct these costs, sole proprietors must show that the education (1) maintains or improves the skills required in their business or (2) is required by law to keep their status in the profession. The rules for deducting education expenses for self-employed taxpayers are essentially the same as those presented in Chapter 6 for employees. Monroe deducts $780 for educational courses taken in 2005.

Sole proprietors can deduct the costs of business gifts to customers and clients. The maximum deduction cannot exceed $25 for business gifts given to any one individual during the tax year. Gifts not subject to the $25 limit include:

1. A widely distributed item costing $4 or less on which the donor's company name is permanently imprinted. Examples include pens and key chains.
2. Signs, display racks, and other promotional material used on the recipient's business premises.
3. Incidental costs, such as engraving, packaging, insuring, and mailing.

> Employees can deduct the costs of business gifts to clients and customers using these same rules. They can deduct the cost of gifts made to subordinates, but not the cost of gifts to superiors. Employees deduct these costs as miscellaneous itemized deductions subject to the 2% rule.

Any item that can be considered either a gift or entertainment generally is considered entertainment. A taxpayer who gives a business client tickets to an event but does not attend the event with the client can treat the tickets either as a gift or as entertainment. However, if the taxpayer goes with the client to the event, the tickets must be treated as entertainment. Employers may also deduct gifts of property valued at up to $400 awarded to employees for their length of service or safety achievement.

Taxpayers deduct bad debts that result from business operations. Bad debts may result from credit sales to customers. They also may result from loans to suppliers, clients, employees, or distributors. Sole proprietors deduct bad debts when a receivable, or a portion of a receivable, becomes uncollectible. The tax law does not permit the use of the "reserve" method, which is an acceptable financial accounting practice. For a bad debt to be deductible, a true creditor-debtor relationship must exist between the taxpayer (creditor) and the debtor. Also, the taxpayer must incur an actual loss of money or have previously reported the amount owed in gross income (direct write-off method). Thus, a cash basis taxpayer who renders services cannot take a bad debt deduction when a customer's receivable becomes uncollectible because no income was ever reported.

To deduct a business bad debt, the taxpayer must show a dominant business reason for making the loan or sale. Only the uncollectible portion of a receivable qualifies as a business bad debt. A business bad debt is deductible in the year it becomes partially or completely worthless. Should the IRS challenge the bad debt deduction, the taxpayer must prove that the debt is worthless and will remain worthless. Doing so may involve going to court, which taxpayers can avoid by showing that the court would rule that the receivable was uncollectible. This usually occurs in the case of a bankrupt debtor.

Total Expenses, $65,237 (Line 28)

Monroe subtracts total expenses from gross income (line 7) to arrive at tentative profit (loss) of $91,684 (line 29).

Business Use of the Home

Chapter 6 presented the rules for the home office deduction for employees. Sole proprietors who use part of their home as a place of business can deduct expenses for part of the home.

Although the rules for employees and sole proprietors overlap in several ways, sole proprietors must complete Form 8829, Expenses for Business Use of Your Home, to support the home office deduction.

Sole proprietors may deduct expenses related to an office located in the home only if they use that part of the home regularly and exclusively as either (1) the principal place of business or (2) a place to meet or deal with patients, clients, or customers in the normal course of business. In contrast, sole proprietors can deduct expenses for using part of the home as a day-care facility or as a place to store inventory sold in the business even if they sometimes use that part of the home for personal purposes.

To claim a home office deduction, the taxpayer usually must be able to demonstrate that, relative to the work done outside the office, the work done in the office is more important to the business. However, taxpayers who use their home office exclusively and regularly for administrative or management activities and have no other location to perform these duties qualify for the home office deduction even if the most important aspect of their business takes place outside of the home. For example, a self-employed plumber who spends several hours each week scheduling appointments, preparing bills, and performing other administrative activities qualifies for the home office deduction, provided that the office is used regularly and exclusively for business purposes.

EXAMPLE 13

Stan Smith, a self-employed writer, uses an office located in his home exclusively and regularly to write. Smith conducts most of his interviews outside of the office. He also spends many hours doing research at the library. Although doing research and conducting interviews are important to the business, the most important part is writing. Since Smith does his writing at the office located in his home, he qualifies for the home office deduction.

To allocate expenses to the home office, taxpayers divide the square feet of the room used as the home office by the total square feet of the home. Taxpayers who provide child care and use part of their home exclusively as a child care facility also use this method to allocate a portion of their expenses of the home to the child care business. However, for areas of the home used to provide child care, but not on an exclusive basis, the deductible costs must be reduced by the ratio of hours the area is used for day care to the total hours in the year. Total hours in 2005 were 8,760 (24 hours × 365 days).

EXAMPLE 14

Betty Glover provides child care in her home. The area of the home used in her child care business is 40% of the total area of the home. For 50 weeks in 2005, Glover provides child care services 10 hours a day, 5 days a week, for a total of 2,500 hours (10 × 5 × 50). Glover can deduct 11.42% (40% × 2,500/8,760) of the expenses of her home against the income she earns providing child care.

Information for Figure 7-2: Filled-In Form 8829

George Monroe (from Figure 7-1) has been operating his consulting business out of his home since 2001. The business portion of the home is 240 square feet. The total square footage of the home is 2,400.

Other Information

  8: Tentative profit from Schedule C, line 29, **$91,684.00**

10b: Mortgage interest, **$4,300.00**

11b: Real estate taxes, **$1,500.00**

17b: Insurance, **$280.00**

18b: Repairs and maintenance, **$950.00**

19b: Utilities, **$1,810.00**

  35: Smaller of the home's adjusted basis ($90,000.00) or its FMV ($128,000.00), **$90,000.00**

  36: Value of land included on line 35, **$12,000.00**

  39: Depreciation percentage, **2.564%** (1/39 years) [explained in Chapter 8]

In Figure 7-2, the income from the business activity exceeded both the business expenses reported on Schedule C, Part II, and the expenses related to the office in the home. With the exception of the business portion of home mortgage interest, real estate taxes, and casualty losses, home office expenses cannot create a loss on Schedule C. Specifically, taxpayers cannot deduct these other types of home office expenses to the extent they exceed the net income derived from the business. **Net income derived from the business** equals tentative profit shown on Schedule C (line 29) minus the home office expenses for home mortgage interest, real estate taxes, and casualty losses. Any disallowed expenses carry over to the next year.

EXAMPLE 15

Neil Morgan conducts a business in his home. The business portion equals 20% of the total square footage of the home. Expenses of operating the home include utilities, $3,500; real estate taxes, $5,000; mortgage interest, $6,000; insurance, $800; general home repairs, $2,000; and depreciation, $4,500. Tentative profit from the business is $3,300. Morgan computes net income derived from the business as follows.

Tentative profit	$3,300
Less business portion of mortgage interest and real estate taxes [20% × ($6,000 + $5,000)]	(2,200)
Net income derived from the business	$1,100

After the business portion of interest and taxes are deducted, taxpayers deduct the other home office expenses (to the extent of net income derived from the business) in the following order:

1. The business portion of expenses (other than depreciation) incurred in operating the business in the home. These expenses include repairs, maintenance, insurance, and utilities.

2. The depreciation on the business portion of the home.

Any home office expenses in excess of net income derived from the business carry over to the next year.

FIGURE 7-2   Filled-In Form 8829

Form **8829**	**Expenses for Business Use of Your Home**	OMB No. 1545-1266
Department of the Treasury Internal Revenue Service (99)	▶ File only with Schedule C (Form 1040). Use a separate Form 8829 for each home you used for business during the year. ▶ See separate instructions.	**2005** Attachment Sequence No. **66**

Name(s) of proprietor(s): George L. Monroe   Your social security number: 139:24:6880

Part I   Part of Your Home Used for Business

1	Area used regularly and exclusively for business, regularly for daycare, or for storage of inventory or product samples (see instructions)	**1**	240
2	Total area of home	**2**	2,400
3	Divide line 1 by line 2. Enter the result as a percentage	**3**	10 %

- For daycare facilities not used exclusively for business, also complete lines 4–6.
- All others, skip lines 4–6 and enter the amount from line 3 on line 7.

4	Multiply days used for daycare during year by hours used per day	**4**	h r.
5	Total hours available for use during the year (365 days × 24 hours) (see instructions)	**5**	8,760 h r.
6	Divide line 4 by line 5. Enter the result as a decimal amount	**6**	
7	Business percentage. For daycare facilities not used exclusively for business, multiply line 6 by line 3 (enter the result as a percentage). All others, enter the amount from line 3 ▶	**7**	10 %

Part II   Figure Your Allowable Deduction

		(a) Direct expenses	(b) Indirect expenses		
8	Enter the amount from Schedule C, line 29, **plus** any net gain or (loss) derived from the business use of your home and shown on Schedule D or Form 4797. If more than one place of business, see instructions			**8**	91,684 00
	See instructions for columns (a) and (b) before completing lines 9–20.				
9	Casualty losses (see instructions)	**9**			
10	Deductible mortgage interest (see instructions)	**10**	4,300 00		
11	Real estate taxes (see instructions)	**11**	1,500 00		
12	Add lines 9, 10, and 11	**12**	5,800 00		
13	Multiply line 12, column (b) by line 7	**13** 580 00			
14	Add line 12, column (a) and line 13			**14**	580 00
15	Subtract line 14 from line 8. If zero or less, enter -0-			**15**	91,104 00
16	Excess mortgage interest (see instructions)	**16**			
17	Insurance	**17**	280 00		
18	Repairs and maintenance	**18**	950 00		
19	Utilities	**19**	1,810 00		
20	Other expenses (see instructions)	**20**			
21	Add lines 16 through 20	**21**	3,040 00		
22	Multiply line 21, column (b) by line 7	**22** 304 00			
23	Carryover of operating expenses from 2004 Form 8829, line 41	**23**			
24	Add line 21 in column (a), line 22, and line 23			**24**	304 00
25	Allowable operating expenses. Enter the **smaller** of line 15 or line 24			**25**	304 00
26	Limit on excess casualty losses and depreciation. Subtract line 25 from line 15			**26**	90,800 00
27	Excess casualty losses (see instructions)	**27**			
28	Depreciation of your home from Part III below	**28** 200 00			
29	Carryover of excess casualty losses and depreciation from 2004 Form 8829, line 42	**29**			
30	Add lines 27 through 29			**30**	200 00
31	Allowable excess casualty losses and depreciation. Enter the **smaller** of line 26 or line 30			**31**	200 00
32	Add lines 14, 25, and 31			**32**	1,084 00
33	Casualty loss portion, if any, from lines 14 and 31. Carry amount to **Form 4684**, Section B			**33**	
34	Allowable expenses for business use of your home. Subtract line 33 from line 32. Enter here and on Schedule C, line 30. If your home was used for more than one business, see instructions ▶			**34**	1,084 00

Part III   Depreciation of Your Home

35	Enter the **smaller** of your home's adjusted basis or its fair market value (see instructions)	**35**	90,000 00
36	Value of land included on line 35	**36**	12,000 00
37	Basis of building. Subtract line 36 from line 35	**37**	78,000 00
38	Business basis of building. Multiply line 37 by line 7	**38**	7,800 00
39	Depreciation percentage (see instructions)	**39**	2.564 %
40	Depreciation allowable (see instructions). Multiply line 38 by line 39. Enter here and on line 28 above	**40**	200 00

Part IV   Carryover of Unallowed Expenses to 2006

41	Operating expenses. Subtract line 25 from line 24. If less than zero, enter -0-	**41**	.
42	Excess casualty losses and depreciation. Subtract line 31 from line 30. If less than zero, enter -0-	**42**	

For Paperwork Reduction Act Notice, see page 4 of separate instructions.   Cat. No. 13232M   Form **8829** (2005)

(handwritten note at left margin: Carried over previous yr. when operating expenses exceed profit)

Morgan computes the rest of the home office deduction and the expenses carried over to the next year as follows.

Business use of other home office expenses:	
Utilities, insurance, repairs (20%)	$1,260
Depreciation on the home office (20%)	900
Total other home office expenses	$2,160
Deductible expenses limited to net income derived from the business	(1,100)
Home office expenses not deductible in the current year, to be carried forward to next year	$1,060

The $1,100 of deductible home office expenses comes from the home office portion of expenses for utilities, insurance, and repairs. The $1,060 of expenses carried over consists of $160 ($1,260 – $1,100) of utilities, insurance, and repairs, and $900 of depreciation.

Schedule C, Part III: Cost of Goods Sold

The calculation of cost of goods sold (line 4), necessary for proprietors in manufacturing, wholesale, or retail businesses, is done on Schedule C, Part III. Cost of goods sold equals beginning inventory plus the cost of net purchases, labor, materials and supplies, and other costs for the year minus ending inventory. Cost of goods sold should include only expenses directly related to obtaining or producing the goods sold.

For merchants, beginning inventory consists of products held for sale. For manufacturers, beginning inventory is the sum of raw materials, work in process, and finished goods. Beginning inventory of one year should be the same as ending inventory of the prior year.

For merchants, purchases include all goods bought for sale during the year. For manufacturers, purchases of raw materials include all materials bought during the year to be used in producing the finished products. Any freight-in paid is added to the costs of purchases. Returns and allowances and trade discounts reduce total purchases. Cash discounts either can be credited to separate discount accounts or deducted from total purchases. The method for handling cash discounts must be used consistently from year to year. Figure 7-4 shows a filled-in Schedule C for a taxpayer in the retail business.

Information for Figure 7-4: Filled-In Schedule C (Form 1040)

Harold R. Wilson is the sole proprietor of Wilson's Hardware Store. Figure 7-3 shows Wilson's income statement for the year ended December 31, 2005. He completes Schedule C (Figure 7-4) using the information from the income statement. His business code is 444130. Wilson materially participates in the business and uses the accrual accounting method and the cost method to value inventory.

Net income from Wilson's income statement is $60,496. Schedule C, however, shows a net profit of $61,131. Part of the $635 difference ($61,131 – $60,496) relates to the $460 of charitable contributions. Although the business paid this amount, the tax laws require charitable contributions of a sole proprietor to be deducted as an itemized deduction on Schedule A. The remaining $175 difference relates to reducing meals and entertainment by 50% on Schedule C.

FIGURE 7-3   Income Statement for Wilson's Hardware Store

WILSON'S HARDWARE STORE
Income Statement
For Year Ended December 31, 2005

Operating revenue:

Sales	$284,280	
Less sales returns and allowances	(2,751)	
Net sales		$281,529

Cost of merchandise sold:

Merchandise inventory, beginning of period		$131,216	
Purchases	$180,716		
Less purchases discount	(3,614)		
Net purchases	$177,102		
Less merchandise withdrawn for personal use	(400)	176,702	
Merchandise available for sale		$307,918	
Less merchandise inventory end of period		(167,546)	
Cost of merchandise sold			(140,372)
Gross profit on sales			$141,157

Operating expenses:

Advertising expense	$ 3,906	
Bad debts from sales or services	1,531	
Charitable contributions	460	
Depreciation expense	1,133	
Entertainment expense	350	
Insurance expense	2,250	
Legal and professional services	6,693	
Miscellaneous expense	15	
Payroll taxes	8,845	
Personal property taxes	960	
Rent expense	10,200	
Repairs to store equipment	2,125	
Supplies expense	3,400	
Telephone expense	1,258	
Travel	184	
Truck rental expense	2,498	
Utilities expense	3,908	
Wages expense	31,297	
Total operating expenses		(81,013)
Operating income		$ 60,144

Other income:

Interest income	584
	$ 60,728

Other expenses:

Interest expense	(232)
Net income	$ 60,496

FIGURE 7-4   Filled-In Schedule C, Form 1040, Page 1

SCHEDULE C (Form 1040)	**Profit or Loss From Business**	OMB No. 1545-0074
	(Sole Proprietorship)	2005
Department of the Treasury Internal Revenue Service	▶ Partnerships, joint ventures, etc., must file Form 1065 or 1065-B. ▶ Attach to Form 1040 or 1041. ▶ See Instructions for Schedule C (Form 1040).	Attachment Sequence No. 09

Name of proprietor	Social security number (SSN)
Harold R. Wilson	272 11 8855

A	Principal business or profession, including product or service (see page C-2 of the instructions)	B Enter code from pages C-7, 8, & 9
	Retail Hardware	▶ 4 4 4 1 3 0

C	Business name. If no separate business name, leave blank.	D Employer ID number (EIN), if any
	Wilson's Hardware Store	9 1 0 6 2 4 4 3 1

E Business address (including suite or room no.) ▶ 27 Main Street
City, town or post office, state, and ZIP code   Madison, WI 53593-3644

F Accounting method: (1) ☐ Cash   (2) ☒ Accrual   (3) ☐ Other (specify) ▶

G Did you "materially participate" in the operation of this business during 2005? If "No," see page C-3 for limit on losses   ☒ Yes ☐ No

H If you started or acquired this business during 2005, check here   ▶ ☐

Part I   Income

1	Gross receipts or sales. **Caution.** If this income was reported to you on Form W-2 and the "Statutory employee" box on that form was checked, see page C-3 and check here ▶ ☐	1	284,280	00
2	Returns and allowances	2	2,751	00
3	Subtract line 2 from line 1	3	281,529	00
4	Cost of goods sold (from line 42 on page 2)	4	140,372	00
5	**Gross profit.** Subtract line 4 from line 3	5	141,157	00
6	Other income, including Federal and state gasoline or fuel tax credit or refund (see page C-3)	6	584	00
7	**Gross income.** Add lines 5 and 6 ▶	7	141,741	00

Part II   Expenses. Enter expenses for business use of your home **only** on line 30.

8	Advertising	8	3,906	00	18	Office expense	18		
9	Car and truck expenses (see page C-3)	9			19	Pension and profit-sharing plans	19		
10	Commissions and fees	10			20	Rent or lease (see page C-5):			
11	Contract labor (see page C-4)	11			a	Vehicles, machinery, and equipment	20a	2,498	00
12	Depletion	12			b	Other business property	20b	10,200	00
13	Depreciation and section 179 expense deduction (not included in Part III) (see page C-4)	13	1,133	00	21	Repairs and maintenance	21	2,125	00
					22	Supplies (not included in Part III)	22	3,400	00
					23	Taxes and licenses	23	9,805	00
14	Employee benefit programs (other than on line 19)	14			24	Travel, meals, and entertainment:			
					a	Travel	24a	184	00
15	Insurance (other than health)	15	2,250	00	b	Deductible meals and entertainment (see page C-5)	24b	175	00
16	Interest:				25	Utilities	25	5,166	00
a	Mortgage (paid to banks, etc.)	16a			26	Wages (less employment credits)	26	31,297	00
b	Other	16b	232	00	27	Other expenses (from line 48 on page 2)	27	1,546	00
17	Legal and professional services	17	6,693	00					

28	**Total expenses** before expenses for business use of home. Add lines 8 through 27 in columns ▶	28	80,610	00
29	Tentative profit (loss). Subtract line 28 from line 7	29	61,131	00
30	Expenses for business use of your home. Attach **Form 8829**	30		
31	**Net profit or (loss).** Subtract line 30 from line 29.			
	• If a profit, enter on **Form 1040, line 12,** and **also** on **Schedule SE, line 2** (statutory employees, see page C-6). Estates and trusts, enter on Form 1041, line 3.	31	61,131	00
	• If a loss, you **must** go to line 32.			
32	If you have a loss, check the box that describes your investment in this activity (see page C-6).			
	• If you checked 32a, enter the loss on **Form 1040, line 12,** and **also** on **Schedule SE, line 2** (statutory employees, see page C-6). Estates and trusts, enter on Form 1041, line 3.	32a ☐ All investment is at risk.		
	• If you checked 32b, you **must** attach **Form 6198.** Your loss may be limited.	32b ☐ Some investment is not at risk.		

For Paperwork Reduction Act Notice, see Form 1040 instructions.	Cat. No. 11334P	Schedule C (Form 1040) 2005

FIGURE 7-4   Filled-In Schedule C, Form 1040, Page 2

Schedule C (Form 1040) 2005   Page **2**

| **Part III** | **Cost of Goods Sold** (see page C-6) |

33 Method(s) used to value closing inventory: **a** ☒ Cost   **b** ☐ Lower of cost or market   **c** ☐ Other (attach explanation)

34 Was there any change in determining quantities, costs, or valuations between opening and closing inventory? If "Yes," attach explanation . . . . ☐ **Yes**   ☒ **No**

35	Inventory at beginning of year. If different from last year's closing inventory, attach explanation . .	**35**	131,216 00
36	Purchases less cost of items withdrawn for personal use	**36**	176,702 00
37	Cost of labor. Do not include any amounts paid to yourself	**37**	
38	Materials and supplies	**38**	
39	Other costs	**39**	
40	Add lines 35 through 39	**40**	307,918 00
41	Inventory at end of year	**41**	167,546 00
42	**Cost of goods sold.** Subtract line 41 from line 40. Enter the result here and on page 1, line 4 . .	**42**	140,372 00

| **Part IV** | **Information on Your Vehicle.** Complete this part **only** if you are claiming car or truck expenses on line 9 and are not required to file Form 4562 for this business. See the instructions for line 13 on page C-4 to find out if you must file Form 4562. |

43 When did you place your vehicle in service for business purposes? (month, day, year) ▶ ...... / ...... / ......

44 Of the total number of miles you drove your vehicle during 2005, enter the number of miles you used your vehicle for:

a Business ....   **b** Commuting (see instructions) ....   **c** Other ....

45 Do you (or your spouse) have another vehicle available for personal use? . . . . ☐ **Yes**   ☐ **No**

46 Was your vehicle available for personal use during off-duty hours? . . . . ☐ **Yes**   ☐ **No**

47a Do you have evidence to support your deduction? . . . . ☐ **Yes**   ☐ **No**

  b If "Yes," is the evidence written? . . . . ☐ **Yes**   ☐ **No**

| **Part V** | **Other Expenses.** List below business expenses not included on lines 8–26 or line 30. |

Miscellaneous expenses	15	00
Bad debts	1,531	00
48	**Total other expenses.** Enter here and on page 1, line 27 . . . . **48**	1,546	00

♲ *Printed on recycled paper*   **Schedule C (Form 1040) 2005**

SELF-EMPLOYMENT TAX FOR SELF-EMPLOYED INDIVIDUALS

For the government to generate enough funds to pay social security and Medicare benefits, taxpayers who work must pay social security and Medicare taxes (FICA). Employees pay FICA through withholdings from their wages. Their employers match the amounts withheld and send the entire sum to the government. Employers deduct as an ordinary and necessary business expense amounts paid to match employees' FICA contributions.

FICA consists of two parts: social security or OASDI (Old-Age, Survivors, and Disability Insurance) and Medicare or HI (Health Insurance). The OASDI tax rate is 6.2% (12.4% after employer matching). The HI rate is 1.45% (2.9% after employer matching). For 2005, the first $90,000 of a taxpayer's earnings is subject to OASDI. All earnings are subject to HI.

The self-employment tax is similar to FICA withheld from employees' wages. However, instead of having the tax withheld from their wages, self-employed taxpayers pay the tax with their (quarterly) estimated payments. They make up any balance due when they file their Form 1040. Because there is no employer to match their contributions, self-employed taxpayers must pay both halves of FICA (12.4% for OASDI and 2.9% for HI). They can, however, deduct one-half of the self-employment tax (the part that represents the employer's share) from their gross income. They take the deduction on Form 1040, page 1, not on Schedule C.

Unlike employees, whose FICA withholding is based on their gross earnings, self-employed taxpayers are subject to self-employment tax on their *net earnings from self-employment*. Net earnings from self-employment equals self-employment net profit multiplied by .9235. This calculation provides a substitute for what is normally an employer's deduction for one-half of the OASDI and HI taxes. Conceptually, this procedure reduces the net profit figure by approximately one-half of the FICA taxes.

Taxpayers pay self-employment tax only on self-employment net profit. Taxpayers reporting net losses from self-employment do not pay self-employment tax. Computing self-employment net profit involves adding the following:

1. Net profit (or loss) an individual derives from any trade or business reported on Schedule C (line 31) or net profit reported on Schedule C-EZ (line 3).
2. Net profit (or loss) an individual derives from farming reported on Schedule F.
3. The individual's distributive share of the ordinary net income (or loss) from a partnership or joint venture. (Most advanced tax textbooks cover this topic.)

EXAMPLE 16

Jessica Whitten owns two businesses. Whitten uses a separate Schedule C to report the net profit (or loss) from each business. Net profit from the first business is $45,000, net profit from the second business is $5,000. Whitten's self-employment net profit is $50,000.

EXAMPLE 17

Assume the same facts as in Example 16, except that Whitten reports a net loss of $5,000 from the second business. Whitten's self-employment net profit is $40,000.

EXAMPLE 18

Assume the same facts as in Example 17, except that Whitten is married and her spouse owns the second business. Jessica's self-employment net profit is $45,000. Because her spouse reports a net loss, he has no self-employment net profit. Only Jessica pays self-employment tax on her $45,000 of net profit.

Once self-employment net profit has been computed, net earnings from self-employment equals 92.35% of self-employment net profit.

EXAMPLE 19

Todd Avery reports $10,000 of self-employment net profit. Avery's net earnings from self-employment equals $9,235 ($10,000 × .9235). Avery pays $1,413 ($9,235 × 15.3%) of self-employment tax and deducts one-half of this amount ($707) on Form 1040, page 1.

Only taxpayers with more than $400 of net earnings from self-employment (92.35% of self-employment net profit) must pay self-employment tax. For self-employed taxpayers who are also employees, their wages subject to social security tax reduce the maximum earnings subject to OASDI.

EXAMPLE 20

Same facts as in Example 19, except that in addition to the $10,000 of self-employment net profit, Avery has FICA withheld on $83,400 of wages earned as an employee in 2005. The first $90,000 of earnings is subject to OASDI. Through withholding on wages, Avery has paid OASDI on $83,400. All $9,235 of net earnings from self-employment is subject to HI, but only $6,600 ($90,000 − $83,400) is subject to OASDI. Avery's self-employment tax equals $1,086 [($6,600 × 12.4%) + ($9,235 × 2.9%)]. Avery deducts one-half of this amount ($543) from gross income on Form 1040, page 1.

Short Schedule SE

Taxpayers compute self-employment tax on Schedule SE. Self-employed taxpayers who do not have wages subject to FICA use the short schedule (Section A) to compute their self-employment tax. Taxpayers whose net earnings from self-employment plus their wages and tips subject to social security tax do not exceed $90,000 also use the short schedule. Taxpayers using the short schedule report their self-employment net profit (lines 1, 2, and 3). They compute their net earnings from self-employment (line 4) by multiplying self-employment net profit (line 3) by 92.35%. They compute self-employment tax (line 5) by multiplying the first $90,000 of net earnings from self-employment by 15.3% and the rest by 2.9%. Taxpayers then enter one-half of this amount on Schedule SE (line 6) and then deduct it for AGI on Form 1040, page 1. Figure 7-5 shows Schedule SE, Section A, for Harold R. Wilson (from Figure 7-4).

Information for Figure 7-5: Filled-In Schedule SE (Section A)

Show only the name of person with self-employment income.

Other Information

    2:    Net profit from Schedule C, line 31, **$61,131.00**

FIGURE 7-5   Filled-In Schedule SE (Section A)

SCHEDULE SE		OMB No. 1545-0074
(Form 1040)	**Self-Employment Tax**	**2005**
Department of the Treasury Internal Revenue Service	▶ Attach to Form 1040. ▶ See Instructions for Schedule SE (Form 1040).	Attachment Sequence No. **17**

Name of person with **self-employment** income (as shown on Form 1040) Harold R. Wilson	Social security number of person with **self-employment** income ▶	272 ¦11 ¦8855

Who Must File Schedule SE

You must file Schedule SE if:

- You had net earnings from self-employment from **other than** church employee income (line 4 of Short Schedule SE or line 4c of Long Schedule SE) of $400 or more **or**
- You had church employee income of $108.28 or more. Income from services you performed as a minister or a member of a religious order **is not** church employee income (see page SE-1).

Note. Even if you had a loss or a small amount of income from self-employment, it may be to your benefit to file Schedule SE and use either "optional method" in Part II of Long Schedule SE (see page SE-3).

Exception. If your only self-employment income was from earnings as a minister, member of a religious order, or Christian Science practitioner **and** you filed Form 4361 and received IRS approval not to be taxed on those earnings, **do not** file Schedule SE. Instead, write "Exempt–Form 4361" on Form 1040, line 58.

May I Use Short Schedule SE or Must I Use Long Schedule SE?

Section A—Short Schedule SE. Caution. Read above to see if you can use Short Schedule SE.

1	Net farm profit or (loss) from Schedule F, line 36, and farm partnerships, Schedule K-1 (Form 1065), box 14, code A	**1**	
2	Net profit or (loss) from Schedule C, line 31; Schedule C-EZ, line 3; Schedule K-1 (Form 1065), box 14, code A (other than farming); and Schedule K-1 (Form 1065-B), box 9. Ministers and members of religious orders, see page SE-1 for amounts to report on this line. See page SE-2 for other income to report	**2**	61,131 | 00
3	Combine lines 1 and 2	**3**	61,131 | 00
4	**Net earnings from self-employment.** Multiply line 3 by 92.35% (.9235). If less than $400, **do not** file this schedule; you do not owe self-employment tax . . . . ▶	**4**	56,454 | 00
5	**Self-employment tax.** If the amount on line 4 is: • $90,000 or less, multiply line 4 by 15.3% (.153). Enter the result here and on **Form 1040, line 58.** • More than $90,000, multiply line 4 by 2.9% (.029). Then, add $11,160.00 to the result. Enter the total here and on **Form 1040, line 58.**	**5**	8,637 | 00
6	**Deduction for one-half of self-employment tax.** Multiply line 5 by 50% (.5). Enter the result here and on **Form 1040, line 27** . . . . | **6** | 4,319 | 00		

For Paperwork Reduction Act Notice, see Form 1040 instructions.   Cat. No. 11358Z   **Schedule SE (Form 1040) 2005**

Long Schedule SE

Taxpayers whose net earnings from self-employment plus their wages and tips subject to social security tax exceed $90,000 cannot use the Short Schedule SE. They instead must use Section B—Long Schedule SE to compute their self-employment tax. As in Section A, taxpayers first compute their self-employment net profit (lines 1 through 3) and their net earnings from self-employment (lines 4 through 6). Taxpayers then report the amount of their wages for the year subject to social security withholding (line 8). If this amount exceeds $90,000, the taxpayer is not subject to the 12.4% OASDI. If the amount does not exceed $90,000 then the taxpayer multiplies 12.4% by the lesser of the difference (line 9) or net earnings from self-employment (line 6). The taxpayer adds this amount to 2.9% of net earnings from self-employment to compute the self-employment tax (line 12). The taxpayer then enters one-half of the self-employment tax on line 13 and again on Form 1040, page 1.

Information for Figure 7-6: Filled-In Schedule SE (Section B)

This filled-in Schedule SE is prepared for **Todd Avery** in Example 20.

Other Information
 2: Net profit from Schedule C, line 31, **$10,000.00**
8a: Total social security wages, **$83,400.00** (Source: box 3 on Form W-2)

RETIREMENT PLANS FOR SELF-EMPLOYED INDIVIDUALS

Sole proprietors can establish retirement plans for themselves and deduct the contributions from their gross income on Form 1040, page 1. Thus, any contributions sole proprietors make to their own retirement plans do not reduce their Schedule C net profits, but will reduce their AGI. Sole proprietors who set up retirement plans for themselves also may have to provide retirement plans for qualified employees. They deduct any contributions they make to their employees' retirement plans on Schedule C.

Self-employed taxpayers have several retirement plan options. They can set up defined benefit and defined contribution plans. When set up for self-employed taxpayers, these plans are commonly referred to as Keoghs. They can also set up SEP, 401(k), and SIMPLE plans. Whichever retirement plan they choose, they must also make it available to all eligible employees.

The same contribution limits that apply to employees apply to sole proprietors. For defined contribution plans, the maximum contribution is the lesser of $42,000 or 25% of the participant's compensation. **Compensation** for a self-employed taxpayer equals self-employment net profit minus both the deduction for one-half of the self-employment tax and the contribution made to the retirement plan.

In computing their maximum allowable contribution, self-employed taxpayers first complete Schedule C to determine net profit. They then compute their self-employment tax on Schedule SE and deduct one-half of the SE tax from their net profit. Self-employed taxpayers may contribute up to 20% of the remaining amount to a defined contribution plan. This percentage is less than that allowed for employees because net profit must be reduced by the amount of the contribution to determine compensation. Example 21 shows how the 20% is determined.

FIGURE 7-6 Filled-In Schedule SE (Section B)

Schedule SE (Form 1040) 2005   Attachment Sequence No. **17**   Page **2**

Name of person with **self-employment** income (as shown on Form 1040)	Social security number of person with **self-employment** income ▶	692 43 1922
Todd Avery		

Section B—Long Schedule SE

Part I	**Self-Employment Tax**

Note. If your only income subject to self-employment tax is **church employee income,** skip lines 1 through 4b. Enter -0- on line 4c and go to line 5a. Income from services you performed as a minister or a member of a religious order **is not** church employee income. See page SE-1.

A   If you are a minister, member of a religious order, or Christian Science practitioner **and** you filed Form 4361, but you had $400 or more of **other** net earnings from self-employment, check here and continue with Part I . . . . . . ▶ ☐

1	Net farm profit or (loss) from Schedule F, line 36, and farm partnerships, Schedule K-1 (Form 1065), box 14, code A. **Note.** Skip this line if you use the farm optional method (see page SE-4)		**1**	
2	Net profit or (loss) from Schedule C, line 31; Schedule C-EZ, line 3; Schedule K-1 (Form 1065), box 14, code A (other than farming); and Schedule K-1 (Form 1065-B), box 9. Ministers and members of religious orders, see page SE-2 for amounts to report on this line. See page SE-2 for other income to report. **Note.** Skip this line if you use the nonfarm optional method (see page SE-4)		**2**	10,000 00
3	Combine lines 1 and 2		**3**	10,000 00
4a	If line 3 is more than zero, multiply line 3 by 92.35% (.9235). Otherwise, enter amount from line 3		**4a**	9,235 00
b	If you elect one or both of the optional methods, enter the total of lines 15 and 17 here . .		**4b**	
c	Combine lines 4a and 4b. If less than $400, **stop;** you do not owe self-employment tax. **Exception.** If less than $400 and you had **church employee income,** enter -0- and continue. . . . . . ▶		**4c**	9,235 00
5a	Enter your **church employee income** from Form W-2. See page SE-1 for definition of church employee income	**5a**		
b	Multiply line 5a by 92.35% (.9235). If less than $100, enter -0-		**5b**	
6	**Net earnings from self-employment.** Add lines 4c and 5b		**6**	9,235 00
7	Maximum amount of combined wages and self-employment earnings subject to social security tax or the 6.2% portion of the 7.65% railroad retirement (tier 1) tax for 2005		**7**	90,000 00
8a	Total social security wages and tips (total of boxes 3 and 7 on Form(s) W-2) and railroad retirement (tier 1) compensation. If $90,000 or more, skip lines 8b through 10, and go to line 11	**8a**	83,400 00	
b	Unreported tips subject to social security tax (from Form 4137, line 9)	**8b**		
c	Add lines 8a and 8b.		**8c**	83,400 00
9	Subtract line 8c from line 7. If zero or less, enter -0- here and on line 10 and go to line 11 . ▶		**9**	6,600 00
10	Multiply the **smaller** of line 6 or line 9 by 12.4% (.124)		**10**	818 00
11	Multiply line 6 by 2.9% (.029)		**11**	268 00
12	**Self-employment tax.** Add lines 10 and 11. Enter here and on **Form 1040, line 58**		**12**	1,086 00
13	**Deduction for one-half of self-employment tax.** Multiply line 12 by 50% (.5). Enter the result here and on **Form 1040, line 27**	**13**	543 00	

Part II	**Optional Methods To Figure Net Earnings** (see page SE-3)

Farm Optional Method. You may use this method **only** if **(a)** your gross farm income[1] was not more than $2,400 **or (b)** your net farm profits[2] were less than $1,733.

14	Maximum income for optional methods		**14**	1,600 00
15	Enter the **smaller** of: two-thirds (⅔) of gross farm income[1] (not less than zero) **or** $1,600. Also include this amount on line 4b above		**15**	

Nonfarm Optional Method. You may use this method **only** if **(a)** your net nonfarm profits[3] were less than $1,733 and also less than 72.189% of your gross nonfarm income[4] **and (b)** you had net earnings from self-employment of at least $400 in 2 of the prior 3 years.

Caution. You may use this method no more than five times.

16	Subtract line 15 from line 14		**16**	
17	Enter the **smaller** of: two-thirds (⅔) of gross nonfarm income[4] (not less than zero) **or** the amount on line 16. Also include this amount on line 4b above		**17**	

[1] From Sch. F, line 11, and Sch. K-1 (Form 1065), box 14, code B.

[2] From Sch. F, line 36, and Sch. K-1 (Form 1065), box 14, code A.

[3] From Sch. C, line 31; Sch. C-EZ, line 3; Sch. K-1 (Form 1065), box 14, code A; and Sch. K-1 (Form 1065-B), box 9.

[4] From Sch. C, line 7; Sch. C-EZ, line 1; Sch. K-1 (Form 1065), box 14, code C; and Sch. K-1 (Form 1065-B), box 9.

Schedule SE (Form 1040) 2005

Keogh Plans

EXAMPLE 21

Lloyd Mills, a self-employed taxpayer, has Schedule C net profit of $60,000. Mills's Keogh plan requires a 25% contribution each year. Net earnings from self-employment are $55,410 ($60,000 × 92.35%). Self-employment tax is $8,478 ($55,410 × 15.3%). Mills deducts one-half of this amount, or $4,239 (½ × $8,478) on Form 1040, page 1. Mills contributes $11,152 to his Keogh. He deducts this amount for AGI on Form 1040, page 1.

Using the required percentage of 25% of his compensation, Mills sets up a formula to solve for the required contribution (C):

$$25\% \times (\text{Schedule C net profit} - \tfrac{1}{2} \text{ of SE tax} - C) = C$$

For Mills, this equation is:

$$25\% \times (\$60,000 - \$4,239 - C) = C$$

which reduces to:

$$25\% \times (\$55,761 - C) = C$$

which reduces to:

$$\$13,940 = 125\% \times C$$

solving for C:

$$\$11,152 = C$$

As shown in Example 21, 20% of the Schedule C net profit minus one-half of the self-employment tax [20% × ($60,000 – $4,239) = $11,152] is the same as 25% of the Schedule C net profit minus one-half of the self-employment tax and the contribution [25% × ($60,000 – $4,239 – $11,152) = $11,152]. Another way to compute the 20% is to divide the required percentage by the sum of 100% and the required percentage (25%/125% = 20%). This short cut is used in Example 22.

EXAMPLE 22

Assume the same facts as in Example 21, except that the plan requires a 10% contribution. Using the short cut approach, Mills computes his deductible contribution as follows.

$$10\%/110\% = .0909 \times \$55,761 = \$5,069$$

The maximum Keogh plan contribution can be made only if the plan specifies 25% as the percentage. If the required percentage is less than 25%, then either the formula from Example 21 or the short cut approach from Example 22 determines the maximum contribution.

KEOGH REQUIREMENTS FOR 2005

1. The plan must be established before the end of the tax year.

2. The plan must be in writing and employees must be provided a summary description including the rules on discrimination and vesting.

3. The plan should be intended as a permanent plan.

4. The plan must have a designated trustee.

5. The maximum annual contribution for a self-employed taxpayer is $42,000, which must be made by the due date of the tax return (including extensions).

Taxpayers can make contributions to qualified retirement plans until the due date of the tax return (including extensions). The big benefit of a Keogh plan is the ability to deduct the contributions each year plus postpone paying taxes on the accrued earnings until the funds are withdrawn. For this reason, the sooner the taxpayer contributes to the plan, the sooner the contributions begin earning tax-deferred (postponed) income.

For example, on January 2, 20x1, a self-employed taxpayer makes a $30,000 contribution to a Keogh plan. During 20x1, $2,000 of earnings accrue on the $30,000. The income tax on that $2,000 is postponed until retirement. Had the taxpayer held the $30,000 in a taxable investment account and waited until December 31, 20x1, to make the Keogh contribution, the $2,000 earned by the taxable investment during 20x1 would be taxable in 20x1.

Simplified Employee Pension (SEP) Plans

Another retirement plan option for sole proprietors is the SEP plan. A SEP is a defined contribution plan, so the maximum contribution self-employed taxpayers can make to a SEP is the lesser of $42,000 or 25% of the participant's compensation. This is the same as the lesser of $42,000 or 20% of self-employment net profit after it is reduced by one-half of the self-employment tax. As with a Keogh, self-employed taxpayers may contribute to a SEP until the due date of the return, including extensions. However, unlike a Keogh, a SEP does not need to be set up before the end of the tax year. Self-employed taxpayers have until the due date of their tax returns (including extensions) to set up a SEP plan. SEP plans have another advantage—they have no annual reporting requirements. Keoghs have annual reporting requirements, even if the taxpayer is the only participant. (These requirements are beyond the scope of this textbook.)

The choice of a retirement plan will depend on the extent of compliance requirements, administrative and other costs contribution limits, and flexibility. Sole proprietors considering setting up retirement plans should carefully review the requirements and limitations of each type of plan and determine the type of plan best suited to their needs. Since most plans require that all eligible employees be allowed to participate, proprietors with employees may want to consider the potential costs of matching contributions when deciding on a retirement plan for themselves.

SEP REQUIREMENTS FOR 2005

1. Each employee has an individual account.
2. Contributions must be made for all full-time employees who are at least age 21, have worked for the employer for three of the last five years, and have received at least $450 of wages during 2005.
3. The employer must contribute the same percentage of compensation for each employee.
4. Employees must be able to withdraw the employer's contributions without restriction.

Savings Incentive Match Plan for Employees (SIMPLE)

Sole proprietors can set up a SIMPLE plan for themselves and their employees. The maximum that sole proprietors can contribute in 2005 to their SIMPLE plan is $10,000 or 100% of their compensation, whichever is less. (Sole proprietors age 50 and older can contribute up to $12,000 or 100% of their compensation). An advantage to having a SIMPLE plan is that it is not subject to the nondiscrimination and top-heavy rules associated with other retirement plans. A disadvantage is that employer matching is required with a SIMPLE plan. Neither of these are issues for sole proprietors with no employees. Due to the $10,000 limit ($12,000 for those age 50 and older), sole proprietors with no employees may want to consider a SEP plan, which has a higher contribution limit.

SIMPLE REQUIREMENTS FOR 2005

1. There must be 100 or fewer employees in the previous year.
2. The SIMPLE plan is the only retirement plan offered.
3. All employees who had at least $5,000 of compensation in the previous year and expect to have at least $5,000 of compensation in the current year must be allowed to participate.

QUESTIONS AND PROBLEMS

1. **Cash vs. Accrual Method.** Ramon S. Torres is an attorney. Torres wants to know how reporting each of the following items would differ if he used the cash method versus the accrual method. In the space provided with each item, enter the correct amount to be included on Schedule C assuming the cash method is used. Then enter the correct amount assuming the use of the accrual method. If there is no amount to be reported, enter a zero.

		Included on Schedule C	
		Cash Method	*Accrual Method*
a.	Cash received from last year's fees	$7,200	$ *7200*	$ *0* (reported as income from prior yr)
b.	Cash received from current year's fees	49,000	*49000*	*49000*
c.	Fees billed for current year for which cash has not been received	10,200	*0*	*10,200*
d.	Cash received for computer with book value of $200	200	*0*	*0*
e.	Cash received from bank loan	2,500	*0*	*0*
f.	Cash received from client to repay loan made last year	500	*0*	*0*
g.	Cash received for retainer from client for whom work is to be done next year	3,800	*3800*	*0*

(handwritten margin notes: selling price 200 (2007); book value 0; taxable 0; depr... liability credited)

2. **Cash vs. Accrual Method.** Lis Schultz is a CPA. Schultz wants to know how reporting each of the following items would differ if she uses the cash method versus the accrual method. In the space provided with each item, enter the correct amount to include on Schedule C assuming the cash method is used. Then enter the correct amount assuming the use of the accrual method. If there is no amount to be reported, enter a zero.

		Included on Schedule C	
		Cash Method	*Accrual Method*
a.	Repaid loan at bank:			
	Principal	$1,000	$ *0*	$ *0*
	Interest	60	*60*	*60*
b.	Paid contribution pledged to church	1,000	*0*	*0*
c.	Paid for supplies used last year	150	*150*	*0*
d.	Paid for supplies used during current year	850	*850*	*850*
e.	Paid for professional journals	200	*200*	*200*
f.	Supplies not used during current year and not paid for	40	*0*	*0*
g.	Paid for new computer	1,564	*0*	*0*

(handwritten margin notes: person Schedule A; must be business related)

7-33

3. **Cash vs. Accrual Method.** Andrew Taylor is a dentist. Taylor wants to know how report-
    ing each of the following items would differ if he uses the cash method versus the accrual
    method. In the space provided with each item, enter the correct amount to include on
    Schedule C assuming the cash method is used. Then enter the correct amount assuming
    the use of the accrual method. If there is no amount to be reported, enter a zero.

			Included on Schedule C	
			Cash Method	*Accrual Method*
a.	Salary paid to receptionist	$12,500	$_____	$_____
b.	Paid for long-distance phone charges made during last year	4	_____	_____
c.	Written-off client billing for fees; work performed in current year	150	_____	_____
d.	Written-off client billing for fees; work performed last year	135	_____	_____
e.	Paid annual subscription to magazines for office	50	_____	_____
f.	Paid life insurance premium on the owner's life	516	_____	_____

4. **Prepaid Income.** Scott Williams operates a fitness center as a sole proprietorship. On
    May 1, 2005, Williams sells a 24-month membership for $1,200. How much of the $1,200
    must Williams report on his 2005, 2006, and 2007 tax returns?

5. **Prepaid Expenses.** A sole proprietor who operates a warehouse purchases insurance for
    his building and equipment in three-year increments to get a good insurance premium
    rate. The insurance policy in force was acquired on October 1, 2003, for $4,800 and will
    be in effect until September 30, 2006. The premium on this policy was paid on July 1,
    2003.

    a. What amount of insurance premium can the taxpayer include as an expense on Sched-
        ule C for 2005, assuming the taxpayer uses the cash method of accounting? Show
        calculations.

    b. What amount of insurance premium is deductible in 2005 if the taxpayer uses the
        accrual method?

6. **Self-Employment Income.** Indicate with Y (yes) or N (no) if the following items are net earnings from self-employment:

    Item

    _N_ ___ a. Net earnings from an apartment building *(passive income)*
    _N_ ___ b. Net income from an accounting practice
    _N_ ___ c. Interest income on a loan
    _N_ ___ d. Share of net income from a manufacturing partnership
    _N_ ___ e. Net income for services as a minister
    _N_ ___ f. Dividends from domestic corporations

7. **Self-Employment Income.** Indicate with Y (yes) or N (no) if the following items are net earnings from self-employment:

    Item

    _N_ ___ a. Gross rent received on an office building
    _N_ ___ b. Gross profit from a doctor's practice — *not gross profit but net income is*
    _N_ ___ c. Prize for winning an essay contest
    _N_ ___ d. Salary for a secretary
    _N_ ___ e. Net gain on the sale of property — *sale of property gain is not subject to self-emplymt tax*
    _N_ ___ f. Director's fees

8. **Self-Employment Income.** Indicate whether each statement is T (true) or F (false):

    Item

    _____ a. Interest on accounts receivable received in a trade or business is treated as self-employment income.
    _____ b. Babysitters who provide child care in the parents' homes must treat their earnings as self-employment income.
    _____ c. Registered nurses who are hired directly by patients to provide private nursing services are treated as self-employed individuals.
    _____ d. Licensed real estate agents working out of a real estate agency are generally treated as employees of the real estate agency.
    _____ e. Amway, Avon, Shaklee, and Tupperware distributors are treated as self-employed individuals.
    _____ f. All executors of estates are treated as self-employed.

9. **Pension Plans.** Three common pension plans employers can provide to their employees are SEP, 401(k) and SIMPLE plans. For each of the following statements, identify the plan or plans having the described characteristics.

    _____ a. This plan allows employees under age 50 to contribute up to $10,000 of their wages to their plan in 2005.
    _____ b. This plan allows only employers to make contributions to employees' plans.
    _____ c. Employers are required to make matching contributions to this plan.
    _____ d. The maximum contribution to this plan is the lesser of $42,000 or 25% of the employee's compensation.
    _____ e. Employees can contribute pre-tax earnings to this plan.

10. **Accountable vs. Nonaccountable Plans.** Robin Clark owns a business that she operates as a sole proprietorship. Clark's business has two full-time employees. The business reimburses each employee at the rate of $250 per month for meals and entertainment ($6,000 per year) without any specific accounting. Assuming that the employees incur meal expenses of $2,000 and entertainment expenses of $4,900 during 2005, answer the following questions about the way the $6,000 should be reported on Clark's 2005 tax return.

a. How much and where on Schedule C should Clark deduct the reimbursements?

b. How would your answer to Part a. differ if Clark required her employees to make an adequate accounting of their meals and entertainment expenses and also required them to return any excess reimbursement?

11. **Schedule C Expenses.** Robert Applewood works as a cost accountant for the Craft Manufacturing Company. He also moonlights at night and on weekends preparing tax returns for a regular set of clients. He does not have a regular office in his home, so he does not take a deduction for a home office. However, he does prepare a Schedule C to reflect the income from his tax practice. He has asked you to review his Schedule C to determine whether he is properly reporting the operating expenses of his business in relation to other aspects of his tax return. He has included the following expenses on Schedule C:

Supplies and postage	$ 72
Professional dues paid to AICPA tax division	120
Professional dues to the Institute of Management Accountants (IMA)	175
Meals ($80) and entertainment ($120) for tax clients	200
Automobile expenses for tax clients (163 miles @ $.405*)	66
Contribution to State Accounting Society's Political Action Committee	100
CPE course fees to meet the annual requirements to be a member of AICPA and the state society	600
Cost of new printer for use with tax clients (shown under repairs and maintenance)	650
Long-distance telephone charges related to tax clients	44
Interest paid on bank loan used to buy computer for tax and personal use (used for tax clients 60% of the time during the tax year)	400

*All business miles were driven before September 1, 2005.

Of these expenses, indicate what amounts, if any, can not be deducted on Schedule C, and explain why in each case.

12. **Home Office Expense.** Rita Porter operates a child care service in her home. The rooms used for this purpose constitute 30% of the total living space of the home. Expenses of operating the home during the year included electricity, $480; water, $340; heating, $3,600; property taxes, $4,000; and home repairs, $800. The depreciation on the rooms and related equipment used for child care amounted to $1,800.

    What is the total amount of expenses that Porter can deduct for using her own home to provide the child care services if she uses these rooms 2,000 hours in 2005 for her child care business?

13. **Form 8829.** Elaine Gerber conducts a business in her home. Tentative profit from Schedule C (line 29) was $9,600. Complete Form 8829 on page 7-38.

14. **Schedule C, Part III, Cost of Goods Sold.** Roger Harkin operates a novelty shop as a sole proprietor. You have been asked to compute the Cost of Goods Sold section of Schedule C for his 2005 income tax return since he is unfamiliar with detailed accounting concepts. You have been given the following information from his records to help meet his request:

Sales revenue	$200,000
Purchases	80,000
Cash operating expenses	40,000
Depreciation expense	15,000
Beginning inventory	60,000
Ending inventory	54,000
Bad debts written off	3,200

    Using the appropriate information from Harkin's books, prepare the Cost of Goods Sold section of Schedule C for 2005. Harkin uses the cost method to value inventory.

15. **Self-Employment Tax.** Determine the self-employment tax that would be paid for 2005 by each of the following taxpayers. If there is no self-employment tax, explain why.

    Taxpayer A: Age, 42; net business profit, $39,000; dividend income, $300; wages subject to social security, $5,000; gross rental income, $6,000; net rental income, $1,500

    Taxpayer B: Age, 71; net business profit, $29,000; dividend income, $500; wages subject to social security, $48,000

    Taxpayer C: Age, 35; net business profit, $70,000; dividend income, $200

    Taxpayer D: Age, 27; net business profit, $15,000; dividend income, $100; wages subject to social security, $86,000

    Taxpayer E: Age, 56; net business profit, $3,000; dividend income, $450; net rental income, ($500)

    Taxpayer F: Age, 64; net business profit, $420; dividend income, $50; wages subject to social security, $400

(Use for Problem 13.)

Form **8829**	**Expenses for Business Use of Your Home**	OMB No. 1545-1266

Department of the Treasury
Internal Revenue Service (99)

► File only with Schedule C (Form 1040). Use a separate Form 8829 for each home you used for business during the year.

► See separate instructions.

2005

Attachment
Sequence No. **66**

Name(s) of proprietor(s)
Elaine Gerber

Your social security number
243 : 56 : 7182

Part I   Part of Your Home Used for Business

1	Area used regularly and exclusively for business, regularly for daycare, or for storage of inventory or product samples (see instructions)	**1**	240
2	Total area of home	**2**	3,000
3	Divide line 1 by line 2. Enter the result as a percentage	**3**	%

- For daycare facilities not used exclusively for business, also complete lines 4–6.
- All others, skip lines 4–6 and enter the amount from line 3 on line 7.

4	Multiply days used for daycare during year by hours used per day	**4**	hr.
5	Total hours available for use during the year (365 days × 24 hours) (see instructions)	**5**	8,760 hr.
6	Divide line 4 by line 5. Enter the result as a decimal amount	**6**	.
7	Business percentage. For daycare facilities not used exclusively for business, multiply line 6 by line 3 (enter the result as a percentage). All others, enter the amount from line 3. ►	**7**	%

Part II   Figure Your Allowable Deduction

		(a) Direct expenses	(b) Indirect expenses	
8	Enter the amount from Schedule C, line 29, **plus** any net gain or (loss) derived from the business use of your home and shown on Schedule D or Form 4797. If more than one place of business, see instructions			**8**
	See instructions for columns (a) and (b) before completing lines 9–20.			
9	Casualty losses (see instructions)	9		
10	Deductible mortgage interest (see instructions)	10	1,800 00	
11	Real estate taxes (see instructions)	11	1,500 00	
12	Add lines 9, 10, and 11	12		
13	Multiply line 12, column (b) by line 7		13	
14	Add line 12, column (a) and line 13			**14**
15	Subtract line 14 from line 8. If zero or less, enter -0-			**15**
16	Excess mortgage interest (see instructions)	16		
17	Insurance	17	500 00	
18	Repairs and maintenance	18		
19	Utilities	19	750 00	
20	Other expenses (see instructions)	20		
21	Add lines 16 through 20	21		
22	Multiply line 21, column (b) by line 7		22	
23	Carryover of operating expenses from 2004 Form 8829, line 41		23	
24	Add line 21 in column (a), line 22, and line 23			**24**
25	Allowable operating expenses. Enter the **smaller** of line 15 or line 24			**25**
26	Limit on excess casualty losses and depreciation. Subtract line 25 from line 15			**26**
27	Excess casualty losses (see instructions)		27	
28	Depreciation of your home from Part III below		28	
29	Carryover of excess casualty losses and depreciation from 2004 Form 8829, line 42		29	
30	Add lines 27 through 29			**30**
31	Allowable excess casualty losses and depreciation. Enter the **smaller** of line 26 or line 30			**31**
32	Add lines 14, 25, and 31			**32**
33	Casualty loss portion, if any, from lines 14 and 31. Carry amount to **Form 4684**, Section B			**33**
34	Allowable expenses for business use of your home. Subtract line 33 from line 32. Enter here and on Schedule C, line 30. If your home was used for more than one business, see instructions ►			**34**

Part III   Depreciation of Your Home

35	Enter the **smaller** of your home's adjusted basis or its fair market value (see instructions)	**35**	60,000 00
36	Value of land included on line 35	**36**	10,000 00
37	Basis of building. Subtract line 36 from line 35	**37**	
38	Business basis of building. Multiply line 37 by line 7	**38**	
39	Depreciation percentage (see instructions)	**39**	2.564 %
40	Depreciation allowable (see instructions). Multiply line 38 by line 39. Enter here and on line 28 above	**40**	

Part IV   Carryover of Unallowed Expenses to 2006

41	Operating expenses. Subtract line 25 from line 24. If less than zero, enter -0-	**41**	
42	Excess casualty losses and depreciation. Subtract line 31 from line 30. If less than zero, enter -0-	**42**	

For Paperwork Reduction Act Notice, see page 4 of separate instructions.   Cat. No. 13232M   Form **8829** (2005)

(Use for Problem 14.)

Schedule C (Form 1040) 2005						Page **2**

Part III   **Cost of Goods Sold** (see page C-6)

33	Method(s) used to value closing inventory:	**a** ☐ Cost	**b** ☐ Lower of cost or market		**c** ☐ Other (attach explanation)	
34	Was there any change in determining quantities, costs, or valuations between opening and closing inventory? If "Yes," attach explanation				☐ **Yes**	☐ **No**
35	Inventory at beginning of year. If different from last year's closing inventory, attach explanation . .				**35**	
36	Purchases less cost of items withdrawn for personal use				**36**	
37	Cost of labor. Do not include any amounts paid to yourself				**37**	
38	Materials and supplies				**38**	
39	Other costs				**39**	
40	Add lines 35 through 39				**40**	
41	Inventory at end of year				**41**	
42	**Cost of goods sold.** Subtract line 41 from line 40. Enter the result here and on page 1, line 4 . .				**42**	

16. Self-Employment Tax. Rosemary R. James is employed as an attorney and also operates a consulting business on the side. If her net profit reported on Schedule C (consulting business) in 2005 was $425, how much self-employment tax would James pay?

17. Self-Employment Tax. Dennis Connor has Schedule C net profit of $10,000. Compute Connor's self-employment tax if his salary as a CPA was $96,000.

18. Self-Employment Tax. Theodore Williams reports net profit on Schedule C of $130,000. How much self-employment tax would he pay if his salary as an accountant were $47,500?

19. Retirement Plans.

a. Assume that Louise Bell (SSN 304-16-1059) earned $14,000 from self-employment in 2005 and wants to make the maximum contribution to a defined contribution retirement plan for a self-employed person. Prepare Schedule SE on page 7-41 to determine the amount of self-employment tax that Bell owes on her self-employment income.

b. What is the maximum Bell can contribute to a SEP plan that would be fully deducted from gross income on her 2005 income tax return? Where on the tax return is the deduction claimed?

c. If Bell wants to contribute to a SEP plan, by what date must she make a contribution for 2005?

20. Retirement Plans. Diana Smith, a self-employed individual, operates a consulting practice. She has no employees. For the 2005 tax year, Smith's gross consulting revenue was $140,000, and her operating expenses, not including retirement plan contributions, totaled $30,000. In addition to her consulting income, Smith also received $5,000 of earned income in 2005 for writing a chapter in a book about management consulting. During 2005 Smith established a Keogh plan. The Keogh plan stipulates a fixed percentage of 10% of compensation as the amount of the required annual contribution.

a. What is the amount of self-employment tax that Smith must pay in 2005 on the basis of her self-employment income?

b. What is the required dollar contribution that Smith must make to her Keogh plan for 2005?

c. By what date must the Keogh plan be established in order for Smith to take a deduction for the contributions on her 2005 tax return?

d. By what date must the contributions be paid into the Keogh plan in order for Smith to take a deduction on her 2005 tax return?

(Use for Problem 19.)

SCHEDULE SE		OMB No. 1545-0074
(Form 1040)	**Self-Employment Tax**	**2005**
Department of the Treasury Internal Revenue Service	▶ Attach to Form 1040. ▶ See Instructions for Schedule SE (Form 1040).	Attachment Sequence No. **17**

Name of person with **self-employment** income (as shown on Form 1040)	Social security number of person with **self-employment** income ▶

Who Must File Schedule SE

You must file Schedule SE if:

● You had net earnings from self-employment from **other than** church employee income (line 4 of Short Schedule SE or line 4c of Long Schedule SE) of $400 or more **or**

● You had church employee income of $108.28 or more. Income from services you performed as a minister or a member of a religious order **is not** church employee income (see page SE-1).

Note. Even if you had a loss or a small amount of income from self-employment, it may be to your benefit to file Schedule SE and use either "optional method" in Part II of Long Schedule SE (see page SE-3).

Exception. If your only self-employment income was from earnings as a minister, member of a religious order, or Christian Science practitioner **and** you filed Form 4361 and received IRS approval not to be taxed on those earnings, **do not** file Schedule SE. Instead, write "Exempt–Form 4361" on Form 1040, line 58.

May I Use Short Schedule SE or Must I Use Long Schedule SE?

You May Use Short Schedule SE Below

You Must Use Long Schedule SE on page 2

Section A—Short Schedule SE. Caution. Read above to see if you can use Short Schedule SE.

1	Net farm profit or (loss) from Schedule F, line 36, and farm partnerships, Schedule K-1 (Form 1065), box 14, code A	**1**	
2	Net profit or (loss) from Schedule C, line 31; Schedule C-EZ, line 3; Schedule K-1 (Form 1065), box 14, code A (other than farming); and Schedule K-1 (Form 1065-B), box 9. Ministers and members of religious orders, see page SE-1 for amounts to report on this line. See page SE-2 for other income to report	**2**	
3	Combine lines 1 and 2	**3**	
4	**Net earnings from self-employment.** Multiply line 3 by 92.35% (.9235). If less than $400, **do not** file this schedule; you do not owe self-employment tax . . . . ▶	**4**	
5	**Self-employment tax.** If the amount on line 4 is: ● $90,000 or less, multiply line 4 by 15.3% (.153). Enter the result here and on **Form 1040, line 58.** ● More than $90,000, multiply line 4 by 2.9% (.029). Then, add $11,160.00 to the result. Enter the total here and on **Form 1040, line 58.**	**5**	
6	**Deduction for one-half of self-employment tax.** Multiply line 5 by 50% (.5). Enter the result here and on **Form 1040, line 27** **6**		

For Paperwork Reduction Act Notice, see Form 1040 instructions.	Cat. No. 11358Z	Schedule SE (Form 1040) 2005

21. **Internet Problem: Researching Publication 560.**

   Normally a 10% penalty is assessed when employees and self-employed taxpayers take distributions from a retirement plan before reaching age 59½. However, exceptions do exist.

   What are the various circumstances under which individuals can take early distributions from the various retirement plans for small business discussed in Chapter 7 and not have to pay the 10% penalty?

   Go to the IRS Web site. Locate Publication 560, and find the answer to the above question regarding exceptions to the 10% penalty. Print out a copy of the page where you found your answer. Underline or highlight the pertinent information.

   See Appendix A for instructions on use of the IRS Web site.

22. **Business Entity Problem: This problem is designed for those using the "business entity" approach. The solution may require information from Chapter 14.**

   Tom Jones is a partner in a partnership that reports ordinary income of $80,000 for the current year. His distributive share of partnership ordinary income is $40,000. During the year his guaranteed salary payments were $30,000. In addition, he withdrew $25,000 from the partnership.

   a. What amount would be subject to social security and Medicare taxes? Explain.

   b. Is the partnership responsible for withholding income taxes and FICA taxes on the partner's earnings? Explain how these taxes are paid to the government.

   c. How would your answers to Parts a. and b. change if the business was operated as an S Corporation?

COMPREHENSIVE PROBLEM

23. Marie A. Lopez (SSN 318-01-6921) lives at 190 Glenn Drive, Grand Rapids, Michigan 49527-2005. Lopez (age 45 and single) claims her aunt, Selda Ray (SSN 282-61-4011), as a dependent. Ray lives with Lopez. Lopez owns and operates the Reliable Drug Company at 1816 First Street in Grand Rapids, Michigan 49503-1902, in which she actively participates the entire year. Her EIN is 38-9654321. Employer quarterly payroll tax returns were filed as required, and Lopez values inventory at cost. The income statement for 2005 is reproduced in this problem. Lopez reports on the accrual method, but uses the "direct write-off" method to compute bad debt expense. Her business code is 446110. She does not deduct expenses for an office in her home.

An examination of Lopez's business records reveals that the depreciable property includes furniture and fixtures, a heavy-duty delivery truck, and store equipment. The depreciation expense shown on the 2005 income statement meets the income tax requirements for depreciation for using the mentioned assets during 2005. Lopez rounds calculations to the nearest dollar. Miscellaneous expenses include the following:

Reimbursement to Ms. Lopez for actual expenses of a purchasing trip ($256 for airfare and lodging, $70 for meals)	$326
Contributions to Red Cross and United Way	350
Chamber of Commerce dues	125
Personal electric bill for August	80
Total miscellaneous expenses	$881

Other income for Lopez included a salary of $100 each month for her services as a member of a working committee of the Drug Association. Her Form W-2 from the association showed gross wages of $1,200 and federal income tax withheld of $296. Lopez also earned $320 in interest. Lopez made federal estimated tax payments totaling $6,300 during 2005. This amount is reported on Form 1040 (line 65).

Prepare Form 1040, and Schedules C and SE for Lopez using the forms provided on pages 7-45 through 7-49.

[Handwritten notes:]

Book income   30,290
+ Donation   350
+ Personal electric bill   80
+ 50% of meals   35
                 30,755

RELIABLE DRUG COMPANY
Income Statement for Year Ended December 31, 2005

Operating revenue:		
Sales		$324,200
Less sales returns and allowances		(3,390)
Net sales		$320,810
Cost of merchandise sold:		
Merchandise inventory, beginning (FIFO)	$ 68,920	
Purchases	$198,240	
Less purchases returns and allowances	(8,100)	
Net purchases	$190,140	
Merchandise available for sale	$259,060	
Less merchandise inventory, ending (FIFO)	(69,185)	
Cost of merchandise sold		(189,875)
Gross profit on sales		$130,935
Operating expenses:		
Advertising expense	$ 6,541	
Bad debt expense	850	
Car and truck expense	7,967[1]	
Depreciation expense	3,396	
Insurance expense (other than health)	644	
Miscellaneous expense	881	
Payroll taxes	3,471	
Rent expense (other business property)	12,000	
Telephone and utilities expense	2,395	
Wages expense	62,500	
Total operating expenses		(100,645)
Net income		$ 30,290

[1]Lopez drove her personal automobile for 19,053 business miles during the year (3,133 after August 31, 2005). Total miles for the year were 32,815. There were 1,300 commuting miles. This is Lopez's only car. She has kept a written log documenting her business miles. Lopez first used the car in her business on May 4, 2004.

(Use for Problem 23.)

Form **1040** Department of the Treasury—Internal Revenue Service **U.S. Individual Income Tax Return** 20**05** (99) IRS Use Only—Do not write or staple in this space.

For the year Jan. 1–Dec. 31, 2005, or other tax year beginning _____ , 2005, ending _____ , 20 ___ OMB No. 1545-0074

Label
(See instructions on page 16.)
Use the IRS label. Otherwise, please print or type.

L A B E L H E R E	
Your first name and initial	Last name
If a joint return, spouse's first name and initial	Last name
Home address (number and street). If you have a P.O. box, see page 16.	Apt. no.
City, town or post office, state, and ZIP code. If you have a foreign address, see page 16.	

Your social security number

Spouse's social security number

▲ You **must** enter your SSN(s) above. ▲

Presidential Election Campaign ▶ Check here if you, or your spouse if filing jointly, want $3 to go to this fund (see page 16) ▶   ☐ **You** ☐ **Spouse**

Checking a box below will not change your tax or refund.

Filing Status
Check only one box.

1 ☐ Single
2 ☐ Married filing jointly (even if only one had income)
3 ☐ Married filing separately. Enter spouse's SSN above and full name here. ▶
4 ☐ Head of household (with qualifying person). (See page 17.) If the qualifying person is a child but not your dependent, enter this child's name here. ▶
5 ☐ Qualifying widow(er) with dependent child (see page 17)

Exemptions

6a ☐ **Yourself.** If someone can claim you as a dependent, **do not** check box 6a
b ☐ **Spouse**
c **Dependents:**

(1) First name Last name	(2) Dependent's social security number	(3) Dependent's relationship to you	(4) ✓ if qualifying child for child tax credit (see page 18)
	:		☐
	:		☐
	:		☐
	:		☐

If more than four dependents, see page 18.

d Total number of exemptions claimed

Boxes checked on 6a and 6b ____
No. of children on 6c who:
• lived with you ____
• did not live with you due to divorce or separation (see page 18) ____
Dependents on 6c not entered above ____
Add numbers on lines above ▶

Income

Attach Form(s) W-2 here. Also attach Forms W-2G and 1099-R if tax was withheld.

If you did not get a W-2, see page 19.

Enclose, but do not attach, any payment. Also, please use Form 1040-V.

7	Wages, salaries, tips, etc. Attach Form(s) W-2		7
8a	**Taxable** interest. Attach Schedule B if required		8a
b	Tax-exempt interest. **Do not** include on line 8a	8b	
9a	Ordinary dividends. Attach Schedule B if required		9a
b	Qualified dividends (see page 20)	9b	
10	Taxable refunds, credits, or offsets of state and local income taxes (see page 20)		10
11	Alimony received		11
12	Business income or (loss). Attach Schedule C or C-EZ		12
13	Capital gain or (loss). Attach Schedule D if required. If not required, check here ▶ ☐		13
14	Other gains or (losses). Attach Form 4797		14
15a	IRA distributions	15a	
b	Taxable amount (see page 22)		15b
16a	Pensions and annuities	16a	
b	Taxable amount (see page 22)		16b
17	Rental real estate, royalties, partnerships, S corporations, trusts, etc. Attach Schedule E		17
18	Farm income or (loss). Attach Schedule F		18
19	Unemployment compensation		19
20a	Social security benefits	20a	
b	Taxable amount (see page 24)		20b
21	Other income. List type and amount (see page 24)		21
22	Add the amounts in the far right column for lines 7 through 21. This is your **total income** ▶		22

Adjusted Gross Income

23	Educator expenses (see page 26)	23
24	Certain business expenses of reservists, performing artists, and fee-basis government officials. Attach Form 2106 or 2106-EZ	24
25	Health savings account deduction. Attach Form 8889	25
26	Moving expenses. Attach Form 3903	26
27	One-half of self-employment tax. Attach Schedule SE	27
28	Self-employed SEP, SIMPLE, and qualified plans	28
29	Self-employed health insurance deduction (see page XX)	29
30	Penalty on early withdrawal of savings	30
31a	Alimony paid b Recipient's SSN ▶	31a
32	IRA deduction (see page XX)	32
33	Student loan interest deduction (see page XX)	33
34	Tuition and fees deduction (see page XX)	34
35	Domestic production activities deduction. Attach Form 8903	35
36	Add lines 23 through 31a and 32 through 35	36
37	Subtract line 36 from line 22. This is your **adjusted gross income** ▶	37

For Disclosure, Privacy Act, and Paperwork Reduction Act Notice, see page 75. Cat. No. 11320B Form **1040** (2005)

(Use for Problem 23.)

Form 1040 (2005)   Page **2**

Tax and Credits	**38**	Amount from line 37 (adjusted gross income)	**38**	
	39a	Check if: ☐ **You** were born before January 2, 1941, ☐ Blind. ☐ **Spouse** was born before January 2, 1941, ☐ Blind. } Total boxes checked ▶ **39a**		
Standard Deduction for—	**b**	If your spouse itemizes on a separate return or you were a dual-status alien, see page 31 and check here ▶ **39b** ☐		
	40	**Itemized deductions** (from Schedule A) **or** your **standard deduction** (see left margin) .	**40**	
• People who checked any box on line 39a or 39b **or** who can be claimed as a dependent, see page 31.	**41**	Subtract line 40 from line 38	**41**	
	42	If line 38 is $109,475 or less, multiply $3,200 by the total number of exemptions claimed on line 6d. If line 38 is over $109,475, see the worksheet on page 33 . . .	**42**	
	43	**Taxable income.** Subtract line 42 from line 41. If line 42 is more than line 41, enter -0- .	**43**	
• All others:	**44**	**Tax** (see page 33). Check if any tax is from: **a** ☐ Form(s) 8814 **b** ☐ Form 4972 . .	**44**	
Single or Married filing separately, $5,000	**45**	**Alternative minimum tax** (see page 35). Attach Form 6251	**45**	
	46	Add lines 44 and 45 . . . . ▶	**46**	
Married filing jointly or Qualifying widow(er), $10,000	**47**	Foreign tax credit. Attach Form 1116 if required	**47**	
	48	Credit for child and dependent care expenses. Attach Form 2441	**48**	
	49	Credit for the elderly or the disabled. Attach Schedule R .	**49**	
Head of household, $7,300	**50**	Education credits. Attach Form 8863	**50**	
	51	Retirement savings contributions credit. Attach Form 8880 .	**51**	
	52	Child tax credit (see page 37). Attach Form 8901 if required	**52**	
	53	Adoption credit. Attach Form 8839	**53**	
	54	Credits from: **a** ☐ Form 8396 **b** ☐ Form 8859 .	**54**	
	55	Other credits. Check applicable box(es): **a** ☐ Form 3800 **b** ☐ Form 8801 **c** ☐ Specify _____	**55**	
	56	Add lines 47 through 55. These are your **total credits**	**56**	
	57	Subtract line 56 from line 46. If line 56 is more than line 46, enter -0- . . . . . ▶	**57**	
Other Taxes	**58**	Self-employment tax. Attach Schedule SE	**58**	
	59	Social security and Medicare tax on tip income not reported to employer. Attach Form 4137	**59**	
	60	Additional tax on IRAs, other qualified retirement plans, etc. Attach Form 5329 if required	**60**	
	61	Advance earned income credit payments from Form(s) W-2	**61**	
	62	Household employment taxes. Attach Schedule H	**62**	
	63	Add lines 57 through 62. This is your **total tax** . . . . ▶	**63**	
Payments	**64**	Federal income tax withheld from Forms W-2 and 1099 . .	**64**	
	65	2005 estimated tax payments and amount applied from 2004 return	**65**	
If you have a qualifying child, attach Schedule EIC.	**66a**	Earned income credit (EIC)	**66a**	
	b	Nontaxable combat pay election ▶ **66b**		
	67	Excess social security and tier 1 RRTA tax withheld (see page 54)	**67**	
	68	Additional child tax credit. Attach Form 8812	**68**	
	69	Amount paid with request for extension to file (see page 54)	**69**	
	70	Payments from: **a** ☐ Form 2439 **b** ☐ Form 4136 **c** ☐ Form 8885	**70**	
	71	Add lines 64, 65, 66a, and 67 through 70. These are your **total payments** . . . . ▶	**71**	
Refund Direct deposit? See page 54 and fill in 73b, 73c, and 73d.	**72**	If line 71 is more than line 63, subtract line 63 from line 71. This is the amount you **overpaid**	**72**	
	73a	Amount of line 72 you want **refunded to you**	**73a**	
	▶ **b**	Routing number ▢▢▢▢▢▢▢▢▢ ▶ **c** Type: ☐ Checking ☐ Savings		
	▶ **d**	Account number ▢▢▢▢▢▢▢▢▢		
	74	Amount of line 72 you want **applied to your 2006 estimated tax** ▶ **74**		
Amount You Owe	**75**	**Amount you owe.** Subtract line 71 from line 63. For details on how to pay, see page 55 ▶	**75**	
	76	Estimated tax penalty (see page 55) **76**		

Third Party Designee	Do you want to allow another person to discuss this return with the IRS (see page 56)? ☐ **Yes.** Complete the following. ☐ **No**
	Designee's name ▶ _____ Phone no. ▶ ( ) _____ Personal identification number (PIN) ▶ ▢▢▢▢▢

Sign Here Joint return? See page 17. Keep a copy for your records.	Under penalties of perjury, I declare that I have examined this return and accompanying schedules and statements, and to the best of my knowledge and belief, they are true, correct, and complete. Declaration of preparer (other than taxpayer) is based on all information of which preparer has any knowledge.		
	Your signature	Date	Your occupation	Daytime phone number ( )
	Spouse's signature. If a joint return, **both** must sign.	Date	Spouse's occupation	

Paid Preparer's Use Only	Preparer's signature ▶	Date	Check if self-employed ☐	Preparer's SSN or PTIN
	Firm's name (or yours if self-employed), address, and ZIP code ▶		EIN	
			Phone no. ( )	

Form **1040** (2005)

✪ Printed on recycled paper

(Use for Problem 23.)

SCHEDULE C (Form 1040) Department of the Treasury Internal Revenue Service	**Profit or Loss From Business** (Sole Proprietorship) ▶ Partnerships, joint ventures, etc., must file Form 1065 or 1065-B. ▶ Attach to Form 1040 or 1041. ▶ See Instructions for Schedule C (Form 1040).	OMB No. 1545-0074 20**05** Attachment Sequence No. **09**

Name of proprietor | Social security number (SSN)

A Principal business or profession, including product or service (see page C-2 of the instructions) | **B** Enter code from pages C-7, 8, & 9 ▶

C Business name. If no separate business name, leave blank. | **D** Employer ID number (EIN), if any

E Business address (including suite or room no.) ▶
City, town or post office, state, and ZIP code

F Accounting method: **(1)** ☐ Cash **(2)** ☐ Accrual **(3)** ☐ Other (specify) ▶

G Did you "materially participate" in the operation of this business during 2005? If "No," see page C-3 for limit on losses ☐ Yes ☐ No

H If you started or acquired this business during 2005, check here . . . . ▶ ☐

Part I Income

1	Gross receipts or sales. **Caution.** If this income was reported to you on Form W-2 and the "Statutory employee" box on that form was checked, see page C-3 and check here ▶ ☐	1	
2	Returns and allowances	2	
3	Subtract line 2 from line 1	3	
4	Cost of goods sold (from line 42 on page 2)	4	
5	**Gross profit.** Subtract line 4 from line 3	5	
6	Other income, including Federal and state gasoline or fuel tax credit or refund (see page C-3) . . .	6	
7	**Gross income.** Add lines 5 and 6 . . . . ▶	7	

Part II Expenses. Enter expenses for business use of your home **only** on line 30.

8	Advertising	8		18	Office expense	18	
9	Car and truck expenses (see page C-3)	9		19	Pension and profit-sharing plans	19	
10	Commissions and fees . .	10		20	Rent or lease (see page C-5):		
11	Contract labor (see page C-4)	11		a	Vehicles, machinery, and equipment .	20a	
12	Depletion	12		b	Other business property . . .	20b	
13	Depreciation and section 179 expense deduction (not included in Part III) (see page C-4)	13		21	Repairs and maintenance . .	21	
				22	Supplies (not included in Part III) .	22	
				23	Taxes and licenses	23	
				24	Travel, meals, and entertainment:		
				a	Travel	24a	
14	Employee benefit programs (other than on line 19) . .	14		b	Deductible meals and entertainment (see page C-5)	24b	
15	Insurance (other than health) .	15		25	Utilities	25	
16	Interest:			26	Wages (less employment credits) .	26	
a	Mortgage (paid to banks, etc.) .	16a		27	Other expenses (from line 48 on page 2)	27	
b	Other	16b					
17	Legal and professional services	17					

28	**Total expenses** before expenses for business use of home. Add lines 8 through 27 in columns . ▶	28	
29	Tentative profit (loss). Subtract line 28 from line 7	29	
30	Expenses for business use of your home. Attach **Form 8829**	30	
31	**Net profit or (loss).** Subtract line 30 from line 29. • If a profit, enter on **Form 1040, line 12,** and **also** on **Schedule SE, line 2** (statutory employees, see page C-6). Estates and trusts, enter on Form 1041, line 3. • If a loss, you **must** go to line 32.	31	
32	If you have a loss, check the box that describes your investment in this activity (see page C-6). • If you checked 32a, enter the loss on **Form 1040, line 12,** and **also** on **Schedule SE, line 2** (statutory employees, see page C-6). Estates and trusts, enter on Form 1041, line 3. • If you checked 32b, you **must** attach **Form 6198.** Your loss may be limited.	32a ☐ All investment is at risk. 32b ☐ Some investment is not at risk.	

For Paperwork Reduction Act Notice, see Form 1040 instructions. | Cat. No. 11334P | Schedule C (Form 1040) 2005

(Use for Problem 23.)

Schedule C (Form 1040) 2005   Page **2**

Part III   **Cost of Goods Sold** (see page C-6)

33	Method(s) used to value closing inventory: **a** ☐ Cost **b** ☐ Lower of cost or market **c** ☐ Other (attach explanation)	
34	Was there any change in determining quantities, costs, or valuations between opening and closing inventory? If "Yes," attach explanation . . . . ☐ **Yes** ☐ **No**	
35	Inventory at beginning of year. If different from last year's closing inventory, attach explanation . .	35
36	Purchases less cost of items withdrawn for personal use	36
37	Cost of labor. Do not include any amounts paid to yourself	37
38	Materials and supplies	38
39	Other costs	39
40	Add lines 35 through 39	40
41	Inventory at end of year	41
42	**Cost of goods sold.** Subtract line 41 from line 40. Enter the result here and on page 1, line 4 . .	42

Part IV   **Information on Your Vehicle.** Complete this part **only** if you are claiming car or truck expenses on line 9 and are not required to file Form 4562 for this business. See the instructions for line 13 on page C-4 to find out if you **must** file Form 4562.

43   When did you place your vehicle in service for business purposes? (month, day, year) ▶ _____ / _____ / _____ .

44   Of the total number of miles you drove your vehicle during 2005, enter the number of miles you used your vehicle for:

a   Business _____   **b** Commuting (see instructions) _____   **c** Other _____

45	Do you (or your spouse) have another vehicle available for personal use? . . . . ☐ **Yes** ☐ **No**	
46	Was your vehicle available for personal use during off-duty hours? . . . . ☐ **Yes** ☐ **No**	
47a	Do you have evidence to support your deduction? . . . . ☐ **Yes** ☐ **No**	
b	If "Yes," is the evidence written? . . . . ☐ **Yes** ☐ **No**	

Part V   **Other Expenses.** List below business expenses not included on lines 8–26 or line 30.

_____	
_____	
_____	
_____	
_____	
_____	
_____	
_____	
_____	

48	**Total other expenses.** Enter here and on page 1, line 27	48

✪ *Printed on recycled paper*   **Schedule C (Form 1040) 2005**

Draft as of 05/31/2005

(Use for Problem 23.)

SCHEDULE SE		OMB No. 1545-0074
(Form 1040)	**Self-Employment Tax**	**20**05
Department of the Treasury Internal Revenue Service	▶ Attach to Form 1040. ▶ See Instructions for Schedule SE (Form 1040).	Attachment Sequence No. **17**

Name of person with **self-employment** income (as shown on Form 1040)	Social security number of person with **self-employment** income ▶

Who Must File Schedule SE

You must file Schedule SE if:

- You had net earnings from self-employment from **other than** church employee income (line 4 of Short Schedule SE or line 4c of Long Schedule SE) of $400 or more **or**
- You had church employee income of $108.28 or more. Income from services you performed as a minister or a member of a religious order **is not** church employee income (see page SE-1).

Note. Even if you had a loss or a small amount of income from self-employment, it may be to your benefit to file Schedule SE and use either "optional method" in Part II of Long Schedule SE (see page SE-3).

Exception. If your only self-employment income was from earnings as a minister, member of a religious order, or Christian Science practitioner **and** you filed Form 4361 and received IRS approval not to be taxed on those earnings, **do not** file Schedule SE. Instead, write "Exempt–Form 4361" on Form 1040, line 58.

May I Use Short Schedule SE or Must I Use Long Schedule SE?

```
                        ┌───────────────────────────────────────────┐
                        │ Did You Receive Wages or Tips in 2005?     │
                        └───────────────────────────────────────────┘
            No │                                              │ Yes

┌────────────────────────────────────────┐          ┌────────────────────────────────────────┐
│ Are you a minister, member of a        │  Yes     │ Was the total of your wages and tips    │ Yes
│ religious order, or Christian          │─────▶    │ subject to social security or railroad  │─────▶
│ Science practitioner who received IRS  │          │ retirement tax plus your net earnings   │
│ approval not to be taxed on earnings   │          │ from self-employment more than $90,000? │
│ from these sources, but you owe        │          └────────────────────────────────────────┘
│ self-employment tax on other earnings? │                        │ No
└────────────────────────────────────────┘
            No │
┌────────────────────────────────────────┐  Yes     ┌────────────────────────────────────────┐
│ Are you using one of the optional      │─────▶     │ Did you receive tips subject to social  │ Yes
│ methods to figure your net earnings    │     No ◀──│ security or Medicare tax that you did    │─────▶
│ (see page SE-3)?                       │           │ not report to your employer?            │
└────────────────────────────────────────┘           └────────────────────────────────────────┘
            No │
┌────────────────────────────────────────┐  Yes
│ Did you receive church employee income │─────▶
│ reported on Form W-2 of $108.28 or     │
│ more?                                  │
└────────────────────────────────────────┘
            No │
┌────────────────────────────────────────┐          ┌────────────────────────────────────────┐
│ You May Use Short Schedule SE Below    │─────────▶│ You Must Use Long Schedule SE on page 2 │
└────────────────────────────────────────┘          └────────────────────────────────────────┘
```

Section A—Short Schedule SE. Caution. Read above to see if you can use Short Schedule SE.

1	Net farm profit or (loss) from Schedule F, line 36, and farm partnerships, Schedule K-1 (Form 1065), box 14, code A	**1**	
2	Net profit or (loss) from Schedule C, line 31; Schedule C-EZ, line 3; Schedule K-1 (Form 1065), box 14, code A (other than farming); and Schedule K-1 (Form 1065-B), box 9. Ministers and members of religious orders, see page SE-1 for amounts to report on this line. See page SE-2 for other income to report	**2**	
3	Combine lines 1 and 2	**3**	
4	**Net earnings from self-employment.** Multiply line 3 by 92.35% (.9235). If less than $400, **do not** file this schedule; you do not owe self-employment tax . . . . ▶	**4**	
5	**Self-employment tax.** If the amount on line 4 is: • $90,000 or less, multiply line 4 by 15.3% (.153). Enter the result here and on **Form 1040, line 58.** • More than $90,000, multiply line 4 by 2.9% (.029). Then, add $11,160.00 to the result. Enter the total here and on **Form 1040, line 58.**	**5**	
6	**Deduction for one-half of self-employment tax.** Multiply line 5 by 50% (.5). Enter the result here and on **Form 1040, line 27**	**6**	

For Paperwork Reduction Act Notice, see Form 1040 instructions.	Cat. No. 11358Z	Schedule SE (Form 1040) 2005

TAX ETHICS CASE*

24. The date is April 14, and Helen Baldwin, CPA tax practitioner, sits at her desk, pondering the tax return before her. Helen has spent plenty of time pondering during the past year since moving from her home in a large eastern city to set up her new tax practice in a small western town. Clients in this small town have not exactly beaten a path to Helen's door to take advantage of her services. Building a client base has proven much more difficult than she had anticipated.

      The return in front of Helen was completed on behalf of her newest client, Billy Joe Carter, who owns Honest Bill's Used Car Lot. He is a cousin of half of the members of the town council and is very influential in the local business community. Establishing a client relationship with Billy is the break that Helen has been looking for. In fact, Billy has made it clear that if Helen can complete and file his return before the April 15 deadline, Helen will receive his tax return business, as well as that of his family, for years to come.

      Of concern to Helen, however, are several items on Billy's return. Billy insists that he is entitled to a business deduction for his new four-wheel-drive truck, since he uses it 100% of the time for business errands (such as traveling to car auctions, picking up parts, etc.). Helen thinks she has seen Billy driving the truck a number of times on what appeared to be personal trips. Also, Billy insists that the expenses associated with several trips to Las Vegas are deductible since the trips were "primarily of a business nature." Billy also claims several other large deductions without offering what Helen would consider to be "substantial documentation." As if anticipating Helen's skepticism, Billy said, "I don't know how things were in the big city where you came from, but around here people believe that a person's word is worth something. You'll just have to trust good old 'Honest Bill' this year, and next year I'll try to keep some better records."

a. What are the ethical issues in this case?

b. Who and what are the stakeholders who will be affected directly or indirectly by an inappropriate decision on Helen's part?

c. What are Helen's options in this situation

d. What do you recommend that Helen do?

*Case adapted from ethics cases prepared for publication by the American Accounting Association.

8

Depreciation and Amortization

CHAPTER CONTENTS

■ ■ CHAPTER OVERVIEW

Chapter 7 covered the reporting requirements for sole proprietors. Sole proprietors report most of their business activities on Schedule C. The filled-in Schedule Cs shown in Chapter 7 (Figures 7–1 and 7–4) reported amounts for depreciation expense but did not explain where those amounts came from. This chapter presents the depreciation rules for business property and provides the supporting data for the 2005 depreciation deduction. This chapter also introduces Form 4562, Depreciation and Amortization, which supports the amount deducted as depreciation on Schedule C.

DEPRECIATION OF BUSINESS PROPERTY

When taxpayers buy business property with a useful life of more than one year, they recover the cost over several years by taking annual deductions from gross income. These annual deductions, called **depreciation expense,** represent the portion of the property's cost written off each year because of wear and tear, deterioration, and normal obsolescence. How quickly taxpayers depreciate business property depends on (1) whether the property is real property or tangible personal property and (2) when the property is placed in service.

Taxpayers recover the costs of tangible personal property more quickly than the costs of real property. Also, they can use more accelerated methods to depreciate the costs of tangible personal property. **Real property** includes all real estate, such as office buildings, apartment buildings, manufacturing plants, and warehouses. Land is not depreciated, even though it is real property. **Tangible personal property** includes tangible property other than real estate, such as furniture, machinery, equipment, and vehicles. The depreciation methods taxpayers can use depend on when the property was placed in service. Different depreciation methods apply to property placed in service before 1981, property placed in service from 1981 to 1986, and property placed in service after 1986.

FIGURE 8-1 Overview of the Depreciation Rules

Property Placed in Service before 1981
Cost minus salvage value is recovered over the useful life of the asset. Acceptable depreciation methods include straight-line, declining balance, and sum-of-the-years' digits.

Property Placed in Service Between 1981–1986,
Accelerated Cost Recovery System (ACRS)
The cost of the property (ignoring salvage value) is written off over government-specified recovery periods. Most personal property is written off over a 3- or 5-year recovery period using the double declining balance method. Real property is recovered over 15, 18, or 19 years using the 175% declining balance method.

Property Placed in Service After 1986,
Modified ACRS (MACRS)
The cost of the property (ignoring salvage value) is written off over government-specified recovery periods. MACRS differs from ACRS in that most MACRS recovery periods are longer than under ACRS. In addition, the accelerated depreciation method applies only to personal property. Real property (but not land) is depreciated using the straight-line method.

The rules in effect when the asset is placed in service continue to apply during the entire time the taxpayer owns the property. For example, to compute the 2005 depreciation expense for a building placed in service in 2001, the taxpayer uses the rules that applied to property placed in service in 2001.

Taxpayers need to understand how to depreciate property correctly. Depreciation expense reduces a property's "adjusted basis," even if the taxpayer fails to deduct it on the tax return. Thus, the adjusted basis must be reduced by depreciation "allowed or allowable," meaning depreciation that is deducted or that which the taxpayer is entitled to deduct. A taxpayer can claim overlooked depreciation expense by deducting it on an amended return. An amended return must be filed within three years of the due date of the original return on which the expense was not claimed. After three years, overlooked depreciation cannot be claimed, but it still reduces the taxpayer's basis in the property.

Taxpayers can place in service property acquired by purchase, exchange, gift, or inheritance. This chapter focuses on business property acquired by purchase. It also focuses on the rules that apply to the depreciation of property placed in service after 1986, since most property placed in service before 1987 is fully depreciated by 2005. Those interested in learning more about ACRS should refer to IRS Publication 534. The depreciation rules for tangible personal property are presented first, followed by the rules for real property.

DEPRECIATION OF TANGIBLE PERSONAL PROPERTY

Additional "Bonus" First-Year Depreciation

To encourage purchases of new property after the events of September 11, 2001, Congress enacted a "bonus" depreciation in the first year for purchases of new personal property used for business or investment acquired after September 10, 2001, and placed in service by December 31, 2004. Taxpayers were required to deduct the bonus depreciation for all eligible purchases unless they made an election not to take it. After deducting the bonus depreciation from the cost of the property, taxpayers depreciated the remaining cost using the MACRS rules discussed in the next section. For property placed in service on or before May 5, 2003, the bonus percentage was 30%. After that date, it increased to 50%. Although bonus depreciation is not allowed for property placed in service after December 31, 2004, to be able to continue depreciating property on which bonus depreciation was taken, it is important to learn how bonus depreciation affected the basis in such property.

EXAMPLE 1

On August 1, 2004, Victor Myers paid $20,000 for new personal property to be used in his business. Myers deducted $10,000 ($20,000 × 50%) of bonus depreciation in 2004, and used MACRS to depreciate the remaining $10,000 ($20,000 – $10,000) starting in 2004.

EXAMPLE 2

Same as in Example 1, except that Myers purchased the property in 2005. Since property placed in service after December 31, 2004 is not eligible for the bonus depreciation, Myers depreciates the $20,000 using MACRS starting in 2005.

Modified Accelerated Cost Recovery System (MACRS)

To calculate depreciation expense using MACRS, taxpayers multiply the cost of the property (reduced by any bonus depreciation taken) by a percentage taken from an IRS-provided table. Under MACRS, personal property is assigned a life of 3, 5, 7, 10, or 15 years, regardless of its actual useful life. MACRS assigns the more common business properties a 5-year or 7-year life. The 5-year-life class includes automobiles, office equipment (copiers, typewriters, fax machines, computers, and printers), and cellular phones. The 7-year-life class includes furniture and fixtures, machinery, and equipment other than the office equipment listed above.

MACRS uses the 200% declining balance method to recover the costs of 3-, 5-, 7-, and 10-year property. The 150% declining balance method is used to recover the cost of 15-year property. However, MACRS switches to the straight-line method when straight-line yields a greater deduction.

MACRS ignores salvage value. Instead, taxpayers multiply the percentage from the table by the property's unadjusted basis to compute their MACRS deduction. The unadjusted basis equals the total cost of preparing the property for use at its operating location. This amount includes the purchase price, sales tax, plus any delivery and installation costs. Any bonus depreciation taken in the first year is subtracted from the unadjusted basis before computing the MACRS deduction. The unadjusted basis of nonbusiness property that a taxpayer converts to business use equals the lesser of (1) the fair market value of the property on the conversion date or (2) the taxpayer's adjusted basis in the property on the conversion date. Special rules also apply for determining the unadjusted basis of property acquired by exchange, gift, or inheritance. These rules are discussed in Chapter 10.

FIGURE 8-2 Cost Recovery Periods for Property under MACRS

Recovery Class	Rate and Method	Special Rules for Each Asset Class
3-year	200% D.B.*	Includes tractor units for over-the-road use and race horses over 2 years old
5-year	200% D.B.	Includes automobiles, light trucks, computers, printers, copiers, typewriters, fax machines, cellular phones, and residential rental furnishings
7-year	200% D.B.	Includes office furniture and fixtures, railroad tracks, and property not assigned to another class (machinery and equipment)
10-year	200% D.B.	Includes vessels, barges, tugs, similar water transportation equipment, and single-purpose agricultural and horticultural structures
15-year	150% D.B.	Includes shrubbery, fences, roads, and bridges

*D.B. stands for declining balance

Averaging Conventions

Two averaging conventions determine the date when taxpayers can begin depreciating personal property. These two conventions are the half-year convention and the mid-quarter convention. The half-year convention applies when at least 60% of the MACRS depreciable basis of personal property for the year is placed in service during the first nine months of the year. The mid-quarter convention applies when more than 40% of all personal property is placed in service during the last three months of the year.

Half-Year Convention

When at least 60% of all personal property is placed in service during the first three quarters of the year, all personal property placed in service during the year is depreciated using the half-year convention. When using the half-year convention, the actual date on which personal property is placed in service is ignored. Instead, the **half-year convention** assumes that taxpayers place personal property in service halfway through the tax year. The half-year convention also assumes that taxpayers dispose of (e.g., sell) such property halfway through the tax year. Thus, under the half-year convention, taxpayers get one-half year's depreciation in the first and last years, regardless of how long the taxpayer actually owned the property in those years. Figure 8-3 shows the MACRS percentages for 3-, 5-, 7-, and 10-year classes under the half-year convention. To compute MACRS on property depreciated under the half-year convention, taxpayers multiply these percentages by the cost of the property (reduced by any bonus depreciation taken).

FIGURE 8-3   MACRS Table for 3-, 5-, 7-, and 10-Year Classes Using the Half-Year Convention (from Appendix A in IRS Publication 946)

Recovery Period

Year	3-Year	5-Year	7-Year	10-Year
1	33.33%	20.00%	14.29%	10.00%
2	44.45	32.00	24.49	18.00
3	14.81*	19.20	17.49	14.40
4	7.41	11.52*	12.49	11.52
5		11.52	8.93*	9.22
6		5.76	8.92	7.37
7			8.93	6.55*
8			4.46	6.55
9				6.56
10				6.55
11				3.28

*Switching to straight-line results in the maximum depreciation deduction

The Year 1 percentages from Figure 8-3 reflect a half year's depreciation. Using the 200% declining balance method, taxpayers should deduct 40% of the cost of 5-year property in the first year (1/5 × 200%). However, because the half-year convention assumes taxpayers place property in service halfway through the year, the MACRS percentage for Year 1 is one-half of the full-year percentage, or 20% for 5-year property. Starting in Year 2, the percentages shown in Figure 8-3 reflect a full year of depreciation under the 200% declining balance method. An asterisk shows the switch to the straight-line method when straight-line yields a greater deduction. Figure 8-3 also shows that the rest of the first year's depreciation is deducted in the year after the recovery period ends. This is the sixth year for 5-year property and the eighth year for 7-year property.

EXAMPLE 3

On March 2, 2004, a taxpayer placed in service new 5-year property costing $10,000. After deducting $5,000 ($10,000 × 50%) of bonus depreciation, the remaining $5,000 ($10,000 − $5,000) is depreciated using the 5-year column in Figure 8-3. Total depreciation deductions using the half-year convention are shown below. Note that in 2004, the taxpayer deducted depreciation totalling $6,000 ($5,000 + $1,000). At the end of 2005, the taxpayer's adjusted basis in the property is $2,400 ($10,000 − $6,000 − $1,600).

Year	Depreciation	
2004	$5,000	($10,000 × 50%) bonus depreciation
2004	1,000	($5,000 × 20%) MACRS depreciation
2005	1,600	($5,000 × 32%) MACRS depreciation
2006	960	($5,000 × 19.2%) MACRS depreciation
2007	576	($5,000 × 11.52%) MACRS depreciation
2008	576	($5,000 × 11.52%) MACRS depreciation
2009	288	($5,000 × 5.76%) MACRS depreciation
	$10,000	

Except in the last year of the recovery period, when taxpayers dispose of property under the half-year convention, they multiply the MACRS percentage from the table by one-half. In the last year of the recovery period (for example, year 6 for 5-year property), taxpayers use the full MACRS percentage even if they dispose of the property in that year.

EXAMPLE 4

On April 10, 2001, Kate Roberts placed in service 5-year property costing $10,000. In 2005, Roberts sells the property. Under the half-year convention, the annual depreciation for the property is shown below.

Year	MACRS	
2001	$2,000*	($10,000 × 20%)
2002	3,200	($10,000 × 32%)
2003	1,920	($10,000 × 19.2%)
2004	1,152	($10,000 × 11.52%)
2005	576	($10,000 × 11.52% × ½)
	$8,848	

*No bonus depreciation was taken in 2001 since the property was purchased before September 11, 2001.

It does not matter when in 2005 Roberts actually sells the property. The half-year convention assumes that she sells the property on June 30, 2005, halfway through the tax year.

Mid-Quarter Convention

During the first few years after the half-year convention was enacted, many taxpayers took advantage of it by purchasing assets near the end of the year and taking a half-year's depreciation in the first year. To counter this strategy, the government now imposes a mid-quarter convention. Taxpayers who purchase over 40% of their personal property (equipment, furniture, etc.) during the last quarter of the year must use the mid-quarter convention to depreciate all personal property placed in service during that year.

Like the half-year convention, the mid-quarter convention ignores the actual date personal property is placed in service. Instead, the **mid-quarter convention** assumes that taxpayers placed the personal property in service in the middle of the quarter. Thus, taxpayers who place personal property in service between January 1 and March 31 are assumed to place it in service on February 15. This means that, in the first year, they can depreciate the property from February 15 until December 31 (10.5 months). Figure 8-4 shows the four mid-quarter tables for 3-, 5-, and 7-year classes.

The Year 1 percentages in Figure 8-4 reflect the portion of the year in which the property is assumed to be placed in service. For property placed in service in the first quarter, depreciation on the property begins on February 15. For 5-year property, the first-year percentage equals 35% ($1/5 \times 200\% \times 10.5/12$). For 7-year property placed in service in the fourth quarter (deemed placed in service on November 15), the first-year percentage equals 3.57% ($1/7 \times 200\% \times 1.5/12$). Starting in Year 2, the percentages reflect a full year of depreciation under the 200% declining balance method, switching to straight-line at the most opportune time.

The mid-quarter convention also assumes that taxpayers dispose of property halfway through the quarter. Thus, all personal property sold during October, November, and December is deemed to have been sold on November 15, regardless of the quarter in which the property was purchased. Likewise, all personal property sold during April, May, and June is deemed sold on May 15. In the year taxpayers dispose of personal property depreciated using the mid-quarter convention, the percentage from the table must be reduced to reflect the portion of the year the property was assumed to be in service. This would be from January 1 until the middle of the quarter in which the property is sold.

FIGURE 8-4   MACRS Table for 3-, 5-, and 7-Year Classes Using the Mid-Quarter Convention (from Appendix A in IRS Publication 946)

Property Placed in Service				Years				
1st quarter	1	2	3	4	5	6	7	8
3-year	58.33%	27.78%	12.35%	1.54%				
5-year	35.00	26.00	15.60	11.01	11.01%	1.38%		
7-year	25.00	21.43	15.31	10.93	8.75	8.74	8.75%	1.09%
2nd quarter								
3-year	41.67	38.89	14.14	5.30				
5-year	25.00	30.00	18.00	11.37	11.37	4.26		
7-year	17.85	23.47	16.76	11.97	8.87	8.87	8.87	3.34
3rd quarter								
3-year	25.00	50.00	16.67	8.33				
5-year	15.00	34.00	20.40	12.24	11.30	7.06		
7-year	10.71	25.51	18.22	13.02	9.30	8.85	8.86	5.53
4th quarter								
3-year	8.33	61.11	20.37	10.19				
5-year	5.00	38.00	22.80	13.68	10.94	9.58		
7-year	3.57	27.55	19.68	14.06	10.04	8.73	8.73	7.64

EXAMPLE 5

In March 2001, George Rodgers placed in service 5-year property that cost $10,000. Rodgers sold the property in June 2005. Under the mid-quarter convention, depreciation for the property is as follows.

Year	MACRS	
2001	$3,500	($10,000 × 35%)
2002	2,600	($10,000 × 26%)
2003	1,560	($10,000 × 15.6%)
2004	1,101	($10,000 × 11.01%)
2005	413	($10,000 × 11.01% × 4.5/12)
	$9,174	

The MACRS first-quarter percentages apply since Rodgers placed the property in service during the first quarter. Although Rodgers actually sold the property in June, the property is deemed sold halfway through the second quarter (May 15). Rodgers multiplies the Year 5 MACRS percentage by 4.5/12 to reflect the property's depreciation from January 1 through May 15. Notice that Rodgers uses the 5-year percentages for the 1st quarter for all years that he depreciates the property. Also, there is no bonus depreciation taken in 2001 since the property was placed in service before September 11, 2001.

Each year taxpayers must determine whether the half-year or mid-quarter convention applies to personal property placed in service that year. If the mid-quarter convention applies, then taxpayers may need to use four different tables to compute depreciation on personal property placed in service that year. (Under the half-year convention, taxpayers use one table to depreciate all personal property placed in service during the year.) The mid-quarter convention applies when the taxpayer placed in service in the fourth quarter more than 40% of the total personal property placed in service that year. Otherwise, the half-year convention applies.

It is important to note that real property placed in service during the year is not used when determining whether more than 40% of all personal property placed in service during the year is done so in the fourth quarter. The relevant percentage is fourth quarter personal property purchases divided by total personal property purchases during the year.

EXAMPLE 6

On June 21, 2005, Jean Nelson placed in service 7-year property that costs $20,000. On October 10, 2005, she placed in service 5-year property that costs $15,000. These are the only properties placed in service in 2005. Since Nelson placed in service 42.9% ($15,000/$35,000) of the personal property in the fourth quarter, the mid-quarter convention applies to all personal property placed in service in 2005. Depreciation for 2005 on the 7-year property equals $3,570 ($20,000 × 17.85%); on the 5-year property it equals $750 ($15,000 × 5%).

EXAMPLE 7

Assume the same facts as in Example 6, except that Nelson placed the 5-year property in service on September 30, 2005. Since 40% or less of the personal property placed in service in 2005 was placed in service in the fourth quarter, the half-year convention applies to both properties. Depreciation on the 7-year property would be $2,858 ($20,000 × 14.29%). Depreciation on the 5-year property would be $3,000 ($15,000 × 20%).

Election Choices

Taxpayers who do not wish to use the regular MACRS (accelerated) method can elect to use either the alternate MACRS method or the Alternative Depreciation System (ADS).

Alternate MACRS

Alternate MACRS uses the straight-line method instead of the accelerated method. Straight-line depreciation spreads the cost evenly over the recovery period. When the taxpayer elects the straight-line method, the recovery periods and averaging conventions continue to apply. For example, using alternative MACRS, 7-year property would be depreciated over seven years using the straight-line method. Assuming the half-year convention applied, first year depreciation on property costing $10,000 would be $714 ($10,000 × ⅟₇ × ½). This same amount would be the depreciation in the year the furniture is sold. For the years in between, depreciation would be $1,429 ($10,000 × ⅟₇).

The election to use the straight-line method can be made annually for each class of property. For example, a taxpayer who elects the straight-line method in 2005 for 5-year property must use the straight-line method to depreciate all 5-year property placed in service in 2005. However, the taxpayer can use the regular (accelerated) MACRS for 7-year property purchased in 2005. This is called an election on a **class-by-class basis.** A taxpayer who uses the straight-line method to depreciate 5-year property placed in service in 2005 does not have to use it to depreciate 5-year property placed in service in 2006.

Alternative Depreciation System (ADS)

The **Alternative Depreciation System (ADS)** differs from MACRS in that most properties have longer recovery periods. For most property, the taxpayer can choose between the straight-line method and the 150% declining balance method. The half-year and mid-quarter conventions apply to personal property depreciated under the ADS method. Separate tables are available for this method. The IRS provides these tables in Publication 946. The following comparison shows the recovery periods under MACRS and ADS.

	MACRS	ADS
Office furniture, fixtures, and equipment	7 years	10 years
Automobiles, light general purpose trucks, computers, and printers	5 years	5 years
Copiers, calculators, and typewriters	5 years	6 years
Heavy general purpose trucks	5 years	6 years

Personal property with no designated class life has a recovery period of 12 years under ADS. The taxpayer makes the election to use ADS annually on a class-by-class basis. Once a taxpayer elects to depreciate specific property using ADS, that election for that property cannot be revoked.

Example 8 illustrates the four different options available for depreciating personal property. ADS must be used to depreciate property used less than 50 percent for business. It also is used to compute a corporation's "earnings and profits."

> ### EXAMPLE 8
>
> In 2005, Natalie Brown places in service a desk. To recover the cost of the desk and all other 7-year property placed in service during 2005, Brown can choose from the following methods:
>
> 1. MACRS:
>   a. 200% declining balance over 7 years (regular MACRS)
>   b. Straight-line over 7 years (alternate MACRS)
> 2. ADS:
>   a. Straight-line over 10 years
>   b. 150% declining balance over 10 years
>
> No matter which method Brown selects, the percentage of all personal property placed in service in the fourth quarter will determine whether the half-year or mid-quarter convention applies. Also, the method Brown selects will apply to all 7-year property placed in service in 2005. Regardless of which depreciation method Brown selects, she must continue to depreciate the desk (plus all other 7-year property placed in service in 2005) using this method in all future years.

In determining the depreciation deduction for a given tax year, it is often assumed that the taxpayer should take the maximum deduction allowed at the earliest possible time. However, this may not always be the best policy. For example, a taxpayer currently in a low tax bracket may expect to be in a higher tax bracket in future years. This taxpayer will benefit most by delaying the large depreciation deductions until the higher tax bracket years. This can be accomplished by electing alternative MACRS or ADS to depreciate property.

Section 179 Expense Election

Taxpayers that qualify can elect to take an up-front deduction in the year certain personal property is placed in service. For 2005, taxpayers can expense up to $105,000 of Section 179 property placed in service during 2005. The Code defines **Section 179 property** as *tangible personal property purchased* by the taxpayer and *used in a trade or business*. Thus, real property and property acquired by means other than a purchase are not Section 179 property. Likewise, depreciable personal property used for investment is not Section 179 property. However, used property that the taxpayer purchases for use in the taxpayer's business is eligible for Section 179 expensing.

The amount of Section 179 property that taxpayers can expense in the first year is reduced dollar for dollar when more than $420,000 of Section 179 property is placed in service during 2005. For example, taxpayers who place in service $469,000 of Section 179 property during 2005 would be allowed to expense up to $56,000 [$105,000 − ($469,000 − $420,000)] of the Section 179 property in that year. Taxpayers compute the maximum Section 179 expense they can take each year on Form 4562, Part I (lines 1 to 5).

Taxpayers can elect Section 179 expense only in the year they place the property in service. Once taxpayers determine the amount of Section 179 expense they wish to elect,

[handwritten margin notes: "phaseout", "no taxable loss can be created", "max"]

they allocate it among one or more of the Section 179 properties. Taxpayers must identify on the tax return the property (or properties) they elect to expense under Section 179. Taxpayers make this election on Form 4562, Part I (line 6). After selecting the property (or properties) to expense under Section 179, they can recover the rest of the unadjusted basis of the property (or properties) using regular MACRS, alternate MACRS, or ADS.

For Section 179 property placed in service between 2003 and 2007, taxpayers can make or revoke a Section 179 election on an amended return. An amended return must be filed within three years of the due date of the original tax return (including extensions). See Chapter 12 for more details.

EXAMPLE 9

On February 10, 2005, Lowe Enterprises placed in service personal property that costs $504,000, which includes $80,000 of equipment (7-year property). The half-year convention applies to personal property placed in service in 2005. Lowe elects to expense part of the equipment under Section 179. Since in 2005 Lowe placed in service more than $420,000 of Section 179 property, it can elect to expense up to $21,000 under Section 179 [$105,000 − ($504,000 − $420,000)]. Lowe can then deduct regular MACRS on the remaining $59,000 ($80,000 − $21,000). In 2005, total depreciation on the equipment equals $29,431 [$21,000 Section 179 expense + $8,431 MACRS ($59,000 × 14.29%)].

Section 179 expense cannot exceed a taxpayer's taxable income from any trade or business after regular depreciation has been taken. Taxpayers can carry over to the next tax year any Section 179 expense disallowed because of the taxable income limit. However, this carryover is subject to the Section 179 limit that applies to the next year(s). For purposes of MACRS, taxpayers must reduce the basis in the property by the total amount they *elect* to expense under Section 179.

EXAMPLE 10

Assume the same facts as in Example 9, except that Lowe's taxable income from the business (after regular depreciation) is $5,000. Although Lowe can elect up to $21,000 of Section 179 expense, only $5,000 can be deducted in 2005. The $16,000 of disallowed expense can be carried over to 2006 and later years.

For purposes of computing MACRS on the equipment, Lowe reduces its basis by the amount it elects to expense under Section 179, even though part of the expense must be postponed to 2006. If Lowe does not do this, over the next eight years Lowe will deduct $21,000 under Section 179 ($5,000 in 2005 and $16,000 in a future year) and $75,000 ($80,000 − $5,000) as MACRS depreciation. The total deductions of $96,000 would exceed the $80,000 cost of the equipment.

Figure 8-5 illustrates how Lowe from Example 10 elects Section 179 for $21,000 of the equipment.

In determining whether the half-year or mid-quarter convention applies to personal property placed in service during the year, the 40% test is applied after Section 179 expensing.

FIGURE 8-5 Filled-In Form 4562, Part I

Form **4562**	**Depreciation and Amortization** (Including Information on Listed Property)	OMB No. 1545-0172
Department of the Treasury Internal Revenue Service	▶ See separate instructions. ▶ Attach to your tax return.	20**05** Attachment Sequence No. **67**

Name(s) shown on return	Business or activity to which this form relates	Identifying number
Lowe Enterprises		71-6928490

Part I **Election To Expense Certain Property Under Section 179**
Note: *If you have any listed property, complete Part V before you complete Part I.*

1	Maximum amount. See the instructions for a higher limit for certain businesses	**1**	$105,000
2	Total cost of section 179 property placed in service (see instructions)	**2**	504,000
3	Threshold cost of section 179 property before reduction in limitation	**3**	$420,000
4	Reduction in limitation. Subtract line 3 from line 2. If zero or less, enter -0-	**4**	84,000
5	Dollar limitation for tax year. Subtract line 4 from line 1. If zero or less, enter -0-. If married filing separately, see instructions	**5**	21,000

	(a) Description of property	**(b)** Cost (business use only)	**(c)** Elected cost	
6	Equipment	80,000	21,000	

7	Listed property. Enter the amount from line 29 . . . . **7**		
8	Total elected cost of section 179 property. Add amounts in column (c), lines 6 and 7	**8**	21,000
9	Tentative deduction. Enter the **smaller** of line 5 or line 8.	**9**	21,000
10	Carryover of disallowed deduction from line 13 of your 2004 Form 4562	**10**	
11	Business income limitation. Enter the smaller of business income (not less than zero) or line 5 (see instructions)	**11**	5,000
12	Section 179 expense deduction. Add lines 9 and 10, but do not enter more than line 11 . . .	**12**	5,000
13	Carryover of disallowed deduction to 2006. Add lines 9 and 10, less line 12 ▶ **13**	16,000	

Note: *Do not use Part II or Part III below for listed property. Instead, use Part V.*

Listed Property Limitations

Special rules apply to property *suitable for personal use.* Such property, referred to as **listed property**, commonly includes automobiles, cellular phones, computers, and printers. Listed property that the taxpayer does not use more than 50% of the time for business does not qualify for regular (accelerated) MACRS or Section 179 first-year expense. Instead, such property must be depreciated under ADS using the straight-line method. The half-year and mid-quarter provisions apply to listed property.

PROPERTY SUITABLE FOR PERSONAL USE

Property used for transportation

- Passenger automobiles and motorcycles
- Trucks, buses, boats, and airplanes

Property used for entertainment, recreation, or amusement

- Cameras and VCRs
- Communication and stereo equipment

Computers and related equipment (but not if used only at the taxpayer's regular business establishment, including a qualified home office)

Cellular telephones

For property used for transportation (like passenger automobiles), the 50% test should be based on *miles used for business* in relation to total miles used. For other types of listed property, taxpayers should use the appropriate *units of time* (hours) to allocate between business use and other use. Although any investment use of the property is not considered in meeting the more-than-50% test, taxpayers can depreciate the portion of the property's cost that involves investment use. Whichever depreciation method (regular MACRS or ADS) is chosen, that method is used to depreciate both the business and the investment use portions of the property.

Part V of Form 4562 is where taxpayers report the depreciation of listed property. In Part V, taxpayers confirm that they have written evidence to support the business or investment use of the property. They then separate the listed property used more than 50% of the time for business from property not used more than 50% of the time for business. Only property used more than 50% for business can be expensed under Section 179 and depreciated using regular (accelerated) MACRS.

EXAMPLE 11

On August 9, 2005, Tom Richards placed in service a computer that costs $4,000. This is the only property Richards placed in service in 2005, so the half-year convention applies. Richards uses the computer 60% of the time for business, 15% of the time for investment purposes, and 25% of the time for personal use. Since the business use of the computer exceeds 50%, MACRS can be taken on the 75% combined business and investment use ($4,000 × 75% = $3,000 business/investment basis). MACRS for 2005 equals $600 ($3,000 × 20%). MACRS on the business use alone is $1,440 ($1,800 × 60/75).

Since business use exceeds 50%, Richards could elect to expense $2,400 ($4,000 × 60%) under Section 179 and deduct MACRS on the $600 ($4,000 × 15%) investment basis.

EXAMPLE 12

Assume the same facts as in Example 11, except that Richards uses the computer 40% for business, 15% for investment purposes, and 45% for personal use. Because business use does not exceed 50%, Section 179 cannot be elected and regular (accelerated) MACRS cannot be used. Richards must use ADS and the half-year convention to depreciate the 55% combined business/investment basis.

Figure 8-6 shows where Richards from Example 12 reports the depreciation on his computer. Richards has written evidence to support his 40% business use and 15% investment use. He enters the information on line 27 because his business use alone does not exceed 50%. The $220 depreciation deduction on line 27(h) reflects the straight-line methods and half-year convention ($2,200 × 1/5 × 1/2).

If the business usage of listed property drops below 50% in a future year and the taxpayer has used Section 179, bonus depreciation or regular (accelerated) MACRS to depreciate the property, the taxpayer must permanently switch to the straight-line method. Also, the taxpayer must recompute what depreciation would have been in all prior years for that property using only the straight-line method. The difference between accumulated depreciation taken on the property (including any bonus depreciation and Section 179 expense) and what accumulated depreciation would have been under the straight-line method must be included in the taxpayer's income in the year business usage drops below 50%.

FIGURE 8-6   Filled-In Form 4562, Part V

Form 4562 (2005)   Page **2**

Part V	**Listed Property** (Include automobiles, certain other vehicles, cellular telephones, certain computers, and property used for entertainment, recreation, or amusement.)

Note: *For any vehicle for which you are using the standard mileage rate or deducting lease expense, complete only 24a, 24b, columns (a) through (c) of Section A, all of Section B, and Section C if applicable.*

Section A—Depreciation and Other Information (Caution: *See the instructions for limits for passenger automobiles.***)**

24a Do you have evidence to support the business/investment use claimed? ☒ Yes ☐ No	24b If "Yes," is the evidence written? ☒ Yes ☐ No

(a) Type of property (list vehicles first)	(b) Date placed in service	(c) Business/ investment use percentage	(d) Cost or other basis	(e) Basis for depreciation (business/investment use only)	(f) Recovery period	(g) Method/ Convention	(h) Depreciation deduction	(i) Elected section 179 cost
25 Special allowance for qualified New York Liberty Zone listed property placed in service during the tax year and used more than 50% in a qualified business use (see instructions)						**25**		
26 Property used more than 50% in a qualified business use:								
		%						
		%						
		%						
27 Property used 50% or less in a qualified business use:								
Computer	8-9-05	55 %	4,000	2,200	5 yr	S/L –	220	
		%				S/L –		
		%				S/L –		
28 Add amounts in column (h), lines 25 through 27. Enter here and on line 21, page 1. . .						**28**	220	
29 Add amounts in column (i), line 26. Enter here and on line 7, page 1.							**29**	

EXAMPLE 13

Fred Newman paid $3,000 for a computer on April 3, 2003. Newman elected out of taking bonus depreciation on all 5-year property placed in service in 2003. He uses the computer 60% for business and 40% for personal use during both 2003 and 2004. Newman used regular (accelerated) MACRS and the half-year convention to depreciate the computer. On his 2003 and 2004 tax returns, Newman deducted $360 ($3,000 × 60% × .2) and $576 ($3,000 × 60% × .32), respectively. In 2005, Newman's business usage drops to 45%. Beginning in 2005, Newman must permanently switch to the straight-line method. His 2005 depreciation expense deduction is $270 ($3,000 × 45% × ⅕). In addition, Newman must compute what his depreciation expense would have been in 2003 and 2004 using the straight-line method. His depreciation would have been $180 ($3,000 × 60% × ⅕ × ½) in 2003 and $360 ($3,000 × 60% × ⅕) in 2004. Newman must include in 2005 income the $396 difference between the $936 ($360 + $576) actually deducted in 2003 and 2004 and the $540 ($180 + $360) that would have been deducted using the straight-line method.

Taxpayers must be able to substantiate the amount, time, place, and business purpose of transportation expenses. For automobiles and other vehicles, they must establish both the business/ investment miles and total miles the vehicle was driven during the year. They do this by keeping adequate records or by producing evidence that supports statements they prepare. Mileage records created at or around the time the vehicle was used for business/investment/ have a higher degree of credibility than records prepared at a later date. The Tax Court has disallowed unsubstantiated transportation expenses primarily because the mileage summary did not contain odometer readings entered at the time the vehicle was used. Instead, the business miles had been computed from figures in a computer atlas database.

Luxury Automobile Limits

MACRS limits the depreciation of luxury automobiles used for business, even those used 100% for business. Figure 8-7 shows the luxury automobile depreciation limits for the years 2001 to 2005. Due to the bonus depreciation allowed from September 11, 2001 until December 31, 2004, the first year MACRS limits for these years are considerably higher than the limit for 2005.

FIGURE 8-7   Luxury Automobile Depreciation Limits for the Years 2001–2005

	Automobiles Placed in Service During				
Year	**2001**	**2002**	**2003**	**2004**	**2005**
1*	$7,660	$7,660	$7,660/$10,710	$10,610	$2,960
2	4,900	4,900	4,900	4,800	4,700
3	2,950	2,950	2,950	2,850	2,850
4 and on	1,775	1,775	1,775	1,675	1,675

*The $10,710/$10,610 limit applied to new automobiles purchased after May 5, 2003, when the 50% bonus was used. The $7,660 limit applied to new automobiles after September 10, 2001, when the 30% bonus was used. From 2001–2003, the limit was $3,060 for automobiles placed in service before September 11, 2001; for any used automobile; and for any automobile used 50% or less for business. For 2004, the limit for used automobiles and automobiles used 50% or less for business was $2,960.

The limits in Figure 8-7 apply only to passenger automobiles. A passenger automobile is any four-wheeled vehicle made primarily for use on public streets, roads, and highways and whose unloaded gross vehicle weight is 6,000 pounds or less. Slightly higher limits apply to light trucks and vans (including minivans and sports utility vehicles (SUVs)). Ambulances, hearses, taxis, and limousines are not subject to the luxury automobile rules. Neither are trucks and vans placed in service after July 6, 2003, that have been specially modified so that they are not likely to be used for personal use.

When the luxury automobile rules were first enacted, the rules applied to "passenger automobiles" that did not weigh over 6,000 pounds. Since then, many sport-utility vehicles (SUVs) now weigh over 6,000 pounds and taxpayers could avoid the luxury automobile limits by purchasing these heavier SUVs and using them in their businesses. This allowed them to expense the SUV's cost (up to $105,000 in 2005) under Section 179 (assuming 100% business use).

Congress addressed this issue by enacting tax rules that now limit the amount of Section 179 expense allowed on SUVs weighing between 6,000 and 14,000 pounds to a maximum of $25,000 (based on 100% business use). Amounts not expensed under Section 179 are depreciated using the MACRS rules discussed in this chapter. The new limits apply to SUVs placed in service after October 22, 2004. Under this tax rule, only SUVs weighing more than 14,000 pounds are exempt from the $25,000 Section 179 limit. SUVs placed in service on or before this date are subject to the same luxury automobile rules as trucks and vans (thus SUVs weighing over 6,000 pounds would be exempt from these rules).

The amounts in Figure 8-7 show the limits imposed for automobiles used 100% of the time for business. Taxpayers must reduce these amounts for automobiles used less than 100% for business. The Year 1 limit also applies to the bonus depreciation and Section 179 expense. (Recall that bonus depreciation was allowed for new vehicles placed in service between September 11, 2001 and December 31, 2004.) Figure 8-8 shows that if there were no limits, simply by using regular MACRS, a taxpayer could deduct the entire cost of a $25,000 automobile in the first six years of use (assuming 100% business use). However, the luxury automobile limits allow only $15,535 in the first six years. In Year 7, taxpayers can continue to deduct $1,675 each year a deduction of the remaining cost is recovered.

FIGURE 8-8 2005 Depreciation Limitations for a 25,000 Luxury Automobile

Year	Depreciation Using Potential MACRS Deduction		Luxury Automobile Limitation
2005	$ 5,000	($25,000 × 20%)	$ 2,960
2006	8,000	($25,000 × 32%)	4,700
2007	4,800	($25,000 × 19.2%)	2,850
2008	2,880	($25,000 × 11.52%)	1,675
2009	2,880	($25,000 × 11.52%)	1,675
2010	1,440	($25,000 × 5.76%)	1,675
	$25,000		$15,535
2011			1,675
2012			1,675
2013			1,675
2014			1,675
2015			1,675
2016			1,090
			$25,000

For a luxury automobile used partially for business, the taxpayer must combine the rules for listed property with those for luxury automobiles.

EXAMPLE 14

On August 2, 2004, Paula Hendricks placed in service a new automobile that cost $40,000. The half-year convention applied to personal property Hendricks placed in service in 2004. Hendricks uses the car 70% of the time for business. Since Hendricks's business use exceeds 50%, both bonus depreciation and regular MACRS were taken on the automobile. She uses the 2004 column from Figure 8-7 to compute her luxury automobile limits. In 2004, Hendricks deducted $7,427 [the lesser of $16,800 (($40,000 × 70% business use × 50% bonus) + ($20,000 × 70% × .20 MACRS)) or $7,427 ($10,610 × 70%)]. In 2005, she deducts $3,360 [the lesser of ($20,000 × 70% × .32 MACRS) or ($4,800 × 70%)].

EXAMPLE 15

On July 15, 2005, Anne Jones placed in service an automobile that cost $30,000. The half-year convention applies to 5-year property Jones placed in service in 2005. Jones uses the car 80% of the time for business. Jones uses the 2005 column from Figure 8-7 to compute her first-year luxury automobile limit. Jones is limited to $2,368 ($2,960 × 80%) of depreciation in 2005, since it is less than $4,800 ($30,000 × 80% × .20).

Leased Automobiles

Taxpayers leasing automobiles can either use the standard mileage rate (in 2005, 40.5 cents per mile before September 1; 48.5 cents per mile after August 31) or deduct the business portion of their lease payments. To prevent taxpayers who choose to deduct their lease payments from getting around the luxury automobile limits by leasing expensive cars, the government reduces the amount taxpayers can deduct for their lease payments. They do this by reducing the deduction by a gross income "inclusion amount." The inclusion amount is based on the fair market value (FMV) of the car. Taxpayers multiply the inclusion amount from the IRS table by the business use percentage. In the first and last years of the lease, the amount is further reduced to reflect the portion of the year the car was leased.

The IRS publishes inclusion amounts for leased cars in Publication 463. Figure 8-9 shows the portion of the table for cars with a FMV between $35,000 and $40,000 that were first leased during 2004. Inclusion amounts for trucks, vans, and electric cars are slightly lower. These amounts, along with inclusion amounts for car values not listed in Figure 8-9, can be found in IRS Publication 463, Appendix A.

FIGURE 8-9   Inclusion Amounts for Cars First Leased in 2004

Fair Market Value		Tax Year of Lease				
Over	Not Over	1st	2nd	3rd	4th	5th and later
$35,000	$36,000	$ 75	$165	$244	$294	$340
36,000	37,000	79	173	256	308	357
37,000	38,000	83	181	268	322	373
38,000	39,000	86	189	280	337	389
39,000	40,000	90	197	292	351	405

EXAMPLE 16

On September 1, 2004, Janet Lane began leasing a car for $400 a month. Lane leased the car for 122 days during 2004 (September 1 to December 31). The FMV of the car was $37,200 and Lane's business usage is 70%. In 2004, Lane's lease deduction initially equals 70% of her lease payments, or $1,120 ($400 × 4 × 70%). From Figure 8-9, the inclusion amount for 2004 (1st year of the lease) is $83. Lane reduces her 2004 lease deduction by $19 ($83 × 70% × 122/366) and deducts $1,101 ($1,120 – $19) on Schedule C (line 20a). In 2005, Lane's vehicle lease deduction is $3,233 [$3,360 for her lease payments ($400 × 12 × 70%) – $127 ($181 inclusion amount × 70%)].

DEPRECIATION OF REAL PROPERTY

MACRS

Under MACRS, taxpayers depreciate real property using the straight-line method. The recovery period for real property under MACRS depends on whether the property is residential or nonresidential real property. Taxpayers recover the cost of residential rental property, such as apartment buildings and rental vacation homes, over 27.5 years. The recovery period for nonresidential (commercial and industrial) real estate, such as office buildings, manufacturing plants, and warehouses, is 31.5 years if placed in service before May 13, 1993. For nonresidential property placed in service after May 12, 1993, the recovery period is 39 years. Although land is real property, it is not depreciated.

The **mid-month convention** applies to real property depreciated under MACRS. The mid-month convention assumes taxpayers place real property in service in the middle of the month they actually place it in service. The mid-month convention also assumes that taxpayers dispose of real property in the middle of a month.

EXAMPLE 17

On March 1, 1993, Vicky Mathews placed in service residential real property that cost $100,000. Mathews sells the property on December 5, 2005. Mathews's annual cost recovery for the property follows.

Year	MACRS	
1993	$ 2,879	($100,000 × 1/27.5 × 9.5/12)
1994–2004	40,000	($100,000 × 1/27.5 × 11 years)
2005	3,485	($100,000 × 1/27.5 × 11.5/12)
	$46,364	

EXAMPLE 18

Assume the same facts as in Example 17, except that on March 1, 1993, Mathews placed in service nonresidential real property.

Year	MACRS	
1993	$ 2,513	($100,000 × 1/31.5 × 9.5/12)
1994–2004	34,921	($100,000 × 1/31.5 × 11 years)
2005	3,042	($100,000 × 1/31.5 × 11.5/12)
	$40,476	

EXAMPLE 19

Assume the same facts as in Example 18, except that Mathews placed the nonresidential real property in service on July 1, 1993.

Year	MACRS	
1993	$ 1,175	($100,000 × 1/39 × 5.5/12)
1994–2004	28,205	($100,000 × 1/39 × 11 years)
2005	2,457	($100,000 × 1/39 × 11.5/12)
	$31,837	

Optional Recovery Periods

Instead of using MACRS recovery periods of 27.5 (for residential realty) and 31.5 or 39 years (for nonresidential realty), taxpayers can elect under the Alternative Depreciation System (ADS) to depreciate both residential and nonresidential real realty over 40 years. Those who elect ADS continue to use the straight-line method and the mid-month convention. Taxpayers can elect to use the optional 40-year recovery period on a **property-by-property** basis.

This allows them to depreciate one piece of real property over 40 years and another over the regular MACRS recovery period.

Depreciation of a Business in the Home

Taxpayers who use part of their home for business purposes can depreciate the business portion of the home. Chapter 7 discussed the rules regarding deductions for the business use of the home. To compute the depreciation deduction, the taxpayer first computes the percentage of the total square footage of the home used for business. If the rooms are all of approximately equal size, the taxpayer can divide the number of rooms used for business by the total number of rooms in the home. The taxpayer uses the business-use percentage of the home to compute depreciation on the home.

The depreciable basis for the home is the lesser of the home's adjusted basis or its fair market value (FMV) at the time the home office was placed in service. In determining the depreciable basis, the cost of the land must be removed from the adjusted basis. Likewise, the value of the land cannot be included when computing the FMV of the residence. The value of the land often is shown separately from the value of the building on a professional appraisal of property. Taxpayers report the allowable depreciation deduction for a business in the home for a sole proprietor on Form 8829, Expenses for Business Use of Your Home, Part III. Figure 8-10 shows the calculation of the depreciation deduction.

Information for Figure 8-10: Filled-In Form 8829

In 1994 Darryl Collins bought a home for $320,000 (includes $80,000 for the land). On March 1, 1998, when the FMV of the home was $340,000 (includes $80,000 for the land), Collins began using one room exclusively as a business office. The square footage of the office is 200; the total square footage of the home is 4,000. Since Collins uses the business portion of the home as an office, it meets the definition of nonresidential real property. Thus, a depreciation percentage of 2.564% (1/39 applies to nonresidential realty placed in service after May 12, 1993).

Chapter 7 discussed the order in which taxpayers deduct home office expenses:

1. All non–home office expenses from Schedule C. This amount includes depreciation on personal and real property (other than the home office).
2. The portion of mortgage interest, real estate taxes, and casualty losses taken on Form 8829 that relates to the home office.
3. The portion of operating expenses that relates to the business use of the home. These amounts include repairs, maintenance, utilities, and insurance.
4. The business portion of depreciation on the home.

Expenses listed in items 3 and 4 cannot create or increase a business loss. Any expenses disallowed because they create or increase a business loss do not reduce business income on Schedule C. The disallowed expenses may be carried forward and included on Form 8829 in the following year. Form 8829, Part IV, computes the expenses carried over to 2006. Form 8829 (line 23) reports the disallowed operating expenses (insurance, utilities, etc.) from 2004. Form 8829 (line 29) reports the disallowed depreciation from 2004.

FIGURE 8-10   Filled-In Form 8829

Form **8829**	**Expenses for Business Use of Your Home**	OMB No. 1545-1266
Department of the Treasury Internal Revenue Service (99)	▶ File only with Schedule C (Form 1040). Use a separate Form 8829 for each home you used for business during the year. ▶ See separate instructions.	**2005** Attachment Sequence No. **66**

Name(s) of proprietor(s)	Your social security number
Darryl Collins	531 64 9923

Part I   Part of Your Home Used for Business

1	Area used regularly and exclusively for business, regularly for daycare, or for storage of inventory or product samples (see instructions)	**1**	200
2	Total area of home	**2**	4,000
3	Divide line 1 by line 2. Enter the result as a percentage	**3**	5 %

● **For daycare facilities not used exclusively for business, also complete lines 4–6.**

● **All others, skip lines 4–6 and enter the amount from line 3 on line 7.**

4	Multiply days used for daycare during year by hours used per day	**4**		h r.
5	Total hours available for use during the year (365 days × 24 hours) (see instructions)	**5**	8,760	h r.
6	Divide line 4 by line 5. Enter the result as a decimal amount	**6**	.	
7	Business percentage. For daycare facilities not used exclusively for business, multiply line 6 by line 3 (enter the result as a percentage). All others, enter the amount from line 3. ▶	**7**		5 %

Part II   Figure Your Allowable Deduction

		(a) Direct expenses	(b) Indirect expenses		
8	Enter the amount from Schedule C, line 29, **plus** any net gain or (loss) derived from the business use of your home and shown on Schedule D or Form 4797. If more than one place of business, see instructions			**8**	
	See instructions for columns (a) and (b) before completing lines 9–20.				
9	Casualty losses (see instructions)	**9**			
10	Deductible mortgage interest (see instructions)	**10**			
11	Real estate taxes (see instructions)	**11**			
12	Add lines 9, 10, and 11	**12**			
13	Multiply line 12, column (b) by line 7		**13**		
14	Add line 12, column (a) and line 13			**14**	
15	Subtract line 14 from line 8. If zero or less, enter -0-			**15**	
16	Excess mortgage interest (see instructions)	**16**			
17	Insurance	**17**			
18	Repairs and maintenance	**18**			
19	Utilities	**19**			
20	Other expenses (see instructions)	**20**			
21	Add lines 16 through 20	**21**			
22	Multiply line 21, column (b) by line 7		**22**		
23	Carryover of operating expenses from 2004 Form 8829, line 41		**23**		
24	Add line 21 in column (a), line 22, and line 23			**24**	
25	Allowable operating expenses. Enter the **smaller** of line 15 or line 24			**25**	
26	Limit on excess casualty losses and depreciation. Subtract line 25 from line 15			**26**	
27	Excess casualty losses (see instructions)	**27**			
28	Depreciation of your home from Part III below	**28**	308 00		
29	Carryover of excess casualty losses and depreciation from 2004 Form 8829, line 42	**29**			
30	Add lines 27 through 29			**30**	
31	Allowable excess casualty losses and depreciation. Enter the **smaller** of line 26 or line 30			**31**	
32	Add lines 14, 25, and 31			**32**	
33	Casualty loss portion, if any, from lines 14 and 31. Carry amount to **Form 4684**, Section B			**33**	
34	Allowable expenses for business use of your home. Subtract line 33 from line 32. Enter here and on Schedule C, line 30. If your home was used for more than one business, see instructions ▶			**34**	

Part III   Depreciation of Your Home

35	Enter the **smaller** of your home's adjusted basis or its fair market value (see instructions)	**35**	320,000 00
36	Value of land included on line 35	**36**	80,000 00
37	Basis of building. Subtract line 36 from line 35	**37**	240,000 00
38	Business basis of building. Multiply line 37 by line 7	**38**	12,000 00
39	Depreciation percentage (see instructions)	**39**	2.564 %
40	Depreciation allowable (see instructions). Multiply line 38 by line 39. Enter here and on line 28 above	**40**	308 00

Part IV   Carryover of Unallowed Expenses to 2006

41	Operating expenses. Subtract line 25 from line 24. If less than zero, enter -0-	**41**	
42	Excess casualty losses and depreciation. Subtract line 31 from line 30. If less than zero, enter -0-	**42**	

For Paperwork Reduction Act Notice, see page 4 of separate instructions.	Cat. No. 13232M	Form **8829** (2005)

EXAMPLE 20

In 2005 John MacDonald reports $1,600 as tentative profit on Schedule C. He uses 10% of his home exclusively as an office. Expenses for the 10% business portion of the home include mortgage interest and real estate taxes of $420, operating expenses (insurance, maintenance, and utilities) of $1,000, and depreciation of $650. MacDonald's deduction on Form 8829 for the business use of his home follows:

Tentative profit (line 8)	$1,600
Less interest and taxes (line 14)	(420)
Net income derived from the business	$1,180
Less operating expenses (line 25)	(1,000)
Limit on depreciation (line 26)	$ 180
Depreciation	(650)
Depreciation expense not deductible in 2005 (show on line 42 and carry forward to 2006)	($ 470)

All the business expenses except $470 of the depreciation expense offset 2005 income. Since MacDonald cannot deduct $470 of depreciation expense in 2005, he reduces the basis of the home office by the $180 deducted in 2005. The basis in the home will be reduced for the rest of the $470 of depreciation expense in the year MacDonald deducts it.

Information for Figure 8-12: Filled-In Form 4562

Figure 7-3 in Chapter 7, the income statement from Wilson's Hardware Store gave an amount of $1,133 for depreciation expense. Figure 8-11 shows how to compute Wilson's depreciation expense. The half-year convention applies to the 5-year property placed in service in 2004. Wilson has written evidence to support the business use of the computer.

FIGURE 8-11 Calculation of Depreciation for Wilson's Hardware Store

Property	Date Acquired	Basis for Depreciation	Recovery Period	% or Method	Depreciation in 2005
Computer (80% Business)	8-01-04	$ 480[1]	5	200% DB	$ 154[2]
Paint mixer	3-01-05	1,546	7	200% DB	221[3]
Tool cabinet	3-14-05	1,400	7	200% DB	200[4]
Small tools	7-16-05	441	7	200% DB	63[5]
Wet/dry vac	11-03-05	357	7	200% DB	51[6]
Table saw	1-15-00	516	12*	ADS/SL	43
Jointer/planer	6-29-00	420	12*	ADS/SL	35
Storage shed	2-06-99	14,274	39	SL	366
Total cost recovery					$1,133

*Since no designated class life applies to the equipment, the recovery period is 12 years.
[1] $600 cost × 80% = $480
[2] $480 × 32%
[3] $1,546 × 14.29%
[4] $1,400 × 14.29%
[5] $441 × 14.29%
[6] $357 × 14.29%

Because computers are listed property, the depreciation deduction is first recorded in Part V, and then is entered on Part IV (line 21). See Figure 8-12.

Other Information

26(c):	Business/investment use percentage, **80%**
26(d):	Cost or other basis, **$600**
26(e):	Basis for depreciation, **$480** ($600 × 80%)
26(h):	Depreciation deduction, **$154** ($480 × 32%)
16:	Other depreciation, **$78** (ADS property, $516/12 + $420/12)
17:	MACRS on pre-2005 assets, **$366** (storage shed, $14,274/39)
19c(c):	Basis for depreciation, **$3,744** ($1,546 + $1,400 + $441 + $357)
19c(e):	Convention, **HY** (half-year, since $357 ÷ $3,744 = 9.5%, which is ≤ 40%)
19c(g):	Depreciation deduction, **$535** ($3,744 × 14.29%)

AMORTIZATION OF INTANGIBLE PROPERTY

Depreciation applies to the cost recovery of real and tangible personal business property. Amortization applies to the cost recovery of intangible personal property. Amortization recovers certain costs through annual deductions over a fixed period of time (similar to the straight-line method). Section 197 intangible personal property acquired after August 10, 1993 in the purchase of a business must be amortized over 15 years using the straight-line method, starting with the month of acquisition. Certain intangibles acquired separately, like patents and copyrights, are amortized the lesser of 15 years or their remaining useful lives. Computer software not acquired in the purchase of a business is amortized over 3 years beginning in the month the software is placed in service. Leasehold improvements acquired between September 11, 2001, and December 31, 2006, are amortized over 5 years. Taxpayers report the amortization of intangible property on Part VI of Form 4562, Depreciation and Amortization.

ITEMS INCLUDED AS SECTION 197 INTANGIBLE PERSONAL PROPERTY

- Business books and records, operating systems, or any other information base
- Covenant not to compete entered into in connection with the acquisition of a business
- Customer-based intangibles, including customer lists
- Franchise (other than a sports franchise), trademark, or trade name
- Goodwill
- Patent, copyright, formula, process design, or similar item
- Supplier-based intangibles

The amortization of intangibles applies only to purchased intangibles. It does not apply to self-created intangibles, like self-created goodwill, or self-created copyrights. Although self-created goodwill provides value to the business, there is no cost basis to amortize.

FIGURE 8-12 Filled-In Form 4562, Page 1

Form **4562**	**Depreciation and Amortization**	OMB No. 1545-0172
Department of the Treasury Internal Revenue Service	**(Including Information on Listed Property)** ▶ See separate instructions. ▶ Attach to your tax return.	20**05** Attachment Sequence No. **67**

Name(s) shown on return	Business or activity to which this form relates	Identifying number
Harold R. Wilson	Wilson's Hardware Store	272-11-8855

Part I **Election To Expense Certain Property Under Section 179**
Note: *If you have any listed property, complete Part V before you complete Part I.*

1	Maximum amount. See the instructions for a higher limit for certain businesses	**1**	$105,000
2	Total cost of section 179 property placed in service (see instructions)	**2**	
3	Threshold cost of section 179 property before reduction in limitation	**3**	$420,000
4	Reduction in limitation. Subtract line 3 from line 2. If zero or less, enter -0-	**4**	
5	Dollar limitation for tax year. Subtract line 4 from line 1. If zero or less, enter -0-. If married filing separately, see instructions	**5**	

(a) Description of property	**(b)** Cost (business use only)	**(c)** Elected cost	
6			

7	Listed property. Enter the amount from line 29 . . . . **7**		
8	Total elected cost of section 179 property. Add amounts in column (c), lines 6 and 7	**8**	
9	Tentative deduction. Enter the **smaller** of line 5 or line 8	**9**	
10	Carryover of disallowed deduction from line 13 of your 2004 Form 4562	**10**	
11	Business income limitation. Enter the smaller of business income (not less than zero) or line 5 (see instructions)	**11**	
12	Section 179 expense deduction. Add lines 9 and 10, but do not enter more than line 11	**12**	
13	Carryover of disallowed deduction to 2006. Add lines 9 and 10, less line 12 ▶ **13**		

Note: *Do not use Part II or Part III below for listed property. Instead, use Part V.*

Part II **Special Depreciation Allowance and Other Depreciation (Do not** include listed property.) (See instructions.)

14	Special allowance for certain aircraft, certain property with a long production period, and qualified New York Liberty Zone property (other than listed property) placed in service during the tax year	**14**	
15	Property subject to section 168(f)(1) election	**15**	
16	Other depreciation (including ACRS)	**16**	78

Part III **MACRS Depreciation (Do not** include listed property.) (See instructions.)

Section A

17	MACRS deductions for assets placed in service in tax years beginning before 2005	**17**	366
18	If you are electing to group any assets placed in service during the tax year into one or more general asset accounts, check here ▶ ☐		

Section B—Assets Placed in Service During 2005 Tax Year Using the General Depreciation System

(a) Classification of property	**(b)** Month and year placed in service	**(c)** Basis for depreciation (business/investment use only—see instructions)	**(d)** Recovery period	**(e)** Convention	**(f)** Method	**(g)** Depreciation deduction
19a 3-year property						
b 5-year property						
c 7-year property		3,744	7 yr.	HY	DDB	535
d 10-year property						
e 15-year property						
f 20-year property						
g 25-year property			25 yrs.		S/L	
h Residential rental property			27.5 yrs.	MM	S/L	
			27.5 yrs.	MM	S/L	
i Nonresidential real property			39 yrs.	MM	S/L	
				MM	S/L	

Section C—Assets Placed in Service During 2005 Tax Year Using the Alternative Depreciation System

20a Class life					S/L	
b 12-year			12 yrs.		S/L	
c 40-year			40 yrs.	MM	S/L	

Part IV **Summary** (see instructions)

21	Listed property. Enter amount from line 28	**21**	154
22	**Total.** Add amounts from line 12, lines 14 through 17, lines 19 and 20 in column (g), and line 21. Enter here and on the appropriate lines of your return. Partnerships and S corporations—see instr.	**22**	1,133
23	For assets shown above and placed in service during the current year, enter the portion of the basis attributable to section 263A costs . . **23**		

For Paperwork Reduction Act Notice, see separate instructions.   Cat. No. 12906N   Form **4562** (2005)

FIGURE 8-12 Filled-In Form 4562, Page 2

Form 4562 (2005) | Page **2**

Part V **Listed Property** (Include automobiles, certain other vehicles, cellular telephones, certain computers, and property used for entertainment, recreation, or amusement.)

Note: *For any vehicle for which you are using the standard mileage rate or deducting lease expense, complete **only** 24a, 24b, columns (a) through (c) of Section A, all of Section B, and Section C if applicable.*

Section A—Depreciation and Other Information (Caution: *See the instructions for limits for passenger automobiles.***)**

24a Do you have evidence to support the business/investment use claimed? ☒ **Yes** ☐ **No** **24b** If "Yes," is the evidence written? ☒ **Yes** ☐ **No**

(a) Type of property (list vehicles first)	(b) Date placed in service	(c) Business/ investment use percentage	(d) Cost or other basis	(e) Basis for depreciation (business/investment use only)	(f) Recovery period	(g) Method/ Convention	(h) Depreciation deduction	(i) Elected section 179 cost
25 Special allowance for qualified New York Liberty Zone listed property placed in service during the tax year and used more than 50% in a qualified business use (see instructions)					**25**			
26 Property used more than 50% in a qualified business use:								
Computer	8-01-04	80 %	600	480	5yrs	DDB/HY	154	
		%						
		%						
27 Property used 50% or less in a qualified business use:								
		%				S/L –		
		%				S/L –		
		%				S/L –		
28 Add amounts in column (h), lines 25 through 27. Enter here and on line 21, page 1. . .					**28**		154	
29 Add amounts in column (i), line 26. Enter here and on line 7, page 1.							**29**	

Section B—Information on Use of Vehicles

Complete this section for vehicles used by a sole proprietor, partner, or other "more than 5% owner," or related person.

If you provided vehicles to your employees, first answer the questions in Section C to see if you meet an exception to completing this section for those vehicles.

		(a) Vehicle 1		(b) Vehicle 2		(c) Vehicle 3		(d) Vehicle 4		(e) Vehicle 5		(f) Vehicle 6	
30	Total business/investment miles driven during the year (**do not** include commuting miles)												
31	Total commuting miles driven during the year												
32	Total other personal (noncommuting) miles driven												
33	Total miles driven during the year. Add lines 30 through 32												
34	Was the vehicle available for personal use during off-duty hours?	Yes	No	Yes	No	Yes	No	Yes	No	Yes	No	Yes	No
35	Was the vehicle used primarily by a more than 5% owner or related person?												
36	Is another vehicle available for personal use?												

Section C—Questions for Employers Who Provide Vehicles for Use by Their Employees

Answer these questions to determine if you meet an exception to completing Section B for vehicles used by employees who **are not** more than 5% owners or related persons (see instructions).

		Yes	No
37	Do you maintain a written policy statement that prohibits all personal use of vehicles, including commuting, by your employees?		
38	Do you maintain a written policy statement that prohibits personal use of vehicles, except commuting, by your employees? See the instructions for vehicles used by corporate officers, directors, or 1% or more owners		
39	Do you treat all use of vehicles by employees as personal use?		
40	Do you provide more than five vehicles to your employees, obtain information from your employees about the use of the vehicles, and retain the information received?		
41	Do you meet the requirements concerning qualified automobile demonstration use? (See instructions.)		

Note: *If your answer to 37, 38, 39, 40, or 41 is "Yes," do not complete Section B for the covered vehicles.*

Part VI **Amortization**

(a) Description of costs	(b) Date amortization begins	(c) Amortizable amount	(d) Code section	(e) Amortization period or percentage	(f) Amortization for this year
42 Amortization of costs that begins during your 2005 tax year (see instructions):					
43 Amortization of costs that began before your 2005 tax year.				**43**	
44 **Total.** Add amounts in column (f). See the instructions for where to report.				**44**	

♻ *Printed on recycled paper* | Form **4562** (2005)

QUESTIONS AND PROBLEMS

1. **MACRS Recovery Periods.** For each of the following types of properties depreciated under MACRS, state the IRS-specified useful life, depreciation method, and averaging convention(s).

	Useful Life in Years	Depreciation Method	Averaging Convention
Automobiles	_____	_____	_____
Light trucks	_____	_____	_____
Computers	_____	_____	_____
Furniture and fixtures	_____	_____	_____
Machinery and equipment	_____	_____	_____
Commercial buildings	_____	_____	_____
Residential buildings	_____	_____	_____

2. **Mid-Quarter vs. Half-Year Convention.** Quentin Miller, a calendar-year taxpayer, acquired the following four new machines in 2005 on the dates indicated.

February 1	$25,000
April 1	35,000
October 1	30,000
December 1	40,000

[handwritten: since 40% in last qtr (70,000/130,000 = 54%) use mid-qtr convention]

a. Compute Miller's total depreciation deduction for 2005 that would be reported on Schedule C, using MACRS with the appropriate averaging convention.

*[handwritten: *(Oct 1st considered 4th qtr because Sales bets. 10/1-12/31)*

25,000 × 25% = 6250
35,000 × 17.85% = 6248
30,000 × 3.57% = 1071
40,000 × 3.57% = 1428

Total depreciation 2005 = $14,997]*

b. Compute the total depreciation for 2005 had the $30,000 machine been acquired on September 30. Comment on the significance of the difference between this amount and the answer to Part a.

*[handwritten: 130,000 × 14.29 = $18,577

difference 18,577 - 14,997 = $3580]*

3. **MACRS, Year of Sale.** Bradford Company sold the following properties in 2005. Compute the allowable depreciation deduction for 2005 for each property.

Property	Date Acquired	MACRS Basis	Depreciation Method	Averaging Convention	Date of Sale
Computer	7-1-02	$ 4,200*	DDB	HY	3-5-05
Automobile	4-1-03	12,000*	DDB	HY	9-1-05
Furniture	7-10-00	24,000	DDB	MQ	8-1-05

*After subtracting bonus depreciation from the original cost

4. **ADS and MACRS.** Peter Baker uses the following properties in his business.

Equipment:	Acquired in 2000 at a cost of $72,000
Furniture:	Acquired in 2002 at a cost of $60,000
Computer:	Acquired in 2003 at a cost of $10,000

a. Compute the 2005 depreciation deduction. In 2000 Baker elected the ADS straight-line method with a ten-year life for the equipment. He used regular (accelerated) MACRS for the furniture and the computer. He did not elect Section 179 for any of the properties. In 2002, he took the 30% bonus depreciation on the furniture, thereby reducing its MACRS basis to $42,000. In 2003, the computer qualified for the 50% bonus depreciation, thereby reducing its MACRS basis to $5,000. The half-year convention applies to all three properties.

b. Now assume that Peter Baker purchased each of these properties new in January 2005. Compute depreciation for each of these properties for 2005 using the maximum depreciation allowed for each property without electing Section 179 expense.

5. **Section 179.** Sands Corporation purchases one asset in 2005—machinery costing $450,000. The machine was placed in service on June 2, 2005. Sands wants to elect the maximum Section 179 possible, even if some must be carried over to 2006. Sands's 2005 taxable income before Section 179 is $67,000.

a. Compute the maximum Section 179 Sands can elect in 2005 and the Section 179 carryover to 2006.

b. Compute the maximum total depreciation on the machine for 2005.

[handwritten: $120,558 [67,000 Sect 179 + 53,558 MACRS = ((450,000 − 75,000) × 14.29% (half yr percentage)]

[handwritten: (all $53,588 can be used unlike Sect 179)]

6. **Listed Property, Section 179.** Dewey Terrell is a self-employed personal financial adviser. In March 2005, Terrell purchased a computer for $2,800. During 2005 he used the computer 60% of the time in providing financial advice to clients, 15% of the time for his own investments, and 25% of the time for personal use.

   a. What is the maximum amount of depreciation Terrell is entitled to take in 2005 for the computer, assuming he does not elect Section 179?

   b. How much total depreciation is Terrell entitled to take in 2005 for the computer assuming he elects to take the maximum Section 179 deduction?

7. **Listed Property.** During 2005, Tim Simon (self-employed) pays $14,500 for an automobile that he uses 45% of the time for business, 25% of the time for investment purposes, and 30% of the time for personal use. The half-year convention applies to the automobile. How much depreciation is Simon entitled to deduct in 2005?

8. **MACRS, Section 179.** The Redwood Company, a calendar-year corporation, acquired the following new properties during 2005.

Item	Cost	Date Acquired
Automobile	$ 18,500	July 2, 2005
Copier	14,200	March 1, 2005
Furniture	42,000	June 1, 2005
Equipment	128,000	June 30, 2005
Warehouse	110,250	July 9, 2005

   a. Compute the maximum depreciation deduction that Redwood can take on each of these properties assuming no Section 179 is elected.

b. Assume that Redwood elects to take the maximum allowed Section 179 expense on the equipment acquired on June 30, 2005. The company uses regular (accelerated) MACRS for the remainder of the cost. Redwood's taxable income before Section 179 expense is $250,000. Compute the maximum total depreciation deduction for the equipment for 2005 and 2006.

9. **Luxury Automobiles.** Charlotte Milone helps install computer systems for a variety of clients. Since Milone often drives considerable distances to work in client offices, she decides to buy a new automobile to use in her work. She purchased the car on March 1, 2005, for $30,000 and uses it 80% of the time for business purposes. Prepare a schedule for Milone that shows the maximum depreciation she will be entitled to take in each of the years 2005 through 2010, assuming that she uses the automobile 80% of the time for business each year.

10. **Luxury Automobiles.** On September 13, 2005, Dolly Martin places in service a new automobile costing $25,000. This is Martin's only acquisition during 2005. She uses the automobile 90% of the time for business. What is the maximum total depreciation Martin can deduct in 2005?

11. **Leased Automobiles.** On March 1, 2004, Casey Stukel enters into a 36-month lease for a car valued at $36,400. Her monthly lease payment is $470, and she uses the car 75% for business. What amount will Stukel deduct in 2004 and 2005?

12. MACRS and Averaging Conventions. Jan Stephenson purchased the following new properties during 2005.

Description	Date Placed in Service	Cost
Computer	March 9, 2005	$ 3,000
Machinery	July 17, 2005	35,000
Office building	September 6, 2005	270,000
Equipment	December 27, 2005	42,000

Handwritten annotations:

(3.5 mths in use) (39 yrs for depreciation)

In

2005
$3,000 × 35% = $1,050
35,000 × 10.70% = $3,749
270,000/39 × 3.5 × 12 = $2019
42,000 × 3.57 = $1499

2006
× 26%
× 25.31%
÷ 39 × 4.13
× 27.55%

$780
$8929
$6923
$11,571

Compute Stephenson's depreciation for each of these properties for 2005 and 2006 using the maximum depreciation allowed without taking Section 179.

(42,000/80,000 = 53%)
midmonth convention applies to office building
midqtr applies to personal property

13. MACRS and Averaging Conventions. Howard Fields (SSN 748-29-4631) operates the H.B. Fields Company as a sole proprietorship. Fields acquires the following new properties in 2005. The automobile is used 100% for business. Fields has written evidence of the business use, which was 19,280 miles in 2005. Fields has another vehicle he uses for personal use. He does not elect Section 179.

Date of Acquisition	Item	Cost
January 30	Automobile	$18,000
March 10	Garage for auto	39,000
November 6	Machine	1,246
December 1	Office desk	910

a. Compute Fields's depreciation deduction reported on Schedule C for 2005, using regular (accelerated) MACRS.

b. Complete Form 4562, Depreciation and Amortization, on pages 8-30 and 8-31 to report the depreciation deduction reported on Schedule C as computed in Part a.

14. MACRS, Realty, Year of Acquisition. In January 2005, a taxpayer purchased an office building for $320,000 and an apartment building for $400,000. These amounts include only the buildings, not the land. Compute the 2005 depreciation for each building.

39 yrs   27½ yrs

(320,000 / 39) × (11.5/12) = 7863
(400,000 / 27.5) × (11.5/12) = 13,939

15. MACRS, Realty, Year of Sale. In 1991, a taxpayer purchased an office building for $250,000. On August 2, 2005, the taxpayer sold the office building. Compute MACRS on the building for 2005.

owned for 14 yrs   2/31.5   14   26.5

mid-month convention

(250,800 / 31.5 × 7.5/12) = $4960

purchase amt   # of yrs depreciation   # of mth owned   # of mths in yr

(Use for Problem 13.)

Form **4562**	**Depreciation and Amortization**	OMB No. 1545-0172
Department of the Treasury Internal Revenue Service	**(Including Information on Listed Property)** ▶ See separate instructions. ▶ Attach to your tax return.	20**05** Attachment Sequence No. **67**

Name(s) shown on return	Business or activity to which this form relates	Identifying number

Part I   **Election To Expense Certain Property Under Section 179**
Note: *If you have any listed property, complete Part V before you complete Part I.*

1	Maximum amount. See the instructions for a higher limit for certain businesses	**1**	$105,000
2	Total cost of section 179 property placed in service (see instructions)	**2**	
3	Threshold cost of section 179 property before reduction in limitation	**3**	$420,000
4	Reduction in limitation. Subtract line 3 from line 2. If zero or less, enter -0-	**4**	
5	Dollar limitation for tax year. Subtract line 4 from line 1. If zero or less, enter -0-. If married filing separately, see instructions	**5**	

(a) Description of property	(b) Cost (business use only)	(c) Elected cost
6		

7	Listed property. Enter the amount from line 29	**7**	
8	Total elected cost of section 179 property. Add amounts in column (c), lines 6 and 7	**8**	
9	Tentative deduction. Enter the **smaller** of line 5 or line 8	**9**	
10	Carryover of disallowed deduction from line 13 of your 2004 Form 4562	**10**	
11	Business income limitation. Enter the smaller of business income (not less than zero) or line 5 (see instructions)	**11**	
12	Section 179 expense deduction. Add lines 9 and 10, but do not enter more than line 11 . . .	**12**	
13	Carryover of disallowed deduction to 2006. Add lines 9 and 10, less line 12 ▶	**13**	

Note: *Do not use Part II or Part III below for listed property. Instead, use Part V.*

Part II   **Special Depreciation Allowance and Other Depreciation (Do not** include listed property.) (See instructions.)

14	Special allowance for certain aircraft, certain property with a long production period, and qualified New York Liberty Zone property (other than listed property) placed in service during the tax year	**14**	
15	Property subject to section 168(f)(1) election	**15**	
16	Other depreciation (including ACRS)	**16**	

Part III   **MACRS Depreciation (Do not** include listed property.) (See instructions.)

Section A

17	MACRS deductions for assets placed in service in tax years beginning before 2005	**17**	
18	If you are electing to group any assets placed in service during the tax year into one or more general asset accounts, check here . . . . ▶ ☐		

Section B—Assets Placed in Service During 2005 Tax Year Using the General Depreciation System

(a) Classification of property	(b) Month and year placed in service	(c) Basis for depreciation (business/investment use only—see instructions)	(d) Recovery period	(e) Convention	(f) Method	(g) Depreciation deduction
19a 3-year property						
b 5-year property						
c 7-year property						
d 10-year property						
e 15-year property						
f 20-year property						
g 25-year property			25 yrs.		S/L	
h Residential rental property			27.5 yrs.	MM	S/L	
			27.5 yrs.	MM	S/L	
i Nonresidential real property			39 yrs.	MM	S/L	
				MM	S/L	

Section C—Assets Placed in Service During 2005 Tax Year Using the Alternative Depreciation System

20a Class life					S/L	
b 12-year			12 yrs.		S/L	
c 40-year			40 yrs.	MM	S/L	

Part IV   **Summary** (see instructions)

21	Listed property. Enter amount from line 28	**21**	
22	**Total.** Add amounts from line 12, lines 14 through 17, lines 19 and 20 in column (g), and line 21. Enter here and on the appropriate lines of your return. Partnerships and S corporations—see instr.	**22**	
23	For assets shown above and placed in service during the current year, enter the portion of the basis attributable to section 263A costs . .	**23**	

For Paperwork Reduction Act Notice, see separate instructions.   Cat. No. 12906N   Form **4562** (2005)

(Use for Problem 13.)

Form 4562 (2005)   Page **2**

Part V   **Listed Property** (Include automobiles, certain other vehicles, cellular telephones, certain computers, and property used for entertainment, recreation, or amusement.)

Note: *For any vehicle for which you are using the standard mileage rate or deducting lease expense, complete **only** 24a, 24b, columns (a) through (c) of Section A, all of Section B, and Section C if applicable.*

Section A—Depreciation and Other Information (Caution: See the instructions for limits for passenger automobiles.)

24a Do you have evidence to support the business/investment use claimed? ☐ Yes ☐ No	24b If "Yes," is the evidence written? ☐ Yes ☐ No

(a) Type of property (list vehicles first)	(b) Date placed in service	(c) Business/ investment use percentage	(d) Cost or other basis	(e) Basis for depreciation (business/investment use only)	(f) Recovery period	(g) Method/ Convention	(h) Depreciation deduction	(i) Elected section 179 cost
25 Special allowance for qualified New York Liberty Zone listed property placed in service during the tax year and used more than 50% in a qualified business use (see instructions)					25			
26 Property used more than 50% in a qualified business use:								
		%						
		%						
		%						
27 Property used 50% or less in a qualified business use:								
		%				S/L –		
		%				S/L –		
		%				S/L –		
28 Add amounts in column (h), lines 25 through 27. Enter here and on line 21, page 1.					28			
29 Add amounts in column (i), line 26. Enter here and on line 7, page 1.							29	

Section B—Information on Use of Vehicles

Complete this section for vehicles used by a sole proprietor, partner, or other "more than 5% owner," or related person.

If you provided vehicles to your employees, first answer the questions in Section C to see if you meet an exception to completing this section for those vehicles.

	(a) Vehicle 1		(b) Vehicle 2		(c) Vehicle 3		(d) Vehicle 4		(e) Vehicle 5		(f) Vehicle 6	
30 Total business/investment miles driven during the year (**do not** include commuting miles)												
31 Total commuting miles driven during the year												
32 Total other personal (noncommuting) miles driven												
33 Total miles driven during the year. Add lines 30 through 32												
34 Was the vehicle available for personal use during off-duty hours?	Yes	No	Yes	No	Yes	No	Yes	No	Yes	No	Yes	No
35 Was the vehicle used primarily by a more than 5% owner or related person?												
36 Is another vehicle available for personal use?												

Section C—Questions for Employers Who Provide Vehicles for Use by Their Employees

Answer these questions to determine if you meet an exception to completing Section B for vehicles used by employees who **are not** more than 5% owners or related persons (see instructions).

		Yes	No
37	Do you maintain a written policy statement that prohibits all personal use of vehicles, including commuting, by your employees?		
38	Do you maintain a written policy statement that prohibits personal use of vehicles, except commuting, by your employees? See the instructions for vehicles used by corporate officers, directors, or 1% or more owners		
39	Do you treat all use of vehicles by employees as personal use?		
40	Do you provide more than five vehicles to your employees, obtain information from your employees about the use of the vehicles, and retain the information received?		
41	Do you meet the requirements concerning qualified automobile demonstration use? (See instructions.)		

Note: *If your answer to 37, 38, 39, 40, or 41 is "Yes," do not complete Section B for the covered vehicles.*

Part VI   **Amortization**

(a) Description of costs	(b) Date amortization begins	(c) Amortizable amount	(d) Code section	(e) Amortization period or percentage	(f) Amortization for this year
42 Amortization of costs that begins during your 2005 tax year (see instructions):					
43 Amortization of costs that began before your 2005 tax year.			43		
44 **Total.** Add amounts in column (f). See the instructions for where to report.			44		

✶ *Printed on recycled paper*   Form **4562** (2005)

16. **MACRS, Realty.** What depreciation method and useful life are used to depreciate a home office placed in service in 2005?

17. **Amortization of Intangibles.** For each of the following intangibles, which ones can be amortized and what method should be used to amortize them?

a. A customer list purchased as part of a business acquired during the year

b. A copyright purchased from an author

c. Self-created goodwill

d. A trademark purchased as part of a business acquired during the year; the trademark has a 10 year remaining life

e. A patent created internally by an employee

18. **Internet Problem: Researching Publication 463.**

On August 29, 2003, Renee Woodby entered into a 36-month lease for a car valued at $40,220. Woodby's monthly lease payment is $590. She uses the car 65% for business.

a. What affect does this lease arrangement have on the amount Woodby must include in gross income in 2005?

b. How much of the lease payment can be deducted?

c. How is this information presented on the tax return?

Go to the IRS Web site. Locate Publication 463 and find the appropriate page in Appendix A to answer the above question regarding Woodby's inclusion amount. Print out a copy of the page where you found your answer. Underline or highlight the pertinent information.

See Appendix A for instructions on use of the IRS Web site.

19. **Business Entity Problem: This problem is designed for those using the "business entity" approach. The solution may require information from Chapter 14.**

MSO Corporation owns a residential apartment building that it depreciates over 27.5 years. The building originally cost $550,000.

a. How much depreciation expense can the company claim on its tax return in the fifth year of ownership?

b. Earnings and profits serves as the source of taxable dividends. By what amount does depreciation reduce the corporation's earnings and profits in the fifth year of ownership?

COMPREHENSIVE PROBLEM

20. Patrick A. and Danielle R. Beckman file a joint return for 2005. The Beckmans rent a three-bedroom apartment located at 529 W. Maywood #4, Aurora, IL 60505. They provide over half of the support for Danielle's mother, Ellen Tyler (SSN 384-58-7338), who qualifies as their dependent. Ellen lives in a nursing home in Peoria, Illinois. The Beckmans claim their 20-year-old daughter, Susan (SSN 487-58-3957) as a dependent. Susan lives with the Beckmans while attending college full-time.

Danielle (SSN 394-59-3948) works full-time as an employee for an advertising firm. In 2005, Danielle earned wages of $34,000, from which her employer withheld $4,800 in federal income taxes and $1,020 in state income taxes.

Patrick (SSN 549-82-2497) began operating a carpet cleaning service in 2003. The business code for Schedule C is 812990. The guest bedroom doubles as Patrick's office. Patrick uses the office periodically to schedule appointments and keep track of his business records. Patrick uses the cash method, and during 2005 he earned $18,000 from his business. He paid $2,928 for cleaning chemicals and supplies. He also paid $300 for advertising and $50 for office expenses.

On November 10, 2003, Patrick purchased carpet cleaning equipment for $24,000. This was the only acquisition of depreciable property Patrick made during 2003. Patrick did not elect Section 179, but took the 50% bonus depreciation on the equipment. He deducts regular (accelerated) MACRS on the remaining $12,000 basis [$24,000 − ($24,000 × 50%)].

On June 8, 2004, Patrick purchased a computer for $1,600 and a printer for $400. During 2004 and 2005, Patrick used the computer and printer 60% for business and 40% for personal use. This was Patrick's only acquisition during 2004. Patrick has written evidence to support the 60% business use. In 2004, Patrick took the 50% bonus depreciation on both the computer and printer. This left him with a MACRS depreciable basis of $480 for the computer ($1,600 × 60% business use × 50% after the bonus). His MACRS depreciable basis for the printer is $120 ($400 × 60% × 50%).

Patrick uses his van to get to and from customers' homes. During the year Patrick drove his van 2,496 miles for business and keeps a written log as evidence of these miles. Of these 2,496 business miles, 388 were driven after August 31, 2005. Total miles for the year on the van were 10,540. Danielle has her own car that she uses to get to and from work. Patrick bought the van on March 5, 2003. He used the standard mileage method in 2003 and 2004. Patrick incurred no business-related parking or tolls in 2005.

Prepare the Beckmans' 2005 Form 1040 and accompanying Schedules C and SE, and Form 4562. Be sure to complete lines 26 and 30–36 on Form 4562 for Patrick's business automobile.

(Use for Problem 20.)

Form 1040 Department of the Treasury—Internal Revenue Service	**2005**	(99) IRS Use Only—Do not write or staple in this space.
U.S. Individual Income Tax Return		

For the year Jan. 1–Dec. 31, 2005, or other tax year beginning _____ , 2005, ending _____ , 20 ____   OMB No. 1545-0074

Label (See instructions on page 16.)

Use the IRS label. Otherwise, please print or type.

L A B E L   H E R E

Your first name and initial   Last name   **Your social security number**

If a joint return, spouse's first name and initial   Last name   **Spouse's social security number**

Home address (number and street). If you have a P.O. box, see page 16.   Apt. no.   ▲ You **must** enter your SSN(s) above. ▲

City, town or post office, state, and ZIP code. If you have a foreign address, see page 16.

Checking a box below will not change your tax or refund.

Presidential Election Campaign ► Check here if you, or your spouse if filing jointly, want $3 to go to this fund (see page 16) ► ☐ You ☐ Spouse

Filing Status

Check only one box.

1 ☐ Single
2 ☐ Married filing jointly (even if only one had income)
3 ☐ Married filing separately. Enter spouse's SSN above and full name here. ►
4 ☐ Head of household (with qualifying person). (See page 17.) If the qualifying person is a child but not your dependent, enter this child's name here. ►
5 ☐ Qualifying widow(er) with dependent child (see page 17)

Exemptions

If more than four dependents, see page 18.

6a ☐ **Yourself.** If someone can claim you as a dependent, **do not** check box 6a
b ☐ **Spouse**
c Dependents:

(1) First name Last name	(2) Dependent's social security number	(3) Dependent's relationship to you	(4) ✓ if qualifying child for child tax credit (see page 18)
			☐
			☐
			☐
			☐

Boxes checked on 6a and 6b ____

No. of children on 6c who:
• lived with you ____
• did not live with you due to divorce or separation (see page 18) ____

Dependents on 6c not entered above ____

d Total number of exemptions claimed

Add numbers on lines above ► ____

Income

Attach Form(s) W-2 here. Also attach Forms W-2G and 1099-R if tax was withheld.

If you did not get a W-2, see page 19.

Enclose, but do not attach, any payment. Also, please use **Form 1040-V.**

7	Wages, salaries, tips, etc. Attach Form(s) W-2	7	
8a	**Taxable** interest. Attach Schedule B if required	8a	
b	**Tax-exempt** interest. **Do not** include on line 8a	8b	
9a	Ordinary dividends. Attach Schedule B if required	9a	
b	Qualified dividends (see page 20)	9b	
10	Taxable refunds, credits, or offsets of state and local income taxes (see page 20)	10	
11	Alimony received	11	
12	Business income or (loss). Attach Schedule C or C-EZ	12	
13	Capital gain or (loss). Attach Schedule D if required. If not required, check here ► ☐	13	
14	Other gains or (losses). Attach Form 4797	14	
15a	IRA distributions 15a	b Taxable amount (see page 22)	15b	
16a	Pensions and annuities 16a	b Taxable amount (see page 22)	16b	
17	Rental real estate, royalties, partnerships, S corporations, trusts, etc. Attach Schedule E	17	
18	Farm income or (loss). Attach Schedule F	18	
19	Unemployment compensation	19	
20a	Social security benefits 20a	b Taxable amount (see page 24)	20b	
21	Other income. List type and amount (see page 24)	21	
22	Add the amounts in the far right column for lines 7 through 21. This is your **total income** ►	22	

Adjusted Gross Income

23	Educator expenses (see page 26)	23	
24	Certain business expenses of reservists, performing artists, and fee-basis government officials. Attach Form 2106 or 2106-EZ	24	
25	Health savings account deduction. Attach Form 8889	25	
26	Moving expenses. Attach Form 3903	26	
27	One-half of self-employment tax. Attach Schedule SE	27	
28	Self-employed SEP, SIMPLE, and qualified plans	28	
29	Self-employed health insurance deduction (see page XX)	29	
30	Penalty on early withdrawal of savings	30	
31a	Alimony paid b Recipient's SSN ►	31a	
32	IRA deduction (see page XX)	32	
33	Student loan interest deduction (see page XX)	33	
34	Tuition and fees deduction (see page XX)	34	
35	Domestic production activities deduction. Attach Form 8903	35	
36	Add lines 23 through 31a and 32 through 35	36	
37	Subtract line 36 from line 22. This is your **adjusted gross income** ►	37	

For Disclosure, Privacy Act, and Paperwork Reduction Act Notice, see page 75.   Cat. No. 11320B   Form **1040** (2005)

(Use for Problem 20.)

Form 1040 (2005) | Page **2**

Tax and Credits

38	Amount from line 37 (adjusted gross income)	38	

39a Check if: ☐ **You** were born before January 2, 1941, ☐ Blind. ☐ **Spouse** was born before January 2, 1941, ☐ Blind. Total boxes checked ▶ 39a

Standard Deduction for—

b If your spouse itemizes on a separate return or you were a dual-status alien, see page 31 and check here ▶ 39b ☐

40	**Itemized deductions** (from Schedule A) **or** your **standard deduction** (see left margin)	40	
41	Subtract line 40 from line 38	41	
42	If line 38 is $109,475 or less, multiply $3,200 by the total number of exemptions claimed on line 6d. If line 38 is over $109,475, see the worksheet on page 33	42	
43	**Taxable income.** Subtract line 42 from line 41. If line 42 is more than line 41, enter -0-	43	
44	**Tax** (see page 33). Check if any tax is from: **a** ☐ Form(s) 8814 **b** ☐ Form 4972	44	
45	**Alternative minimum tax** (see page 35). Attach Form 6251	45	
46	Add lines 44 and 45 ▶	46	

- People who checked any box on line 39a or 39b **or** who can be claimed as a dependent, see page 31.
- All others:

Single or Married filing separately, $5,000

Married filing jointly or Qualifying widow(er), $10,000

Head of household, $7,300

47	Foreign tax credit. Attach Form 1116 if required	47	
48	Credit for child and dependent care expenses. Attach Form 2441	48	
49	Credit for the elderly or the disabled. Attach Schedule R	49	
50	Education credits. Attach Form 8863	50	
51	Retirement savings contributions credit. Attach Form 8880	51	
52	Child tax credit (see page 37). Attach Form 8901 if required	52	
53	Adoption credit. Attach Form 8839	53	
54	Credits from: **a** ☐ Form 8396 **b** ☐ Form 8859	54	
55	Other credits. Check applicable box(es): **a** ☐ Form 3800 **b** ☐ Form 8801 **c** ☐ Specify	55	
56	Add lines 47 through 55. These are your **total credits**	56	
57	Subtract line 56 from line 46. If line 56 is more than line 46, enter -0- ▶	57	

Other Taxes

58	Self-employment tax. Attach Schedule SE	58	
59	Social security and Medicare tax on tip income not reported to employer. Attach Form 4137	59	
60	Additional tax on IRAs, other qualified retirement plans, etc. Attach Form 5329 if required	60	
61	Advance earned income credit payments from Form(s) W-2	61	
62	Household employment taxes. Attach Schedule H	62	
63	Add lines 57 through 62. This is your **total tax** ▶	63	

Payments

If you have a qualifying child, attach Schedule EIC.

64	Federal income tax withheld from Forms W-2 and 1099	64	
65	2005 estimated tax payments and amount applied from 2004 return	65	
66a	**Earned income credit (EIC)**	66a	
b	Nontaxable combat pay election ▶ 66b		
67	Excess social security and tier 1 RRTA tax withheld (see page 54)	67	
68	Additional child tax credit. Attach Form 8812	68	
69	Amount paid with request for extension to file (see page 54)	69	
70	Payments from: **a** ☐ Form 2439 **b** ☐ Form 4136 **c** ☐ Form 8885	70	
71	Add lines 64, 65, 66a, and 67 through 70. These are your **total payments** ▶	71	

Refund

Direct deposit? See page 54 and fill in 73b, 73c, and 73d.

72	If line 71 is more than line 63, subtract line 63 from line 71. This is the amount you **overpaid**	72	
73a	Amount of line 72 you want **refunded to you** ▶	73a	
b	Routing number		
	▶ c Type: ☐ Checking ☐ Savings		
d	Account number		
74	Amount of line 72 you want **applied to your 2006 estimated tax** ▶ 74		

Amount You Owe

75	**Amount you owe.** Subtract line 71 from line 63. For details on how to pay, see page 55 ▶	75	
76	Estimated tax penalty (see page 55) 76		

Third Party Designee

Do you want to allow another person to discuss this return with the IRS (see page 56)? ☐ **Yes.** Complete the following. ☐ **No**

Designee's name ▶ Phone no. ▶ ( ) Personal identification number (PIN) ▶

Sign Here

Joint return? See page 17. Keep a copy for your records.

Under penalties of perjury, I declare that I have examined this return and accompanying schedules and statements, and to the best of my knowledge and belief, they are true, correct, and complete. Declaration of preparer (other than taxpayer) is based on all information of which preparer has any knowledge.

Your signature | Date | Your occupation | Daytime phone number ( )

Spouse's signature. If a joint return, **both** must sign. | Date | Spouse's occupation

Paid Preparer's Use Only

Preparer's signature | Date | Check if self-employed ☐ | Preparer's SSN or PTIN

Firm's name (or yours if self-employed), address, and ZIP code | EIN | Phone no. ( )

Form **1040** (2005)

Printed on recycled paper

(Use for Problem 20.)

SCHEDULE C (Form 1040) Department of the Treasury Internal Revenue Service	**Profit or Loss From Business** (Sole Proprietorship) ▶ Partnerships, joint ventures, etc., must file Form 1065 or 1065-B. ▶ Attach to Form 1040 or 1041.　▶ See Instructions for Schedule C (Form 1040).	OMB No. 1545-0074 20**05** Attachment Sequence No. **09**

Name of proprietor | Social security number (SSN)

A Principal business or profession, including product or service (see page C-2 of the instructions) | **B** Enter code from pages C-7, 8, & 9 ▶

C Business name. If no separate business name, leave blank. | **D** Employer ID number (EIN), if any

E Business address (including suite or room no.) ▶ ....
City, town or post office, state, and ZIP code

F Accounting method: **(1)** ☐ Cash **(2)** ☐ Accrual **(3)** ☐ Other (specify) ▶ ....

G Did you "materially participate" in the operation of this business during 2005? If "No," see page C-3 for limit on losses ☐ Yes ☐ No

H If you started or acquired this business during 2005, check here .... ▶ ☐

Part I Income

1	Gross receipts or sales. **Caution.** If this income was reported to you on Form W-2 and the "Statutory employee" box on that form was checked, see page C-3 and check here ▶ ☐	**1**	
2	Returns and allowances	**2**	
3	Subtract line 2 from line 1	**3**	
4	Cost of goods sold (from line 42 on page 2)	**4**	
5	**Gross profit.** Subtract line 4 from line 3	**5**	
6	Other income, including Federal and state gasoline or fuel tax credit or refund (see page C-3)	**6**	
7	**Gross income.** Add lines 5 and 6 ▶	**7**	

Part II Expenses. Enter expenses for business use of your home **only** on line 30.

8	Advertising	**8**		18	Office expense	**18**	
9	Car and truck expenses (see page C-3)	**9**		19	Pension and profit-sharing plans	**19**	
10	Commissions and fees	**10**		20	Rent or lease (see page C-5):		
11	Contract labor (see page C-4)	**11**		**a**	Vehicles, machinery, and equipment	**20a**	
12	Depletion	**12**		**b**	Other business property	**20b**	
13	Depreciation and section 179 expense deduction (not included in Part III) (see page C-4)	**13**		21	Repairs and maintenance	**21**	
				22	Supplies (not included in Part III)	**22**	
				23	Taxes and licenses	**23**	
				24	Travel, meals, and entertainment:		
14	Employee benefit programs (other than on line 19)	**14**		**a**	Travel	**24a**	
15	Insurance (other than health)	**15**		**b**	Deductible meals and entertainment (see page C-5)	**24b**	
16	Interest:			25	Utilities	**25**	
a	Mortgage (paid to banks, etc.)	**16a**		26	Wages (less employment credits)	**26**	
b	Other	**16b**		27	Other expenses (from line 48 on page 2)	**27**	
17	Legal and professional services	**17**					

28	**Total expenses** before expenses for business use of home. Add lines 8 through 27 in columns ▶	**28**	
29	Tentative profit (loss). Subtract line 28 from line 7	**29**	
30	Expenses for business use of your home. Attach **Form 8829**	**30**	
31	**Net profit or (loss).** Subtract line 30 from line 29.		
	● If a profit, enter on **Form 1040, line 12,** and **also** on **Schedule SE, line 2** (statutory employees, see page C-6). Estates and trusts, enter on Form 1041, line 3.	**31**	
	● If a loss, you **must** go to line 32.		
32	If you have a loss, check the box that describes your investment in this activity (see page C-6).		
	● If you checked 32a, enter the loss on **Form 1040, line 12,** and **also** on **Schedule SE, line 2** (statutory employees, see page C-6). Estates and trusts, enter on Form 1041, line 3.	**32a** ☐ All investment is at risk.	
	● If you checked 32b, you **must** attach **Form 6198.** Your loss may be limited.	**32b** ☐ Some investment is not at risk.	

For Paperwork Reduction Act Notice, see Form 1040 instructions. 　Cat. No. 11334P 　**Schedule C (Form 1040) 2005**

Draft as of 05/31/2005

(Use for Problem 20.)

Schedule C (Form 1040) 2005   Page **2**

| **Part III** | **Cost of Goods Sold** (see page C-6) |

33 Method(s) used to value closing inventory: **a** ☐ Cost   **b** ☐ Lower of cost or market   **c** ☐ Other (attach explanation)

34 Was there any change in determining quantities, costs, or valuations between opening and closing inventory? If "Yes," attach explanation . . . . ☐ **Yes**   ☐ **No**

35	Inventory at beginning of year. If different from last year's closing inventory, attach explanation . .	**35**
36	Purchases less cost of items withdrawn for personal use	**36**
37	Cost of labor. Do not include any amounts paid to yourself	**37**
38	Materials and supplies	**38**
39	Other costs	**39**
40	Add lines 35 through 39	**40**
41	Inventory at end of year	**41**
42	**Cost of goods sold.** Subtract line 41 from line 40. Enter the result here and on page 1, line 4 . .	**42**

| **Part IV** | **Information on Your Vehicle.** Complete this part **only** if you are claiming car or truck expenses on line 9 and are not required to file Form 4562 for this business. See the instructions for line 13 on page C-4 to find out if you must file Form 4562. |

43 When did you place your vehicle in service for business purposes? (month, day, year) ▶ ..../......../....... .

44 Of the total number of miles you drove your vehicle during 2005, enter the number of miles you used your vehicle for:

a Business ....   **b** Commuting (see instructions) ....   **c** Other ....

45 Do you (or your spouse) have another vehicle available for personal use?. . . . . ☐ **Yes**   ☐ **No**

46 Was your vehicle available for personal use during off-duty hours? . . . . ☐ **Yes**   ☐ **No**

47a Do you have evidence to support your deduction? . . . . ☐ **Yes**   ☐ **No**

  b If "Yes," is the evidence written? . . . . ☐ **Yes**   ☐ **No**

| **Part V** | **Other Expenses.** List below business expenses not included on lines 8–26 or line 30. |

48	**Total other expenses.** Enter here and on page 1, line 27	**48**

✳ *Printed on recycled paper*   **Schedule C (Form 1040) 2005**

(Use for Problem 20.)

SCHEDULE SE (Form 1040) Department of the Treasury Internal Revenue Service	**Self-Employment Tax** ▶ Attach to Form 1040. ▶ See Instructions for Schedule SE (Form 1040).	OMB No. 1545-0074 2005 Attachment Sequence No. **17**

Name of person with **self-employment** income (as shown on Form 1040)	Social security number of person with **self-employment** income ▶

Who Must File Schedule SE

You must file Schedule SE if:

- You had net earnings from self-employment from **other than** church employee income (line 4 of Short Schedule SE or line 4c of Long Schedule SE) of $400 or more **or**
- You had church employee income of $108.28 or more. Income from services you performed as a minister or a member of a religious order **is not** church employee income (see page SE-1).

Note. Even if you had a loss or a small amount of income from self-employment, it may be to your benefit to file Schedule SE and use either "optional method" in Part II of Long Schedule SE (see page SE-3).

Exception. If your only self-employment income was from earnings as a minister, member of a religious order, or Christian Science practitioner **and** you filed Form 4361 and received IRS approval not to be taxed on those earnings, **do not** file Schedule SE. Instead, write "Exempt–Form 4361" on Form 1040, line 58.

May I Use Short Schedule SE or Must I Use Long Schedule SE?

Did You Receive Wages or Tips in 2005?

No →

Are you a minister, member of a religious order, or Christian Science practitioner who received IRS approval **not** to be taxed on earnings from these sources, **but** you owe self-employment tax on other earnings? — Yes →

No ↓

Are you using one of the optional methods to figure your net earnings (see page SE-3)? — Yes →

No ↓

Did you receive church employee income reported on Form W-2 of $108.28 or more? — Yes →

No ↓

Yes →

Was the total of your wages and tips subject to social security or railroad retirement tax **plus** your net earnings from self-employment more than $90,000? — Yes →

No ↓

Did you receive tips subject to social security or Medicare tax that you **did not** report to your employer? — Yes →

No ←

You May Use Short Schedule SE Below

You Must Use Long Schedule SE on page 2

Section A—Short Schedule SE. Caution. Read above to see if you can use Short Schedule SE.

1 Net farm profit or (loss) from Schedule F, line 36, and farm partnerships, Schedule K-1 (Form 1065), box 14, code A	**1**	
2 Net profit or (loss) from Schedule C, line 31; Schedule C-EZ, line 3; Schedule K-1 (Form 1065), box 14, code A (other than farming); and Schedule K-1 (Form 1065-B), box 9. Ministers and members of religious orders, see page SE-1 for amounts to report on this line. See page SE-2 for other income to report	**2**	
3 Combine lines 1 and 2	**3**	
4 **Net earnings from self-employment.** Multiply line 3 by 92.35% (.9235). If less than $400, **do not** file this schedule; you do not owe self-employment tax . . . . ▶	**4**	
5 **Self-employment tax.** If the amount on line 4 is: • $90,000 or less, multiply line 4 by 15.3% (.153). Enter the result here and on **Form 1040, line 58.** • More than $90,000, multiply line 4 by 2.9% (.029). Then, add $11,160.00 to the result. Enter the total here and on **Form 1040, line 58.**	**5**	
6 **Deduction for one-half of self-employment tax.** Multiply line 5 by 50% (.5). Enter the result here and on **Form 1040, line 27**	**6**	

For Paperwork Reduction Act Notice, see Form 1040 instructions. Cat. No. 11358Z **Schedule SE (Form 1040) 2005**

(Use for Problem 20.)

Form **4562**	**Depreciation and Amortization**	OMB No. 1545-0172
Department of the Treasury Internal Revenue Service	**(Including Information on Listed Property)** ▶ See separate instructions. ▶ Attach to your tax return.	**2005** Attachment Sequence No. **67**

Name(s) shown on return	Business or activity to which this form relates	Identifying number

Part I Election To Expense Certain Property Under Section 179
Note: *If you have any listed property, complete Part V before you complete Part I.*

1	Maximum amount. See the instructions for a higher limit for certain businesses	**1**	$105,000
2	Total cost of section 179 property placed in service (see instructions)	**2**	
3	Threshold cost of section 179 property before reduction in limitation	**3**	$420,000
4	Reduction in limitation. Subtract line 3 from line 2. If zero or less, enter -0-	**4**	
5	Dollar limitation for tax year. Subtract line 4 from line 1. If zero or less, enter -0-. If married filing separately, see instructions	**5**	

(a) Description of property	**(b)** Cost (business use only)	**(c)** Elected cost
6		

7	Listed property. Enter the amount from line 29	**7**	
8	Total elected cost of section 179 property. Add amounts in column (c), lines 6 and 7	**8**	
9	Tentative deduction. Enter the **smaller** of line 5 or line 8	**9**	
10	Carryover of disallowed deduction from line 13 of your 2004 Form 4562	**10**	
11	Business income limitation. Enter the smaller of business income (not less than zero) or line 5 (see instructions)	**11**	
12	Section 179 expense deduction. Add lines 9 and 10, but do not enter more than line 11	**12**	
13	Carryover of disallowed deduction to 2006. Add lines 9 and 10, less line 12 ▶	**13**	

Note: *Do not use Part II or Part III below for listed property. Instead, use Part V.*

Part II Special Depreciation Allowance and Other Depreciation (Do not include listed property.) (See instructions.)

14	Special allowance for certain aircraft, certain property with a long production period, and qualified New York Liberty Zone property (other than listed property) placed in service during the tax year	**14**	
15	Property subject to section 168(f)(1) election	**15**	
16	Other depreciation (including ACRS)	**16**	

Part III MACRS Depreciation (Do not include listed property.) (See instructions.)

Section A

17	MACRS deductions for assets placed in service in tax years beginning before 2005	**17**	
18	If you are electing to group any assets placed in service during the tax year into one or more general asset accounts, check here ▶ ☐		

Section B—Assets Placed in Service During 2005 Tax Year Using the General Depreciation System

(a) Classification of property	**(b)** Month and year placed in service	**(c)** Basis for depreciation (business/investment use only—see instructions)	**(d)** Recovery period	**(e)** Convention	**(f)** Method	**(g)** Depreciation deduction
19a 3-year property						
b 5-year property						
c 7-year property						
d 10-year property						
e 15-year property						
f 20-year property						
g 25-year property			25 yrs.		S/L	
h Residential rental property			27.5 yrs.	MM	S/L	
			27.5 yrs.	MM	S/L	
i Nonresidential real property			39 yrs.	MM	S/L	
				MM	S/L	

Section C—Assets Placed in Service During 2005 Tax Year Using the Alternative Depreciation System

20a Class life					S/L	
b 12-year			12 yrs.		S/L	
c 40-year			40 yrs.	MM	S/L	

Part IV Summary (see instructions)

21	Listed property. Enter amount from line 28	**21**	
22	**Total.** Add amounts from line 12, lines 14 through 17, lines 19 and 20 in column (g), and line 21. Enter here and on the appropriate lines of your return. Partnerships and S corporations—see instr.	**22**	
23	For assets shown above and placed in service during the current year, enter the portion of the basis attributable to section 263A costs **23**		

For Paperwork Reduction Act Notice, see separate instructions.   Cat. No. 12906N   Form **4562** (2005)

(Use for Problem 20.)

Form 4562 (2005)   Page **2**

Part V   **Listed Property** (Include automobiles, certain other vehicles, cellular telephones, certain computers, and property used for entertainment, recreation, or amusement.)

Note: *For any vehicle for which you are using the standard mileage rate or deducting lease expense, complete only 24a, 24b, columns (a) through (c) of Section A, all of Section B, and Section C if applicable.*

Section A—Depreciation and Other Information (Caution: *See the instructions for limits for passenger automobiles.***)**

24a Do you have evidence to support the business/investment use claimed? ☐ Yes ☐ No   **24b** If "Yes," is the evidence written? ☐ Yes ☐ No

(a) Type of property (list vehicles first)	(b) Date placed in service	(c) Business/ investment use percentage	(d) Cost or other basis	(e) Basis for depreciation (business/investment use only)	(f) Recovery period	(g) Method/ Convention	(h) Depreciation deduction	(i) Elected section 179 cost
25 Special allowance for qualified New York Liberty Zone listed property placed in service during the tax year and used more than 50% in a qualified business use (see instructions)							**25**	
26 Property used more than 50% in a qualified business use:								
		%						
		%						
		%						
27 Property used 50% or less in a qualified business use:								
		%				S/L –		
		%				S/L –		
		%				S/L –		
28 Add amounts in column (h), lines 25 through 27. Enter here and on line 21, page 1.						**28**		
29 Add amounts in column (i), line 26. Enter here and on line 7, page 1.							**29**	

Section B—Information on Use of Vehicles

Complete this section for vehicles used by a sole proprietor, partner, or other "more than 5% owner," or related person.

If you provided vehicles to your employees, first answer the questions in Section C to see if you meet an exception to completing this section for those vehicles.

	(a) Vehicle 1		(b) Vehicle 2		(c) Vehicle 3		(d) Vehicle 4		(e) Vehicle 5		(f) Vehicle 6	
30 Total business/investment miles driven during the year (**do not** include commuting miles)												
31 Total commuting miles driven during the year												
32 Total other personal (noncommuting) miles driven												
33 Total miles driven during the year. Add lines 30 through 32												
34 Was the vehicle available for personal use during off-duty hours?	Yes	No	Yes	No	Yes	No	Yes	No	Yes	No	Yes	No
35 Was the vehicle used primarily by a more than 5% owner or related person?												
36 Is another vehicle available for personal use?												

Section C—Questions for Employers Who Provide Vehicles for Use by Their Employees

Answer these questions to determine if you meet an exception to completing Section B for vehicles used by employees who **are not** more than 5% owners or related persons (see instructions).

	Yes	No
37 Do you maintain a written policy statement that prohibits all personal use of vehicles, including commuting, by your employees?		
38 Do you maintain a written policy statement that prohibits personal use of vehicles, except commuting, by your employees? See the instructions for vehicles used by corporate officers, directors, or 1% or more owners		
39 Do you treat all use of vehicles by employees as personal use?		
40 Do you provide more than five vehicles to your employees, obtain information from your employees about the use of the vehicles, and retain the information received?		
41 Do you meet the requirements concerning qualified automobile demonstration use? (See instructions.)		

Note: *If your answer to 37, 38, 39, 40, or 41 is "Yes," do not complete Section B for the covered vehicles.*

Part VI   **Amortization**

(a) Description of costs	(b) Date amortization begins	(c) Amortizable amount	(d) Code section	(e) Amortization period or percentage	(f) Amortization for this year
42 Amortization of costs that begins during your 2005 tax year (see instructions):					
43 Amortization of costs that began before your 2005 tax year.				**43**	
44 **Total.** Add amounts in column (f). See the instructions for where to report.				**44**	

Printed on recycled paper   Form **4562** (2005)

9

Rental Activities

CHAPTER CONTENTS

■■ CHAPTER OVERVIEW

*I*n addition to earning income from their jobs, many individuals earn income from property they own. For instance, taxpayers who own stocks often earn dividend income. Likewise, those who own bonds earn interest income. Taxpayers also can earn income by renting their property. Chapters 3 and 4 described the tax consequences of interest and dividend income. This chapter focuses on the income and expenses from rental activities. Taxpayers report rental income and expenses on their tax returns. However, in cases where rental expenses exceed rental income, the vacation home rules, at-risk rules, or passive loss rules may limit the losses taxpayers can deduct on their tax returns. The chapter begins with a discussion of rental income and expenses. The focus then shifts to the areas of the tax law that may limit deductions for losses from rental activities.

RENTAL INCOME AND EXPENSES

Although taxpayers can rent both personal and real property, this chapter focuses on the tax aspects of owning residential rental property. **Residential rental property** is rental property where at least 80% of the income comes from the rental of dwelling units. In general, a **dwelling unit** is property that provides the basic living accommodations—kitchen, sleeping, and toilet facilities. Dwelling units include houses, apartments, condominiums, and mobile homes because they are residential property. They do not include hotels, motels, and similar establishments.

Rental Income *Recorded on Sch E*

Rental income includes the payments taxpayers receive for allowing others to *use or occupy* their property. Usually rent payments are received in cash. However, when a tenant performs services in exchange for the use of the taxpayer's property, rental income includes the value of those services. Rental income includes payments a tenant makes to cancel a lease. It also includes the value of improvements a tenant makes to the taxpayer's property in lieu of rent.

EXAMPLE 1

Jay Haas rents property to a tenant for $500 a month. In November the tenant installs a ceiling fan valued at $100. Haas then reduces the tenant's December rent by $100. Haas's rental income equals $6,000 ($500 × 11 months + $400 for December + $100 improvement substituted for rent). Haas then capitalizes and depreciates the ceiling fan.

Cash basis taxpayers report rental income the year they receive it, even when it applies to a prior or future tax year. Accrual basis taxpayers usually report rental income in the year it is due to them, but must report rent received in advance in the year they receive it. Therefore, if on December 26, 20x1, the taxpayer receives $600 from a tenant for January 20x2 rent, the $600 would be reported as rental income in 20x1 under both the cash and accrual methods. A security deposit is considered rent received in advance when the deposit represents the tenant's final rent payment. It is not considered rent received in advance if the taxpayer intends to return the deposit at the end of the lease. However, should the tenant forfeit any part of the deposit in a future year (for example, to cover late charges), the forfeited amount is rental income to the taxpayer in the year forfeited.

EXAMPLE 2

Connie Esmond enters into a 5-year lease to rent property she owns. On July 1, 2005, Esmond receives $6,000 for the first year's rent and $6,000 of rent in advance for the final year of the lease. Esmond also receives a $1,000 security deposit that she intends to return to the tenant at the end of the lease. Esmond's 2005 rental income equals $12,000, regardless of whether she uses the cash or accrual method of accounting.

Rental Expenses

Taxpayers can deduct against rental income all ordinary expenses related to the rental property. Examples of common rental expenses include advertising, cleaning, maintenance, utilities, real estate taxes, mortgage interest, insurance premiums, management fees, and necessary travel and transportation. Other rental expenses include repairs and depreciation. Accrual basis taxpayers take deductions in the year that services are received or assets are used. Cash basis taxpayers generally deduct rental expenses in the year the expenses are paid.

Repairs

Repairs and maintenance keep the rental property in good operating condition. Taxpayers can deduct the costs to repair rental property as a rental expense. Examples of repairs to rental property include painting the property (inside and out), fixing gutters or leaks, and replacing broken windows. Repairs are minor costs and should not be confused with improvements, which add value to the rental property or prolong its useful life. Improvements to rental property include such items as adding a bathroom, paving a driveway, installing new cabinets, or replacing the roof. Improvements increase the taxpayer's investment (basis) in the rental property. Taxpayers recover the cost of improvements through the depreciation methods described in Chapter 8.

EXAMPLE 3

Jake Dugan spends $15,000 to replace the roof and $3,000 to repaint the exterior of an apartment building he owns. Dugan can deduct the $3,000 spent on repairs from rental income in the current year. Dugan adds the $15,000 of improvements to his cost basis in the apartment building and depreciates this amount using the depreciation rules from Chapter 8.

Depreciation

Taxpayers depreciate furniture, appliances, and carpeting used in rental property over 5 years under MACRS (9 years if ADS is elected). Section 179 expense cannot be taken on rental property. However, the 50% bonus depreciation was allowed on new furnishings placed in service on or before December 31, 2004. Taxpayers depreciate residential realty placed in service after 1986 using the straight-line method over 27.5 years (MACRS) or 40 years (ADS). They cannot depreciate the land associated with rental realty.

Special Rules When Only Part of the Property Is Rented

The rules previously described assume that the rental property is used exclusively by or available for use by rent-paying tenants. Sometimes the taxpayer rents only part of the property, as is the case when an owner of a duplex rents one unit and lives in the other. In such instances, the taxpayer must allocate expenses between rental and personal use. The taxpayer then deducts the rental portion of each expense against rental income and can deduct the personal portion of the mortgage interest and real estate taxes as itemized deductions.

Some expenses are easy to split between rental and personal use. For example, taxpayers can fully deduct the cost of repairs performed on rental units but cannot deduct the cost to repair their own personal units. Other expenses, like real estate taxes and depreciation, are harder to divide between rental and personal use. For these expenses, taxpayers can use any reasonable method to divide expenses between rental and personal use. The number of rooms or the relative square footage are two widely used methods for allocating these types of expenses.

EXAMPLE 4

Marvin Greene rents one room in his home. The area of the rented room is 140 square feet. The area of the entire home is 1,400 square feet. Greene deducts against rental income 10% (140/1,400) of the expenses related to the home during the year. Thus, if Greene's real estate taxes are $2,000, he can deduct $200 against rental income and the rest ($1,800) as an itemized deduction.

Converting a Personal Residence to Rental Use

When taxpayers convert their personal residence to rental property, they must divide the expenses for the year of the conversion between the two uses. Rental use begins when the property is offered for rent. Taxpayers deduct the rental portion of these expenses against rental income. They can deduct the personal portion of the interest and taxes as itemized deductions.

EXAMPLE 5

In September, Sylvia Black moved out of her home. Black listed her home for rent on October 1, and on November 1, she entered into a 2-year lease. Black can deduct 25% (October–December) of the annual expenses (real estates taxes, insurance, depreciation) against the rental income she receives during the year. She also can deduct any other expenses (interest, utilities, etc.) allocated to the last three months of the year. Black can deduct the personal portion (the other 75%) of the interest and taxes as itemized deductions.

RENTAL OF VACATION HOMES

The previous section dealt with situations where the rental income was derived from rental property used solely by the tenant. Special rules apply when taxpayers rent out vacation homes for part of the year and personally use the property during other parts of the year. The tax treatment of this type of rental activity depends on the number of rental and personal days during the year.

Property Rented Less Than 15 Days

When taxpayers rent their vacation home or principal residence for less than 15 days during the year, they do not report the rental income and do not deduct any rental expenses. However, home mortgage interest (but only for a principal residence or second residence), real estate taxes, and casualty losses may be deducted as itemized deductions.

EXAMPLE 6

Darren Benton rents his vacation home for 12 days during the year and personally uses it for 80 days. Benton collects rents of $1,200 and incurs the following expenses.

Home mortgage interest	$ 6,000
Real estate taxes	1,800
Utilities	400
Depreciation	2,000
Total expenses	$10,200

Since Benton rents the property for less than 15 days, he does not report the $1,200 of rental income. Benton can deduct as itemized deductions the $6,000 of home mortgage interest as his second residence and the $1,800 of real estate taxes.

Congress has failed on several occasions to get rid of the loophole in the tax law that allows taxpayers to rent out their residences for up to two weeks each year and not report the rental income to the IRS. This loophole made the headlines during the 1984 summer Olympics, when Los Angeles–area residents rented out their mansions for over $10,000 a day. Although the most they could rent their homes for was for 14 days, at more than $10,000 a day, they could generate over $140,000 in tax-free income.

Property Rented More Than 14 Days

Taxpayers who rent their vacation homes or principal residence for more than 14 days during the year report the rental income on their tax returns. They then allocate the expenses related to the property between rental and personal use and deduct the rental portion of the expenses against their rental income. The Internal Revenue Code states that taxpayers allocate expenses other than interest, taxes, and casualty losses on the basis of the days the property is used during the year. To compute the rental portion of expenses like utilities, repairs, and depreciation, taxpayers multiply the expense by the ratio of the number of days rented at fair rental value to the number of days used during the year.

$$\text{Percent allocated to rental activity} = \frac{\text{Number of days rented at fair rental value during the year}}{\text{Number of days used during the year}}$$

The Code does not address how to allocate interest, taxes, and casualty losses between rental and personal use. In Publication 527, the IRS suggests that taxpayers use the same method used to allocate other expenses. The courts, however, have allowed interest and taxes to be allocated based on the days rented to the number of days in the year. For purposes of this chapter, the same ratio (days rented/days used) is used to allocate all expenses to rental use.

EXAMPLE 7

Dan Walsh rents out his vacation home for 120 days during the year. He personally uses it for 80 days. Walsh collects rents of $12,000 and incurs the following expenses.

Home mortgage interest	$ 8,000
Real estate taxes	2,500
Utilities	800
Depreciation	3,000
Total expenses	$14,300

Walsh allocates 60% of the expenses (120 rental days/200 total days used during the year) to rental use. Walsh deducts $8,580 ($14,300 × 60%) as rental expense. He can deduct the rest of the home mortgage interest of $3,200 ($8,000 × 40%) and real estate taxes of $1,000 ($2,500 × 40%) as itemized deductions.

Before taxpayers can allocate expenses between rental and personal use, they first must determine what days count as rental days and what days count as personal days. Personal use includes days when the taxpayer donates use of the property to a charitable organization. Personal use also includes days when the property is used by:

1. The owner, unless the owner is working full time to repair or maintain the property.
2. A member of an owner's family, unless the family member pays a fair rental price *and* the family member uses the property as a principal residence. Family members include siblings (brothers and sisters), ancestors (parents, grandparents, etc.), and lineal descendants (children, grandchildren, etc.).
3. Anyone who has a reciprocal agreement that allows the owner to use some other dwelling unit.
4. Anyone who pays less than fair rental to use the property.

A rental day is any day the taxpayer rents the property for a fair rental price (however, see 2. above for special rules for family members). Days that the property is offered for rental but is not actually rented do not count as rental days.

WHAT IS A FAIR RENTAL PRICE?

A fair rental price is the amount of rent that an *unrelated person* would be willing to pay to use the property. If the rent charged is substantially less than the rents received on *similar* properties, it might not be considered a fair rental price. The following questions can be used to determine whether two properties are *similar:*

- Are the properties used for the same purpose?
- Are the properties about the same size?
- Are the properties in about the same condition?
- Do the properties have similar furnishings?
- Are the properties in similar locations?

Generally, answering "No" to any of these questions means that the two properties are not similar.

EXAMPLE 8

Jane Sherman owns a house that she rents to her son. The son pays a fair rental price to use the home as his principal residence. The son's use of the home is not considered personal use by Sherman since the son is using the home as his principal residence and paying fair rental.

EXAMPLE 9

Bruce Reynolds rents his vacation home for 200 days during the year. On 40 of the 200 days, Reynolds's sister paid fair rental to use the house. The other 160 days also were rented at fair rental. Reynolds treats the days his sister rents the house as personal days, since she does not use the house as her principal residence. Thus, Reynolds's rental days equal 160. Reynolds allocates 80% (160 rental days/200 days used) of the expenses related to the house to rental use. He deducts these amounts against rental income.

Expenses Limited for Certain Vacation Homes

When the property is considered a "residence," rental expenses are deductible only to the extent of rental income. Disallowed expenses carry over to offset rental income in future tax years. A vacation home qualifies as a **residence** if the number of personal days exceeds the greater of 14 days or 10% of the days the property is rented at fair rental. Thus, if the taxpayer's personal days exceed *both* (1) 14 days and (2) 10% of the number of days rented at fair rental, then the property is considered a residence. When the property is treated as a residence, the personal portion of the interest can be deducted as an itemized deduction if the property is chosen as the taxpayer's second residence. When the property does not qualify as a residence, the personal portion of the interest cannot be deducted.

EXAMPLE 10

From June 1 through October 31 (153 days), Denise Miller rents her cabin (used as a vacation home) and receives fair rental. Miller uses the cabin 5 days during the year. Miller's parents stayed at the cabin for 12 days in May. In deciding whether the cabin qualifies as a residence, personal days include days the parents used the cabin (12 days). Thus, the total number of personal days equals 17 (5 + 12).

Miller treats the cabin as a residence since her 17 personal days exceed the greater of: (1) 14 days or (2) 15.3 days (10% of the 153 days rented at fair rental). Thus, Miller can deduct the rental portion of the expenses on the cabin only to the extent of rental income. She carries over any excess rental expense to the next year. In allocating expenses between rental and personal use, Miller allocates 90% (153 rental days/170 days used) of the expenses to the rental activity.

When renting out a vacation home, the owner's personal use of the property will determine whether the vacation home rules apply. The vacation home rules cannot take effect until the owner's personal days exceed 14. Thus, to avoid having the vacation home rules limit the deduction for rental expenses, owners might consider limiting their personal usage of the home to two weeks a year.

If the rental property qualifies as a residence and the taxpayer's rental expenses exceed rental income, the taxpayer deducts the expenses in the following order:

1. Home mortgage interest, real estate taxes, casualty and theft losses, and rent expenses not directly related to the rental property (management fees, advertising, etc.)
2. All other rental expenses other than depreciation on the rental property
3. Depreciation of the rental property

EXAMPLE 11

Jan Lehman rents her vacation home at fair rental to an unrelated party for 35 days during the year. Lehman personally uses the home for 15 days. The property is not used during any other time. During the year, Lehman collects $6,000 in rents and has the following expenses:

Home mortgage interest	$ 6,000
Real estate taxes	1,500
Utilities	300
Depreciation	3,000
Total expenses	$10,800

Lehman allocates 70% (35 rental days/50 total days used) of the expenses to the rental use. The rental portion of the expenses related to the home equals $7,560 ($10,800 × 70%). Because Lehman's personal use (15 days) exceeds the greater of (1) 14 days or (2) 10% of the days rented at fair rental (35 × 10% = 3.5), the vacation home qualifies as a residence. Thus, Lehman's rental expenses cannot exceed rental income. Lehman deducts the rental expenses in the following order:

Rental income	$6,000
Less rental portion of interest and taxes ($7,500 × 70%)	(5,250)
Rental income left to cover rent expenses other than interest and taxes	$ 750
Less rent expenses other than depreciation ($300 × 70%)	(210)
Rental income left to cover depreciation expense	$ 540
Less depreciation ($3,000 × 70% = $2,100)	(540)
Net rental income	$ 0

Because the vacation home qualifies as a residence, Lehman can deduct only $540 of the $2,100 of depreciation allocated to rental use. Lehman carries over the disallowed depreciation of $1,560 ($2,100 − $540) to the next year. She adds this amount to next year's depreciation expense.

REPORTING RENTAL ACTIVITIES ON SCHEDULE E

Taxpayers use Schedule E (Form 1040), Supplemental Income and Loss, to report income and expenses from rental activities. In Part I (line 1), taxpayers describe the rental realty and provide its location. In Part I (line 2), taxpayers answer a question that determines whether the property qualifies as a residence. Taxpayers also report in Part I rental income (line 3) and expenses (lines 5 through 20) in computing their overall income or loss from the rental activity (line 22). For taxpayers who answer "Yes" to the question in Part I (line 2), total expenses (line 21) cannot exceed rental income (line 3). For taxpayers who answer "No" to this question, the vacation home rules do not apply and there is no limit on the total expenses. However, the expenses may be limited under either the *at-risk* or *passive loss* rules (discussed later in the chapter).

Information for Figure 9-1: Filled-In Schedule E

During 2005, Kurt F. and Heather M. Reding received rents of **$38,168** from an eight-unit apartment complex. The Redings paid $375,000 for the apartment building in 1996, which includes $100,000 for the land. They depreciate the building using MACRS (straight-line over 27.5 years). Expenses related to the building include **$250** advertising, **$2,500** cleaning and maintenance, **$1,227** insurance, **$300** legal fees, **$14,329** mortgage interest, **$3,262** supplies, **$4,290** real estate taxes, and **$1,800** utilities.

The Redings also own a condominium in Naples, Florida, that they used for 30 days in 2005. The Redings rented the condo for 90 days and received fair rentals totaling **$12,000.** None of the tenants were members of the Redings' family. The Redings paid $220,000 for the condo in 1995 and depreciate it using MACRS (straight-line over 27.5 years). The expenses related to the condo include $9,200 home mortgage interest, $3,400 real estate taxes, $1,000 utilities, $300 insurance, and $100 cleaning and maintenance.

Other Information

1A: Description: 8-unit apartment building, 505 West Street, Verona, WI

1B: Description: Condominium, 1500 Vanderbelt Beach Road, Naples, FL

2A: **No.** Personal use did not exceed the greater of 14 days or 10% of the days rented at fair rental.

2B: **Yes.** The Redings's 30 days of personal use exceeds the greater of (1) 14 days or (2) 9 days (10% of the 90 days rented at fair rental). Therefore, total rental expenses cannot exceed rental income.

7B: Cleaning and maintenance, **$75.00** (90 rental days/120 total days used × $100)

9B: Insurance, **$225.00** (90/120 × $300)

12B: Mortgage interest, **$6,900.00** (90/120 × $9,200)

16B: Taxes, **$2,550.00** (90/120 × $3,400)

17B: Utilities, **$750.00** (90/120 × $1,000)

20A: Depreciation expense, **$10,000.00** ($275,000/27.5)

20B: Depreciation expense, **$1,500.00** ($220,000/27.5 × 90/120 = $6,000; however, total rental expenses cannot exceed rental income of $12,000. Expenses other than depreciation total $10,500 [line 19B]; therefore depreciation is limited to $1,500).

FIGURE 9-1 Filled-In Schedule E, Page 1

SCHEDULE E (Form 1040)	Supplemental Income and Loss	OMB No. 1545-0074
Department of the Treasury Internal Revenue Service (99)	(From rental real estate, royalties, partnerships, S corporations, estates, trusts, REMICs, etc.) ► Attach to Form 1040 or Form 1041. ► See Instructions for Schedule E (Form 1040).	2005 Attachment Sequence No. 13

Name(s) shown on return
Kurt F. and Heather M. Reding

Your social security number
885 : 46 : 5566

Part I   **Income or Loss From Rental Real Estate and Royalties**   **Note.** If you are in the business of renting personal property, use Schedule C or C-EZ (see page E-3). Report farm rental income or loss from **Form 4835** on page 2, line 40.

1 List the type and location of each **rental real estate property:**

A   8-unit apartment building
     505 West Street, Vernoa, WI

B   Condominim
     1500 Vanderbelt Beach Road, Naples, FL

C

2 For each rental real estate property listed on line 1, did you or your family use it during the tax year for personal purposes for more than the greater of:
- 14 days **or**
- 10% of the total days rented at fair rental value?

(See page E-3.)

	Yes	No
A		X
B	X	
C		

Draft as of 05/24/2005

Income:		Properties				Totals (Add columns A, B, and C.)	
		A	B	C			
3 Rents received	3	38,168 00	12,000 00		**3**	50,168	00
4 Royalties received	4				**4**		
Expenses:							
5 Advertising	5	250 00					
6 Auto and travel (see page E-4)	6						
7 Cleaning and maintenance	7	2,500 00	75 00				
8 Commissions	8						
9 Insurance	9	1,227 00	225 00				
10 Legal and other professional fees	10	300 00					
11 Management fees	11						
12 Mortgage interest paid to banks, etc. (see page E-4)	12	14,329 00	6,900 00		**12**	21,229	00
13 Other interest	13						
14 Repairs	14						
15 Supplies	15	3,262 00					
16 Taxes	16	4,290 00	2,550 00				
17 Utilities	17	1,800 00	750 00				
18 Other (list) ►	18						
19 Add lines 5 through 18	19	27,958 00	10,500 00		**19**	38,458	00
20 Depreciation expense or depletion (see page E-4)	20	10,000 00	1,500 00		**20**	11,500	00
21 Total expenses. Add lines 19 and 20	21	37,958 00	12,000 00				
22 Income or (loss) from rental real estate or royalty properties. Subtract line 21 from line 3 (rents) or line 4 (royalties). If the result is a (loss), see page E-4 to find out if you must file **Form 6198**	22	210 00	0				
23 Deductible rental real estate loss. **Caution.** Your rental real estate loss on line 22 may be limited. See page E-4 to find out if you must file **Form 8582.** Real estate professionals must complete line 43 on page 2	23	( )	( )	( )			

24   **Income.** Add positive amounts shown on line 22. **Do not** include any losses   **24**   210 00

25   **Losses.** Add royalty losses from line 22 and rental real estate losses from line 23. Enter total losses here   **25** ( )

26   **Total rental real estate and royalty income or (loss).** Combine lines 24 and 25. Enter the result here. If Parts II, III, IV, and line 40 on page 2 do not apply to you, also enter this amount on Form 1040, line 17. Otherwise, include this amount in the total on line 41 on page 2   **26**   210 00

For Paperwork Reduction Act Notice, see Form 1040 instructions.   Cat. No. 11344L   **Schedule E (Form 1040) 2005**

LOSS LIMITATIONS

When rental expenses exceed rental income and the rental property is considered a "residence," the vacation home rules limit the amount of rental expenses taxpayers can deduct against rental income. For rental property not subject to the vacation home limitation rules, two other sets of rules may affect the taxpayer's ability to deduct losses arising from rental activities: the at-risk rules and the passive activity loss rules. These rules not only affect rental activities but can affect losses arising from any trade, business, or income-producing activity. Because this chapter focuses on rental activities, the discussion will focus on these activities.

AT-RISK RULES

The at-risk rules limit a taxpayer's loss to the amount the taxpayer could actually lose from the activity. This is known as the amount the taxpayer is "at-risk." The at-risk rules apply to any activity carried on as a trade or business (reported on Schedule C) or for the production of income (reported on Schedule E).

Amounts at Risk *mortgage generally apply*

A taxpayer's risk in any activity equals the following:

1. The money and adjusted basis (cost + improvements − accumulated depreciation) of any property contributed to the activity, **plus**
2. Amounts borrowed for use in the activity if the taxpayer either is personally liable for the loan or pledges personal assets as security for the loan.

Disallowed Losses

Taxpayers determine the amount of their deductible loss on Form 6198, At-Risk Limitations. They file this form with their tax return if they have a loss from an at-risk activity and some of their investment in the activity is not at risk. A net loss limited because of the at-risk rules is treated as a deduction for the activity in the next year. When taxpayers sell or dispose of property used in an activity where the at-risk rules apply, they include any gain or loss from the disposal in computing the activity's overall profit or loss for the year.

PASSIVE ACTIVITY LOSSES

After applying the at-risk rules, taxpayers must consider the passive activity loss rules. Losses generated by activities of a passive nature can only offset income and gains generated from passive activities. Taxpayers carry over excess losses to offset passive income in future tax years. When the taxpayer disposes of the entire interest in a passive activity, any suspended losses left on that activity are fully deductible in that year.

Passive Activity Income Defined

The passive activity rules classify all income and losses into one of three categories: active, portfolio, or passive. **Active income** consists of wages, salaries, and income from material participation in a trade or business. **Portfolio income** comes from investments that generate dividends and interest. Portfolio income also includes gains from the sale of securities (stocks and bonds). **Passive income** generally comes from (1) a trade or business in which the taxpayer does not materially participate, (2) rental activities, and (3) limited partnerships. Any of these activities may produce losses. Losses from portfolio investments are treated as capital losses. However, losses not classified as portfolio are either active or passive. The distinction is important, as taxpayers can offset losses from active activities against both portfolio and passive income. They can only offset losses from passive activities against income from other passive activities.

(rental income & losses offset each other)

Phase out

$25,000 losses avail to taxpayers w/ property btw.

Material participation in a trade or business produces active income and losses. **Material participation** occurs when the taxpayer is involved in the operations of the activity on a regular, continuous, and substantial basis. Except for real estate rental activities (which must meet a stricter test, discussed later), the material participation requirement can be met if the taxpayer participates in the activity for more than 500 hours during the year. (Participation by the owner's spouse is considered participation by the owner.) Another way to meet this requirement is for the taxpayer to participate in the activity for more than 100 hours during the year and for the taxpayer's participation to be at least as much as the participation of any other individual, including employees. IRS Publication 925 describes other ways to meet the material participation requirement.

The tax laws usually treat all rental activities as passive activities. However, exceptions do exist. One exception applies to taxpayers involved in the business of renting real property. This situation is described in the next section. Other exceptions include rental activities where: (1) the average rental period is less than 8 days (for example, a video rental store); (2) the average rental period is less than 31 days and significant personal services are provided (for example, motels and hotels); and (3) the rental activity is incidental to the taxpayer's business. If one of these three exceptions applies, taxpayers need only meet the material participation requirements to avoid the passive loss rules. This will allow them to treat the income and losses from these rental activities as active income and losses.

LOSSES FROM RENTAL REAL ESTATE

Real Estate Trade or Business

Real estate rental activities usually are treated as "passive," even if the taxpayer meets one of the seven tests described in IRS Publication 925. However, a real estate rental activity may qualify as an active trade or business if the taxpayer satisfies both of the following conditions:

1. More than 50% of the personal services rendered during the year are performed in a trade or business involving real estate, **and**
2. At a minimum, the taxpayer performs more than 750 hours of personal service in the real property trade or business.

If the taxpayer meets both conditions, then the income or loss from the real estate rental activity is considered active, and all rental expenses are deductible, even if they exceed rental income. A married couple passes the two tests only if one spouse separately satisfies both tests. In other words, couples cannot pool their time and efforts in meeting the material participation test for real estate rental activities. If these conditions are not met, then the real estate rental activity is considered a passive activity. Accordingly, expenses related to the taxpayer's passive activities are deductible only to the extent that the taxpayer's passive activities generate passive income.

> The taxpayer has the burden of providing proof that any personal service tests have been met. To do this, taxpayers should keep a weekly log of their hours spent on the activity as evidence of their participation.

$25,000 Special Deduction for Active Participants

Taxpayers who are not in a "real estate trade or business" and have losses from rental real estate activities may deduct up to $25,000 of rental real estate losses from active and portfolio income. The deduction limit is $12,500 for married taxpayers filing separately and living apart at all times during the year. No special deduction is allowed for married taxpayers filing separately if the couple lived together at any time during the year. To qualify for this special deduction, the taxpayer must meet both of the following requirements:

1. The taxpayer actively participates in the rental real estate activity, **and**
2. The taxpayer owns at least 10% of the value of all interests in the activity throughout the entire year.

Active participation and material participation are two different concepts. **Active participation** requires less involvement than material participation. Active participation does not require regular, continuous, and substantial involvement. However, it does require that the taxpayer participate in management decisions in a significant and real sense. Examples of this level of involvement include approving new tenants, deciding on rental terms, approving improvements or repairs, or arranging for others to provide services such as repairs.

Phase-Out of the $25,000 Deduction

The $25,000 annual deduction is reduced by 50% of the taxpayer's modified AGI in excess of $100,000 ($50,000 for married taxpayers who file separately). Thus, the deduction is completely phased out when modified AGI reaches $150,000 ($75,000 for married taxpayers filing separately). Modified AGI is computed the same as AGI except that it does not include the following:

1. Taxable social security and railroad retirement payments
2. Deductible contributions to individual retirement accounts (IRAs) and self-employed retirement plans
3. The deduction for one-half of self-employment taxes
4. The interest exclusion for educational savings bonds (Series EE bonds)
5. Passive losses in excess of passive income

EXAMPLE 12

Rachel Phillips, a single taxpayer, earned $110,000 from her job, $15,000 of passive income from a non–real estate activity, and $20,000 of interest income. Phillips also incurred a $50,000 loss from a rental real estate activity in which she actively participates. Phillips made a $4,000 deductible IRA contribution in 2005. Under the general rule, passive losses usually can offset only passive income. Therefore, Phillips can use $15,000 of her $50,000 rental real estate loss to offset the $15,000 of the income from the non–real estate passive activity. Because Phillips is actively involved in the rental real estate activities, she may be able to deduct more than $15,000 of her loss. Phillips computes the additional deduction and passive loss carryover to 2006 as follows.

Modified AGI (does not include the $4,000 IRA deduction or the $35,000 of passive losses in excess of passive income):

Wages	$110,000	
Interest income	20,000	
Passive income	15,000	
Passive losses allowed under the general rule	(15,000)	$130,000
Less AGI threshold for the phase-out		(100,000)
Amount subject to phase-out		$ 30,000
		× 50%
Amount of deduction lost due to phase-out		$ 15,000
Passive loss from rental real estate in excess of passive income ($50,000 – $15,000)		$ 35,000
Additional passive loss deduction for active participation in rental real estate ($25,000 initial deduction – $15,000 lost due to phase-out)		(10,000)
Passive loss carried forward to 2006		$ 25,000

Phillips will deduct a total of $25,000 of passive activity losses ($15,000 under the general rule and $10,000 special deduction) against passive activity income of $15,000.

SUSPENDED LOSSES

Passive activity losses not deducted in the current tax year carry forward to the next year. However, taxpayers must reduce their basis in the passive activity by all allowable deductions. This includes those losses not deductible on the current tax return because of the passive loss rule.

Multiple Activities

When multiple passive activities exist, taxpayers must determine the suspended loss for each separate activity through an allocation process. The following is the formula for the loss allocation process:

$$\text{Total \textbf{disallowed} loss} \times \frac{\text{Loss from separate activity}}{\text{Sum of \textbf{all} losses}}$$

EXAMPLE 13

Dick White reports the following income and losses from his four passive activities for 2005.

Activity A	($40,000)
Activity B	30,000
Activity C	(32,000)
Activity D	(8,000)
Net passive loss	($50,000)

White allocates his net passive loss of $50,000 to activities A, C, and D (the activities producing a total of $80,000 of losses) as follows:

Activity A ($50,000 × $40,000/$80,000)	($25,000)
Activity C ($50,000 × $32,000/$80,000)	(20,000)
Activity D ($50,000 × $8,000/$80,000)	(5,000)
Total suspended losses	($50,000)

These suspended losses carry forward indefinitely as deductions associated with the activity to which each relates. Thus, the $25,000 passive loss carryover associated with Activity A is added to/netted against any passive income (loss) generated by Activity A in 2006. This net amount becomes White's passive income (loss) from Activity A for 2006. The same process is applied to Activities C and D.

DISPOSING OF A PASSIVE ACTIVITY

When taxpayers dispose of a passive activity, any suspended losses relating to that activity are deductible in full. To qualify for this treatment, taxpayers must dispose of their entire interest in the activity in a fully taxable transaction. Also, the new property owner cannot be the taxpayer's sibling (sister or brother), ancestor (parent, grandparent, etc.), or descendent (child, grandchild, etc.). Special rules apply when taxpayers dispose of a passive activity by way of gift or inheritance. These rules are beyond the scope of this book.

The gain or loss from the sale of a passive activity receives special treatment. If a loss results, the loss is either an ordinary loss or capital loss depending on the circumstances. The loss is not treated as a passive loss, so it is not limited to passive income. Chapter 11 explains the difference between ordinary and capital losses in greater detail.

REPORTING PASSIVE ACTIVITY LOSSES

Taxpayers with income or loss from passive activities complete Form 8582, Passive Activity Loss Limitations, to compute the amount of passive loss allowed from such activities. Taxpayers then report the passive loss allowed on the appropriate tax form or schedule. For example, taxpayers report the passive loss allowed from rental activities on Schedule E.

Form 8582

Regardless of the number or complexity of passive activities, taxpayers file only one Form 8582, Passive Activity Loss Limitations. Taxpayers prepare Form 8582 to determine whether the passive loss rules disallow any of the losses shown on those forms.

Form 8582 consists of three parts. In Part I, taxpayers report net income (line 1a), net loss (line 1b), and prior year carry forwards (line 1c) from rental real estate activities with active participation. They also report in Part I net income (line 3a), net loss (line 3b), and prior year carry forwards (line 3c) from all other passive activities. Taxpayers then combine these amounts (line 4). If net income results, taxpayers enter the net amount on the appropriate form/schedule to which the activity relates (for example, Schedule E for rental real estate). If a net loss results, then taxpayers proceed to Part II to see whether they can utilize any of the $25,000 special allowance for active participation in rental real estate activities.

In Part II, taxpayers determine the amount of net loss available for the $25,000 special allowance (line 5). They then compute their modified adjusted gross income and determine the amount of phase-out, if any, that applies (lines 6–8). In Part IV, taxpayers compute the passive income and loss reported on that year's tax return. Deductible passive losses (line 16) equal the total passive income (from lines 1a and 3a) plus the special allowance amount from Part II (line 10).

Information for Figure 9-2: Filled-In Form 8582

Derrick Smart earned $120,000 from his job, $15,000 of interest income, $10,000 from a passive activity (non–real estate), and a $20,000 loss from a rental real estate activity in which he actively participates (see accompanying Schedule E). Smart has no other income and no passive loss carryovers from prior years. Form 8582 shows that Smart has deductible passive losses of $17,500. He deducts this amount on Schedule E (line 23). Smart's passive loss carryover to 2006 is $2,500 ($20,000 – $17,500).

Other Information

1b: Activities with net loss (Rental Real Estate Activities With Active Participation), **$20,000.00**

3a: Activities with net income (All Other Passive Activities), **$10,000.00**

7: Modified adjusted gross income, **$135,000.00** [$120,000 + $15,000 + $10,000 (non–real estate passive net income) – $10,000 (rental real estate passive loss to the extent of passive net income)]

FIGURE 9-2 Filled-In Form 8582

Form **8582**	**Passive Activity Loss Limitations**	OMB No. 1545-1008

Department of the Treasury
Internal Revenue Service (99)

▶ See separate instructions.
▶ Attach to Form 1040 or Form 1041.

2005
Attachment Sequence No. **88**

Name(s) shown on return: Derrick Smart

Identifying number: 421-68-5546

Part I   2005 Passive Activity Loss

Caution: *Complete Worksheets 1, 2, and 3 on page 2 before completing Part I.*

Rental Real Estate Activities With Active Participation (For the definition of active participation see **Special Allowance for Rental Real Estate Activities** on page 3 of the instructions.)

1a	Activities with net income (enter the amount from Worksheet 1, column (a))	**1a**	
b	Activities with net loss (enter the amount from Worksheet 1, column (b))	**1b** (20,000 00)	
c	Prior years unallowed losses (enter the amount from Worksheet 1, column (c))	**1c** ( )	
d	Combine lines 1a, 1b, and 1c		**1d** (20,000 00)

Commercial Revitalization Deductions From Rental Real Estate Activities

2a	Commercial revitalization deductions from Worksheet 2, column (a)	**2a** ( )	
b	Prior year unallowed commercial revitalization deductions from Worksheet 2, column (b)	**2b** ( )	
c	Add lines 2a and 2b		**2c** ( )

All Other Passive Activities

3a	Activities with net income (enter the amount from Worksheet 3, column (a))	**3a** 10,000 00	
b	Activities with net loss (enter the amount from Worksheet 3, column (b))	**3b** ( )	
c	Prior years unallowed losses (enter the amount from Worksheet 3, column (c))	**3c** ( )	
d	Combine lines 3a, 3b, and 3c		**3d** 10,000 00

4	Combine lines 1d, 2c, and 3d. If the result is net income or zero, all losses are allowed, including any prior year unallowed losses entered on line 1c, 2b, or 3c. **Do not** complete Form 8582. Report the losses on the forms and schedules normally used	**4**	(10,000 00)

If line 4 is a loss and: • Line 1d is a loss, go to Part II.
• Line 2c is a loss (and line 1d is zero or more), skip Part II and go to Part III.
• Line 3d is a loss (and lines 1d and 2c are zero or more), skip Parts II and III and go to line 15.

Caution: *If your filing status is married filing separately and you lived with your spouse at any time during the year, **do not** complete Part II or Part III. Instead, go to line 15.*

Part II   Special Allowance for Rental Real Estate With Active Participation

Note: *Enter all numbers in Part II as positive amounts. See page 8 of the instructions for an example.*

5	Enter the **smaller** of the loss on line 1d or the loss on line 4		**5** 10,000 00
6	Enter $150,000. If married filing separately, see page 8	**6** 150,000 00	
7	Enter modified adjusted gross income, but not less than zero (see page 8)	**7** 135,000 00	
	Note: *If line 7 is greater than or equal to line 6, skip lines 8 and 9, enter -0- on line 10. Otherwise, go to line 8.*		
8	Subtract line 7 from line 6	**8** 15,000 00	
9	Multiply line 8 by 50% (.5). **Do not** enter more than $25,000. If married filing separately, see page 8		**9** 7,500 00
10	Enter the **smaller** of line 5 or line 9		**10** 7,500 00

If line 2c is a loss, go to Part III. Otherwise, go to line 15.

Part III   Special Allowance for Commercial Revitalization Deductions From Rental Real Estate Activities

Note: *Enter all numbers in Part III as positive amounts. See the example for Part II on page 8 of the instructions.*

11	Enter $25,000 reduced by the amount, if any, on line 10. If married filing separately, see instructions	**11**
12	Enter the loss from line 4	**12**
13	Reduce line 12 by the amount on line 10	**13**
14	Enter the **smallest** of line 2c (treated as a positive amount), line 11, or line 13	**14**

Part IV   Total Losses Allowed

15	Add the income, if any, on lines 1a and 3a and enter the total	**15** 10,000 00
16	**Total losses allowed from all passive activities for 2005.** Add lines 10, 14, and 15. See pages 10 and 11 of the instructions to find out how to report the losses on your tax return	**16** 17,500 00

For Paperwork Reduction Act Notice, see page 12 of the instructions.   Cat. No. 63704F   Form **8582** (2005)

FIGURE 9-2   Schedule E to Accompany Filled-In Form 8582

SCHEDULE E (Form 1040) Department of the Treasury Internal Revenue Service (99)	**Supplemental Income and Loss** (From rental real estate, royalties, partnerships, S corporations, estates, trusts, REMICs, etc.) ► Attach to Form 1040 or Form 1041. ► See Instructions for Schedule E (Form 1040).	OMB No. 1545-0074 2005 Attachment Sequence No. **13**

Name(s) shown on return: Derrick Smart   Your social security number: 421 68 5546

Part I   **Income or Loss From Rental Real Estate and Royalties**   Note. If you are in the business of renting personal property, use **Schedule C** or **C-EZ** (see page E-3). Report farm rental income or loss from **Form 4835** on page 2, line 40.

1 List the type and location of each **rental real estate property**:

A   Condominium, 1802 Eighth Street #207
    Danville, IL 60529

B

C

2 For each rental real estate property listed on line 1, did you or your family use it during the tax year for personal purposes for more than the greater of:
- 14 days **or**
- 10% of the total days rented at fair rental value?
(See page E-3.)

	Yes	No
A		X
B		
C		

Income:			**Properties**				**Totals** (Add columns A, B, and C.)
		A	B	C			
3 Rents received	3	7,800 00			3	7,800 00
4 Royalties received	4				4	
Expenses:						
5 Advertising	5					
6 Auto and travel (see page E-4)	6					
7 Cleaning and maintenance	7	1,600 00				
8 Commissions	8					
9 Insurance	9	140 00				
10 Legal and other professional fees	10					
11 Management fees	11					
12 Mortgage interest paid to banks, etc. (see page E-4)	12	11,700 00			12	11,700 00
13 Other interest	13					
14 Repairs	14	3,100 00				
15 Supplies	15					
16 Taxes	16	2,950 00				
17 Utilities	17	1,620 00				
18 Other (list) ► Condo Association Fees	18	1,880 00				
19 Add lines 5 through 18	19	22,990 00			19	22,990 00
20 Depreciation expense or depletion (see page E-4)	20	4,810 00			20	4,810 00
21 Total expenses. Add lines 19 and 20	21	27,800 00				
22 Income or (loss) from rental real estate or royalty properties. Subtract line 21 from line 3 (rents) or line 4 (royalties). If the result is a (loss), see page E-4 to find out if you must file **Form 6198**	22	(20,000 00)				
23 Deductible rental real estate loss. **Caution.** Your rental real estate loss on line 22 may be limited. See page E-4 to find out if you must file **Form 8582**. Real estate professionals must complete line 43 on page 2	23	(17,500 00)	( )	( )		

24 **Income.** Add positive amounts shown on line 22. **Do not** include any losses .... | 24 |

25 **Losses.** Add royalty losses from line 22 and rental real estate losses from line 23. Enter total losses here | 25 | (17,500 00) |

26 **Total rental real estate and royalty income or (loss).** Combine lines 24 and 25. Enter the result here. If Parts II, III, IV, and line 40 on page 2 do not apply to you, also enter this amount on Form 1040, line 17. Otherwise, include this amount in the total on line 41 on page 2 .... | 26 | (17,500 00) |

For Paperwork Reduction Act Notice, see Form 1040 instructions.   Cat. No. 11344L   Schedule E (Form 1040) 2005

QUESTIONS AND PROBLEMS

1. **Rental Income.** State the amount of rental income that must be reported on Schedule E for 2005 by each of the following taxpayers.

Taxpayer	Description	Amount
A	On November 30, 2005, the taxpayer receives $1,000 as a security deposit, $1,000 for the December rent, and an advance payment of $5,000 for an additional five months' of rent.	$_____
B	The taxpayer normally receives rent of $300 per month on the first of each month. In 2005, the tenant made $600 of improvements in lieu of two months' rent.	$_____
C	Rent of $1,200 is received when the taxpayer rents a personal residence to friends for 12 days during the Mardi Gras festivities.	$_____

2. **Rental Expenses.** State the maximum amount of rental expenses attributable to the property that can be claimed by each of the following taxpayers.

Taxpayer	Description	Amount
A	A dwelling unit is rented to a friend for $100 per month for two months and to an unrelated party for $275 per month for three months. Fair rental value is $275 per month.	$_____
B	A personal residence rented for 12 days during 2005 for a total of $300.	$_____

3. **Net Rental Income.** Derek Quinn owns a two-family home. He rents out the first floor and resides on the second floor. Each floor is of equal size. He incurred the following expenses attributable to the building for the year.

	Expenses For		
	Entire Building	First Floor	Second Floor
Depreciation	$4,000		
Real estate taxes	2,000		
Mortgage interest	1,600		
Utilities	1,200		
Repairs		$500	
Painting			$400

a. What portion of the expenses can Quinn deduct on Schedule E of Form 1040?

b. What portion of the expenses can Quinn take as itemized deductions on Schedule A of Form 1040?

4. **Net Rental Income.** Sandee Scott, a cash basis taxpayer, owns a house with two identical apartments. Scott resides in one apartment and rents out the other. The tenant made timely monthly rental payments of $500 for the months of January through November 2005. Rents for December 2005 and January 2006 were paid by the tenant on January 5, 2006. Scott incurred the following expenses relating to the building in 2005.

Utilities	$3,600
Depreciation of building	3,000
Maintenance and repairs (rental apartment)	400
Insurance on building	600

What amount should Scott report as net rental income for 2005?

5. **Vacation Homes.** Henry Schuller owns a fishing cabin in Wisconsin. Schuller offered the cabin for rent from June 1 through September 30, except for 16 days in August when his family used it. Schuller was unable to rent the cabin for two weeks (14 days) during the remaining rental period. At all other times, the cabin was rented.

a. Will Schuller's cabin be treated as a residence? Explain.

b. For purposes of allocating expenses, how many days of rental use and personal use does Schuller have?

6. **Vacation Homes.**

a. What is the tax advantage to having a vacation home treated as a residence?

b. What is the disadvantage to having a vacation home considered a residence?

7. **Vacation Homes.** During the year, Barry Barone (SSN 839-62-1444) rents his vacation home for 90 days and spends 60 days there. The vacation home is a townhome located at 610 Oak St. in Boulder, Colorado. Gross rental income from the property totals $6,000. Barone's expenses for the property are shown below.

Mortgage interest	$3,000
Real estate taxes	1,500
Utilities	800
Maintenance	900
Depreciation	4,000

Compute Barone's net rental income for the vacation home and complete his Schedule E.

8. **At-risk.**

   a. What is the significance of the at-risk rules?

   b. What activities are subject to the at-risk loss limitations?

9. **Passive Activities.**

   a. What types of trade or business activities are considered passive activities?

   b. Distinguish between material participation and active participation in rental activities. Explain the significance of this difference.

   c. Historically, dividend income and interest income have been treated as passive income. How are these categories of income treated in relation to the passive loss limitations?

(Use for Problem 7.)

SCHEDULE E	Supplemental Income and Loss	OMB No. 1545-0074
(Form 1040)	(From rental real estate, royalties, partnerships, S corporations, estates, trusts, REMICs, etc.)	**2005**
Department of the Treasury Internal Revenue Service (99)	▶ Attach to Form 1040 or Form 1041. ▶ See Instructions for Schedule E (Form 1040).	Attachment Sequence No. **13**

Name(s) shown on return   Your social security number

Part I   Income or Loss From Rental Real Estate and Royalties **Note.** If you are in the business of renting personal property, use **Schedule C** or **C-EZ** (see page E-3). Report farm rental income or loss from **Form 4835** on page 2, line 40.

1 List the type and location of each **rental real estate property:**

A ....

B ....

C ....

2 For each rental real estate property listed on line 1, did you or your family use it during the tax year for personal purposes for more than the greater of:
- 14 days **or**
- 10% of the total days rented at fair rental value?

(See page E-3.)

		Yes	No
A			
B			
C			

Income:

		Properties			Totals (Add columns A, B, and C.)
		A	B	C	
3	Rents received	3			3
4	Royalties received	4			4

Expenses:

5	Advertising	5				
6	Auto and travel (see page E-4)	6				
7	Cleaning and maintenance	7				
8	Commissions	8				
9	Insurance	9				
10	Legal and other professional fees	10				
11	Management fees	11				
12	Mortgage interest paid to banks, etc. (see page E-4)	12				12
13	Other interest	13				
14	Repairs	14				
15	Supplies	15				
16	Taxes	16				
17	Utilities	17				
18	Other (list) ▶	18				
19	Add lines 5 through 18	19				19
20	Depreciation expense or depletion (see page E-4)	20				20
21	Total expenses. Add lines 19 and 20	21				
22	Income or (loss) from rental real estate or royalty properties. Subtract line 21 from line 3 (rents) or line 4 (royalties). If the result is a (loss), see page E-4 to find out if you must file **Form 6198**	22				
23	Deductible rental real estate loss. **Caution.** Your rental real estate loss on line 22 may be limited. See page E-4 to find out if you must file **Form 8582.** Real estate professionals must complete line 43 on page 2	23 (	)(	)(	)	
24	**Income.** Add positive amounts shown on line 22. **Do not** include any losses					24
25	**Losses.** Add royalty losses from line 22 and rental real estate losses from line 23. Enter total losses here					25 ( )
26	**Total rental real estate and royalty income or (loss).** Combine lines 24 and 25. Enter the result here. If Parts II, III, IV, and line 40 on page 2 do not apply to you, also enter this amount on Form 1040, line 17. Otherwise, include this amount in the total on line 41 on page 2					26

For Paperwork Reduction Act Notice, see Form 1040 instructions.   Cat. No. 11344L   Schedule E (Form 1040) 2005

10. Passive Activities. A taxpayer owned four passive activities. Net income (loss) for each activity is shown below.

Passive Activity	Gross Income	Deductions	Net Income (or Loss)
A	$12,000	$ 8,000	$14,000
B	20,000	32,000	(12,000)
C	3,000	6,000	(3,000)
D	14,000	12,000	2,000

a. What is the amount of passive loss that can offset passive income in the current year?

b. What is the amount of passive loss that can be carried forward for each activity?

11. Rental Real Estate. Mark and Martha Matthews report $130,000 of AGI before considering a $22,000 loss from rental real estate activities in which they actively participate. The Matthewses own more than 10% of the activity. What amount of the loss can the Matthewses deduct on their joint return?

12. Rental Real Estate. Bobby Southworth actively participates in three different rental real estate activities. His ownership in each activity exceeds 10%. Southworth's income and losses from these activities are shown below.

Activity	Income (or Loss)
X	($10,000)
Y	(30,000)
Z	9,000

Southworth has AGI of $80,000 before consideration of the rental real estate activities. Calculate his loss allowed and any suspended losses.

a. Loss allowed   _____

b. Suspended loss   _____

13. **Passive Activities.** Bob Jefferson owns three passive activities, none of which involve rental real estate. As of January 1, 2005, the suspended losses on these activities included the following:

Activity	Suspended Losses
X	($20,000)
Y	(30,000)
Z	0

In 2005 his passive activities generated the following income and losses during the year:

Activity	Income (or Loss)
X	$ 10,000
Y	(10,000)
Z	20,000

How will Jefferson report the results of his activities for 2005?

14. **Rental Real Estate, Active Participation.** In 1990, Jeremy L. Schultz (SSN 678-88-5244) paid $90,000 for a townhouse purchased as an investment. The townhouse is located at 812 E. Locust, Springfield, MO. During 2005, Schultz received $9,600 in rental income from the tenants and paid the following expenses:

Association dues	$ 400
Insurance	130
Mortgage interest	6,200
Real estate taxes	1,100
Repairs	320
Utilities	440

Schultz actively participates in the rental of the townhome. Schultz's AGI before considering the income and expenses from the rental property is $140,000. He depreciates the townhouse using MACRS (straight-line over 27.5 years). Prepare Schedule E and Form 8582 using the forms provided on pages 9–25 and 9–26.

15. **Internet Problem: Researching Publication 925.**

The chapter discussed two ways to meet the material participation test: (1) participate in the activity for more than 500 hours during the year, and (2) participate in the activity for more than 100 hours during the year and have that participation be at least as much as the participation by all other individuals, including employees. There are several other ways in which to meet the material participation test.

Go to the IRS Web site. Locate Publication 925 and find the appropriate page that lists all the various ways to meet the material participation test. Print out a copy of the page where you found your answer. Underline or highlight the pertinent information.

See Appendix A for instructions on use of the IRS Web site.

(Use for Problem 14:)

SCHEDULE E (Form 1040)	Supplemental Income and Loss	OMB No. 1545-0074

SCHEDULE E (Form 1040)
Department of the Treasury
Internal Revenue Service (99)

Supplemental Income and Loss
(From rental real estate, royalties, partnerships, S corporations, estates, trusts, REMICs, etc.)
► **Attach to Form 1040 or Form 1041.**   ► See Instructions for Schedule E (Form 1040).

OMB No. 1545-0074
2005
Attachment Sequence No. **13**

Name(s) shown on return

Your social security number

Part I   **Income or Loss From Rental Real Estate and Royalties**   **Note.** If you are in the business of renting personal property, use **Schedule C** or **C-EZ** (see page E-3). Report farm rental income or loss from **Form 4835** on page 2, line 40.

1 List the type and location of each **rental real estate property:**
A
B
C

2 For each rental real estate property listed on line 1, did you or your family use it during the tax year for personal purposes for more than the greater of:
● 14 days **or**
● 10% of the total days rented at fair rental value?
(See page E-3.)

	Yes	No
A		
B		
C		

Income:

		Properties A	B	C	Totals (Add columns A, B, and C.)
3 Rents received	3				3
4 Royalties received	4				4

Expenses:

5 Advertising	5				
6 Auto and travel (see page E-4)	6				
7 Cleaning and maintenance	7				
8 Commissions	8				
9 Insurance	9				
10 Legal and other professional fees	10				
11 Management fees	11				
12 Mortgage interest paid to banks, etc. (see page E-4)	12				12
13 Other interest	13				
14 Repairs	14				
15 Supplies	15				
16 Taxes	16				
17 Utilities	17				
18 Other (list) ►	18				
19 Add lines 5 through 18	19				19
20 Depreciation expense or depletion (see page E-4)	20				20
21 Total expenses. Add lines 19 and 20	21				
22 Income or (loss) from rental real estate or royalty properties. Subtract line 21 from line 3 (rents) or line 4 (royalties). If the result is a (loss), see page E-4 to find out if you must file **Form 6198**	22				
23 Deductible rental real estate loss. **Caution.** Your rental real estate loss on line 22 may be limited. See page E-4 to find out if you must file **Form 8582**. Real estate professionals must complete line 43 on page 2	23	( )(	)(	)	

24 **Income.** Add positive amounts shown on line 22. **Do not** include any losses | **24** | |
25 **Losses.** Add royalty losses from line 22 and rental real estate losses from line 23. Enter total losses here | **25** | ( )|
26 **Total rental real estate and royalty income or (loss).** Combine lines 24 and 25. Enter the result here. If Parts II, III, IV, and line 40 on page 2 do not apply to you, also enter this amount on Form 1040, line 17. Otherwise, include this amount in the total on line 41 on page 2 | **26** | |

For Paperwork Reduction Act Notice, see Form 1040 instructions.   Cat. No. 11344L   Schedule E (Form 1040) 2005

(Use for Problem 14.)

Form **8582**	Passive Activity Loss Limitations	OMB No. 1545-1008
Department of the Treasury Internal Revenue Service (99)	► See separate instructions. ► Attach to Form 1040 or Form 1041.	**2005** Attachment Sequence No. **88**

Name(s) shown on return		Identifying number

Part I — **2005 Passive Activity Loss**
Caution: *Complete Worksheets 1, 2, and 3 on page 2 before completing Part I.*

Rental Real Estate Activities With Active Participation (For the definition of active participation see **Special Allowance for Rental Real Estate Activities** on page 3 of the instructions.)

1a Activities with net income (enter the amount from Worksheet 1, column (a))	**1a**		
b Activities with net loss (enter the amount from Worksheet 1, column (b))	**1b** ( )		
c Prior years unallowed losses (enter the amount from Worksheet 1, column (c))	**1c** ( )		
d Combine lines 1a, 1b, and 1c.		**1d**	

Commercial Revitalization Deductions From Rental Real Estate Activities

2a Commercial revitalization deductions from Worksheet 2, column (a)	**2a** ( )	
b Prior year unallowed commercial revitalization deductions from Worksheet 2, column (b)	**2b** ( )	
c Add lines 2a and 2b		**2c** ( )

All Other Passive Activities

3a Activities with net income (enter the amount from Worksheet 3, column (a))	**3a**	
b Activities with net loss (enter the amount from Worksheet 3, column (b))	**3b** ( )	
c Prior years unallowed losses (enter the amount from Worksheet 3, column (c))	**3c** ( )	
d Combine lines 3a, 3b, and 3c.		**3d**

4 Combine lines 1d, 2c, and 3d. If the result is net income or zero, all losses are allowed, including any prior year unallowed losses entered on line 1c, 2b, or 3c. **Do not** complete Form 8582. Report the losses on the forms and schedules normally used . . . . | **4** |

If line 4 is a loss and:
- Line 1d is a loss, go to Part II.
- Line 2c is a loss (and line 1d is zero or more), skip Part II and go to Part III.
- Line 3d is a loss (and lines 1d and 2c are zero or more), skip Parts II and III and go to line 15.

Caution: *If your filing status is married filing separately and you lived with your spouse at any time during the year, do not complete Part II or Part III. Instead, go to line 15.*

Part II — **Special Allowance for Rental Real Estate With Active Participation**
Note: *Enter all numbers in Part II as positive amounts. See page 8 of the instructions for an example.*

5 Enter the **smaller** of the loss on line 1d or the loss on line 4	**5**	
6 Enter $150,000. If married filing separately, see page 8 . . .	**6**	
7 Enter modified adjusted gross income, but not less than zero (see page 8)	**7**	
Note: *If line 7 is greater than or equal to line 6, skip lines 8 and 9, enter -0- on line 10. Otherwise, go to line 8.*		
8 Subtract line 7 from line 6	**8**	
9 Multiply line 8 by 50% (.5). **Do not** enter more than $25,000. If married filing separately, see page 8	**9**
10 Enter the **smaller** of line 5 or line 9	**10**
If line 2c is a loss, go to Part III. Otherwise, go to line 15.	

Part III — **Special Allowance for Commercial Revitalization Deductions From Rental Real Estate Activities**
Note: *Enter all numbers in Part III as positive amounts. See the example for Part II on page 8 of the instructions.*

11 Enter $25,000 reduced by the amount, if any, on line 10. If married filing separately, see instructions	**11**
12 Enter the loss from line 4	**12**
13 Reduce line 12 by the amount on line 10	**13**
14 Enter the **smallest** of line 2c (treated as a positive amount), line 11, or line 13	**14**

Part IV — **Total Losses Allowed**

15 Add the income, if any, on lines 1a and 3a and enter the total.	**15**
16 **Total losses allowed from all passive activities for 2005.** Add lines 10, 14, and 15. See pages 10 and 11 of the instructions to find out how to report the losses on your tax return .	**16**

For Paperwork Reduction Act Notice, see page 12 of the instructions.   Cat. No. 63704F   Form **8582** (2005)

16. Business Entity Problem: This problem is designed for those using the "business entity" approach. The solution may require information from Chapter 14.

The Hampton-Lewis Partnership owns an apartment building. Gross income from the apartments was $200,000. Total deductions were $260,000. The two partners share profits and losses equally.

a. How will the partnership report the resulting $60,000 loss?

b. If Hampton-Lewis was an S corporation, how would the loss be reported?

c. If Hampton-Lewis was a regular C corporation, how would the loss be reported?

COMPREHENSIVE PROBLEM

17. On January 2, 1995, Janis R. Jetson (SSN 344-46-5768), a cash basis taxpayer, purchased a two-unit apartment building at 1626 Flat Street, Detroit, Michigan 48270-8224. The costs of the land and building were $10,000 and $41,250, respectively. Jetson depreciates the building using the straight-line method over 27.5 years. Both apartments are the same size, with one on the ground floor and the other upstairs. Jetson has lived in the upstairs apartment since she acquired the building. The tenant in the ground-floor apartment at the time the building was purchased has continued to rent from Jetson. The tenant pays $350 a month in rent. On June 30 the tenant moved out. The apartment was vacant until August 1, even though Jetson advertised and attempted to rent it. On August 1, a new tenant moved in, paying rent of $400 per month. Rent is due on the first day of the month. Information on the apartment follows:

Revenue

Rent from the first tenant (6 months @ $350)	$2,100
Rent from the second tenant (5 months @ $400)	2,000
Total revenue	$4,100

Expenses

Entire house:

Real estate taxes	$1,700
Janitor and yard work	160
Electricity and water	440
Repairs	300
Heat (gas)	800
Interest on mortgage	1,100
Insurance	376
Expenses other than depreciation	$4,876

Ground-floor apartment:

Advertising	100
Painting and papering	420
Repairs	70
	$ 590

Upstairs apartment:

Repairs	$ 90
Cleaning and maintenance	480
	$ 570

In addition to the rental property, Jetson works as an administrative assistant and earned $17,600 in wages. From this amount, $1,080 of federal income tax was withheld. Jetson also earned $147 in interest from Bank of America. Jetson is single and has no dependents. She does not want to contribute $3 to the presidential campaign fund.

Prepare Form 1040 and Schedule E, Supplemental Income and Loss, reproduced on pages 9-29 to 9-31.

(Use for Problem 17.)

Form 1040 Department of the Treasury—Internal Revenue Service
U.S. Individual Income Tax Return **2005** (99) IRS Use Only—Do not write or staple in this space.

For the year Jan. 1–Dec. 31, 2005, or other tax year beginning , 2005, ending , 20 | OMB No. 1545-0074

Label (See instructions on page 16.) **Use the IRS label.** Otherwise, please print or type.

L A B E L   H E R E

Your first name and initial | Last name | Your social security number

If a joint return, spouse's first name and initial | Last name | Spouse's social security number

Home address (number and street). If you have a P.O. box, see page 16. | Apt. no.

▲ You **must** enter your SSN(s) above. ▲

City, town or post office, state, and ZIP code. If you have a foreign address, see page 16.

Checking a box below will not change your tax or refund.

Presidential Election Campaign ▶ Check here if you, or your spouse if filing jointly, want $3 to go to this fund (see page 16) ▶ ☐ **You** ☐ **Spouse**

Filing Status

Check only one box.

1 ☐ Single
2 ☐ Married filing jointly (even if only one had income)
3 ☐ Married filing separately. Enter spouse's SSN above and full name here. ▶
4 ☐ Head of household (with qualifying person). (See page 17.) If the qualifying person is a child but not your dependent, enter this child's name here. ▶
5 ☐ Qualifying widow(er) with dependent child (see page 17)

Exemptions

6a ☐ **Yourself.** If someone can claim you as a dependent, **do not** check box 6a
b ☐ **Spouse**

c **Dependents:**

(1) First name Last name	(2) Dependent's social security number	(3) Dependent's relationship to you	(4) ✓ if qualifying child for child tax credit (see page 18)
			☐
			☐
			☐
			☐

If more than four dependents, see page 18.

Boxes checked on 6a and 6b
No. of children on 6c who:
• lived with you
• did not live with you due to divorce or separation (see page 18)
Dependents on 6c not entered above
Add numbers on lines above ▶

d Total number of exemptions claimed

Income

Attach Form(s) W-2 here. Also attach Forms W-2G and 1099-R if tax was withheld.

If you did not get a W-2, see page 19.

Enclose, but do not attach, any payment. Also, please use Form 1040-V.

7 Wages, salaries, tips, etc. Attach Form(s) W-2 | 7
8a Taxable interest. Attach Schedule B if required | 8a
b Tax-exempt interest. **Do not** include on line 8a | 8b
9a Ordinary dividends. Attach Schedule B if required | 9a
b Qualified dividends (see page 20) | 9b
10 Taxable refunds, credits, or offsets of state and local income taxes (see page 20) | 10
11 Alimony received | 11
12 Business income or (loss). Attach Schedule C or C-EZ | 12
13 Capital gain or (loss). Attach Schedule D if required. If not required, check here ▶ ☐ | 13
14 Other gains or (losses). Attach Form 4797 | 14
15a IRA distributions | 15a | b Taxable amount (see page 22) | 15b
16a Pensions and annuities | 16a | b Taxable amount (see page 22) | 16b
17 Rental real estate, royalties, partnerships, S corporations, trusts, etc. Attach Schedule E | 17
18 Farm income or (loss). Attach Schedule F | 18
19 Unemployment compensation | 19
20a Social security benefits | 20a | b Taxable amount (see page 24) | 20b
21 Other income. List type and amount (see page 24) | 21
22 Add the amounts in the far right column for lines 7 through 21. This is your **total income** ▶ | 22

Adjusted Gross Income

23 Educator expenses (see page 26) | 23
24 Certain business expenses of reservists, performing artists, and fee-basis government officials. Attach Form 2106 or 2106-EZ | 24
25 Health savings account deduction. Attach Form 8889 | 25
26 Moving expenses. Attach Form 3903 | 26
27 One-half of self-employment tax. Attach Schedule SE | 27
28 Self-employed SEP, SIMPLE, and qualified plans | 28
29 Self-employed health insurance deduction (see page XX) | 29
30 Penalty on early withdrawal of savings | 30
31a Alimony paid b Recipient's SSN ▶ | 31a
32 IRA deduction (see page XX) | 32
33 Student loan interest deduction (see page XX) | 33
34 Tuition and fees deduction (see page XX) | 34
35 Domestic production activities deduction. Attach Form 8903 | 35
36 Add lines 23 through 31a and 32 through 35 | 36
37 Subtract line 36 from line 22. This is your **adjusted gross income** ▶ | 37

For Disclosure, Privacy Act, and Paperwork Reduction Act Notice, see page 75. | Cat. No. 11320B | Form **1040** (2005)

(Use for Problem 17.)

Form 1040 (2005)   Page **2**

Tax and Credits	38	Amount from line 37 (adjusted gross income)		38	
	39a	Check if: ☐ **You** were born before January 2, 1941, ☐ Blind. ☐ **Spouse** was born before January 2, 1941, ☐ Blind. **Total boxes checked** ▶ 39a			
Standard Deduction for—	b	If your spouse itemizes on a separate return or you were a dual-status alien, see page 31 and check here ▶ 39b ☐			
	40	**Itemized deductions** (from Schedule A) **or** your **standard deduction** (see left margin) .		40	
• People who checked any box on line 39a or 39b **or** who can be claimed as a dependent, see page 31.	41	Subtract line 40 from line 38		41	
	42	If line 38 is $109,475 or less, multiply $3,200 by the total number of exemptions claimed on line 6d. If line 38 is over $109,475, see the worksheet on page 33		42	
	43	**Taxable income.** Subtract line 42 from line 41. If line 42 is more than line 41, enter -0- .		43	
	44	**Tax** (see page 33). Check if any tax is from: **a** ☐ Form(s) 8814 **b** ☐ Form 4972 . .		44	
	45	**Alternative minimum tax** (see page 35). Attach Form 6251		45	
• All others:	46	Add lines 44 and 45 . . . . ▶		46	
Single or Married filing separately, $5,000	47	Foreign tax credit. Attach Form 1116 if required . . .	47		
	48	Credit for child and dependent care expenses. Attach Form 2441	48		
Married filing jointly or Qualifying widow(er), $10,000	49	Credit for the elderly or the disabled. Attach Schedule R	49		
	50	Education credits. Attach Form 8863	50		
	51	Retirement savings contributions credit. Attach Form 8880 .	51		
	52	Child tax credit (see page 37). Attach Form 8901 if required	52		
Head of household, $7,300	53	Adoption credit. Attach Form 8839	53		
	54	Credits from: **a** ☐ Form 8396 **b** ☐ Form 8859 . .	54		
	55	Other credits. Check applicable box(es): **a** ☐ Form 3800 **b** ☐ Form 8801 **c** ☐ Specify	55		
	56	Add lines 47 through 55. These are your **total credits**		56	
	57	Subtract line 56 from line 46. If line 56 is more than line 46, enter -0- . . . . . ▶		57	
Other Taxes	58	Self-employment tax. Attach Schedule SE		58	
	59	Social security and Medicare tax on tip income not reported to employer. Attach Form 4137 . .		59	
	60	Additional tax on IRAs, other qualified retirement plans, etc. Attach Form 5329 if required		60	
	61	Advance earned income credit payments from Form(s) W-2		61	
	62	Household employment taxes. Attach Schedule H		62	
	63	Add lines 57 through 62. This is your **total tax** . . . . ▶		63	
Payments	64	Federal income tax withheld from Forms W-2 and 1099 . .	64		
	65	2005 estimated tax payments and amount applied from 2004 return	65		
If you have a qualifying child, attach Schedule EIC.	66a	**Earned income credit (EIC)**	66a		
	b	Nontaxable combat pay election ▶	66b		
	67	Excess social security and tier 1 RRTA tax withheld (see page 54)	67		
	68	Additional child tax credit. Attach Form 8812	68		
	69	Amount paid with request for extension to file (see page 54)	69		
	70	Payments from: **a** ☐ Form 2439 **b** ☐ Form 4136 **c** ☐ Form 8885	70		
	71	Add lines 64, 65, 66a, and 67 through 70. These are your **total payments** . . . . ▶		71	
Refund Direct deposit? See page 54 and fill in 73b, 73c, and 73d.	72	If line 71 is more than line 63, subtract line 63 from line 71. This is the amount you **overpaid**		72	
	73a	Amount of line 72 you want **refunded to you** . . . . ▶		73a	
	▶ b	Routing number ⎹⎹⎹⎹⎹⎹⎹⎹⎹ ▶ **c** Type: ☐ Checking ☐ Savings			
	▶ d	Account number ⎹⎹⎹⎹⎹⎹⎹⎹⎹⎹⎹⎹⎹⎹⎹⎹			
	74	Amount of line 72 you want **applied to your 2006 estimated tax** ▶	74		
Amount You Owe	75	**Amount you owe.** Subtract line 71 from line 63. For details on how to pay, see page 55 ▶		75	
	76	Estimated tax penalty (see page 55)	76		

Third Party Designee	Do you want to allow another person to discuss this return with the IRS (see page 56)? ☐ **Yes.** Complete the following. ☐ **No**
	Designee's name ▶ Phone no. ▶ ( ) Personal identification number (PIN) ▶ ⎹⎹⎹⎹⎹

Sign Here Joint return? See page 17. Keep a copy for your records.	Under penalties of perjury, I declare that I have examined this return and accompanying schedules and statements, and to the best of my knowledge and belief, they are true, correct, and complete. Declaration of preparer (other than taxpayer) is based on all information of which preparer has any knowledge.
	Your signature Date Your occupation Daytime phone number ( )
	Spouse's signature. If a joint return, **both** must sign. Date Spouse's occupation

Paid Preparer's Use Only	Preparer's signature ▶ Date Check if self-employed ☐ Preparer's SSN or PTIN
	Firm's name (or yours if self-employed), address, and ZIP code ▶ EIN Phone no. ( )

Form **1040** (2005)

♻ *Printed on recycled paper*

(Use for Problem 17.)

SCHEDULE E (Form 1040) Department of the Treasury Internal Revenue Service (99)	Supplemental Income and Loss (From rental real estate, royalties, partnerships, S corporations, estates, trusts, REMICs, etc.) ► Attach to Form 1040 or Form 1041. ► See Instructions for Schedule E (Form 1040).	OMB No. 1545-0074 **2005** Attachment Sequence No. **13**

Name(s) shown on return | Your social security number

Part I   **Income or Loss From Rental Real Estate and Royalties**   **Note.** If you are in the business of renting personal property, use **Schedule C** or **C-EZ** (see page E-3). Report farm rental income or loss from **Form 4835** on page 2, line 40.

1 List the type and location of each **rental real estate property:**

A _____
B _____
C _____

2 For each rental real estate property listed on line 1, did you or your family use it during the tax year for personal purposes for more than the greater of:
- 14 days **or**
- 10% of the total days rented at fair rental value?

(See page E-3.)

	Yes	No
A		
B		
C		

Income:

		Properties A	B	C	Totals (Add columns A, B, and C.)
3	Rents received	3			3
4	Royalties received	4			4

Expenses:

5	Advertising	5			
6	Auto and travel (see page E-4)	6			
7	Cleaning and maintenance	7			
8	Commissions	8			
9	Insurance	9			
10	Legal and other professional fees	10			
11	Management fees	11			
12	Mortgage interest paid to banks, etc. (see page E-4)	12			12
13	Other interest	13			
14	Repairs	14			
15	Supplies	15			
16	Taxes	16			
17	Utilities	17			
18	Other (list) ► _____ _____ _____ _____	18			
19	Add lines 5 through 18	19			19
20	Depreciation expense or depletion (see page E-4)	20			20
21	Total expenses. Add lines 19 and 20	21			
22	Income or (loss) from rental real estate or royalty properties. Subtract line 21 from line 3 (rents) or line 4 (royalties). If the result is a (loss), see page E-4 to find out if you must file **Form 6198**	22			
23	Deductible rental real estate loss. **Caution.** Your rental real estate loss on line 22 may be limited. See page E-4 to find out if you must file **Form 8582.** Real estate professionals must complete line 43 on page 2	23 (	)(	)(	)
24	**Income.** Add positive amounts shown on line 22. **Do not** include any losses			24	
25	**Losses.** Add royalty losses from line 22 and rental real estate losses from line 23. Enter total losses here			25 (	)
26	**Total rental real estate and royalty income or (loss).** Combine lines 24 and 25. Enter the result here. If Parts II, III, IV, and line 40 on page 2 do not apply to you, also enter this amount on Form 1040, line 17. Otherwise, include this amount in the total on line 41 on page 2			26	

For Paperwork Reduction Act Notice, see Form 1040 instructions.   Cat. No. 11344L   Schedule E (Form 1040) 2005

10

Property: Basis and Nontaxable Exchanges

CHAPTER CONTENTS

■■ CHAPTER OVERVIEW

When taxpayers sell or otherwise dispose of property, a gain or loss usually results. This chapter explains how taxpayers compute gains and losses when they dispose of property. It also explains which gains and losses taxpayers report on the tax return. The chapter begins by presenting the formula used to compute realized gains and losses when disposing of property. Realized gains and losses reflect the taxpayer's economic gain or loss from the transaction. To compute the realized gain or loss, taxpayers compare the amount realized from the transaction to their adjusted basis in the property. When the amount realized exceeds the adjusted basis, a realized gain results. A realized loss occurs when the amount realized is less than the adjusted basis. The rules for computing amount realized and adjusted basis are presented in the chapter.

Although disposing of property results in a realized gain or loss, not all realized gains and losses are reported on the tax return. As a general rule, taxpayers are taxed on all realized gains but can deduct only realized losses that result from the disposal of investment or business property. One exception to this rule involves property destroyed in a casualty or a theft. Although the general rule does not allow taxpayers to deduct losses from the disposal of personal-use property, Chapter 5 presented the rules for the (itemized) deduction for nonbusiness casualty or theft losses. Other exceptions are described later in the chapter.

REALIZED GAIN OR LOSS

Realized gains or losses occur when taxpayers sell, exchange, or otherwise dispose of property. They also occur when the government takes the taxpayer's property in a condemnation. When the amount realized from the transaction exceeds the adjusted basis in the property given up, the difference is a **realized gain.** When the adjusted basis exceeds the amount realized, the difference is a **realized loss.** Stated another way,

$$\text{Realized gain (loss)} = \text{Amount realized} - \text{Adjusted basis}$$

Amount Realized

The **amount realized** equals the sales price minus selling expenses. Selling expenses include commissions, legal fees, and other costs related to the sale. The sales price is the sum of the fair market value (FMV) of the property (which includes cash) and services received in return for the property given up. It also includes any debt of the taxpayer that the buyer assumes or pays off. (When the buyer assumes the taxpayer's debt, it is similar to the buyer giving the taxpayer cash that the taxpayer uses to pay off the debt.)

EXAMPLE 1

Howard Trier sells stock for $12,000 cash plus a car valued at $5,000. Trier's amount realized is $17,000 ($12,000 + $5,000).

EXAMPLE 2

Martha Simms exchanges land for a building that has a FMV of $90,000. The land is subject to a $50,000 mortgage, which the other party assumes. Simms's amount realized is $140,000 ($90,000 + $50,000).

Adjusted Basis

When disposing of property, the tax laws allow taxpayers to recover their investment in property tax free. **Basis** is the term used to describe the taxpayer's investment in property. Taxpayers realize a gain when the amount realized exceeds their basis in the property. If the entire basis is not recovered, taxpayers realize a loss for the unrecovered amount.

Between the time taxpayers acquire property and the time they dispose of it, events may occur that require taxpayers to adjust their basis in property. **Adjusted basis** is the term for the taxpayer's investment in property after making those adjustments. Adjusted basis can be stated as follows:

Adjusted basis = Initial basis in property + Capital additions − Capital recoveries

The initial basis of purchased property usually is its cost. However, taxpayers can acquire property in other ways, such as through gift or inheritance. The initial basis of a property depends on how the taxpayer acquired it. The rules for computing initial basis are presented later in the chapter.

Capital Additions

Capital additions include costs incurred in transferring or defending title to the property. Examples of such costs include commissions and legal fees. Capital additions also include the cost of improvements that increase the property's value, lengthen its useful life, or convert it to a different use. Improvements have a useful life that exceeds one year. Maintenance and repairs are not improvements since they are routine and recurring costs.

EXAMPLES OF IMPROVEMENTS

- Installing a new furnace
- Putting up a fence
- Paving a driveway
- Rebuilding a car engine
- Landscaping
- Building a recreation room in an unfinished basement
- Paying special assessments for sidewalks, roads, etc.
- Adding a room onto a house

Capital Recoveries

Capital recoveries are a return of the taxpayer's investment in property. They occur when taxpayers receive money or take tax deductions in connection with the property. Any time taxpayers recover part of their investment in property prior to disposing of it, they must reduce their basis in the property accordingly. When property is damaged in a casualty, taxpayers reduce their basis in the property by the amount of proceeds they receive from the insurance company. The basis then increases by amounts spent to restore the property. The same basis reduction rule applies to amounts taxpayers receive from the government for the right to use part of their property (known as an easement). The amounts taxpayers receive from the insurance company or from the government represent a return of their initial investment in the property. After receiving these amounts, the taxpayer has less invested in the property. Thus, the taxpayer's basis (investment) in the property must be reduced accordingly.

EXAMPLE 3

In 1990 Ralph Cuthbert paid $120,000 for land. In the current year, Cuthbert receives $20,000 from the government in exchange for the right to use part of the land. Cuthbert must reduce his basis in the land by $20,000. Although Cuthbert initially paid $120,000 for the land, after receiving $20,000 from the government, his net investment is $100,000. Cuthbert's adjusted basis in the land equals $100,000 ($120,000 initial basis − $20,000 capital recovery).

Taxpayers also reduce the basis in property by amounts deducted on the tax return in connection with the property. This includes amounts deducted for casualty or theft losses. It also includes amounts deducted for Section 179 and depreciation expense.

EXAMPLE 4

In 1993 Lisa Lee paid $62,000 for a building. Lee spent $10,000 in 1999 for a new roof. In 2005 a fire damaged the building. The insurance company paid Lee $20,000 for the loss. Lee claimed a $10,000 casualty loss deduction on her 2005 tax return for the unreimbursed portion of the loss. In 2005 Lee spent $29,000 to rebuild the part of the building destroyed in the fire. Over the years, Lee has deducted $22,000 for depreciation on the building. Lee computes the adjusted basis in the building as follows.

Initial basis in the building		$62,000
Plus capital additions:		
Improvements	$10,000	
Restoration costs	29,000	39,000
Less capital recoveries:		
Depreciation	$22,000	
Insurance proceeds	20,000	
Casualty loss	10,000	(52,000)
Adjusted basis in the building		$49,000

INITIAL BASIS

When computing their adjusted basis in property, taxpayers start with the initial basis. The initial basis of purchased property is its cost. However, taxpayers can acquire property through other means, such as through gifts, inheritances, and divorce settlements.

Property Acquired by Purchase

The initial basis of purchased property is its cost (what the taxpayer gives up to buy the property). It includes amounts taxpayers borrow to buy the property. It also includes any costs incurred to acquire clear title or make the property ready for use. Examples of such costs include the following:

1. Sales or excise taxes paid on the purchase
2. Title insurance and survey costs
3. Expenses paid to deliver, install, and test the property
4. Recording, legal, and accounting fees

EXAMPLE 5

Burt Compall buys real estate, paying $50,000 cash and assuming the seller's $75,000 mortgage on the property. Compall's initial basis is $125,000 ($50,000 + $75,000).

EXAMPLE 6

Kelly Hall purchases a machine for $10,000. Hall pays $600 in sales tax and $400 for delivery and installation. Hall's initial basis in the machine equals $11,000 ($10,000 + $600 + $400).

When the taxpayer performs services in exchange for property, the initial basis in the property is the value of the services the taxpayer includes in income.

EXAMPLE 7

Al Barkin received ten shares of stock in exchange for services he rendered. The market value of the shares is $300. Barkin is taxed on $300 for his services. His initial basis in the shares is $300.

Bargain Purchases

Sometimes companies sell goods or other property to their employees for less than FMV. Often the employee reports the difference between the FMV and the purchase price as income on the tax return. In such cases, the employee's initial basis ends up the same as the FMV of the property since the initial basis includes amounts taxed as income. If the employee does not have to report any income from the bargain purchase (as in a qualified employee discount), then the employee's initial basis equals the amount paid for the property.

EXAMPLE 8

Frank Morgan pays $60 for property from a company where he is an employee. The FMV of the property is $100. Morgan reports the $40 difference between FMV and the purchase price on his tax return. Morgan's initial basis in the property equals $100 ($60 purchase price + $40 reported in income).

Basket Purchases

Sometimes a single purchase price buys more than one property. As we learned in Chapter 8, different depreciation rules can apply to different properties. Also, taxpayers may sell the properties at various times in the future. For these reasons, the purchase price must be allocated among the properties acquired. Taxpayers allocate the purchase price among the properties on the basis of their relative FMVs. The amount allocated to one property equals the purchase price times the ratio of the FMV of that property to the total FMV of all properties.

$$\text{Initial basis} = \text{Purchase price} \times \frac{\text{FMV of the property}}{\text{FMV of all properties}}$$

EXAMPLE 9

George Casteil pays $90,000 for land and a building. At the time of the purchase, the FMV of the land and building are $80,000 and $40,000, respectively. Casteil's basis in the land equals $60,000 [$90,000 × ($80,000/$120,000)]. The basis in the building equals $30,000 [$90,000 × ($40,000/$120,000)].

Property Received from a Spouse

When a taxpayer receives property from a spouse, the spouse's adjusted basis in the property carries over to the taxpayer. No tax consequences occur when property is transferred between spouses (or ex-spouses when the transfer is part of a divorce settlement).

Inherited Property

When a person dies, an executor is assigned to handle the decedent's property (known as the estate). Before distributing the estate to the decedent's heirs, the executor first computes the estate tax due. Estate tax is computed on the total fair market value of the decedent's estate. Estate tax is due only when the value of the estate exceeds a certain amount.

In computing the estate tax, the executor usually values the estate on the date of the decedent's death. However, under certain conditions, the executor can elect to value the estate six months later (known as the alternative valuation date). When the value of the estate is small enough such that no estate tax return is required, the heir's initial basis in the property is its FMV on the decedent's date of death (DOD). The heir's initial basis also is the FMV on the DOD if an estate tax return is required and the executor uses the DOD to value the estate. If an estate tax return is required and the executor values the estate on the alternative valuation date (AVD), then the heir's initial basis in the property is its FMV on the AVD or on the date it is distributed to the heir, whichever occurs first.

EXAMPLE 10

Rhonda Valdez inherited land from her grandfather, who died on April 5, 2005. On April 5, 2005, the land was valued at $45,000. On October 5, 2005, its value was $42,000. The land was distributed to Valdez on March 2, 2006. Valdez's basis in the land is $45,000 if either no estate tax return is required or the executor uses the DOD to value the grandfather's estate. If the AVD is used, Valdez's basis is $42,000 (since the AVD occurs before the date of distribution).

EXAMPLE 11

Assume the same facts as in Example 10, except that the land was distributed to Valdez on August 22, 2005, when its value was $43,000. If no estate tax return is filed or if the executor uses DOD to value the grandfather's estate, Valdez's basis in the land is $45,000. If the AVD is used, Valdez's basis is $43,000 (since the distribution date occurs first).

Gifted Property

Two sets of rules apply to property received as a gift. One set applies when, at the time of the gift, the FMV of the property exceeds the donor's adjusted basis in the property. Another set applies when the donor's adjusted basis exceeds the FMV of the property.

FMV Less Than Donor's Basis

If at the time of the gift the FMV of the property is less than the donor's (adjusted) basis, then the donee's basis in the property is not known until the donee (the person receiving the gifted property) disposes of the property. If the donee realizes a gain (the amount realized exceeds the donor's basis), then the donee's basis equals the donor's basis. If the donee realizes a loss (the amount realized is less than the FMV of the property at the time of the gift), then the donee's basis equals the FMV at the time of the gift. When the amount realized falls between the donor's basis and the FMV at the time of the gift, there is no gain or loss and the donee's basis equals the amount realized.

EXAMPLE 12

Joan Kemp receives stock as a gift. At the time of the gift, the stock was worth $15,000. The donor paid $20,000 for the stock. Kemp sells the stock for $23,000. Since Kemp sells the stock for a gain (more than the donor's $20,000 basis), Kemp's basis in the stock is $20,000. Kemp realizes a $3,000 gain ($23,000 – $20,000).

EXAMPLE 13

Same facts as in Example 12, except that Kemp sells the stock for $13,000. Kemp sells the stock for a loss (less than the $15,000 FMV). Thus, her basis in the stock is $15,000, and she realizes a $2,000 loss ($13,000 – $15,000).

EXAMPLE 14

Same facts as in Example 12, except that Kemp sells the stock for $17,000. Here, Kemp realizes neither a gain nor a loss. Her basis in the stock equals $17,000.

When the gifted property is depreciable property to the donee, the donee uses the donor's basis to compute depreciation on the property. This rule applies regardless of which basis (donor's basis or FMV at the time of the gift) the donee uses to compute the realized gain or loss at the time of the sale.

FMV Exceeds Donor's Basis

If at the time of the gift the FMV of the property exceeds the donor's basis, the donee assumes the donor's basis. If the donor paid gift tax on the transfer, then the donee adds a portion of the gift tax to the basis. The portion of the gift tax added to the donee's basis depends on when the gift was made. For gifts made prior to 1977, 100% of the gift tax is added to the donee's basis. For gifts made after 1976, only a fraction of the gift tax is added to the donee's basis. This fraction equals the ratio of the amount the property appreciated in value while owned by the donor (FMV at the time of the gift – donor's basis) to its FMV at the time of the gift. In both cases, the donee's basis cannot exceed the FMV of the property at the time of the gift.

EXAMPLE 15

In 1993 Sue Miller received property from her uncle worth $75,000. The uncle paid $15,000 in gift tax on the transfer. The uncle's adjusted basis in the property was $30,000. Since the FMV exceeds the uncle's basis, Miller assumes her uncle's $30,000 basis. While her uncle owned the property, it appreciated in value by $45,000 ($75,000 − $30,000). Therefore, Miller adds 60% ($45,000/$75,000) of the gift tax to her basis. Miller's initial basis in the gifted property equals $39,000 [$30,000 + (60% × $15,000)].

EXAMPLE 16

Assume the same facts as in Example 15, except that the gift occurred in 1973. Miller still takes her uncle's basis in the property but adds 100% of the gift tax to arrive at her initial basis in the property. Miller's initial basis equals $45,000 ($30,000 + $15,000).

DONEE'S INITIAL BASIS IN GIFTED PROPERTY

When FMV < donor's basis and the donee disposes of the property for

- a gain: donee's basis = donor's basis
- a loss: donee's basis = FMV at time of gift
- no gain or loss: donee's basis = amount realized

When FMV > donor's basis,

Donee's basis = Donor's basis + Percentage of the gift tax

Percentage for pre-1977 gifts: 100%

Percentage for post-1976 gifts: $\dfrac{\text{FMV at time of gift} - \text{Donor's basis}}{\text{FMV at time of gift}}$

Property Converted to Business or Rental Use

Instead of buying new property to use in a business or rental activity, taxpayers can convert their personal belongings to such use. For example, taxpayers can convert their principal residences to rental property, or they can start using their personal automobiles or their personal computers in their businesses. As with gifted property, two sets of rules apply to the basis of converted property. The first set applies if the FMV of the property at the time of conversion exceeds the taxpayer's adjusted basis. Another set applies if the adjusted basis exceeds the FMV.

FMV Exceeds Adjusted Basis (Appreciated Property)

When taxpayers convert appreciated property, they use the general rule to compute the adjusted basis: Initial basis + Capital additions − Capital recoveries. If the converted property is depreciable property, taxpayers use the adjusted basis at the time of conversion to compute depreciation expense.

FMV Less Than Adjusted Basis

When taxpayers convert property that has declined in value, the adjusted basis of the property is determined when they dispose of it. To compute realized gains, taxpayers use the general rule for computing adjusted basis: Initial basis + Capital additions − Capital recoveries. To compute realized losses, they use: FMV at conversion + Postconversion capital additions − Postconversion capital recoveries. If the converted property is depreciable property, taxpayers use the FMV of property at the time of the conversion to compute depreciation.

ADJUSTED BASIS IN CONVERTED PROPERTY

When at conversion FMV > adjusted basis,

- Adjusted basis = Initial basis + Capital additions − Capital recoveries
- Depreciable basis = Adjusted basis

When at conversion FMV < adjusted basis,

- Adjusted basis for gains = Initial basis + Capital additions − Capital recoveries
- Adjusted basis for losses = FMV at conversion + Postconversion capital additions − Postconversion capital recoveries
- Depreciable basis = FMV at conversion

EXAMPLE 17

On January 1, 2000, Emily Connors converted her home to rental property. At the time of the conversion, the FMV of the home was $50,000. Connors paid $56,000 for the home and made $4,000 of capital improvements prior to 2000. After converting the property, Connors deducted $6,000 for depreciation and made $3,000 in capital improvements. Connors sells the property in 2005 for $59,000. Since at the time of conversion the FMV ($50,000) is less than the adjusted basis ($56,000 + $4,000 preconversion improvements = $60,000), Connors computes an adjusted basis for gain and an adjusted basis for loss.

Initial basis		$56,000
Plus capital additions	$4,000	
	3,000	7,000
Less capital recoveries		(6,000)
Adjusted basis for gain		$57,000
FMV at conversion		$50,000
Plus postconversion capital additions		3,000
Less postconversion capital recoveries		(6,000)
Adjusted basis for loss		$47,000

Because the amount realized exceeds the adjusted basis for gain, Connors sells the property for a gain. Using an adjusted basis of $57,000, Connors realizes a $2,000 gain ($59,000 − $57,000). Had Connors sold the property for a loss (an amount realized less than $47,000), her adjusted basis would have been $47,000. Had the amount realized been between $47,000 and $57,000, Connors would have realized no gain or loss, and her adjusted basis would have equaled the amount realized.

Special Rules for Stock Ownership

When taxpayers buy stock, their basis in the shares equals the purchase price plus commissions or transfer fees paid. If taxpayers acquire stock through other means (gift, inheritance, etc.), the rules presented in this chapter for computing adjusted basis apply.

Identification of Shares

Taxpayers can acquire identical shares of stock in the same company at various times for different amounts. When taxpayers sell stock in that company, they should identify which shares they are selling at the time of the sale. If no identification is made, then taxpayers must use the first-in, first-out method. To illustrate, assume that in 2000 a taxpayer paid $10,000 for 1,000 shares of common stock. In 2001 the taxpayer paid $12,500 for another 1,000 common shares in the same company. In 2005 the taxpayer sells 1,000 shares for $11,000. By identifying which shares are being sold, the taxpayer could create either a $1,000 gain ($11,000 – $10,000) or a $1,500 loss ($11,000 – $12,500). However, if the taxpayer does not identify which shares were sold at the time of the sale, it is assumed that the shares acquired in 2000 were the ones sold.

To identify shares sold, taxpayers should deliver the stock certificates to the broker or agent. If a broker or agent holds the stock certificates, then taxpayers should instruct the broker in writing which shares they wish to sell. Taxpayers should then request written confirmation from the broker to document that the instructions were followed.

Stock Splits

Taxpayers owning stock may later acquire additional shares either through a stock split or a stock dividend. In a stock split, the corporation distributes to its shareholders a ratable portion of additional shares. This results in more shares outstanding without affecting the ownership percentages. With a stock split, taxpayers prorate the adjusted basis in the original shares to all shares held. Thus, the basis for a taxpayer who pays $1,000 for 100 shares is $10 a share. In a two-for-one stock split, the taxpayer receives an additional 100 shares. After the stock split, the taxpayer's basis is reduced to $5 a share ($1,000 ÷ 200). No income is realized on a stock split.

Stock Dividends

Shareholders receive a stock dividend when the corporation pays them a dividend with shares of stock instead of cash. If shareholders have the option to receive either a stock or a cash dividend, then the cash or FMV of the stock (whichever they choose) must be included as income on the tax return. If they choose to receive a stock dividend, then the FMV of the stock becomes their basis in the newly acquired shares.

When the corporation pays shareholders a stock dividend without giving them the option of a cash dividend, it is a nontaxable stock dividend. As with stock splits, taxpayers must allocate some basis from the original shares to the shares acquired in a nontaxable stock dividend. When the stock dividend is of the same class, the taxpayer prorates the original basis among the total number of shares. An example of a *same class of stock* dividend would be a common stock shareholder receiving a common stock dividend. When the stock dividend is not of the same class, the taxpayer allocates the basis in the original shares using the relative FMV of the total shares. Taxpayers use the same formula to allocate the purchase price among properties acquired in a basket purchase. An example of a stock dividend *not of the same class* would be a common stock shareholder's receiving a preferred stock dividend.

EXAMPLE 18

Pat Brown paid $1,100 for 50 shares of common stock. This year Brown received 5 shares of common stock as a nontaxable stock dividend. Brown's basis in 55 shares of common stock is $1,100, or $20 a share.

Return-of-Capital

Corporations pay dividends from earnings and profits (E&P). E&P is roughly the same as retained earnings on the corporate balance sheet. When a corporation with no E&P distributes property (including cash) to its shareholders, the distribution is treated as a return of the shareholder's investment. The amount distributed is not taxable, but as with other capital recoveries, the shareholder reduces the basis in the stock by the amount distributed. If the amount distributed exceeds the shareholder's basis in the stock, then the shareholder realizes a gain for the excess amount.

Corporations report their distributions to shareholders on Form 1099-DIV. On this form, the corporation reports the taxable dividends paid to the shareholder during the year (distributions from the corporation's E&P), as well as distributions made to the shareholder during the year that represent a return of the shareholder's investment. Shareholders report the taxable dividends on Schedule B and reduce their basis (investment) in the stock by the nontaxable distributions.

RECOGNIZED GAINS AND LOSSES

Recognized gains and losses are realized gains and losses taxpayers report on their tax returns. Not all realized gains and losses result in taxable gains and losses. As a general rule, taxpayers recognize all realized gains but recognize losses only from the disposal of business or investment property. Chapter 5 described an exception to this rule that allows taxpayers to deduct casualty or theft losses on personal-use property. This chapter covers the following six additional exceptions to the general rule.

- Losses involving wash sales
- Losses from sales between related parties
- Gains from qualified small business stock
- Gains and losses from like-kind exchanges
- Most gains from the sale of a principal residence
- Certain gains from involuntary conversions

WASH SALES

Because securities (stocks and bonds) are an investment, the taxpayer usually recognizes any realized loss on the sale of securities. However, no loss is allowed when the taxpayer repurchases "substantially identical" securities within 30 days before or after the sale. The term used to describe these sales and repurchases is **wash sales.**

Substantially identical securities are securities *in the same company* that have similar features. For stocks, substantially identical would be the same class of stock with the same voting rights. For bonds, substantially identical would be bonds with similar interest rates and maturity dates. If the taxpayer repurchases only a fraction of the securities within the 61-day period surrounding the sale, then only that fraction of the loss is denied.

EXAMPLE 19

On January 5, 2005, Tom Mathy sold 1,000 shares of common stock in Omega Co. for $5,000. Mathy's purchases of Omega common stock follow:

1,000 shares on June 6, 2003	$8,000
600 shares on November 6, 2004	4,500
250 shares on December 17, 2004	2,000
350 shares on January 10, 2005	3,000

Assuming Mathy does not identify which shares were sold, he is assumed to sell the 1,000 shares purchased on June 6, 2003. The sale results in a $3,000 realized loss ($5,000 − $8,000), which normally would be recognized for tax purposes. However, since Mathy repurchased 600 (250 + 350) of the 1,000 shares between December 6, 2004, and February 4, 2005 (61 days surrounding January 5, 2005), 60% (600/1,000) of the loss is disallowed ($3,000 × 60% = $1,800). Mathy recognizes a $1,200 loss ($3,000 − $1,800) for the 40% of the shares sold and not repurchased.

Any disallowed loss due to a wash sale is merely postponed and will be allowed when the taxpayer later sells the (repurchased) shares. To postpone the loss, the taxpayer adds the disallowed loss to the basis of the repurchased shares.

EXAMPLE 20

In Example 19, Mathy allocates the $1,800 disallowed loss among the 600 shares that caused the wash sale ($1,800/600 = $3 a share). The basis in the 250 shares purchased on December 17, 2004, equals $2,750 [$2,000 + ($3 × 250)]. The basis in the 350 shares purchased on January 10, 2005, equals $4,050 [$3,000 + ($3 × 350)]. The basis in the 600 shares purchased on November 6, 2004, is their $4,500 cost since the shares were not involved in the wash sale.

SALES BETWEEN RELATED PARTIES

The sale of investment or business property for less than its adjusted basis usually results in a recognized loss. However, taxpayers cannot recognize losses when they sell business or investment property to a related party. For tax purposes, individuals and their family members are related parties. **Family members** include spouses, siblings (brothers and sisters), descendants (children, grandchildren, etc.), and ancestors (parents, grandparents, etc.). Unlike wash sales, the disallowed loss does not increase the (related) buyer's basis in the property. Instead, the buyer can use the disallowed loss to offset any realized gain when the property is later sold. The buyer cannot use the disallowed loss to create or increase a loss.

EXAMPLE 21

Pete sold stock to his son, Stan, for $10,000. Pete bought the stock several years ago for $16,000. Although stock is investment property, Pete cannot recognize the $6,000 realized loss ($10,000 − $16,000) since he sold the stock to a related party. Stan's basis in the stock is $10,000, the amount he paid for it.

   If Stan later sells the stock for $12,000, Stan uses Pete's disallowed loss to offset his $2,000 realized gain ($12,000 − $10,000). Since the disallowed loss can only reduce realized gains and cannot create a loss, Stan can use only $2,000 of the disallowed loss. The rest of the disallowed loss will never be used.

EXAMPLE 22

Assume the same facts as in Example 21, except that Stan sells the stock for $9,000. Stan realizes a $1,000 loss ($9,000 − $10,000). Since a disallowed loss cannot create or increase a loss, Stan cannot use any of Pete's disallowed loss. Stan recognizes the $1,000 loss from the sale, and Pete's entire $6,000 disallowed loss is gone.

Besides individuals and their family members, related parties also involve individuals and corporations when an individual owns more than 50% of the voting stock in the corporation. Stock owned by family members counts as stock owned by the individual. This indirect ownership of stock is known as **constructive ownership.**

EXAMPLE 23

Henry owns 30% of Alpha Corporation. The following people own the rest of the stock:

Henry's aunt   35%
Henry's brother   25%
Henry's father   10%

   Henry owns 30% of Alpha outright. He constructively owns the 35% owned by his brother (25%) and father (10%). Henry's actual plus constructive ownership exceeds 50%. Should Henry sell investment or business property to Alpha, any realized loss would be disallowed.

QUALIFIED SMALL BUSINESS STOCK

Individuals can exclude 50% of the gain realized on the sale of Section 1202 qualified small business stock, provided the stock is held for more than five years. To qualify for the 50% exclusion, the stock purchased must have been part of the corporation's original issuance of stock. Only certain corporations are able to issue qualified small business stock. These restrictions are beyond the scope of this textbook.

EXAMPLE 24

On September 6, 1996, Philip Markel acquires $100,000 of Section 1202 qualified small business stock from Alpha Corporation. On November 19, 2005, Markel sells the stock for $230,000. Markel's realized gain from the sale is $130,000 ($230,000 – $100,000). However, since he held the stock for more than five years, Markel recognizes 50% of the gain, or $65,000.

The ability to exclude 50% of the gain on the sale of Section 1202 qualified small business stock provides taxpayers with a great incentive to buy stock in a new corporation that qualifies under Section 1202. Shareholders can continue to exclude 50% of the gains until the total excluded gains on the sale of Section 1202 stock equals the greater of $10 million or 10 times the shareholder's aggregate adjusted basis in the Section 1202 stock disposed of during the year.

TAX-DEFERRED EXCHANGES

Taxpayers usually must recognize any gain realized on the exchange of property. However, certain exchanges do not result in taxable gain (or deductible loss). Instead, these realized gains and losses are postponed (deferred) to a future tax year. Like-kind exchanges are one example of a tax-deferred exchange.

LIKE-KIND EXCHANGES

Instead of selling property for cash, taxpayers can exchange property they own for other property. When this occurs, a realized gain or loss results from the difference between the FMV of the property received and the adjusted basis of the property given up. Under the general rule, taxpayers recognize all gains from such exchanges but recognize losses only from exchanges that involve business or investment property. One exception to the general rule exists when the exchange involves like-kind property. In a like-kind exchange, taxpayers generally do not recognize gains or losses. Instead, realized gains and losses are postponed. To postpone the gains and losses until such time that the property is disposed of in a non-like-kind exchange, taxpayers adjust the basis of the property they receive in the like-kind exchange. This new basis is also used to depreciate depreciable property.

Basis of the new property = FMV of the new property + Postponed losses – Postponed gains

EXAMPLE 25

Joan Wright exchanges property with an adjusted basis of $100,000 for like-kind property valued at $60,000. Wright realizes a $40,000 loss ($60,000 – $100,000) but does not recognize the loss on her tax return. Wright's basis in the new property equals $100,000 ($60,000 FMV of new property + $40,000 postponed loss). If the new property is depreciable property, the basis in the property for purposes of depreciation is $100,000.

Like-Kind Property

The rules just described apply only to exchanges involving like-kind property. To qualify as like-kind property, four conditions must be met.

1. A direct exchange must occur. Certain exchanges involving three parties can qualify as a direct exchange. Also, a direct exchange can occur if the property to be received is identified within 45 days and received within 180 days after the taxpayer transfers the property.
2. Both the property traded and the property received must be business or investment property.
3. Real property must be exchanged for other real property. Personal property must be exchanged for similar personal property.
4. The property exchanged cannot be inventory, foreign real property, securities, or partnership interests.

The like-kind rules are not elective. When all four conditions are met, taxpayers must postpone any realized gain or loss resulting from the like-kind exchange.

> The like-kind exchange rules are mandatory. If the taxpayer exchanges like-kind property that results in a loss, the loss must be postponed. To deduct the loss, the taxpayer needs to fail at least one of the four requirements. For example, the taxpayer could fail to meet the requirements for a direct exchange.

LIKE-KIND EXCHANGES OF BUSINESS OR INVESTMENT PERSONAL PROPERTY

To qualify as a like-kind exchange, taxpayers must exchange personal property held for business or investment for similar personal property to be held for business or investment. Similar personal property is that which is *nearly identical*. The following are five examples of like-kind personal property.

- Office furniture, fixtures, and office equipment are all like-kind
- All automobiles are like-kind
- Computers, printers, and peripheral equipment are like-kind
- All light general-purpose trucks are like-kind
- All heavy general-purpose trucks are nearly identical, but are different from light general-purpose trucks.

Exchanging office furniture for office equipment qualifies as a like-kind exchange since both are like-kind. However, exchanging a computer for office equipment does not qualify as a like-kind exchange since the two are not like-kind.

LIKE-KIND EXCHANGES OF BUSINESS OR INVESTMENT REAL PROPERTY

The like-kind exchange rules are more lenient for exchanges of real property. To qualify as a like-kind exchange, real property used for business or investment must be exchanged for any other real property to be used for business or investment. Thus, unimproved land held for investment can be exchanged for a warehouse used in the taxpayer's business. Likewise, an office building used in the taxpayer's business can be exchanged for an apartment building to be held as an investment.

Boot

Not all like-kind exchanges involve properties of equal value. When exchanging properties of unequal value, the one receiving property of lesser value will require more property from the other party. The non-like-kind property thrown in to even up the deal is known as **boot.** Often boot involves cash, but it can involve other property. Boot occurs when one party takes over the other party's debt. The party who assumes the debt is treated as giving boot. The party relieved of debt is treated as receiving boot. When both parties assume each other's debt, only the net (excess) liability counts as boot. The amount of gain or loss recognized on like-kind exchanges involving boot depends on whether the taxpayer gave or received boot.

EXAMPLE 26

Elaine Dorn exchanges land valued at $100,000 for Bill Lane's building valued at $80,000. Both properties qualify as like-kind. To even up the deal, Lane agrees to assume Dorn's $20,000 liability on the land. Dorn's release from debt is similar to her receiving $20,000 cash and using it to pay off the debt. Thus, Dorn receives $20,000 boot; Lane gives $20,000 boot.

EXAMPLE 27

Sam Hackman exchanges land valued at $80,000 for Diane Glover's building valued at $100,000. Both properties qualify as like-kind. Hackman owes $40,000 on the land; Glover owes $60,000 on the building. Both parties agree to assume each other's debt.

In this exchange, each party receives property worth $140,000. Hackman receives a building worth $100,000 and is relieved of $40,000 of debt. Glover receives land valued at $80,000 and is relieved of $60,000 of debt. Because the parties assume each other's debt, only the net liability of $20,000 ($60,000 − $40,000) is treated as boot. Hackman takes on more debt than he is relieved of; therefore, Hackman gives $20,000 of boot. Glover is relieved of more debt than she assumed; therefore, Glover receives $20,000 of boot.

Receipt of Boot

Receiving boot has no affect on realized losses from the like-kind exchange. Those losses are postponed and increase the taxpayer's basis in the like-kind property received. However, taxpayers recognize gains to the extent of the FMV of the boot received.

EXAMPLE 28

Ken Hart exchanges a machine with an adjusted basis of $47,000 for a machine valued at $45,000 and $5,000 cash. Hart's realized gain equals $3,000 ($50,000 amount realized − $47,000 adjusted basis). Hart receives boot of $5,000; therefore, he recognizes the entire $3,000 gain. Hart's basis in the new machine is its FMV of $45,000 since there is no postponed gain.

EXAMPLE 29

Assume the same facts as in Example 28, except that Hart's adjusted basis in the old machine is $42,000. Hart realizes an $8,000 gain ($50,000 − $42,000). Hart recognizes the gain to the extent of the boot received. Therefore, Hart reports a $5,000 gain on his tax return and postpones the rest. Hart reduces the basis in the new machine by the postponed gain ($45,000 FMV − $3,000 postponed gain = $42,000 basis in the new machine).

EXAMPLE 30

Assume the same facts as in Example 28, except that Hart's adjusted basis in the old machine is $52,000. Hart realizes a $2,000 loss ($50,000 – $52,000). Since the receipt of boot has no affect on his realized losses, Hart postpones the entire loss by increasing the basis in the new machine to $47,000 ($45,000 FMV + $2,000 postponed loss).

Boot Given

When boot is received in a like-kind exchange, any realized gain is recognized to the extent of the boot received. Realized losses are never recognized when boot is received. When the taxpayer gives boot in a like-kind exchange, no gain or loss is recognized as long as the FMV of the boot equals the taxpayer's basis in the boot. This occurs when the taxpayer gives cash or assumes the other party's debt. When the FMV of the boot is different from the taxpayer's basis in the boot given, the taxpayer is treated as having sold the boot to the other party and the taxpayer has a realized gain or loss for the difference between the FMV and basis. Under the general rule, the taxpayer will recognize a gain to the extent that the FMV of the boot exceeds its basis. However, the taxpayer will recognize a loss if the FMV is less than the basis in the boot only if the boot was business or investment property.

Exchanges between Related Parties

Related parties can use the like-kind exchange rules. However, if either (related) party disposes of the like-kind property within two years after the exchange, any postponed gain or loss must be recognized in the disposal year. The basis of the like-kind property is increased by the recognized gain or reduced by the recognized loss.

SALE OF A PRINCIPAL RESIDENCE

Since taxpayers own and use a principal residence for personal purposes, usually they would recognize the gain from the sale of a principal residence but would not recognize a loss. However, the tax law allows taxpayers to exclude up to $250,000 of the gain. Married couples who file a joint tax return can exclude up to $500,000. To qualify for the exclusion, taxpayers must use the home as their principal residence for two of the previous five years. Partial exclusions are available to taxpayers who fail to meet the two-out-of-five-year requirement because of change in employment location, health, or other specified reasons.

Since taxpayers can exclude up to $250,000 of gain ($500,000 if MFJ) from the sale of their principal residence, very few taxpayers will report gain when selling their home. However, taxpayers still will want to keep track of their basis in their home to show that the gain from the sale does not exceed the exclusion amount. This includes keeping a copy of the closing statement and receipts for all capital improvements made to the home. Keeping good records is also important in casualty loss situations. In addition, when some or all of the home is converted to income-producing property, basis becomes important in determining depreciation deductions.

EXAMPLE 31

On September 11, 2005, the Duncans sell their principal residence for $200,000. Selling expenses are $10,000. The Duncans paid $50,000 for the home. The Duncans do not recognize any of the $140,000 ($200,000 – $10,000 – $50,000) gain.

EXAMPLE 32

On July 11, 2005, Dale Lincoln (a single taxpayer) sells his principal residence for $450,000. Selling expenses are $25,000. Lincoln paid $115,000 for the home in 1982. In 1988 he paid $15,000 to finish the basement. In 1990, he paid $5,000 for landscaping. Of the $290,000 realized gain, Lincoln recognizes $40,000.

Sales price	$450,000
Less selling expenses	(25,000)
Amount realized	$425,000
Less adjusted basis ($115,000 + $15,000 + $5,000)	(135,000)
Realized gain	$290,000
Less $250,000 exclusion for single taxpayers	(250,000)
Recognized gain	$ 40,000

INVOLUNTARY CONVERSIONS

Taxpayers realize a gain or loss on property involved in an involuntary conversion. The most common involuntary conversions are casualties, thefts, and condemnations.

Condemnation Gains and Losses

When the government takes the taxpayer's real property (known as a condemnation), the taxpayer often receives cash in exchange for the condemned property. Occasionally the taxpayer will receive property other than cash. Taxpayers realize a gain when the amount received from the government exceeds the adjusted basis in the condemned property. They realize a loss when the amount received is less than the adjusted basis of the property. Under the general rule, taxpayers pay tax on all recognized gains resulting from condemnations but deduct losses only on condemned business or investment property. There is no deduction for condemnation losses on personal-use property, even though it is an involuntary event.

Casualty or Theft Gains and Losses

Taxpayers realize a casualty or theft loss when the amount of the loss exceeds the amount reimbursed by insurance. The amount of the loss for *personal-use property* and for *partially destroyed business or investment property* equals the lesser of the property's adjusted basis or its decline in FMV. Decline in FMV is measured as the difference between the FMV before and after the casualty or theft. The amount of the loss for *completely destroyed (includes stolen) business or investment property* equals the adjusted basis in the property, even if the decline in FMV is less. When the insurance proceeds exceed the amount of the loss, the taxpayer does not realize a casualty or theft loss. Instead, the taxpayer realizes a casualty or theft gain when the insurance proceeds exceed the *adjusted basis* in the property.

| | | | | **Insurance** |
| EXAMPLE 33 | | | | |

In March, Scott Talbot's business auto was damaged in an accident. In June, Talbot's business computer was stolen. Information about the properties is shown below.

	FMV Before	FMV After	Adjusted Basis	Insurance Proceeds
Auto	$22,000	$8,000	$15,000	$16,000
Computer	3,000	0	1,000	2,900

The business auto was partially destroyed; therefore, Talbot computes his casualty loss using the lesser of the decline in value ($22,000 − $8,000 = $14,000) or the adjusted basis ($15,000). However, because the insurance proceeds ($16,000) exceed the amount of the loss ($14,000), Talbot does not incur a casualty loss on the auto. Instead, Talbot realizes a $1,000 casualty gain ($16,000 insurance proceeds − $15,000 adjusted basis).

The business computer was completely destroyed; therefore, Talbot measures the loss using the adjusted basis ($1,000). Talbot does not realize a theft loss on the computer since the insurance proceeds ($2,900) exceed the amount of the loss. Talbot realizes a $1,900 business theft gain on the computer ($2,900 insurance proceeds − $1,000 adjusted basis).

Generally, taxpayers recognize both gains and losses from casualty or theft events. Chapter 5 discussed the special rules for calculating an itemized deduction for casualty or theft losses on personal-use property. It should be noted that casualty and theft losses are the only deductible losses that an individual may claim on personal-use property.

Election to Postpone Realized Gains

Under the general rule, taxpayers recognize gains from property involved in an involuntary conversion. However, taxpayers can postpone these gains if they invest the *entire* proceeds in qualified replacement property within a specified period of time. This provision is elective if the taxpayer receives cash for the converted property. If the election is made, taxpayers recognize a gain (up to the amount of realized gain) for amounts not reinvested.

EXAMPLE 34

The local government condemns Tracy Kraig's property. The government pays Kraig $200,000 for the property. The property has an adjusted basis of $170,000. Kraig can avoid recognizing the $30,000 realized gain ($200,000 − $170,000) if she reinvests at least $200,000 in qualified replacement property within the required time period. Assuming Kraig buys qualified replacement property costing $190,000, she recognizes $10,000 of the gain ($200,000 − $190,000) and could elect to postpone the rest ($30,000 − $10,000 = $20,000).

When the election is made to postpone gains, taxpayers reduce the basis in the new property by the amount of postponed gain. In Example 34, if Kraig made the election, her basis in the qualified replacement property would equal $170,000 ($190,000 cost − $20,000 postponed gain).

Qualified Replacement Property

Qualified replacement property for property involved in an involuntary conversion normally is property related in service or use. Thus, taxpayers usually must replace an office building with another office building. Likewise, they must replace equipment with similar functioning equipment. Two exceptions to this rule follow.

The first exception applies to taxpayers who lease property involved in an involuntary conversion. Qualified replacement property for these taxpayers involves investing in other rental property. The rental property need not be of the same type. Thus, taxpayers who lease an office building can replace it with an apartment building or any other rental real estate that they lease out.

The second exception allows taxpayers to replace condemned business or investment realty with any other business or investment realty. Taxpayers can replace a condemned office building with land to be held for investment. Alternatively, they could replace it with an apartment building, a warehouse, or any other business or investment realty.

Replacement Period

Taxpayers who want to postpone the gain from an involuntary conversion must replace the converted property within a specified period. The replacement period begins on the date the property was damaged, destroyed, condemned, or stolen. However, for condemned property, the period starts when the government officially threatens to condemn the property. Taxpayers then have until two years after the close of the tax year (December 31 for calendar year taxpayers) in which they realize any part of the gain to replace converted property. They have one additional year to replace condemned business or investment realty.

EXAMPLE 35

On October 19, 2004, Jim Rollins's business property was completely destroyed in a fire. At the time of the fire, the property was worth $40,000. Rollins paid $80,000 for the property in 1992, and its adjusted basis at the time of the fire was $30,000. In 2005 the insurance company paid Rollins $40,000. Rollins's business casualty gain equals $10,000 ($40,000 − $30,000 adjusted basis). If Rollins wants to postpone the entire gain, he must reinvest at least $40,000 in qualified replacement property between October 19, 2004, and December 31, 2007 (two years after 2005, the year in which Rollins receives the proceeds and realizes the gain).

EXAMPLE 36

Assume the same facts as in Example 35, except that Rollins's business property was condemned and in 2005 the government paid Rollins $40,000 for the property. Rollins's realized gain equals $10,000 ($40,000 proceeds − $30,000 adjusted basis). To avoid recognition of any gain, Rollins has from October 19, 2004 (or the official date of threat, if earlier) until December 31, 2008 (three years after 2005) to buy qualified replacement property costing at least $40,000.

Taxpayers with business or investment property located in the Hurricane Katrina disaster area that was involuntarily converted due to Hurricane Katrina on or after August 25, 2005, have an additional three years to replace such property with qualified replacement property as long as substantially all of the use of the replacement property is in the Hurricane Katrina disaster area.

QUESTIONS AND PROBLEMS

1. **Amount Realized, Realized Gain.** Jane Barnett sells land that has a $60,000 mortgage. In return for the land, Barnett receives cash of $40,000 and stock with a FMV of $30,000. The buyer also assumes the mortgage. Barnett's adjusted basis in the land is $80,000.

   a. What is Barnett's amount realized?

   b. What is Barnett's realized gain?

   c. How would these amounts change if the buyer had not assumed the mortgage but instead had paid Barnett an additional $60,000 to pay off the mortgage before the transfer of the land took place?

2. **Basket Purchase.** Leo Small purchased an apartment building. Small paid $300,000 in cash, assumed a $200,000 mortgage, and paid the following:

   Brokerage commission $35,000
   Attorney's fee to acquire title   2,000

   What is Small's basis for depreciation on this building if the FMV of the land and building are $100,000 and $400,000, respectively?

3. **Bargain Purchase.** George O'Brien, president of Sugarman Corporation, was given the opportunity to buy 1,000 shares of the corporation's stock for $120 per share. The par value of the stock was $100. O'Brien took advantage of this offer and purchased 100 shares of stock at a time when the stock was selling for $150 per share. O'Brien includes as income the difference between the FMV of the stock and his cost. The company also gave O'Brien an additional 100 shares of stock as a bonus when the stock was selling for $160 per share.

   a. What amount of income must O'Brien recognize as a result of these stock acquisitions?

   b. What is O'Brien's per-share basis in the stock he acquired?

4. **Property Received in a Divorce.** Hal and Wendy are divorced. Under the terms of the divorce agreement, Hal transferred 100 shares of Big Rig stock (cost $30,000, market value $45,000) to Wendy in satisfaction of Wendy's property rights. If Wendy sells the stock for $50,000, what is her recognized gain?

5. **Inherited Property.** Sharon Bedford inherited 10 shares of Alpha Corporation stock when her aunt died. Her aunt paid $10,000 for the stock, but it was worth only $7,000 at the date of her death. No estate tax return was required. Bedford sold the stock this year for $8,000. What is Bedford's recognized gain or loss from the sale?

6. **Inherited Property.** Terry Taylor purchased 5,000 shares of Ferrero Corporation stock in 1980 for $60,000. Terry died on August 1, 2004, leaving the stock to his daughter, Tina. Tina received the stock on November 1, 2004. The alternate valuation date was elected for Terry's estate. The FMV of the stock for various dates follows:

August 1, 2004	$80,000
November 1, 2004	78,000
February 1, 2005	77,000

    a. Tina sold the stock for $75,000 on March 10, 2005. What is Tina's recognized gain or loss from the sale?

    b. Assume instead that Tina received the stock on March 1, 2005, when the FMV of the stock was $79,000. What is Tina's recognized gain or loss?

7. **Gifted Property.** Max Fisher purchased 100 shares of XQM stock in 1998 for $10,000. In 2002 Fisher gave the stock to his daughter, Linda, when the FMV of the stock was $8,000. No gift tax was paid.

    a. What is Linda's basis in the stock if she sells it in the current year for $11,000?

    b. What is Linda's basis in the stock if she sells it in the current year for $9,000?

    c. What is Linda's recognized gain or loss if she sells the stock in the current year for $7,000?

8. **Gifted Property.** In 1975, Sam Smythe gave his son, Al, land worth $80,000. Smythe paid $60,000 for the land in 1970. He paid $12,000 in gift tax on the transfer. What is Al's basis in the land?

9. **Gifted Property.** In 1999, Bruce Fogg gave Shirley Hayes a house worth $100,000. Fogg's adjusted basis in the house was $80,000. Fogg paid $8,000 in gift tax on the transfer. What is Hayes's initial basis in the house?

10. **Converted Property.** In 1999, Parker Lewis converted his personal residence to rental property. The FMV of the home at the time of conversion was $85,000, Lewis paid $90,000 for the home ten years ago.

    a. If Parker sells the property for $100,000 after taking depreciation deductions of $10,000, what is his recognized gain or loss?

    b. If Parker sells the property for $70,000 after taking depreciation deductions of $10,000, what is his recognized gain or loss?

    c. If Parker sells the property for $78,000 after taking depreciation deductions of $10,000, what is his recognized gain or loss?

11. **Sale of Stock.** Ima O. Witch had the following purchases of common stock of Halloween Tricks, Inc.

1980	400 shares at $10 per share
1983	100 shares at $20 per share
1986	300 shares at $30 per share
1988	200 shares at $40 per share

    a. In 2005 Witch sold 500 shares at $35 per share. Assuming that Witch kept incomplete records and did not identify which blocks of stock were sold, compute Witch's recognized gain or loss on the sale.

    b. If Witch's objective is to minimize taxes and she could adequately identify which stock she was selling, which stock should she sell, and what is the recognized gain or loss that would result?

12. **Stock Splits.** Diane Watkins owned 100 shares of common stock in the Delta Corporation when it had a two-for-one-stock split. The original 100 shares cost $50 each, for a total cost of $5,000. After the split, Watkins had 200 shares that were valued at $30 each, for a total value of $6,000. As a result of the stock split, what is Watkins's basis in each share of stock, and how much income must she recognize?

13. **Stock Dividends.** In 1995, Debra Hopkins paid $1,200 for 100 shares of UPI common stock. In the current year, UPI offers Hopkins the choice between a $50 cash dividend or 8 additional shares of common stock valued at $9 a share. Hopkins opts for the stock dividend.

    a. What is Hopkins's basis in each of the 108 shares she now owns?

    b. How would your answer to Part a. change if Hopkins did not have the option of a cash dividend?

14. **Wash Sales.**

    a. An individual taxpayer, not a dealer or trader in securities, completed the following transactions in Micro Products Company common stock:

    September 15, 2005, purchased 100 shares at a cost of $4,800
    December 10, 2005, sold the above shares for $3,200
    January 4, 2006, purchased 60 shares at a cost of $1,800

    (1) What is the total taxable capital gain or deductible capital loss from the sale on December 10?

    (2) What is the basis of the stock purchased on January 4?

    b. Assume that the sales price of the 100 shares sold on December 10 was $5,300; all other facts stated in Part a. remain the same.

    (1) What is the total capital gain or deductible capital loss from the sale on December 10?

    (2) What is the basis of the stock purchased on January 4?

c. Assume that the sales price of the shares sold on December 10 was $3,200 and that the original 100 shares of stock had been inherited by the taxpayer from the taxpayer's father on September 15, 2005, when they were valued at $2,500. The stock had been purchased by the taxpayer's father two months earlier for $2,000. No estate tax return was filed.

    (1) What is the total capital gain or deductible loss from the sale on December 10?

    (2) What is the basis of the stock purchased on January 4?

15. **Sale to a Related Party.** Fred sold common stock, which cost him $12,000, to his sister, Sara, for $9,000. Three years later Sara sold the stock for $14,000 to an unrelated party.

  a. What was Fred's recognized loss when he sold the stock to Sara?

  b. What is Sara's basis in the stock she purchased from Fred?

  c. What is Sara's recognized gain or loss when she sells the stock?

  d. If Sara had sold the stock for $11,000, what would be her recognized gain or loss?

  e. If Sara had sold the stock for $7,000, what would be her recognized gain or loss?

16. **Qualified Small Business Stock.** Van Jenson pays $30,000 for Section 1202 qualified small business stock on February 6, 1998. In October 2005, Jenson sells the stock for $80,000. Compute Jenson's realized and recognized gain on the sale of the stock.

17. **Like-Kind Exchange.** Which of the following transactions qualify as like-kind exchanges?

  a. Grocery store for rental house
  b. Apartment building for parking lot
  c. GM common stock for land to be held for investment
  d. 100 shares of Ford common stock for 100 shares of Chrysler common stock
  e. Duplex apartment (investment property) for personal residence

18. **Like-Kind Exchange.** Which of the following transactions qualify as like-kind exchanges?

    a. Old computer for new computer (both used in business)

    b. Inventory traded for computer (used in business)

    c. Old personal auto for new business auto

    d. Office furniture for office equipment (both used in business)

    e. Automobile for machinery (both used in business)

19. **Like-Kind Exchange.** Dottie Packard exchanges real estate held for investment for other real estate to be held for investment. The following facts relate to the exchange.

Adjusted basis of old property	$ 75,000
FMV of new property	100,000
Cash received by Packard	10,000
Mortgage on old property assumed by other party	30,000

    a. What is the amount of Packard's realized and recognized gain?

    b. What is Packard's basis in the new property?

20. **Like-Kind Exchange.** For each of the following nontaxable exchanges, compute the realized gain or loss, the recognized gain or loss, and the basis of the new property acquired.

	Basis of Old Asset	FMV of New Asset	Cash Received or Paid
Exchange a:	$ 8,000	$ 5,000	$ 0
Exchange b:	6,000	10,000	5,000 paid
Exchange c:	6,000	10,000	2,000 paid
Exchange d:	10,000	7,000	2,000 received
Exchange e:	10,000	7,000	5,000 received
Exchange f:	10,000	11,000	2,000 received

21. **Like-Kind Exchange.** Jim Bates wanted Jack McKean's farm as a site for an amusement park and offered him $200,000 for the farm. McKean did not want to sell his farm, which had a basis of $50,000. Bates is now considering acquiring another farm for $170,000 and then offering this farm plus $20,000 in cash to McKean in exchange for McKean's farm. If McKean accepts this offer, what tax consequences does he face?

22. **Sale of a Principal Residence.** Adam Hodges, who is single, sold his principal residence for $440,000. He paid $28,000 in selling expenses. Hodges paid $107,000 for the house 17 years ago. Over the years Hodges made capital improvements to the house totaling $42,000. Compute Hodges's recognized gain on the sale of his home.

23. **Involuntary Conversion.** The Wholesale Dress Shop was destroyed by fire in January. The adjusted basis of the store was $150,000. In March, the insurance company paid $140,000 to cover the loss. Shortly thereafter a new shop was purchased for $200,000.

    a. What, if any, is the recognized gain or loss?

    b. What is the basis of the new dress shop?

24. **Involuntary Conversion.** Duffy & Co.'s warehouse, which had an adjusted basis of $1,100,000, was destroyed by fire. Duffy received insurance in the amount of $2,000,000. Duffy immediately invested $1,800,000 in a new warehouse and elected to postpone as much of the gain as possible.

    a. What is the amount of gain recognized for income tax purposes?

    b. What is the basis of the new warehouse?

25. **Involuntary Conversion.** On February 17, 2005, Kari Baker was notified by the state that the land she owned as an investment was needed for a state park and that the land would be condemned. The state took possession of the land on January 15, 2006, and Baker received her condemnation award on January 20, 2006.

   a. If Baker elects to postpone recognition of her gain, by what date must she purchase replacement property?

   b. What type of property could Baker purchase and still postpone recognition of her gain?

26. **Internet Problem: Researching Publication 550.**

   Beta Corporation is a C Corporation whose total gross assets have never exceeded $35 million. Donald Adams purchased stock from Beta Corporation in March 1995 as part of Beta's initial issuance. Adams is interested in selling his stock in Beta Corporation and wants to know whether Beta Corporation meets the requirements of a qualified small business corporation under Section 1202.

   Go to the IRS Web site. Locate Publication 550 and find the appropriate page that discusses the requirements for a qualified small business corporation under Section 1202. Print out a copy of the page where you found your answer. Underline or highlight the pertinent information. Comment on whether you can answer Adams's question with the information that has been provided.

   See Appendix A for instructions on use of the IRS Web site.

27. **Business Entity Problem: This problem is designed for those using the "business entity" approach. The solution may require information from Chapter 14.**

   Judy Davis converts her sole proprietorship into a regular C corporation. The basis of the assets she transfers into the corporation is $225,000. The fair market value is $265,000. In return for these assets, Davis received all of the corporation's stock—50,000 shares.

   a. What is the basis of these assets to the corporation?

   b. What is Davis's basis in stock she receives?

Property: Capital Gains and Losses, and Depreciation Recapture

CHAPTER CONTENTS

■■ CHAPTER OVERVIEW

*C*hapter 10 covered the calculation of realized gains and losses from the sale, *exchange, or other disposal of property. It also covered which realized gains and losses taxpayers recognize for tax purposes. This chapter examines the nature of those gains and losses. Recognized gains may be capital gains or ordinary income. Recognized losses may be treated as capital losses or ordinary deductions. The distinction is important because capital gains and losses are treated differently than ordinary gains and losses. This chapter explains which gains and losses are capital and which are ordinary. It also shows where taxpayers report gains and losses on the tax return.*

CAPITAL GAINS AND LOSSES

The tax laws treat capital gains and losses differently from ordinary gains and losses. Individual taxpayers are limited on the amount of capital losses they can deduct each year, whereas reduced tax rates can apply to capital gains. There are several ways gains and losses can be classified as capital gains and losses. The most common way is through the sale or exchange of a capital asset.

Capital Assets Defined

All property that taxpayers own is a capital asset unless it falls into one of the following five categories:

1. Inventory held primarily for sale to customers. This includes property that will become part of inventory, such as materials and work-in-process.
2. Business receivables, including accounts and notes receivable.
3. Depreciable property and land used in a trade or business.
4. Copyrights; literary, musical, or artistic compositions; letters; memorandums; etc., created by the taxpayer, or letters and memorandums prepared or produced for the taxpayer.
5. U.S. government publications purchased for less than the normal sales price.

A closer look at the five categories reveals that the first three involve business property. Thus, except for items described in the last two categories, capital assets can be defined as the taxpayer's personal belongings and investment property. Common examples of capital assets include the taxpayer's clothing, residence, and automobile (personal-use property). Other examples include stock, bonds, and land held for speculation (investment property).

Using the rules from Chapter 10, taxpayers compute the realized gains and losses that result from the sale or exchange of capital assets. Next, they determine which realized gains and losses they recognize for tax purposes. (Recall from Chapter 10 that not all realized gains and losses are recognized on the tax return.) Taxpayers then classify the recognized gains and losses as short-term or long-term capital gains and losses.

Short-term capital gains and losses result from the sale or exchange of capital assets held for one year or less. **Long-term capital gains and losses** result if the capital asset was held for more than one year. In determining whether property has been held for more than one year, the date taxpayers acquire property does not count, but the disposal date does.

EXAMPLE 1

On June 3, 2004, Joel Thomas buys 100 shares of common stock. Thomas's holding period begins on June 4, 2004. On June 4, 2005, Thomas will have held the shares for more than one year. If Thomas sells the shares after June 3, 2005, he will recognize a long-term capital gain or loss. This, of course, assumes that neither the wash sale rules nor the related party rules from Chapter 10 prevent Thomas from recognizing a loss on the sale.

Holding Periods for Property

Not all holding periods begin the day after the taxpayer physically acquires property. Special rules apply to inherited property and to property with a carryover basis.

Inherited Property

The holding period for inherited property usually begins the day after the decedent dies. However, when taxpayers dispose of inherited property, a long-term gain or loss results, regardless of the actual holding period. Thus, if the property inherited is a capital asset, any recognized gain or loss upon its sale or exchange results in a long-term capital gain or loss.

Carryover Basis

When property has a carryover basis, the holding period also carries over. A carryover basis and holding period can occur one of three ways.

1. The taxpayer uses the previous owner's basis to compute the basis in property. This occurs with transfers of property between spouses and gifted property where the taxpayer uses the donor's basis. In these cases, the previous owner's holding period carries over to the taxpayer.
2. The taxpayer allocates part of the basis in existing property to the basis of newly acquired property. This happens with nontaxable stock dividends and stock splits. When this occurs, the holding period of the original property carries over to the new property.
3. The taxpayer adjusts the basis in property to reflect a postponed gain or loss from previously owned property. This can occur with like-kind exchanges, involuntary conversions, and wash sales. In these cases, the holding period of the old property becomes the holding period of the new property.

EXAMPLE 2

On July 11, 2004, Tara Reynolds gave her nephew, Chris Adams, stock worth $6,000. Reynolds paid $7,000 for the stock on May 9, 1982. Adams sells the stock on February 5, 2005, for $7,500.

   Recall from Chapter 10 that when the FMV of gifted property is less than the donor's basis, the donee's basis is determined when the donee disposes of the property. The donee uses the donor's basis to compute gains, and the FMV of the property at the time of the gift to compute losses. Because Adams sells the stock for a gain (more than the donor's basis), his basis in the stock is the donor's basis. Using his aunt's basis, Adams realizes a $500 gain ($7,500 – $7,000). Since Adams uses the donor's basis as his basis in the stock, his holding period begins on May 10, 1982 (the day after the day his aunt bought the stock). Therefore, Adams recognizes a $500 long-term capital gain.

EXAMPLE 3

On March 10, 2005, Doug Simpson exchanges land for a building in a like-kind exchange. Simpson purchased the land on August 18, 1991. Simpson is treated as having owned the building acquired in the like-kind exchange since August 18, 1991.

Netting Capital Gains and Losses

The netting process begins by separating short-term gains and losses from long-term capital gains and losses. The netting process continues by offsetting these gains and losses within each of these two groups. The result is a *net short-term capital gain or loss* and a *net long-term capital gain or loss.*

EXAMPLE 4

Janice Altman sold the following capital assets during the year.

Description	Gain (Loss)	Group
Stock held 6 months	$5,000	short-term
Stock held 8 months	(7,000)	short-term
Stock held 3 years	(14,000)	long-term
Stock held 6 years	21,000	long-term

The first step in the netting process involves separating the gains and losses into two groups (see the column **Group** above). Altman then begins netting within each group.

Short-Term	Long-Term
$5,000	($14,000)
(7,000)	21,000
($2,000)	$ 7,000

The netting process produces a $2,000 net short-term capital loss and a $7,000 net long-term capital gain.

When a net gain results in both groups, the netting process is complete. Likewise, the netting process is complete when both groups show a net loss. Otherwise, netting losses against gains between the two groups occurs. Examples 5, 6 and 7 demonstrate netting between groups.

EXAMPLE 5

Continuing with Example 4, Altman offsets the $2,000 net short-term loss against the $7,000 net long-term gain. This leaves Altman with a $5,000 overall net long-term capital gain.

Short-Term	Long-Term
$5,000	($14,000)
(7,000)	21,000
($2,000)	$7,000
⎿———————→	(2,000)
	$ 5,000

EXAMPLE 6

Jim Brooks sold four capital assets during the year. After separating the gains and losses into two groups, Brooks nets the gains and losses within each group. This netting within groups produces a $2,000 net short-term loss and a $3,000 net long-term loss. Since both groups result in a loss, the netting process is complete.

Short-Term	Long-Term
$6,000	$1,000
(8,000)	(4,000)
($2,000)	($3,000)

EXAMPLE 7

Lynda Tymes sold five capital assets during the year. After separating the gains and losses into two groups, Tymes nets the gains and losses within each group. This netting within groups produces a $5,000 net short-term capital gain, and a $1,000 net long-term capital loss. Tymes uses the $1,000 net long-term capital loss to offset the net short-term gain. Tymes has a $4,000 net short-term capital gain.

Short-Term	Long-Term
($13,000)	$3,000
7,000	(4,000)
11,000	
$5,000	($1,000)
(1,000) ← ┘	
$ 4,000	

Once the netting process is complete, individual taxpayers with a *net capital gain* pay a reduced tax rate on the net capital gain. **Net capital gain** equals the excess of net long-term capital gain over net short-term capital loss. If there is both a net long-term capital gain and a net short-term capital gain, then net capital gain equals the net long-term capital gain. Taxpayers with a net capital gain compute their tax liability by subtracting the net capital gain from taxable income and computing tax on the remaining amount. They then add to this amount the tax on the net capital gain. The tax rate on net capital gain is 5% for taxpayers in the 10% and 15% tax brackets. For taxpayers in the 25% and higher tax brackets, the tax rate on net capital gain is 15%.

EXAMPLE 8

The taxable income for Janice Altman from Examples 4 and 5 is $95,000 for 2005. Altman's filing status is single. Altman computes her 2005 tax liability as follows.

Tax on $90,000 ($95,000 – $5,000 net capital gain)	$19,714
Plus $5,000 × 15%	750
Tax liability on $95,000	$20,464

EXAMPLE 9

Same as in Example 8, except that Altman's taxable income is $25,000.

Tax on $20,000 ($25,000 – $5,000)	$2,639
Plus $5,000 × 5% (Altman is in the 15% bracket)	250
Tax liability on $25,000	$2,889

> The lowest tax rate on net capital gains does not always extend to net gains from the sale of collectibles and to gains on the sale of Section 1202 qualified small business stock. Net gains from the sale of these assets are taxed at a higher 28% rate for taxpayers in the 28% or higher tax brackets. Collectibles include any work of art, rugs, antiques and gemstones, plus the taxpayer's stamp and coin collections. Those interested in learning more about how the sale of these assets fits into the netting process should refer to the Instructions to Form 1040, Schedule D, Capital Gains and Losses.

Net Capital Losses

When capital losses exceed capital gains, the excess is a net capital loss. Each year, individual taxpayers can use up to $3,000 of net capital losses to offset ordinary income. Ordinary income includes wages, interest, dividends, and net profit from a business. Any net capital loss in excess of $3,000 can be carried forward indefinitely. Should the netting process produce both a net short-term and a net long-term capital loss, taxpayers first use up the net short-term capital loss, and then net long-term capital loss. Any unused short-term capital loss is carried over to the next year to offset next year's short-term capital gains. Any unused long-term capital loss is carried over to the next year to offset next year's long-term capital gains.

EXAMPLE 10

In 2005, Meg Fortin sold three capital assets that produced a $4,000 short-term gain, a $13,000 short-term capital loss, and a $2,000 long-term capital loss.

Short-Term	Long-Term
$4,000	($2,000)
(13,000)	
($9,000)	($2,000)

Fortin's capital losses exceed capital gains by $11,000. Fortin uses $3,000 of the net short-term capital loss to offset ordinary income on her 2005 tax return. Fortin carries over to 2006 a $6,000 short-term capital loss ($9,000 – $3,000) and a $2,000 long-term capital loss.

EXAMPLE 11

Mary Hill sells three capital assets in 2005 that produce a $5,000 short-term gain, a $1,000 long-term gain, and a $4,000 long-term capital loss. Hill has a $6,000 short-term capital loss carryover and a $2,000 long-term capital loss carryover from 2004. She nets these amounts against her 2005 capital gains and losses. This results in a $1,000 net short-term capital loss and a $5,000 net long-term capital loss.

	Short-Term	**Long-Term**
carryover	($6,000)	($2,000)
	$5,000	1,000
		(4,000)
	($1,000)	($5,000)

Hill uses the $1,000 net short-term capital loss and $2,000 of the net long-term capital loss to offset ordinary income on her 2005 tax return. She carries over to 2006 a $3,000 long-term capital loss ($5,000 – $2,000).

Schedule D

Individual taxpayers report capital gains and losses on Schedule D (Form 1040), Capital Gains and Losses. They report short-term capital gains and losses in Part I. Taxpayers report long-term capital gains and losses in Part II. All gains and losses are reported in column (f).

In Part III, taxpayers combine the net short-term capital gain or loss (line 7) and the net long-term capital gain or loss (line 15). If combining these amounts results in an overall net loss, the taxpayer enters up to $3,000 of the net loss (1,500 if married filing separately) on Schedule D (line 21) and transfers this amount to Form 1040. When an overall net gain results, the taxpayer completes lines 17–20, which may involve completing a worksheet to pay a reduced the tax rate on net capital gain. Even if the taxpayer does not report a net capital gain, when the taxpayer reports qualified dividends on Form 1040 (line 9b), line 22 of Schedule D is answered **Yes**. The taxpayer then completes the **Qualified Dividends and Capital Gains Tax Worksheet** located in the Instructions to Form 1040 to pay a 15% tax rate on the qualified dividends (5% for taxpayers in the 10% and 15% tax brackets). This worksheet is shown on page 11-10 in an unofficial form reflecting the authors' revisions. It is included for illustration purposes only. The official version was not released at press time.

Information for Figure 11-1: Filled-In Schedule D

On November 20, 2005, Curt R. Stevens sold 100 shares of Comco Corporation common stock for $2,975. Stevens paid a $20 commission on the sale. Stevens purchased the stock on June 27, 2005, for $750.

On September 3, 2005, Stevens sold 100 shares of Wilcox Industries preferred stock for $6,000. Stevens paid a $120 commission on the sale. Stevens received the stock as a gift from his father on May 8, 1994. The FMV of the stock on May 8, 1994, was $9,000. His father paid $3,192 for the stock on February 7, 1981. The father did not pay gift tax on the transfer.

In 2004, Stevens's capital losses exceeded his capital gains by $4,000. Stevens used $3,000 of the excess of the net capital loss to offset ordinary income and carried over to 2005 a $1,000 short-term capital loss.

Other Information

1(d): Sales price, **$2,955.00** ($2,975 – $20 selling expenses)

6: Short-term capital loss carryover, **$1,000.00**

8(b): Date acquired, **2/7/81** (donor's holding period carries over since donor's basis is used)

8(d): Sales price, **$5,880.00** ($6,000 – $120)

8(e): Cost or other basis, **$3,192.00** (donor's basis carries over since donor's basis < FMV at the time of the gift)

FIGURE 11-1 Filled-In Schedule D, Page 1

SCHEDULE D (Form 1040) Department of the Treasury Internal Revenue Service (99)	**Capital Gains and Losses** ▶ Attach to Form 1040. ▶ See Instructions for Schedule D (Form 1040). ▶ Use Schedule D-1 to list additional transactions for lines 1 and 8.	OMB No. 1545-0074 20**05** Attachment Sequence No. **12**

Name(s) shown on Form 1040: Curtis R. Stevens   Your social security number: 992 84 5922

Part I Short-Term Capital Gains and Losses—Assets Held One Year or Less

(a) Description of property (Example: 100 sh. XYZ Co.)	(b) Date acquired (Mo., day, yr.)	(c) Date sold (Mo., day, yr.)	(d) Sales price (see page D-6 of the instructions)	(e) Cost or other basis (see page D-6 of the instructions)	(f) Gain or (loss) Subtract (e) from (d)
1 100 shares Comco Corp.	6/27/05	11/20/05	2,955 00	750 00	2,205 00

2 Enter your short-term totals, if any, from Schedule D-1, line 2	**2**		
3 **Total short-term sales price amounts.** Add lines 1 and 2 in column (d)	**3**	2,955 00	
4 Short-term gain from Form 6252 and short-term gain or (loss) from Forms 4684, 6781, and 8824	**4**		
5 Net short-term gain or (loss) from partnerships, S corporations, estates, and trusts from Schedule(s) K-1	**5**		
6 Short-term capital loss carryover. Enter the amount, if any, from line 8 of your **Capital Loss Carryover Worksheet** on page D-6 of the instructions	**6**	(1,000 00)	
7 **Net short-term capital gain or (loss).** Combine lines 1 through 6 in column (f)	**7**	1,205 00	

Part II Long-Term Capital Gains and Losses—Assets Held More Than One Year

(a) Description of property (Example: 100 sh. XYZ Co.)	(b) Date acquired (Mo., day, yr.)	(c) Date sold (Mo., day, yr.)	(d) Sales price (see page D-6 of the instructions)	(e) Cost or other basis (see page D-6 of the instructions)	(f) Gain or (loss) Subtract (e) from (d)
8 100 Shares Wilcox Industries	2/7/81	9/3/05	5,880 00	3,192 00	2,688 00

9 Enter your long-term totals, if any, from Schedule D-1, line 9	**9**		
10 **Total long-term sales price amounts.** Add lines 8 and 9 in column (d)	**10**	5,880 00	
11 Gain from Form 4797, Part I; long-term gain from Forms 2439 and 6252; and long-term gain or (loss) from Forms 4684, 6781, and 8824	**11**		
12 Net long-term gain or (loss) from partnerships, S corporations, estates, and trusts from Schedule(s) K-1	**12**		
13 Capital gain distributions. See page D-1 of the instructions	**13**		
14 Long-term capital loss carryover. Enter the amount, if any, from line 13 of your **Capital Loss Carryover Worksheet** on page D-6 of the instructions	**14**	( )	
15 **Net long-term capital gain or (loss).** Combine lines 8 through 14 in column (f). Then go to Part III on the back	**15**	2,688 00	

For Paperwork Reduction Act Notice, see Form 1040 instructions.   Cat. No. 11338H   Schedule D (Form 1040) 2005

FIGURE 11-1   Filled-In Schedule D, Page 2

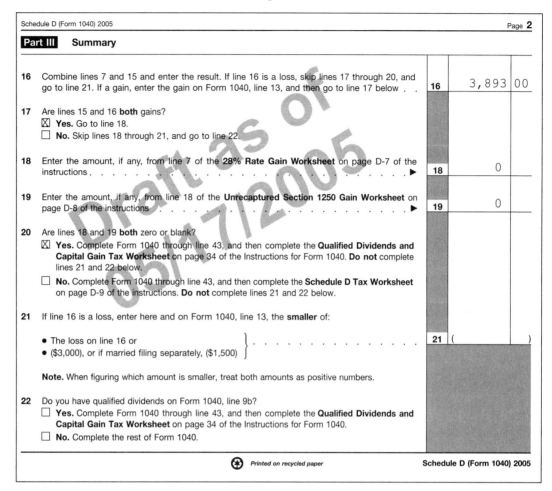

Other Information

18: Stevens has no amount from line 7 of the **28% Rate Gain Worksheet**

19: Stevens has no amount from line 18 of the **Unrecaptured Section 1250 Gain Worksheet**

20: Stevens answers **Yes** to this question. He transfers the $3,893 total capital gain from Schedule D (line 16) to Form 1040 (line 13). He then calculates his tax by completing the **Qualified Dividends and Capital Gain Tax Worksheet** from the IRS Instructions to Form 1040 to pay a reduced tax rate on his $2,688 net capital gain. An unofficial copy of this worksheet can be found on the next page.

Unofficial
Qualified Dividends and Capital Gain Tax Worksheet—Line 44

Keep for Your Records

| **Before you begin:** | √ | See the instructions for line 44 to see if you can use this worksheet to figure your tax. |
| | √ | If you do not have to file Schedule D and you received capital gain distributions, be sure you checked the box on line 13 of Form 1040. |

1. Enter the amount from Form 1040, line 43 . . . . **1.** _____

2. Enter the amount from Form 1040, line 9b . . . . **2.** _____

3. Are you filing Schedule D?
   ☐ **Yes.** Enter the **smaller** of line 15 or 16 of Schedule D, but do not enter less than -0-
   ☐ **No.** Enter the amount from Form 1040, line 13 } **3.** _____

4. Add lines 2 and 3 . . . . **4.** _____

5. If you are claiming investment interest expense on Form 4952, enter the amount from line 4g of that form. Otherwise, enter -0- . . . . **5.** _____

6. Subtract line 5 from line 4. If zero or less, enter -0- . . . . **6.** _____

7. Subtract line 6 from line 1. If zero or less, enter -0- . . . . **7.** _____

8. Enter the **smaller** of:
   • The amount on line 1, or
   • $29,700 if single or married filing separately, $59,400 if married filing jointly or qualifying widow(er), $39,800 if head of household. } . . . . **8.** _____

9. Is the amount on line 7 equal to or more than the amount on line 8?
   ☐ **Yes.** Skip lines 9 through 11; go to line 12 and check the "No" box.
   ☐ **No.** Enter the amount from line 7 . . . . **9.** _____

10. Subtract line 9 from line 8 . . . . **10.** _____

11. Multiply line 10 by 5% (.05) . . . . **11.** _____

12. Are the amounts on lines 6 and 10 the same?
    ☐ **Yes.** Skip lines 12 through 15; go to line 16.
    ☐ **No.** Enter the **smaller** of line 1 or line 6 . . . . **12.** _____

13. Enter the amount from line 10 (if line 10 is blank, enter -0-) . . . . **13.** _____

14. Subtract line 13 from line 12 . . . . **14.** _____

15. Multiply line 14 by 15% (.15) . . . . **15.** _____

16. Figure the tax on the amount on line 7. Use the Tax Table or Tax Computation Worksheet, whichever applies . . . . **16.** _____

17. Add lines 11, 15, and 16 . . . . **17.** _____

18. Figure the tax on the amount on line 1. Use the Tax Table or Tax Computation Worksheet, whichever applies . . . . **18.** _____

19. **Tax on all taxable income.** Enter the **smaller** of line 17 or line 18. Also include this amount on Form 1040, line 44 . . . . **19.** _____

*Note: The worksheet shown above is unofficial and reflects the authors' revisions. It is included for illustration purposes only. The official version was not yet released at press time.

Special Rules

Special rules apply to losses from worthless securities and from the sale of Section 1244 stock. Special rules also apply to gains from sales between certain related parties and from sales of subdivided real estate.

Worthless Securities

In the year securities become worthless, the taxpayer is treated as having sold the securities for $0 on the last day of the tax year. For most taxpayers, securities are capital assets. Hence, worthless securities produce a capital loss. A long-term capital loss results if, on the last day of the tax year, the taxpayer held the securities for more than one year.

EXAMPLE 12

On April 3, 2004, Randy Harmon pays $10,000 for stock. On January 23, 2005, the stock is declared worthless. Harmon is deemed to have sold the stock for $0 on December 31, 2005. Since the period from April 4, 2004 (the day after the purchase) until December 31, 2005 (the "sales date") exceeds one year, Harmon recognizes a $10,000 long-term capital loss. He reports the loss in Part II on Schedule D (line 8) and identifies the loss as coming from a worthless security by writing "worthless" in the columns for date sold and sales price.

Section 1244 Stock

For most people, stock is an investment. A loss on the sale of an investment normally produces a capital loss. However, each year individuals can deduct as ordinary losses up to $50,000 ($100,000 on a joint return) of the loss on the sale, exchange, or worthlessness of *qualified small business stock* (Section 1244 stock). Annual losses in excess of $50,000 ($100,000 on a joint return) are capital losses. Although both common and preferred stock qualify as Section 1244 stock, only the original owner of the stock qualifies for the ordinary loss treatment. To qualify as Section 1244 stock, the corporation issuing the stock must meet certain requirements. Two main requirements are:

1. The corporation's contributed capital plus paid-in-surplus cannot exceed $1,000,000 at the time the stock is issued.
2. The corporation must be primarily an operating company rather than an investment company.

EXAMPLE 13

Page Walters, a single taxpayer, sells Section 1244 stock for $17,000. Walters purchased the stock several years ago for $80,000. Walters's realized loss equals $63,000 ($17,000 − $80,000). Walters recognizes a $50,000 ordinary loss and a $13,000 long-term capital loss. She enters the long-term capital loss into the netting process and uses the ordinary loss to offset ordinary income such as wages and dividends. If Walters has no other capital gains or losses, only $3,000 of the $13,000 long-term capital loss can be used to offset ordinary income in the current year. Had the stock not qualified as Section 1244 stock, Walters would have recognized a $63,000 long-term capital loss.

Each year taxpayers are allowed up to $50,000 ($100,000 for MFJ) of ordinary losses from the sale of Section 1244 stock. Taxpayers whose Section 1244 stock has declined in value more than $50,000 ($100,000 MFJ) from when they bought it should plan on selling their stock over more than one tax year to take advantage of the $50,000 ($100,000) of ordinary losses allowed each year.

Gains from Sales between Certain Related Parties

When individuals sell capital assets to a corporation, they should recognize capital gains or losses. However, for individuals who own (directly or constructively) more than 50% of the value of the corporation's outstanding stock, capital gain treatment does not apply if the property is depreciable property to the corporation. Instead, the individual recognizes ordinary income. The same rule applies to individuals who sell capital assets to a partnership in which they own (directly or constructively) more than a 50% interest. If the property is depreciable property to the partnership, then capital gain treatment does not apply, and the individual recognizes ordinary income. Note that this rule applies only to gains between certain related parties. See Chapter 10 for rules disallowing losses between related parties, as well as the rules governing constructive ownership.

Subdivided Property

Although a capital gain or loss usually results when investors sell parcels of land, special rules apply to *gains* on the sale of subdivided property. To receive capital gain treatment, taxpayers must first meet the following four conditions.

1. The taxpayer cannot be a real estate dealer.
2. The taxpayer cannot be a corporation.
3. The taxpayer cannot make substantial improvements to the lots sold. Filling, draining, clearing, and leveling activities normally are not considered substantial improvements.
4. The taxpayer must hold the lots for at least five years before selling them. Inherited property has no minimum holding requirement.

Taxpayers who meet these four conditions recognize capital gain on the sale of all lots sold until the tax year in which they sell the sixth lot. Starting with the tax year in which the sixth lot is sold, taxpayers recognize ordinary income for up to 5% of the sales price. Gain not taxed as ordinary income is taxed as long-term capital gain. All selling expenses are first absorbed by the ordinary income.

EXAMPLE 14

Eric Marmoll bought a tract of land in 1995. Marmoll, who is not a real estate dealer, subdivides the land in 2004 and sells four lots for $12,000 each. The adjusted basis of each lot is $9,000. There were no selling expenses. Marmoll recognizes a $3,000 long-term capital gain on the sale of each lot ($12,000 – $9,000).

EXAMPLE 15

Continuing with Example 14, in 2005 Marmoll sells two more lots for $12,000 each. The adjusted basis of each lot is $9,000. There were no selling expenses. Marmoll recognizes a $3,000 gain on the sale of each lot. Because Marmoll sells the sixth lot in 2005, he recognizes $600 ($12,000 × 5%) of ordinary income and $2,400 ($3,000 – $600) of long-term capital gain for each lot sold in 2005. Marmoll will recognize up to 5% of the sales price as ordinary income on lots sold in future years.

EXAMPLE 16

Assume the same facts as in Example 15, except that Marmoll incurred $500 of selling expenses for each lot. The selling expenses reduce the recognized gain for each lot to $2,500 ($3,000 – $500). The selling expenses are first absorbed by the ordinary income. Thus, for each lot sold Marmoll recognizes $100 ($600 – $500 selling expenses) of ordinary income and $2,400 ($2,500 – $100) of long-term capital gain. Had the selling expenses exceeded $600, the entire recognized gain would have been long-term capital gain.

Other Ways of Producing Capital Gains and Losses

Besides the sale or exchange of capital assets, other activities can produce capital gains and losses. These activities include nonbusiness bad debts, net casualty or theft gains on personal-use property, and disposing of business property.

Nonbusiness Bad Debts

Chapter 7 described the rules for deducting business bad debts. A nonbusiness bad debt is a bona fide debt that does not qualify as a business bad debt. A nonbusiness bad debt is reported as a short-term capital loss, regardless of how long the debt was held. This differs from business bad debts, which sole proprietors deduct on Schedule C. Also, unlike a business bad debt, which taxpayers can start deducting in the year the debt becomes partially worthless, taxpayers cannot deduct a nonbusiness bad debt until it becomes completely worthless.

In the year taxpayers claim a nonbusiness bad debt, they enter the name of the debtor and the words *statement attached* on Schedule D, Part I [line 1(a)]. They then report the amount of the loss on line 1(f). Finally, they attach to the tax return a statement describing the following:

1. The amount of the debt and the date it was due
2. Their business or family relationship with the debtor
3. Their efforts to collect the debt
4. Their reason for concluding the debt was worthless

EXAMPLE 17

Pam McMillan lent a friend $10,000 in 2003. A bona fide debtor-creditor relationship existed between McMillan and her friend. In 2004 the friend filed for bankruptcy, and McMillan was told to expect 60¢ on the dollar for her loan. The friend completed bankruptcy proceedings in 2005, and McMillan received $4,500. McMillan recognizes a $5,500 ($10,000 – $4,500) short-term capital loss in 2005, the year in which the loan became completely worthless.

Net Personal Casualty or Theft Gains

Chapters 5 and 10 discussed the calculation of casualty or theft gains and losses on personal-use property. A casualty or theft gain occurs when the insurance proceeds exceed the taxpayer's adjusted basis in the property. A casualty or theft loss occurs when the amount of the loss exceeds the insurance reimbursement. For *personal-use property,* the amount of the loss is measured as the lesser of the property's adjusted basis or its decline in value.

Sometimes the taxpayer incurs just one personal casualty or theft during the year. When this happens, the taxpayer determines the gain or loss from each property damaged or destroyed in the casualty or theft. The taxpayer then nets the gains and losses to compute a *net personal casualty or theft gain or loss.* If the result is a net gain, then all personal casualty or theft gains and losses are treated as capital gains and losses. If the result is a net loss, then the taxpayer reduces the loss by $100 and by 10% of AGI. Any remaining loss is deducted as an itemized deduction (Chapter 5).

| | EXAMPLE 18 | | | |

Martha Voit's home was burglarized. A family heirloom and a TV were stolen. Information about the items reveals the following:

	FMV Before	FMV After	Adjusted Basis	Insurance Proceeds
TV	$ 500	$0	$ 700	$ 0
Heirloom	3,000	0	1,000	2,900

Since Voit did not insure the TV, the theft of the TV produces a $500 casualty or theft loss (the lesser of adjusted basis or decline in value). Voit insured the heirloom, which results in a $1,900 casualty or theft gain ($2,900 insurance proceeds – $1,000 adjusted basis). Voit's net casualty or theft gain equals $1,400 ($1,900 – $500). Assuming Voit held both the TV and the heirloom long-term, she treats the $1,400 as a long-term capital gain.

When several personal casualties and thefts occur during the year, the taxpayer first computes a net personal casualty or theft gain or loss for each casualty or theft. If a single casualty or theft results in a net personal casualty or theft loss, the taxpayer reduces the loss by $100 (Chapter 5). A net personal casualty gain is not reduced by $100. The taxpayer then nets the gains and losses from the various personal casualties and thefts. If the result is an overall net gain, all personal casualty or theft gains and losses for the year are treated as capital gains and losses.

Taxpayers compute their net personal casualty or theft gain or loss on Form 4684 (Section A), Casualties and Thefts. If a net loss results, the taxpayer attaches Form 4684 to the tax return to support the itemized deduction for the amount that exceeds 10% of AGI. If the result is a net gain, the taxpayer transfers the personal casualty or theft gains and losses to the appropriate short-term/long-term parts on Schedule D.

BUSINESS GAINS AND LOSSES

Disposing of real and depreciable business property can produce a long-term capital gain, even though the definition of a capital asset specifically excludes business property. To understand how and when this can happen, it is necessary to examine the tax laws regarding the disposal of real and depreciable business property.

By definition, real and depreciable business property are not capital assets. However, under certain conditions, disposing of real and depreciable business property held for over one year can produce a long-term capital gain. (The disposal of real and depreciable business property held one year or less always produces ordinary income or loss). Real and depreciable business property held long-term is known as **Section 1231 property.** The sale, exchange, or condemnation of Section 1231 property produces a Section 1231 gain or loss. If Section 1231 gains for the year exceed Section 1231 losses, the net Section 1231 gain may be treated as long-term capital gain. If Section 1231 losses exceed Section 1231 gains, the net Section 1231 loss is treated as an ordinary loss.

EXAMPLE 19

For the year, Jerry Novak reports a $12,000 Section 1231 gain and a $5,000 Section 1231 loss. Novak's net Section 1231 gain equals $7,000 ($12,000 – $5,000). Novak enters this amount as long-term capital gain in the netting process.

EXAMPLE 20

For the year, Nancy Morris reports a $10,000 Section 1231 gain and a $23,000 Section 1231 loss. Morris's net Section 1231 loss equals $13,000 ($10,000 – $23,000). Morris deducts this amount as an ordinary loss.

Business Casualty or Theft Gains and Losses

Chapter 10 presented the rules for computing business casualty or theft gains and losses. At the end of the year, taxpayers sum all casualty or theft gains and losses from Section 1231 property (business property held long-term). When gains exceed losses, the excess is a *net business casualty or theft gain.* A net business casualty or theft gain is treated as a Section 1231 gain. When losses exceed gains, the difference is a *net business casualty or theft loss.* A net business casualty or theft loss is treated as an ordinary loss. Casualty or theft gains and losses from business property held short-term produce ordinary income and losses.

EXAMPLE 21

For the year, Leslie Burton recognizes a $10,000 business casualty gain and a $4,000 business casualty loss from properties held long-term. Burton also recognizes a $2,000 Section 1231 loss. Burton treats the $6,000 net business casualty or theft gain ($10,000 – $4,000) as a Section 1231 gain. Burton's net Section 1231 gain equals $4,000 ($6,000 – $2,000). Burton includes the $4,000 as a long-term capital gain in the netting process.

EXAMPLE 22

In the current year, Mary Clark has a $6,000 business casualty gain, a $13,000 business casualty loss, and a $5,000 Section 1231 gain. Clark's net business casualty or theft loss equals $7,000 ($6,000 – $13,000). Clark deducts the $7,000 as an ordinary loss. Clark treats the $5,000 net Section 1231 gain as a long-term capital gain.

Section 1231 provides taxpayers with the best of both situations: long-term capital gains for net Section 1231 gains and ordinary losses for net Section 1231 losses. For this reason, Congress did not want taxpayers taking unfair advantage of the Section 1231 rules. Over the years, Congress identified two situations where taxpayers might take advantage of the rules for Section 1231 property. The first situation involves the sale or exchange of depreciable property for a gain. The second situation involves unrecaptured Section 1231 losses.

Depreciation Recapture

Because net Section 1231 gain becomes long-term capital gain, depreciating property as quickly as possible increases the chance of recognizing long-term capital gain when the property is sold. This results in larger depreciation deductions (where the tax benefits are computed using the taxpayer's marginal tax rate) and possibly greater long-term capital gains (where net capital gain is taxed at a lower tax rate). Example 23 illustrates this point.

EXAMPLE 23

In March 2004, Henry Wallace paid $20,000 for a machine that he used in his business. Wallace elected to expense the entire machine under Section 179, therefore his adjusted basis in the machine is $0 at the end of 2004. On October 12, 2005, Wallace sold the machine for $12,000, resulting in a $12,000 Section 1231 gain. If Wallace had no other Section 1231 or capital gains and losses in 2005, the entire $12,000 becomes long-term capital gain, which is taxed at no more than 15%.

Assume instead that Wallace had not elected Section 179, but chose to depreciate the machine using regular (accelerated) MACRS without any bonus depreciation. He would have deducted $2,858 in 2004 ($20,000 × 14.29%) and $2,449 in 2005 ($20,000 × 24.49% × ½). His adjusted basis in the machine at the time of the sale would have been $14,693 ($20,000 − $2,858 − $2,449) and he would have recognized a $2,693 Section 1231 loss on the sale ($12,000 − $14,693). Again assuming no other Section 1231 gains or losses, Wallace would deduct the $2,693 as an ordinary loss.

In both scenarios, Wallace's overall deduction equals $8,000. In the first case, Wallace deducts $20,000 for depreciation expense but reports a $12,000 gain on the sale. In the second case, he deducts $5,307 for depreciation plus another $2,693 for the loss on the sale, for a total of $8,000.

Now assume that Wallace's marginal tax rate in both years is 28%. In the first case, Wallace receives a $5,600 tax benefit from the depreciation expense ($20,000 × 28%) but pays tax of $1,800 ($12,000 × 15%) on the gain from the sale. The net tax benefit equals $3,800 ($5,600 − $1,800). In the second case, everything is taxed at the marginal tax rate, so Wallace's tax benefit is only $2,240 ($8,000 × 28%).

As you see from Example 23, an incentive existed for taxpayers to use the fastest depreciation method possible. To limit this opportunity, Congress introduced the concept of **depreciation recapture.** Under the Section 1245 depreciation recapture rules, part or all of the gains on the disposal of depreciable personal property may be taxed as ordinary income. Gain not taxed as ordinary income is Section 1231 gain. [Note that depreciation recapture only affects gains on the disposal of depreciable Section 1231 property. Losses on the disposal of Section 1231 property are always treated as Section 1231 losses.]

For personal property, all depreciation taken (including Section 179 expense and bonus depreciation) is subject to depreciation recapture. Even when the taxpayer uses the straight-line method to depreciate personal property, the entire amount of straight-line depreciation is subject to recapture.

EXAMPLE 24

Tony Bonnell bought a business machine on January 3, 2003, for $20,000. Bonnell sold the machine on April 25, 2005, for $21,000. In 2003, 2004, and 2005, Bonnell deducted depreciation totaling $9,505. Bonnell's adjusted basis in the machine equals $10,495 ($20,000 – $9,505). Bonnell recognizes a $10,505 gain ($21,000 – $10,495), of which $9,505 is ordinary income and $1,000 is Section 1231 gain.

Depreciation recapture only applies to real property when an accelerated depreciation method is used to depreciate the realty. Since the only depreciation method for realty under MACRS is the straight-line method, there is no depreciation recapture on the sale of real property placed in service after 1986.

Recapture of Section 1231 Losses

The tax treatment of Section 1231 gains and losses gives taxpayers the opportunity to treat net Section 1231 gains as long-term capital gains and net Section 1231 losses as ordinary losses. To keep taxpayers from bunching all Section 1231 gains in one year to get long-term capital gain treatment, and then bunching Section 1231 losses in the next year to deduct them as ordinary losses, Congress introduced Section 1231 recapture.

Before net Section 1231 gain can become long-term capital gain, taxpayers must look back over the past five years and compute the amount of unrecaptured Section 1231 losses. Unrecaptured Section 1231 losses act like depreciation recapture. That is, net Section 1231 gain is taxed as ordinary income to the extent of unrecaptured Section 1231 losses. Unrecaptured Section 1231 losses equal the excess of the net Section 1231 losses (deducted as ordinary losses) over the Section 1231 gains taxed as ordinary income.

EXAMPLE 25

In 2005, Jose Mandella has Section 1231 gains of $30,000 and Section 1231 losses of $12,000. Mandella also has unrecaptured Section 1231 losses from 2000-2004 of $7,000. Mandella's net Section 1231 gains for 2005 equals $18,000 ($30,000 – $12,000). He reports $7,000 of this gain as ordinary income and the rest, $11,000 ($18,000 – $7,000), as long-term capital gain.

Unrecaptured Section 1250 Gain

When real property placed in service after 1986 is sold at a gain, individual taxpayers treat the gain as Section 1231 gain. When Section 1231 gains exceed Section 1231 losses for the year (a net Section 1231 gain), such gain may be treated as long-term capital gain. However, the tax law requires that any unrecaptured Section 1250 gain be taxed at the higher 25% for taxpayers in the 25% or higher tax brackets.

Unrecaptured Section 1250 gain equals the lesser of the gain or the depreciation taken on the property. Unrecaptured Section 1250 gain applies only to real property sold at a gain. It does not apply to realty sold at a loss. It also applies only to individual taxpayers, not corporations.

EXAMPLE 26

Jane Everett sold residential realty during 2005 for $400,000. Everett paid $520,000 for the building in 1995. Depreciation taken on the building from 1995–2005 totaled $193,818. Thus, Everett's basis in the building is $326,182 ($520,000 – $193,818). Her recognized gain is $73,818 ($400,000 – $326,182). Everett's unrecaptured Section 1250 gain equals $73,818 (lesser of the gain, $73,818, or depreciation taken, $193,818).

EXAMPLE 27

Same as in Example 26, except that Everett sold the property for $600,000. Unrecaptured Section 1250 gain equals $193,818 [lesser of the $273,818 gain ($600,000 – $326,182) or $193,818 depreciation taken]. When Everett goes to transfer net Section 1231 gain to long-term capital gain, she will report the first $193,818 of the net gain as 25% long-term gain and the rest as 15% long-term gain.

Taxpayers with unrecaptured Section 1250 gain report this gain in the netting process between the short-term and long-term columns. When unrecaptured Section 1250 gain exists, netting of gains and losses is done as follows.

1. If the amount in the 15% long-term column is a net loss, use it to offset any 25% long-term gain first, followed by any short-term gain. If there is no net 15% long-term loss, proceed to Step 2.

2. Use any net short-term capital loss to offset any 25% long-term gain, and then any net 15% long-term gain. The netting process is complete when only all gains or all losses remain.

EXAMPLE 28

Brook and Jerry Daniels sold several assets during 2005. Their taxable income is $142,125, which does not include any qualified dividends. The netting within the groups resulted in a $2,000 net short-term loss; a $6,000 25% long-term gain; and a $7,000 net 15% long-term gain. The netting process within and between groups is as follows.

	Long-Term	
Short-Term	**25%**	**15%**
$ 6,000	$6,000	$18,000
(8,000)		(11,000)
($2,000) ⟶	(2,000)	$7,000
	$4,000	

Since there is no net 15% long-term loss, the Daniels begin the netting process between groups by offsetting the $2,000 net short-term loss against the net 25% long-term gain (Step 2). This results in a $4,000 25% long-term gain and a $7,000 net 15% long-term gain. The Daniels compute their tax liability as follows.

Tax on $131,125 ($142,125 – $11,000 net capital gain)	$26,447
Plus $4,000 × 25% (the Daniels are in the 28% bracket)	1,000
Plus $7,000 × 15%	1,050
Tax liability on $142,125	$28,497

EXAMPLE 29

Kelli Rogers sold several capital assets during 2005. These assets produced a $9,000 net short-term loss; a $4,000 25% long-term gain; and a $13,000 net 15% long-term gain. Rogers files as head of household and her 2005 taxable income is $64,230 (no qualified dividends). The netting process between groups is as follows.

	Long-Term	
Short-Term	**25%**	**15%**
$6,000	$4,000	$14,000
(15,000)		(1,000)
($9,000)		$13,000
→	(4,000) →	(5,000)
	$ 0	$ 8,000

Rogers skips Step 1 and uses the $9,000 net short-term loss to offset first the 25% long-term gain and then the net 15% long-term gain. Rogers is left with $8,000 net 15% long-term gain. Her tax liability is computed as follows.

Tax on $56,230 ($64,230 – $8,000)	$ 9,554
Plus $8,000 × 15%	1,200
Tax liability on $64,230	$10,774

EXAMPLE 30

Jim and Erin Stegall sold several assets during 2005. These assets produced a $6,000 net short-term loss; a $15,000 25% long-term gain; and a $2,000 net 15% long-term loss. The Stegalls file a joint return for 2005 and report taxable income of $129,230 (including $2,200 of qualified dividends). The netting process between groups is as follows.

	Long-Term	
Short-Term	**25%**	**15%**
($13,000)	$15,000	($3,000)
7,000		1,000
($ 6,000)	(2,000) ←	($2,000)
	$13,000	
→	(6,000)	
	$ 7,000	

The Stegalls offset the net 15% long-term loss against the 25% gain (Step 1). They then use the short-term loss to offset more of the 25% gain (Step 2). The Stegalls are left with a $7,000 net 25% long-term capital gain. They compute their tax liability as follows.

Tax on $120,030 ($129,230 – $7,000 net gain – $2,200 qualified dividends)	$23,340
Plus $7,000 × 25% (the Stegalls are in the 28% bracket)	1,750
Plus $2,200 × 15%	330
Tax liability on $129,230	$25,420

A special rule applies to corporations. When corporations sell depreciable real property, they are not entitled to treat the entire gain as Section 1231 gain. Instead, 20% of the lesser of (1) depreciation taken or (2) the recognized gain is taxed as ordinary income. Any remaining gain is treated as Section 1231 gain. For example, a building is purchased for $100,000 and over the years, $20,000 of MACRS is deducted, resulting in an $80,000 adjusted basis. If the property is sold for $120,000, then $4,000 (20% × $20,000, which is the lesser of the MACRS or the gain) of the $40,000 gain ($120,000 – $80,000) is taxed as ordinary income; the rest ($40,000 – $4,000 = $36,000) is taxed as Section 1231 gain.

REPORTING BUSINESS GAINS AND LOSSES ON THE TAX RETURN

In the end, all recognized gains and losses appear on Form 1040. However, only gains and losses that appear on Schedule D, Capital Gains and Losses, receive capital gain and loss treatment. Taxpayers report the gain and loss on the sale, exchange, or condemnation of business property on Form 4797, Sales of Business Property. They report the gains and losses resulting from casualties and thefts of business property on Form 4684 (Section B), Casualties and Thefts. (Taxpayers also use Form 4684 [Section B] to report casualty or theft gains and losses from investment property. However, the scope of this chapter is limited to business casualties or thefts. Those interested in casualty or theft gains and losses on investment property should refer to IRS Publication 547.) Net gains and losses from Form 4684 (Section B) flow through to Form 4797. Therefore, taxpayers should begin by completing Form 4684.

Form 4684 (Section B), Casualties and Thefts

Taxpayers compute business casualty or theft gains and losses on Form 4684 (Section B), Casualties and Thefts. Taxpayers with more than one business casualty or theft during the year complete a separate Form 4684, Part I, for each casualty or theft. In Part II, taxpayers separate gains and losses involving Section 1231 property from gains and losses involving business property held short-term. They transfer a net business casualty or theft gain to Form 4797, Part I (line 3), and treat it as a gain from the sale of Section 1231 property. They transfer a net business casualty or theft loss to Form 4797, Part II (line 14), and deduct it as an ordinary loss. A net casualty or theft gain or loss from business property held short-term is also transferred to Form 4797, Part II (line 14), and deducted as an ordinary gain or loss.

Information for Figure 11-2: Filled-In Form 4684 (Section B)

On October 15, 2005, Jonathan Miller's laptop computer and laser printer were stolen from his office. Miller purchased both properties on December 4, 2003. Before the theft, the FMV of the computer and printer were $1,500 and $1,800, respectively. The insurance company reimbursed Miller $1,500 for the computer (adjusted basis, $2,200) and $2,150 for the printer (adjusted basis, $2,000).

Other Information

26:    **$2,200.00** is entered since the property was completely destroyed. See **Note:** below line 26. Miller transfers the $550 net business casualty or theft loss to Form 4797 (line 14).

FIGURE 11-2   Filled-In Form 4684 (Section B), Casualties and Thefts

Form 4684 (2005) — Attachment Sequence No. **26** — Page **2**

Name(s) shown on tax return. Do not enter name and identifying number if shown on other side.
Jonathan L. Miller

Identifying number **668-58-9977**

SECTION B—Business and Income-Producing Property

Part I   Casualty or Theft Gain or Loss (Use a separate Part I for each casualty or theft.)

19 Description of properties (show type, location, and date acquired for each property). Use a separate line for each property lost or damaged from the same casualty or theft.

Property **A** Laptop Computer, acquired December 4, 2003
Property **B** Laser Printer, acquired December 4, 2003
Property **C**
Property **D**

		A	B	C	D
20	Cost or adjusted basis of each property	2,200 00	2,000 00		
21	Insurance or other reimbursement (whether or not you filed a claim). See the instructions for line 3. Note: If line 20 is more than line 21, skip line 22	1,500 00	2,150 00		
22	Gain from casualty or theft. If line 21 is more than line 20, enter the difference here and on line 29 or line 34, column (c)...		150 00		
23	Fair market value before casualty or theft	1,500 00			
24	Fair market value after casualty or theft	0 00			
25	Subtract line 24 from line 23	1,500 00			
26	Enter the smaller of line 20 or line 25	2,200 00			
27	Subtract line 21 from line 26. If zero or less, enter -0-	700 00			
28	Casualty or theft loss. Add the amounts on line 27. Enter the total here and on line 29 or line 34 (see instructions)	28	(700 00)		

Part II   Summary of Gains and Losses (from separate Parts I)

	(a) Identify casualty or theft	(b) Losses from casualties or thefts (i) Trade, business, rental or royalty property	(ii) Income-producing and employee property	(c) Gains from casualties or thefts includible in income
	Casualty or Theft of Property Held One Year or Less			
29		( )	( )	
30	Totals. Add the amounts on line 29	( )	( )	
31	Combine line 30, columns (b)(i) and (c). Enter the net gain or (loss) here and on Form 4797, line 14...		31	
32	Enter the amount from line 30, column (b)(ii) here...		32	
	Casualty or Theft of Property Held More Than One Year			
33	Casualty or theft gains from Form 4797, line 32		33	150 00
34		(700 00)	( )	
35	Total losses. Add amounts on line 34, columns (b)(i) and (b)(ii)	35 (700 00)	( )	
36	Total gains. Add lines 33 and 34, column (c)		36	150 00
37	Add amounts on line 35, columns (b)(i) and (b)(ii)		37	700 00
38	If the loss on line 37 is more than the gain on line 36:			
a	Combine line 35, column (b)(i) and line 36, and enter the net gain or (loss) here...		38a	(550 00)
b	Enter the amount from line 35, column (b)(ii) here...		38b	
39	If the loss on line 37 is less than or equal to the gain on line 36, combine lines 36 and 37 and enter here...		39	

Note: Partnerships, enter the amount from line 38a, 38b, or line 39 on Form 1065, Schedule K, line 11.
S corporations, enter the amount from line 38a or 38b on Form 1120S, Schedule K, line 10.

Printed on recycled paper   Form **4684** (2005)

Form 4797

Taxpayers use Form 4797, Sales of Business Property, to report gains and losses from the sale, exchange, or condemnation of business property. Form 4797 consists of three parts. Part I summarizes Section 1231 gains and losses. Part II summarizes ordinary gains and losses. Part III separates the gain from the sale or exchange of property subject to depreciation recapture between ordinary income and Section 1231 gain.

Part I

In Part I, taxpayers report gains and losses from Section 1231 property not subject to depreciation recapture. Also included in Part I are net business casualty gains from Form 4684 and Section 1231 gains from the sale of depreciable property from Form 4797, Part III. After entering all Section 1231 gains and losses in Part I, taxpayers compute their net Section 1231 gain or loss (line 7). They transfer a net Section 1231 loss to Part II (line 11) so that it can be treated as an ordinary loss. A net Section 1231 gain is first reduced by the nonrecaptured net Section 1231 losses from the past five years (line 8), and the rest is reported as a long-term capital gain on Schedule D (line 11). Taxpayers report the recaptured gain as ordinary income in Part II (line 12).

Part II

Taxpayers report gains and losses from the sale, exchange, or condemnation of business property held one year or less in Part II (line 10). Taxpayers also report in Part II (line 14) net business casualty or theft losses and casualty or theft gains and losses from business property held short-term. Net Section 1231 losses and recaptured Section 1231 gains from Part I also appear in Part II. After netting the ordinary gains and losses (line 17), the taxpayer transfers the net amount to Form 1040 (line 14).

Part III

This chapter introduced the concept of depreciation recapture. The recapture where gain is taxed as ordinary income to the extent of the *accumulated depreciation* taken is referred to as **Section 1245 recapture.** Section 1245 applies to tangible personal property sold for a gain. Taxpayers report property subject to Section 1245 depreciation recapture on Form 4797, Part III (line 25).

In Part III, total gains from the disposition of property subject to recapture are separated between amounts recaptured as ordinary income (line 31) and Section 1231 gain (line 32). Taxpayers report the ordinary income on Part II (line 13) and the Section 1231 gain on Part I (line 6).

Information for Figure 11-3: Filled-In Form 4797

On July 3, 2001, Teresa F. Lohman placed in service equipment costing $36,000. On May 10, 2005, she sold the equipment for $15,000. Depreciation taken on the equipment was $26,361. On January 3, 2005, Lohman sold land used in her business for $22,800. Commissions paid on the sale were $1,000. Lohman bought the land on February 6, 1978, for $14,000.

In 2005 the government notified Lohman that land she held for investment was to be condemned. Lohman paid $33,200 for the land on March 5, 1983. She received $30,200 from the government for the land on May 2, 2005. Lohman has $2,500 of unrecaptured Section 1231 losses from the past five years.

Other Information

1: Gross proceeds from the sale or exchange of real estate reported on Forms 1099-S and included on lines 2, 10, and 20, **$53,000** ($22,800 + $30,200)

2(f): Cost or other basis plus improvements and expenses of sale, **$15,000** ($14,000 + $1,000)

2(a): Description of property, **Land (involuntary conversion)**

8: Nonrecaptured net section 1231 losses from prior years, **$2,500**

25a: Depreciation allowed or allowable,* **$26,361**

*Taxpayers are required to reduce their basis in the property by the amount of depreciation they are entitled to deduct over the years, even if they fail to take the deduction on their tax returns.

Lohman transfers the $2,300 net Section 1231 gain to Schedule D (line 11). She transfers the $7,861 ordinary gain to Form 1040 (line 14).

INSTALLMENT SALES

When property is sold, the seller may collect the sales price in full at the time of sale. Alternatively, the sales price may be collected over a number of months or years. If the full sales price is collected in the year of sale, recognized gain or loss is reported in that year. When collections extend beyond the year of sale, any gain (but not loss) may be recognized on the installment method. The installment method allows taxpayers to report the gain (and pay the related taxes) as they collect payments on the installment obligation. To use the installment sales method, at least one payment must be received in the tax year following the year of the sale. Taxpayers, however, may elect not to use the installment method. They make this election by reporting the entire gain in the year of sale. The election must be made before the due date of the return (including extensions) for the year of the sale.

The installment sales method is intended for casual sales of personal and real property by nondealers. It cannot be used by most dealers. A dealer is someone who regularly sells personal or real property in the ordinary course of a trade or business. The installment method cannot be used to report gain from the sale of publicly traded stock or securities.

Computing Installment Gain

The amount of gain that must be reported in a given tax year is computed as follows:

$$\text{Gain recognized} = \text{payments received} \times (\text{gross profit} \div \text{contract price})$$

Payments Received

As payments on the sales price are collected, a portion of the profit is reported (recognized). Payments include cash and property the seller receives. Payments do not include notes or other obligations received from the buyer.

Gross Profit

Gross profit equals the amount realized less the adjusted basis of the property. Gross profit is the amount of gain that would be recognized in the year of sale if the installment method were not used. The amount realized includes cash and other property received. It also includes notes received from the buyer or mortgages the buyer assumes. It does not include any interest to be received from the transaction.

FIGURE 11-3 Filled-In Form 4797, Page 1

Form **4797**	**Sales of Business Property**	OMB No. 1545-0184
Department of the Treasury Internal Revenue Service (99)	(Also Involuntary Conversions and Recapture Amounts Under Sections 179 and 280F(b)(2)) ▶Attach to your tax return. ▶See separate instructions.	**2005** Attachment Sequence No. **27**

Name(s) shown on return	Identifying number
Teresa F. Lohman	271-57-2696

1 Enter the gross proceeds from sales or exchanges reported to you for 2005 on Form(s) 1099-B or 1099-S (or substitute statement) that you are including on line 2, 10, or 20 (see instructions). **1** 53,000

Part I Sales or Exchanges of Property Used in a Trade or Business and Involuntary Conversions From Other Than Casualty or Theft—Most Property Held More Than 1 Year (see instructions)

(a) Description of property	(b) Date acquired (mo., day, yr.)	(c) Date sold (mo., day, yr.)	(d) Gross sales price	(e) Depreciation allowed or allowable since acquisition	(f) Cost or other basis, plus improvements and expense of sale	(g) Gain or (loss) Subtract (f) from the sum of (d) and (e)
2 Land	2/6/78	1/3/05	22,800		15,000	7,800
Land (involuntary conversion)	3/5/83	5/2/05	30,200		33,200	(3,000)

3 Gain, if any, from Form 4684, line 42 . . . . **3**

4 Section 1231 gain from installment sales from Form 6252, line 26 or 37 . . . . **4**

5 Section 1231 gain or (loss) from like-kind exchanges from Form 8824 . . . . **5**

6 Gain, if any, from line 32, from other than casualty or theft **6** 0

7 Combine lines 2 through 6. Enter the gain or (loss) here and on the appropriate line as follows: **7** 4,800

Partnerships (except electing large partnerships) and S corporations. Report the gain or (loss) following the instructions for Form 1065, Schedule K, line 10, or Form 1120S, Schedule K, line 9. Skip lines 8, 9, 11, and 12 below.

Individuals, partners, S corporation shareholders, and all others. If line 7 is zero or a loss, enter the amount from line 7 on line 11 below and skip lines 8 and 9. If line 7 is a gain and you did not have any prior year section 1231 losses, or they were recaptured in an earlier year, enter the gain from line 7 as a long-term capital gain on the Schedule D filed with your return and skip lines 8, 9, 11, and 12 below.

8 Nonrecaptured net section 1231 losses from prior years (see instructions) **8** 2,500

9 Subtract line 8 from line 7. If zero or less, enter -0-. If line 9 is zero, enter the gain from line 7 on line 12 below. If line 9 is more than zero, enter the amount from line 8 on line 12 below and enter the gain from line 9 as a long-term capital gain on the Schedule D filed with your return (see instructions). **9** 2,300

Part II Ordinary Gains and Losses (see instructions)

10 Ordinary gains and losses not included on lines 11 through 16 (include property held 1 year or less):

11 Loss, if any, from line 7 . . . . **11** ( )

12 Gain, if any, from line 7 or amount from line 8, if applicable **12** 2,500

13 Gain, if any, from line 31 . . . . **13** 5,361

14 Net gain or (loss) from Form 4684, lines 34 and 41a **14**

15 Ordinary gain from installment sales from Form 6252, line 25 or 36 . . . . **15**

16 Ordinary gain or (loss) from like-kind exchanges from Form 8824 . . . . **16**

17 Combine lines 10 through 16 . . . . **17** 7,861

18 For all except individual returns, enter the amount from line 17 on the appropriate line of your return and skip lines a and b below. For individual returns, complete lines a and b below:

a If the loss on line 11 includes a loss from Form 4684, line 38, column (b)(ii), enter that part of the loss here. Enter the part of the loss from income-producing property on Schedule A (Form 1040), line 27, and the part of the loss from property used as an employee on Schedule A (Form 1040), line 22. Identify as from "Form 4797, line 18a." See instructions **18a**

b Redetermine the gain or (loss) on line 17 excluding the loss, if any, on line 18a. Enter here and on Form 1040, line 14 . . . . **18b** 7,861

For Paperwork Reduction Act Notice, see separate instructions. Cat. No. 13086I Form **4797** (2005)

FIGURE 11-3   Filled-In Form 4797, Page 2

Form 4797 (2005)   Page **2**

Part III   Gain From Disposition of Property Under Sections 1245, 1250, 1252, 1254, and 1255
(see instructions)

19	(a) Description of section 1245, 1250, 1252, 1254, or 1255 property:	(b) Date acquired (mo., day, yr.)	(c) Date sold (mo., day, yr.)
A	Equipment	7/3/01	5/10/05
B			
C			
D			

	These columns relate to the properties on lines 19A through 19D. ▶		Property A	Property B	Property C	Property D
20	Gross sales price (**Note:** *See line 1 before completing.*)	20	15,000			
21	Cost or other basis plus expense of sale	21	36,000			
22	Depreciation (or depletion) allowed or allowable	22	26,361			
23	Adjusted basis. Subtract line 22 from line 21	23	9,639			
24	Total gain. Subtract line 23 from line 20	24	5,361			
25	**If section 1245 property:**					
a	Depreciation allowed or allowable from line 22	25a	26,361			
b	Enter the **smaller** of line 24 or 25a	25b	5,361			
26	**If section 1250 property:** If straight line depreciation was used, enter -0- on line 26g, except for a corporation subject to section 291.					
a	Additional depreciation after 1975 (see instructions)	26a				
b	Applicable percentage multiplied by the **smaller** of line 24 or line 26a (see instructions)	26b				
c	Subtract line 26a from line 24. If residential rental property **or** line 24 is not more than line 26a, skip lines 26d and 26e	26c				
d	Additional depreciation after 1969 and before 1976	26d				
e	Enter the **smaller** of line 26c or 26d	26e				
f	Section 291 amount (corporations only)	26f				
g	Add lines 26b, 26e, and 26f	26g				
27	**If section 1252 property:** Skip this section if you did not dispose of farmland or if this form is being completed for a partnership (other than an electing large partnership).					
a	Soil, water, and land clearing expenses	27a				
b	Line 27a multiplied by applicable percentage (see instructions)	27b				
c	Enter the **smaller** of line 24 or 27b	27c				
28	**If section 1254 property:**					
a	Intangible drilling and development costs, expenditures for development of mines and other natural deposits, and mining exploration costs (see instructions)	28a				
b	Enter the **smaller** of line 24 or 28a	28b				
29	**If section 1255 property:**					
a	Applicable percentage of payments excluded from income under section 126 (see instructions)	29a				
b	Enter the **smaller** of line 24 or 29a (see instructions)	29b				

Summary of Part III Gains. Complete property columns A through D through line 29b before going to line 30.

30	Total gains for all properties. Add property columns A through D, line 24	30	5,361
31	Add property columns A through D, lines 25b, 26g, 27c, 28b, and 29b. Enter here and on line 13	31	5,361
32	Subtract line 31 from line 30. Enter the portion from casualty or theft on Form 4684, line 36. Enter the portion from other than casualty or theft on Form 4797, line 6	32	0

Part IV   Recapture Amounts Under Sections 179 and 280F(b)(2) When Business Use Drops to 50% or Less
(see instructions)

			(a) Section 179	(b) Section 280F(b)(2)
33	Section 179 expense deduction or depreciation allowable in prior years	33		
34	Recomputed depreciation (see instructions)	34		
35	Recapture amount. Subtract line 34 from line 33. See the instructions for where to report	35		

♻ *Printed on recycled paper*   Form **4797** (2005)

EXAMPLE 31

In 2005, Ellen Brown sells land held for investment and receives $18,000. Brown paid $11,200 for the land and over the years made $1,400 worth of improvements. The gross profit is determined as follows.

Amount realized		$18,000
Less adjusted basis		
Cost	$11,200	
Improvements	1,400	(12,600)
Gross profit		$ 5,400

Contract Price

The contract price is the amount realized less mortgages the buyer assumes. It is usually the sum of the principal payments, excluding interest, that the seller expects to receive. In Example 31, Brown's gross profit ratio equals 30% [$5,400 (gross profit) ÷ $18,000 (contract price)].

Taxpayers compute the current year's recognized gain by multiplying the amounts received on the principal during the year by the gross profit ratio. Keep in mind that payments on notes normally include interest as well as principal. Interest received by the seller is ordinary income reported on Schedule B.

EXAMPLE 32

Assume the same facts as in Example 31, except that the purchaser gives Brown a $4,000 down payment plus an interest-bearing note for the rest ($14,000). From this note, $12,000 of principal is due in 2005, and $2,000 is due in 2006. If the notes are paid when due, Brown reports the gain as follows.

2005	($4,000 + $12,000) × 30%	$4,800
2006	$2,000 × 30%	600
Total		$5,400

A special rule applies to the sale of nondepreciable property to a related party. If nondepreciable property is sold to a related party (descendant, ancestor, sibling, or spouse) in an installment sale AND the related party sells the property within two years of the sale, the rest of the installment gain is taxable to the seller in the year that the related party sells the property. Thus, the subsequent sale by a related party accelerates the gain reported by the original seller.

Depreciation Recapture

If property sold as an installment sale is subject to depreciation recapture, the recapture must be recognized as ordinary income in the year of the sale, regardless of the payments received during the year. The gain reported in the first year as a recapture of depreciation reduces gross profit used in computing the gross profit ratio. Likewise, it reduces the amount of each installment gain to be included in income as capital gain or Section 1231 gain.

EXAMPLE 33

Mark Jamar sells depreciable personal property for $180,000, accepting five equal installments of $36,000 plus interest. Jamar realizes gross profit of $120,000 on the sale.

Amount realized		$180,000
Less adjusted basis		
Cost	$90,000	
Accumulated depreciation	(30,000)	(60,000)
Gross profit		$120,000

Gain on the sale of personal property is recaptured as ordinary income to the extent of depreciation taken on the property. Thus, Jamar recognizes the $30,000 of accumulated depreciation as ordinary income in the year of the sale. In addition, a portion of each year's receipts is recognized as section 1231 gain. The portion of gain recognized each year is computed by reducing Jamar's gross profit by $30,000 and recalculating the gross profit ratio.

Income Recognized in Year 1

Ordinary income (depreciation recapture)	$30,000
Recomputing the gross profit ratio:	
($120,000 – $30,000) ÷ $180,000 = 50% gross profit ratio	
Section 1231 gain reportable in Year 1 (50% × $36,000)	18,000
Total gain recognized in Year 1	$48,000

Income Recognized in Years 2–5

Section 1231 gain (50% × $36,000 = $18,000 × 4 years)	72,000
Total gain recognized in the five years	$120,000

QUESTIONS AND PROBLEMS

1. **Capital Assets.** Are the following properties capital assets? (Indicate your answer by writing *yes* or *no* in the column at the right.)

   Item   *Answer*

   a. House occupied as a residence by the owner   _____
   b. Delivery truck used in a contractor's business   _____
   c. Corporate stocks owned by a doctor   _____
   d. Valuable jewelry held for sale by Jones Jewelers   _____
   e. Land held for speculation by an accountant   _____
   f. Automobile used for personal purposes by the owner   _____
   g. Business suits worn only to work   _____
   h. House used strictly as a summer residence   _____
   i. Musical copyright owned by the composer   _____

2. **Capital Gains and Losses.**

   a. Distinguish between long-term capital gain and short-term capital gain for capital assets acquired January 10, 2004.

   b. If an individual has gains and losses from the sale of stocks and other investments, what schedule is used to supplement Form 1040 in reporting this gain or loss?

3. **Holding Period.** State the time when the holding period begins on capital assets acquired by the following methods:

   a. Capital asset acquired by gift, if sold at a gain

   b. Capital asset acquired by gift, if sold at a loss (FMV < donor's basis at time of the gift)

   c. Inherited property

4. **Capital Gains and Losses.** For each of the following cases, determine whether the gain should be classified in the netting process as short-term capital gain, long-term capital gain taxed at 15%, or long-term capital gain taxed at 5%. Assume that in each case the taxpayer files as single.

   a. On February 3, 2005, stock held for four years is sold for a gain. The taxpayer has taxable income of $25,000 in 2005.

b. On March 13, 2005, stock held for eight months is sold for a gain. The taxpayer has taxable income of $25,000 in 2005.

c. On June 2, 2005, stock held for four years is sold for a gain. The taxpayer has taxable income of $20,000 in 2005.

d. On August 5, 2005, stock held for four years is sold for a gain. The taxpayer has taxable income of $70,000 in 2005.

e. On October 30, 2005, stock held four months is sold for a gain. The taxpayer has taxable income of $70,000 in 2005.

5. **Netting Capital Gains and Losses.** In each of the following cases, use the netting process between groups to determine how much capital gain is taxed at 15%.

   a. A $2,000 loss on the sale of a capital asset held six months; a $9,000 gain on the sale of a capital asset held for three years. The taxpayer is in the 25% tax bracket.

   b. Same as Part a., except that the taxpayer is in the 15% bracket.

   c. A $6,000 gain on the sale of a capital asset held nine months; a $5,000 gain on the sale of a capital asset held four years. The taxpayer is in the 28% tax bracket.

   d. Same as Part c., except that the taxpayer is in the 10% bracket.

6. **Stock Sales.** A taxpayer sold 100 shares of stock on August 13, 2005, for $7,500 cash. Before this sale, the taxpayer owned shares in the company as evidenced by the following certificates:

Certificate Number	Date Acquired	Number of Shares	Cost
CR642	4-11-77	300	$15,000
DO111	9-10-82	100	9,000
EA002	8-13-84	100	6,000

   Which certificate should be delivered to the broker to cover the stock sold, and what are the tax consequences of this selection?

7. **Capital Gains Tax.** In March of 2005, Shirley Thompson sold stock of the Wingate Corporation for $15,000. She had acquired the stock three years earlier at a cost of $11,600. Exclusive of this gain she expects to have a taxable income of $34,000 (after deductions and exemptions) for the year. Thompson files a joint return with her husband, who has no income. In December 2005 she contemplated selling stock of the Roberts Printing Company, which she acquired on January 15, 2004, for $18,000 and which had since declined in value to $13,000.

   a. Compute Thompson's total tax liability for 2005, assuming that she did not sell the Roberts stock in 2005.

   b. Compute Thompson's total tax liability for 2005, assuming that she did sell the Roberts stock for $13,000 in 2005. What amount of tax savings would result from the sale?

8. **Capital Losses.** What capital loss deduction can be claimed in 2005 for each of the following taxpayers? Also, what is the capital loss carryover to 2006 by type of loss? If none, insert *None*.

Gains and Losses	A	B	C	D	E
Short-term capital gains	$ 900	$ 800	$ 0	$ 400	$3,200
Short-term capital losses	(6,200)	(1,200)	(400)	(2,400)	(8,600)
Long-term capital gains	800	2,200	800	1,600	1,400
Long-term capital losses	(600)	(800)	(1,150)	(4,200)	(2,600)
Capital loss deduction in 2005	$_____	$_____	$_____	$_____	$_____
Short-term loss carryover to 2006	$_____	$_____	$_____	$_____	$_____
Long-term loss carryover to 2006	$_____	$_____	$_____	$_____	$_____

9. **Section 1244 Stock.**

    a. Roger Razaki sells 1,000 shares of his Section 1244 stock ("small business corporation" stock) at a loss of $200,000. If Roger and his wife file a joint return, how will this loss be treated on the tax return?

    b. If Roger were single, how would he treat the loss on his tax return?

    c. How might Roger have better planned for the sale of his Section 1244 stock?

10. **Subdivided Realty.** Juan Alvarez, a farmer, subdivided an unimproved tract of land that he acquired 20 years ago. In 2005, he sold four lots for $10,000 each. The basis of each lot is $2,000, and the selling expenses are $400 per lot.

    a. What is the gain or loss on these transactions, and how will these transactions be taxed?

    b. Assuming that Alvarez sells five more lots in 2006 at the same price with selling expenses of $400 per lot, what will be the gain or loss, and how will these transactions be taxed?

11. **Subdivided Realty.** Benji Baba, a real estate dealer, purchased two lots for $12,000 each in May 2003. On August 30, 2005, Baba sold the tracts of land for $20,000 each. Compute the gain and describe how it will be treated on the tax return.

12. **Bad Debts.** Rita loaned her brother, Richard, $7,500 on February 14, 2004. The loan represents a bona fide loan. Richard filed for bankruptcy in 2005, and Rita learned that she could expect to receive only $.70 on the dollar on the personal loan that she had made to him. On May 17, 2006, Rita received a final settlement of $4,000.

    a. How much loss can Rita deduct in 2005?

    b. How much loss can Rita deduct in 2006?

    c. How will this loss be treated on Rita's tax return?

13. **Section 1231 and Capital Gains and Losses.** Use the following information to answer Parts a. through c.

	Period Property Was Held	Amount of Gain or Loss
Nonbusiness bad debt	Three years	($2,600)
Sale of equipment used in business	Two months	(1,500)
Sale of equipment used in business	Two years	(3,000)
Sale of corporate stock	Five years	2,500
Sale of land used in business	Four years	5,000

a. What, if any, is the amount of net short-term capital loss?

b. What, if any, is the amount of net Section 1231 gain or (loss)?

c. What, if any, is the ordinary loss deduction?

14. **Sale of Business Property.** Carlotta Sanchez purchased computer equipment for her business in 2003 for $50,000. In 2005 she sold the computers for $30,000. Depreciation information follows:

Regular (accelerated) MACRS deduction claimed	$30,800
Straight-line depreciation would have been	$20,000

What is Sanchez's gain or loss on the sale of the computers, and how will it be treated?

15. **Unrecaptured Section 1250 Gain.** Victor Soto purchased a warehouse in 1995 for $1,000,000. Soto sold the warehouse in July of 2005 for $1,200,000. Soto claimed $309,524 of depreciation during the period when he owned the building. How will this transaction be reported on the tax return? How will the gain on this transaction be taxed?

16. **Unrecaptured Section 1250 Gain.** On November 10, 2005, Beverly Peterman sold residential realty for $300,000. Peterman purchased the realty on August 5, 1997, for $275,000. She depreciated the property over 27.5 years using the straight-line method. Compute Peterman's unrecaptured Section 1250 (amount taxed at 25%).

17. **Sale of Business Property.** In 2005 Virginia Banks, SSN 364-25-8153, had the following transactions involving property used in her manufacturing business.

a. Machinery purchased for $50,000 on August 6, 2002 was sold on April 6, 2005 for $22,000. Total depreciation taken on the machine was $31,258.

b. Land used in Banks' business was sold for $23,000 on June 6, 2005. The land was purchased for $16,000 on May 3, 1989.

c. A small tool shed was destroyed by fire during 2005. The loss was not covered by insurance. The shed had been used for several years and had an adjusted basis of $2,500 at the time of the fire. The loss was initially reported on Form 4684. (Enter loss on Form 4797 [line 14]).

d. A warehouse purchased for $50,000 on August 10, 1996, was condemned by the city in order to acquire the land upon which it stood for a new highway. Banks was paid $45,000 for the building on May 1, 2005. Depreciation totaled $10,897.

e. Banks received $36,000 for the condemned land. The land had a basis of $30,000.

Banks will not reinvest any of the proceeds from the condemned land or building in qualified replacement property and wants to report the gain on her 2005 return. Banks' nonrecaptured net section 1231 losses the previous five years are $3,500. Prepare Form 4797, Sales of Business Property, using the blank forms provided.

18. **Installment Sales.** Yvonne Saburo, a consulting engineer and cash basis taxpayer, decided to close her office and go back to college and study business. One of her business assets was an automobile that she had purchased in 2004 for $12,000. She still owed $5,000 on the car when she sold it for $10,600 on January 10, 2005. The buyer agreed to assume the $5,000 note. Further, the buyer agreed to pay $1,600 as a down payment and pay $2,000 (plus 12% interest) on January 10, 2006, and $2,000 (plus 12% interest on the remaining balance) on January 10, 2007. Under the MACRS rules, Saburo took $2,400 of depreciation on the automobile. Assume that Saburo has no other liabilities.

a. What is the realized gain to Saburo on the sale of the automobile?

b. If the realized gain is reported on the installment basis, how much and what type of gain will Saburo report as income in 2005, 2006, and 2007?

c. How much interest income will Saburo report in 2006 and 2007?

(Use for Problem 17.)

Form **4797**		**Sales of Business Property**		OMB No. 1545-0184

Form **4797**
Department of the Treasury
Internal Revenue Service (99)

Sales of Business Property
(Also Involuntary Conversions and Recapture Amounts
Under Sections 179 and 280F(b)(2))
►Attach to your tax return. ►See separate instructions.

OMB No. 1545-0184

2005

Attachment
Sequence No. **27**

Name(s) shown on return   Identifying number

1 Enter the gross proceeds from sales or exchanges reported to you for 2005 on Form(s) 1099-B or 1099-S (or substitute statement) that you are including on line 2, 10, or 20 (see instructions) **1**

Part I Sales or Exchanges of Property Used in a Trade or Business and Involuntary Conversions From Other Than Casualty or Theft—Most Property Held More Than 1 Year (see instructions)

(a) Description of property	(b) Date acquired (mo., day, yr.)	(c) Date sold (mo., day, yr.)	(d) Gross sales price	(e) Depreciation allowed or allowable since acquisition	(f) Cost or other basis, plus improvements and expense of sale	(g) Gain or (loss) Subtract (f) from the sum of (d) and (e)
2						

3 Gain, if any, from Form 4684, line 42 . . . . **3**
4 Section 1231 gain from installment sales from Form 6252, line 26 or 37 . . . . **4**
5 Section 1231 gain or (loss) from like-kind exchanges from Form 8824 . . . . **5**
6 Gain, if any, from line 32, from other than casualty or theft **6**
7 Combine lines 2 through 6. Enter the gain or (loss) here and on the appropriate line as follows: **7**

Partnerships (except electing large partnerships) and S corporations. Report the gain or (loss) following the instructions for Form 1065, Schedule K, line 10, or Form 1120S, Schedule K, line 9. Skip lines 8, 9, 11, and 12 below.

Individuals, partners, S corporation shareholders, and all others. If line 7 is zero or a loss, enter the amount from line 7 on line 11 below and skip lines 8 and 9. If line 7 is a gain and you did not have any prior year section 1231 losses, or they were recaptured in an earlier year, enter the gain from line 7 as a long-term capital gain on the Schedule D filed with your return and skip lines 8, 9, 11, and 12 below.

8 Nonrecaptured net section 1231 losses from prior years (see instructions) **8**
9 Subtract line 8 from line 7. If zero or less, enter -0-. If line 9 is zero, enter the gain from line 7 on line 12 below. If line 9 is more than zero, enter the amount from line 8 on line 12 below and enter the gain from line 9 as a long-term capital gain on the Schedule D filed with your return (see instructions). **9**

Part II Ordinary Gains and Losses (see instructions)

10 Ordinary gains and losses not included on lines 11 through 16 (include property held 1 year or less):

11 Loss, if any, from line 7 . . . . **11** ( )
12 Gain, if any, from line 7 or amount from line 8, if applicable **12**
13 Gain, if any, from line 31 . . . . **13**
14 Net gain or (loss) from Form 4684, lines 34 and 41a **14**
15 Ordinary gain from installment sales from Form 6252, line 25 or 36 . . . . **15**
16 Ordinary gain or (loss) from like-kind exchanges from Form 8824 . . . . **16**
17 Combine lines 10 through 16 . . . . **17**
18 For all except individual returns, enter the amount from line 17 on the appropriate line of your return and skip lines a and b below. For individual returns, complete lines a and b below:
a If the loss on line 11 includes a loss from Form 4684, line 38, column (b)(ii), enter that part of the loss here. Enter the part of the loss from income-producing property on Schedule A (Form 1040), line 27, and the part of the loss from property used as an employee on Schedule A (Form 1040), line 22. Identify as from "Form 4797, line 18a." See instructions **18a**
b Redetermine the gain or (loss) on line 17 excluding the loss, if any, on line 18a. Enter here and on Form 1040, line 14 . . . . **18b**

For Paperwork Reduction Act Notice, see separate instructions.   Cat. No. 13086I   Form **4797** (2005)

(Use for Problem 17.)

Form 4797 (2005)   Page **2**

| Part III | Gain From Disposition of Property Under Sections 1245, 1250, 1252, 1254, and 1255 (see instructions) |

19	**(a)** Description of section 1245, 1250, 1252, 1254, or 1255 property:	**(b)** Date acquired (mo., day, yr.)	**(c)** Date sold (mo., day, yr.)
A			
B			
C			
D			

	These columns relate to the properties on lines 19A through 19D. ▶		Property A	Property B	Property C	Property D
20	Gross sales price (**Note:** *See line 1 before completing.*)	20				
21	Cost or other basis plus expense of sale	21				
22	Depreciation (or depletion) allowed or allowable	22				
23	Adjusted basis. Subtract line 22 from line 21	23				
24	Total gain. Subtract line 23 from line 20	24				
25	**If section 1245 property:**					
a	Depreciation allowed or allowable from line 22	25a				
b	Enter the **smaller** of line 24 or 25a	25b				
26	**If section 1250 property:** If straight line depreciation was used, enter -0- on line 26g, except for a corporation subject to section 291.					
a	Additional depreciation after 1975 (see instructions)	26a				
b	Applicable percentage multiplied by the **smaller** of line 24 or line 26a (see instructions)	26b				
c	Subtract line 26a from line 24. If residential rental property **or** line 24 is not more than line 26a, skip lines 26d and 26e	26c				
d	Additional depreciation after 1969 and before 1976	26d				
e	Enter the **smaller** of line 26c or 26d	26e				
f	Section 291 amount (corporations only)	26f				
g	Add lines 26b, 26e, and 26f	26g				
27	**If section 1252 property:** Skip this section if you did not dispose of farmland or if this form is being completed for a partnership (other than an electing large partnership).					
a	Soil, water, and land clearing expenses	27a				
b	Line 27a multiplied by applicable percentage (see instructions)	27b				
c	Enter the **smaller** of line 24 or 27b	27c				
28	**If section 1254 property:**					
a	Intangible drilling and development costs, expenditures for development of mines and other natural deposits, and mining exploration costs (see instructions)	28a				
b	Enter the **smaller** of line 24 or 28a	28b				
29	**If section 1255 property:**					
a	Applicable percentage of payments excluded from income under section 126 (see instructions)	29a				
b	Enter the **smaller** of line 24 or 29a (see instructions)	29b				

Summary of Part III Gains. Complete property columns A through D through line 29b before going to line 30.

30	Total gains for all properties. Add property columns A through D, line 24	30	
31	Add property columns A through D, lines 25b, 26g, 27c, 28b, and 29b. Enter here and on line 13	31	
32	Subtract line 31 from line 30. Enter the portion from casualty or theft on Form 4684, line 36. Enter the portion from other than casualty or theft on Form 4797, line 6	32	

| Part IV | Recapture Amounts Under Sections 179 and 280F(b)(2) When Business Use Drops to 50% or Less (see instructions) |

			(a) Section 179	**(b)** Section 280F(b)(2)
33	Section 179 expense deduction or depreciation allowable in prior years	33		
34	Recomputed depreciation (see instructions)	34		
35	Recapture amount. Subtract line 34 from line 33. See the instructions for where to report	35		

♻ *Printed on recycled paper*

Form **4797** (2005)

19. **Installment Sales.** Virginia Mann sold depreciable personal property for $70,000 on August 4, 2005. The buyer agreed to pay $10,000 at the time of sale and $20,000 on August 4 in each of the next three years. In addition, interest at the current market rate will be paid on the remaining installment balance. Mann bought the property several years ago for $43,000. Its adjusted basis at the time of the sale was $25,000. Depreciation totalling $18,000 was taken on the property.

    a. Compute the total gain from the sale.

    b. How much gain and what type of gain must be reported in the year of sale?

    c. How much gain and what type of gain must be reported in each of the next three years?

20. **Internet Problem: Researching Publication 537.**

    During 2005, Leo Hunt, a cash basis taxpayer, sold land at a gain to an unrelated party. Leo received part of the proceeds in 2005 and will receive the rest of the proceeds in 2006 and 2007. Leo is fairly sure he would like to elect out of the installment sales method and has asked for advice on how to accomplish this. He also wants to know if he elects out of the installment method whether he can later change his mind and use the installment method to report the gain on the sale.

    Go to the IRS Web site. Locate Publication 537. Print out a copy of the page where the answer to Leo's questions can be found. Underline or highlight the pertinent information. Prepare a brief discussion of the answer to Leo's questions.

    See Appendix A for instructions on use of the IRS Web site.

21. **Business Entity Problem: This problem is designed for those using the "business entity" approach. The solution may require information from Chapter 14.**

    Kazoo Corporation purchased a commercial building ten years ago for $390,000. The building was sold in the current year for $450,000. Straight-line depreciation over the period of ownership was $100,000.

    a. How much of the gain from the sale of the building is ordinary income?

    b. How will the remaining gain be treated?

COMPREHENSIVE PROBLEM

22. Michael L. (SSN 374-47-7774) and Joyce A. (SSN 642-81-9982) Sea, married taxpayers filing a joint return, sold the following securities in 2005:

No. of Shares	Company	Date Acquired	Cost or Other Basis	Date Sold	Sales Price
20	Red Corporation	7-1-94	$1,661	12–6-05	$2,311
50	Lee Corporation	9-15-94	5,820	11-14-05	4,320
60	Alf Corporation	6-10-05	850	10-15-05	715
100	RST Corporation	5-10-83	4,600	8-5-05	2,430
—	$1,000 par value bond, TF Company	5-5-05	800	10-15-05	900

A short-term capital loss of $260 and a long-term capital loss of $2,500 were carried over from 2004.

In addition, the Seas report total wages of $41,920. From this amount $1,190 was withheld for federal income taxes. This represents the Seas' only other item of income during 2005.

Prepare the 2005 tax return for Mr. and Mrs. Sea using the forms on the pages that follow. The Seas live at 1319 Mayfair Drive, Champaign, IL 61821. The Seas claim one dependent, their 13-year-old son, Tad (SSN 629-43-7881). The Seas both elect to have $3 go to the presidential election campaign fund.

(Use for Problem 22.)

Form **1040**

Department of the Treasury—Internal Revenue Service
U.S. Individual Income Tax Return 2005 (99) IRS Use Only—Do not write or staple in this space.

For the year Jan. 1–Dec. 31, 2005, or other tax year beginning _____ , 2005, ending _____ , 20 ___   OMB No. 1545-0074

Label
(See instructions on page 16.)
Use the IRS label.
Otherwise, please print or type.

Presidential Election Campaign ▶ Check here if you, or your spouse if filing jointly, want $3 to go to this fund (see page 16) ▶   ☐ **You** ☐ **Spouse**

Your first name and initial | Last name | Your social security number

If a joint return, spouse's first name and initial | Last name | Spouse's social security number

Home address (number and street). If you have a P.O. box, see page 16. | Apt. no.

▲ You **must** enter your SSN(s) above. ▲

City, town or post office, state, and ZIP code. If you have a foreign address, see page 16.

Checking a box below will not change your tax or refund.

Filing Status

Check only one box.

1 ☐ Single
2 ☐ Married filing jointly (even if only one had income)
3 ☐ Married filing separately. Enter spouse's SSN above and full name here. ▶
4 ☐ Head of household (with qualifying person). (See page 17.) If the qualifying person is a child but not your dependent, enter this child's name here. ▶
5 ☐ Qualifying widow(er) with dependent child (see page 17)

Exemptions

6a ☐ **Yourself.** If someone can claim you as a dependent, **do not** check box 6a
b ☐ **Spouse**
c **Dependents:**

(1) First name Last name	(2) Dependent's social security number	(3) Dependent's relationship to you	(4) ✓ if qualifying child for child tax credit (see page 18)
			☐
			☐
			☐
			☐

If more than four dependents, see page 18.

Boxes checked on 6a and 6b ____
No. of children on 6c who:
• lived with you ____
• did not live with you due to divorce or separation (see page 18) ____
Dependents on 6c not entered above ____
Add numbers on lines above ▶ ____

d Total number of exemptions claimed

Income

Attach Form(s) W-2 here. Also attach Forms W-2G and 1099-R if tax was withheld.

If you did not get a W-2, see page 19.

Enclose, but do not attach, any payment. Also, please use **Form 1040-V.**

7 Wages, salaries, tips, etc. Attach Form(s) W-2 | 7
8a **Taxable** interest. Attach Schedule B if required | 8a
b **Tax-exempt** interest. **Do not** include on line 8a | 8b
9a Ordinary dividends. Attach Schedule B if required | 9a
b Qualified dividends (see page 20) | 9b
10 Taxable refunds, credits, or offsets of state and local income taxes (see page 20) | 10
11 Alimony received | 11
12 Business income or (loss). Attach Schedule C or C-EZ | 12
13 Capital gain or (loss). Attach Schedule D if required. If not required, check here ▶ ☐ | 13
14 Other gains or (losses). Attach Form 4797 | 14
15a IRA distributions | 15a | b Taxable amount (see page 22) | 15b
16a Pensions and annuities | 16a | b Taxable amount (see page 22) | 16b
17 Rental real estate, royalties, partnerships, S corporations, trusts, etc. Attach Schedule E | 17
18 Farm income or (loss). Attach Schedule F | 18
19 Unemployment compensation | 19
20a Social security benefits | 20a | b Taxable amount (see page 24) | 20b
21 Other income. List type and amount (see page 24) | 21
22 Add the amounts in the far right column for lines 7 through 21. This is your **total income** ▶ | 22

Adjusted Gross Income

23 Educator expenses (see page 26) | 23
24 Certain business expenses of reservists, performing artists, and fee-basis government officials. Attach Form 2106 or 2106-EZ | 24
25 Health savings account deduction. Attach Form 8889 | 25
26 Moving expenses. Attach Form 3903 | 26
27 One-half of self-employment tax. Attach Schedule SE | 27
28 Self-employed SEP, SIMPLE, and qualified plans | 28
29 Self-employed health insurance deduction (see page XX) | 29
30 Penalty on early withdrawal of savings | 30
31a Alimony paid   b Recipient's SSN ▶ | 31a
32 IRA deduction (see page XX) | 32
33 Student loan interest deduction (see page XX) | 33
34 Tuition and fees deduction (see page XX) | 34
35 Domestic production activities deduction. Attach Form 8903 | 35
36 Add lines 23 through 31a and 32 through 35 | 36
37 Subtract line 36 from line 22. This is your **adjusted gross income** ▶ | 37

For Disclosure, Privacy Act, and Paperwork Reduction Act Notice, see page 75.   Cat. No. 11320B   Form **1040** (2005)

(Use for Problem 22.)

Form 1040 (2005)   Page **2**

Tax and Credits	38	Amount from line 37 (adjusted gross income)	38
	39a	Check if: { You were born before January 2, 1941, ☐ Blind. / Spouse was born before January 2, 1941, ☐ Blind. } Total boxes checked ▶ 39a	
Standard Deduction for—	b	If your spouse itemizes on a separate return or you were a dual-status alien, see page 31 and check here ▶ 39b ☐	
	40	**Itemized deductions** (from Schedule A) **or** your **standard deduction** (see left margin) .	40
• People who checked any box on line 39a or 39b **or** who can be claimed as a dependent, see page 31.	41	Subtract line 40 from line 38	41
	42	If line 38 is $109,475 or less, multiply $3,200 by the total number of exemptions claimed on line 6d. If line 38 is over $109,475, see the worksheet on page 33	42
	43	**Taxable income.** Subtract line 42 from line 41. If line 42 is more than line 41, enter -0-	43
• All others:	44	**Tax** (see page 33). Check if any tax is from: a ☐ Form(s) 8814 b ☐ Form 4972	44
Single or Married filing separately, $5,000	45	**Alternative minimum tax** (see page 35). Attach Form 6251	45
	46	Add lines 44 and 45 . . . . ▶	46
Married filing jointly or Qualifying widow(er), $10,000	47	Foreign tax credit. Attach Form 1116 if required	47	
	48	Credit for child and dependent care expenses. Attach Form 2441	48	
	49	Credit for the elderly or the disabled. Attach Schedule R	49	
	50	Education credits. Attach Form 8863	50	
Head of household, $7,300	51	Retirement savings contributions credit. Attach Form 8880 .	51	
	52	Child tax credit (see page 37). Attach Form 8901 if required	52	
	53	Adoption credit. Attach Form 8839	53	
	54	Credits from: a ☐ Form 8396 b ☐ Form 8859 .	54	
	55	Other credits. Check applicable box(es): a ☐ Form 3800 b ☐ Form 8801 c ☐ Specify	55	
	56	Add lines 47 through 55. These are your **total credits**	56
	57	Subtract line 56 from line 46. If line 56 is more than line 46, enter -0- . . . . ▶	57
Other Taxes	58	Self-employment tax. Attach Schedule SE	58
	59	Social security and Medicare tax on tip income not reported to employer. Attach Form 4137 . .	59
	60	Additional tax on IRAs, other qualified retirement plans, etc. Attach Form 5329 if required	60
	61	Advance earned income credit payments from Form(s) W-2	61
	62	Household employment taxes. Attach Schedule H	62
	63	Add lines 57 through 62. This is your **total tax** . . . . . ▶	63
Payments	64	Federal income tax withheld from Forms W-2 and 1099 . .	64	
	65	2005 estimated tax payments and amount applied from 2004 return	65	
If you have a qualifying child, attach Schedule EIC.	66a	**Earned income credit (EIC)**	66a	
	b	Nontaxable combat pay election ▶	66b	
	67	Excess social security and tier 1 RRTA tax withheld (see page 54)	67	
	68	Additional child tax credit. Attach Form 8812	68	
	69	Amount paid with request for extension to file (see page 54)	69	
	70	Payments from: a ☐ Form 2439 b ☐ Form 4136 c ☐ Form 8885	70	
	71	Add lines 64, 65, 66a, and 67 through 70. These are your **total payments** . . . . ▶	71
Refund	72	If line 71 is more than line 63, subtract line 63 from line 71. This is the amount you **overpaid**	72
Direct deposit? See page 54 and fill in 73b, 73c, and 73d.	73a	Amount of line 72 you want **refunded to you** . . . . ▶	73a
	▶ b	Routing number ▶ c Type: ☐ Checking ☐ Savings	
	▶ d	Account number	
	74	Amount of line 72 you want **applied to your 2006 estimated tax** ▶	74	
Amount You Owe	75	**Amount you owe.** Subtract line 71 from line 63. For details on how to pay, see page 55 ▶	75
	76	Estimated tax penalty (see page 55)	76	

Third Party Designee	Do you want to allow another person to discuss this return with the IRS (see page 56)? ☐ **Yes.** Complete the following. ☐ **No** Designee's name ▶ Phone no. ▶ ( ) Personal identification number (PIN)
Sign Here Joint return? See page 17. Keep a copy for your records.	Under penalties of perjury, I declare that I have examined this return and accompanying schedules and statements, and to the best of my knowledge and belief, they are true, correct, and complete. Declaration of preparer (other than taxpayer) is based on all information of which preparer has any knowledge. Your signature Date Your occupation Daytime phone number ( ) Spouse's signature. If a joint return, **both** must sign. Date Spouse's occupation
Paid Preparer's Use Only	Preparer's signature ▶ Date Check if self-employed ☐ Preparer's SSN or PTIN Firm's name (or yours if self-employed), address, and ZIP code ▶ EIN Phone no. ( )

Form **1040** (2005)

✿ Printed on recycled paper

(Use for Problem 22.)

| **SCHEDULE D**
(Form 1040)

Department of the Treasury
Internal Revenue Service   (99) | **Capital Gains and Losses**

▶ Attach to Form 1040. ▶ See Instructions for Schedule D (Form 1040).

▶ Use Schedule D-1 to list additional transactions for lines 1 and 8. | OMB No. 1545-0074

20**05**

Attachment
Sequence No. **12** |

Name(s) shown on Form 1040 | Your social security number

Part I Short-Term Capital Gains and Losses—Assets Held One Year or Less

(a) Description of property (Example: 100 sh. XYZ Co.)	**(b)** Date acquired (Mo., day, yr.)	**(c)** Date sold (Mo., day, yr.)	**(d)** Sales price (see page D-6 of the instructions)	**(e)** Cost or other basis (see page D-6 of the instructions)	**(f)** Gain or (loss) Subtract (e) from (d)
1					

2 Enter your short-term totals, if any, from Schedule D-1, line 2	**2**	
3 **Total short-term sales price amounts.** Add lines 1 and 2 in column (d)	**3**	
4 Short-term gain from Form 6252 and short-term gain or (loss) from Forms 4684, 6781, and 8824	**4**	
5 Net short-term gain or (loss) from partnerships, S corporations, estates, and trusts from Schedule(s) K-1	**5**	
6 Short-term capital loss carryover. Enter the amount, if any, from line 8 of your **Capital Loss Carryover Worksheet** on page D-6 of the instructions	**6**	( )
7 **Net short-term capital gain or (loss).** Combine lines 1 through 6 in column (f)	**7**	

Part II Long-Term Capital Gains and Losses—Assets Held More Than One Year

(a) Description of property (Example: 100 sh. XYZ Co.)	**(b)** Date acquired (Mo., day, yr.)	**(c)** Date sold (Mo., day, yr.)	**(d)** Sales price (see page D-6 of the instructions)	**(e)** Cost or other basis (see page D-6 of the instructions)	**(f)** Gain or (loss) Subtract (e) from (d)
8					

9 Enter your long-term totals, if any, from Schedule D-1, line 9	**9**	
10 **Total long-term sales price amounts.** Add lines 8 and 9 in column (d)	**10**	
11 Gain from Form 4797, Part I; long-term gain from Forms 2439 and 6252; and long-term gain or (loss) from Forms 4684, 6781, and 8824	**11**	
12 Net long-term gain or (loss) from partnerships, S corporations, estates, and trusts from Schedule(s) K-1	**12**	
13 Capital gain distributions. See page D-1 of the instructions	**13**	
14 Long-term capital loss carryover. Enter the amount, if any, from line 13 of your **Capital Loss Carryover Worksheet** on page D-6 of the instructions	**14**	( )
15 **Net long-term capital gain or (loss).** Combine lines 8 through 14 in column (f). Then go to Part III on the back	**15**	

For Paperwork Reduction Act Notice, see Form 1040 instructions.   Cat. No. 11338H   **Schedule D (Form 1040) 2005**

(Use for Problem 22.)

Schedule D (Form 1040) 2005   Page **2**

Part III   **Summary**

16   Combine lines 7 and 15 and enter the result. If line 16 is a loss, skip lines 17 through 20, and go to line 21. If a gain, enter the gain on Form 1040, line 13, and then go to line 17 below . . **16**

17   Are lines 15 and 16 **both** gains?
     ☐ **Yes.** Go to line 18.
     ☐ **No.** Skip lines 18 through 21, and go to line 22.

18   Enter the amount, if any, from line 7 of the **28% Rate Gain Worksheet** on page D-7 of the instructions . . . . ▶ **18**

19   Enter the amount, if any, from line 18 of the **Unrecaptured Section 1250 Gain Worksheet** on page D-8 of the instructions . . . . ▶ **19**

20   Are lines 18 and 19 **both** zero or blank?
     ☐ **Yes.** Complete Form 1040 through line 43, and then complete the **Qualified Dividends and Capital Gain Tax Worksheet** on page 34 of the Instructions for Form 1040. **Do not** complete lines 21 and 22 below.
     ☐ **No.** Complete Form 1040 through line 43, and then complete the **Schedule D Tax Worksheet** on page D-9 of the instructions. **Do not** complete lines 21 and 22 below.

21   If line 16 is a loss, enter here and on Form 1040, line 13, the **smaller** of:

     ● The loss on line 16 or
     ● ($3,000), or if married filing separately, ($1,500)   . . . . **21**   (   )

     Note. When figuring which amount is smaller, treat both amounts as positive numbers.

22   Do you have qualified dividends on Form 1040, line 9b?
     ☐ **Yes.** Complete Form 1040 through line 43, and then complete the **Qualified Dividends and Capital Gain Tax Worksheet** on page 34 of the Instructions for Form 1040.
     ☐ **No.** Complete the rest of Form 1040.

♻ *Printed on recycled paper*   **Schedule D (Form 1040) 2005**

12

NOL, AMT, and Business Tax Credits

CHAPTER CONTENTS

■ ■

CHAPTER OVERVIEW

This chapter describes the tax rules for net operating losses and the alternative minimum tax. It also discusses the various business credits available to business owners and lessors of real property. Consideration is also given to both the audit and the appeals processes, as well as filing an amended tax return.

NET OPERATING LOSS (NOL)

A special rule applies when business owners report a loss in one year and profits in other years. It would be unfair if business profits were always taxed, but no tax relief was available when the business suffered a loss. The net operating loss (NOL) provisions allow business losses to offset income from other tax years. An NOL generated in 2005 offsets taxable income of the 2 previous years and then is carried forward to offset income in the next 20 years.

A 5-year carryback period applied to NOLs generated in 2001 and 2002. NOLs generated during 2001 or 2002 could elect a 5-year carryback, a 2-year carryback, or forego the carryback of the NOL. The 20-year carryforward also applied to these NOLs.

Calculating NOL

The NOL is not the same as negative taxable income on Form 1040. In fact, it is not computed anywhere on the tax return for the year in which it occurs. Instead, the NOL is computed on Form 1045, Schedule A (not shown). Filed separately from Form 1040, Form 1045 is the application for a refund of prior year income taxes. In computing the NOL, the following adjustments are made to negative taxable income.

1. The deduction for personal and dependency exemptions is added back.
2. Nonbusiness capital losses can offset only nonbusiness capital gains. Nonbusiness capital gains and losses arise from transactions involving nonbusiness property (for example, investment property). Thus, any nonbusiness net capital loss is added back.
3. The NOL of a preceding or a succeeding year is added back.
4. Nonbusiness deductions in excess of nonbusiness income are added back. Nonbusiness deductions include all itemized deductions except casualty and theft losses. Taxpayers who do not itemize deductions treat their standard deduction as a nonbusiness deduction. Nonbusiness income comes from sources other than the taxpayer's business. Examples include interest, dividends, and net gains from the sale of nonbusiness property. Salaries, net gains from the sale of business property, and rental income are treated as business income.

EXAMPLE 1

Chris and Dana Bosky are married and file a joint tax return. Chris operates a business that generated $120,000 of gross revenues and $150,000 of operating expenses during 2005. The Boskys show a negative taxable income of $28,600.

Salary		$15,000
Business loss ($120,000 – $150,000)		(30,000)
Net business capital gains		3,000
Net nonbusiness capital gains		4,000
Interest income		1,500
AGI		($6,500)
Less itemized deductions:		
Mortgage interest	$9,500	
Casualty loss	6,200	(15,700)
Less personal exemptions		(6,400)
Taxable income (loss)		($28,600)

Using this information, the Bosky's $18,200 NOL for 2005 is computed:

Taxable loss			($28,600)
Add back:			
Personal exemptions		$6,400	
Net nonbusiness deductions (mortgage interest)	$9,500		
Nonbusiness income ($4,000 + $1,500)	(5,500)	4,000	10,400
NOL for 2005			($18,200)

NOL Deduction

Once determined, an NOL generated in 2005 is carried back 2 years, then carried forward 20 years. Alternatively, taxpayers can elect to forgo the carryback and carry forward an NOL 20 years. When carried to another year, an NOL deduction is treated as a *deduction for AGI.* An NOL carried forward is entered as a negative amount on the Other Income line of Form 1040, page 1.

In Example 1, the Boskys could have applied the NOL to their 2003 taxable income and recomputed their 2003 tax liability. The difference between the Bosky's original tax liability and the recomputed tax liability would be refunded to them. Alternatively, the Boskys could elect to forgo the carryback and use the $18,200 as a deduction for AGI when filing their 2006 tax return.

Taxpayers elect to forego the carryback period by attaching a statement to the tax return that produced the NOL. Once made, the election to forego the carryback of an NOL is final. When a 2005 tax return showing an NOL is filed without such a statement, the IRS assumes the taxpayer is carrying back the NOL to the 2003 tax year.

ALTERNATIVE MINIMUM TAX (AMT)

The tax law contains many exclusions, deductions, and other tax incentives that allow individuals to reduce their tax liabilities. In the past, some individuals with high incomes used these tax benefits so much that they paid little or no income tax. In order to redistribute the tax burden, Congress enacted an alternative minimum tax (AMT). The AMT works with the regular income tax to ensure that taxpayers with high economic incomes pay some amount of income tax.

The AMT operates as a completely separate tax system. If subject to the AMT, the taxpayer will pay the AMT plus the regular income tax. Following is the basic format for computing the AMT.

> Regular taxable income
> ± Tax preferences and positive adjustments
> − Negative adjustments
> − Allowed net operating losses
> = Alternative minimum taxable income (AMTI)
> − Allowable exemption
> = Amount subject to tax (AMT Base)
> × AMT tax rate
> = Tentative minimum tax
> − Regular income tax
> = AMT (if positive)

Preferences and Adjustments

Alternative minimum taxable income (AMTI) is regular taxable income modified by preferences and adjustments. Preferences and adjustments allow taxpayers to receive large exclusions and deductions in computing regular taxable income. The AMT computation reduces the benefits of these tax incentives by limiting the exclusions or the amounts currently deductible. The amounts disallowed for AMT are added back to the regular taxable income in computing AMTI.

Preferences are added back to regular taxable income in arriving at AMTI. Thus, preferences increase income subject to the AMT. Adjustments, on the other hand, can be positive or negative. Adjustments generally arise from timing differences. **Timing differences** occur when a deduction is allowed for regular income tax in a year before it is allowed for the AMT. Thus, adjustments tend to be positive in the first years to which they apply (the deduction for regular tax is greater than the deduction for AMT) and become negative in later years when they reverse (the deduction for regular tax is less than the deduction for AMT). When adjustments are negative, they reduce the amount subject to the AMT.

For the most part, the adjustments and preferences used in computing the AMT fall into four categories: (1) preferences and adjustments related to the recovery of costs, (2) income recognition adjustments, (3) tax shelter losses, and (4) tax-exempt or excluded items.

Recovery of Costs

The adjustments and preferences in this category involve costs that are capital in nature. The regular income tax system allows taxpayers to immediately expense (Section 179) and/or use an accelerated method (200% declining balance) to recover the costs of tangible personal property. AMT also allows Section 179 expensing, but can require slower recovery methods or longer recovery periods. Two of the more common cost recovery adjustments, are:

1. **Cost recovery on real property.** Real property placed in service between 1987 and 1998 must be recovered using straight-line depreciation over 40 years for AMT. In computing regular income tax, MACRS allows recovery over 27.5, 31.5, or 39 years using the straight-line method. The difference in the two methods is the AMT adjustment. There is no AMT depreciation adjustment for realty placed in service after 1998.

2. **Cost recovery on personal property.** AMTI uses the 150% declining balance (DB) method over the longer alternative depreciation system (ADS) lives. For computing regular taxable income, both the 200% DB and straight-line methods are allowed. The difference in the allowable cost recovery between the methods used for computing regular tax and computing AMT is an adjustment for AMT. However, there is no AMT adjustment required for personal property on which bonus depreciation was taken. (See Chapter 8 for a discussion of bonus depreciation allowed on personal property placed in service between September 11, 2001 and December 31, 2004.)

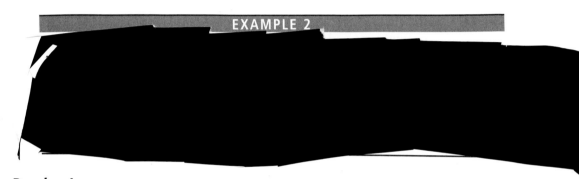

Passive Losses

Neither the regular tax nor the AMT system allows for passive losses in excess of passive income to be deducted in the year they occur. Such losses carry forward and offset passive income in future years. Any losses carried forward are deducted in full when the taxpayer disposes of the entire interest in the activity. While the loss recognition for both tax calculations is deferred, the amount of the loss to be deferred will generally differ. The difference occurs because the loss for AMT purposes is determined using all required AMT tax adjustments rather than the regular income tax deductions.

For example, MACRS depreciates residential realty over 27.5 years using the straight-line method. For AMT, this property is depreciated over 40 years. Because this difference affects the amount of passive loss carryover for regular tax versus AMT, it will affect the amount of passive loss deduction allowed when the property is sold.

Tax-Exempt and Excluded Income

Three other items of income may result in adjustments for AMT. First, AMTI includes tax-exempt interest from private activity bonds. Such interest is not taxable in computing regular taxable income. Thus, any interest from private activity bonds is added to taxable income in computing AMTI. Second, when exercising an incentive stock option, the excess of the FMV of the stock over the exercise price is income for purposes of computing AMT. Since exercising an incentive stock option does not affect regular taxable income, the excess amount is added to taxable income in computing AMTI. Third, 7% of the 50% excluded gain on the sale of Section 1202 small business stock is a preference item, and is added to taxable income to compute AMTI.

The tax law allows taxpayers to earn tax-free interest income when they invest in state and local government bonds (municipal bonds) under the assumption that municipalities would use the bond proceeds for various government purposes. However, sometimes municipalities issue bonds and then loan the proceeds to private parties, or alternatively, they raise funds to construct facilities to be used for private purposes. Bonds of this nature are referred to as private activity bonds. For private activity bonds issued after May 15, 1997, the tax law still allows the interest earned on such bonds to be tax-free from regular income taxes, but requires taxpayers to report the interest as a preference item for purposes of computing AMT.

AMT Itemized Deductions

The AMTI calculation disallows certain itemized deductions used to compute the regular taxable income. Taxpayers adjust regular taxable income for the following itemized deductions:

1. Taxes
2. Miscellaneous deductions subject to the 2% AGI limit
3. Medical expenses
4. Interest

AGI in excess of ting the itemized

All state and local income sales tax deducted on Schedule A must be added back in computing AMTI. Any state income tax refunds included in regular taxable income are not included in AMTI, and therefore must be subtracted from taxable income in computing AMTI. Also, any miscellaneous itemized deductions in excess of the 2% AGI limit deduction on Schedule A are added back when computing AMTI.

Medical Expenses

Only medical expenses that exceed 10% of AGI may be deducted for purposes of computing AMTI. In computing regular taxable income, medical expenses in excess of 7.5% of AGI are deductible. The taxpayer recomputes the medical expense deduction using a 10% AGI "floor." The taxpayer then adds back to regular taxable income the difference between the medical expense deduction in excess of 7.5% AGI and the recomputed medical expense deduction using 10% AGI.

EXAMPLE 3

Tom Rosen's AGI is $120,000 and he has $10,000 of unreimbursed medical expenses. When computing his itemized deductions, Rosen deducts $1,000 of medical expenses ($10,000 − (7.5% × $120,000)). When computing AMTI, he only can deduct medical expenses in excess of $12,000 (10% × $120,000). Since no medical expense deduction would be allowed in computing AMTI, Rosen must add back $1,000 to taxable income when computing AMTI.

Investment Credit

The investment credit consists of two separate credits: the business energy investment credit and the credit for substantial rehabilitation expenditures.

Business Energy Investment Credit

A 10% tax credit is available for qualified investment in *solar* and *geothermal* energy property. Any energy credit taken reduces the basis of the energy property by 50% of the credit. Taxpayers may either construct or purchase the energy property. However, the taxpayer must be the original user of the property. The credit is not available for public utility property. Taxpayers calculate business energy credits on Form 3468, Investment Credit.

Credit for Substantial Rehabilitation Expenditures

The purpose of the credit for rehabilitation expenditures is to encourage businesses to stay in economically distressed areas and to preserve historical structures. The credit equals a percentage of the costs incurred in substantially rehabilitating qualified buildings and certified historic structures. Only the costs to substantially rehabilitate a building qualify for the credit. A building is substantially rehabilitated when the rehabilitation costs during a 24-month period exceed the *greater of* (i) the building's adjusted basis before the rehabilitation, or (ii) $5,000. The percentage used in computing the credit is as follows:

Type of Property Credit	*Credit*
Certified historical structures (both nonresidential and residential)	20%
Nonresidential and residential buildings originally placed in service before 1936	10%

When taxpayers make capital expenditures to property, they normally increase their basis in the property by such costs. A special rule requires that taxpayers reduce their basis by the amount of the rehabilitation credit.

EXAMPLE 5

Barry Tamblyn pays $50,000 for a certified historical structure. Tamblyn spends $60,000 to restore the structure. The $60,000 qualifies for the rehabilitation credit since it exceeds $50,000 (the greater of (i) the $50,000 adjusted basis in the building before the rehabilitation, or (ii) $5,000). Tamblyn's credit for rehabilitation expenditures equals $12,000 ($60,000 × 20%). His basis in the building increases by $48,000 ($60,000 − $12,000) to $98,000 ($50,000 + $48,000).

Taxpayers who dispose of the property within five years of taking the credit for rehabilitation expenditures must recapture 20% of the credit taken for each year shy of five years. Any recaptured amount is added to the adjusted basis of the building.

Work Opportunity Credit

Employers who hire certain individuals may qualify for the work opportunity credit. To qualify for this credit, the individuals must be hired prior to January 1, 2006, and be from one of the following eight specified targeted groups.

1. Qualified Aid to Families with Dependent Children (AFDC) recipients
2. Qualified veterans

3. Qualified ex-felons
4. High-risk youths (age 18 to 24 when hired) who live in an empowerment zone or enterprise community (as specified by the federal government)
5. Vocational rehabilitation referrals
6. Qualified summer youth employees
7. Qualified food stamp recipients
8. Qualified SSI recipients

> A provision in the Katrina Emergency Tax Relief Act of 2005 added "Hurricane Katrina employees" to the list of eligible persons for whom the work opportunity credit could be taken. A **Hurricane Katrina employee** is a person who on August 28, 2005 had a principal place of abode in the core disaster area (as specified by the federal government), who was displaced from such abode by the hurricane, and who is hired between August 28, 2005 and December 31, 2005. It also includes any person who on August 28, 2005 had a principal place of abode in the core disaster area and who is hired between August 28, 2005 and August 27, 2007 to work at a business located within the core disaster area. This provision rewards employers with tax breaks for hiring persons who lived in core disaster areas at the time of the hurricane. If the employer's business is located outside the core disaster area, the wages of qualified employees hired by the end of 2005 qualify for the work opportunity credit. For employers whose businesses are located in the core disaster area, the wages of any qualified employee hired before August 28, 2007 qualify for the work opportunity credit.

The credit equals 40% of up to $6,000 of qualified first-year wages for each qualified employee. The percentage drops to 25% for employees who work at least 120 hours, but less than 400 hours during their first year. No credit is allowed for wages of employees who have worked less than 120 hours during their first year. If the employee's first 12 months of employment spans over two of the employer's tax years, the employer can take the credit over two tax years. Employers who claim this credit must reduce their wage expense deduction by the amount of the credit claimed.

EXAMPLE 6

On April 10, 2005, Joe Oliver hired two qualified employees to help him out in his shop. Both employees worked more than 400 hours for Oliver during their first year. Each employee was paid $9,000 of wages in their first year. Of this amount $5,500 was paid in 2005 and $3,500 in 2006.

Oliver is entitled to a work opportunity credit for 40% of the employees' first-year wages. Oliver's work opportunity credit for 2005 equals $4,400 [40% × ($5,500 × 2)]. Only the first $6,000 of qualified first-year wages are used in computing the work opportunity credit. Therefore in 2006 his work opportunity credit is $400 [40% × ($500 × 2)].

A qualified summer youth employee is a 16- or 17-year old that the employer hires to work between May 1 and September 15. The youth must live in an empowerment zone or enterprise community for his or her wages to qualify for the work opportunity credit. The youth need only work 90 days during the May 1 to September 15 period, and only the first $3,000 of wages qualify for the credit.

Low-Income Housing Credit

The low-income rental housing credit is available to certain owners of residential rental property who provide low-income housing. The credit may be taken each year for a period of 10 years. The IRS sets the credit rate monthly to reflect changes in the applicable federal rate (AFR). Once determined, however, the rate remains constant for that property. The credit has a number of special requirements and interrelationships with other federal programs. The project must continue to meet requirements for 15 years, or recapture of a portion of the credit may occur. The credit can be claimed on Form 8586, Low-Income Housing Credit.

Disabled Access Credit

This nonrefundable credit is an incentive to small businesses to make themselves more accessible to disabled persons. The credit is claimed on Form 8826, Disabled Access Credit. The credit equals 50% of the eligible expenditures for the year that exceed $250 but do not exceed $10,250. Thus, the maximum credit available is $5,000 [50% × ($10,250 – $250)]. A business qualifies for the credit if it satisfies one of the following criteria in the previous tax year:

1. The business did not have gross receipts in excess of $1 million, or
2. The business did not employ more than 30 full-time employees.

Expenditures eligible for the credit include those that lead to the removal of architectural, communication, physical, or transportation barriers on buildings placed in service before November 1990. Qualifying barriers prevent a business from being accessible to, or usable by, disabled individuals. Amounts paid for qualified interpreters or readers to effect the communication of materials to hearing- and visually-impaired individuals also qualify. The depreciable basis of the property is increased by the amount of the improvements and reduced by the amount of credit.

EXAMPLE 7

Jenny Bandos owns a small business that she reports on Schedule C. During the year Bandos pays $8,500 to make her office building more accessible to disabled persons. The building was placed in service in 1987. Bandos's disabled access credit equals $4,125 [50% × ($8,500 – $250)]. Bandos completes Form 8826 to claim this credit. Bandos's basis in the building increases by $4,375 ($8,500 – $4,125).

FICA Tax Credit

Food and beverage establishments are allowed a tax credit for the employer's FICA tax contribution on qualifying employee cash tips. These are tips the employee reports to the employer that are in excess of the amount required to satisfy the federal minimum wage requirements. No wage deduction can be taken on any amount used in computing the credit calculation.

Empowerment Zone Employment Credit

An employer whose business is located in a designated empowerment zone may receive a 20% tax credit on the first $15,000 of wages paid to each qualified employee. The $15,000 limit is reduced by any wages used in computing the work opportunity credit for a qualified employee. Qualified employees are individuals who live within the empowerment zone and who work primarily within the zone in the employer's trade or business. The amount of the credit claimed reduces the employer's wage expense deduction.

EXAMPLE 8

Tony Silver's business is located in a designated empowerment zone. During 2005 Silver hired two people who live in the empowerment zone. Neither person belongs to a work opportunity credit–targeted group. During 2005 one employee was paid wages of $12,000. The other was paid wages of $13,000. Silver's empowerment zone employment credit equals $5,000 [($12,000 + $13,000) × 20%].

EXAMPLE 9

Continuing with Example 8, assume that in 2006 each of these two employees is paid wages of $16,000. During 2006 Silver does not hire anyone else who lives in the empowerment zone. Only the first $15,000 of wages are used in computing the credit. Thus, only $3,000 of wages from the first employee ($15,000 – $12,000 wages paid in 2005) and $2,000 ($15,000 – $13,000) from the second employee are used in computing Silver's 2006 empowerment zone employment credit. Silver's 2006 credit equals $1,000 [$5,000 × 20%].

Welfare-to-Work Credit

The welfare-to-work credit is designed to encourage employers to hire and continue to employ persons on welfare. The credit equals 35% of qualified first-year wages plus 50% of qualified second year wages. The maximum wages that can be used in computing the credit in each year is $10,000. Thus, the maximum credit for each employee is $8,500 ($3,500 in the first year plus $5,000 in the second year). When the employee's first two years of employment span over three of the employer's tax years, the employer can take the credit over three tax years.

Qualified wages are wages paid to long-term family assistance recipients. Such recipients include members of a family who have been receiving family assistance for at least 18 months prior to being hired. It also includes wages paid to recipients within two years after welfare payments stop because of the length of time the family has been receiving welfare payments. In order to include an employee's wages in computing the welfare-to-work credit, the employee must have worked for an employer for a least 180 days or have completed 400 hours of service. Employers who take the welfare-to-work credit for a worker cannot claim the work opportunity credit for the same worker. Also, only qualified wages of employees hired before January 1, 2006 are eligible for this credit.

EXAMPLE 10

On January 1, 2005, Bob Sanford hired one employee who qualified for the welfare-to-work credit. Qualified wages for this employee were $7,000 in 2005 and $12,000 in 2006. Sanford's 2005 welfare-to-work credit is $2,450 ($7,000 × 35%). His credit for 2006 is $5,000 ($10,000 maximum wages for the second year × 50%).

Employer-Provided Child Care Credit

Employers can take a tax credit for providing child care to their employees. The amount of the credit is the sum of (i) 25% of qualified child care expenses plus (ii) 10% of qualified child care resources or referral expenses. The maximum credit allowed each year is $150,000.

Qualified child care expenses include amounts paid to acquire or construct property used as part of a qualified child care facility. It also includes costs incurred to operate a qualified child care facility and amounts paid to a qualified child care facility that provides child care services to employees. **Qualified child care resource and referral expenses** are amounts paid under a contract to provide child care resource and referral services to an employee. However, these services cannot discriminate in favor of highly-paid employees.

EXAMPLE 11

In 2004, Stanley Emory started a qualified child care program for his employees. During 2005, Emory pays $7,000 in qualified child care expenses and $1,000 in qualified child care resource and referral expenses. Emory's employer-provided child care credit for 2005 is $1,850 ([$7,000 × 25%] + [$1,000 × 10%]). He includes this amount as part of the General Business Credit when he files his 2005 tax return.

Small Employer Pension Plan Startup Credit

Certain employers can take a tax credit equal to 50% of qualified startup costs when they establish a new defined benefit plan, defined contribution plan (including a 401(k) plan), SIMPLE plan, or SEP plan for their employees. However, the new pension plan must cover at least one employee who is not a highly compensated employee. The tax credit is limited to $500 in each of the first three years the pension plan is offered. **Qualified startup costs** include amounts paid to establish or administer the new plan, as well as amounts paid to educate employees about retirement planning. Only employers who employed no more than 100 employees earning at least $5,000 in the prior year can claim to this credit. Furthermore, the credit is available only to employers who have not maintained a qualified plan during any of the previous three tax years.

The Katrina Emergency Tax Relief Act of 2005 added a new (temporary) general business credit aimed at giving tax breaks to certain employers who continued to pay their employees while their businesses were inoperable due to damages sustained during Hurricane Katrina. The **Employee Retention Credit** allows small business employers a tax credit equal to 40% of an employee's wages (up to $6,000) paid between August 29, 2005 and the date on which they reopened their businesses, or December 31, 2005, whichever occurs first. A small business employer is one that averages during the year 200 or fewer employees. Only employers that were conducting an active trade or business in the core disaster area (as specified by the federal government) on August 28, 2005 are eligible for the credit. In addition, only the wages paid to employees who were working for the employer on August 28, 2005 are included when computing this credit. The wages of any employee whose wages are used in computing the work opportunity credit during this same time are not included in computing the employee retention credit.

TAX PENALTIES

When people fail to file a tax return or fail to pay the proper amount of tax, a penalty applies. Other acts may also invoke a penalty. Tax penalties are generally based on the amount of tax due on the tax return (tax liability – credits and prepayments = tax due). Having a "reasonable cause" for not complying with the law may save the taxpayer from a penalty.

Type of Penalty	*Amount of Penalty*
Failure to file	5% of the amount due for each month or fraction of month that the return is late (maximum penalty = 25%)
Failure to pay	.5% of the amount due for each month or fraction of month that the payment is late (maximum penalty = 25%)
Accuracy-related (negligence, substantial understatement of income tax, or substantial valuation misstatement)	20% of the tax due
Fraud	75% of the tax due (accuracy-related penalties will not be applied)
Frivolous return filing	$500
Preparer penalties	From $5 to $500 for each wrongful act
Improper disclosure of information acquired from a taxpayer by a tax preparer	$1,000 and/or one year in prison

Reasonable Cause

Taxpayers may avoid a penalty if failure to comply was due to reasonable cause. The IRS lists the following circumstances as reasonable causes for failing to comply with the tax laws.

1. Death or serious illness
2. Unavoidable absence
3. Destruction of certain facilities or records
4. Timely mailing
5. Wrong filing place
6. Reliance on competent tax advisor
7. Unobtainable records
8. IRS office visit in which an IRS employee was unable to be seen for reasons beyond taxpayer control
9. Erroneous IRS information

Other reasonable causes may exist. The IRS judges each case on its merits.

INFORMATION RETURNS

Information returns play an important part in the IRS computerized taxpayer compliance program. Persons and organizations making specific types of payments must report them to the IRS and the taxpayer. Taxpayers must then report these payments on their income tax returns. This reporting process makes it possible for the IRS to determine whether taxpayers have reported the appropriate amounts on their tax returns. The taxpayer's identification number (SSN or EIN), shown on both the information return and the income tax return, is the basis for comparing reported data. Unlike Forms W-2 and W-2G, filed with the income tax return, taxpayers do not attach information returns to the tax return. They should, however, retain copies of the information returns for their records.

Most organizations or persons required to file information returns use magnetic media to transmit the data to the IRS. However, some payers still report this data in paper form. They must use a separate transmittal Form 1096, Annual Summary and Transmittal of U.S. Information Returns, for each different type of information return.

IRS Comparisons

The IRS routinely examines the amounts reported on information returns filed by the payers of interest, dividends, and other types of payments. It compares these amounts to those reported by the taxpayer on the income tax return. Taxpayers should report all amounts received on their returns as separate items. Combining amounts is unwise. For example, the taxpayer may receive two Forms 1099-DIV from ABC Company. One is for a $300 dividend on stock held personally by the taxpayer. The other is for a $176 dividend on stock held by a trustee for a dividend reinvestment plan. The taxpayer should enter both amounts separately on Schedule B. If only one Form 1099-DIV is received for the $476 total, then only one amount is reported on Schedule B. When taxpayers detect an error on an information return, they should request the payer to correct the mistake and issue a corrected information return.

AVOIDING DEFICIENCY NOTICES

The computer may detect a difference between the amounts reported on the information returns and the amounts reported by the taxpayer. It may then generate a deficiency notice that will require an explanation by the taxpayer. The differences may be easily explained by the taxpayer with no penalty assessed. However, much time and effort can be saved if the taxpayer carefully reports the amounts as shown on the information returns.

Penalty for Failure to File Information Returns

The penalty for failure to furnish a required return or statement to a taxpayer in a timely manner is $50 for each statement not furnished. The maximum penalty for any calendar year is $100,000.

A penalty also applies for filing late, incorrect, or incomplete information returns with the IRS. The following penalty structure applies.

1. Any reporting failure corrected within 30 days after the due date—$15 per return, with a yearly maximum of $75,000 ($25,000 for small businesses)
2. Any reporting failure corrected after the 30-day period up to August 1—$30 per return, with a yearly maximum of $150,000 ($50,000 for small businesses)
3. Any reporting failure corrected after August 1—$50 per return, with a yearly maximum of $250,000 ($100,000 for small businesses)

These penalties also apply to companies that fail to file by means of magnetic media when required to do so. However, the penalty applies only on the number of returns in excess of 250. "**Small businesses**" are those having average annual gross receipts of less than $5 million for the last three years.

The IRS imposes a penalty of $50 for each failure to provide certain specified information, such as taxpayer identification numbers. The maximum penalty is $100,000 a year.

No penalty applies if it can be shown that the reporting failure was due to reasonable cause and not to willful neglect. Also, a penalty waiver is available when only a small number of returns contain incomplete or incorrect information. To apply, correction of the errors must take place by August 1. In addition, the waiver limits the benefits to the greater of:

1. Ten returns, or
2. One-half of 1% of the total number of information returns required to be filed.

COMMON INFORMATION RETURNS

Form 1098, Mortgage Interest Statement

Form 1099-B, Proceeds from Broker and Barter Exchange Transactions

Form 1099-DIV, Dividends and Distributions

Form 1099-INT, Interest Income

Form 1099-G, Certain Government Payments

Form 1099-MISC, Miscellaneous Income

Form 1099-R, Distributions from Pensions, Annuities, Retirement or Profit-Sharing Plans, IRAs, Insurance Contracts, Etc.

Form 1099-S, Proceeds from Real Estate Transactions

Form 5498, Individual Retirement Arrangement Information

Form 8027, Employer's Annual Information Return of Tip Income and Allocated Tips

THE AUDIT PROCESS

When returns reach the IRS service centers, a computer makes an initial check for mathematical or clerical errors. These errors are defined as:

1. An error in arithmetic shown on the return
2. Incorrect use of any IRS table, if such use is apparent from the existence of other information on the return
3. Inconsistent entries on the return
4. Omission of information necessary to substantiate a return entry
5. Entry of a deduction or credit item that exceeds a statutory limit based on information appearing on the return

The IRS corrects these mathematical errors and sends a notice of the correction to the taxpayer. It either requests payment for additional tax or encloses a refund for an overpayment.

Returns most in need of examination are identified by computer, using mathematical formulas developed by the IRS to single out returns that are likely to have errors. The system focuses on those returns that stand the best chance of producing enough additional tax revenue to justify the audit.

Examples of factors that could affect a return's selection for audit include:

1. Large gross income
2. Self-employed taxpayers with high incomes and large deductions

3. Cash businesses (e.g., restaurants, businesses that provide services)

4. Excessive itemized deductions in relation to income level

5. Claims for large refunds

6. Disagreement between reported income and information returns (e.g., Form 1099, Form W-2)

7. A large increase in exemptions

8. A major decrease in rental income

9. Informant information

10. Prior tax deficiencies

Returns containing minor items that need clarification go to the audit division at the Regional Service Center for correction by *correspondence.* Such returns may contain questionable charitable contributions or medical expenses, for example.

Returns having the greatest audit possibility are sent to the district audit division to be examined. Within the district audit division, there are two types of audits. One is the *office audit* which usually takes place in an IRS office and is limited in scope. A short discussion may be all that is needed to clear up any questions. The other is the *field audit* which normally takes place on the taxpayer's premises. This is typically a much more extensive audit involving a number of major issues.

Facing budget constraints, the IRS audits less than 1% of the tax returns.

Burden of Proof

Historically, the burden of proof for most tax disputes has rested with the taxpayer. During the mid-1980s, the IRS came under scrutiny for the way taxpayers were being treated during the audit process. Congress responded by enacting tax laws that shift the burden of proof to the IRS in court proceedings over factual issues when:

1. The taxpayer has provided the IRS with relevant, credible evidence,

2. The taxpayer has complied with the IRS's substantiation and record-keeping requirements, and

3. The taxpayer has maintained proper records and cooperates with any reasonable IRS request for witnesses, information, documents, meetings, and interviews.

To illustrate these new rules, take a situation where the taxpayer uses the standard business mileage method to deduct automobile expenses on Schedule C. As discussed in Chapter 7, the tax laws require that the taxpayer maintain contemporaneous records to support the number of business miles driven during the year. Thus, if the taxpayer provides the IRS with the mileage log used to record the number of business miles driven during the tax year in question, the burden of proving that the deduction is not valid rests with the IRS.

In addition to the situations Congress recently added, the IRS has the burden of proof whenever it (i) uses statistics to reconstruct the taxpayer's income, (ii) assesses the taxpayer with a penalty or other addition to tax, or (iii) accuses the taxpayer of fraud with intent to evade taxes. The IRS also has the burden or proof in any case that involves hobby losses (Chapter 6) or the accumulated earnings tax (Chapter 14).

THE APPEAL PROCESS

After the audit, the taxpayer will receive a report of the findings, along with a *30-day-letter* describing the taxpayer's appeal rights. A taxpayer who does not agree with the findings of an audit may appeal. The taxpayer has a right to request a conference with the examining officer to work out their differences. This request should be made within 15 days from the date of the letter. Taxpayers not desiring a conference should either start the formal appeal process or make arrangements to pay the tax within 30 days.

An *Appeals Office* headed by a Regional Director of Appeals is established in each of the seven Internal Revenue Service regions. Each office has the authority to fully settle cases. When the amount involved does not exceed $2,500, the taxpayer will be granted an Appeals Office conference merely by requesting it. However, when the amount exceeds $2,500, an Appeals Office conference is available only to taxpayers who file a written protest stating the facts upon which the appeal is based.

If the taxpayer and the Appeals Office cannot agree on the issues in dispute, the taxpayer receives a *90-day deficiency notice.* This must be mailed to the taxpayer within three years of the date that the income tax return was filed. The taxpayer may petition for a review in the Tax Court within 90 days after the deficiency notice is mailed.

Either the taxpayer or the IRS can petition the Circuit Court of Appeals to review the Tax Court's decision. Final disposition of the case may be taken to the United States Supreme Court. The Supreme Court will hear only those cases it chooses to review. All of these steps may take years. However, final assessment of the tax due from a taxpayer may not be made until the case is closed. The IRS Commissioner then has 60 days from the final decision to make an assessment of the tax.

TAXPAYER RIGHTS

Taxpayers have the right to plan their business and personal affairs so they will pay the least amount of tax due under the law. They also have the right to be treated fairly, professionally, promptly, and courteously by the IRS.

The law entitles taxpayers to information and IRS assistance in complying with the tax laws. The IRS provides a wide variety of informational material, educational programs, and tax assistance programs to aid people in understanding and complying with the tax laws. IRS Publication 910, *Guide to Free Tax Services,* is a catalog of free IRS services and publications.

Taxpayers who need a copy of a prior year tax return may receive it by completing Form 4506, Request for Copy of Tax Form. This form is sent to the IRS along with a small fee. If only certain information is needed, such as reported income from a prior year, the taxpayer may get this information for free. To receive this information, the taxpayer should write, visit, or call an IRS office.

Special assistance programs are available to people who cannot resolve their tax problems through normal channels. Help is also available to those whose tax problems cause significant hardship (that is, the inability to provide necessities).

People who have a complaint about the IRS may write to the district director or the service center director for their area. Additional information on taxpayer rights may be found in IRS Publication 1, *Your Rights as a Taxpayer.*

TAX PREPARERS' RESPONSIBILITIES

Currently, over one-half of all individuals have someone else prepare their tax returns. The tax laws consider anyone receiving compensation in exchange for preparing an income tax return as an **income tax return preparer.** In the tax law, there are standards that must be adhered to by all income tax return preparers. Penalties that may be assessed for failing to adhere to these standards include the following.

- A $50 penalty each time the tax preparer fails to sign the tax return as a paid preparer. The maximum annual penalty is $25,000.
- A $50 penalty each time the tax preparer fails to provide the taxpayer with a copy of his or her tax return. The maximum annual penalty is $25,000.
- A $50 penalty each time the tax preparer fails to keep a copy of the taxpayer's tax return. The maximum annual penalty is $25,000.
- A $250 penalty for any tax return in which the tax preparer allows a position to be taken that is either frivolous or does not have a realistic possibility of being sustained on its merits. A position has a realistic possibility of being sustained if it has at least a one-in-three chance of prevailing in court, should the IRS challenge it.
- A $1,000 penalty for any tax return where the tax preparer intentionally disregards the rules and regulations, or willfully understates the taxpayer's tax liability.

Neither the tax law nor the IRS have minimum education or experience requirements to prepare another person's tax return. However, only professional tax preparers can represent taxpayers before the IRS. **Professional tax preparers** prepare tax returns, provide tax planning and give tax advice to their clients. They include attorneys, certified public accountants (CPAs) and enrolled agents. Attorneys and CPAs who prepare tax returns have met certain educational standards, passed a standardized exam, and met specific experience requirements that allow them to be licensed to practice in their respective professions. Enrolled agents, while neither CPAs nor attorneys, have passed an IRS exam and have been granted the authority to represent taxpayers before the IRS. Other paid preparers can receive compensation for their services, but are not allowed to communicate with the IRS on behalf of their clients.

The IRS imposes additional standards for professional tax preparers. Failure to adhere to these standards may result in penalties being assessed, including disbarment from practicing before the IRS. Those interested in learning more about the additional standards for professional tax preparers should refer to IRS Circular 230, which can be obtained from the IRS website. (See the back inside cover of the book for instructions on how to access the IRS website.)

AMENDED RETURNS

Form 1040X, Amended U.S. Individual Income Tax Return, is available to amend an individual income tax return. Taxpayers may file an amended return up until three years after the date the original return was due or filed, whichever was later. Use of Form 1040X is not mandatory, but the IRS prefers its use over a regular Form 1040 or 1040A marked "Revised." The design of Form 1040X expedites processing by the IRS. Thus, use of Form 1040X could speed up a claim for a refund. Taxpayers use Form 1040X only after filing an original return.

Information for Figure 12-3:
Filled-In Form 1040X, Pages 1 and 2

Steven and Sarah Martin failed to claim a **$300** contribution made during 2004 to the General Hospital, Peoria, Illinois, a qualifying charity. Accordingly, they amend their Form 1040 for 2004 and claim a refund by filing a Form 1040X on **June 15, 2006.** The following 2004 information is used.

Other Information

   1: Adjusted gross income, **$49,094**

2A: Itemized deductions, **$11,200**

   4: Exemptions, **$9,300** ($3,100 exemption for 2004 × 3)

   6: Tax, **$3,571** (corrected tax, **$3,526,** from 2004 Tax Table)

   9: Other taxes, **$4,177** (self-employment tax on net profits from Sarah's business)

 11: Federal income withheld, **$856**

 12: Estimated payments, **$9,500**

 19: Overpayment, reported on original return, **$2,608** [$10,356 payments ($856 withheld + $9,500 estimated payments) minus $7,748 total tax ($3,571 regular tax + $4,177 self-employment tax)]

FIGURE 12-3 Filled-In Form 1040X, Page 1

Form **1040X** (Rev. November 2005)	Department of the Treasury—Internal Revenue Service **Amended U.S. Individual Income Tax Return** ▶ See separate instructions.	OMB No. 1545-0091

This return is for calendar year ▶ 2004 , or fiscal year ended ▶ _____ , _____ .

		Your social security number
Your first name and initial: Steven M.	Last name: Martin	471 91 0417
If a joint return, spouse's first name and initial: Sarah J.	Last name: Martin	Spouse's social security number: 916 38 2124
Home address (no. and street) or P.O. box if mail is not delivered to your home: 2886 Linwood Ct.	Apt. no.	Phone number: (309) 721-0846
City, town or post office, state, and ZIP code. If you have a foreign address, see page 2 of the instructions. Peoria, IL 61064-5417		For Paperwork Reduction Act Notice, see page 6.

Please print or type

Draft as of 06/07/2005

A If the address shown above is different from that shown on your last return filed with the IRS and you would like us to change it, check here . . . . ▶ ☐

B Filing status. Be sure to complete this line. **Note.** You cannot change from joint to separate returns after the due date.

On original return ▶ ☐ Single ☒ Married filing jointly ☐ Married filing separately ☐ Head of household ☐ Qualifying widow(er)

On this return ▶ ☐ Single ☒ Married filing jointly ☐ Married filing separately ☐ Head of household* ☐ Qualifying widow(er)

* If the qualifying person is a child but not your dependent, see page 2 of the instructions.

Use Part II on the back to explain any changes

Income and Deductions (see instructions)		A. Original amount or as previously adjusted (see page 3)	B. Net change—amount of increase or (decrease)—explain in Part II	C. Correct amount
1 Adjusted gross income (see page 3)	**1**	49,094		49,094
2 Itemized deductions or standard deduction (see page 3). .	**2**	11,200	300	11,500
3 Subtract line 2 from line 1	**3**	37,894		37,594
4 Exemptions. If changing, fill in Parts I and II on the back	**4**	9,300		9,300
5 Taxable income. Subtract line 4 from line 3	**5**	28,594		28,294
6 Tax (see page 4). Method used in col. C_____	**6**	3,571		3,526
7 Credits (see page 4)	**7**	0		0
8 Subtract line 7 from line 6. Enter the result but not less than zero .	**8**	3,571		3,526
9 Other taxes (see page 4)	**9**	4,177		4,177
10 Total tax. Add lines 8 and 9	**10**	7,748		7,703

Tax Liability

11 Federal income tax withheld and excess social security and tier 1 RRTA tax withheld. If changing, see page 4	**11**	856		856
12 Estimated tax payments, including amount applied from prior year's return	**12**	9,500		9,500
13 Earned income credit (EIC)	**13**			
14 Additional child tax credit from Form 8812	**14**			
15 Credits from Form 2439, Form 4136, or Form 8885 . . .	**15**			
16 Amount paid with request for extension of time to file (see page 5)	**16**			
17 Amount of tax paid with original return plus additional tax paid after it was filed	**17**			
18 Total payments. Add lines 11 through 17 in column C	**18**			10,356

Payments

Refund or Amount You Owe

19 Overpayment, if any, as shown on original return or as previously adjusted by the IRS . . .	**19**		2,608
20 Subtract line 19 from line 18 (see page 5)	**20**		7,748
21 **Amount you owe.** If line 10, column C, is more than line 20, enter the difference and see page 5 .	**21**		
22 If line 10, column C, is less than line 20, enter the difference	**22**		45
23 Amount of line 22 you want **refunded to you**	**23**		45
24 Amount of line 22 you want **applied to your** estimated tax | **24** |			

Sign Here

Joint return? See page 2. Keep a copy for your records.

Under penalties of perjury, I declare that I have filed an original return and that I have examined this amended return, including accompanying schedules and statements, and to the best of my knowledge and belief, this amended return is true, correct, and complete. Declaration of preparer (other than taxpayer) is based on all information of which the preparer has any knowledge.

Steven M. Martin	6/15/06	*Sarah J. Martin*	6/15/06
Your signature	Date	Spouse's signature. If a joint return, **both** must sign.	Date

Paid Preparer's Use Only

Preparer's signature ▶	Date	Check if self-employed ☐	Preparer's SSN or PTIN
Firm's name (or yours if self-employed), address, and ZIP code ▶		EIN	
		Phone no. ( )	

Cat. No. 11360L   Form **1040X** (Rev. 11-2005)

FIGURE 12-3 Filled-In Form 1040X, Page 2

Form 1040X (Rev. 11-2005)   Page **2**

Part I Exemptions. See Form 1040 or 1040A instructions.	A. Original number of exemptions reported or as previously adjusted	B. Net change	C. Correct number of exemptions
If you are **not changing your exemptions**, do not complete this part. If claiming **more exemptions**, complete lines 25–31. If claiming **fewer exemptions**, complete lines 25–30.			

25	Yourself and spouse	**25**		
	Caution. If someone can claim you as a dependent, you cannot claim an exemption for yourself.			
26	Your dependent children who lived with you	**26**		
27	Your dependent children who did not live with you due to divorce or separation	**27**		
28	Other dependents.	**28**		
29	Total number of exemptions. Add lines 25 through 28	**29**		
30	Multiply the number of exemptions claimed on line 29 by the amount listed below for the tax year you are amending. Enter the result here and on line 4.			

Tax year	Exemption amount	But see the instructions for line 4 on page 3 if the amount on line 1 is over:
2005	$3,200	$109,475
2004	3,100	107,025
2003	3,050	104,625
2002	3,000	103,000

30

31 Dependents (children and other) not claimed on original (or adjusted) return:

No. of children on 31 who:

(a) First name Last name	(b) Dependent's social security number	(c) Dependent's relationship to you	(d) ✓ if qualifying child for child tax credit (see page 5)
			☐
			☐
			☐
			☐
			☐

- lived with you . . . ☐
- **did not** live with you due to divorce or separation (see page 5) . ▶ ☐
- Dependents on 31 not entered above ▶

Part II Explanation of Changes

Enter the line number from the front of the form for each item you are changing and give the reason for each change. Attach only the supporting forms and schedules for the items changed. If you do not attach the required information, your Form 1040X may be returned. Be sure to include your name and social security number on any attachments.

If the change relates to a net operating loss carryback or a general business credit carryback, attach the schedule or form that shows the year in which the loss or credit occurred. See page 2 of the instructions. Also, check here. . . . . . ▶ ☐

Line 2: Contribution of $300 paid to

General Hospital, Peoria, Illinois,

on July 15, 2004 was omitted

in error on line 15,

Schedule A, Form 1040.

Part III Presidential Election Campaign Fund. Checking below will not increase your tax or reduce your refund.

If you did not previously want $3 to go to the fund but now want to, check here . . . . ▶ ☐
If a joint return and your spouse did not previously want $3 to go to the fund but now wants to, check here . . . . . ▶ ☐

Form **1040X** (Rev. 11-2005)

QUESTIONS AND PROBLEMS

1. **Net Operating Loss.**

   a. What is meant by an NOL?

   b. Can an individual who does not operate a business have an NOL? Explain.

   c. For what taxable years may an NOL created in 2005 be used as a deduction for AGI?

2. **Net Operating Loss.**

   a. What types of adjustments must be made in order to convert negative taxable income into an NOL?

   b. Jamie Wang (single) has business income amounting to $70,000 and negative taxable income of $36,200. Wang has allowable business deductions of $98,000, took the standard deduction, and claimed one personal exemption. What is the amount of Wang's 2005 NOL, assuming that no other adjustments are necessary?

c. What would be the amount of the NOL if, in Part b., Wang's gross income included net nonbusiness long-term capital gains of $6,000 and business income of $64,000?

3. **Net Operating Loss.** Chris Robin, a single lawyer, has opened his own law office. The following summarizes Robin's 2005 net loss.

Business income	$54,500	
Nonbusiness income (dividends and interest)	2,300	
Long-term capital gain (nonbusiness income)	1,800	
Total income		$58,600
Business deductions	$58,800	
Ordinary nonbusiness deductions (includes a $400 theft loss)	5,670	
Personal and dependency exemption	3,200	
Total deductions		(67,670)
Net loss as computed by Robin		($ 9,070)

Compute Robin's NOL.

4. **AMT.** Explain in general the computation of the alternative minimum tax and how the computation differs from the regular tax computation.

5. **AMT.**

   a. How must depreciation expense for real and personal property be determined in computing the alternative minimum tax (AMT)?

b. Explain the *types* of adjustments that must be made to regular taxable income in order to compute the AMT income.

6. **AMT.** James M. (SSN 346-57-4657) and Tammy S. (SSN 465-46-3647) Livingston prepared a joint income tax return for 2005 and claimed four exemptions. Their regular taxable income and tax liability were computed as follows:

Salaries	$40,000
Schedule C net profit	52,000
Dividend income	4,700
Interest income	2,350
Adjusted gross income	$99,050
Itemized deductions	(18,000)
	$81,050
Personal exemptions	(12,800)
Taxable income	$68,250
Tax liability	$10,399

The Livingstons received $15,000 of tax-exempt interest from private activity bonds. In computing taxable income, the Livingstons took $7,000 depreciation on Schedule C, using the MACRS 200% declining balance method on property with a five-year class life. AMT allows $5,500 of depreciation for the same property. Itemized deductions include charitable contributions of $9,000, state and local property taxes of $4,712, casualty losses of $775 (after 10% AGI floor), and state income taxes of $3,513. Compute the Livingstons' AMT.

7. **General Business Tax Credit.**

   a. Which credits discussed in the text are combined into the general business credit?

   b. What option is available to taxpayers who are unable to deduct all of the general business credit from their tax liability in the current year?

   c. When the general business credit is carried to other tax years, in what year order are the carryover credits used? If general business credits from more than one year are carried over, in what order are they used?

8. **Rehabilitation Credit.** Harriet Glanville purchased an office building in 2005 that had originally been placed in service in 1932. Glanville paid $100,000 for the building and spent an additional $150,000 to rehabilitate it. The building was placed in service in May.

   a. Compute Glanville's credit for rehabilitation expenditures.

   b. Compute Glanville's basis in the building for depreciation purposes if she elects to take the rehabilitation credit.

9. **Work Opportunity Credit.** During 2005, RST, Inc., hired three people (Albertson, Baines, and Cantella), all of whom qualified RST for the work opportunity credit. During 2005, RST, Inc., paid first-year wages as follows: Albertson, $4,000; Baines, $2,000; and Cantella, $1,800.

   a. Compute RST's work opportunity credit for 2005.

   b. Assuming that RST paid a total of $180,000 to its employees during the year for wages, compute the amount deductible for wage expense in 2005 if the work opportunity credit is taken.

c. Compute RST's work opportunity credit for 2006 if it paid first year wages during 2006 as follows: Albertson, $3,000; Baines, $3,500; and Cantella, $4,500.

10. **Disabled Access Credit.**

   a. Can a company with $5,000,000 in gross receipts qualify for the disabled access credit? Explain.

   b. Can a company with 40 full-time employees qualify for the disabled access credit? Explain.

   c. What is the maximum disabled access credit?

11. **Empowerment Zone Employment Credit.** Ambly Inc. is located in a qualified empowerment zone. During 2005, Ambly hired two people who live in the empowerment zone. These two employees were paid $3,500 and $2,000, respectively. Neither worker was from one of the eight groups targeted for purposes of the work opportunity credit. Compute Ambly's 2005 empowerment zone employment credit.

12. **Welfare-to-Work Credit.** Back in 2004, Teresa Somner hired two employees who qualified for the welfare-to-work credit. Qualified first-year wages paid during 2005 for these two employees totalled $7,500. Qualified second-year wages paid during 2005 totalled $20,000. Compute Somner's 2005 welfare-to-work credit.

13. **Employer-Provided Child Care Credit.** In 2005, Sarah Peterson started a qualified child care program for her employees. During 2005, Peterson paid $8,000 in qualified child care expenditures and $12,000 in qualified child care resource and referral expenses. Compute Peterson's employer-provided child care credit for 2005.

14. **Small Employer Pension Plan Startup Credit.** Certain employers are entitled to a tax credit for costs associated with establishing a new pension plan for their employees.

   a. Which employers qualify for this credit?

   b. Are there restrictions on the types of pension plans that are eligible for this credit?

   c. How is the credit computed? For how many years can the credit be taken?

15. **Audits and Penalties.** Insert the answer to each of the following questions in the space provided.

   a. What is the monthly penalty for failure to file a tax return?   _____
   b. What is the monthly penalty for late payment of taxes?   _____
   c. What is the penalty for filing a frivolous return?   _____
   d. What is the penalty for each information statement that is filed late?   _____
   e. What is the penalty assessed on a tax preparer for failing to provide a copy of the tax return to the taxpayer?   _____
   f. Within the district audit division, there are two types of audits. One is the field audit. What is the other?   _____
   g. After receiving a *30-day letter,* how long does the taxpayer have to request a conference with the examining officer?   _____
   h. After a tax return is filed, how many years does the IRS have to issue a *90-day deficiency?*   _____

16. **Form 1040X.** Eight months after filing their Form 1040 for 2005 with the IRS Center in Memphis, Tennessee, Jack L. (SSN 347-47-5784) and Judith K. (SSN 457-58-4758) Keith, 1618 Redford Lane, Kingsport, Tennessee 37664-3322, discovered several items that had been omitted from their original return. These items are as follows.

   • A contribution of 20 shares of stock in the ABC Corporation to the Building Fund of the Second Church on January 7, 2005, that had not been claimed. Mrs. Keith purchased the stock for $600 on August 6, 2000. Its FMV on January 7, 2005 was $950.

   • Qualified dividends received during 2005 that had not been reported:
   Wye Corporation (owned by Mr. Keith) $46
   ABC Corporation (owned by Mrs. Keith)
      Dividend had been declared on December 22, 2004, to shareholders of record January 2, 2005. Paid February 1, 2005   52

Information available from the 2005 Form 1040 that had been filed by Mr. and Mrs. Keith is shown below.

Married filing jointly, claiming two personal
    and one dependency exemptions

Total income and AGI (no dividends or capital gains)	$71,000
Itemized deductions	14,370
Taxable income	47,030
Total tax liability	6,324
Federal income tax withheld	6,600
Amount refunded from original return	276

The Keiths have not been advised that their 2005 income tax return is under audit. Prepare an Amended U.S. Individual Income Tax Return, Form 1040X, for Mr. and Mrs. Keith, using the form on pages 12-32–12-33. The amended return was filed November 6, 2006.

17. **Internet Problem: Researching Instructions to Form 8882**

The employer-provided child care credit allows a tax credit for 25% of qualified child care expenses, which includes amounts paid to a qualified child care facility that provides child care services to employees.

Go to the IRS Web site and locate the Instructions to Form 8882, Employer-Provided Child Care Credit. Find the information in the instructions that describes what constitutes a qualified child care facility. Print out that page from the instructions.

See Appendix A for instructions on use of the IRS Web site.

18. **Business Entity Problem: This problem is designed for those using the "business entity" approach. The solution may require information from Chapter 14.**

a. Budget Corporation has a net operating loss (NOL) of $150,000 in 2005. What may the corporation do with this loss?

b. If the business was operated as a partnership, how would the loss be treated?

c. If Budget was an S corporation, how would the loss be treated?

(Use for Problem 16.)

Form 1040X
(Rev. November 2005)

Department of the Treasury—Internal Revenue Service

Amended U.S. Individual Income Tax Return
▶ See separate instructions.

OMB No. 1545-0091

This return is for calendar year ▶ , or fiscal year ended ▶

Your first name and initial	Last name	Your social security number
If a joint return, spouse's first name and initial	Last name	Spouse's social security number
Home address (no. and street) or P.O. box if mail is not delivered to your home	Apt. no.	Phone number ( )
City, town or post office, state, and ZIP code. If you have a foreign address, see page 2 of the instructions.		For Paperwork Reduction Act Notice, see page 6.

A If the address shown above is different from that shown on your last return filed with the IRS and you would like us to change it, check here . . . . ▶ ☐

B Filing status. Be sure to complete this line. **Note.** You cannot change from joint to separate returns after the due date.

On original return ▶ ☐ Single ☐ Married filing jointly ☐ Married filing separately ☐ Head of household ☐ Qualifying widow(er)

On this return ▶ ☐ Single ☐ Married filing jointly ☐ Married filing separately ☐ Head of household* ☐ Qualifying widow(er)

* If the qualifying person is a child but not your dependent, see page 2 of the instructions.

Use Part II on the back to explain any changes

Income and Deductions (see instructions)

		A. Original amount or as previously adjusted (see page 3)	**B. Net change**—amount of increase or (decrease)—explain in Part II	**C. Correct amount**
1 Adjusted gross income (see page 3)	**1**			
2 Itemized deductions or standard deduction (see page 3). .	**2**			
3 Subtract line 2 from line 1	**3**			
4 Exemptions. If changing, fill in Parts I and II on the back	**4**			
5 Taxable income. Subtract line 4 from line 3	**5**			

Tax Liability

6 Tax (see page 4). Method used in col. C_____	**6**			
7 Credits (see page 4).	**7**			
8 Subtract line 7 from line 6. Enter the result but not less than zero .	**8**			
9 Other taxes (see page 4)	**9**			
10 Total tax. Add lines 8 and 9	**10**			

Payments

11 Federal income tax withheld and excess social security and tier 1 RRTA tax withheld. If changing, see page 4	**11**			
12 Estimated tax payments, including amount applied from prior year's return	**12**			
13 Earned income credit (EIC)	**13**			
14 Additional child tax credit from Form 8812	**14**			
15 Credits from Form 2439, Form 4136, or Form 8885 . . .	**15**			
16 Amount paid with request for extension of time to file (see page 5)	**16**			
17 Amount of tax paid with original return plus additional tax paid after it was filed	**17**			
18 Total payments. Add lines 11 through 17 in column C	**18**			

Refund or Amount You Owe

19 Overpayment, if any, as shown on original return or as previously adjusted by the IRS . . .	**19**			
20 Subtract line 19 from line 18 (see page 5)	**20**			
21 **Amount you owe.** If line 10, column C, is more than line 20, enter the difference and see page 5 . .	**21**			
22 If line 10, column C, is less than line 20, enter the difference	**22**			
23 Amount of line 22 you want **refunded to you**	**23**			
24 Amount of line 22 you want **applied to your** estimated tax	**24**			

Sign Here

Joint return?
See page 2.
Keep a copy for your records.

Under penalties of perjury, I declare that I have filed an original return and that I have examined this amended return, including accompanying schedules and statements, and to the best of my knowledge and belief, this amended return is true, correct, and complete. Declaration of preparer (other than taxpayer) is based on all information of which the preparer has any knowledge.

▶ Your signature   Date   ▶ Spouse's signature. If a joint return, **both** must sign.   Date

Paid Preparer's Use Only

Preparer's signature ▶	Date	Check if self-employed ☐	Preparer's SSN or PTIN
Firm's name (or yours if self-employed), address, and ZIP code ▶		EIN Phone no. ( )	

Cat. No. 11360L

Form **1040X** (Rev. 11-2005)

(Use for Problem 16.)

Form 1040X (Rev. 11-2005)   Page **2**

Part I   Exemptions. See Form 1040 or 1040A instructions.

If you are **not changing your exemptions,** do not complete this part.
If claiming **more exemptions,** complete lines 25–31.
If claiming **fewer exemptions,** complete lines 25–30.

		A. Original number of exemptions reported or as previously adjusted	**B. Net change**	**C. Correct number** of exemptions
25	Yourself and spouse			
	Caution. If someone can claim you as a dependent, you cannot claim an exemption for yourself.			
26	Your dependent children who lived with you			
27	Your dependent children who did not live with you due to divorce or separation			
28	Other dependents.			
29	Total number of exemptions. Add lines 25 through 28			
30	Multiply the number of exemptions claimed on line 29 by the amount listed below for the tax year you are amending. Enter the result here and on line 4.			

Tax year	Exemption amount	**But see the instructions for line 4 on page 3 if the amount on line 1 is over:**
2005	$3,200	$109,475
2004	3,100	107,025
2003	3,050	104,625
2002	3,000	103,000

31 Dependents (children and other) not claimed on original (or adjusted) return:

(a) First name Last name	(b) Dependent's social security number	(c) Dependent's relationship to you	(d) ✓ if qualifying child for child tax credit (see page 5)
			☐
			☐
			☐
			☐
			☐

No. of children on 31 who:
● lived with you . . ▶ ☐
● **did not** live with you due to divorce or separation (see page 5) . . ▶ ☐
Dependents on 31 not entered above ▶ ☐

Part II   Explanation of Changes

Enter the line number from the front of the form for each item you are changing and give the reason for each change. Attach only the supporting forms and schedules for the items changed. If you do not attach the required information, your Form 1040X may be returned. Be sure to include your name and social security number on any attachments.

If the change relates to a net operating loss carryback or a general business credit carryback, attach the schedule or form that shows the year in which the loss or credit occurred. See page 2 of the instructions. Also, check here. . . . . ▶ ☐

Part III   Presidential Election Campaign Fund. Checking below will not increase your tax or reduce your refund.

If you did not previously want $3 to go to the fund but now want to, check here . . . . ▶ ☐
If a joint return and your spouse did not previously want $3 to go to the fund but now wants to, check here . . . . . ▶ ☐

Form **1040X** (Rev. 11-2005)

✪ *Printed on recycled paper*

COMPREHENSIVE PROBLEM

19. Ted R. Langley (SSN 556-89-8227) lives at 118 Oxford Ave., Oak Park, IL 60725. In 2005, he has the following income and deductions.

Income:

Salary	$105,000
Tax-exempt interest from private activity bonds	20,000
Interest from Bank of America	10,600

Deductions:

Cash contributions to the American Red Cross	$ 2,000
Home mortgage interest	11,520
Real estate taxes	3,850
State income taxes withheld	3,000
State income taxes paid when filing 2004 taxes	160

In addition to the above, Langley had federal income taxes withheld of $23,908 during the year. He also paid $25,000 for $37,000 of stock through an incentive stock option plan at work. Langley is divorced and claims his 15-year-old daughter, Teresa Langley (SSN 882-94-6648), as a dependent. Teresa lived with her father 10 months during 2005.

Based on this information, complete Langley's 2005 tax return, including Form 6251 to compute his AMT. Langley does not want to contribute $3 to the Presidential Campaign Fund. He does not have a foreign bank account nor did he receive a distribution from a foreign trust. Langley signs his return on April 15, 2006.

(Use for Problem 19.)

Form 1040   Department of the Treasury—Internal Revenue Service
U.S. Individual Income Tax Return **2005** (99) IRS Use Only—Do not write or staple in this space.

For the year Jan. 1–Dec. 31, 2005, or other tax year beginning , 2005, ending , 20 | OMB No. 1545-0074

Label
(See instructions on page 16.)
Use the IRS label. Otherwise, please print or type.

L A B E L   H E R E

Your first name and initial | Last name | Your social security number

If a joint return, spouse's first name and initial | Last name | Spouse's social security number

Home address (number and street). If you have a P.O. box, see page 16. | Apt. no.

▲ You **must** enter your SSN(s) above. ▲

City, town or post office, state, and ZIP code. If you have a foreign address, see page 16.

Checking a box below will not change your tax or refund.

Presidential Election Campaign ▶ Check here if you, or your spouse if filing jointly, want $3 to go to this fund (see page 16) ▶ ☐ You ☐ Spouse

Filing Status
Check only one box.

1 ☐ Single
2 ☐ Married filing jointly (even if only one had income)
3 ☐ Married filing separately. Enter spouse's SSN above and full name here. ▶
4 ☐ Head of household (with qualifying person). (See page 17.) If the qualifying person is a child but not your dependent, enter this child's name here. ▶
5 ☐ Qualifying widow(er) with dependent child (see page 17)

Exemptions

6a ☐ **Yourself.** If someone can claim you as a dependent, **do not** check box 6a
b ☐ **Spouse**
c **Dependents:**

(1) First name Last name	(2) Dependent's social security number	(3) Dependent's relationship to you	(4) ✓ If qualifying child for child tax credit (see page 18)
			☐
			☐
			☐
			☐

If more than four dependents, see page 18.

Boxes checked on 6a and 6b _____
No. of children on 6c who:
• lived with you _____
• did not live with you due to divorce or separation (see page 18) _____
Dependents on 6c not entered above _____
Add numbers on lines above ▶ _____

d Total number of exemptions claimed

Income

Attach Form(s) W-2 here. Also attach Forms W-2G and 1099-R if tax was withheld.

If you did not get a W-2, see page 19.

Enclose, but do not attach, any payment. Also, please use **Form 1040-V.**

7 Wages, salaries, tips, etc. Attach Form(s) W-2 | 7
8a **Taxable** interest. Attach Schedule B if required | 8a
b **Tax-exempt** interest. **Do not** include on line 8a | 8b
9a Ordinary dividends. Attach Schedule B if required | 9a
b Qualified dividends (see page 20) | 9b
10 Taxable refunds, credits, or offsets of state and local income taxes (see page 20) | 10
11 Alimony received | 11
12 Business income or (loss). Attach Schedule C or C-EZ | 12
13 Capital gain or (loss). Attach Schedule D if required. If not required, check here ▶ ☐ | 13
14 Other gains or (losses). Attach Form 4797 | 14
15a IRA distributions | 15a | b Taxable amount (see page 22) | 15b
16a Pensions and annuities | 16a | b Taxable amount (see page 22) | 16b
17 Rental real estate, royalties, partnerships, S corporations, trusts, etc. Attach Schedule E | 17
18 Farm income or (loss). Attach Schedule F | 18
19 Unemployment compensation | 19
20a Social security benefits | 20a | b Taxable amount (see page 24) | 20b
21 Other income. List type and amount (see page 24) | 21
22 Add the amounts in the far right column for lines 7 through 21. This is your **total income** ▶ | 22

Adjusted Gross Income

23 Educator expenses (see page 26) | 23
24 Certain business expenses of reservists, performing artists, and fee-basis government officials. Attach Form 2106 or 2106-EZ | 24
25 Health savings account deduction. Attach Form 8889 | 25
26 Moving expenses. Attach Form 3903 | 26
27 One-half of self-employment tax. Attach Schedule SE | 27
28 Self-employed SEP, SIMPLE, and qualified plans | 28
29 Self-employed health insurance deduction (see page XX) | 29
30 Penalty on early withdrawal of savings | 30
31a Alimony paid b Recipient's SSN ▶ | 31a
32 IRA deduction (see page XX) | 32
33 Student loan interest deduction (see page XX) | 33
34 Tuition and fees deduction (see page XX) | 34
35 Domestic production activities deduction. Attach Form 8903 | 35
36 Add lines 23 through 31a and 32 through 35 | 36
37 Subtract line 36 from line 22. This is your **adjusted gross income** ▶ | 37

For Disclosure, Privacy Act, and Paperwork Reduction Act Notice, see page 75. Cat. No. 11320B Form **1040** (2005)

(Use for Problem 19.)

Form 1040 (2005)   Page **2**

Tax and Credits	38	Amount from line 37 (adjusted gross income)	38	
	39a	Check if: ☐ **You** were born before January 2, 1941, ☐ Blind. ☐ **Spouse** was born before January 2, 1941, ☐ Blind. Total boxes checked ▶ 39a		
Standard Deduction for—	b	If your spouse itemizes on a separate return or you were a dual-status alien, see page 31 and check here ▶ 39b ☐		
	40	**Itemized deductions** (from Schedule A) **or** your **standard deduction** (see left margin)	40	
• People who checked any box on line 39a or 39b **or** who can be claimed as a dependent, see page 31.	41	Subtract line 40 from line 38	41	
	42	If line 38 is $109,475 or less, multiply $3,200 by the total number of exemptions claimed on line 6d. If line 38 is over $109,475, see the worksheet on page 33	42	
	43	**Taxable income.** Subtract line 42 from line 41. If line 42 is more than line 41, enter -0-	43	
	44	**Tax** (see page 33). Check if any tax is from: **a** ☐ Form(s) 8814 **b** ☐ Form 4972	44	
• All others:	45	**Alternative minimum tax** (see page 35). Attach Form 6251	45	
Single or Married filing separately, $5,000	46	Add lines 44 and 45 ▶	46	
	47	Foreign tax credit. Attach Form 1116 if required	47	
Married filing jointly or Qualifying widow(er), $10,000	48	Credit for child and dependent care expenses. Attach Form 2441	48	
	49	Credit for the elderly or the disabled. Attach Schedule R	49	
	50	Education credits. Attach Form 8863	50	
Head of household, $7,300	51	Retirement savings contributions credit. Attach Form 8880	51	
	52	Child tax credit (see page 37). Attach Form 8901 if required	52	
	53	Adoption credit. Attach Form 8839	53	
	54	Credits from: **a** ☐ Form 8396 **b** ☐ Form 8859	54	
	55	Other credits. Check applicable box(es): **a** ☐ Form 3800 **b** ☐ Form 8801 **c** ☐ Specify	55	
	56	Add lines 47 through 55. These are your **total credits**	56	
	57	Subtract line 56 from line 46. If line 56 is more than line 46, enter -0- ▶	57	
Other Taxes	58	Self-employment tax. Attach Schedule SE	58	
	59	Social security and Medicare tax on tip income not reported to employer. Attach Form 4137	59	
	60	Additional tax on IRAs, other qualified retirement plans, etc. Attach Form 5329 if required	60	
	61	Advance earned income credit payments from Form(s) W-2	61	
	62	Household employment taxes. Attach Schedule H	62	
	63	Add lines 57 through 62. This is your **total tax** ▶	63	
Payments	64	Federal income tax withheld from Forms W-2 and 1099	64	
	65	2005 estimated tax payments and amount applied from 2004 return	65	
If you have a qualifying child, attach Schedule EIC.	66a	**Earned income credit (EIC)**	66a	
	b	Nontaxable combat pay election ▶ 66b		
	67	Excess social security and tier 1 RRTA tax withheld (see page 54)	67	
	68	Additional child tax credit. Attach Form 8812	68	
	69	Amount paid with request for extension to file (see page 54)	69	
	70	Payments from: **a** ☐ Form 2439 **b** ☐ Form 4136 **c** ☐ Form 8885	70	
	71	Add lines 64, 65, 66a, and 67 through 70. These are your **total payments** ▶	71	
Refund Direct deposit? See page 54 and fill in 73b, 73c, and 73d.	72	If line 71 is more than line 63, subtract line 63 from line 71. This is the amount you **overpaid**	72	
	73a	Amount of line 72 you want **refunded to you** ▶	73a	
	▶ b	Routing number ▶ c Type: ☐ Checking ☐ Savings		
	▶ d	Account number		
	74	Amount of line 72 you want **applied to your 2006 estimated tax** ▶ 74		
Amount You Owe	75	**Amount you owe.** Subtract line 71 from line 63. For details on how to pay, see page 55 ▶	75	
	76	Estimated tax penalty (see page 55) 76		

Third Party Designee
Do you want to allow another person to discuss this return with the IRS (see page 56)? ☐ **Yes.** Complete the following. ☐ **No**

Designee's name ▶   Phone no. ▶ ( )   Personal identification number (PIN) ▶

Sign Here
Joint return? See page 17.
Keep a copy for your records.

Under penalties of perjury, I declare that I have examined this return and accompanying schedules and statements, and to the best of my knowledge and belief, they are true, correct, and complete. Declaration of preparer (other than taxpayer) is based on all information of which preparer has any knowledge.

Your signature | Date | Your occupation | Daytime phone number ( )

Spouse's signature. If a joint return, **both** must sign. | Date | Spouse's occupation

Paid Preparer's Use Only
Preparer's signature ▶ | Date | Check if self-employed ☐ | Preparer's SSN or PTIN

Firm's name (or yours if self-employed), address, and ZIP code ▶ | EIN | Phone no. ( )

Form **1040** (2005)

♺ *Printed on recycled paper*

(Use for Problem 19.)

SCHEDULES A&B	Schedule A—Itemized Deductions	OMB No. 1545-0074
(Form 1040)	(Schedule B is on back)	**2005**
Department of the Treasury Internal Revenue Service (99)	► **Attach to Form 1040.** ► **See Instructions for Schedules A and B (Form 1040).**	Attachment Sequence No. **07**

Name(s) shown on Form 1040 | Your social security number

Medical and Dental Expenses

Caution. Do not include expenses reimbursed or paid by others.
1 Medical and dental expenses (see page A-2) . . . | **1**
2 Enter amount from Form 1040, line 38 | **2** |
3 Multiply line 2 by 7.5% (.075). . . . . . . | **3**
4 Subtract line 3 from line 1. If line 3 is more than line 1, enter -0- . . . . . | **4**

Taxes You Paid

(See page A-2.)

5 State and local **(check only one box):**
 a ☐ Income taxes, **or**
 b ☐ General sales taxes (see page A-2) | **5**
6 Real estate taxes (see page A-3) . . . | **6**
7 Personal property taxes . . . . . | **7**
8 Other taxes. List type and amount ► | **8**
9 Add lines 5 through 8 . . . . | **9**

Interest You Paid

(See page A-3.)

Note. Personal interest is not deductible.

10 Home mortgage interest and points reported to you on Form 1098 | **10**
11 Home mortgage interest not reported to you on Form 1098. If paid to the person from whom you bought the home, see page A-4 and show that person's name, identifying no., and address ► | **11**
12 Points not reported to you on Form 1098. See page A-4 for special rules . . . . | **12**
13 Investment interest. Attach Form 4952 if required. (See page A-4.) . . . . | **13**
14 Add lines 10 through 13 . . . . | **14**

Gifts to Charity

If you made a gift and got a benefit for it, see page A-4.

15 Gifts by cash or check. If you made any gift of $250 or more, see page A-4 | **15**
16 Other than by cash or check. If any gift of $250 or more, see page A-4. You **must** attach Form 8283 if over $500 | **16**
17 Carryover from prior year . . . . | **17**
18 Add lines 15 through 17 . . . . | **18**

Casualty and Theft Losses

19 Casualty or theft loss(es). Attach Form 4684. (See page A-5.) . . . . | **19**

Job Expenses and Most Other Miscellaneous Deductions

(See page A-5.)

20 Unreimbursed employee expenses—job travel, union dues, job education, etc. Attach Form 2106 or 2106-EZ if required. (See page A-6.) ► | **20**
21 Tax preparation fees . . . . | **21**
22 Other expenses—investment, safe deposit box, etc. List type and amount ► | **22**
23 Add lines 20 through 22 . . . . | **23**
24 Enter amount from Form 1040, line 38 | **24** |
25 Multiply line 24 by 2% (.02) . . . . | **25**
26 Subtract line 25 from line 23. If line 25 is more than line 23, enter -0- . . . . | **26**

Other Miscellaneous Deductions

27 Other—from list on page A-6. List type and amount ► | **27**

Total Itemized Deductions

28 Is Form 1040, line 38, over $145,950 (over $72,975 if married filing separately)?
 ☐ **No.** Your deduction is not limited. Add the amounts in the far right column for lines 4 through 27. Also, enter this amount on Form 1040, line 40. ►
 ☐ **Yes.** Your deduction may be limited. See page A-6 for the amount to enter. | **28**
29 If you elect to itemize deductions even though they are less than your standard deduction, check here ► ☐

For Paperwork Reduction Act Notice, see Form 1040 instructions. Cat. No. 11330X **Schedule A (Form 1040) 2005**

(Use for Problem 19.)

Schedules A&B (Form 1040) 2005   OMB No. 1545-0074   Page **2**

Name(s) shown on Form 1040. Do not enter name and social security number if shown on other side.   **Your social security number**

Schedule B—Interest and Ordinary Dividends

Attachment Sequence No. **08**

Part I Interest (See page B-1 and the instructions for Form 1040, line 8a.)	**1** List name of payer. If any interest is from a seller-financed mortgage and the buyer used the property as a personal residence, see page B-1 and list this interest first. Also, show that buyer's social security number and address ▶	**Amount**

Note. If you received a Form 1099-INT, Form 1099-OID, or substitute statement from a brokerage firm, list the firm's name as the payer and enter the total interest shown on that form.

	1	
2 Add the amounts on line 1	**2**	
3 Excludable interest on series EE and I U.S. savings bonds issued after 1989. Attach Form 8815	**3**	
4 Subtract line 3 from line 2. Enter the result here and on Form 1040, line 8a ▶	**4**	

Note. If line 4 is over $1,500, you must complete Part III.

Part II Ordinary Dividends (See page B-2 and the instructions for Form 1040, line 9a.)	**5** List name of payer ▶	**Amount**

Note. If you received a Form 1099-DIV or substitute statement from a brokerage firm, list the firm's name as the payer and enter the ordinary dividends shown on that form.

	5	
6 Add the amounts on line 5. Enter the total here and on Form 1040, line 9a . ▶	**6**	

Note. If line 6 is over $1,500, you must complete Part III.

Part III Foreign Accounts and Trusts (See page B-2.)	You must complete this part if you **(a)** had over $1,500 of taxable interest or ordinary dividends; or **(b)** had a foreign account; or **(c)** received a distribution from, or were a grantor of, or a transferor to, a foreign trust.	**Yes**	**No**
	7a At any time during 2005, did you have an interest in or a signature or other authority over a financial account in a foreign country, such as a bank account, securities account, or other financial account? See page B-2 for exceptions and filing requirements for Form TD F 90-22.1.		
	b If "Yes," enter the name of the foreign country ▶		
	8 During 2005, did you receive a distribution from, or were you the grantor of, or transferor to, a foreign trust? If "Yes," you may have to file Form 3520. See page B-2		

For Paperwork Reduction Act Notice, see Form 1040 instructions.   Schedule B (Form 1040) 2005

✹ *Printed on recycled paper*

(Use for Problem 19.)

Form **6251**	**Alternative Minimum Tax—Individuals**	OMB No. 1545-0227
Department of the Treasury Internal Revenue Service (99)	▶ See separate instructions. ▶ Attach to Form 1040 or Form 1040NR.	**2005** Attachment Sequence No. **32**

Name(s) shown on Form 1040	Your social security number

Part I — Alternative Minimum Taxable Income (See instructions for how to complete each line.)

1	If filing Schedule A (Form 1040), enter the amount from Form 1040, line 41, and go to line 2. Otherwise, enter the amount from Form 1040, line 38, and go to line 7. (If less than zero, enter as a negative amount.)	**1**
2	Medical and dental. Enter the **smaller** of Schedule A (Form 1040), line 4, **or** 2½% of Form 1040, line 38 .	**2**
3	Taxes from Schedule A (Form 1040), line 9	**3**
4	Enter the home mortgage interest adjustment, if any, from line 6 of the worksheet on page 2 of the instructions	**4**
5	Miscellaneous deductions from Schedule A (Form 1040), line 26	**5**
6	If Form 1040, line 38, is over $145,950 (over $72,975 if married filing separately), enter the amount from line 9 of the **Itemized Deductions Worksheet** on page B-1 of the Instructions for Schedules A & B (Form 1040)	**6** ( )
7	Tax refund from Form 1040, line 10 or line 21	**7** ( )
8	Investment interest expense (difference between regular tax and AMT)	**8**
9	Depletion (difference between regular tax and AMT)	**9**
10	Net operating loss deduction from Form 1040, line 21. Enter as a positive amount .	**10**
11	Interest from specified private activity bonds exempt from the regular tax . . .	**11**
12	Qualified small business stock (7% of gain excluded under section 1202) . . .	**12**
13	Exercise of incentive stock options (excess of AMT income over regular tax income) . . .	**13**
14	Estates and trusts (amount from Schedule K-1 (Form 1041), box 12, code A) . .	**14**
15	Electing large partnerships (amount from Schedule K-1 (Form 1065-B), box 6) . .	**15**
16	Disposition of property (difference between AMT and regular tax gain or loss) . .	**16**
17	Depreciation on assets placed in service after 1986 (difference between regular tax and AMT) . .	**17**
18	Passive activities (difference between AMT and regular tax income or loss) . . .	**18**
19	Loss limitations (difference between AMT and regular tax income or loss) . . .	**19**
20	Circulation costs (difference between regular tax and AMT)	**20**
21	Long-term contracts (difference between AMT and regular tax income)	**21**
22	Mining costs (difference between regular tax and AMT)	**22**
23	Research and experimental costs (difference between regular tax and AMT) . . .	**23**
24	Income from certain installment sales before January 1, 1987	**24** ( )
25	Intangible drilling costs preference	**25**
26	Other adjustments, including income-based related adjustments	**26**
27	Alternative tax net operating loss deduction	**27** ( )
28	**Alternative minimum taxable income.** Combine lines 1 through 27. (If married filing separately and line 28 is more than $191,000, see page 6 of the instructions.)	**28**

Part II — Alternative Minimum Tax

29	Exemption. (If this form is for a child under age 14, see page 6 of the instructions.)	

IF your filing status is . . .	AND line 28 is not over . . .	THEN enter on line 29 . . .	
Single or head of household	$112,500	$40,250	
Married filing jointly or qualifying widow(er) . .	150,000	58,000	**29**
Married filing separately	75,000	29,000	

If line 28 is **over** the amount shown above for your filing status, see page 6 of the instructions.

30	Subtract line 29 from line 28. If zero or less, enter -0- here and on lines 33 and 35 and stop here . .	**30**
31	● If you reported capital gain distributions directly on Form 1040, line 13; you reported qualified dividends on Form 1040, line 9b; **or** you had a gain on both lines 15 and 16 of Schedule D (Form 1040) (as refigured for the AMT, if necessary), complete Part III on the back and enter the amount from line 55 here. ● **All others:** If line 30 is $175,000 or less ($87,500 or less if married filing separately), multiply line 30 by 26% (.26). Otherwise, multiply line 30 by 28% (.28) and subtract $3,500 ($1,750 if married filing separately) from the result.	**31**
32	Alternative minimum tax foreign tax credit (see page 7 of the instructions)	**32**
33	Tentative minimum tax. Subtract line 32 from line 31	**33**
34	Tax from Form 1040, line 44 (minus any tax from Form 4972 and any foreign tax credit from Form 1040, line 47). If you used Schedule J to figure your tax, the amounts for lines 44 and 47 of Form 1040 must be refigured without using Schedule J (see page 8 of the instructions)	**34**
35	**Alternative minimum tax.** Subtract line 34 from line 33. If zero or less, enter -0-. Enter here and on Form 1040, line 45	**35**

For Paperwork Reduction Act Notice, see page 8 of the instructions.	Cat. No. 13600G	Form **6251** (2005)

Draft as of 06/29/2005

CUMULATIVE PROBLEM (CHAPTERS 1–12)

This problem is suitable for manual preparation or computer software application.
Using the following information, prepare a joint federal income tax return for Jerry and Janet Apps.

Jerry R. (SSN 367-83-9403) and Janet K. (SSN 361-73-4098) Apps, married, under age 65, file a joint return. They reside at 410 E. Vernon Avenue, Carlock, Illinois 61725-1287. Both elect to have $3 go to the presidential campaign fund.

Their household includes David A. Apps, their 12-year-old son (SSN 965-26-4381), and Edwin R. Apps (SSN 157-43-2587), Jerry's 70-year-old father. Janet and Jerry provide over half of the support of both David and Edwin. David has no income of his own; Edwin received $4,500 in nontaxable social security benefits during the year.

Jerry, who works as a carpenter for Evergreen Enterprises, received the following information on his Form W-2. Jerry does not participate in an employer-sponsored pension plan.

Gross wages	$42,000
Social security and Medicare tax withheld	3,213
Federal income tax withheld	2,160
State income tax withheld	950

Janet owns and operates J&J Networking, a Dolmore distributorship. The principal business code is 454390. Janet has no employer ID number. She is a cash basis taxpayer but uses the accrual basis in her business. She uses the cost method for valuing the inventory. No changes have been made in the inventory system. Janet operated her business for all 12 months and had an office in her home. She materially participated in the business throughout the year.

Information relating to Janet's business operation is shown below.

Gross receipts	$30,200
Returns and allowances	200
Beginning inventory	700
Purchases	22,625
Ending inventory	825

Expenses:

Advertising	$ 100	Office expense	$80
Bank service charges	24	Supplies	50
Car expenses	675	Travel	400
Commissions	1,200	Meals and entertainment	180
Depreciation on equipment		Business seminars	264
placed in service prior		Other business taxes	560
to 2005	625	Miscellaneous expenses	35
Dues and publications	220	Postage expense	260
Insurance (business)	150		

Janet uses her personal car in her business. She keeps good records of her business mileage and uses the standard mileage method. The car was first used in the business on May 1, 2004. During 2005 Janet drove 7,631 miles, of which 1,605 were for business and 6,026 were personal. Of the business miles, 315 were driven after August 31, 2005.

Information relating to the home is shown below.

Total area of home	1,800 square feet
Area used for business	180 square feet
FMV of home, for purposes of Form 8829, line 35	$150,000
Adjusted basis of home, for purposes of Form 8829, line 35	$115,000
Value of land, Form 8829, line 36	$ 20,000
Applicable depreciation percentage, Form 8829, line 39	3.175%
Mortgage interest	$ 6,250
Real estate taxes	$ 2,400
Homeowner's insurance	$ 2,680
Utilities	$ 3,200

The Appses own a four-unit apartment building, which they actively manage. The Appses paid $125,000 for the building in 1994 and depreciate it using MACRS over 27.5 years. The building is located at 19 Sunset Road in Carlock. All units were rented for the entire year.

Information on the apartments is shown below.

Revenue from rents	$33,600
Expenses:	
Real estate taxes	$ 4,800
Utilities	1,780
Insurance	1,550
Cleaning and maintenance	5,200
Legal and professional fees	125
Mortgage interest	7,200
Repairs	827
Supplies	325
Depreciation	4,545

The Appses had other income consisting of the following:

Interest from Champion Savings	$750
Interest on bonds from the State of Illinois	430
Qualified dividends from General Morris Corporation	120
Qualified dividends from Eagle Corporation	150
Qualified dividends from Roper Corporation	70

The Appses have a $4,950 long-term capital loss carryover from 2004. They also sold the following securities during 2005.

Number of Shares	Company	Date Acquired	Cost	Date Sold	Sales Price
100	Roper Corp.	5-1-00	$5,000	6-12-05	$7,500
50	Fastco Corp.	2-14-05	3,250	7-20-05	2,950
200	Eagle Corp.	3-16-99	6,200	8-10-05	8,100
100	South Corp.	3-14-04	1,500	1-24-05	6,500

Neither Jerry nor Janet had any interest in a foreign trust or account.

The Appses made the following payments during the year:

Medical expenses (unreimbursed):

	Jerry	Janet	David	Edwin	Total
Prescription medicines	$ 50	$ 200	$ 25	$ 100	$ 375
Doctor bills	60	500	30	200	790
Dentist bills	150	40	200	0	390
Hospital bills	0	1,800	0	2,100	3,900
Transportation	8	72	24	16	120
Eyeglasses	0	0	125	0	125
Over-the-counter medicine	0	50	30	70	150

Taxes:

Sales tax	$1,200
Balance due on 2004 state income tax return	625
Balance due on 2004 federal income tax return	725
Estimated federal income tax payments	1,000
Real estate taxes	2,400

Interest:

Mortgage interest	$6,250
Personal interest	975

Contributions:

Church	$1,200
United Way	100
Presidential election campaign	50

In addition to these cash contributions, the Appses donated five shares of S&W common stock to their church on July 30. The stock had been purchased on December 15, 2003, for $200. The fair market value of the stock on July 30 was $400.

Other payments the Appses made in 2005 are as follows.

Rental of safe deposit box for securities	$ 24
2004 tax preparation fee (personal return)	300
Union dues for Jerry	1,200
Automobile license	50
IRA for Jerry	1,800
IRA for Janet	500

(Use for Cumulative Problem.)

Form **1040**	Department of the Treasury—Internal Revenue Service **U.S. Individual Income Tax Return** 2005	(99) IRS Use Only—Do not write or staple in this space.

For the year Jan. 1–Dec. 31, 2005, or other tax year beginning , 2005, ending , 20   OMB No. 1545-0074

Label
(See instructions on page 16.)
Use the IRS label. Otherwise, please print or type.

L A B E L   **H E R E**

Your first name and initial   Last name   Your social security number

If a joint return, spouse's first name and initial   Last name   Spouse's social security number

Home address (number and street). If you have a P.O. box, see page 16.   Apt. no.   ▲ You **must** enter ▲ your SSN(s) above.

City, town or post office, state, and ZIP code. If you have a foreign address, see page 16.

Presidential Election Campaign ▶ Checking a box below will not change your tax or refund. Check here if you, or your spouse if filing jointly, want $3 to go to this fund (see page 16) ▶ ☐ You ☐ Spouse

Filing Status
Check only one box.

1 ☐ Single
2 ☐ Married filing jointly (even if only one had income)
3 ☐ Married filing separately. Enter spouse's SSN above and full name here. ▶
4 ☐ Head of household (with qualifying person). (See page 17.) If the qualifying person is a child but not your dependent, enter this child's name here. ▶
5 ☐ Qualifying widow(er) with dependent child (see page 17)

Exemptions

6a ☐ **Yourself.** If someone can claim you as a dependent, **do not** check box 6a
b ☐ **Spouse**
c **Dependents:**

(1) First name Last name	(2) Dependent's social security number	(3) Dependent's relationship to you	(4) ✓ if qualifying child for child tax credit (see page 18)
			☐
			☐
			☐
			☐

If more than four dependents, see page 18.

Boxes checked on 6a and 6b _____
No. of children on 6c who:
• lived with you _____
• did not live with you due to divorce or separation (see page 18) _____
Dependents on 6c not entered above _____
Add numbers on lines above ▶ ☐

d Total number of exemptions claimed

Income

Attach Form(s) W-2 here. Also attach Forms W-2G and 1099-R if tax was withheld.

If you did not get a W-2, see page 19.

Enclose, but do not attach, any payment. Also, please use **Form 1040-V.**

7	Wages, salaries, tips, etc. Attach Form(s) W-2	7
8a	**Taxable** interest. Attach Schedule B if required	8a
b	Tax-exempt interest. **Do not** include on line 8a 8b	
9a	Ordinary dividends. Attach Schedule B if required	9a
b	Qualified dividends (see page 20) 9b	
10	Taxable refunds, credits, or offsets of state and local income taxes (see page 20)	10
11	Alimony received	11
12	Business income or (loss). Attach Schedule C or C-EZ	12
13	Capital gain or (loss). Attach Schedule D if required. If not required, check here ▶ ☐	13
14	Other gains or (losses). Attach Form 4797	14
15a	IRA distributions 15a b Taxable amount (see page 22)	15b
16a	Pensions and annuities 16a b Taxable amount (see page 22)	16b
17	Rental real estate, royalties, partnerships, S corporations, trusts, etc. Attach Schedule E	17
18	Farm income or (loss). Attach Schedule F	18
19	Unemployment compensation	19
20a	Social security benefits 20a b Taxable amount (see page 24)	20b
21	Other income. List type and amount (see page 24)	21
22	Add the amounts in the far right column for lines 7 through 21. This is your **total income** ▶	22

Adjusted Gross Income

23	Educator expenses (see page 26)	23
24	Certain business expenses of reservists, performing artists, and fee-basis government officials. Attach Form 2106 or 2106-EZ	24
25	Health savings account deduction. Attach Form 8889	25
26	Moving expenses. Attach Form 3903	26
27	One-half of self-employment tax. Attach Schedule SE	27
28	Self-employed SEP, SIMPLE, and qualified plans	28
29	Self-employed health insurance deduction (see page XX)	29
30	Penalty on early withdrawal of savings	30
31a	Alimony paid b Recipient's SSN ▶	31a
32	IRA deduction (see page XX)	32
33	Student loan interest deduction (see page XX)	33
34	Tuition and fees deduction (see page XX)	34
35	Domestic production activities deduction. Attach Form 8903	35
36	Add lines 23 through 31a and 32 through 35	36
37	Subtract line 36 from line 22. This is your **adjusted gross income** ▶	37

For Disclosure, Privacy Act, and Paperwork Reduction Act Notice, see page 75.   Cat. No. 11320B   Form **1040** (2005)

(Use for Cumulative Problem.)

Form 1040 (2005)			Page **2**

Tax and Credits	38	Amount from line 37 (adjusted gross income)	38	
	39a	Check if: ☐ **You** were born before January 2, 1941, ☐ Blind. ☐ **Spouse** was born before January 2, 1941, ☐ Blind. } Total boxes checked ▶ 39a		
Standard Deduction for—	b	If your spouse itemizes on a separate return or you were a dual-status alien, see page 31 and check here ▶ 39b ☐		
	40	**Itemized deductions** (from Schedule A) **or** your **standard deduction** (see left margin) . .	40	
• People who checked any box on line 39a or 39b **or** who can be claimed as a dependent, see page 31.	41	Subtract line 40 from line 38	41	
	42	If line 38 is $109,475 or less, multiply $3,200 by the total number of exemptions claimed on line 6d. If line 38 is over $109,475, see the worksheet on page 33	42	
	43	**Taxable income.** Subtract line 42 from line 41. If line 42 is more than line 41, enter -0-	43	
	44	**Tax** (see page 33). Check if any tax is from: **a** ☐ Form(s) 8814 **b** ☐ Form 4972	44	
• All others:	45	**Alternative minimum tax** (see page 35). Attach Form 6251 . . .	45	
Single or Married filing separately, $5,000	46	Add lines 44 and 45 . . . . ▶	46	
	47	Foreign tax credit. Attach Form 1116 if required . . .	47	
	48	Credit for child and dependent care expenses. Attach Form 2441	48	
Married filing jointly or Qualifying widow(er), $10,000	49	Credit for the elderly or the disabled. Attach Schedule R .	49	
	50	Education credits. Attach Form 8863	50	
	51	Retirement savings contributions credit. Attach Form 8880 .	51	
	52	Child tax credit (see page 37). Attach Form 8901 if required .	52	
Head of household, $7,300	53	Adoption credit. Attach Form 8839	53	
	54	Credits from: **a** ☐ Form 8396 **b** ☐ Form 8859 . .	54	
	55	Other credits. Check applicable box(es): **a** ☐ Form 3800 **b** ☐ Form 8801 **c** ☐ Specify	55	
	56	Add lines 47 through 55. These are your **total credits** . .		56	
	57	Subtract line 56 from line 46. If line 56 is more than line 46, enter -0- . . . . . ▶	57	

Other Taxes	58	Self-employment tax. Attach Schedule SE	58	
	59	Social security and Medicare tax on tip income not reported to employer. Attach Form 4137 . .	59	
	60	Additional tax on IRAs, other qualified retirement plans, etc. Attach Form 5329 if required	60	
	61	Advance earned income credit payments from Form(s) W-2	61	
	62	Household employment taxes. Attach Schedule H	62	
	63	Add lines 57 through 62. This is your **total tax** . . . . ▶	63	

Payments	64	Federal income tax withheld from Forms W-2 and 1099 . .	64	
	65	2005 estimated tax payments and amount applied from 2004 return	65	
If you have a qualifying child, attach Schedule EIC.	66a	**Earned income credit (EIC)**	66a	
	b	Nontaxable combat pay election ▶ 66b		
	67	Excess social security and tier 1 RRTA tax withheld (see page 54)	67	
	68	Additional child tax credit. Attach Form 8812 . . .	68	
	69	Amount paid with request for extension to file (see page 54)	69	
	70	Payments from: **a** ☐ Form 2439 **b** ☐ Form 4136 **c** ☐ Form 8885 .	70	
	71	Add lines 64, 65, 66a, and 67 through 70. These are your **total payments** . . . . ▶	71	

Refund	72	If line 71 is more than line 63, subtract line 63 from line 71. This is the amount you **overpaid**	72	
Direct deposit? See page 54 and fill in 73b, 73c, and 73d.	73a	Amount of line 72 you want **refunded to you** . . . . ▶	73a	
	▶ b	Routing number	▶ c Type: ☐ Checking ☐ Savings	
	▶ d	Account number		
	74	Amount of line 72 you want **applied to your 2006 estimated tax** ▶	74	

Amount You Owe	75	**Amount you owe.** Subtract line 71 from line 63. For details on how to pay, see page 55 ▶	75	
	76	Estimated tax penalty (see page 55)	76	

Third Party Designee	Do you want to allow another person to discuss this return with the IRS (see page 56)? ☐ **Yes.** Complete the following. ☐ **No**
	Designee's name ▶ Phone no. ▶ ( ) Personal identification number (PIN) ▶

Sign Here	Under penalties of perjury, I declare that I have examined this return and accompanying schedules and statements, and to the best of my knowledge and belief, they are true, correct, and complete. Declaration of preparer (other than taxpayer) is based on all information of which preparer has any knowledge.			
Joint return? See page 17.	Your signature	Date	Your occupation	Daytime phone number ( )
Keep a copy for your records.	Spouse's signature. If a joint return, **both** must sign.	Date	Spouse's occupation	

Paid Preparer's Use Only	Preparer's signature ▶	Date	Check if self-employed ☐	Preparer's SSN or PTIN
	Firm's name (or yours if self-employed), address, and ZIP code ▶		EIN	
			Phone no. ( )	

Form **1040** (2005)

♻ *Printed on recycled paper*

(Use for Cumulative Problem.)

SCHEDULES A&B	Schedule A—Itemized Deductions	OMB No. 1545-0074

(Form 1040) — (Schedule B is on back) — **20 05**

Department of the Treasury
Internal Revenue Service (99) ▶ **Attach to Form 1040.** ▶ **See Instructions for Schedules A and B (Form 1040).** — Attachment Sequence No. **07**

Name(s) shown on Form 1040 — Your social security number

Medical and Dental Expenses		**Caution.** Do not include expenses reimbursed or paid by others.		
	1	Medical and dental expenses (see page A-2) . . .	1	
	2	Enter amount from Form 1040, line 38 ⌐2⌐		
	3	Multiply line 2 by 7.5% (.075). . . .	3	
	4	Subtract line 3 from line 1. If line 3 is more than line 1, enter -0-		4
Taxes You Paid (See page A-2.)	5	State and local **(check only one box):** **a** ☐ Income taxes, **or** **b** ☐ General sales taxes (see page A-2)	5	
	6	Real estate taxes (see page A-3)	6	
	7	Personal property taxes	7	
	8	Other taxes. List type and amount ▶	8	
	9	Add lines 5 through 8		9
Interest You Paid (See page A-3.)	10	Home mortgage interest and points reported to you on Form 1098	10	
	11	Home mortgage interest not reported to you on Form 1098. If paid to the person from whom you bought the home, see page A-4 and show that person's name, identifying no., and address ▶	11	
Note. Personal interest is not deductible.	12	Points not reported to you on Form 1098. See page A-4 for special rules	12	
	13	Investment interest. Attach Form 4952 if required. (See page A-4.)	13	
	14	Add lines 10 through 13		14
Gifts to Charity If you made a gift and got a benefit for it, see page A-4.	15	Gifts by cash or check. If you made any gift of $250 or more, see page A-4	15	
	16	Other than by cash or check. If any gift of $250 or more, see page A-4. You **must** attach Form 8283 if over $500	16	
	17	Carryover from prior year	17	
	18	Add lines 15 through 17		18
Casualty and Theft Losses	19	Casualty or theft loss(es). Attach Form 4684. (See page A-5.)		19
Job Expenses and Most Other Miscellaneous Deductions (See page A-5.)	20	Unreimbursed employee expenses—job travel, union dues, job education, etc. Attach Form 2106 or 2106-EZ if required. (See page A-6.) ▶	20	
	21	Tax preparation fees.	21	
	22	Other expenses—investment, safe deposit box, etc. List type and amount ▶	22	
	23	Add lines 20 through 22	23	
	24	Enter amount from Form 1040, line 38 ⌐24⌐		
	25	Multiply line 24 by 2% (.02)	25	
	26	Subtract line 25 from line 23. If line 25 is more than line 23, enter -0-		26
Other Miscellaneous Deductions	27	Other—from list on page A-6. List type and amount ▶		27
Total Itemized Deductions	28	Is Form 1040, line 38, over $145,950 (over $72,975 if married filing separately)? ☐ **No.** Your deduction is not limited. Add the amounts in the far right column for lines 4 through 27. Also, enter this amount on Form 1040, line 40. ☐ **Yes.** Your deduction may be limited. See page A-6 for the amount to enter.		28
	29	If you elect to itemize deductions even though they are less than your standard deduction, check here ▶ ☐		

For Paperwork Reduction Act Notice, see Form 1040 instructions. — Cat. No. 11330X — **Schedule A (Form 1040) 2005**

(Use for Cumulative Problem.)

SCHEDULE C **(Form 1040)** Department of the Treasury Internal Revenue Service	**Profit or Loss From Business** (Sole Proprietorship) ► Partnerships, joint ventures, etc., must file Form 1065 or 1065-B. ► Attach to Form 1040 or 1041. ► See Instructions for Schedule C (Form 1040).	OMB No. 1545-0074 **2005** Attachment Sequence No. **09**

Name of proprietor | Social security number (SSN)

A Principal business or profession, including product or service (see page C-2 of the instructions) | **B** Enter code from pages C-7, 8, & 9 ►

C Business name. If no separate business name, leave blank. | **D** Employer ID number (EIN), if any

E Business address (including suite or room no.) ► ....
City, town or post office, state, and ZIP code

F Accounting method: **(1)** ☐ Cash **(2)** ☐ Accrual **(3)** ☐ Other (specify) ►
G Did you "materially participate" in the operation of this business during 2005? If "No," see page C-3 for limit on losses ☐ **Yes** ☐ **No**
H If you started or acquired this business during 2005, check here . . . . ► ☐

Part I   Income

1	Gross receipts or sales. **Caution.** If this income was reported to you on Form W-2 and the "Statutory employee" box on that form was checked, see page C-3 and check here . . . . . ► ☐	**1**
2	Returns and allowances	**2**
3	Subtract line 2 from line 1	**3**
4	Cost of goods sold (from line 42 on page 2)	**4**
5	**Gross profit.** Subtract line 4 from line 3	**5**
6	Other income, including Federal and state gasoline or fuel tax credit or refund (see page C-3) . . .	**6**
7	**Gross income.** Add lines 5 and 6 . . . . ►	**7**

Part II   Expenses. Enter expenses for business use of your home **only** on line 30.

8	Advertising	**8**	**18** Office expense	**18**	
9	Car and truck expenses (see page C-3)	**9**	**19** Pension and profit-sharing plans	**19**	
10	Commissions and fees . .	**10**	**20** Rent or lease (see page C-5):		
11	Contract labor (see page C-4)	**11**	**a** Vehicles, machinery, and equipment	**20a**	
12	Depletion	**12**	**b** Other business property . .	**20b**	
13	Depreciation and section 179 expense deduction (not included in Part III) (see page C-4)	**13**	**21** Repairs and maintenance . .	**21**	
			22 Supplies (not included in Part III)	**22**	
			23 Taxes and licenses	**23**	
			24 Travel, meals, and entertainment:		
14	Employee benefit programs (other than on line 19) .	**14**	**a** Travel	**24a**	
15	Insurance (other than health) .	**15**	**b** Deductible meals and entertainment (see page C-5)	**24b**	
16	Interest:		**25** Utilities	**25**	
a	Mortgage (paid to banks, etc.) .	**16a**	**26** Wages (less employment credits) .	**26**	
b	Other	**16b**	**27** Other expenses (from line 48 on page 2)	**27**	
17	Legal and professional services	**17**			

28	**Total expenses** before expenses for business use of home. Add lines 8 through 27 in columns . ►	**28**
29	Tentative profit (loss). Subtract line 28 from line 7	**29**
30	Expenses for business use of your home. Attach **Form 8829**	**30**
31	**Net profit or (loss).** Subtract line 30 from line 29. ● If a profit, enter on **Form 1040, line 12,** and **also** on **Schedule SE, line 2** (statutory employees, see page C-6). Estates and trusts, enter on Form 1041, line 3. ● If a loss, you **must** go to line 32.	**31**
32	If you have a loss, check the box that describes your investment in this activity (see page C-6). ● If you checked 32a, enter the loss on **Form 1040, line 12,** and **also** on **Schedule SE, line 2** (statutory employees, see page C-6). Estates and trusts, enter on Form 1041, line 3. ● If you checked 32b, you **must** attach **Form 6198.** Your loss may be limited.	**32a** ☐ All investment is at risk. **32b** ☐ Some investment is not at risk.

For Paperwork Reduction Act Notice, see Form 1040 instructions. | Cat. No. 11334P | Schedule C (Form 1040) 2005

(Use for Cumulative Problem.)

Schedule C (Form 1040) 2005 — Page **2**

Part III — Cost of Goods Sold (see page C-6)

33 Method(s) used to value closing inventory: **a** ☐ Cost **b** ☐ Lower of cost or market **c** ☐ Other (attach explanation)

34 Was there any change in determining quantities, costs, or valuations between opening and closing inventory? If "Yes," attach explanation . . . . ☐ Yes ☐ No

35 Inventory at beginning of year. If different from last year's closing inventory, attach explanation . . | **35** |

36 Purchases less cost of items withdrawn for personal use . . . . | **36** |

37 Cost of labor. Do not include any amounts paid to yourself . . . . . . | **37** |

38 Materials and supplies . . . . | **38** |

39 Other costs . . . . | **39** |

40 Add lines 35 through 39 . . . . | **40** |

41 Inventory at end of year . . . . | **41** |

42 **Cost of goods sold.** Subtract line 41 from line 40. Enter the result here and on page 1, line 4 . . | **42** |

Part IV — Information on Your Vehicle. Complete this part **only** if you are claiming car or truck expenses on line 9 and are not required to file Form 4562 for this business. See the instructions for line 13 on page C-4 to find out if you must file Form 4562.

43 When did you place your vehicle in service for business purposes? (month, day, year) ▶ ..../......../....... .

44 Of the total number of miles you drove your vehicle during 2005, enter the number of miles you used your vehicle for:

a Business .... **b** Commuting (see instructions) .... **c** Other ....

45 Do you (or your spouse) have another vehicle available for personal use?. . . . . ☐ Yes ☐ No

46 Was your vehicle available for personal use during off-duty hours? . . . . ☐ Yes ☐ No

47a Do you have evidence to support your deduction? . . . . ☐ Yes ☐ No

 b If "Yes," is the evidence written? . . . . ☐ Yes ☐ No

Part V — Other Expenses. List below business expenses not included on lines 8–26 or line 30.

48 **Total other expenses.** Enter here and on page 1, line 27 . . . . | **48** |

Printed on recycled paper

Schedule C (Form 1040) 2005

(Use for Cumulative Problem.)

SCHEDULE D
(Form 1040)

Department of the Treasury
Internal Revenue Service (99)

Capital Gains and Losses

► Attach to Form 1040. ► See Instructions for Schedule D (Form 1040).

► Use Schedule D-1 to list additional transactions for lines 1 and 8.

OMB No. 1545-0074

2005

Attachment
Sequence No. **12**

Name(s) shown on Form 1040

Your social security number

Part I   Short-Term Capital Gains and Losses—Assets Held One Year or Less

(a) Description of property (Example: 100 sh. XYZ Co.)	(b) Date acquired (Mo., day, yr.)	(c) Date sold (Mo., day, yr.)	(d) Sales price (see page D-6 of the instructions)	(e) Cost or other basis (see page D-6 of the instructions)	(f) Gain or (loss) Subtract (e) from (d)
1					

2 Enter your short-term totals, if any, from Schedule D-1, line 2	**2**		
3 **Total short-term sales price amounts.** Add lines 1 and 2 in column (d)	**3**		
4 Short-term gain from Form 6252 and short-term gain or (loss) from Forms 4684, 6781, and 8824		**4**	
5 Net short-term gain or (loss) from partnerships, S corporations, estates, and trusts from Schedule(s) K-1		**5**	
6 Short-term capital loss carryover. Enter the amount, if any, from line 8 of your **Capital Loss Carryover Worksheet** on page D-6 of the instructions		**6**	( )
7 **Net short-term capital gain or (loss).** Combine lines 1 through 6 in column (f)		**7**	

Part II   Long-Term Capital Gains and Losses—Assets Held More Than One Year

(a) Description of property (Example: 100 sh. XYZ Co.)	(b) Date acquired (Mo., day, yr.)	(c) Date sold (Mo., day, yr.)	(d) Sales price (see page D-6 of the instructions)	(e) Cost or other basis (see page D-6 of the instructions)	(f) Gain or (loss) Subtract (e) from (d)
8					

9 Enter your long-term totals, if any, from Schedule D-1, line 9	**9**		
10 **Total long-term sales price amounts.** Add lines 8 and 9 in column (d)	**10**		
11 Gain from Form 4797, Part I; long-term gain from Forms 2439 and 6252; and long-term gain or (loss) from Forms 4684, 6781, and 8824		**11**	
12 Net long-term gain or (loss) from partnerships, S corporations, estates, and trusts from Schedule(s) K-1		**12**	
13 Capital gain distributions. See page D-1 of the instructions		**13**	
14 Long-term capital loss carryover. Enter the amount, if any, from line 13 of your **Capital Loss Carryover Worksheet** on page D-6 of the instructions		**14**	( )
15 **Net long-term capital gain or (loss).** Combine lines 8 through 14 in column (f). Then go to Part III on the back		**15**	

For Paperwork Reduction Act Notice, see Form 1040 instructions.   Cat. No. 11338H   **Schedule D (Form 1040) 2005**

(Use for Cumulative Problem.)

Schedule D (Form 1040) 2005   Page **2**

Part III	**Summary**

16 Combine lines 7 and 15 and enter the result. If line 16 is a loss, skip lines 17 through 20, and go to line 21. If a gain, enter the gain on Form 1040, line 13, and then go to line 17 below . . **16**

17 Are lines 15 and 16 **both** gains?
☐ **Yes.** Go to line 18.
☐ **No.** Skip lines 18 through 21, and go to line 22.

18 Enter the amount, if any, from line 7 of the **28% Rate Gain Worksheet** on page D-7 of the instructions . . . . ▶ **18**

19 Enter the amount, if any, from line 18 of the **Unrecaptured Section 1250 Gain Worksheet** on page D-8 of the instructions . . . . ▶ **19**

20 Are lines 18 and 19 **both** zero or blank?
☐ **Yes.** Complete Form 1040 through line 43, and then complete the **Qualified Dividends and Capital Gain Tax Worksheet** on page 34 of the Instructions for Form 1040. **Do not** complete lines 21 and 22 below.
☐ **No.** Complete Form 1040 through line 43, and then complete the **Schedule D Tax Worksheet** on page D-9 of the instructions. **Do not** complete lines 21 and 22 below.

21 If line 16 is a loss, enter here and on Form 1040, line 13, the **smaller** of:

● The loss on line 16 or
● ($3,000), or if married filing separately, ($1,500)
. . . . **21** ( )

Note. When figuring which amount is smaller, treat both amounts as positive numbers.

22 Do you have qualified dividends on Form 1040, line 9b?
☐ **Yes.** Complete Form 1040 through line 43, and then complete the **Qualified Dividends and Capital Gain Tax Worksheet** on page 34 of the Instructions for Form 1040.
☐ **No.** Complete the rest of Form 1040.

✪ *Printed on recycled paper*   **Schedule D (Form 1040) 2005**

(Use for Cumulative Problem.)

SCHEDULE E (Form 1040) Department of the Treasury Internal Revenue Service (99)	**Supplemental Income and Loss** (From rental real estate, royalties, partnerships, S corporations, estates, trusts, REMICs, etc.) ► **Attach to Form 1040 or Form 1041.** ► **See Instructions for Schedule E (Form 1040).**	OMB No. 1545-0074 **2005** Attachment Sequence No. **13**

Name(s) shown on return | | Your social security number

Part I   Income or Loss From Rental Real Estate and Royalties   **Note.** If you are in the business of renting personal property, use **Schedule C** or **C-EZ** (see page E-3). Report farm rental income or loss from **Form 4835** on page 2, line 40.

1 List the type and location of each **rental real estate property:**

A ....

B ....

C ....

2 For each rental real estate property listed on line 1, did you or your family use it during the tax year for personal purposes for more than the greater of:
- 14 days **or**
- 10% of the total days rented at fair rental value?
(See page E-3.)

	Yes	No
A		
B		
C		

Income:		**Properties**			**Totals** (Add columns A, B, and C.)
		A	**B**	**C**	
3 Rents received	**3**				**3**
4 Royalties received	**4**				**4**
Expenses:					
5 Advertising	**5**				
6 Auto and travel (see page E-4) . .	**6**				
7 Cleaning and maintenance . . .	**7**				
8 Commissions	**8**				
9 Insurance	**9**				
10 Legal and other professional fees	**10**				
11 Management fees	**11**				
12 Mortgage interest paid to banks, etc. (see page E-4)	**12**				**12**
13 Other interest	**13**				
14 Repairs	**14**				
15 Supplies	**15**				
16 Taxes	**16**				
17 Utilities	**17**				
18 Other (list) ►	**18**				
19 Add lines 5 through 18	**19**				**19**
20 Depreciation expense or depletion (see page E-4)	**20**				**20**
21 Total expenses. Add lines 19 and 20	**21**				
22 Income or (loss) from rental real estate or royalty properties. Subtract line 21 from line 3 (rents) or line 4 (royalties). If the result is a (loss), see page E-4 to find out if you must file **Form 6198**	**22**				
23 Deductible rental real estate loss. **Caution.** Your rental real estate loss on line 22 may be limited. See page E-4 to find out if you must file **Form 8582.** Real estate professionals must complete line 43 on page 2	**23** (	)(	)(	)	
24 **Income.** Add positive amounts shown on line 22. **Do not** include any losses					**24**
25 **Losses.** Add royalty losses from line 22 and rental real estate losses from line 23. Enter total losses here					**25** (	)
26 **Total rental real estate and royalty income or (loss).** Combine lines 24 and 25. Enter the result here. If Parts II, III, IV, and line 40 on page 2 do not apply to you, also enter this amount on Form 1040, line 17. Otherwise, include this amount in the total on line 41 on page 2					**26**

For Paperwork Reduction Act Notice, see Form 1040 instructions.   Cat. No. 11344L   **Schedule E (Form 1040) 2005**

(Use for Cumulative Problem.)

SCHEDULE SE		OMB No. 1545-0074
(Form 1040)	**Self-Employment Tax**	**20**05
Department of the Treasury Internal Revenue Service	▶ **Attach to Form 1040.** ▶ **See Instructions for Schedule SE (Form 1040).**	Attachment Sequence No. **17**

Name of person with **self-employment** income (as shown on Form 1040)	Social security number of person with **self-employment** income ▶

Who Must File Schedule SE

You must file Schedule SE if:

- You had net earnings from self-employment from **other than** church employee income (line 4 of Short Schedule SE or line 4c of Long Schedule SE) of $400 or more **or**
- You had church employee income of $108.28 or more. Income from services you performed as a minister or a member of a religious order **is not** church employee income (see page SE-1).

Note. Even if you had a loss or a small amount of income from self-employment, it may be to your benefit to file Schedule SE and use either "optional method" in Part II of Long Schedule SE (see page SE-3).

Exception. If your only self-employment income was from earnings as a minister, member of a religious order, or Christian Science practitioner **and** you filed Form 4361 and received IRS approval not to be taxed on those earnings, **do not** file Schedule SE. Instead, write "Exempt–Form 4361" on Form 1040, line 58.

May I Use Short Schedule SE or Must I Use Long Schedule SE?

Did You Receive Wages or Tips in 2005?

No → Are you a minister, member of a religious order, or Christian Science practitioner who received IRS approval **not** to be taxed on earnings from these sources, **but** you owe self-employment tax on other earnings? — Yes →

No ↓

Are you using one of the optional methods to figure your net earnings (see page SE-3)? — Yes →

No ↓

Did you receive church employee income reported on Form W-2 of $108.28 or more? — Yes →

No ↓

Yes → Was the total of your wages and tips subject to social security or railroad retirement tax **plus** your net earnings from self-employment more than $90,000? — Yes →

No ↓

No ← Did you receive tips subject to social security or Medicare tax that you **did not** report to your employer? — Yes →

You May Use Short Schedule SE Below

You Must Use Long Schedule SE on page 2

Section A—Short Schedule SE. Caution. Read above to see if you can use Short Schedule SE.

1	Net farm profit or (loss) from Schedule F, line 36, and farm partnerships, Schedule K-1 (Form 1065), box 14, code A	**1**	
2	Net profit or (loss) from Schedule C, line 31; Schedule C-EZ, line 3; Schedule K-1 (Form 1065), box 14, code A (other than farming); and Schedule K-1 (Form 1065-B), box 9. Ministers and members of religious orders, see page SE-1 for amounts to report on this line. See page SE-2 for other income to report	**2**	
3	Combine lines 1 and 2	**3**	
4	**Net earnings from self-employment.** Multiply line 3 by 92.35% (.9235). If less than $400, **do not** file this schedule; you do not owe self-employment tax . . . . ▶	**4**	
5	**Self-employment tax.** If the amount on line 4 is: ● $90,000 or less, multiply line 4 by 15.3% (.153). Enter the result here and on **Form 1040, line 58.** ● More than $90,000, multiply line 4 by 2.9% (.029). Then, add $11,160.00 to the result. Enter the total here and on **Form 1040, line 58.**	**5**	
6	**Deduction for one-half of self-employment tax.** Multiply line 5 by 50% (.5). Enter the result here and on **Form 1040, line 27**	**6**	

For Paperwork Reduction Act Notice, see Form 1040 instructions.   Cat. No. 11358Z   **Schedule SE (Form 1040) 2005**

(Use for Cumulative Problem.)

Form **4562**	**Depreciation and Amortization** (Including Information on Listed Property)	OMB No. 1545-0172 **2005**
Department of the Treasury Internal Revenue Service	▶ See separate instructions. ▶ Attach to your tax return.	Attachment Sequence No. **67**
Name(s) shown on return	Business or activity to which this form relates	Identifying number

Part I **Election To Expense Certain Property Under Section 179**
Note: *If you have any listed property, complete Part V before you complete Part I.*

1	Maximum amount. See the instructions for a higher limit for certain businesses	**1**	$105,000
2	Total cost of section 179 property placed in service (see instructions)	**2**	
3	Threshold cost of section 179 property before reduction in limitation	**3**	$420,000
4	Reduction in limitation. Subtract line 3 from line 2. If zero or less, enter -0-	**4**	
5	Dollar limitation for tax year. Subtract line 4 from line 1. If zero or less, enter -0-. If married filing separately, see instructions	**5**	

(a) Description of property	(b) Cost (business use only)	(c) Elected cost
6		

7	Listed property. Enter the amount from line 29	**7**	
8	Total elected cost of section 179 property. Add amounts in column (c), lines 6 and 7	**8**	
9	Tentative deduction. Enter the **smaller** of line 5 or line 8	**9**	
10	Carryover of disallowed deduction from line 13 of your 2004 Form 4562	**10**	
11	Business income limitation. Enter the smaller of business income (not less than zero) or line 5 (see instructions)	**11**	
12	Section 179 expense deduction. Add lines 9 and 10, but do not enter more than line 11	**12**	
13	Carryover of disallowed deduction to 2006. Add lines 9 and 10, less line 12 ▶ **13**		

Note: *Do not use Part II or Part III below for listed property. Instead, use Part V.*

Part II **Special Depreciation Allowance and Other Depreciation (Do not** include listed property.) (See instructions.)

14	Special allowance for certain aircraft, certain property with a long production period, and qualified New York Liberty Zone property (other than listed property) placed in service during the tax year	**14**	
15	Property subject to section 168(f)(1) election	**15**	
16	Other depreciation (including ACRS)	**16**	

Part III **MACRS Depreciation (Do not** include listed property.) (See instructions.)

Section A

17	MACRS deductions for assets placed in service in tax years beginning before 2005	**17**	
18	If you are electing to group any assets placed in service during the tax year into one or more general asset accounts, check here ▶ ☐		

Section B—Assets Placed in Service During 2005 Tax Year Using the General Depreciation System

(a) Classification of property	(b) Month and year placed in service	(c) Basis for depreciation (business/investment use only—see instructions)	(d) Recovery period	(e) Convention	(f) Method	(g) Depreciation deduction
19a 3-year property						
b 5-year property						
c 7-year property						
d 10-year property						
e 15-year property						
f 20-year property						
g 25-year property			25 yrs.		S/L	
h Residential rental property			27.5 yrs.	MM	S/L	
			27.5 yrs.	MM	S/L	
i Nonresidential real property			39 yrs.	MM	S/L	
				MM	S/L	

Section C—Assets Placed in Service During 2005 Tax Year Using the Alternative Depreciation System

20a Class life					S/L	
b 12-year			12 yrs.		S/L	
c 40-year			40 yrs.	MM	S/L	

Part IV **Summary** (see instructions)

21	Listed property. Enter amount from line 28	**21**	
22	**Total.** Add amounts from line 12, lines 14 through 17, lines 19 and 20 in column (g), and line 21. Enter here and on the appropriate lines of your return. Partnerships and S corporations—see instr.	**22**	
23	For assets shown above and placed in service during the current year, enter the portion of the basis attributable to section 263A costs **23**		

For Paperwork Reduction Act Notice, see separate instructions.   Cat. No. 12906N   Form **4562** (2005)

(Use for Cumulative Problem.)

Form 4562 (2005) | Page **2**

Part V — Listed Property (Include automobiles, certain other vehicles, cellular telephones, certain computers, and property used for entertainment, recreation, or amusement.)

Note: *For any vehicle for which you are using the standard mileage rate or deducting lease expense, complete **only** 24a, 24b, columns (a) through (c) of Section A, all of Section B, and Section C if applicable.*

Section A—Depreciation and Other Information (Caution: *See the instructions for limits for passenger automobiles.***)**

24a Do you have evidence to support the business/investment use claimed? ☐ Yes ☐ No | 24b If "Yes," is the evidence written? ☐ Yes ☐ No

(a) Type of property (list vehicles first)	(b) Date placed in service	(c) Business/ investment use percentage	(d) Cost or other basis	(e) Basis for depreciation (business/investment use only)	(f) Recovery period	(g) Method/ Convention	(h) Depreciation deduction	(i) Elected section 179 cost
25 Special allowance for qualified New York Liberty Zone listed property placed in service during the tax year and used more than 50% in a qualified business use (see instructions)					25			
26 Property used more than 50% in a qualified business use:								
		%						
		%						
		%						
27 Property used 50% or less in a qualified business use:								
		%				S/L –		
		%				S/L –		
		%				S/L –		

28 Add amounts in column (h), lines 25 through 27. Enter here and on line 21, page 1 . . | 28 |
29 Add amounts in column (i), line 26. Enter here and on line 7, page 1 . . . . | 29 |

Section B—Information on Use of Vehicles

Complete this section for vehicles used by a sole proprietor, partner, or other "more than 5% owner," or related person.
If you provided vehicles to your employees, first answer the questions in Section C to see if you meet an exception to completing this section for those vehicles.

	(a) Vehicle 1		(b) Vehicle 2		(c) Vehicle 3		(d) Vehicle 4		(e) Vehicle 5		(f) Vehicle 6	
30 Total business/investment miles driven during the year (**do not** include commuting miles)												
31 Total commuting miles driven during the year												
32 Total other personal (noncommuting) miles driven												
33 Total miles driven during the year. Add lines 30 through 32												
34 Was the vehicle available for personal use during off-duty hours?	Yes	No	Yes	No	Yes	No	Yes	No	Yes	No	Yes	No
35 Was the vehicle used primarily by a more than 5% owner or related person?												
36 Is another vehicle available for personal use?												

Section C—Questions for Employers Who Provide Vehicles for Use by Their Employees

Answer these questions to determine if you meet an exception to completing Section B for vehicles used by employees who **are not** more than 5% owners or related persons (see instructions).

	Yes	No
37 Do you maintain a written policy statement that prohibits all personal use of vehicles, including commuting, by your employees?		
38 Do you maintain a written policy statement that prohibits personal use of vehicles, except commuting, by your employees? See the instructions for vehicles used by corporate officers, directors, or 1% or more owners		
39 Do you treat all use of vehicles by employees as personal use?		
40 Do you provide more than five vehicles to your employees, obtain information from your employees about the use of the vehicles, and retain the information received?		
41 Do you meet the requirements concerning qualified automobile demonstration use? (See instructions.)		

Note: *If your answer to 37, 38, 39, 40, or 41 is "Yes," do not complete Section B for the covered vehicles.*

Part VI — Amortization

(a) Description of costs	(b) Date amortization begins	(c) Amortizable amount	(d) Code section	(e) Amortization period or percentage	(f) Amortization for this year
42 Amortization of costs that begins during your 2005 tax year (see instructions):					

43 Amortization of costs that began before your 2005 tax year . . . . | 43 |
44 **Total.** Add amounts in column (f). See the instructions for where to report . . . . | 44 |

⊛ *Printed on recycled paper* | Form **4562** (2005)

(Use for Cumulative Problem.)

Form **4562**	**Depreciation and Amortization** (Including Information on Listed Property)	OMB No. 1545-0172 **2005**
Department of the Treasury Internal Revenue Service	▶ See separate instructions. ▶ Attach to your tax return.	Attachment Sequence No. **67**
Name(s) shown on return	Business or activity to which this form relates	Identifying number

Part I   Election To Expense Certain Property Under Section 179
Note: *If you have any listed property, complete Part V before you complete Part I.*

1	Maximum amount. See the instructions for a higher limit for certain businesses	**1**	$105,000
2	Total cost of section 179 property placed in service (see instructions)	**2**	
3	Threshold cost of section 179 property before reduction in limitation	**3**	$420,000
4	Reduction in limitation. Subtract line 3 from line 2. If zero or less, enter -0-	**4**	
5	Dollar limitation for tax year. Subtract line 4 from line 1. If zero or less, enter -0-. If married filing separately, see instructions	**5**	

(a) Description of property	(b) Cost (business use only)	(c) Elected cost	
6			

7	Listed property. Enter the amount from line 29	**7**	
8	Total elected cost of section 179 property. Add amounts in column (c), lines 6 and 7	**8**	
9	Tentative deduction. Enter the **smaller** of line 5 or line 8	**9**	
10	Carryover of disallowed deduction from line 13 of your 2004 Form 4562	**10**	
11	Business income limitation. Enter the smaller of business income (not less than zero) or line 5 (see instructions)	**11**	
12	Section 179 expense deduction. Add lines 9 and 10, but do not enter more than line 11	**12**	
13	Carryover of disallowed deduction to 2006. Add lines 9 and 10, less line 12 ▶	**13**	

Note: *Do not use Part II or Part III below for listed property. Instead, use Part V.*

Part II   Special Depreciation Allowance and Other Depreciation (Do not include listed property.) (See instructions.)

14	Special allowance for certain aircraft, certain property with a long production period, and qualified New York Liberty Zone property (other than listed property) placed in service during the tax year	**14**	
15	Property subject to section 168(f)(1) election	**15**	
16	Other depreciation (including ACRS)	**16**	

Part III   MACRS Depreciation (Do not include listed property.) (See instructions.)

Section A

17	MACRS deductions for assets placed in service in tax years beginning before 2005	**17**	
18	If you are electing to group any assets placed in service during the tax year into one or more general asset accounts, check here ▶ ☐		

Section B—Assets Placed in Service During 2005 Tax Year Using the General Depreciation System

(a) Classification of property	(b) Month and year placed in service	(c) Basis for depreciation (business/investment use only—see instructions)	(d) Recovery period	(e) Convention	(f) Method	(g) Depreciation deduction
19a 3-year property						
b 5-year property						
c 7-year property						
d 10-year property						
e 15-year property						
f 20-year property						
g 25-year property			25 yrs.		S/L	
h Residential rental property			27.5 yrs.	MM	S/L	
			27.5 yrs.	MM	S/L	
i Nonresidential real property			39 yrs.	MM	S/L	
				MM	S/L	

Section C—Assets Placed in Service During 2005 Tax Year Using the Alternative Depreciation System

20a Class life					S/L	
b 12-year			12 yrs.		S/L	
c 40-year			40 yrs.	MM	S/L	

Part IV   Summary (see instructions)

21	Listed property. Enter amount from line 28	**21**	
22	**Total.** Add amounts from line 12, lines 14 through 17, lines 19 and 20 in column (g), and line 21. Enter here and on the appropriate lines of your return. Partnerships and S corporations—see instr.	**22**	
23	For assets shown above and placed in service during the current year, enter the portion of the basis attributable to section 263A costs	**23**	

For Paperwork Reduction Act Notice, see separate instructions.   Cat. No. 12906N   Form **4562** (2005)

(Use for Cumulative Problem.)

Form 4562 (2005)   Page **2**

Part V   Listed Property (Include automobiles, certain other vehicles, cellular telephones, certain computers, and property used for entertainment, recreation, or amusement.)

Note: *For any vehicle for which you are using the standard mileage rate or deducting lease expense, complete **only** 24a, 24b, columns (a) through (c) of Section A, all of Section B, and Section C if applicable.*

Section A—Depreciation and Other Information (Caution: *See the instructions for limits for passenger automobiles.***)**

24a   Do you have evidence to support the business/investment use claimed? ☐ Yes ☐ No   24b   If "Yes," is the evidence written? ☐ Yes ☐ No

(a) Type of property (list vehicles first)	(b) Date placed in service	(c) Business/ investment use percentage	(d) Cost or other basis	(e) Basis for depreciation (business/investment use only)	(f) Recovery period	(g) Method/ Convention	(h) Depreciation deduction	(i) Elected section 179 cost
25 Special allowance for qualified New York Liberty Zone listed property placed in service during the tax year and used more than 50% in a qualified business use (see instructions) **25**								
26 Property used more than 50% in a qualified business use:								
		%						
		%						
		%						
27 Property used 50% or less in a qualified business use:								
		%				S/L –		
		%				S/L –		
		%				S/L –		
28 Add amounts in column (h), lines 25 through 27. Enter here and on line 21, page 1. . . **28**								
29 Add amounts in column (i), line 26. Enter here and on line 7, page 1. . . . . **29**								

Section B—Information on Use of Vehicles

Complete this section for vehicles used by a sole proprietor, partner, or other "more than 5% owner," or related person.

If you provided vehicles to your employees, first answer the questions in Section C to see if you meet an exception to completing this section for those vehicles.

	(a) Vehicle 1		(b) Vehicle 2		(c) Vehicle 3		(d) Vehicle 4		(e) Vehicle 5		(f) Vehicle 6	
30 Total business/investment miles driven during the year (**do not** include commuting miles)												
31 Total commuting miles driven during the year												
32 Total other personal (noncommuting) miles driven												
33 Total miles driven during the year. Add lines 30 through 32												
34 Was the vehicle available for personal use during off-duty hours?	Yes	No	Yes	No	Yes	No	Yes	No	Yes	No	Yes	No
35 Was the vehicle used primarily by a more than 5% owner or related person?												
36 Is another vehicle available for personal use?												

Section C—Questions for Employers Who Provide Vehicles for Use by Their Employees

Answer these questions to determine if you meet an exception to completing Section B for vehicles used by employees who **are not** more than 5% owners or related persons (see instructions).

		Yes	No
37	Do you maintain a written policy statement that prohibits all personal use of vehicles, including commuting, by your employees?		
38	Do you maintain a written policy statement that prohibits personal use of vehicles, except commuting, by your employees? See the instructions for vehicles used by corporate officers, directors, or 1% or more owners		
39	Do you treat all use of vehicles by employees as personal use?		
40	Do you provide more than five vehicles to your employees, obtain information from your employees about the use of the vehicles, and retain the information received?		
41	Do you meet the requirements concerning qualified automobile demonstration use? (See instructions.)		

Note: *If your answer to 37, 38, 39, 40, or 41 is "Yes," do not complete Section B for the covered vehicles.*

Part VI   Amortization

(a) Description of costs	(b) Date amortization begins	(c) Amortizable amount	(d) Code section	(e) Amortization period or percentage	(f) Amortization for this year
42 Amortization of costs that begins during your 2005 tax year (see instructions):					
43 Amortization of costs that began before your 2005 tax year. **43**					
44 **Total.** Add amounts in column (f). See the instructions for where to report. **44**					

✪ Printed on recycled paper   Form **4562** (2005)

(Use for Cumulative Problem.)

Form **8829**	**Expenses for Business Use of Your Home**	OMB No. 1545-1266
Department of the Treasury Internal Revenue Service (99)	▶ File only with Schedule C (Form 1040). Use a separate Form 8829 for each home you used for business during the year. ▶ See separate instructions.	**2005** Attachment Sequence No. **66**

Name(s) of proprietor(s)   Your social security number

Part I   Part of Your Home Used for Business

1	Area used regularly and exclusively for business, regularly for daycare, or for storage of inventory or product samples (see instructions)	**1**	
2	Total area of home	**2**	
3	Divide line 1 by line 2. Enter the result as a percentage	**3**	%

- For daycare facilities not used exclusively for business, also complete lines 4–6.
- All others, skip lines 4–6 and enter the amount from line 3 on line 7.

4	Multiply days used for daycare during year by hours used per day	**4**		h r .
5	Total hours available for use during the year (365 days × 24 hours) (see instructions)	**5**	8,760	h r .
6	Divide line 4 by line 5. Enter the result as a decimal amount	**6**	.	
7	Business percentage. For daycare facilities not used exclusively for business, multiply line 6 by line 3 (enter the result as a percentage). All others, enter the amount from line 3. . . . . ▶	**7**		%

Part II   Figure Your Allowable Deduction

8	Enter the amount from Schedule C, line 29, **plus** any net gain or (loss) derived from the business use of your home and shown on Schedule D or Form 4797. If more than one place of business, see instructions		**8**	
	See instructions for columns (a) and (b) before completing lines 9–20.	**(a)** Direct expenses **(b)** Indirect expenses		
9	Casualty losses (see instructions)	**9**		
10	Deductible mortgage interest (see instructions)	**10**		
11	Real estate taxes (see instructions)	**11**		
12	Add lines 9, 10, and 11.	**12**		
13	Multiply line 12, column (b) by line 7		**13**	
14	Add line 12, column (a) and line 13		**14**	
15	Subtract line 14 from line 8. If zero or less, enter -0-		**15**	
16	Excess mortgage interest (see instructions) . .	**16**		
17	Insurance	**17**		
18	Repairs and maintenance	**18**		
19	Utilities	**19**		
20	Other expenses (see instructions)	**20**		
21	Add lines 16 through 20	**21**		
22	Multiply line 21, column (b) by line 7		**22**	
23	Carryover of operating expenses from 2004 Form 8829, line 41 . .		**23**	
24	Add line 21 in column (a), line 22, and line 23	**24**		
25	Allowable operating expenses. Enter the **smaller** of line 15 or line 24	**25**		
26	Limit on excess casualty losses and depreciation. Subtract line 25 from line 15	**26**		
27	Excess casualty losses (see instructions)	**27**		
28	Depreciation of your home from Part III below	**28**		
29	Carryover of excess casualty losses and depreciation from 2004 Form 8829, line 42	**29**		
30	Add lines 27 through 29		**30**	
31	Allowable excess casualty losses and depreciation. Enter the **smaller** of line 26 or line 30 . .		**31**	
32	Add lines 14, 25, and 31		**32**	
33	Casualty loss portion, if any, from lines 14 and 31. Carry amount to **Form 4684**, Section B . .		**33**	
34	Allowable expenses for business use of your home. Subtract line 33 from line 32. Enter here and on Schedule C, line 30. If your home was used for more than one business, see instructions ▶		**34**	

Part III   Depreciation of Your Home

35	Enter the **smaller** of your home's adjusted basis or its fair market value (see instructions) . .	**35**		
36	Value of land included on line 35	**36**		
37	Basis of building. Subtract line 36 from line 35	**37**		
38	Business basis of building. Multiply line 37 by line 7	**38**		
39	Depreciation percentage (see instructions)	**39**		%
40	Depreciation allowable (see instructions). Multiply line 38 by line 39. Enter here and on line 28 above	**40**		

Part IV   Carryover of Unallowed Expenses to 2006

41	Operating expenses. Subtract line 25 from line 24. If less than zero, enter -0-	**41**	
42	Excess casualty losses and depreciation. Subtract line 31 from line 30. If less than zero, enter -0-	**42**	

For Paperwork Reduction Act Notice, see page 4 of separate instructions.   Cat. No. 13232M   Form **8829** (2005)

13

Withholding, Payroll, and Estimated Taxes

CHAPTER CONTENTS

■ ■   CHAPTER OVERVIEW

*O*n January 1, 1943, the income of most wage earners became subject to pay-as-you-go *withholding. Under this system, the government collects tax revenue by having the payer withhold taxes before distributing the income. This gives the government a steady cash flow and reduces tax collection problems. Withholding also lessens the cash burdens of taxpayers when they file their tax returns. This chapter provides background information about the tax withholding process.*

Large depositors of payroll taxes, withheld income taxes, estimated income taxes, and various excise taxes must use the Treasury's electronic funds transfer (EFT) system to make their deposits. Since the rules do not affect small and medium-size depositors (those who deposit less than $200,000 a year), this chapter does not discuss the mechanics of the EFT system but instead focuses on the existing paper system.

ELECTRONIC DEPOSIT OF PAYROLL AND OTHER TAXES

The Treasury has developed an Electronic Funds Transfer (EFT) System for depositing the following:

- Payroll taxes
- Various excise taxes
- Withheld income taxes
- Corporate income and estimated taxes

Businesses with deposits in the previous year in excess of $200,000 must start making EFT deposits on January 1 of the next year. For example, businesses with more than $200,000 of deposits in 2004 must start making EFT deposits on January 1, 2006. Likewise, businesses with more than $200,000 of deposits in 2005 must start making EFT deposits on January 1, 2007.

WITHHOLDING SYSTEM

Under the pay-as-you-go system, *employers* withhold taxes from *employees'* wages that approximate their tax liabilities. Employers deposit these withholdings with a specified depository. To credit withholdings to the proper taxpayer accounts, each employee must have an identification number.

Identification Numbers

The IRS uses computer programs to process withholding data and taxpayer returns. Taxpayer identification numbers (TINs) provide the key to unlock related data. Individual taxpayers use their SSN (social security number) as their TIN. By law, employers request, receive, and enter a taxpayer's TIN on tax withholding and reporting forms.

Individuals

Individuals who need a SSN apply for one by filing Form SS-5, Application for a Social Security Card. Individuals can get Form SS-5 from any social security office. U.S. citizens as young as age 1 should obtain a SSN. This allows them to be claimed as a dependent on another's tax return. Also, taxpayers who claim the child tax credit must provide a SSN for each eligible child.

Businesses

Employers use an employer identification number (EIN) on payroll tax reporting forms, tax returns, and other government reports. Employers apply for an EIN by filing Form SS-4, Application for Employer Identification Number. Employers can get Form SS-4 from the IRS.

Withholding from Income

Withholding is based primarily on the employee's gross income from employment. Gross income from employment includes wages, salaries, fees, tips, bonuses, and commissions. From gross pay, an employer withholds income and payroll taxes (social security and Medicare taxes).

Withholding Allowance Certificate

Form W-4, Employee's Withholding Allowance Certificate, is the focal point of the income tax withholding system. The amount of income tax withheld from an employee's gross pay depends on the employee's filing status and the number of withholding allowances claimed on Form W-4. The more allowances claimed, the less tax withheld.

Employees receive withholding allowances for the personal and dependency exemptions they expect to claim in the current tax year. They also receive withholding allowances for anticipated deductions and adjustments to income.

Employers request a Form W-4 from each employee. If an employee fails to furnish Form W-4, the employer withholds the maximum amount of taxes allowed for single taxpayers. Thus, married employees must complete Form W-4 to take advantage of the lower withholding rates.

Employees complete and sign Form W-4 but give only the Employee's Withholding Allowance Certificate (bottom part of page 1) to their employer. They keep the top portion for their records.

Employers generally do not file Forms W-4 with the IRS. The only send in Forms W-4 if directed to do so by the IRS.

Form W-4 has four sections:

1. Personal Allowances Worksheet
2. Employee's Withholding Allowance Certificate
3. Deductions and Adjustments Worksheet
4. Two-Earner/Two-Job Worksheet (including Tables 1 and 2)

Each of these sections is described in the text that follows.

Personal Withholding Allowances

On the Personal Allowances Worksheet, employees enter whole numbers for personal withholding allowances (lines A through G). Single employees with more than one job, but no dependents, claim only one withholding allowance. They should claim this allowance with the employer that pays them the highest wage. At the other job(s), they should claim zero withholding allowances. Figure 13-1 describes the calculation of the withholding allowance on the Personal Allowances Worksheet for 2005.

An employee with more than one job or may want to request that an additional amount be withheld from each paycheck if combined wages exceed $35,000. This helps ensure that the employee will not be underwithheld for the year. Likewise, if the employee is married and both spouses work, each spouse may want to have additional amounts withheld from their respective paychecks when their combined wages exceed $25,000. Alternatively, they could ask their respective employers to withhold taxes at the single rate. They do this by marking an "X" in the box on the Form W-4 (line 3), "Married, but withhold at higher Single rate."

FIGURE 13-1   Personal Allowances Worksheet

A. One exemption allowance for the employee, as long as the employee does not qualify as a dependent on another person's return.

B. One additional exemption allowance for employees who are:

   1. Single and have only one job;

   2. Married, have one job, and their spouse does not work; or

   3. Married and their spouse's wages plus their second job wages (if any) do not exceed $1,000.

C. One exemption for the employee's spouse. However, the IRS recommends that married employees who have more than one job, or have spouses who work, claim a zero spousal allowance. This may avoid being underwithheld for the year.

D. One exemption for each person (other than the employee's spouse) who qualifies as the employee's dependent.

E. One exemption if the employee files as head of household.

F. One exemption if the employee plans to claim the child or dependent care credit for at least $1,500 of expenses.

G. One or more exemptions are available to employees who plan to claim the child tax credit.

   • For single employees, two exemptions are allowed for each eligible child if the employee expects total income to be less than $54,000. If total income between $54,000 and $84,000 is expected, one exemption is allowed for each eligible child, plus one additional exemption is allowed when there are more than three eligible children.

   • For married employees, two exemptions are allowed for each eligible child if total income is expected to be less than $79,000. If total income between $79,000 and $119,000 is expected, one exemption is allowed for each eligible child, plus one additional exemption is allowed when there are more than three eligible children.

Married couples with dependents can choose how to divide their withholding allowances among their employers. If the husband claims withholding allowances for a particular child on his Form W-4, the wife should not claim an allowance for that same child.

Employee's Withholding Allowance Certificate

After completing the other three parts of Form W-4, employees complete and sign Form W-4. They then clip the bottom portion of Form W-4 and give the Employee's Withholding Allowance Certificate to their employer. They keep the top portion for their records.

Deductions and Adjustments Allowances

The Deduction and Adjustments Worksheet helps employees compute additional allowances based on their expected itemized deductions and other adjustments to income. The employee estimates itemized deductions for the current year. To the extent the itemized deductions exceed the standard deduction, the excess is added to other adjustments the employee might have. The other adjustments include (1) IRA deductions, (2) the tuition and fees deduction, (3) moving expenses, (4) alimony paid, (5) penalties on early withdrawals of savings, (6) student loan interest, (7) educator expenses, and (8) deductions for self-employed individuals. The total of excess itemized deductions and adjustments equals the employee's estimate of reductions for the year (line 5).

Next, the employee estimates the amount of nonwage income for the current year. Nonwage income includes (1) interest, (2) dividends, (3) taxable payments from retirement plans, (4) income or losses from passive activities, and (5) capital gains and losses. The nonwage income (line 6) is subtracted from the excess income reductions (line 5), resulting in the net reductions (line 7). A positive net reduction is divided by $3,200. This number (use whole numbers and round down any fraction) represents additional withholding allowances that the employee claims. A negative net reduction results in no additional allowances.

Use of the additional allowance helps bring withholdings more into line with the employee's actual tax liability. The employee adds the personal withholding allowances (page 1, line H) to the additional withholding allowances. Employees who do not use the Two-Earner/Two-Job Worksheet enter the total on page 1 of Form W-4 (line 5). Employees who use the Two-Earner/Two-Job Worksheet enter this total on the Two-Earner/Two Job Worksheet (line 1).

Additional Withholding for Two-Earner/Two-Job Employees

Employees who are married and whose spouses also work use the Two-Earner/Two-Job Worksheet (page 2) when combined earnings exceed $25,000. The same rule applies to unmarried employees with more than one job and combined earnings in excess of $35,000. The goal of this worksheet is to compute additional amounts employees should have withheld. The extra withholding helps employees avoid being underwithheld for the year.

Information for Figure 13-2: Filled-In Form W-4

Jerry J. Page starts a new job in January, 2005. Jerry must complete Form W-4 for his new employer. He expects to file a joint tax return for 2005 with his wife Belle. For 2005 Jerry expects to earn $46,000; Belle expects to earn $23,000. The Pages provide all the support for their two children, who have no income. Both are eligible children for purposes of the child tax credit. They decide that Jerry will claim all withholding allowances. The Pages estimate that they will pay or receive the following amounts during 2005.

Deductible IRA payment for Belle	$4,000
Deductible IRA payment for Jerry	4,000
Child and dependent care expenses	2,300
Interest income on corporate bonds	500
Dividend income	250
Home mortgage interest	6,460
Property taxes	2,750
State income taxes	2,300
Charitable contributions	540

Personal Allowances Worksheet, page 1

Other Information

C: The Pages choose to enter -0- because both spouses work

F: Enter **1** because the Pages have at least $1,500 of child care expenses

G: Enter **4.** The Pages expect their total income to be less than $79,000, so they enter two exemptions for each eligible child.

Deductions and Adjustments Worksheet, page 2

Other Information

1: Estimate of itemized deductions, **$12,050** ($6,460 + $2,750 + $2,300 + $540)

4: Estimate of adjustments to income, **$8,000** ($4,000 + $4,000 IRA deductions)

6: Nonwage income, **$750** ($500 + $250)

8: $9,300 ÷ $3,200 = **2** when the fraction is dropped

Two-Earner/Two-Job Worksheet, page 2

Other Information

1: Number from line 10 of the Deduction and Adjustments Worksheet, **10**

2: Table 1 number that applies to $46,000 and $23,000, **4**

Changing Withholding Allowances

Employees are not required to file a new Form W-4 with their employer each year. However, the employee should make sure that the form on file indicates the proper number of allowances for the year. While the IRS does not assess penalties for being overwithheld, it does assess a penalty for being underwithheld. Therefore, when an employee's withholding allowances decrease, a new Form W-4 should be filed within ten days of the changing event (such as divorce). When an employee's withholding allowances increase, the employee can file a new Form W-4 or leave the old Form W-4 in effect. When a continuing employee files an updated Form W-4, the employer places it in effect at the beginning of the next payroll period or 30 days after an employer receives the new Form W-4, whichever is later.

The death of a spouse or dependent in the current year does not change an employee's withholding allowances. However, an employee should file a new Form W-4 by December 1 to ensure that it becomes effective at the start of the next tax year. For the two years after a spouse's death, a surviving spouse with a qualifying child can use the married filing jointly tax rates and standard deduction. However, the surviving spouse cannot claim a withholding allowance for the deceased spouse. A surviving spouse should take these facts into consideration when completing the Deductions and Adjustments Worksheet on Form W-4.

Exemption from Withholding

Certain employees can claim exemption from federal income tax withholding on Form W-4. However, social security and Medicare taxes must still be withheld. The provision to claim exemption from withholding of federal income taxes helps people who work short periods or earn small amounts. Without this provision, employers would withhold taxes from employees with no tax liability. If an employer does withhold taxes, the employee would need to file a tax return just to get back the amounts withheld.

To claim exemption from withholding in 2005, an employee must have had no federal income tax liability in 2004. Also, the employee must not expect to owe any federal income taxes for 2005.

FIGURE 13-2 Filled-In Form W-4, Employee's Withholding Allowance Certificate, Page 1

Form W-4 (2005)

Purpose. Complete Form W-4 so that your employer can withhold the correct federal income tax from your pay. Because your tax situation may change, you may want to refigure your withholding each year.

Exemption from withholding. If you are exempt, complete only lines 1, 2, 3, 4, and 7 and sign the form to validate it. Your exemption for 2005 expires February 16, 2006. See Pub. 505, Tax Withholding and Estimated Tax.

Note. You cannot claim exemption from withholding if (a) your income exceeds $800 and includes more than $250 of unearned income (for example, interest and dividends) and (b) another person can claim you as a dependent on their tax return.

Basic instructions. If you are not exempt, complete the **Personal Allowances Worksheet** below. The worksheets on page 2 adjust your withholding allowances based on itemized deductions, certain credits, adjustments to income, or two-earner/two-job situations. Complete all worksheets that apply. However, you may claim fewer (or zero) allowances.

Head of household. Generally, you may claim head of household filing status on your tax return only if you are unmarried and pay more than 50% of the costs of keeping up a home for yourself and your dependent(s) or other qualifying individuals. See line **E** below.

Tax credits. You can take projected tax credits into account in figuring your allowable number of withholding allowances. Credits for child or dependent care expenses and the child tax credit may be claimed using the **Personal Allowances Worksheet** below. See Pub. 919, How Do I Adjust My Tax Withholding? for information on converting your other credits into withholding allowances.

Nonwage income. If you have a large amount of nonwage income, such as interest or dividends, consider making estimated tax payments using Form 1040-ES, Estimated Tax for Individuals. Otherwise, you may owe additional tax.

Two earners/two jobs. If you have a working spouse or more than one job, figure the total number of allowances you are entitled to claim on all jobs using worksheets from only one Form W-4. Your withholding usually will be most accurate when all allowances are claimed on the Form W-4 for the highest paying job and zero allowances are claimed on the others.

Nonresident alien. If you are a nonresident alien, see the Instructions for Form 8233 before completing this Form W-4.

Check your withholding. After your Form W-4 takes effect, use Pub. 919 to see how the dollar amount you are having withheld compares to your projected total tax for 2005. See Pub. 919, especially if your earnings exceed $125,000 (Single) or $175,000 (Married).

Recent name change? If your name on line 1 differs from that shown on your social security card, call 1-800-772-1213 to initiate a name change and obtain a social security card showing your correct name.

Personal Allowances Worksheet (Keep for your records.)

A Enter "1" for **yourself** if no one else can claim you as a dependent . . . . **A** __1__

B Enter "1" if: {
- You are single and have only one job; or
- You are married, have only one job, and your spouse does not work; or
- Your wages from a second job or your spouse's wages (or the total of both) are $1,000 or less.
} . . **B** ____

C Enter "1" for your **spouse.** But, you may choose to enter "-0-" if you are married and have either a working spouse or more than one job. (Entering "-0-" may help you avoid having too little tax withheld.) . . . . **C** __0__

D Enter number of **dependents** (other than your spouse or yourself) you will claim on your tax return . . . . . . **D** __2__

E Enter "1" if you will file as **head of household** on your tax return (see conditions under **Head of household** above) . **E** ____

F Enter "1" if you have at least $1,500 of **child or dependent care expenses** for which you plan to claim a credit . . **F** __1__

   (**Note.** Do **not** include child support payments. See **Pub. 503,** Child and Dependent Care Expenses, for details.)

G **Child Tax Credit** (including additional child tax credit):
- If your total income will be less than $54,000 ($79,000 if married), enter "2" for each eligible child.
- If your total income will be between $54,000 and $84,000 ($79,000 and $119,000 if married), enter "1" for each eligible child plus "1" **additional** if you have four or more eligible children. . . . . **G** __4__

H Add lines A through G and enter total here. (**Note.** This may be different from the number of exemptions you claim on your tax return.) ▶ **H** __8__

| For accuracy, complete all worksheets that apply. | { | • If you plan to **itemize or claim adjustments to income** and want to reduce your withholding, see the **Deductions and Adjustments Worksheet** on page 2.
 • If you have **more than one job** or are **married and you and your spouse both work** and the combined earnings from all jobs exceed $35,000 ($25,000 if married) see the **Two-Earner/Two-Job Worksheet** on page 2 to avoid having too little tax withheld.
 • If **neither** of the above situations applies, **stop here** and enter the number from line H on line 5 of Form W-4 below. |

--------------------- **Cut here and give Form W-4 to your employer. Keep the top part for your records.** ---------------------

Form **W-4**

Department of the Treasury
Internal Revenue Service

Employee's Withholding Allowance Certificate

▶ Whether you are entitled to claim a certain number of allowances or exemption from withholding is subject to review by the IRS. Your employer may be required to send a copy of this form to the IRS.

OMB No. 1545-0010

2005

1 Type or print your first name and middle initial	Last name	2 Your social security number
Jerry J.	Page	432 16 8410

Home address (number and street or rural route) 1222 West Main Street	**3** ☐ Single ☒ Married ☐ Married, but withhold at higher Single rate. **Note.** If married, but legally separated, or spouse is a nonresident alien, check the "Single" box.
City or town, state, and ZIP code San Diego, CA 91344-8135	**4** If your last name differs from that shown on your social security card, check here. You must call 1-800-772-1213 for a new card. ▶ ☐

5 Total number of allowances you are claiming (from line **H** above **or** from the applicable worksheet on page 2) **5** __6__

6 Additional amount, if any, you want withheld from each paycheck . . . . **6** $ __0__

7 I claim exemption from withholding for 2005, and I certify that I meet **both** of the following conditions for exemption.
- Last year I had a right to a refund of **all** federal income tax withheld because I had **no** tax liability **and**
- This year I expect a refund of **all** federal income tax withheld because I expect to have **no** tax liability.

If you meet both conditions, write "Exempt" here . . . . ▶ **7**

Under penalties of perjury, I declare that I have examined this certificate and to the best of my knowledge and belief, it is true, correct, and complete.

Employee's signature
(Form is not valid
unless you sign it.) ▶ *Jerry J. Page*

Date ▶ January 15, 2005

8 Employer's name and address (Employer: Complete lines 8 and 10 only if sending to the IRS.)	9 Office code (optional)	10 Employer identification number (EIN)

For Privacy Act and Paperwork Reduction Act Notice, see page 2.　　　Cat. No. 10220Q　　　Form **W-4** (2005)

FIGURE 13-2: Filled-In Form W-4, Employee's Withholding Allowance Certificate, Page 2

Form W-4 (2005)   Page **2**

Deductions and Adjustments Worksheet

Note. Use this worksheet *only* if you plan to itemize deductions, claim certain credits, or claim adjustments to income on your 2005 tax return.

1. Enter an estimate of your 2005 itemized deductions. These include qualifying home mortgage interest, charitable contributions, state and local taxes, medical expenses in excess of 7.5% of your income, and miscellaneous deductions. (For 2005, you may have to reduce your itemized deductions if your income is over $145,950 ($72,975 if married filing separately). See *Worksheet 3* in Pub. 919 for details.) . . . **1** $ 12,050

2. Enter: { $10,000 if married filing jointly or qualifying widow(er) / $ 7,300 if head of household / $ 5,000 if single or married filing separately } . . . . . . **2** $ 10,000

3. **Subtract** line 2 from line 1. If line 2 is greater than line 1, enter "-0-" . . . **3** $ 2,050

4. Enter an estimate of your 2005 adjustments to income, including alimony, deductible IRA contributions, and student loan interest **4** $ 8,000

5. **Add** lines 3 and 4 and enter the total. (Include any amount for credits from *Worksheet 7* in Pub. 919) . **5** $ 10,050

6. Enter an estimate of your 2005 nonwage income (such as dividends or interest) . . . . **6** $ 750

7. **Subtract** line 6 from line 5. Enter the result, but not less than "-0-" . . . . **7** $ 9,300

8. **Divide** the amount on line 7 by $3,200 and enter the result here. Drop any fraction . . . **8** 2

9. Enter the number from the **Personal Allowances Worksheet,** line H, page 1 . . . . **9** 8

10. **Add** lines 8 and 9 and enter the total here. If you plan to use the **Two-Earner/Two-Job Worksheet,** also enter this total on line 1 below. Otherwise, **stop here** and enter this total on Form W-4, line 5, page 1 . **10** 10

Two-Earner/Two-Job Worksheet (See *Two earners/two jobs* on page 1.)

Note. Use this worksheet *only* if the instructions under line H on page 1 direct you here.

1. Enter the number from line H, page 1 (or from line 10 above if you used the **Deductions and Adjustments Worksheet**) **1** 10

2. Find the number in **Table 1** below that applies to the **LOWEST** paying job and enter it here **2** 4

3. If line 1 is **more than or equal to** line 2, subtract line 2 from line 1. Enter the result here (if zero, enter "-0-") and on Form W-4, line 5, page 1. **Do not** use the rest of this worksheet **3** 6

Note. If line 1 is *less than* line 2, enter "-0-" on Form W-4, line 5, page 1. Complete lines 4–9 below to calculate the additional withholding amount necessary to avoid a year-end tax bill.

4. Enter the number from line 2 of this worksheet . . . . **4** _____

5. Enter the number from line 1 of this worksheet . . . . **5** _____

6. **Subtract** line 5 from line 4 . . . . **6** _____

7. Find the amount in **Table 2** below that applies to the **HIGHEST** paying job and enter it here . . . . **7** $ _____

8. **Multiply** line 7 by line 6 and enter the result here. This is the additional annual withholding needed . . **8** $ _____

9. Divide line 8 by the number of pay periods remaining in 2005. For example, divide by 26 if you are paid every two weeks and you complete this form in December 2004. Enter the result here and on Form W-4, line 6, page 1. This is the additional amount to be withheld from each paycheck . . . . **9** $ _____

Table 1: Two-Earner/Two-Job Worksheet

Married Filing Jointly						**All Others**	
If wages from **HIGHEST** paying job are—	AND, wages from **LOWEST** paying job are—	Enter on line 2 above	If wages from **HIGHEST** paying job are—	AND, wages from **LOWEST** paying job are—	Enter on line 2 above	If wages from **LOWEST** paying job are—	Enter on line 2 above
$0 - $40,000	$0 - $4,000	0	$40,001 and over	30,001 - 36,000	6	$0 - $6,000	0
	4,001 - 8,000	1		36,001 - 45,000	7	6,001 - 12,000	1
	8,001 - 18,000	2		45,001 - 50,000	8	12,001 - 18,000	2
	18,001 and over	3		50,001 - 60,000	9	18,001 - 24,000	3
				60,001 - 65,000	10	24,001 - 31,000	4
$40,001 and over	$0 - $4,000	0		65,001 - 75,000	11	31,001 - 45,000	5
	4,001 - 8,000	1		75,001 - 90,000	12	45,001 - 60,000	6
	8,001 - 18,000	2		90,001 - 100,000	13	60,001 - 75,000	7
	18,001 - 22,000	3		100,001 - 115,000	14	75,001 - 80,000	8
	22,001 - 25,000	4		115,001 and over	15	80,001 - 100,000	9
	25,001 - 30,000	5				100,001 and over	10

Table 2: Two-Earner/Two-Job Worksheet

Married Filing Jointly		**All Others**	
If wages from **HIGHEST** paying job are—	Enter on line 7 above	If wages from **HIGHEST** paying job are—	Enter on line 7 above
$0 - $60,000	$480	$0 - $30,000	$480
60,001 - 110,000	800	30,001 - 70,000	800
110,001 - 160,000	900	70,001 - 140,000	900
160,001 - 280,000	1,060	140,001 - 320,000	1,060
280,001 and over	1,120	320,001 and over	1,120

Privacy Act and Paperwork Reduction Act Notice. We ask for the information on this form to carry out the Internal Revenue laws of the United States. The Internal Revenue Code requires this information under sections 3402(f)(2)(A) and 6109 and their regulations. Failure to provide a properly completed form will result in your being treated as a single person who claims no withholding allowances; providing fraudulent information may also subject you to penalties. Routine uses of this information include giving it to the Department of Justice for civil and criminal litigation, to cities, states, and the District of Columbia for use in administering their tax laws, and using it in the National Directory of New Hires. We may also disclose this information to other countries under a tax treaty, to federal and state agencies to enforce federal nontax criminal laws, or to federal law enforcement and intelligence agencies to combat terrorism.

You are not required to provide the information requested on a form that is subject to

the Paperwork Reduction Act unless the form displays a valid OMB control number. Books or records relating to a form or its instructions must be retained as long as their contents may become material in the administration of any Internal Revenue law. Generally, tax returns and return information are confidential, as required by Code section 6103.

The time needed to complete this form will vary depending on individual circumstances. The estimated average time is: Recordkeeping, 45 min.; Learning about the law or the form, 12 min.; Preparing the form, 58 min. If you have comments concerning the accuracy of these time estimates or suggestions for making this form simpler, we would be happy to hear from you. You can write to: Internal Revenue Service, Tax Products Coordinating Committee, SE:W:CAR:MP:T:T:SP, 1111 Constitution Ave. NW, IR-6406, Washington, DC 20224. **Do not** send Form W-4 to this address. Instead, give it to your employer.

 Printed on recycled paper

The exemption from withholding for a given year expires on February 15 of the next year. Employees who wish to continue a withholding exemption for the next year must file a new Form W-4 by February 15. They must revoke the exemption within 10 days of an event that causes them to no longer qualify as exempt.

FICA TAXES

FICA provides for an old age, survivors, and disability insurance (OASDI) tax. FICA also provides for a health insurance (HI) tax. On Form W-2, the IRS calls the OASDI portion the **social security tax.** It calls the HI portion the **Medicare tax.** The government assesses an equal amount of FICA taxes on employers and employees. Each employer withholds the employee's share of FICA from the employee's wages, then matches that amount using the employer's funds, and deposits both shares (employer and employee) with a specified depository.

Social Security and Medicare Taxes

The social security or OASDI tax rate equals 6.2%. For 2005, employers apply the rate to each employee's wages up to $90,000. This includes employees who have reached the maximum wage base with another employer. However, an employee's total OASDI tax for 2005 cannot exceed $5,580 (6.2% × $90,000). Thus, an employee who works for two or more employers may qualify to get a refund. This refund is claimed in the "Payments" section of Form 1040, page 2. The Medicare or HI tax rate equals 1.45%. The HI rate applies to employees' total wages. This includes employees who work for another employer.

Special FICA Situations

Not all wages nor are all employees subject to FICA withholding requirements. Moreover, certain types of income receive special FICA withholding treatment.

Family Employees of a Business

Taxpayers do not withhold FICA on wages paid to their children under the age of 18 who work for them in their businesses. This rule applies only when the parent's business is operated as a sole proprietorship. Once the child turns 18, the child's wages are subject to FICA withholding. Wages paid to a spouse who works for the taxpayer's business are subject to FICA withholding.

Household Employees

Household employees can include maids, babysitters, private nurses, yard workers, and nannies. These employees are subject to FICA withholding if they are paid $1,400 or more during 2005. This rule does not apply to individuals who are under age 18 at any time during the calendar year and are not full-time employees. It also does not apply to wages paid to a spouse, the taxpayer's child under age 21, and in most instances, a parent. Employers of household workers report both their share and their employee's share of the social security and Medicare taxes they withheld on their Form 1040. Schedule H documents the amount reported in the "Other Taxes" section of Form 1040, page 2.

Employee Fringe Benefits

Nontaxable fringe benefits are not subject to FICA taxes. However, taxable fringe benefits may be subject to FICA withholding. For example, personal use of a company car and group term life insurance purchased for the employee in excess of the excludable amount are subject to FICA withholding.

Penalty for Failure to Collect or Deposit Taxes

The IRS can assess a 100% penalty against employers who fail to collect or deposit FICA taxes. The 100% penalty does not apply to direct taxes (federal unemployment tax or employer's share of FICA taxes). The IRS can assess the penalty against (1) employers who willfully try to avoid withholding income and payroll taxes by classifying employees as independent contractors and (2) employees responsible for an employer's tax withholdings. However, the employee must have the authority to decide which creditors receive payment when a shortage of funds exists.

REPORTING TO EMPLOYEES AND THE GOVERNMENT

In January, employers prepare a Form W-2, Wage and Tax Statement, for each employee. Thus, in January 2006, employers prepare a 2005 Form W-2 for each employee. Form W-2 shows an employee's gross wages, wages subject to OASDI withholding and wages subject to HI withholding. Form W-2 also shows the income taxes withheld as well as amounts withheld for OASDI and HI. Form W-2 can show an employee's pension plan contributions, state income taxes withheld, and other items. When filing their tax return, employees attach one copy of Form W-2 (Copy B) to their tax return.

Distribution of Forms W-2

Employers prepare six copies of Form W-2 for each employee. Employers send Copy A, along with Form W-3, Transmittal of Wage and Tax Statements, to the Social Security Administration before March 1. If applicable, they file Copy 1 with the proper state or local government agency. Employers send Copies B, C, and 2 to each employee before February 1. The employer keeps Copy D.

When employment ends before the close of a calendar year, employers still send former employees their copies of Form W-2 before February 1 of the next year. Former employees can request a Form W-2 before this date. When requested, employers must give former employees their Form W-2 by the later of 30 days after the request or 30 days after the last wage payment.

Form W-2

A machine usually reads Copy A of Form W-2. Therefore, if possible, the forms should be typed and without erasures, whiteouts, or strikeovers. The employer should make all dollar entries without dollar signs or commas, but with decimal points (00000.00). The rest of this section describes the information contained on Form W-2. Not all boxes are covered since many are self-explanatory. For a full description of all boxes on Form W-2, see the *Instructions for Form W-2* provided by the IRS.

Control Number (Box a)

Employers can assign control numbers of up to seven digits to identify individual Forms W-2. Employers should include this number on any correspondence with the Social Security Administration regarding an individual Form W-2.

Void

Employers mark this box when a form contains an incorrect entry. The employer cannot simply discard a Form W-2 containing a mistake. The government printing office prints two Forms W-2 on a single sheet of paper. Copy A, sent to the Social Security Administration, cannot be cut or separated. Therefore, Forms W-2 with errors also get sent to the Social Security Administration.

Box 12

This box has no title. Employers complete this box to report up to four items of information. For each item, a code and the dollar amount are listed. Examples of items reported in this box include the following:

1. Taxable amounts for providing the employee with more than $50,000 of group life insurance (Code C)
2. Elective deferrals to a section 401(k) plan (Code D)
3. Elective deferrals under a salary reduction SEP (Code F)
4. Nontaxable sick pay (Code J)
5. Per diem or employee mileage reimbursements in excess of amounts substantiated under IRS rules (Code L)
6. Excludable moving expense reimbursements (Code P)
7. Employee salary reduction contributions under a SIMPLE plan not part of a 401(k) plan (Code S)
8. Amounts received under an adoption assistance program (Code T)

Statutory Employee, Retirement Plan, Third-Party Sick Pay (Box 13)

Employers place an *X* in the proper square (box 13) to identify the employee or Form W-2 situation.

Statutory Employee. Employers withhold FICA taxes, but not federal income taxes, from **statutory employee** wages. Statutory employees include certain employees from one of four occupation groups. Group 1 includes drivers who are agents of the employer or those who deliver laundry, dry-cleaning, and food products (other than milk) to customers and who are paid on commission. Group 2 includes full-time life insurance salespersons. Group 3 includes workers who work at home using materials provided by and returned to the employer. Group 4 includes traveling or city salespersons who take orders on behalf of the employer. To qualify as statutory employees, group members must meet the three tests shown below.

1. Work under a service contract that states or implies that they will provide most of the services,
2. Work in a continuing (ongoing) employment relationship, and
3. Have little or no investment in the equipment or property used to perform the contracted services (other than transportation facilities).

Retirement Plan. This square identifies active participants in the employer's retirement plan. Recall from Chapter 4 that limits may apply to the deduction for IRA contributions for taxpayers who are active participants in an employer's retirement plan. Employers do not mark this square for contributions to nonqualified pension plans or Section 457 plans. Section 457 covers the deferred compensation plans of state and local governments.

Third-Party Sick Pay. This square is checked only if the payer is a third-party sick pay provider filing Form W-2 for an insured's employee.

Other (Box 14)

Employers use this box to provide any other information they feel is necessary to their employees. Each amount is labeled by its type. Items that may be listed include union dues, health insurance premiums deducted, nontaxable income, voluntary after-tax contributions to retirement plans, and educational assistance payments.

CASES WHEN EMPLOYEES SHOULD RECEIVE A FORM W-2, WAGE AND TAX STATEMENT

1. When they had income tax or FICA taxes withheld from wages
2. When they would have had income taxes withheld from wages had they not claimed more than one withholding allowance exemption or had not claimed exemption from withholding

Information for Figure 13-3: Filled-In Form W-2

Harriet R. Shawver works for Anderson, Berger, and Green (ABG). ABG assigns control number 004 to Shawver's Form W-2. From Shawver's $43,500 of wages, ABG withheld $7,356 for federal; $2,039 for state; $2,697 for social security (OASDI); and $630.75 for Medicare (HI) taxes.

Form W-3

Employers send to the Social Security Administration Copy A, Form W-2, for all employees along with Form W-3, Transmittal of Income and Tax Statements. These forms must reach the employer's regional Social Security Administration Data Operations Center by March 1. When completing Form W-3, employers type all data entries, omitting dollar signs and commas but using decimal points and zeros to show cents (00000.00). The amounts on Form W-3 represent the totals from all the amounts on all Copies A of Forms W-2 attached (except Forms W-2 that were voided). The actual person who completes Form W-3 signs it, certifying the correctness and completeness of it and of the accompanying Forms W-2.

This section describes the data contained on Form W-3. However, it does not cover every box since most boxes contain clear descriptive headings. The instructions for Form W-3 describe the data needs of all boxes.

FIGURE 13-3   Filled-In Form W-2, Wage and Tax Statement

a Control number			For Official Use Only ▶	
004	22222	Void ☐	OMB No. 1545-0008	

b Employer identification number (EIN)	1 Wages, tips, other compensation	2 Federal income tax withheld
92-0446587	43500.00	7356.00

c Employer's name, address, and ZIP code	3 Social security wages	4 Social security tax withheld
Anderson, Berger, and Green	43500.00	2697.00

	5 Medicare wages and tips	6 Medicare tax withheld
2700 South Park Avenue	43500.00	630.75

	7 Social security tips	8 Allocated tips
Milwaukee, WI 53202-2645		

d Employee's social security number	9 Advance EIC payment	10 Dependent care benefits
364-74-6560		

e Employee's first name and initial	Last name	11 Nonqualified plans	12a See instructions for box 12
Harriet R.	Shawver		

13 Statutory employee ☐   Retirement plan ☐   Third-party sick pay ☐
12b

2123 Fairmount Drive
14 Other   12c
Milwaukee, WI 53209-3685

12d

f Employee's address and ZIP code

15 State Employer's state ID number	16 State wages, tips, etc.	17 State income tax	18 Local wages, tips, etc.	19 Local income tax	20 Locality name
WI 104693	43500.00	2039.00			

Form **W-2** Wage and Tax Statement   **2005**   Department of the Treasury—Internal Revenue Service
For Privacy Act and Paperwork Reduction Act Notice, see back of Copy D.

Copy A For Social Security Administration — Send this entire page with Form W-3 to the Social Security Administration; photocopies are **not** acceptable.   Cat. No. 10134D

Do Not Cut, Fold, or Staple Forms on This Page — Do Not Cut, Fold, or Staple Forms on This Page

Control Number (Box a)

As with Form W-2, employers can assign a *control* number of up to seven digits or leave the box blank.

Kind of Payer (Box b)

Employers check one of the following six groups:

1. *941.* Check this square when filing Form 941 and no other group applies.
2. *Military.* Check this square when sending Forms W-2 for members of the armed forces.
3. *943.* Check this square when filing Forms 943 for agricultural employees. Employers of agricultural and nonagricultural workers send a separate Form W-3.
4. *CT-1.* Check this square when sending Forms W-2 for employees under the Railroad Retirement Tax Act (RRTA).
5. *Hshld. emp.* Check this square when sending Forms W-2 for household workers. Employers of household workers and nonhousehold workers send a separate Form W-3 with each group of Forms W-2.
6. *Medicare gov't. emp.* Check this box for government and local agency employees subject to the 1.45% Medicare (HI) tax.
7. *Third-party sick pay.* Check this box if the payer is a third-party sick pay provider filing Form W-2 for an insured's employee.

Total Number of Forms W-2 (Box c)

Employers enter the number of individual Forms W-2 they are sending with Form W-3. However, they exclude voided forms from the count.

Establishment Number (Box d)

Employers enter a four-digit number to identify separate establishments of their business. For each establishment, employers file a separate Form W-3 with related Forms W-2. They file a separate Form W-3 even though each establishment has the same EIN.

Employer's State I.D. Number (Box 15)

A state in which an employer does business may assign a state I.D. number. Employers that report in two states enter one state's I.D. number in each box.

Information for Figure 13-4: Filled-In Form W-3

Martinez Enterprises, Inc., sends two Forms W-2 (Copy A) to the Social Security Administration with Form W-3. The wages for the two employees total $87,560. For both employees, social security (OASDI) and Medicare (HI) wages were the same as overall wages. Federal income tax withheld for the two employees was $13,518.40. Social security and Medicare withheld were $5,428.72 and $1,269.62, respectively. Since Florida does not have a state income tax, lines 15–19 are blank.

FIGURE 13-4   Filled-In Form W-3, Transmittal of Wage and Tax Statements

DO NOT STAPLE OR FOLD		
a Control number 01	33333 For Official Use Only ▶ OMB No. 1545-0008	
b Kind of Payer: 941 [X] Military [ ] 943 [ ] CT-1 [ ] Hshld. emp. [ ] Medicare govt. emp. [ ] Third-party sick pay [ ]	**1** Wages, tips, other compensation 87560.00	**2** Federal income tax withheld 13518.40
	3 Social security wages 87560.00	**4** Social security tax withheld 5428.72
c Total number of Forms W-2 2 **d** Establishment number	**5** Medicare wages and tips 87560.00	**6** Medicare tax withheld 1269.62
e Employer identification number (EIN) 91-0118224	**7** Social security tips	**8** Allocated tips
f Employer's name Martinez Enterprises, Inc. 64 Bay Road Miami, FL 33139-5670	**9** Advance EIC payments	**10** Dependent care benefits
	11 Nonqualified plans	**12** Deferred compensation
	13 For third-party sick pay use only	
	14 Income tax withheld by payer of third-party sick pay	
g Employer's address and ZIP code		
h Other EIN used this year		
15 State Employer's state ID number	**16** State wages, tips, etc.	**17** State income tax
	18 Local wages, tips, etc.	**19** Local income tax
Contact person Edward L. Martinez	Telephone number (305) 555-3544	For Official Use Only
Email address	Fax number ( )	

Under penalties of perjury, I declare that I have examined this return and accompanying documents, and, to the best of my knowledge and belief, they are true, correct, and complete.

Signature ▶ *Edward L. Martinez*   Title ▶ President   Date ▶ 1/29/2006

UNEMPLOYMENT TAXES

In conjunction with state unemployment systems, the Federal Unemployment Tax Act (FUTA) furnishes payments to workers who have lost their jobs. The funds for the unemployment compensation come solely from employers. Employers make no withholdings from employees for this tax. Most employers pay taxes into both the state and the federal systems.

Rate and Base

Employers pay a maximum unemployment tax of 6.2% on the first $7,000 of each employee's taxable wages in the calendar year. For computing FUTA taxes, employees do not include the following:

1. Children under age 21 who work for their parents
2. Spouses working for the other spouse
3. Parents working for their children
4. Statutory employees who work at home
5. Domestic workers (nannies, gardeners, housekeepers, etc.) who earn less than $1,500 each quarter in both the current and preceding calendar years

Employers generally reduce the FUTA tax rate by the lesser of 5.4% or the rate paid to their state unemployment tax fund. Thus, after the reduction for the state, the net FUTA rate may be as low as 0.8% (6.2% − 5.4%). Employers who pay a proper state unemployment rate but do not pay the state tax on time reduce their state credit by 10%.

Without an extension of the FUTA filing date, employers must file their FUTA returns by January 31 of the next year. Depending on the situation, employers use either Form 940 or Form 940EZ, Employer's Annual Federal Unemployment (FUTA) Tax Return. Both forms have the same name. If employers make all tax deposits on a timely basis, they may file the Form 940 or 940EZ by February 10.

EXAMPLE 1

Wild Card has two employees, Susan and Mike Thompson. During 2005 Susan and Mike earned taxable gross wages of $10,000 and $5,000, respectively. The Thompsons live and work in a state with a 5.4% unemployment tax. Wild Card pays the state unemployment tax by January 31, 2006. For 2005 Wild Card pays $96 of FUTA tax ($56 for Susan and $40 for Mike).

	Susan	Mike
1. Gross wages	$10,000	$ 5,000
2. Lesser of $7,000 or gross wages	$ 7,000	$ 5,000
3. Times net FUTA rate (6.2% − 5.4%)	× 0.8%	× 0.8%
4. FUTA tax	$ 56	$ 40

Depositing FUTA Taxes

Employers deposit FUTA taxes with an authorized depository when their debt exceeds $500. The FUTA tax is due on the last day of the month that follows the end of a quarter. When an employer's FUTA debt for any quarter does not exceed $500, the deposit due carries over to the next quarter. Employers with a fourth-quarter FUTA tax of $500 or less can either pay the tax when they file their FUTA return or make a deposit. If the fourth-quarter FUTA tax exceeds $500, they deposit the tax with an authorized depository by January 31. Making a timely deposit extends the due date for filing the FUTA return until February 10. When a deposit date falls on a Saturday, Sunday, or banking holiday, the deposit is timely if made by the next business banking day.

FUTA TAX DEPOSIT DUE DATES

Quarter Ending	Due Date
March 31	April 30
June 30	July 31
September 30	October 31
December 31	January 31

EXAMPLE 2

After reduction by the state unemployment credit, the Bucket Company's quarterly FUTA taxes for 2006 are: first, $235; second, $250; third, $245; and fourth, $200. No deposits are needed for the first and second quarters since the cumulative debt does not exceed $500 until the third quarter. Bucket must deposit $730 ($235 + $250 + $245) by October 31, 2006. For the fourth quarter, Bucket can either deposit the tax by January 31, 2007, or include the payment when filing its FUTA return. If Bucket makes timely deposits of its 2006 FUTA taxes, the due date for its FUTA tax return is extended to February 10, 2007.

WITHHOLDING ON PENSIONS, ANNUITIES, AND DEFERRED INCOME

Withholding of income taxes also applies to the taxable part of distributions from pensions, profit-sharing plans, individual retirement accounts, annuities, and deferred compensation plans. Unless recipients of pension and annuity payments ask for no withholding, payers must withhold taxes. Recipients can request nonwithholding for any reason. They do so by filing Form W-4P, Withholding Certificate for Pension or Annuity Payments, with their pension or annuity payer.

By filing a Form W-4P with the payer of an annuity or pension, payees may request withholding on the basis of their marital status and withholding allowances. They make this request by entering the proper number of withholding allowances on Form W-4P. Payees can request that the payer withhold an additional amount. The format of Form W-4P is similar to that of Form W-4.

EMPLOYER'S QUARTERLY REPORT

Most employers who withhold income taxes or who owe FICA, file a quarterly Form 941, Employer's Quarterly Federal Tax Return. Seasonal employers who do not pay wages in a quarter do not file a Form 941 for that quarter. On every Form 941 that seasonal employers file, they place an *X* in the seasonal employers' box (line 17).

All depositors complete both pages of Form 941. Semiweekly depositors also complete Schedule B (Form 941), Report of Tax Liability for Semiweekly Depositors, and attach it to Form 941.

Filing the Quarterly Report

Employers must file Form 941 by the last day of the month that follows the close of a calendar quarter. For example, for the quarter ending September 30, 20x1, employers must file a Form 941 by October 31, 20x1. Employers who deposit all taxes before the due dates get an additional ten days to file Form 941. Thus, if the employer deposits all taxes by the required due dates, Form 941 for the quarter ending December 31, 20x1, would be due by February 10, 20x2. Employers cannot use a Form 941 to report taxes from more than one calendar quarter. Instead, each quarter must be reported separately.

Adjusting for Overwithholding or Underwithholding

Employers who find an error in withheld income taxes for an earlier quarter of the same year correct it on Form 941 for the quarter in which the error is discovered. Employers correct FICA tax reporting errors in the same manner. For every correction (adjustment), employers attach a statement explaining and identifying the earlier return with the error(s). Employers who withhold *less* than the correct amount of tax from wages deduct the amounts underwithheld from future wages. When employers withhold *more* than the correct amount, they can repay the excess to the proper employees in any quarter of the same year. Employers keep the employee's dated and signed receipts for the repayment. Also, these employers include excess withholdings not repaid in the withholding quarter on their quarterly Form 941.

Final Returns

A special rule applies when an employer goes out of business. The employer marks an "X" in the box on line 16 and then enters the final date wages were paid in the space provided. Employers who temporarily cease to pay wages continue to file Form 941. They simply check the box on line 4 and complete the rest of Form 941.

Information for Figure 13-5: Filled-In Form 941

Martinez Enterprises, Inc., (from Figure 13-4) reports combined wages for withholding and employment taxes of $22,396 for the first quarter ($6,172.61 in January, $6,714.90 in February, and $9,508.49 in March). Martinez withheld $3,369.49 in federal income taxes from its two employees ($928.31 in January, $1,010.41 in February, and $1,430.77 in March).

Other Information

15: Month 1 liability, **$1,872.71** [($6,172.61 × .124) + ($6,172.61 × .029) + $928.31]
Month 2 liability, **$2,037.79** [($6,714.90 × .124) + ($6,714.90 × .029) + $1,010.41]
Month 3 liability, **$2,885.57** [($9,508.49 × .124) + ($9,508.49 × .029) + $1,430.77]
Total: **$6,796.07** ($1,872.71 + $2,037.79 + $2,885.57)

FIGURE 13-5 Filled-In Form 941, Employer's Quarterly Federal Tax Return, Page 1

Form **941 for 2005:** **Employer's Quarterly Federal Tax Return**   9901
(Rev. January 2005)   Department of the Treasury — Internal Revenue Service   OMB No. 1545-0029

Employer identification number   9 1 – 0 1 1 8 2 2 4

Name *(not your trade name)*   Edward L. Martinez

Trade name *(if any)*   Martinez Enterprises, Inc.

Address   64 Bay Road
           Number   Street   Suite or room number
           Miami   FL   33139
           City   State   ZIP code

Report for this Quarter ...
(Check one.)

[X] **1:** January, February, March
[ ] **2:** April, May, June
[ ] **3:** July, August, September
[ ] **4:** October, November, December

Read the separate instructions before you fill out this form. Please type or print within the boxes.

Part 1: Answer these questions for this quarter.

1 Number of employees who received wages, tips, or other compensation for the pay period
  including: *Mar. 12* (Quarter 1), *June 12* (Quarter 2), *Sept. 12* (Quarter 3), *Dec. 12* (Quarter 4)   1 | 2

2 Wages, tips, and other compensation . . . .   2 | 22,396 . 00

3 Total income tax withheld from wages, tips, and other compensation . . . .   3 | 3,369 . 49

4 If no wages, tips, and other compensation are subject to social security or Medicare tax . . [ ] Check and go to line 6.

5 Taxable social security and Medicare wages and tips:

	Column 1		Column 2
5a Taxable social security wages	22,396 . 00	× .124 =	2,777 . 10
5b Taxable social security tips	.	× .124 =	.
5c Taxable Medicare wages & tips	22,396 . 00	× .029 =	649 . 48

5d Total social security and Medicare taxes (*Column 2*, lines 5a + 5b + 5c = line 5d) . . **5d** | 3,426 . 58

6 Total taxes before adjustments (lines 3 + 5d = line 6) . . . .   **6** | 6,796 . 07

7 Tax adjustments (If your answer is a negative number, write it in brackets.):

7a Current quarter's fractions of cents . . . . | .

7b Current quarter's sick pay . . . . | .

7c Current quarter's adjustments for tips and group-term life insurance | .

7d Current year's income tax withholding (Attach Form 941c) . . | .

7e Prior quarters' social security and Medicare taxes (Attach Form 941c) | .

7f Special additions to federal income tax (reserved use) . . . . . | .

7g Special additions to social security and Medicare (reserved use) | .

7h Total adjustments (Combine all amounts: lines 7a through 7g.) . . . .   **7h** | 0 .

8 Total taxes after adjustments (Combine lines 6 and 7h.) . . . .   **8** | 6,796 . 07

9 Advance earned income credit (EIC) payments made to employees . . . .   **9** | .

10 Total taxes after adjustment for advance EIC (lines 8 – 9 = line 10) . . . .   **10** | 6,796 . 07

11 Total deposits for this quarter, including overpayment applied from a prior quarter . . .   **11** | 6,796 . 07

12 Balance due (lines 10 – 11 = line 12) Make checks payable to the *United States Treasury* . .   **12** | 0 .

13 Overpayment (If line 11 is more than line 10, write the difference here.) | .   Check one [ ] Apply to next return.
                                                                                                        [ ] Send a refund.

Next ➡

For Privacy Act and Paperwork Reduction Act Notice, see the back of the Payment Voucher.   Cat. No. 17001Z   Form **941** (Rev. 1-2005)

FIGURE 13-5   Filled-In Form 941, Employer's Quarterly Federal Tax Return, Page 2

Name *(not your trade name)*	Employer identification number
Edward L. Martinez	91-0118224

Part 2: Tell us about your deposit schedule for this quarter.

If you are unsure about whether you are a monthly schedule depositor or a semiweekly schedule depositor, see *Pub. 15 (Circular E)*, section 11.

14 [F] [L] Write the state abbreviation for the state where you made your deposits OR write "MU" if you made your deposits in *multiple* states.

15 Check one: ☐ Line 10 is less than $2,500. Go to Part 3.

☒ You were a monthly schedule depositor for the entire quarter. Fill out your tax liability for each month. Then go to Part 3.

Tax liability: Month 1   1,872.71

Month 2   2,037.79

Month 3   2,885.57

Total   6,796.07   Total must equal line 10.

☐ You were a semiweekly schedule depositor for any part of this quarter. Fill out *Schedule B (Form 941): Report of Tax Liability for Semiweekly Schedule Depositors*, and attach it to this form.

Part 3: Tell us about your business. If a question does NOT apply to your business, leave it blank.

16 If your business has closed and you do not have to file returns in the future . . . . ☐ Check here, and

enter the final date you paid wages [/   /   ] .

17 If you are a seasonal employer and you do not have to file a return for every quarter of the year . . ☐ Check here.

Part 4: May we contact your third-party designee?

Do you want to allow an employee, a paid tax preparer, or another person to discuss this return with the IRS? See the instructions for details.

☐ Yes. Designee's name _____

Phone ( ) –   Personal Identification Number (PIN) ☐☐☐☐☐

☐ No.

Part 5: Sign here

Under penalties of perjury, I declare that I have examined this return, including accompanying schedules and statements, and to the best of my knowledge and belief, it is true, correct, and complete.

X Sign your name here *Edward L. Martinez*

Print name and title Edward L. Martinez, President

Date 4/26/05   Phone (305) 555-3544

Part 6: For paid preparers only *(optional)*

Preparer's signature		
Firm's name		
Address		EIN
		ZIP code
Date / / Phone ( ) –		SSN/PTIN
☐ Check if you are self-employed.		

Page **2**   Form **941** (Rev. 1-2005)

FEDERAL TAX DEPOSIT SYSTEM

Employers use the federal tax deposit system to transfer payroll taxes to the government. They usually deposit these taxes with a specified depository servicing the employer's area. Under certain conditions, employers send some tax payments directly to the IRS.

Federal Tax Deposit Coupon Book

The IRS issues Form 8109, Federal Tax Deposit Coupon Book, to employers. Each coupon book contains 24 deposit coupons. The sixth and seventh coupons contain an identification number that automatically triggers a coupon reorder request. Thus, depositors do not need to reorder a supply of deposit coupons. For each tax deposit, employers prepare a deposit coupon. They enter the numerical data, omitting dollar signs, leading zeros, commas, and decimal points. Commas and decimal points already appear in the form's entry area. Employers depositing dollars and no cents write zeros in the boxes for cents. At the top right of each deposit coupon, a list of tax period ovals appears. Employers darken one to show the quarter that a deposit covers. To the left of these ovals a list of payment ovals appears with form numbers. Employers darken one to identify the deposit type.

Information for Figure 13-6: Filled-In Form 8109

Martinez Enterprises, Inc. (from Figure 13-5) is a calendar year corporation. Martinez makes a deposit of $6,796.07 with Form 941 (FICA taxes and withheld income taxes) for the first quarter on filled-in Form 8109. The IRS preprints Martinez's EIN and address on its forms.

TAX YEAR MONTH, enter **12** (for December 31 year end)

FIGURE 13-6 Filled-In Form 8109, Federal Tax Deposit Coupon

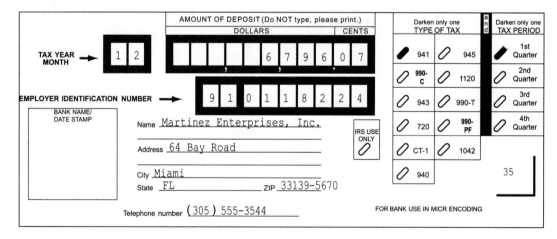

FORM 8109 TAX DEPOSIT TYPES BY FORM NUMBER

Form 720—Excise Tax

Form 940—Federal Unemployment Tax (FUTA)

Form 941—Income Tax and Social Security and Medicare Taxes Withheld

Form 943—Agricultural Withheld Income, Social Security and Medicare Taxes

Form 990C—Farmers' Cooperative Association Income Tax

Form 990PF—Excise Tax on Private Foundation Net Investment Income

Form 990T—Exempt Organization Business Income Tax

Form 1042—Withholding on Foreign Persons

Form 1120—Corporate Income Tax

Form CT-1—Railroad Retirement Taxes

Form 945—Withholding Income Tax from Pensions, Annuities, IRAs, Gambling, Indian Gaming and Backup Withholding

Deposit Frequency

Employers make deposits using either a monthly or semiweekly deposit schedule. The schedule used depends on the total taxes the employer reported in the lookback period.

Lookback Period

Each employer's lookback period is the 12-month period ending on June 30 of the prior year. For 2006, the lookback period ended on June 30, 2005. The employment taxes reported on the four Forms 941, Employer's Quarterly Federal Tax Report, filed during the lookback period are used to determine the employer's deposit schedule. If an employer did not exist during the lookback period, the IRS treats the employer as having zero tax accumulations.

EMPLOYMENT TAXES: WHAT'S INCLUDED?

1. Income and FICA taxes withheld from employees
2. Employer's share of FICA taxes
3. Taxes withheld from pensions, annuities, and some deferred income
4. Taxes withheld under the backup withholding rules

Monthly Depositors

When total employment tax accumulations for an employer's lookback period are $50,000 or less, the employer deposits employment taxes monthly. Monthly depositors deposit each month's employment taxes by the 15th day of the next month.

Semiweekly Depositors

When total employment tax accumulations for an employer's lookback period exceed $50,000, the employer makes semiweekly deposits. Semiweekly depositors deposit employment tax on Wednesday or Friday. Wednesday deposits include tax accumulations for payrolls paid on the previous Wednesday, Thursday, and Friday. Friday deposits include tax accumulations for payrolls paid on the previous Saturday, Sunday, Monday, and Tuesday.

SEMIWEEKLY DEPOSITORS

Deposit Day	Deposit for Payrolls Paid
Wednesday	Prior days
	Wednesday
	Thursday
	Friday
Friday	Prior days
	Saturday
	Sunday
	Monday
	Tuesday

Semiweekly depositors make two deposits when the end of a calendar quarter does not fall on the employer's payday. They make one deposit for the last day(s) in the quarter just ended. They make another deposit for the starting day(s) in the new quarter. Employers must prepare a separate Form 8109, Federal Tax Deposit Coupon, for each deposit and make the deposits by the next regular deposit date.

EXAMPLE 3

The second quarter of 2005 ends on Thursday, June 30. Elete Corporation, a semiweekly depositor, has a payroll period that ends on Friday, June 24, and another that ends on Friday, July 1. Elete makes two deposits. The first is for the Thursday payroll as the last of the second quarter. The other is for the Friday payroll as the first payroll for the second quarter in 2005. Elete uses a separate Form 8109 for each deposit. Both deposits are due on Wednesday, July 6, 2005.

EXAMPLE 4

Assume the same facts as in Example 3, except that Elete pays its employees once a month on the last day of each month. Although Elete is a semiweekly depositor, it makes only one deposit for the month of June. Since June 30, 2005, falls on Thursday, Elete makes the deposit the next Wednesday, July 6, 2005.

One-Day Rule

Whenever an employer's employment taxes reach $100,000 during a deposit period, the one-day rule applies. This rule requires the employer to deposit employment taxes by the close of the next business day. This rule applies whether the employer is a monthly or a semiweekly depositor. Furthermore, once this event occurs for monthly depositors, they switch to being semiweekly depositors for the rest of the current calendar year and for the next year. After that, the lookback period will determine whether the employer qualifies as a monthly or semiweekly depositor.

Semiweekly depositors determine whether they fall under the one-day rule by examining their employment tax accumulations since the last deposit date. They use Wednesday–Friday or Saturday–Tuesday for their examination period. On the day their accumulations reach $100,000, they meet the test for the one-day rule. Monthly depositors can determine if they fall under the one-day rule by examining their accumulations in the current month. They fall under the one-day rule on the day their accumulations reach $100,000. Once the employer deposits the employment taxes, the counting of accumulations starts over again at zero.

EXAMPLE 5

Cambry Company, a monthly depositor, has four payroll periods during the month. The first payroll period accumulates $40,000 of employment taxes. The second has $50,000 of employment taxes, for an accumulation of $90,000 ($40,000 + $50,000). The third payroll period involves $30,000 of payroll taxes. As of the end of the third payroll period, Cambry has accumulated employment taxes of $120,000 ($90,000 + $30,000). Cambry must deposit the $120,000 the next business day. From this day forward, Cambry becomes a semiweekly depositor, and will remain a semiweekly depositor for the rest of the current year and all of next year. Cambry's fourth payroll period for the month ends on a Saturday. As a semiweekly depositor, Cambry deposits its employment taxes by the following Friday.

Weekends and Holidays

When a deposit date falls on a Saturday, Sunday, or other depository holiday, the deposit is timely if made by the next business banking day.

EXAMPLE 6

RSV deposits employment taxes monthly. For March 2006, RSV accumulates $10,000 of employment taxes. RSV normally would deposit these taxes by April 15, 2006. However, April 15, 2006, falls on a Saturday. Thus, RSV must deposit the taxes by Monday, April 17, 2006, the next banking day.

Safe Harbor/De Minimis Rule

An employer satisfies its deposit requirement if the undeposited amount (shortfall) does not exceed the larger of $100 or 2% of a required deposit. **Shortfall** means the required deposit amount less the amount deposited before the end of a deposit date. To use this rule, employers must deposit unplanned shortfalls before the end of their make-up date.

The shortfall make-up date for monthly depositors falls on the due date of the quarterly Form 941 for the period in which the shortfall occurs. The employer sends the shortfall attached to the Form 941 or deposits it by the due date.

A different shortfall make-up date applies to semiweekly and one-day depositors. For these employers, the shortfall must be deposited by the first Wednesday or Friday (whichever is earlier) that falls after the 14th of the month following the month of the shortfall. However, if the quarterly due date of a Form 941 falls before the shortfall make-up date, the shortfall deposit must take place by the earlier Form 941 due date.

EXAMPLE 7

Romano Company, a semiweekly depositor, has a shortfall for January 2006. Romano's make-up period ends on the first Wednesday or Friday after February 14. Since February 14, 2006, falls on a Tuesday, the first Wednesday or Friday after that date would be Wednesday, February 15, 2006.

EXAMPLE 8

Assume the same facts as in Example 7, except that Romano's shortfall occurs on October 10, 2006. Normally, Romano would be required to deposit the shortfall by Wednesday, November 15. However, Romano's third-quarter Form 941 is due on October 31. Thus, Romano must deposit the shortfall by October 31, 2006.

$500 Rule

A special deposit rule applies when the tax accumulations for a quarter do not reach $500. No deposits are necessary, and the employer may send the taxes with Form 941.

A flowchart of the employment tax deposit rules appears in Figure 13-7. It shows how the rules separate employment tax depositors by frequency of deposits.

FIGURE 13-7 A Summary of the Employment Tax Deposit Rules

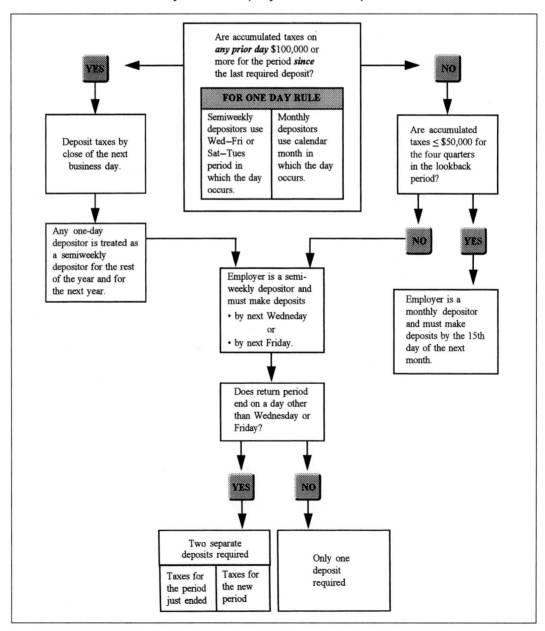

ESTIMATED TAXES

Wage earners pay taxes on their wages through the payroll withholding system. Taxpayers with income from sources other than wages (self-employment profits, interest, dividends, etc.) estimate their taxes and make quarterly payments directly to the IRS. For 2006, quarterly tax payment due dates fall on April 17, 2006; June 15, 2006; September 15, 2006; and January 16, 2007.

To help taxpayers prepare a tax estimate, the IRS provides Form 1040-ES, Estimated Tax for Individuals. The Form 1040-ES package includes four taxpayer-identifying payment vouchers, a tax worksheet, and a schedule of payments.

Who Makes Estimated Payments?

In 2006, when *estimated unpaid tax* for the year equals or exceeds $1,000, taxpayers usually must make estimated tax payments. Unpaid taxes include income tax and self-employment taxes. Employees do not make estimated payments in 2006 unless their tax withholdings and credits for 2006 fall below (1) 90% of the tax on their 2006 tax return or (2) 100% (110% for taxpayers whose 2005 AGI exceeded $150,000) of the tax on their 2005 tax return.

Estimated Tax Worksheet

The IRS provides a worksheet to help taxpayers calculate their estimated tax. The difference between their total estimated tax, net of estimated credits and their employer's withholdings, represents the *estimated unpaid tax*. Taxpayers can make an immediate payment of the balance or pay it in four equal installments.

TAXPAYERS WHO USUALLY MAKE QUARTERLY TAX PAYMENTS

1. Self-employed persons with business or professional income

2. Persons with large dividend, interest, rent, royalty, pension, and capital gain income

3. Wage earners whose income is not subject to withholding

4. Wage earners whose tax credits and withholdings fall short of their tax liability

---

Information for Figure 13-8: Filled-In Estimated Tax Worksheet

Audrey C. McGrath, single, age 25, with good vision and no dependents, prepares an estimated tax worksheet, shown in Figure 13-8. McGrath estimates her 2006 AGI at $22,873 and withholdings at $632. Her AGI estimate is based on the following:

Salary	$11,600
Net rentals from apartment building	9,600
Net income from business	1,800
Total income	$23,000
Less 50% of self-employment tax	(127)
AGI	$22,873

McGrath does not expect to itemize deductions in 2006. Her 2005 income taxes were $1,780.

FIGURE 13-8   Filled-In Estimated Tax Worksheet

1	AGI Expected in 2006		22,873
2	Larger of:		
	Estimated itemized deductions	0	
	Standard deduction (in 2006) for filing class	5,150	5,150
3	Subtract line 2 from line 1		17,723
4	Personal and dependency exemptions (in 2006)		3,300
5	Subtract line 4 from line 3		14,423
6	Tax on amount on line 5 (using the 2006 rates)*		1,786
7	Tax on Accumulation Distributions of Trusts	0	
	Tax on Lump-Sum Distributions	0	0
8	Add lines 6 and 7		1,786
9	Less: Credits		0
10	Subtract line 9 from line 8		1,786
11	Self-employment tax ($1,800 × 92.35% × 15.3%)		254
12	Other taxes (early distribution and AMT tax)		0
13a	Add lines 10 through 12		2,040
13b	Earned Income Credit and fuel credit		0
13c	Subtract line 13b from line 13a.		
	TOTAL 2006 ESTIMATED TAX		2,040
14a	90% of 2006 ESTIMATED TAX	1,836	
14b	100% of tax on 2005 tax return	1,780	
14c	Enter the smaller of line 14a or 14b		
	REQUIRED ANNUAL PAYMENT TO AVOID		
	A PENALTY		1,780
15	Income taxes withheld and estimated to be withheld		
	during 2006.		632
16	Subtract line 15 from 14c		1,148
17	Enter ¼ of line 16 ($1,148 ÷ 4),		
	rounded up to nearest whole dollar		287

* The 2006 tax rates for single taxpayers are 10% on the first $7,550 of taxable income, and 15% on
taxable income in excess of $7,550, but not more than $30,650.

Joint Estimated Tax Payments

A husband and wife can make joint estimated tax payments. Making a joint payment or separate payments does not commit the couple to filing a joint Form 1040. When a husband and wife make joint payments but file separate income tax returns, they can divide the estimate as they choose. One of them could use all the payments as a credit. A couple separated under a decree of divorce or separate maintenance cannot make joint estimated tax payments.

Payment of Estimated Tax

Taxpayers who make estimated tax payments mail their payment vouchers to the IRS Service Center for their district. The annual preprinted Form 1040-ES package contains four dated payment vouchers and mailing envelopes. A taxpayer who files an estimated tax voucher for the first time will receive a preprinted Form 1040-ES package.

For calendar year taxpayers, the vouchers and payments are due April 15, June 15, and September 15 of the current year, and January 15 of the next year. If the due date falls on a weekend or a holiday, the voucher and payment are due the next business day.

Prior-Year Overpayments

If a taxpayer's Form 1040 tax return for the year results in overpayment of taxes, the taxpayer can choose to receive a refund. The taxpayer can also choose to apply the overpayment to any estimated tax due the next year. The taxpayer can use the overpayment either to reduce each subsequent installment until the overpayment is used up or to reduce each installment equally.

EXAMPLE 9

Betty Nystrum overpaid her 2005 taxes by $700. The overpayment was not refunded to her. Nystrum's 2006 tax payments and estimated withholding data are as follows.

Estimated tax for 2006	$14,200
Less estimated income tax withholding during the year	(12,600)
Estimated unpaid tax	$ 1,600

Nystrum's quarterly installment payments equal $400 ($1,600 ÷ 4). Nystrum does not have to pay the first installment because the amount falls below last year's overpayment of $700. When the second installment comes due on June 15, 2006, Nystrum pays $100 (second quarterly installment of $400 less the remaining $300 from her last year's overpayment). The payment due dates and installment amounts for Nystrum are as follows.

April 17, 2006	$ 0
June 15, 2006	100
September 15, 2006	400
January 16, 2007	400

Nystrum could make an election to apply the overpayment evenly against each installment rather than in full against the first and succeeding installments. If she makes this election, Nystrum divides last year's overpayment by the number of installments ($700 ÷ 4) and applies this amount to each installment. Nystrum would pay four installments of $225 each ($400 − $175).

Underpayment of Estimated Tax

No underpayment penalty will be assessed when the amount of tax due after withholding is less than $1,000. Taxpayers who expect to owe more than $1,000 after withholdings should make timely estimated tax payments. One way to avoid the underpayment penalty in 2005 is to make four equal payments that total 90% of 2005 tax liability. A second way to avoid the penalty was to make four equal payments that total 100% of 2004 tax liability (110% for taxpayers whose 2004 AGI exceeded $150,000 [$75,000 for married filing separately]). A third way to avoid the underpayment penalty was to make estimated payments based on 90% of 2005 annualized tax liability. The calculations required in annualizing taxable income and tax liability are rather involved and beyond the scope of this textbook. Those interested in learning more about the annualized method making estimated payments should refer to IRS Publication 505.

Sometimes taxpayers need to make estimated payments, but also have wages subject to withholding. In calculating the amount of each estimated payment, wages are treated as occurring evenly throughout the year. Thus, taxpayers who work only part of the year and have $2,000 withheld from their wages will be treated as having had $500 withheld each quarter.

Determining the Penalty Amount

Taxpayers determine their penalty amount on Form 2210, Underpayment of Estimated Tax by Individuals. Taxpayers enter their penalty on Form 1040 (line 76). Then they add it to any other amounts due the government. Taxpayers may choose not to file Form 2210 and instead have the IRS calculate the penalty and bill them.

The IRS adjusts the underpayment penalty rate quarterly. The rate equals the short-term federal interest rate plus three percentage points. Although the penalty looks like an interest expense, taxpayers cannot deduct it.

QUESTIONS AND PROBLEMS

1. **Withholding Allowances.**

   a. How do employees claim withholding allowances?

   b. If employees do not give their employer a filled-in Form W-4, Employee's Withholding Allowance Certificate, what withholding action must the employer take?

   c. If a taxpayer holds more than one job, can the taxpayer claim withholding allowances with more than one employer?

2. **Withholding Rules.** What tax withholding action, if any, must a taxpayer take for each of the following situations?

   a. Withholding allowances decrease.

   b. Withholding allowances increase.

   c. A qualifying dependent dies on July 23 of the current year.

3. **Withholding Rules.**

   a. An employee files a Form W-4 on June 10, 2006, claiming to be exempt from withholding. For what period does the exempt status apply?

   b. Does an exemption from withholding that an employee claims on Form W-4 apply to both FICA taxes and federal income taxes?

4. **Withholding Allowances.** On the basis of the information given, how many withholding allowances can be claimed for 2005 by each of the following taxpayers? Identify the type of each withholding allowance claimed.

Taxpayer A	A single taxpayer, age 12, is claimed as a dependent on his parents' return. The taxpayer will earn $800 in wages during the year and receive $50 in dividend income.
Taxpayer B	A single taxpayer, age 20, is not claimed as a dependent on another return. The taxpayer will have earned income of $18,500 and interest income of $150. The taxpayer uses the standard deduction and has no adjustments to income.
Taxpayer C	A married taxpayer files jointly. The couple claim four dependent children (ages 3 to 16). The taxpayer has two jobs, and the spouse has one job. The taxpayer's total wages are $69,500, and the spouse's wages are $23,500. Dividend income equals $400. No adjustments to income exist. Child care expenses are $1,200, and expected itemized deductions are $15,000.
Taxpayer D	A single taxpayer has one dependent (age 9) and files as head of household. The taxpayer will earn $44,600 from one job. Expected interest income is $200. The taxpayer claims $2,000 as adjustments to income. Child care expenses equal $3,200, and expected itemized deductions are $5,800.

Taxpayer	Number of Withholding Allowances	Type of Withholding Allowances
A	_____	_____
B	_____	_____
C	_____	_____
D	_____	_____

5. **Form W-4.** Married taxpayers, Ethel P. (SSN 448-47-4747) and Irving J. (SSN 739-33-8990) Mead, file a joint return. They reside at 1001 West Wind Plaza, Fox Lake, Wisconsin 53933-4611. Both are 42 years of age. They have one dependent child, Mary Jean, age 14 (SSN 668-32-1184).

On November 15, 2005, the Meads became aware that their income tax for 2005 will be underpaid. Ethel decides to file a new Form W-4, Employee's Withholding Allowance Certificate, to change the number of withholding allowances to ensure more appropriate withholding in the future. Ethel will not claim an allowance for Irving but will claim Mary Jean. The Meads' estimated income and deductions is as follows.

Wages:	Ethel:	Henry Maintenance Company	$38,000
		Arnold Corporation	12,000
		Total gross wages—Ethel	$50,000
	Irving:	Readers' Specialty Store	8,500
		Total gross wages	$58,500
Dividend income—Ethel			1,316
Interest income—Irving			1,034
Total			$60,850

The Meads estimate their itemized deductions will equal $13,850. In addition, they anticipate the following "adjustments to income" and "other payments."

IRA contributions	$4,000
Fees for Mary Jean's school textbooks	216
Contributions to political party	320
Total	$4,536

Complete the 2005 Form W-4 that Ethel files with her employer, Henry Maintenance Company. Ethel signs and dates the form on November 18, 2005. Also prepare the necessary Form W-4 worksheets to determine the number of withholding allowances. Use the form and worksheet provided on pages 13-32–13-33.

6. **Form W-2.**

   a. By what date must an employer file Copy A of an employee's Form W-2 with the Social Security Administration?

   b. By what date must an employer give an employee Copies B and C of the employee's Form W-2?

7. **Form W-2.** Examine a Form W-2, Wage and Tax Statement.

   a. Explain the special meaning of *Statutory employee* in box 13.

   b. Explain the special meaning of the Void box at the top of the Form W-2.

8. **Form W-2.** Speedy Department Store (EIN is 04-0450523) is located at 2706 Bluff Drive, Boston, Massachusetts 02101-3214. Prepare the original 2005 Form W-2, Wage and Tax Statement, for Susan W. Jenkins, a married employee with no dependents. Use the blank Form W-2 provided on page 13-34. The following data was taken from Speedy's payroll records:

   Susan W. Jenkins, 214 Northrup Street, Boston, Massachusetts 02112-1415, SSN 331-06-4821.

Total wages paid (before payroll deductions)	$45,000.00
Social security tax withheld	Calculate
Medicare tax withheld	Calculate
Federal income tax withheld	6,552.00
State income tax withheld	1,125.75
Form W-2 control number	0623
Employer's state I.D. number	25703

(Use for Problem 5.)

Form W-4 (2005)

Purpose. Complete Form W-4 so that your employer can withhold the correct federal income tax from your pay. Because your tax situation may change, you may want to refigure your withholding each year.

Exemption from withholding. If you are exempt, complete only lines 1, 2, 3, 4, and 7 and sign the form to validate it. Your exemption for 2005 expires February 16, 2006. See Pub. 505, Tax Withholding and Estimated Tax.

Note. You cannot claim exemption from withholding if (a) your income exceeds $800 and includes more than $250 of unearned income (for example, interest and dividends) and (b) another person can claim you as a dependent on their tax return.

Basic instructions. If you are not exempt, complete the **Personal Allowances Worksheet** below. The worksheets on page 2 adjust your withholding allowances based on itemized deductions, certain credits, adjustments to income, or two-

earner/two-job situations. Complete all worksheets that apply. However, you may claim fewer (or zero) allowances.

Head of household. Generally, you may claim head of household filing status on your tax return only if you are unmarried and pay more than 50% of the costs of keeping up a home for yourself and your dependent(s) or other qualifying individuals. See line **E** below.

Tax credits. You can take projected tax credits into account in figuring your allowable number of withholding allowances. Credits for child or dependent care expenses and the child tax credit may be claimed using the **Personal Allowances Worksheet** below. See Pub. 919, How Do I Adjust My Tax Withholding? for information on converting your other credits into withholding allowances.

Nonwage income. If you have a large amount of nonwage income, such as interest or dividends, consider making estimated tax payments using Form 1040-ES, Estimated Tax for Individuals. Otherwise, you may owe additional tax.

Two earners/two jobs. If you have a working spouse or more than one job, figure the total number of allowances you are entitled to claim on all jobs using worksheets from only one Form W-4. Your withholding usually will be most accurate when all allowances are claimed on the Form W-4 for the highest paying job and zero allowances are claimed on the others.

Nonresident alien. If you are a nonresident alien, see the Instructions for Form 8233 before completing this Form W-4.

Check your withholding. After your Form W-4 takes effect, use Pub. 919 to see how the dollar amount you are having withheld compares to your projected total tax for 2005. See Pub. 919, especially if your earnings exceed $125,000 (Single) or $175,000 (Married).

Recent name change? If your name on line 1 differs from that shown on your social security card, call 1-800-772-1213 to initiate a name change and obtain a social security card showing your correct name.

Personal Allowances Worksheet (Keep for your records.)

A   Enter "1" for **yourself** if no one else can claim you as a dependent . . . .   **A** ____

B   Enter "1" if: { • You are single and have only one job; or
• You are married, have only one job, and your spouse does not work; or
• Your wages from a second job or your spouse's wages (or the total of both) are $1,000 or less. } . .   **B** ____

C   Enter "1" for your **spouse**. But, you may choose to enter "-0-" if you are married and have either a working spouse or more than one job. (Entering "-0-" may help you avoid having too little tax withheld.) . . . .   **C** ____

D   Enter number of **dependents** (other than your spouse or yourself) you will claim on your tax return . . . . . .   **D** ____

E   Enter "1" if you will file as **head of household** on your tax return (see conditions under **Head of household** above) .   **E** ____

F   Enter "1" if you have at least $1,500 of **child or dependent care expenses** for which you plan to claim a credit . .   **F** ____
(**Note.** Do **not** include child support payments. See **Pub. 503,** Child and Dependent Care Expenses, for details.)

G   **Child Tax Credit** (including additional child tax credit):
• If your total income will be less than $54,000 ($79,000 if married), enter "2" for each eligible child.
• If your total income will be between $54,000 and $84,000 ($79,000 and $119,000 if married), enter "1" for each eligible child plus "1" **additional** if you have four or more eligible children.   **G** ____

H   Add lines A through G and enter total here. (**Note.** This may be different from the number of exemptions you claim on your tax return.) ▶ **H** ____

For accuracy, complete all worksheets that apply. { • If you plan to **itemize or claim adjustments to income** and want to reduce your withholding, see the **Deductions and Adjustments Worksheet** on page 2.
• If you have **more than one job** or are **married and you and your spouse both work** and the combined earnings from all jobs exceed $35,000 ($25,000 if married) see the **Two-Earner/Two-Job Worksheet** on page 2 to avoid having too little tax withheld.
• If **neither** of the above situations applies, **stop here** and enter the number from line H on line 5 of Form W-4 below. }

-   **Cut here and give Form W-4 to your employer. Keep the top part for your records.**   - - - - - - - - - - - - -

Form **W-4**		**Employee's Withholding Allowance Certificate**	OMB No. 1545-0010
Department of the Treasury Internal Revenue Service		▶ **Whether you are entitled to claim a certain number of allowances or exemption from withholding is subject to review by the IRS. Your employer may be required to send a copy of this form to the IRS.**	**2005**

1 Type or print your first name and middle initial	Last name		**2** Your social security number
Home address (number and street or rural route)		**3** ☐ Single ☐ Married ☐ Married, but withhold at higher Single rate. **Note.** If married, but legally separated, or spouse is a nonresident alien, check the "Single" box.	
City or town, state, and ZIP code		**4** If your last name differs from that shown on your social security card, check here. You must call 1-800-772-1213 for a new card. ▶ ☐	

5   Total number of allowances you are claiming (from line **H** above **or** from the applicable worksheet on page 2)   **5** ____

6   Additional amount, if any, you want withheld from each paycheck . . . .   **6** $ ____

7   I claim exemption from withholding for 2005, and I certify that I meet **both** of the following conditions for exemption.
• Last year I had a right to a refund of **all** federal income tax withheld because I had **no** tax liability **and**
• This year I expect a refund of **all** federal income tax withheld because I expect to have **no** tax liability.
If you meet both conditions, write "Exempt" here . . . . ▶ **7** ____

Under penalties of perjury, I declare that I have examined this certificate and to the best of my knowledge and belief, it is true, correct, and complete.
Employee's signature
(Form is not valid
unless you sign it.) ▶ _____   Date ▶ _____

8 Employer's name and address (Employer: Complete lines 8 and 10 only if sending to the IRS.)	**9** Office code (optional)	**10** Employer identification number (EIN)

For Privacy Act and Paperwork Reduction Act Notice, see page 2.   Cat. No. 10220Q   Form **W-4** (2005)

(Use for Problem 5.)

Form W-4 (2005)   Page **2**

Deductions and Adjustments Worksheet

Note. Use this worksheet *only* if you plan to itemize deductions, claim certain credits, or claim adjustments to income on your 2005 tax return.

1.   Enter an estimate of your 2005 itemized deductions. These include qualifying home mortgage interest, charitable contributions, state and local taxes, medical expenses in excess of 7.5% of your income, and miscellaneous deductions. (For 2005, you may have to reduce your itemized deductions if your income is over $145,950 ($72,975 if married filing separately). See *Worksheet 3* in Pub. 919 for details.) . . .   **1** $ _____

2.   Enter: { $10,000 if married filing jointly or qualifying widow(er) }   **2** $ _____
            { $ 7,300 if head of household }
            { $ 5,000 if single or married filing separately }

3.   **Subtract** line 2 from line 1. If line 2 is greater than line 1, enter "-0-" . . . .   **3** $ _____

4.   Enter an estimate of your 2005 adjustments to income, including alimony, deductible IRA contributions, and student loan interest   **4** $ _____

5.   **Add** lines 3 and 4 and enter the total. (Include any amount for credits from *Worksheet 7* in Pub. 919) .   **5** $ _____

6.   Enter an estimate of your 2005 nonwage income (such as dividends or interest) . . . .   **6** $ _____

7.   **Subtract** line 6 from line 5. Enter the result, but not less than "-0-" . . . .   **7** $ _____

8.   **Divide** the amount on line 7 by $3,200 and enter the result here. Drop any fraction . . . . .   **8**   _____

9.   Enter the number from the **Personal Allowances Worksheet,** line H, page 1 . . . .   **9**   _____

10.   **Add** lines 8 and 9 and enter the total here. If you plan to use the **Two-Earner/Two-Job Worksheet,** also enter this total on line 1 below. Otherwise, **stop here** and enter this total on Form W-4, line 5, page 1 .   **10**   _____

Two-Earner/Two-Job Worksheet (See *Two earners/two jobs* on page 1.)

Note. Use this worksheet *only* if the instructions under line H on page 1 direct you here.

1.   Enter the number from line H, page 1 (or from line 10 above if you used the **Deductions and Adjustments Worksheet**)   **1**   _____

2.   Find the number in **Table 1** below that applies to the **LOWEST** paying job and enter it here . . . .   **2**   _____

3.   If line 1 is **more than or equal to** line 2, subtract line 2 from line 1. Enter the result here (if zero, enter "-0-") and on Form W-4, line 5, page 1. **Do not** use the rest of this worksheet . . . .   **3**   _____

Note. If line 1 is *less than* line 2, enter "-0-" on Form W-4, line 5, page 1. Complete lines 4–9 below to calculate the additional withholding amount necessary to avoid a year-end tax bill.

4.   Enter the number from line 2 of this worksheet   . . . .   **4**   _____

5.   Enter the number from line 1 of this worksheet   . . . .   **5**   _____

6.   **Subtract** line 5 from line 4   . . . .   **6**   _____

7.   Find the amount in **Table 2** below that applies to the **HIGHEST** paying job and enter it here . . . .   **7** $ _____

8.   **Multiply** line 7 by line 6 and enter the result here. This is the additional annual withholding needed . .   **8** $ _____

9.   Divide line 8 by the number of pay periods remaining in 2005. For example, divide by 26 if you are paid every two weeks and you complete this form in December 2004. Enter the result here and on Form W-4, line 6, page 1. This is the additional amount to be withheld from each paycheck . . . .   **9** $ _____

Table 1: Two-Earner/Two-Job Worksheet

Married Filing Jointly						All Others	
If wages from **HIGHEST** paying job are—	AND, wages from **LOWEST** paying job are—	Enter on line 2 above	If wages from **HIGHEST** paying job are—	AND, wages from **LOWEST** paying job are—	Enter on line 2 above	If wages from **LOWEST** paying job are—	Enter on line 2 above
$0 - $40,000	$0 - $4,000	0	$40,001 and over	30,001 - 36,000	6	$0 - $6,000	0
	4,001 - 8,000	1		36,001 - 45,000	7	6,001 - 12,000	1
	8,001 - 18,000	2		45,001 - 50,000	8	12,001 - 18,000	2
	18,001 and over	3		50,001 - 60,000	9	18,001 - 24,000	3
$40,001 and over	$0 - $4,000	0		60,001 - 65,000	10	24,001 - 31,000	4
	4,001 - 8,000	1		65,001 - 75,000	11	31,001 - 45,000	5
	8,001 - 18,000	2		75,001 - 90,000	12	45,001 - 60,000	6
	18,001 - 22,000	3		90,001 - 100,000	13	60,001 - 75,000	7
	22,001 - 25,000	4		100,001 - 115,000	14	75,001 - 80,000	8
	25,001 - 30,000	5		115,001 and over	15	80,001 - 100,000	9
						100,001 and over	10

Table 2: Two-Earner/Two-Job Worksheet

Married Filing Jointly		All Others	
If wages from **HIGHEST** paying job are—	Enter on line 7 above	If wages from **HIGHEST** paying job are—	Enter on line 7 above
$0 - $60,000	$480	$0 - $30,000	$480
60,001 - 110,000	800	30,001 - 70,000	800
110,001 - 160,000	900	70,001 - 140,000	900
160,001 - 280,000	1,060	140,001 - 320,000	1,060
280,001 and over	1,120	320,001 and over	1,120

Privacy Act and Paperwork Reduction Act Notice. We ask for the information on this form to carry out the Internal Revenue laws of the United States. The Internal Revenue Code requires this information under sections 3402(f)(2)(A) and 6109 and their regulations. Failure to provide a properly completed form will result in your being treated as a single person who claims no withholding allowances; providing fraudulent information may also subject you to penalties. Routine uses of this information include giving it to the Department of Justice for civil and criminal litigation, to cities, states, and the District of Columbia for use in administering their tax laws, and using it in the National Directory of New Hires. We may also disclose this information to other countries under a tax treaty, to federal and state agencies to enforce federal nontax criminal laws, or to federal law enforcement and intelligence agencies to combat terrorism.

You are not required to provide the information requested on a form that is subject to the Paperwork Reduction Act unless the form displays a valid OMB control number. Books or records relating to a form or its instructions must be retained as long as their contents may become material in the administration of any Internal Revenue law. Generally, tax returns and return information are confidential, as required by Code section 6103.

The time needed to complete this form will vary depending on individual circumstances. The estimated average time is: Recordkeeping, 45 min.; Learning about the law or the form, 12 min.; Preparing the form, 58 min. If you have comments concerning the accuracy of these time estimates or suggestions for making this form simpler, we would be happy to hear from you. You can write to: Internal Revenue Service, Tax Products Coordinating Committee, SE:W:CAR:MP:T:T:SP, 1111 Constitution Ave. NW, IR-6406, Washington, DC 20224. **Do not** send Form W-4 to this address. Instead, give it to your employer.

 Printed on recycled paper

(Use for Problem 8.)

a Control number	22222	Void ☐	For Official Use Only ▶ OMB No. 1545-0008		
b Employer identification number (EIN)				1 Wages, tips, other compensation	2 Federal income tax withheld
c Employer's name, address, and ZIP code				3 Social security wages	4 Social security tax withheld
				5 Medicare wages and tips	6 Medicare tax withheld
				7 Social security tips	8 Allocated tips
d Employee's social security number				9 Advance EIC payment	10 Dependent care benefits
e Employee's first name and initial / Last name				11 Nonqualified plans	12a See instructions for box 12
			13 Statutory employee ☐ / Retirement plan ☐ / Third-party sick pay ☐		12b
			14 Other		12c
					12d
f Employee's address and ZIP code					
15 State / Employer's state ID number	16 State wages, tips, etc.	17 State income tax	18 Local wages, tips, etc.	19 Local income tax	20 Locality name

Form **W-2** Wage and Tax Statement   **2005**

Department of the Treasury—Internal Revenue Service

For Privacy Act and Paperwork Reduction Act Notice, see back of Copy D.

Copy A For Social Security Administration — Send this entire page with Form W-3 to the Social Security Administration; photocopies are **not** acceptable.

Cat. No. 10134D

Do Not Cut, Fold, or Staple Forms on This Page — Do Not Cut, Fold, or Staple Forms on This Page

9. **Withholding Rules.** Must a taxpayer who receives taxable annuity, pension, or deferred income payments have federal income taxes withheld from the payments? Explain.

10. **Form W-3.**

   a. What documents does an employer transmit with Form W-3 when filing with the Social Security Administration?

   b. By what date must an employer file these documents?

11. **Form W-3.** The Golden Door Company (EIN 39–0630726), 1906 North Avenue, Cheyenne, Wyoming 82001-1222, withheld income and social security taxes from each of its 28 employees during 2005. Golden's telephone number is (619) 438–2444. In 2006 it prepared and sent to each employee a separate Form W-2. All wages paid to employees total $225,250. Total federal income taxes withheld from employees were $36,250. Total social security and Medicare wages equaled $209,850. No employee's wages exceeded $90,000 during 2005. Compute the company's total employment tax liability for 2005, and prepare its Form W-3, Transmittal of Income and Tax Statements. Use blank Form W-3 and control number 01 to prepare the form as of January 21, 2006. If no entry applies to the box, leave it blank. Have Marsha A. Golden, president of Golden, sign the form.

(Use for Problem 11.)

	DO NOT STAPLE OR FOLD	
a Control number 33333	For Official Use Only ▶ OMB No. 1545-0008	
b Kind of Payer — 941 ☐ Military ☐ 943 ☐ CT-1 ☐ Hshld. emp. ☐ Medicare govt. emp. ☐ Third-party sick pay ☐	1 Wages, tips, other compensation	2 Federal income tax withheld
	3 Social security wages	4 Social security tax withheld
c Total number of Forms W-2 **d** Establishment number	5 Medicare wages and tips	6 Medicare tax withheld
e Employer identification number (EIN)	7 Social security tips	8 Allocated tips
f Employer's name	9 Advance EIC payments	10 Dependent care benefits
	11 Nonqualified plans	12 Deferred compensation
	13 For third-party sick pay use only	
	14 Income tax withheld by payer of third-party sick pay	
g Employer's address and ZIP code		
h Other EIN used this year		
15 State Employer's state ID number	16 State wages, tips, etc.	17 State income tax
	18 Local wages, tips, etc.	19 Local income tax
Contact person	Telephone number ( )	For Official Use Only
Email address	Fax number ( )	

Under penalties of perjury, I declare that I have examined this return and accompanying documents, and, to the best of my knowledge and belief, they are true, correct, and complete.

12. FUTA Withholdings.

a. Should employers withhold FUTA taxes from employees? Explain.

b. When must an employer deposit FUTA taxes?

c. What is the FUTA tax rate? What is the effective FUTA tax rate for most taxpayers who are subject to it?

13. Form 941. During the third quarter of 2005, the Fillmore Restaurant (EIN 93-0530660) at 244 North Second Street, Fillmore, New York 14735-0022, withheld income and social security taxes from its five employees. It withheld income taxes of $3,117 from employees' wages and tips of $15,570. In addition, Fillmore withheld $912.95 of social security taxes on $14,725 of social security wages, and $52.39 of social security taxes on $845 of social security tips. It also withheld $225.77 of Medicare taxes on $15,570 of Medicare wages. During the quarter, Fillmore deposited income and employment taxes as follows: August 15, $1,739.50; September 15, $1,962.84; October 15, $1,796.87. Each deposit was accompanied by a federal tax deposit coupon. Data for quarterly wages and reported tips of employees is as follows:

Name	Total Wages	Social Security Wages	Taxable Tips Reported
Barker, J. R.	$ 7,025	$ 7,025	$315
Duwe, H. K.	3,000	3,000	180
Miller, M. M.	2,000	2,000	120
Pressman, R. M.	1,200	1,200	125
Smathers, H. H.	1,500	1,500	105
	$14,725	$14,725	$845

Prepare Form 941, Employer's Quarterly Federal Tax Return, for the Fillmore Restaurant, using the blank form provided on pages 13-37 and 13-38. Fillmore filed Form 941 and M. L. Wright, owner, signed it on October 25, 2005.

(Use for Problem 13.)

Form **941 for 2005:** Employer's Quarterly Federal Tax Return   9901
(Rev. January 2005)   Department of the Treasury — Internal Revenue Service

OMB No. 1545-0029

Employer identification number ☐ ☐ — ☐ ☐ ☐ ☐ ☐ ☐ ☐

Name *(not your trade name)*

Trade name *(if any)*

Address
  Number   Street   Suite or room number

  City   State   ZIP code

Report for this Quarter ...
(Check one.)

☐ **1:** January, February, March

☐ **2:** April, May, June

☐ **3:** July, August, September

☐ **4:** October, November, December

Read the separate instructions before you fill out this form. Please type or print within the boxes.

Part 1: Answer these questions for this quarter.

1 Number of employees who received wages, tips, or other compensation for the pay period including: *Mar. 12* (Quarter 1), *June 12* (Quarter 2), *Sept. 12* (Quarter 3), *Dec. 12* (Quarter 4)   **1**

2 Wages, tips, and other compensation **2**

3 Total income tax withheld from wages, tips, and other compensation **3**

4 If no wages, tips, and other compensation are subject to social security or Medicare tax . . ☐ Check and go to line 6.

5 Taxable social security and Medicare wages and tips:

	Column 1		Column 2
5a Taxable social security wages		× .124 =	
5b Taxable social security tips		× .124 =	
5c Taxable Medicare wages & tips		× .029 =	

5d Total social security and Medicare taxes (*Column 2*, lines 5a + 5b + 5c = line 5d) . . **5d**

6 Total taxes before adjustments (lines 3 + 5d = line 6) **6**

7 Tax adjustments (If your answer is a negative number, write it in brackets.):

7a Current quarter's fractions of cents . . . .

7b Current quarter's sick pay . . . .

7c Current quarter's adjustments for tips and group-term life insurance

7d Current year's income tax withholding (Attach Form 941c) . .

7e Prior quarters' social security and Medicare taxes (Attach Form 941c)

7f Special additions to federal income tax (reserved use) . . . . .

7g Special additions to social security and Medicare (reserved use)

7h Total adjustments (Combine all amounts: lines 7a through 7g.) **7h**

8 Total taxes after adjustments (Combine lines 6 and 7h.) **8**

9 Advance earned income credit (EIC) payments made to employees **9**

10 Total taxes after adjustment for advance EIC (lines 8 – 9 = line 10) **10**

11 Total deposits for this quarter, including overpayment applied from a prior quarter . . . **11**

12 Balance due (lines 10 – 11 = line 12) Make checks payable to the *United States Treasury* . . **12**

13 Overpayment (If line 11 is more than line 10, write the difference here.)   Check one ☐ Apply to next return.
                                                            ☐ Send a refund.

Next ➡

For Privacy Act and Paperwork Reduction Act Notice, see the back of the Payment Voucher.   Cat. No. 17001Z   Form **941** (Rev. 1-2005)

(Use for Problem 13.)

9902

Name *(not your trade name)*	Employer identification number

Part 2: Tell us about your deposit schedule for this quarter.

If you are unsure about whether you are a monthly schedule depositor or a semiweekly schedule depositor, see *Pub. 15 (Circular E)*, section 11.

14 ⬜⬜ Write the state abbreviation for the state where you made your deposits OR write "MU" if you made your deposits in *multiple* states.

15 Check one: ⬜ Line 10 is less than $2,500. Go to Part 3.

⬜ You were a monthly schedule depositor for the entire quarter. Fill out your tax liability for each month. Then go to Part 3.

Tax liability:	Month 1	_____ .
	Month 2	_____ .
	Month 3	_____ .
	Total	_____ . Total must equal line 10.

⬜ You were a semiweekly schedule depositor for any part of this quarter. Fill out *Schedule B (Form 941): Report of Tax Liability for Semiweekly Schedule Depositors,* and attach it to this form.

Part 3: Tell us about your business. If a question does NOT apply to your business, leave it blank.

16 If your business has closed and you do not have to file returns in the future . . . . ⬜ Check here, and

enter the final date you paid wages [/ /] .

17 If you are a seasonal employer and you do not have to file a return for every quarter of the year . . ⬜ Check here.

Part 4: May we contact your third-party designee?

Do you want to allow an employee, a paid tax preparer, or another person to discuss this return with the IRS? See the instructions for details.

⬜ Yes. Designee's name _____

Phone ( ) – Personal Identification Number (PIN) ⬜⬜⬜⬜⬜

⬜ No.

Part 5: Sign here

Under penalties of perjury, I declare that I have examined this return, including accompanying schedules and statements, and to the best of my knowledge and belief, it is true, correct, and complete.

✗ Sign your name here _____

Print name and title _____

Date [/ /] Phone ( ) –

Part 6: For paid preparers only *(optional)*

Preparer's signature	_____		
Firm's name	_____		
Address	_____	EIN	_____
	_____	ZIP code	_____
Date	[/ /] Phone ( ) –	SSN/PTIN	_____
	⬜ Check if you are self-employed.		

Form **941** (Rev. 1-2005)

14. **Form 941.**

    a. When must employers file their Form 941 returns?

    b. Can employers combine data from different quarters on one Form 941 as long as the combined period does not exceed three months?

15. **Form 8109.**

    a. What name has the IRS given Form 8109? Discuss its contents, indicate who uses it, and explain how it is used.

    b. Identify the types of employment taxes that employers usually deposit with a specified depository.

16. **Lookback Period.** Describe the lookback period and discuss its significance for purposes of determining an employer's deposit frequency.

17. **Deposit Dates.** For each of the following situations, determine the employer's required deposit date.

    a. A monthly depositor whose payroll period ends on Friday, October 28.

    b. A semiweekly depositor whose payroll period ends on Wednesday, April 12.

    c. A semiweekly depositor whose payroll period ends on Friday, December 28.

    d. A monthly depositor whose payroll period ends on Tuesday, May 15.

18. **Estimated Taxes.** Indicate whether or not the following individuals are required to pay an estimated tax for 2006. (Check either the "Yes" or the "No" column.)

	Yes	No
a. Single taxpayer with income derived solely from wages subject to withholding expected to equal $6,000. Estimated unpaid tax expected to total $250.	___	___
b. Married couple with husband's income derived solely from wages subject to withholding expected to equal $10,500. Spouse does not receive wages. Estimated unpaid tax expected to total $400.	___	___
c. Qualifying widower with income derived from wages subject to withholding expected to equal $12,500; income from other sources not subject to withholding expected to total $5,000. Estimated unpaid tax expected to total $1,200.	___	___
d. Married couple with husband's income derived solely from wages subject to withholding expected to equal $11,000; spouse expects to receive dividend income totaling $3,000. Estimated unpaid tax expected to total $1,550.	___	___

19. **Estimated Taxes.** Prepare the Estimated Tax Worksheet, reproduced below, for George B. Lewis, 2111 North Second Street, Madison, Wisconsin 53705-4001. Lewis, an unmarried taxpayer, claims one personal exemption and no dependency exemptions. He elects to pay the minimum amount of estimated tax required. The data for the worksheet is as follows.

AGI (includes estimated salary, $18,650; estimated self-employment net profit, $14,000) before deduction for ½ SE tax	$32,650
Itemized deductions estimated	8,000
Estimated income tax withheld	2,216
Credit for overpayment on the 2005 tax return, elected as a credit on the 2006 estimated tax and subtracted evenly from each quarterly payment	250
Income taxes for 2005 as determined by the income tax return	4,200

1	AGI Expected in 2006		_____
2	Larger of:		
	Estimated itemized deductions	_____	
	Standard deduction (in 2006) for filing class	5,150	_____
3	Subtract line 2 from line 1		_____
4	Personal and dependency exemptions (in 2006)		3,300
5	Subtract line 4 from line 3		_____
6	Tax on amount on line 5*		_____
7	Tax on accumulation distributions of trusts	_____	
	Tax on lump-sum distributions	_____	
8	Add lines 6 and 7		_____
9	Less credits		_____
10	Subtract line 9 from line 8		_____
11	Self-employment tax	_____	
12	Other taxes (AMT tax)	_____	_____
13a	Add lines 10 through 12		_____
13b	Earned income credit and fuel credit		_____
13c	Subtract line 13b from line 13a TOTAL 2006 ESTIMATED TAX		_____
14a	90% of 2006 ESTIMATED TAX	_____	
14b	100% of tax on 2005 tax return	_____	
14c	Enter the smaller of line 14a or 14b REQUIRED ANNUAL PAYMENT TO AVOID A PENALTY		_____
15	Income taxes withheld and estimated to be withheld during 2006		_____
16	Subtract line 15 from 14c		_____
17	Enter ¼ of line 16, rounded to nearest whole dollar		_____

*The 2006 tax rates for single taxpayers are 10% on the first $7,550 of taxable income, and 15% on taxable income in excess of $7,550 but not more than $30,650.

20. **Estimated Taxes.** What steps can an unmarried taxpayer with estimated AGI in 2005 of $75,000 take to avoid a penalty for underpayment of estimated taxes in 2006?

21. **Internet Problem: Researching Publication 926.**

Brad and Carol Thomas made an agreement with a neighbor's child to care for their lawn. The neighbor's son, Tad, takes care of the lawns of others in the neighborhood. Tad provides all of his own machinery, tools and necessary supplies. During 2005 the Thomases pay Tad $2,000 for various lawn care services. Since this amount exceeds $1,400, they are worried that they might be required to report Tad as a household employee and be required to withhold employment taxes.

Go to the IRS Web site. Locate Publication 926, *Household Employer's Tax Guide* and use it to answer the Thomas's question. Print out a copy of the page where you find the answer. Underline or highlight the pertinent information. Comment on what you believe to be the answer to the Thomas's question.

See Appendix A for instructions on how to access the IRS Web site.

22. **Business Entity Problem: This problem is designed for those using the "business entity" approach. The solution may require information from Chapter 14.**

a. Sunset Corporation had taxable income of $300,000 last year. To avoid underpayment penalties for the current year, what amount of estimated taxes must the company deposit during the year?

b. If the corporation had taxable income of $3,000,000 last year, what amount of estimated taxes must be deposited in the current year to avoid an underpayment penalty?(Use for Problem 11.)

14

Business Entities

CHAPTER CONTENTS

■■ CHAPTER OVERVIEW

*T*he proprietorship is the most common form of business ownership. Chapter 7 focuses on the taxation of income arising from proprietorship operations. However, partnerships and corporations are also popular ownership structures that are available to carry out business activities. Business owners must weigh the advantages and disadvantages of each when choosing the best entity from which to conduct their business operations. The impact of income taxation on each of these business entities plays a major role in this important choice.

Partnerships are separate legal entities. They can carry on a variety of business activities. However, for tax purposes, partnerships are not separate taxable entities. They file informational tax forms but do not pay taxes. Rather, the results of all their business activities belong to the owners (partners). The partners report their shares of the business activities on their own returns. This means that only one level of tax is levied on partnership profits.

In contrast, a business organized as a corporation is a separate taxable entity. The corporation exists outside of its owners (shareholders), and it must pay a tax on its income. Such companies are called C corporations. The name comes from the location of the governing Code provisions (Subchapter C). However, Congress created another tax entity, called an S corporation, frequently referred to as a tax-option corporation. In S corporations, as in partnerships, the owners (shareholders) pay the tax on the business's income. S corporations have some partnership traits and some corporation traits; they also have some unique tax traits. The S corporation is, therefore, a tax entity with its own tax rules and requirements.

While this chapter provides an overview of the taxation of income generated by partnerships and corporations, some corporations qualify for tax-exempt status. They include religious, charitable, scientific, educational, civic, and literary units operated for society's general benefit. These corporations are called not-for-profit organizations.

THE NATURE OF PARTNERSHIPS

A partnership is an association of two or more persons (or other entities) that conduct business with an intent to share profits or losses. A partnership does not include a joint undertaking merely to share expenses. Each person contributing property or services to the partnership receives an ownership interest. Each becomes a partner. Partners can be individuals, corporations, estates, partnerships, or trusts.

EXAMPLE 1

If Tom Jones and Bessy Smith dig a ditch merely to drain surface water from their properties, they do not create a partnership. If they actively carry on a business and divide the profits, however, they do create a partnership and become partners.

The tax term *partnership* includes a syndicate, group, pool, joint venture, or other entity that exists for the purpose of achieving any business, financial operation, or venture. Any organization that qualifies as a corporation, estate, or trust does not fall within the definition of a partnership.

PARTNERSHIP RETURNS

In a partnership, the individual partners, rather than the partnership, are the taxpayers. All items of partnership income and loss pass through to the partners. These items appear on the partners' personal returns. Partners must pay taxes on their shares of the partnership income regardless of whether or not they receive distributions from the partnership. However, a partnership can choose to be taxed as a corporation.

Every partnership doing business within the United States files the informational return Form 1065, U.S. Partnership Return of Income. The return reports the partnership's revenues and expenses. It also provides each partner's share of all partnership items. The return is due by the fifteenth day of the fourth month after the partnership's year end. For a calendar year partnership, the due date is April 15. A partnership may receive an automatic three-month extension for filing by submitting a Form 8736. This form must be filed by the due date for the original return. The Code imposes a penalty on the partnership (not the partners) for its failure to file a complete Form 1065 in a timely manner. For each month that the failure continues (not to exceed five months), the penalty equals $50 times the number of partners. Thus, the maximum penalty equals $250 times the number of partners.

Year to Report Partnership Income

Partners are taxed on their shares of partnership items in the year in which the partnership's tax year ends. They include the results of all partnership activities on their personal tax returns.

EXAMPLE 2

The partnership and partner Amber Brown have a calendar tax year. Brown reports her share of partnership items for the calendar year 20x1 on her individual 20x1 tax return. Now, suppose the partnership uses a fiscal year from February 1, 20x1, to January 31, 20x2. Brown still uses a calendar tax year. Brown includes the partnership income, most of which was earned in 20x1, on her 20x2 return. Thus, 11 months of income earned by the partnership in 20x1 is not taxed until 20x2. Brown has an 11-month tax deferral on this income.

Partnership Tax Year

To prevent partners from deferring partnership income into the next year (like Brown in Example 2), Congress passed rules limiting a partnership's choice of year ends. The partnership must select the same tax year as the majority partners. Majority partners own in total more than 50% of capital and profits. Because most partners use a calendar year, most partnerships also use the calendar year. However, if the majority partners have different tax years, the partnership must select the same tax year as all of its principal partners. A principal partner owns at least 5% of capital and profits. Partnerships unable to determine a tax year using these rules must adopt a tax year that results in the least aggregate deferral of income. Most partnerships are not affected by this method, and it is not discussed here.

Exceptions

Two exceptions apply to the required tax year rules. The first permits a partnership to select a tax year based on the natural business year of the entity. A natural business year is one in which at least 25% of gross receipts are received in the last two months of a 12-month period. This requirement must be met for three consecutive years *before* the partnership can apply for a natural business year. Thus, the natural business year exception may be adopted only by partnerships that have been in existence for at least three years.

The second exception allows partnerships to select a tax year that provides no more than a three-month deferral for its partners. For partners using a calendar tax year, the partnership could select a tax year ending the last day of September, October, or November. The partnership makes the election by filing Form 8716, Election To Have a Tax Year Other Than a Required Tax Year. This election requires partnerships to make tax deposits approximating the amount of tax deferral due to the difference in the partnership and the partners' tax years. Thus, these tax deposits eliminate any income deferral benefits. Treasury Regulations provide details regarding the computation of the required tax deposits.

Tax Year Change

A partnership wanting to change its tax year must obtain permission from the IRS. Partnerships make the request on Form 8716. A partnership receiving permission to change its tax year files a short-year tax return in the year of change. This return covers the period from its prior year end to its new year end.

EXAMPLE 3

A change from a fiscal year ending March 31 to the calendar year ending December 31 requires a short-year return. The short-year return covers the nine-month period of April 1 to December 31. Suppose that the partnership changes from a calendar year to a March 31 year end. In this case, it files a short-year return covering January 1 to March 31.

Changes in partnership membership or in the relative interests among the partners sometimes terminate the partnership tax year. Normally, the following occurrences will not automatically terminate the partnership tax year: death of a partner, addition of a partner, or a shift of a partial interest in the firm among partners. However, if the cumulative effect of any events during a twelve-month period cause at least a 50% change in ownership, the tax year closes. The tax year also closes when the partnership ceases to carry on any business. Thus, all of the partners must recognize their shares of income/loss items at the time of closing. The rules are slightly different for the individual partner. Here the partnership tax year closes with respect to an individual partner whose entire partnership interest terminates by death or some other event, but it will not close the tax year for the other partners.

Reporting Partnership Income and Deductions

A partnership is not a taxable entity. A partnership *passes through* income and expenses to the individual partners. This pass-through treatment is an application of the *conduit principle.* Many partnership income and expense items receive special tax treatment on the partners' individual tax returns. Therefore, the partnership must report these items separately on its return. This separate reporting enables the partners to determine their shares of these income and expense items which they must separately report on their personal returns. Separately stated items include net income from rental real estate activities, capital gains and losses, portfolio income (dividends, interest income, and royalty income), charitable contributions, and net operating losses (NOLs). Any items that do not require separate reporting are passed through to the partners as ordinary income from partnership operations.

Partners are not employees and no taxes are withheld on their earnings. Therefore, partners must make estimated payments large enough to cover both income and self-employment taxes on their shares of partnership income.

Partnership Ordinary Income

The income resulting from the partnership's business is the starting point for computing ordinary income. Income items such as dividends, interest, rents, and capital gains pass through to the partners as separately stated items. Consequently, ordinary income does not include these items.

From the resulting income the partnership deducts operating expenses. The net result of subtracting operation expenses from nonseparately stated income is income from operations. The partnership reports this amount on its tax return as ordinary income from trade or business activities.

Calculating Ordinary Income

Gross receipts or gross sales	$xx	
Less returns and allowances	(xx)	$xx
Less cost of goods sold		(xx)
Gross profit		$xx
Ordinary income or (loss) from other partnerships and fiduciaries		xx
Net farm profit or (loss)		xx
Net ordinary gain or (loss) from Form 4797		xx
Other income or (loss)		xx
Total income or (loss)		$xx
Less:		
Allowable operating expenses	$xx	
Guaranteed payments to partners	xx	(xx)
Ordinary income or (loss) from trade or business		$xx

Guaranteed Payments to Partners

Partnership agreements frequently provide that some or all partners receive payments as compensation. These payments recognize the varying skills and amounts of time partners devote to partnership business. Also, partners may receive a stated rate of interest on the amount of capital that each has invested in the partnership.

The partnership generally deducts these guaranteed payments in computing partnership ordinary income. To be deductible, the payments must be reasonable and determined without regard to partnership income. Although guaranteed salaries and interest payments to partners are deducted to arrive at ordinary income, they are part of the profit allocation process. Thus, partners report these items as income for the partnership year to which they relate.

EXAMPLE 4

Dave and Bob Blunk are partners in the law firm of Blunk and Blunk which ends its tax year on December 31. Dave, a cash basis taxpayer, uses a fiscal tax year ending June 30. Dave's monthly salary for the calendar year 20x1 is $3,000. For 20x2, this monthly salary is increased to $4,000. Dave's share of the partnership's 20x1 ordinary income (after guaranteed salary reductions) is $40,000.

Dave's June 30, 20x2, tax return will report income from the partnership of $76,000. This includes his guaranteed salary of $36,000 ($3,000 × 12) paid during the partnership year and his share of ordinary income ($40,000). Although Dave is a cash basis taxpayer, the $24,000 guaranteed salary ($4,000 × 6) he receives during the first six months of 20x2 relates to the partnership year ending December 31, 20x2. Thus, this $24,000 will be reported on Dave's June 30, 20x3, tax return.

While partners may receive payments for providing services, they are not considered employees. Therefore, the guaranteed payments are not subject to withholding of social security or income taxes. They are considered earned income and subject to self-employment taxes. The partners must report the guaranteed payments they receive as gross income on Form 1040, Schedule E, Supplemental Income and Loss, as nonpassive income. The partnership also deducts salaries and wages paid to spouses or other members of a partner's family. They are considered wages paid to employees. The deductible amounts must be reasonable for the services rendered. Any unreasonable portion is considered a payment to the related partner.

Separately Stated Items

As previously stated, certain items of income and deductions are separately stated on the partnership return because they can affect partners' personal tax liabilities differently. The partnership return Form 1065, Schedule K, is where these separately stated items are listed. Each partner receives a Form 1065, Schedule K-1, which shows that partner's share of each separately stated item. The following sections present the most common separately stated items.

Income Items

Rental income, interest, dividends, royalties, and gains (losses) from the sale of capital assets or business properties (Section 1231 assets) are separately stated on Schedules K and K-1. In addition, a partnership Form 1065, Schedule D, lists any current long-term or short-term capital gains (losses) of the partnership. The partnership files a Form 4797 to report any gains (losses) on business properties. Partners add each separately stated item on Schedule K-1 to other similar items they have personally. They report these items in total on their individual tax returns. Their shares of partnership capital gains (losses) appear on each partner's own Form 1040, Schedule D. Similarly, partners report gains (losses) from partnership business properties with other such personal business gains (losses) on their own Forms 4797.

Even though state and municipal bond interest is exempt from federal income taxes, it is a separately stated item. The interest may be subject to state income tax, depending on the partner's state of residence. Also, an individual partner must report this income on the Form 1040 for use in the computation of the taxability of social security benefits.

Deduction Items

Relatively few deductions are separately stated on Schedules K and K-1. The partnership deducts most expenses in the computation of ordinary income. The three most common separately stated deductions include Section 179 expense, deductions related to portfolio (investment) income, and charitable contributions. Section 179 provides a special option that allows the immediate expensing of assets purchased in the current year. The partnership decides whether or not to take the Section 179 deduction. Limitations apply to this deduction. These limitations apply at both the partnership level and again at the partner level. Thus, the partners add their distributive shares of this deduction to the amounts they have available from personal businesses in determining their own Section 179 deductions. Individual taxpayers deduct investment interest expense to the extent of their net investment income. Net investment income equals investment income less deductible investment expenses. Individual taxpayers deduct investment expenses as an itemized deduction on Form 1040, Schedule A. Any partnership item affecting this computation must be separately stated. Charitable contributions do not qualify as business expenses. Therefore, the partnership does not claim them as a deduction in computing ordinary income. Instead, the partnership lists the total amount of charitable contributions on Schedule K. Individual partners add their shares of each contribution to their personal contributions and list the totals as itemized deductions on Form 1040, Schedule A, of their tax returns.

Net Operating Losses (NOLs)

A net operating loss (NOL) generally equals the excess of allowable deductions over taxable gross income in any tax year. A NOL from a trade or business may be carried back to the 2 preceding tax years and forward to the 20 succeeding years. A partnership, however, does not carry over its losses to other partnership tax years. Instead, the partners report their shares of the partnership's losses on their individual returns as deductions for AGI. The partnership allocates income and losses to partners only for that portion of the year that the partner is a member of the partnership. Partners cannot be allocated losses for the period before they joined the partnership.

Also, partners may deduct losses only to the extent of the bases of (investment in) their interests in the partnership. These losses reduce their bases in the partnership. However, partners do not reduce their bases below zero. Any disallowed losses remain available to the partners in future years when their bases increase so as to absorb some or all of the loss.

EXAMPLE 5

Janet Monroe has a 40% partnership interest with a basis of $16,000 at the beginning of 20x1. The partnership has an ordinary loss of $60,000 in 20x1. Monroe's share of the loss would be $24,000 ($60,000 × 40%). However, she deducts only $16,000 (equal to her investment) which reduces her basis in the partnership to zero. The $8,000 ($24,000 − $16,000) of the loss not deductible in 20x1 carries forward to offset a future positive partnership basis.

Foreign Taxes

Partnerships engaging in business activities outside the United States may pay taxes to foreign countries. Such taxes receive special treatment on the tax return of an individual and therefore are separately stated. Individual partners report their shares of these foreign taxes on their own tax returns, either as itemized deductions on Form 1040, Schedule A, or as a tax credit.

Credits

Since partnerships pay no income tax, they do not take any credits. The benefits of any credits pass through to the partners as separately stated items. The partnerships make any elections necessary to qualify for the credits. The partners claim the benefits on their personal returns to the extent they meet the limitations on the credits.

EXAMPLES OF SEPARATELY STATED ITEMS

Rental income	Section 179 deductions
Interest income	Investment expenses
Dividend income	Credits and credit recaptures
Royalty income	Self-employment earnings
Short-term capital gains (losses)	AMT adjustments and preferences
Long-term capital gains (losses)	Foreign taxes
Other investment income	Tax-exempt income
Guaranteed payments*	Nondeductible expenses
Section 1231 gains	Personal expenses paid for partners
Charitable contributions	

*Deducted in total in computing ordinary income but separately stated for each partner

Deductions Not Applicable to Partnerships

Partnerships do not include any nonbusiness deductions in the computation of ordinary income. There is no deduction for personal exemptions, the standard deduction, or personal expenses. These benefits apply solely to individuals. Personal expenses of a partner paid directly by the partnership are treated as withdrawals. They are not included in the calculation of partnership income. Withdrawals are generally treated as tax-free reductions in the partner's investment. Usually, partners only pay taxes on partnership income, not withdrawals.

TRANSACTIONS BETWEEN PARTNERSHIPS AND PARTNERS

Factors Affecting Investment (Basis)

Initially, a partner's investment in a partnership is equal to cash plus the partner's basis (investment) in any business assets contributed to a partnership. If personal-use assets are contributed, the partner's investment is the lower of: 1) basis, or 2) FMV of the assets. The partnership's investment in the assets contributed is equal to the partner's investment in the partnership.

Basis Adjustments

Partners adjust their initial basis in the partnership by the following:

1. Ordinary income (loss)
2. Separately stated items
3. Additional capital contributions to the partnership
4. Distributions (withdrawals) from the partnership
5. Partnership liabilities

Ordinary income, separately stated income, and additional contributions increase the partner's basis in the partnership. Ordinary losses, separately stated deductions or losses, and distributions reduce the partner's basis. An additional factor affecting the partner's basis is partnership liabilities. Because partners are personally liable for their share of any debts, a partner's basis increases or decreases as partnership liabilities increase or decrease. This adjustment is based on the partner's interest in the partnership. Thus, a ten percent partner increases her investment by ten percent of the partnership liabilities.

EXAMPLE 6

Jim Peabody and Mary Jones are business partners sharing profits and losses 40% and 60%, respectively. Peabody's basis in the business is $20,000 and Jones's basis is $30,000. The business incurs $10,000 of liabilities. As a result, Peabody's basis increases to $24,000 [$20,000 + ($10,000 × 40%)]. Jones's basis increases to $36,000 [$30,000 + ($10,000 × 60%)].

Partnership Distributions

Distributions to partners are generally tax free to the partners. Partners pay taxes on income, not distributions. In a distribution, partners are simply withdrawing previously taxed income from the partnership. However, distributions (withdrawals) of money or property to the partners decrease their investments in the partnership, but not below zero. Their partnership bases decrease by the adjusted basis of the property distributed. The basis of the property received by the partners is the same as it was while in the hands of the partnership. Generally, no gain or loss is recognized by either party at the time of distribution.

EXAMPLE 7

A partnership purchases stock in 20x1 for $5,000. In 20x3, the partnership distributes the stock to the partners. At this time the stock has a FMV of $23,000. A 50% partner with a partnership basis of $50,000 receives stock with a market value of $11,500. His basis in this stock is only $2,500 ($5,000 × 50%). In addition, his partnership basis is reduced to $47,500. No gain recognition for tax purposes occurs until the partner sells his stock. Upon sale, the partner's basis in computing any gain or loss is $2,500.

LIMITED LIABILITY COMPANIES AND PARTNERSHIPS

Limited liability companies (LLCs) are a popular form of business ownership. All states have laws recognizing this form of business. LLCs provide the owners with the limited personal liability of a corporation but are partnerships for tax purposes. The reason they receive partnership tax treatment is that they tend to lack the corporate characteristics of continuity of life and free transferability of interests. Form 1065, Schedule B, now recognizes limited liability companies as one of the partnership forms along with general partnerships and limited partnerships. The major advantage of the LLC form of partnership over the general and limited partnerships is the limited liability. With a general partnership, all partners become personally liable for the debts of the partnership. Even with a limited partnership, at least one general partner is personally liable. For limited partners to retain their limited liability, they cannot participate in the management of the partnership. The LLC grants personal limited liability for **all** of its owners and still allows each owner to participate in the management of the business. Thus, the LLC combines the corporate legal benefits of limited liability with the partnership tax benefits of a single level of tax.

While an LLC is a formal corporation for state legal purposes, a limited liability partnership (LLP) is a partnership for state legal and income tax purposes. Therefore, LLPs may avoid state taxes placed on corporations, such as franchise taxes. Yet the most important difference between LLCs and LLPs is in the owners' liability. LLC owners have the corporate benefit of limited liability. LLP owners, on the other hand, are liable for commercial debt and for their own malpractice and torts. However, they are not liable for the malpractice or torts of their partners. For this reason, most of the national and regional CPA firms have reorganized as LLPs. Changing from a general partnership to a LLP is not a taxable event. It is considered a continuation of the same partnership in most cases. Nevertheless, an LLP must register with the state to place the liability limitation on public record. The benefits of limited liability with the tax treatment as partnerships make LLCs and LLPs very popular business forms for doing business today.

THE NATURE OF S CORPORATIONS

When a corporation elects S corporation status, the shareholders, rather than the corporation, become the taxpayers. The shareholders include their pro rata shares of the corporate taxable income on their personal tax returns. This inclusion occurs whether or not the corporation makes cash distributions to the shareholders. The corporation files an informational return similar to a partnership's return. Hence, the conduit concept of passing through income and deductions to the owners applies to S corporations and partnerships.

Even though an S corporation generally pays no income tax, it is in all other respects a corporation under state law and must act accordingly. This means that the owners can choose the S corporation form of organization for such nontax reasons as limited liability and still have the benefit of the conduit principle for taxing income. It should be noted that some states do not recognize S corporation status in filing a corporation tax return. In such states, the corporation must file a state corporation tax return and pay a state corporation tax. A state tax must be paid even if the corporation is not required to pay a federal corporation tax.

S CORPORATION STATUS

A corporation must qualify as a "small business corporation" before it can elect S corporation status. The term **small business corporation** may seem misleading because the law provides no limit on the "size" of the corporation. Rather, the law limits the types and number of shareholders and the types of corporations that qualify for S status.

Requirements

A corporation must have the following traits to have small business corporation status.

Domestic Corporation

An S corporation must be a U.S. or U.S. territory corporation. The term *corporation* includes a joint-stock company and an association that has the traits of a corporation. Certain U.S. corporations cannot elect S corporation status. These corporations include DISCs (Domestic International Sales Corporations), financial institutions, insurance companies, and corporations using the Puerto Rico or possessions tax credit.

One Class of Stock

The corporation must have only one class of stock outstanding. One class of stock means that the outstanding shares of the corporation must have identical rights in the distribution of profits and in the liquidation of corporate assets. The articles of incorporation, state law, and binding agreements determine whether all outstanding shares have identical rights. The tax law allows differences in the voting rights within the one class of stock.

Number of Shareholders

An S corporation may have up to 100 shareholders. However, family members may elect to be treated as one shareholder in determining the number of shareholders of an S corporation. "Family" includes a common ancestor and all lineal descendants of the common ancestor as well as the spouses, or former spouses, of these individuals. Thus, the S corporation can actually have more than 100 shareholders when some of the shareholders are family members. All other shareholders are counted separately even if they own the stock jointly with someone else. Finally, when a trust holds stock in an S corporation primarily for voting power, each "non-family" beneficiary of the trust, not the trust itself, counts as a shareholder for the 100 limit.

EXAMPLE 8

John and Mary, a married couple, each own shares in an S corporation. The corporation has 100 shareholders, counting John and Mary as one shareholder under the "family" election. If John and Mary got divorced and each retained shares in the S corporation, the corporation would still have 100 shareholders. Suppose John died and his shares were put in a voting trust for his five children. Using the "family" election, the children would be treated as one shareholder, and the corporation would not lose its S corporation status.

Shareholder Type Limitation

Shareholders in an S corporation must be individuals (other than nonresident aliens), estates, and certain trusts. Partnerships and corporations cannot be shareholders. If they were allowed to be owners, the 100-shareholder limit could easily be avoided. The trusts that can be shareholders include (1) a trust owned by one individual, (2) voting trusts, and (3) a "qualified S corporation trust." A qualified S corporation trust owns stock in one or more S corporations and distributes all of its income to only one qualified individual.

S CORPORATION REQUIREMENTS

To be an S corporation, the entity must have the following traits:

1. Be a domestic corporation

2. Have only one class of stock outstanding

3. Have not more than 100 shareholders

4. Limit shareholders to individuals (other than nonresident aliens), estates, and certain trusts

Election

A corporation meeting the four requirements listed may make an S election with the consent of all shareholders. The corporation makes the election by filing Form 2553, Election by a Small Business Corporation.

Timing of Election

To have the election apply to the corporation's current tax year, the corporation files Form 2553 during the prior tax year or within the first 2½ months of the current year. The corporation must meet the requirements for S status from the beginning of the current year. It must continue meeting the requirements in order to maintain its S election. An election made after the first 2½ months applies to the following tax year. An election becomes effective only at the beginning of the corporation's calendar or fiscal tax year.

EXAMPLE 9

The shareholders elect S corporation status on March 1, 20x1, by filing Form 2553. The corporation has a calendar tax year. The election normally is effective for the calendar year beginning January 1, 20x1. The last date an election can be made for a tax year starting with the current calendar year would be March 15, 20x1. An election made on March 16 or later would not be effective until the beginning of the next calendar year.

Only existing corporations can make elections for S status. Thus, deciding when a corporation comes into existence is important. This is especially true when determining the 2½ month election period. The election period begins in the month the corporation comes into existence. A corporation exists when (1) it begins having business transactions, (2) it acquires assets, or (3) it has shareholders.

Shareholder Consent

All shareholders must consent to the S corporation election. This includes any former shareholders who owned stock in the year the election is effective but prior to the filing of Form 2553.

EXAMPLE 10

Karen Ryzek owned stock in X Corporation on January 1, 20x1. She sold the stock on February 10, 20x1. On March 1, 20x1, X Corporation shareholders elect to be an S corporation effective January 1, 20x1. In order for the election to be valid, Ryzek must consent to the election even though she's no longer a shareholder on March 1, 20x1. Ryzek's consent is necessary because she will report on her 20x1 income tax return her share of income from January 1, 20x1, to February 10, 20x1, while she owned stock in X Corporation.

A shareholder's consent is binding and may be withdrawn only by following prescribed procedures. Shareholders execute a consent by providing all of the required information on Form 2553. Shareholders may also consent by signing a separate consent statement, which should be attached to Form 2553. The separate consent should furnish the following information:

1. The name, address, and identification number of the corporation
2. The name, address, and identification number of the shareholder
3. The number of shares owned by the shareholder and the dates on which the stock was acquired
4. The day and month of the end of the shareholder's tax year

Any consent not filed on time invalidates the corporation's election of S status. Each co-owner, tenant by entirety, tenant in common, and joint tenant must consent. This means that each family member must consent even though treated as one shareholder. The legal representative or guardian may consent for a minor shareholder. The executor or administrator of an estate makes the consent for the estate. The consent of a qualified trust holding stock must be made by each person who is treated as a shareholder. Extensions of time to file a consent may be granted under certain circumstances.

Termination

An S corporation election may be terminated either voluntarily or automatically. An automatic termination occurs when the corporation ceases to meet the S corporation requirements.

Voluntary Termination

An election of S corporation status can be terminated voluntarily. Shareholders holding more than one-half of the shares must consent to end the S status. The corporation then files a statement to this effect with the IRS office where it had previously filed its election. If a timely filed revocation specifies an effective date, the revocation will be effective on that date. From that date forward, the corporation reports as a regular corporation. Thus, even though an election to become an S corporation must be effective on the first day of a tax year, a termination may be effective before the end of the regular tax year. If no specific revocation date is given, a revocation made within the first 2½ months of the corporation's tax year is retroactive to the first day of the tax year. If made after the first 2½ months, the revocation is effective on the first day of the following tax year.

Automatic Termination

S corporation status automatically terminates upon the occurrence of one of the following events:

1. The corporation fails to meet any of the requirements for being an S corporation. These requirements include the number of shareholders, type of stock, being a domestic corporation, and no shareholders other than individuals, estates, and certain trusts.
2. The corporation has passive investment income in excess of 25% of its gross receipts for three consecutive years. This applies only if a corporation has accumulated earnings and profits (AEP) carried over from when it was a regular C corporation. Thus, if the corporation was always an S, passive income cannot trigger termination.

The election terminates as of the date on which the disqualifying event occurs. As a result, the day preceding termination is the last day for the S corporation, and the day of termination becomes the first day of C Corporation status. However, if the election terminates because of excessive passive income, termination is effective beginning with the following tax year.

EXAMPLE 11

Assume an S corporation has been operating on a calendar year basis for several years with 100 shareholders. On July 21, 20x1, one of the shareholders dies, with his 100 shares passing equally to his wife and brother on that date. The status as an S corporation automatically terminates on July 21, 20x1, because of the addition of the 101st shareholder. The S corporation must file a return for the period January 1, 20x1, through July 20, 20x1. On July 21, 20x1, the corporation becomes a C corporation for the remainder of the year ending December 31, 20x1. All income (loss) and separately stated items are prorated between the S corporation tax return and the C corporation tax return on a daily basis.

Reelection

Generally, if an election terminates (either voluntarily or automatically), the corporation may not reelect S status for five years. However, the IRS may allow an earlier election when violations of the S corporation requirements were minor. If the S corporation election was inadvertently terminated, the IRS may even waive termination when the corporation makes a timely correction of the violation.

S CORPORATION RETURNS

An S corporation files an annual informational tax return, Form 1120S, U.S. Income Tax Return for an S Corporation. It is due on the fifteenth day of the third month after the end of the corporation's tax year. For a calendar year corporation, the return is due March 15. An S corporation receives an automatic six-month extension of time to file when it submits a Form 7004, Application for Automatic Extension of Time To File Corporation Income Tax Return. The Form 7004 must be filed by the due date for the original return.

The character of all items of income, deductions, losses, and credits passes through from the corporation to the shareholders in a manner similar to partnerships. The shareholders receive a Form 1120S, Schedule K-1, that reports their shares of the ordinary income and each separately stated item. The law requires companies to furnish this information to owners no later than the filing date for Form 1120S. The S corporation receives a penalty of $50 for each Schedule K-1 not provided to its shareholders in a timely manner.

Tax Year

Like partnerships, S corporations must have the same tax year as the shareholders owning more than 50% of the stock. This is generally a calendar year. Exceptions may apply to this general requirement, however.

One exception involves the natural business year. As described previously in the partnership discussion, in a natural business year 25% of gross receipts are received in the last two months of the fiscal year. Another tax year exception comes under Section 444, which allows an S corporation to elect a tax year that provides no more than a three-month deferral for its shareholders. This same election is available to partnerships. The tax year rules prevent shareholders from deferring S corporation income into a future tax year. The taxation of income could be deferred if rules permitted shareholders to select an S corporation tax year that ended after the shareholders' year ended. This is because S corporation income is included in the shareholder's tax return in the year in which the S corporation's tax year ends.

Shareholders of an S corporation have calendar tax years. If allowed, they would prefer the S corporation to have a January 31 year end. This means that the income earned from February 1, 20x1, to January 31, 20x2, would be taxable on the shareholders' 20x2 tax returns. This confers an 11-month deferral of income taxes. The law, however, requires S corporations have a calendar year end unless they can meet requirements for one of the exceptions to the tax year rule.

Reporting Income and Deductions

To file a Form 1120S, the S corporation must divide its tax items into two categories: (1) separately stated items and (2) ordinary items. The ordinary items not separately stated combine and result in ordinary income or loss. The separately stated items and ordinary income (loss) are collectively known as the pass-through items. These items pass to the shareholders who report them on their personal tax returns.

Separately Stated Items

Separately stated items are income, deductions, and credits that have the possibility of affecting shareholders' personal tax liabilities differently. The most common separately stated items for S corporations are the same as the items separately stated for partnerships. These separately stated items appear on Form 1120S, Schedule K, Shareholders' Share of Income, Credits, Deductions, Etc. The Schedule K-1 provides each shareholder's portion of ordinary income and separately stated items. A copy of each shareholder's Schedule K-1 is attached to the S corporation's Form 1120S. A copy is also given to the shareholder. The shareholders include taxable items from their Schedules K-1 on their personal tax returns.

EXAMPLES OF SEPARATELY STATED ITEMS

- Charitable contributions
- Tax-exempt income and nondeductible expenses
- Foreign taxes
- Investment expenses
- Personal expenses paid for shareholder's benefit
- Net income (loss) from rental real estate activities

- Capital gains (losses)
- Investment income (loss)
- Section 179 expenses deduction
- Section 1231 gains (losses)
- Tax credits
- Tax preferences and adjustments related to the AMT

Ordinary Income or Loss

Ordinary income (loss) is generally the net result of the S corporation's trade or business activities. Its computation includes all items of income or deductions that are not separately stated. These tend to be the same items used in determining partnership ordinary income and sole proprietorship income. The resulting amount of ordinary income (loss) passes through to the shareholders along with the separately stated items on the Schedule K-1. The ordinary income (loss) appears on the shareholder's Form 1040, Schedule E.

In partnerships, limited liability companies, and sole proprietorships, FICA taxes apply to all ordinary income passing to the owners who pay the self-employment taxes. However, in S corporations, FICA taxes apply only to designated salaries, and the corporation is responsible for paying the taxes. No FICA taxes are paid on the remaining ordinary income which passes to the owners.

Deductions Not Allowed

Like partnerships, certain individual deductions are not available to S corporations, such as the standard deduction, personal itemized deductions, and personal exemptions. S corporations also cannot take certain deductions available to regular taxable C corporations. The most notable of these deductions is the dividend received deduction of 70%, 80%, or 100% available to taxable corporations.

Allocation of Tax Items to Shareholders

A shareholder's portion of S corporation income, deductions, losses, and credits is determined on a per-share-per-day basis. The S corporation allocates an equal amount of each item to each share on a per-day basis for the corporation's tax year. The per-share-per-day amount is multiplied by the number of shares the shareholder owned each day of the year. The shareholders' personal tax returns include their allocated yearly totals for each of the S corporation tax items. This allocation concept also applies to partnerships.

EXAMPLE 13

An S corporation is owned equally by Adam Smith, Tom Jones, and James Brown on November 1, 20x1, the first day of a new fiscal year. Brown sells his shares to Shirley Black on August 8, 20x2. The corporation's fiscal year ends on October 31, 20x2. Thus, Brown held the shares for 281 days (76.99% of the year), and Black owned the shares for 84 days (23.01% of the year). Brown is considered to own the shares from November 1, 20x1, through August 8, 20x2. The corporation earns $150,000 of ordinary taxable income and $90,000 of long-term capital gains during its fiscal year ending October 31, 20x2.

On the basis of these facts, the shareholders report on their calendar year 20x2 tax returns the following S corporation income:

	Ordinary Income	*Capital Gains*
Adam Smith	$ 50,000	$30,000
Tom Jones	50,000	30,000
James Brown (76.99%)	38,495	23,097
Shirley Black (23.01%)	11,505	6,903
Totals	$150,000	$90,000

Utilizing Losses

Partnerships and S corporations both operate under the conduit principle (income and separately stated items pass through to the owners). Because the conduit principle applies, one might think that the utilization of operating losses by S corporation shareholders would be similar to that of partners. Both S corporation shareholders and partners may deduct losses only to the extent of their ownership basis. The losses cannot reduce the basis below zero. However, losses available to partners and S shareholders differ because the computation of basis is not the same for the two entities. Partners' basis includes their proportionate share of all partnership liabilities. On the other hand, a liability increases an S corporation shareholder's basis only if a loan is made directly by the shareholder to the corporation. The S corporation's liabilities are not part of the S shareholder's basis because of the limited liability feature of the corporate status. Thus, a partner generally has a larger basis for utilizing operating losses than would an S shareholder.

EXAMPLE 14

Swift, an S corporation, has five shareholders, each owning 100 shares of stock. They each materially participate in Swift. Each shareholder has a stock basis of $25,000. For 20x1 Swift reports an operating loss of $75,000. Each shareholder's portion of the loss ($15,000) is deductible on the shareholder's individual tax return because it does not reduce any shareholder's basis below zero. After the $15,000 loss, each shareholder's basis in Swift is $10,000 ($25,000 – $15,000).

Remember that losses deductible by each S shareholder cannot reduce the shareholder's ownership basis below zero. Further, they must meet the at-risk and passive loss requirements (Chapter 9). Disallowed losses carry forward and are deductible when the shareholder has sufficient basis to cover the losses.

EXAMPLE 15

Su Lin Chang owns a 30% interest in Inco, an S corporation. At the end of 20x1, she has a basis in Inco stock of $15,000 and a basis in loans made to Inco of $12,000. Inco reports an operating loss for 20x1 of $120,000, of which Chang's share is $36,000. She deducts $27,000 of the total loss ($15,000 stock basis + $12,000 loan basis) on her personal tax return. The remaining loss of $9,000 ($36,000 – $27,000) carries over to 20x2 and later years to be offset against future positive ownership basis.

When the lack of basis limits the deductibility of losses, an allocation is necessary. A pro rata share of the ordinary loss and each separately stated loss item appears on the shareholder's tax return. The pro rata percentage equals the shareholder's basis divided by the shareholder's portion of losses for the year. The portion of each item disallowed carries forward.

EXAMPLE 16

Jerry Garcia has a $20,000 basis in his 40% equity interest in an S corporation. Garcia's K-1 indicates that his share of the corporation's ordinary loss is $24,000 and his share of capital losses is $8,000. Garcia can deduct $20,000 of losses (an amount equal to his basis). The specific ordinary loss deducted on Garcia's tax return is $15,000 ($24,000 × $20,000 ÷ $32,000). In computing his personal net capital gain (loss), Garcia includes $5,000 of capital loss ($8,000 × $20,000 ÷ $32,000). Garcia carries forward to future years a total loss of $12,000. The carryover loss consists of an ordinary loss deduction of $9,000 and a capital loss deduction of $3,000.

When an S corporation election terminates, any disallowed loss can be taken if the shareholders restore their stock basis sufficiently to cover their losses. The basis must be restored by a specific date. The mandatory date is the *later* of the following:

1. One year after the effective date of termination or the due date of the last S corporation tax return, whichever is later, or

    2. 120 days after a determination that the corporation's election had terminated for a previous year

TRANSACTIONS BETWEEN S CORPORATIONS AND SHAREHOLDERS

Shareholders' Investment (Basis) in Stock

Shareholders compute their initial basis in S corporation stock using the same rules as for regular C corporation formation. If the requirements are met, their basis in the assets contributed to the corporation becomes the basis of their investment (stock) in the corporation. Thus, shareholders can avoid the taxation of gains or losses on forming an S corporation. Partners receive similar treatment when they transfer property to the partnership. When shareholders purchase their shares, their basis in the stock is its cost.

    Shareholders adjust their initial basis in S corporation stock by the following:

1. Ordinary income (loss)
2. Separately stated items
3. Additional contributions to the S corporation
4. Distributions from the S corporation

    Ordinary income, separately stated income, and additional contributions increase the shareholder's basis in the stock, whereas ordinary loss, separately stated deductions or losses, and distributions reduce the shareholder's basis. Corporate liabilities are generally not a factor affecting basis unless the shareholder personally loans money to the company.

EXAMPLE 17

Jody Ryan acquires 100 shares of S corporation stock at the beginning of the corporation's 20x1 calendar tax year at a cost of $7,500. Her share of income and separately stated items of the S corporation are regular income, $1,500; long-term capital gains, $300; and cash distributions received, $1,000. Ryan's basis in her stock on December 31, 20x1, is $8,300, calculated as follows:

Purchase cost of S shares	$7,500
Add:	
Share of regular income	1,500
Share of capital gains	300
Less distributions received	(1,000)
Ryan's basis at December 31, 20x1	$8,300

    When S corporation shareholders sell stock, the taxable gain or loss cannot be determined until after the end of the corporation's tax year. The shareholders who sell shares must adjust their stock bases by their portion of the S corporation's income, deductions, and separately stated items. This information will not be known until after the S corporation's year end. The unknown effect at the time of sale can be lessened if the seller and the buyer agree to an adjustment of the selling price based on the year-end profit or loss results. As an alternative, the affected shareholders can agree to divide the tax year into two parts for accounting purposes. One part would be from the beginning of the year through the day of sale; the second part would be the remainder of the year. This agreement limits the income or loss of the selling shareholder to the corporation's results up to the date of sale. The stockholders who remain will share income or losses occurring after the date of sale. Even though the tax year is split into two parts for shareholder income (loss) computations, the corporation files only one return for the year.

Distributions to Shareholders

Distributions from S corporations formed after 1983 are generally tax free to the shareholder. The distributions reduce the shareholder's basis in the stock, but not below zero. If the distributions exceed the shareholder's stock basis, the excess is treated as a capital gain.

The S corporation keeps track of all its taxable income and losses in a special account called the **accumulated adjustments account,** or **AAA.** The account can have a positive or negative balance, depending on the income and losses it has sustained. Distributions to shareholders reduce the AAA balance. However, distributions themselves cannot reduce the balance below zero. The distributions from AAA can be thought of as disbursing income that has already been taxed on the shareholders' personal returns. When an S election terminates, shareholders can still receive distributions tax free. The payments cannot exceed the balance of AAA and must be made within an acceptable period (about one year after termination).

EXAMPLE 18

JL corporation, formed on January 1, 20x1, elected S corporation status. Shareholders Jill Jaffy and Lisa Laker each invested $30,000, and each received 50% of the stock. JL's taxable income for 20x1 was $20,000, all ordinary income. The shareholders each received $12,000 in cash distributions during 20x1, a total distribution of $24,000.

In 20x1, Jill and Lisa each report $10,000 of income on their individual income tax returns. The $12,000 distribution to each shareholder is tax free. The basis of the stock to each shareholder at the end of 20x1 is $28,000 ($30,000 + $10,000 − $12,000). The balance in the AAA account is zero ($20,000 income − $20,000 distribution). The distribution cannot reduce AAA below zero.

Distributions from an S corporation that was previously a regular C corporation may be taxable. This occurs when an S corporation has earnings and profits (E&P) carried over from C corporation years. Distributions are first payments out of AAA and not taxable. They reduce the shareholder's basis in the stock. To the extent that the distributions exceed AAA, they are payments out of E&P and taxable as dividends. The shareholders do not reduce their stock basis for these taxable distributions. Any distributions in excess of AAA and E&P are not taxable as long as they do not exceed the shareholder's remaining basis in the stock. Such distributions, however, reduce the shareholder's basis in the stock.

EXAMPLE 19

GY Corporation was a regular corporation until 20x1, when an S election was made. GY carried over $5,000 of E&P from its C corporation years. In 20x1 GY has $16,000 of ordinary income. It distributes $30,000 to its sole shareholder, Gary Gemberling, who has a stock basis of $40,000. The first $16,000 of distributions are out of AAA and not taxable. Gemberling reduces his stock basis by $16,000. The next $5,000 is from E&P and is taxable. No stock basis reduction is made for the $5,000. The last $9,000 of distribution is not taxable. Gemberling reduces his stock basis by the nontaxable distributions, and his ending stock basis is $15,000 ($40,000 − $16,000 − $9,000).

S corporations can elect to have distributions come from E&P first, thus bypassing AAA. The election requires the consent of all shareholders and is irrevocable. The reason S corporations make this election is to remove all prior C corporation E&P at a time when its shareholders can most afford the income. Further, corporations benefit from the election by removing the possibility of being subject to a special tax on excess passive income (details are beyond the scope of this book).

Distributions of Property

Distributions to shareholders may be in cash or property. The FMV of property determines the amount of the distribution. This is the amount by which the AAA balance and the shareholder's stock basis are reduced. The shareholder's basis in the property is its FMV. If an S corporation distributes appreciated property to shareholders, the corporation recognizes gain. The amount of gain recognized is the same as if the property had been sold to the shareholders at the FMV. The gain then passes through to the shareholders. However, the S corporation does not recognize a loss when the FMV of the property distributed is less than its corporate basis. The shareholder's basis in the property is its FMV, and the stock basis is reduced by this amount. Since neither the corporation nor the shareholder recognizes the loss, S corporations should not distribute properties that have declined in value.

EXAMPLE 20

Freda Moon receives a distribution of property from the Flint S Corporation. Moon is the sole shareholder, with a basis in her stock of $75,000. The property she receives has a FMV of $30,000, and Flint's basis in it is $50,000. Moon's basis in the property is $30,000, and she reduces her basis in her Flint stock to $45,000 ($75,000 − $30,000). Flint does not recognize the $20,000 loss ($50,000 − $30,000) and reduces its AAA by $30,000.

THE NATURE OF C CORPORATIONS

Usually, a business organized as a corporation qualifies as a separate tax entity and pays tax on corporate income. However, determination of whether an organization is a corporation for federal tax purposes does not depend strictly on whether the entity is legally a corporation under state law. Rather, the decision is based on the number of tax-defined corporate traits the entity possesses. The law generally taxes a business as a corporation if it has these traits:

1. Business associates
2. A purpose to carry on a business and divide the profits
3. Continuity of life
4. Centralized management
5. Limited liability
6. Free transferability of ownership interests

The first two traits help distinguish a corporation from an estate or trust. Since partnerships and corporations have these first two traits in common, the IRS and the courts focus on the last four to distinguish the entities. The regulations state that entities with more than two of the last four traits are corporations for tax purposes.

Forming a Corporation

Individuals setting up a corporation transfer either cash, property, or services to the corporation in exchange for its stock. Those purchasing the stock have an investment (basis) in the stock equal to the cash paid. However, when people transfer property to the corporation for its stock, it is treated as a type of nontaxable exchange (Chapter 10). No gain or loss is recognized, and the basis of the stock is usually the basis of the property transferred. Additionally, the basis of the property acquired by the corporation is normally the same as that of the transferor. An exception applies if personal-use property is transferred to the corporation. Here, the basis of the investment (stock received) and the property transferred is equal to the lesser of 1) the taxpayer's basis in the property, or 2) the property's FMV at the time of the transfer. This exception also applies to transfers of property to a partnership and an S corporation.

When people perform services in exchange for the corporation's stock, they recognize income equal to the FMV of the stock received. FMV also becomes the basis of their investment (stock) in the company. This same rule regarding income recognition when services are rendered in exchange for an ownership interest also applies to partnerships and to S corporations.

EXAMPLE 21

Cara Bernardi and several business associates decide to set up a corporation. Bernardi transfers the assets of her proprietorship to the new corporation in exchange for 100,000 shares of stock. Bernardi's basis in the assets transferred is $250,000. Her basis in the stock received is $250,000 ($2.50 per share). The basis of the assets to the corporation is also $250,000.

CORPORATE TAX RETURNS AND TAX RATES

Every C corporation must file a tax return, regardless of the amount of its taxable income or loss. Once the corporation computes its taxable income, it applies the appropriate corporate tax rate. Both individual and corporate tax rates are **progressive** (the rates increase as taxable income increases). However, the corporate tax brackets are not indexed for inflation as are the individual tax brackets. The next sections describe the corporate tax return and its tax rates.

Corporate Tax Return

Most C corporations use Form 1120, U.S. Corporation Income Tax Return, to report their taxable income (loss). Under certain conditions, they file Form 1120-A, U.S. Corporation Short-Form Income Tax Return. While Form 1120 has four pages, simplified Form 1120-A has two. Form 1120-A is for small corporations with gross receipts and total assets each under $500,000. Special rules apply to returns for partial years, corporations with no transactions, and bankrupt corporations.

Period Covered by Return

Corporations generally use a 12-month year for tax reporting. Unlike individuals, partnerships, or S corporations, regular C corporations may choose to use a calendar year or a fiscal year. One fiscal year option is a year that starts on the first day of a month and ends 12 months later on the last day of the month. Corporations often use July 1 to June 30 as a fiscal year.

Another fiscal year option that corporations may choose is the 52–53 week year. Corporations select this tax year when they want their tax year to end on the same day of the week each year. The day may be either the last one occurring in the last month of their tax year or the one occurring closest to their normal year end.

Corporations can have a tax year shorter than 12 months in three situations. Newly formed corporations may have a short year for their first taxable year. For example, if a corporation desires a September 30 year end and begins operations on May 16, its first tax year is from May 16 to September 30. This same situation can occur when a corporation ceases doing business and dissolves. Finally, when a corporation changes its tax year, it files a short-period return. This return covers the period between the close of its last year and the start of its new year. Corporations must get permission from the IRS to change their accounting period. They file their change request on Form 1128, Application to Adopt, Change, or Retain a Tax Year.

Due Date

The due date for most corporate returns falls on the fifteenth of the third month after the corporation's year ends. This date also applies to foreign corporations with a U.S. place of business. Other foreign corporations file their returns by the fifteenth day of the sixth month. When a due date falls on a Saturday, Sunday, or holiday, the due date becomes the next business day.

Corporate Tax Rates

Like the rate structure for individual taxpayers, the one for corporations is progressive. At higher income levels, benefits from the low rates phase out. Once the phase-out stops, the rates stay **flat** (same rate for all taxable income). Other than professional service corporations (described later), all regular C corporations compute their tax using the same rate structure, as follows:

Taxable Income	Corporate Tax Rate
$0–50,000	15.0%
$50,001–75,000	25.0
$75,001–100,000	34.0
$100,001–335,000	39.0
$335,001–10,000,000	34.0
$10,000,001–15,000,000	35.0
$15,000,001–18,333,333	38.0
Over $18,333,333	35.0

Rate Structure and Tax Calculation

The tax rate structure contains two phase-out ranges and two phase-out rates. Before and after the first phase-out, the marginal tax rate equals 34%. The marginal tax rate before and after the second phase-out equals 35%. For corporations with taxable income below $75,000, Congress set the rates low (15% and 25%) to stimulate growth. The Code phases out the benefits of the low rates by a 5% additional tax on taxable income between $100,000 and $335,000 (39% rather than 34%). When taxable income reaches $335,000, the government has recovered all low-rate benefits. The amount of these benefits equals $11,750 {[(34% − 15%) × $50,000] + [(34% − 25%) × $25,000]} or [($335,000 − $100,000) × 5%]. The tax rate is then a flat 34% for incomes up to $10 million.

EXAMPLE 22

XYZ corporation, a calendar year corporation, has taxable income of $900,000. The computations for XYZ's income tax of $306,000 follow. Notice that XYZ's tax equals a flat rate of 34% (34% × $900,000 = $306,000).

Income Tax

15% × $50,000	$ 7,500
25% × $25,000	6,250
34% × $25,000	8,500
39% × $235,000	91,650
34% × $565,000	192,100
Income tax	$306,000

A similar phase-out takes place for corporations whose taxable income exceeds $15,000,000. This phase-out eliminates the 1% lower tax benefit (35% − 34%) on incomes below $10 million ($10,000,000 × 1% = $100,000 benefit). Between $15,000,000 and $18,333,333, the Code increases the 35% rate by 3 percentage points. This rate increase produces additional revenues of $100,000 (3% × $3,333,333 = $99,999.99, rounded to $100,000). For taxable incomes in excess of $18,333,333, corporations have a flat rate of 35%.

Personal Service Corporations

Personal service corporations (PSC) are corporations whose shareholders and employees provide professional services for a fee. Doctors, dentists, lawyers, architects, accountants, and others organize as PSCs. Such corporations provide the owners with several tax and nontax benefits. However, these corporations have some tax restrictions. PSCs generally may only use a calendar year as their tax year. This limits any benefits of income deferral. If they use other than a calendar year, the PSCs must make sure that the amount of salaries paid to shareholder-employees in the deferral period is consistent with the salaries paid in the nondeferral periods. Another limitation on PSCs is the tax rate they use for computing tax liability. PSCs have a flat tax rate of 35% on all taxable income. The purpose of this high tax rate on all income is to encourage the PSC to pay out its net earnings to its shareholder-employees as salaries. These salaries are then taxed at the individual tax rates.

CORPORATE TAXABLE INCOME

Corporations compute their taxable income as individuals compute their business profit or loss (Chapter 7). Most of the rules governing income and business deductions apply to both individuals and corporations. The major difference between corporations and individuals concerns the treatment of nonbusiness deductions. Whereas individuals deduct personal expenditures as itemized deductions, corporations have no personal expenses. Thus, corporations do not use the concept of adjusted gross income (AGI) because they have no deductions from AGI (itemized deductions) and no personal or dependency exemptions. Further, corporations have different limitations on capital losses and charitable contributions. They also get a deduction based on the dividends they collect that individuals do not receive. These latter differences are covered in more detail later in this chapter.

Accounting Methods

A corporation must select an accounting method for determining its taxable income. Most corporations use the accrual method of accounting. With the **accrual method,** corporations report income when it is earned even though they may not have received it in cash. Also, they deduct expenses when they are incurred though they may remain unpaid at the end of the tax year.

Besides the accrual method, the other accounting options available to certain corporations are the cash and hybrid methods. With the **cash method,** income is taxable when received, and expenses are deductible when paid. The **hybrid method** combines cash and accrual methods. Here, the corporation uses the accrual method for computing gross profit from the sale of inventory and the cash method for other income and deductions.

The kinds of corporations permitted to use the cash method are limited. Farming and personal service corporations may use the cash method. All other corporations must have average gross receipts for the last three years of no more than $5 million. Even for these corporations, the law requires use of the accrual method for computing the gross profit from the sale of inventory.

Corporate Taxable Income Formula

Corporations compute their taxable income as gross income less business expenses. However, some specific deductions require special computations and therefore cannot be grouped with other business expenses. These include (1) charitable contribution deduction (CC), (2) dividends received deduction (DRD), (3) net operating loss (NOL) carrybacks, and (4) short-term capital loss carrybacks. Following is the formula for computing corporate taxable income:

Gross income
- Deductions (except CC, DRD, NOL carryback, STCL carryback)
= Taxable income for figuring CC
- Charitable contribution (CC) deduction
= Taxable income for figuring DRD
- Dividends received deduction (DRD)
= Taxable income before carrybacks
- NOL carryback
- Short-term capital loss (STCL) carryback
= Taxable income

Income Items

Typically, the same Code provisions determine the tax status of income items for individual taxpayers (Chapters 3 and 4) and corporations. However, in some cases additional provisions apply.

Gross Profit from Sales

Net sales less cost of goods sold equals **gross profit from sales.** Gross sales less returns and allowances equals **net sales.** Corporations can deduct *sales discounts* directly from sales or treat them as a business expense. Corporate inventories usually make a material contribution to income. These inventories can include raw materials, supplies, work in process, and finished goods. Corporations that produce goods for sale include all production costs in inventories. These costs include direct materials, direct labor, and direct and indirect overhead. The term for this process is **full costing.**

To compute **cost of goods sold,** a corporation adds beginning inventories, labor, and overhead. Then, it subtracts ending inventories. An example follows:

Globe Manufacturing Company
Cost of Goods Sold Computations

Beginning inventories	$100,956
Add:	
Purchases	207,858
Labor	74,807
Other costs	30,529
Total	$414,150
Less ending inventories	(90,283)
Cost of goods sold	$323,867

Capital Gains and Losses

Corporations report the sale of capital assets on Schedule D (Form 1120). Unlike individuals, corporations receive no special tax rate treatment of capital gains. They must include the full amount of capital gains in their regular taxable income. However, corporations must record capital gains separately from other income because capital losses can be deducted only from capital gains. They cannot offset any ordinary income as individuals' capital losses can. Any capital losses in excess of capital gains for the year are carried back three years or forward five years. They may offset capital gains only in the carryover years. The corporation treats all carryovers as short-term capital losses. First, the corporation uses capital losses arising in the carryover year, then it uses the carryover capital losses. If it has carry over losses from more than one year, the losses are used on a first-created-first-used basis. If it does not use the losses within the carryover years, the corporation loses the tax benefit of the losses.

Business Deductions

Many corporate deductions are the same as those taken by proprietors (Chapter 7) and partnerships to arrive at their profit or loss. However, within any one deduction group, differences can exist.

Compensation

Corporations deduct payments for personal services as compensation when they pass three tests: (1) the payments represent an ordinary and necessary expense of the business, (2) the payments represent a reasonable amount for services received, and (3) the corporation pays or accrues them in the current tax year under its accounting method. In addition, for publicly held corporations, a special rule limits the deduction for corporate salaries paid to the CEO and the other four most highly paid officers. Generally, the rule limits the compensation deduction for each of these officers to not more than $1 million. However, all compensation paid to an officer is taxable, even though some of it is not deductible.

Bad Debts

Most taxpayers, including corporations, can use only the direct write-off method for bad debts. An exception exists for certain financial institutions. These organizations use the reserve method of accounting (allowance for doubtful accounts).

Organizational Costs

Corporations can elect to permanently capitalize organizational costs or they can elect to amortize these costs over a period of time. The corporation makes an election to amortize by attaching a statement to the corporation's first tax return.

When amortizing, the organizational costs must be amortized over a period of not less than 60 months. The amortization period begins in the month when the corporation begins business. The date a business begins is not always easy to determine. Generally, a corporation begins business when it starts its business operations or purchases operating assets.

The expenses qualifying as organizational costs include any costs related to the creation of the corporation chargeable to a capital account. They must be incurred within the first year of the corporation's operations. These costs include (1) legal expenses for setting up the corporation, (2) state costs of incorporation, (3) necessary accounting services, (4) expenses of temporary directors, and (5) costs of organizational meetings. Organizational expenditures do not include the costs of issuing or selling stocks or other securities or costs associated with transferring assets to the corporation. These latter costs simply reduce the amount of paid-in capital.

Passive Losses

The passive loss limitations (Chapter 9) do not apply to most corporations. Thus, corporations can use passive losses to reduce active or portfolio income. However, closely-held corporations (over 50% owned by 5 or fewer individuals) and personal service corporations (PSCs) are subject to the passive loss limitations.

Special Deductions

The deductions for corporations, for the most part, are treated the same as business deductions for other entities. Nevertheless, some special deductions for corporations receive distinctive treatment. In reviewing the formula for computing taxable income, these special deductions are listed separately. The following paragraphs describe each of these special deductions.

Charitable Contributions

Like individuals, corporations can take a deduction for contributions to charitable organizations. However, the corporate deduction has an upper limit equal to 10% of the corporation's taxable income before certain items. These items include any deductions for charitable contributions, dividend received deductions, NOL carrybacks, and capital loss carrybacks (see taxable income formula).

Ordinarily, a corporation deducts a contribution in the year it transfers property or cash to a charity. A corporation using the accrual method of accounting, however, can choose to deduct a contribution in the year it makes the accrual. To take the deduction in the accrual year, the corporation must pay the contribution within 2½ months after its year ends.

Sometimes, a corporation donates appreciated property to a public charity. The corporation figures the amount of the contribution in the same manner as individuals (Chapter 5).

Dividend Received Deduction

Corporations get a deduction for a certain amount of the dividends they receive. The deduction lessens or avoids triple taxation of the gains of corporations. Triple taxation occurs when a corporation distributes its after-tax profits to corporate shareholders. These corporate shareholders then pay taxes on the dividends before they distribute the proceeds to their shareholders who also pay taxes on the dividends received. The amount of the dividends received deduction (DRD) depends on the corporation's percentage of stock ownership in the dividend-paying corporation.

Percentage Owned	DRD Percentage
Less than 20%	70%
From 20% to less than 80%	80%
From 80% to 100%	100%

EXAMPLE 23

Delta Corporation owns 60% of the total value and outstanding shares of Epsilon Corporation. Epsilon makes a dividend distribution to Delta of $100,000. Delta includes the $100,000 of dividends in income and takes a $80,000 DRD. Thus, the net amount of dividends taxed to Delta is $20,000 ($100,000 – $80,000).

Net Operating Loss (NOL)

When a corporation's deductions exceed its income, the corporation may suffer a net loss for the year. A corporation need make only one adjustment to its taxable income in determining its NOL for the current year. It must add back any NOL carryovers from prior years. Like individuals, corporations carry their NOLs back 2 years and forward 20 (back 3, forward 15 for tax years starting before August 6, 1997). They have the option of not carrying back and just carrying forward the NOL. The carryover provisions reduce the hardship of the 12-month accounting period for those businesses with longer business cycles. It also allows corporations to offset profitable years with unprofitable ones.

Credits

Like individuals, corporations may offset their tax liabilities with available tax credits. Most of the credits available to corporations are also available to other businesses (see Chapter 12). However, corporations cannot use the personal tax credits available to individuals, such as the earned income credit, credit for the elderly, and the child and dependent care credit.

Special Taxes

Besides the regular income tax, corporations may be subject to the accumulated earnings tax (AET), the personal holding company (PHC) tax, and the alternative minimum tax (AMT). The AET and PHC tax are penalty taxes on undistributed earnings. The AMT, on the other hand, is an alternative method of computing taxable income and income taxes. Careful tax planning can eliminate the need to pay these additional taxes. Discussion of these taxes is beyond the scope of this book.

Tax Payments

The IRS has a pay-as-you-go system for corporations. Under this plan, all corporations with an expected tax liability of $500 or more must make estimated tax payments. A corporation computes its estimated payments on Form 1120-W (Worksheet), Corporation Estimated Tax. These payments are due in equal quarterly installments by the following dates:

Date	Percentage of Estimated Tax Due
Fifteenth of fourth month	25%
Fifteenth of sixth month	25%
Fifteenth of ninth month	25%
Fifteenth of twelfth month	25%

For calendar year corporations, the payment dates are normally April 15, June 15, September 15, and December 15. If one of the above dates falls on a weekend or a holiday, the due date becomes the next business day.

The expectation of a $500 tax liability, however, may not materialize until late in the tax year. When this occurs, the law requires proportional payments of the estimated tax over the remaining payment dates. The full amount of any unpaid tax becomes due 2½ months after the end of the tax year (due date of tax return without extensions). Note that corporations must include the effect of the alternative minimum tax (AMT) in their quarterly payments. This complexity may force corporations subject to the AMT to overpay their quarterly taxes to avoid underpayment penalties.

Federal Tax Deposit System

The IRS requires that corporations make estimated tax payments to specified depositories. Form 8109, Federal Tax Deposit Coupon, must accompany the payment. This deposit system applies to estimated tax payments and to actual income tax return payments. To be considered timely, a mailed deposit must be postmarked at least two days before the deposit due date.

Penalty for Underpayment of Estimated Tax: Small Corporations

Failure to pay the minimum amount due at each installment date causes an underpayment penalty. The IRS considers the estimated tax underpaid if payments total less than 100% of the amount due at each payment date. The 100% test applies to the actual tax liability of small corporations for the year prorated over the required payment dates.

Avoiding the Underpayment Penalty

Small corporations may avoid the penalty for underpayment of estimated taxes by making payments equal to the lesser of (1) 100% of the tax shown on the current year's return or (2) 100% of the tax for the preceding year. Corporations use Form 2220, Underpayment of Estimated Tax by Corporations, to determine if an underpayment of taxes occurred. This form also provides for the calculation of any underpayment penalties.

Estimated Payment Requirements: Large Corporations

Large corporations must make estimated tax payments of 100% of the current year's tax liability. Large corporations cannot avoid the penalty for underpayment of taxes by making estimated tax payments that equal or exceed last year's tax liability. A large corporation has a taxable income of $1 million or more for any of its three immediately preceding tax years. A controlled group of corporations divides the $1 million amount equally among its members unless all such members consent to an unequal allocation of such amount.

CORPORATE DISTRIBUTIONS

Shareholders receiving corporate distributions may have taxable dividends, tax-free returns of capital, or capital gain. A given distribution may be subject to all three treatments. Determination of the general nature of a distribution takes place at the corporate level. However, the final taxability of a distribution may depend on shareholder circumstances. Most corporate distributions result in taxable income to the recipient shareholders. However, distributions from corporations in the process of terminating or downsizing operations under a qualified corporate liquidation may receive more favorable tax treatment. Also, some so-called dividends are not true dividends (stock dividends).

Taxable Dividends

Unless affected parties provide contrary evidence, corporate distributions receive ordinary dividend treatment. Shareholders include in gross income the full amounts of any ordinary dividends received. When the distribution involves property, the property's FMV at the distribution date determines the amount of dividend received. Technically, dividends receive ordinary income treatment only if the company has earnings and profits to absorb the distribution. Distributions come first from the current year's earnings and profits (CEP) and then from prior years' accumulated earnings and profits (AEP). When parties to a distribution can prove the lack of earnings and profits (E&P), recipients will avoid dividend treatment. Shareholders treat distributions in excess of E&P as a tax-free recovery of their capital investment. After shareholders recover their capital, any additional distribution is capital gain.

Earnings and Profits

The Internal Revenue Code does not contain a definition of earnings and profits (E&P). Consequently, many people compare E&P with retained earnings. While similarities exist, numerous differences make them very unlike, which causes much confusion. Corporate directors may think they can distribute cash or other property tax free when the corporation has zero retained earnings. Such thinking may be erroneous. If the corporation has E&P, some portion of the distribution will be a dividend. Basically, transactions that increase a corporation's ability to pay a dividend increase E&P. Transactions that decrease a corporation's ability to pay a dividend decrease E&P. Consider the following examples. When a corporation receives tax-exempt interest, the interest is not taxed. However, E&P is increased by the interest received because the interest can serve as a source for dividend distributions. In contrast, the deduction for charitable contributions is limited to 10% of income. When the actual contribution exceeds this limitation, E&P is decreased by the full contribution. The company has reduced its ability to pay a dividend by the full amount contributed to the charity. Also, while there is no definition of E&P, the law may require the use of certain accounting methods in some situations. For example, there are various acceptable methods by which to calculate depreciation expense for the tax return. However, a special Alternative Depreciation System (Chapter 8) is required to calculate depreciation expense for E&P purposes.

Distributions of Property

Corporate distributions may involve either cash or property. For property, FMV determines the amount of the distribution. Like S corporations, C corporations must also recognize a gain on any appreciated property it distributes. Unlike S corporations where the gain is taxed to the shareholders, C corporations pay the tax on the gain. Earnings and profits increase as a result of the gain. They decrease by the FMV of the property distributed. Neither S or C corporations recognize a loss when the FMV of the property distributed is less than its corporate basis. The basis of the property received by shareholders is FMV.

> Because dividends are not deductible, closely held corporations typically find ways to make deductible payments to the owners in the form of salaries, interest, or rent.

QUESTIONS AND PROBLEMS

1. **Partnership Characteristics.** Answer the following questions in the spaces provided:

   a. What tax form do partnerships use? _____

   b. Do partnerships withhold income taxes on guaranteed salaries paid to partners? _____

   c. An LLC is what type of tax entity? _____

   d. A partnership return for a calendar year is due on or before what date? _____

   e. A partnership return for a fiscal year ending April 30 is due on or before what date? _____

2. **Partnership Activities.** Indicate how each of the following items is reported on the partnership tax return by placing a check mark in the appropriate column:

Item	Ordinary Income	Separately Stated
a. Rent received from rental property	_____	_____
b. Sale of partnership capital asset	_____	_____
c. Dividend received from Canadian corporation	_____	_____
d. Contribution to Red Cross	_____	_____
e. Guaranteed payments to partners	_____	_____
f. Business activity income	_____	_____
g. Interest on partners' capital (guaranteed)	_____	_____
h. Fee for membership in local Chamber of Commerce	_____	_____
i. Interest from a municipal bond	_____	_____
j. Property taxes on partnership assets	_____	_____
k. Interest paid on loan from bank	_____	_____

3. **Partnership Income.** Helen Royal is a member of a partnership that reports ordinary income of $68,000 for the current taxable year. Her distributive share of the partnership income is $34,000, of which she withdrew $18,000 during the year. Compute the amount she should report as income from the partnership in preparing her individual return for the year.

4. **Partnership Income.** Fred Pingle and Ken Franz are partners in a business sharing profits and losses 60% and 40% respectively. The partnership adopted a fiscal year ending June 30 at the time of its organization. Franz files his individual return on the basis of

the calendar year. Pingle keeps a personal set of books and files his individual return on the basis of a fiscal year ending on June 30. The partnership's ordinary income for the fiscal year ending June 30, 2005, is $140,000. For the calendar year 2004, each partner received a guaranteed salary of $7,000 per month. For 2005, their guaranteed salaries were increased to $8,000 per month.

a. Compute the amount of partnership income Franz should report on his 2005 tax return.

b. Compute the amount of partnership income Pingle should report on his 2005 tax return.

5. **Partnership Charitable Contributions.** Leona Mendez and Luisa Torres operate a placement service as partners, sharing profits and losses equally. During the current calendar year, the partnership contributes $3,000 to the partners' alma mater, State University. The partnership treats this contribution as an expense in the annual income statement that reports net income of $47,500.

a. Is the partnership entitled to treat the contribution to State University as a deduction from income in the partnership return?

b. What is each partner's distributive share of the taxable income shown by the partnership return?

c. May each partner claim a deduction on her individual return for the partnership contribution to State University? If so, how much?

6. **S Corporation Characteristics.** Answer each of the following questions in relation to an S corporation:

a. How many shareholders may an S corporation have?

b. What is the period during which the shareholders of a corporation may elect S corporation status?

c. What will automatically terminate an S status election?

d. When is the termination of S corporation status effective under voluntary termination and under automatic termination?

7. **Electing S Corporation Status.**

   a. The Sherwin Corporation is a United States corporation owned by 12 shareholders. All of the stock outstanding is common stock. At a regular meeting of the shareholders, all shareholders except one agreed to have the corporation become an S corporation. Can the Sherwin Corporation elect S corporation status? Explain.

   b. What are the tax advantages of S corporation status over C corporation status?

   c. What are the advantages of S corporation status over being a general partnership?

8. **Sale of S Corporation Stock.** Sally Jordan owned a 10% interest in an S corporation for several years. The basis of her stock on January 1, 2005, is $40,000. On April 30, 2005, Jordan sells her entire interest in the S corporation for $58,000. For the calendar year 2005, the S corporation estimated that its ordinary income would be $80,000. No dividends are paid for 2005 prior to the sale of Jordan's stock.

   a. On April 30, 2005, the date of sale, what is the expected gain Jordan will report on her 2005 tax return as the result of the sale of her stock?

   b. At year end, the S corporation determines that its actual ordinary income for 2005 is $100,000. On the basis of this year-end knowledge, does this additional information affect Jordan's 2005 tax return? If so, how is the 2005 tax return affected, and if it is not affected, why not?

9. **S Corporation NOL.** The Viking Corporation, a calendar year corporation, formed and immediately elected to become an S corporation as of January 2, 2003. Terry Trammel has owned 40% of the stock since the corporation's inception, with an original investment of $27,000. In 2003 and 2004, the corporation had NOLs of $45,000 and $30,000,

respectively. During 2005 the corporation had taxable income of $60,000, all ordinary income, and made cash distributions of $40,000.

a. How does Terry Trammel report her share of the 2003 and 2004 NOLs?

b. How does Terry Trammel report her share of the 2005 taxable income and cash distributions of the S corporation?

c. What is the basis of the stock owned by Terry Trammel at December 31, 2005?

10. **S Corporation Income.** The Siegal Management Corporation has operated as an S corporation for the years 2003, 2004, and 2005. The shareholders of the corporation are Tracy Sherman and Flora Shaw. They each own 200 shares of stock of the corporation, for which each paid $25,000 at the beginning of 2003. The corporation's ordinary income and cash distributions for the three years follow:

	2003	2004	2005
Ordinary income	$10,000	$11,000	$16,000
Cash distributions	6,000	11,000	24,000

a. How much do Tracy Sherman and Flora Shaw report as income on their individual income tax returns for 2005?

b. What are Sherman's and Shaw's stock bases at the end of 2005?

11. **S Corporation Losses.** Melbourne Corporation is an S corporation with ten shareholders. Bill Fox owns 100 shares of stock, which represents a 15% equity interest in the corporation. His basis for those 100 shares is $12,000. He also has loaned the corporation $4,000 to support the purchase of a special machine. For the year 2005, the corporation reports an operating loss of $120,000. In addition, the corporation made charitable contributions for the year of $10,000.

a. Explain how Bill Fox reports his share of the S corporation's operating loss and charitable contributions.

b. What is Fox's basis in his S corporation stock at the end of 2005?

c. Compute the amount and type of carryover losses to 2006 that Fox is entitled to, if any.

12. **C Corporation Taxable Income.**

   a. For the current year, the Wish Corporation had ordinary income from operations of $80,000, a net long-term capital gain of $17,000, and a net short-term capital loss of $7,000. What is its taxable income for the year?

   b. For the current year, the BB Corporation had net income from operations of $65,000 and a net long-term capital loss of $9,000. It also had a net short-term capital gain of $7,000. What is its taxable income for the year?

   c. For the current year, before considering capital loss carryovers, the Stitchell Corporation had a net long-term capital loss of $8,000 and a net short-term capital loss of $3,000. Its net capital loss carryover from last year was $2,000. How much is Stitchell's capital loss carryover to the next tax year, and what is its nature (long-term or short-term)? Be specific as to how much of this carryover is long-term and how much is short-term.

13. **Bad Debts.** Corporation ARM uses the accrual method of reporting for income taxes. It is a retail hardware store. On average, 1% of its gross sales on account ($500,000 for the current year) become uncollectable. During the year, ARM actually wrote off $4,700 of accounts receivable that were uncollectable. What is ARM's deduction for bad debts on its tax return?

14. C Corporation Charitable Contributions. The following data relate to the Regal Corporation for the current year:

Gross income includable on the tax return	$115,000
Allowable business deductions, exclusive of contributions	90,000
Contributions to charitable organizations	2,750
Dividends received from domestic corporations (30% ownership and included in the gross income amount of $115,000)	2,000

a. What is the amount of the contributions deduction for the current year?

b. What is the amount of taxable income for the current year?

c. What is the amount of the contributions deduction carryover to the next year, if any?

15. C Corporation Tax Liability. Sanford Corporation had gross income from business operations of $150,000 for the current year. Allowable business expenses were $40,000. In addition, the company received dividends from domestic corporations (less than 20% owned) in the amount of $10,000. What is Sanford's tax liability for the year?

16. Internet Problem: Researching Publication 541.

Tom Wilson owns a hardware store (capital is a material income-producing factor). On January 1, he gave his ten-year old son 40% of the business and appointed a trustee to look after his son's interest. Wilson believes he can split the profits with his son and lower the total income tax liability by reporting the store's income on two tax returns—his and his son's.

For the year, the partnership had a profit of $120,000. Wilson's services to the business were worth $50,000, which is reasonable compensation. The son performed no services. How should the profit be divided between Wilson and his son?

Go to the IRS Web site, locate Publication 541, and find the information needed to answer the above question regarding "family partnerships."

See Appendix A for instructions on use of the IRS Web site.

COMPREHENSIVE PROBLEM

17. Bebop, Inc. (a C corporation) distributes investment property to its shareholders. The property was acquired five years ago and has a basis of $50,000 and a market value of $80,000.

a. How will this distribution be treated for tax purposes at both the corporate and shareholder levels?

b. If Bebop, Inc. was an S corporation, how would you answer Part a. above?

c. If the company was a partnership, how would the distribution be treated for tax purposes at the partnership and partner levels?

Tax Tables

2005 Tax Table

 See the instructions for line 44 that begin on page 33 to see if you must use the Tax Table below to figure your tax.

Example. Mr. and Mrs. Brown are filing a joint return. Their taxable income on Form 1040, line 43, is $25,300. First, they find the $25,300–25,350 taxable income line. Next, they find the column for married filing jointly and read down the column. The amount shown where the taxable income line and filing status column meet is $3,069. This is the tax amount they should enter on Form 1040, line 44.

Sample Table

At least	But less than	Single	Married filing jointly *	Married filing separately	Head of a household
			Your tax is—		
25,200	25,250	3,419	3,054	3,419	3,261
25,250	25,300	3,426	3,061	3,426	3,269
25,300	25,350	3,434	(3,069)	3,434	3,276
25,350	25,400	3,441	3,076	3,441	3,284

If line 43 (taxable income) is— At least	But less than	And you are— Single	Married filing jointly *	Married filing separately	Head of a household
		Your tax is—			
0	5	0	0	0	0
5	15	1	1	1	1
15	25	2	2	2	2
25	50	4	4	4	4
50	75	6	6	6	6
75	100	9	9	9	9
100	125	11	11	11	11
125	150	14	14	14	14
150	175	16	16	16	16
175	200	19	19	19	19
200	225	21	21	21	21
225	250	24	24	24	24
250	275	26	26	26	26
275	300	29	29	29	29
300	325	31	31	31	31
325	350	34	34	34	34
350	375	36	36	36	36
375	400	39	39	39	39
400	425	41	41	41	41
425	450	44	44	44	44
450	475	46	46	46	46
475	500	49	49	49	49
500	525	51	51	51	51
525	550	54	54	54	54
550	575	56	56	56	56
575	600	59	59	59	59
600	625	61	61	61	61
625	650	64	64	64	64
650	675	66	66	66	66
675	700	69	69	69	69
700	725	71	71	71	71
725	750	74	74	74	74
750	775	76	76	76	76
775	800	79	79	79	79
800	825	81	81	81	81
825	850	84	84	84	84
850	875	86	86	86	86
875	900	89	89	89	89
900	925	91	91	91	91
925	950	94	94	94	94
950	975	96	96	96	96
975	1,000	99	99	99	99
1,000					
1,000	1,025	101	101	101	101
1,025	1,050	104	104	104	104
1,050	1,075	106	106	106	106
1,075	1,100	109	109	109	109
1,100	1,125	111	111	111	111
1,125	1,150	114	114	114	114
1,150	1,175	116	116	116	116
1,175	1,200	119	119	119	119
1,200	1,225	121	121	121	121
1,225	1,250	124	124	124	124
1,250	1,275	126	126	126	126
1,275	1,300	129	129	129	129

If line 43 (taxable income) is— At least	But less than	And you are— Single	Married filing jointly *	Married filing separately	Head of a household
		Your tax is—			
1,300	1,325	131	131	131	131
1,325	1,350	134	134	134	134
1,350	1,375	136	136	136	136
1,375	1,400	139	139	139	139
1,400	1,425	141	141	141	141
1,425	1,450	144	144	144	144
1,450	1,475	146	146	146	146
1,475	1,500	149	149	149	149
1,500	1,525	151	151	151	151
1,525	1,550	154	154	154	154
1,550	1,575	156	156	156	156
1,575	1,600	159	159	159	159
1,600	1,625	161	161	161	161
1,625	1,650	164	164	164	164
1,650	1,675	166	166	166	166
1,675	1,700	169	169	169	169
1,700	1,725	171	171	171	171
1,725	1,750	174	174	174	174
1,750	1,775	176	176	176	176
1,775	1,800	179	179	179	179
1,800	1,825	181	181	181	181
1,825	1,850	184	184	184	184
1,850	1,875	186	186	186	186
1,875	1,900	189	189	189	189
1,900	1,925	191	191	191	191
1,925	1,950	194	194	194	194
1,950	1,975	196	196	196	196
1,975	2,000	199	199	199	199
2,000					
2,000	2,025	201	201	201	201
2,025	2,050	204	204	204	204
2,050	2,075	206	206	206	206
2,075	2,100	209	209	209	209
2,100	2,125	211	211	211	211
2,125	2,150	214	214	214	214
2,150	2,175	216	216	216	216
2,175	2,200	219	219	219	219
2,200	2,225	221	221	221	221
2,225	2,250	224	224	224	224
2,250	2,275	226	226	226	226
2,275	2,300	229	229	229	229
2,300	2,325	231	231	231	231
2,325	2,350	234	234	234	234
2,350	2,375	236	236	236	236
2,375	2,400	239	239	239	239
2,400	2,425	241	241	241	241
2,425	2,450	244	244	244	244
2,450	2,475	246	246	246	246
2,475	2,500	249	249	249	249
2,500	2,525	251	251	251	251
2,525	2,550	254	254	254	254
2,550	2,575	256	256	256	256
2,575	2,600	259	259	259	259
2,600	2,625	261	261	261	261
2,625	2,650	264	264	264	264
2,650	2,675	266	266	266	266
2,675	2,700	269	269	269	269

If line 43 (taxable income) is— At least	But less than	And you are— Single	Married filing jointly *	Married filing separately	Head of a household
		Your tax is—			
2,700	2,725	271	271	271	271
2,725	2,750	274	274	274	274
2,750	2,775	276	276	276	276
2,775	2,800	279	279	279	279
2,800	2,825	281	281	281	281
2,825	2,850	284	284	284	284
2,850	2,875	286	286	286	286
2,875	2,900	289	289	289	289
2,900	2,925	291	291	291	291
2,925	2,950	294	294	294	294
2,950	2,975	296	296	296	296
2,975	3,000	299	299	299	299
3,000					
3,000	3,050	303	303	303	303
3,050	3,100	308	308	308	308
3,100	3,150	313	313	313	313
3,150	3,200	318	318	318	318
3,200	3,250	323	323	323	323
3,250	3,300	328	328	328	328
3,300	3,350	333	333	333	333
3,350	3,400	338	338	338	338
3,400	3,450	343	343	343	343
3,450	3,500	348	348	348	348
3,500	3,550	353	353	353	353
3,550	3,600	358	358	358	358
3,600	3,650	363	363	363	363
3,650	3,700	368	368	368	368
3,700	3,750	373	373	373	373
3,750	3,800	378	378	378	378
3,800	3,850	383	383	383	383
3,850	3,900	388	388	388	388
3,900	3,950	393	393	393	393
3,950	4,000	398	398	398	398
4,000					
4,000	4,050	403	403	403	403
4,050	4,100	408	408	408	408
4,100	4,150	413	413	413	413
4,150	4,200	418	418	418	418
4,200	4,250	423	423	423	423
4,250	4,300	428	428	428	428
4,300	4,350	433	433	433	433
4,350	4,400	438	438	438	438
4,400	4,450	443	443	443	443
4,450	4,500	448	448	448	448
4,500	4,550	453	453	453	453
4,550	4,600	458	458	458	458
4,600	4,650	463	463	463	463
4,650	4,700	468	468	468	468
4,700	4,750	473	473	473	473
4,750	4,800	478	478	478	478
4,800	4,850	483	483	483	483
4,850	4,900	488	488	488	488
4,900	4,950	493	493	493	493
4,950	5,000	498	498	498	498

(Continued on page 65)

* This column must also be used by a qualifying widow(er).

If line 43 (taxable income) is—		And you are—				If line 43 (taxable income) is—		And you are—				If line 43 (taxable income) is—		And you are—			
At least	But less than	Single	Married filing jointly *	Married filing separately	Head of a household	At least	But less than	Single	Married filing jointly *	Married filing separately	Head of a household	At least	But less than	Single	Married filing jointly *	Married filing separately	Head of a household
		Your tax is—						Your tax is—						Your tax is—			
5,000						**8,000**						**11,000**					
5,000	5,050	503	503	503	503	8,000	8,050	839	803	839	803	11,000	11,050	1,289	1,103	1,289	1,131
5,050	5,100	508	508	508	508	8,050	8,100	846	808	846	808	11,050	11,100	1,296	1,108	1,296	1,139
5,100	5,150	513	513	513	513	8,100	8,150	854	813	854	813	11,100	11,150	1,304	1,113	1,304	1,146
5,150	5,200	518	518	518	518	8,150	8,200	861	818	861	818	11,150	11,200	1,311	1,118	1,311	1,154
5,200	5,250	523	523	523	523	8,200	8,250	869	823	869	823	11,200	11,250	1,319	1,123	1,319	1,161
5,250	5,300	528	528	528	528	8,250	8,300	876	828	876	828	11,250	11,300	1,326	1,128	1,326	1,169
5,300	5,350	533	533	533	533	8,300	8,350	884	833	884	833	11,300	11,350	1,334	1,133	1,334	1,176
5,350	5,400	538	538	538	538	8,350	8,400	891	838	891	838	11,350	11,400	1,341	1,138	1,341	1,184
5,400	5,450	543	543	543	543	8,400	8,450	899	843	899	843	11,400	11,450	1,349	1,143	1,349	1,191
5,450	5,500	548	548	548	548	8,450	8,500	906	848	906	848	11,450	11,500	1,356	1,148	1,356	1,199
5,500	5,550	553	553	553	553	8,500	8,550	914	853	914	853	11,500	11,550	1,364	1,153	1,364	1,206
5,550	5,600	558	558	558	558	8,550	8,600	921	858	921	858	11,550	11,600	1,371	1,158	1,371	1,214
5,600	5,650	563	563	563	563	8,600	8,650	929	863	929	863	11,600	11,650	1,379	1,163	1,379	1,221
5,650	5,700	568	568	568	568	8,650	8,700	936	868	936	868	11,650	11,700	1,386	1,168	1,386	1,229
5,700	5,750	573	573	573	573	8,700	8,750	944	873	944	873	11,700	11,750	1,394	1,173	1,394	1,236
5,750	5,800	578	578	578	578	8,750	8,800	951	878	951	878	11,750	11,800	1,401	1,178	1,401	1,244
5,800	5,850	583	583	583	583	8,800	8,850	959	883	959	883	11,800	11,850	1,409	1,183	1,409	1,251
5,850	5,900	588	588	588	588	8,850	8,900	966	888	966	888	11,850	11,900	1,416	1,188	1,416	1,259
5,900	5,950	593	593	593	593	8,900	8,950	974	893	974	893	11,900	11,950	1,424	1,193	1,424	1,266
5,950	6,000	598	598	598	598	8,950	9,000	981	898	981	898	11,950	12,000	1,431	1,198	1,431	1,274
6,000						**9,000**						**12,000**					
6,000	6,050	603	603	603	603	9,000	9,050	989	903	989	903	12,000	12,050	1,439	1,203	1,439	1,281
6,050	6,100	608	608	608	608	9,050	9,100	996	908	996	908	12,050	12,100	1,446	1,208	1,446	1,289
6,100	6,150	613	613	613	613	9,100	9,150	1,004	913	1,004	913	12,100	12,150	1,454	1,213	1,454	1,296
6,150	6,200	618	618	618	618	9,150	9,200	1,011	918	1,011	918	12,150	12,200	1,461	1,218	1,461	1,304
6,200	6,250	623	623	623	623	9,200	9,250	1,019	923	1,019	923	12,200	12,250	1,469	1,223	1,469	1,311
6,250	6,300	628	628	628	628	9,250	9,300	1,026	928	1,026	928	12,250	12,300	1,476	1,228	1,476	1,319
6,300	6,350	633	633	633	633	9,300	9,350	1,034	933	1,034	933	12,300	12,350	1,484	1,233	1,484	1,326
6,350	6,400	638	638	638	638	9,350	9,400	1,041	938	1,041	938	12,350	12,400	1,491	1,238	1,491	1,334
6,400	6,450	643	643	643	643	9,400	9,450	1,049	943	1,049	943	12,400	12,450	1,499	1,243	1,499	1,341
6,450	6,500	648	648	648	648	9,450	9,500	1,056	948	1,056	948	12,450	12,500	1,506	1,248	1,506	1,349
6,500	6,550	653	653	653	653	9,500	9,550	1,064	953	1,064	953	12,500	12,550	1,514	1,253	1,514	1,356
6,550	6,600	658	658	658	658	9,550	9,600	1,071	958	1,071	958	12,550	12,600	1,521	1,258	1,521	1,364
6,600	6,650	663	663	663	663	9,600	9,650	1,079	963	1,079	963	12,600	12,650	1,529	1,263	1,529	1,371
6,650	6,700	668	668	668	668	9,650	9,700	1,086	968	1,086	968	12,650	12,700	1,536	1,268	1,536	1,379
6,700	6,750	673	673	673	673	9,700	9,750	1,094	973	1,094	973	12,700	12,750	1,544	1,273	1,544	1,386
6,750	6,800	678	678	678	678	9,750	9,800	1,101	978	1,101	978	12,750	12,800	1,551	1,278	1,551	1,394
6,800	6,850	683	683	683	683	9,800	9,850	1,109	983	1,109	983	12,800	12,850	1,559	1,283	1,559	1,401
6,850	6,900	688	688	688	688	9,850	9,900	1,116	988	1,116	988	12,850	12,900	1,566	1,288	1,566	1,409
6,900	6,950	693	693	693	693	9,900	9,950	1,124	993	1,124	993	12,900	12,950	1,574	1,293	1,574	1,416
6,950	7,000	698	698	698	698	9,950	10,000	1,131	998	1,131	998	12,950	13,000	1,581	1,298	1,581	1,424
7,000						**10,000**						**13,000**					
7,000	7,050	703	703	703	703	10,000	10,050	1,139	1,003	1,139	1,003	13,000	13,050	1,589	1,303	1,589	1,431
7,050	7,100	708	708	708	708	10,050	10,100	1,146	1,008	1,146	1,008	13,050	13,100	1,596	1,308	1,596	1,439
7,100	7,150	713	713	713	713	10,100	10,150	1,154	1,013	1,154	1,013	13,100	13,150	1,604	1,313	1,604	1,446
7,150	7,200	718	718	718	718	10,150	10,200	1,161	1,018	1,161	1,018	13,150	13,200	1,611	1,318	1,611	1,454
7,200	7,250	723	723	723	723	10,200	10,250	1,169	1,023	1,169	1,023	13,200	13,250	1,619	1,323	1,619	1,461
7,250	7,300	728	728	728	728	10,250	10,300	1,176	1,028	1,176	1,028	13,250	13,300	1,626	1,328	1,626	1,469
7,300	7,350	734	733	734	733	10,300	10,350	1,184	1,033	1,184	1,033	13,300	13,350	1,634	1,333	1,634	1,476
7,350	7,400	741	738	741	738	10,350	10,400	1,191	1,038	1,191	1,038	13,350	13,400	1,641	1,338	1,641	1,484
7,400	7,450	749	743	749	743	10,400	10,450	1,199	1,043	1,199	1,043	13,400	13,450	1,649	1,343	1,649	1,491
7,450	7,500	756	748	756	748	10,450	10,500	1,206	1,048	1,206	1,049	13,450	13,500	1,656	1,348	1,656	1,499
7,500	7,550	764	753	764	753	10,500	10,550	1,214	1,053	1,214	1,056	13,500	13,550	1,664	1,353	1,664	1,506
7,550	7,600	771	758	771	758	10,550	10,600	1,221	1,058	1,221	1,064	13,550	13,600	1,671	1,358	1,671	1,514
7,600	7,650	779	763	779	763	10,600	10,650	1,229	1,063	1,229	1,071	13,600	13,650	1,679	1,363	1,679	1,521
7,650	7,700	786	768	786	768	10,650	10,700	1,236	1,068	1,236	1,079	13,650	13,700	1,686	1,368	1,686	1,529
7,700	7,750	794	773	794	773	10,700	10,750	1,244	1,073	1,244	1,086	13,700	13,750	1,694	1,373	1,694	1,536
7,750	7,800	801	778	801	778	10,750	10,800	1,251	1,078	1,251	1,094	13,750	13,800	1,701	1,378	1,701	1,544
7,800	7,850	809	783	809	783	10,800	10,850	1,259	1,083	1,259	1,101	13,800	13,850	1,709	1,383	1,709	1,551
7,850	7,900	816	788	816	788	10,850	10,900	1,266	1,088	1,266	1,109	13,850	13,900	1,716	1,388	1,716	1,559
7,900	7,950	824	793	824	793	10,900	10,950	1,274	1,093	1,274	1,116	13,900	13,950	1,724	1,393	1,724	1,566
7,950	8,000	831	798	831	798	10,950	11,000	1,281	1,098	1,281	1,124	13,950	14,000	1,731	1,398	1,731	1,574

* This column must also be used by a qualifying widow(er).

(Continued on page 66)

T-2

If line 43 (taxable income) is—		And you are—			
At least	But less than	Single	Married filing jointly *	Married filing separately	Head of a household
		Your tax is—			
14,000					
14,000	14,050	1,739	1,403	1,739	1,581
14,050	14,100	1,746	1,408	1,746	1,589
14,100	14,150	1,754	1,413	1,754	1,596
14,150	14,200	1,761	1,418	1,761	1,604
14,200	14,250	1,769	1,423	1,769	1,611
14,250	14,300	1,776	1,428	1,776	1,619
14,300	14,350	1,784	1,433	1,784	1,626
14,350	14,400	1,791	1,438	1,791	1,634
14,400	14,450	1,799	1,443	1,799	1,641
14,450	14,500	1,806	1,448	1,806	1,649
14,500	14,550	1,814	1,453	1,814	1,656
14,550	14,600	1,821	1,458	1,821	1,664
14,600	14,650	1,829	1,464	1,829	1,671
14,650	14,700	1,836	1,471	1,836	1,679
14,700	14,750	1,844	1,479	1,844	1,686
14,750	14,800	1,851	1,486	1,851	1,694
14,800	14,850	1,859	1,494	1,859	1,701
14,850	14,900	1,866	1,501	1,866	1,709
14,900	14,950	1,874	1,509	1,874	1,716
14,950	15,000	1,881	1,516	1,881	1,724
15,000					
15,000	15,050	1,889	1,524	1,889	1,731
15,050	15,100	1,896	1,531	1,896	1,739
15,100	15,150	1,904	1,539	1,904	1,746
15,150	15,200	1,911	1,546	1,911	1,754
15,200	15,250	1,919	1,554	1,919	1,761
15,250	15,300	1,926	1,561	1,926	1,769
15,300	15,350	1,934	1,569	1,934	1,776
15,350	15,400	1,941	1,576	1,941	1,784
15,400	15,450	1,949	1,584	1,949	1,791
15,450	15,500	1,956	1,591	1,956	1,799
15,500	15,550	1,964	1,599	1,964	1,806
15,550	15,600	1,971	1,606	1,971	1,814
15,600	15,650	1,979	1,614	1,979	1,821
15,650	15,700	1,986	1,621	1,986	1,829
15,700	15,750	1,994	1,629	1,994	1,836
15,750	15,800	2,001	1,636	2,001	1,844
15,800	15,850	2,009	1,644	2,009	1,851
15,850	15,900	2,016	1,651	2,016	1,859
15,900	15,950	2,024	1,659	2,024	1,866
15,950	16,000	2,031	1,666	2,031	1,874
16,000					
16,000	16,050	2,039	1,674	2,039	1,881
16,050	16,100	2,046	1,681	2,046	1,889
16,100	16,150	2,054	1,689	2,054	1,896
16,150	16,200	2,061	1,696	2,061	1,904
16,200	16,250	2,069	1,704	2,069	1,911
16,250	16,300	2,076	1,711	2,076	1,919
16,300	16,350	2,084	1,719	2,084	1,926
16,350	16,400	2,091	1,726	2,091	1,934
16,400	16,450	2,099	1,734	2,099	1,941
16,450	16,500	2,106	1,741	2,106	1,949
16,500	16,550	2,114	1,749	2,114	1,956
16,550	16,600	2,121	1,756	2,121	1,964
16,600	16,650	2,129	1,764	2,129	1,971
16,650	16,700	2,136	1,771	2,136	1,979
16,700	16,750	2,144	1,779	2,144	1,986
16,750	16,800	2,151	1,786	2,151	1,994
16,800	16,850	2,159	1,794	2,159	2,001
16,850	16,900	2,166	1,801	2,166	2,009
16,900	16,950	2,174	1,809	2,174	2,016
16,950	17,000	2,181	1,816	2,181	2,024

If line 43 (taxable income) is—		And you are—			
At least	But less than	Single	Married filing jointly *	Married filing separately	Head of a household
		Your tax is—			
17,000					
17,000	17,050	2,189	1,824	2,189	2,031
17,050	17,100	2,196	1,831	2,196	2,039
17,100	17,150	2,204	1,839	2,204	2,046
17,150	17,200	2,211	1,846	2,211	2,054
17,200	17,250	2,219	1,854	2,219	2,061
17,250	17,300	2,226	1,861	2,226	2,069
17,300	17,350	2,234	1,869	2,234	2,076
17,350	17,400	2,241	1,876	2,241	2,084
17,400	17,450	2,249	1,884	2,249	2,091
17,450	17,500	2,256	1,891	2,256	2,099
17,500	17,550	2,264	1,899	2,264	2,106
17,550	17,600	2,271	1,906	2,271	2,114
17,600	17,650	2,279	1,914	2,279	2,121
17,650	17,700	2,286	1,921	2,286	2,129
17,700	17,750	2,294	1,929	2,294	2,136
17,750	17,800	2,301	1,936	2,301	2,144
17,800	17,850	2,309	1,944	2,309	2,151
17,850	17,900	2,316	1,951	2,316	2,159
17,900	17,950	2,324	1,959	2,324	2,166
17,950	18,000	2,331	1,966	2,331	2,174
18,000					
18,000	18,050	2,339	1,974	2,339	2,181
18,050	18,100	2,346	1,981	2,346	2,189
18,100	18,150	2,354	1,989	2,354	2,196
18,150	18,200	2,361	1,996	2,361	2,204
18,200	18,250	2,369	2,004	2,369	2,211
18,250	18,300	2,376	2,011	2,376	2,219
18,300	18,350	2,384	2,019	2,384	2,226
18,350	18,400	2,391	2,026	2,391	2,234
18,400	18,450	2,399	2,034	2,399	2,241
18,450	18,500	2,406	2,041	2,406	2,249
18,500	18,550	2,414	2,049	2,414	2,256
18,550	18,600	2,421	2,056	2,421	2,264
18,600	18,650	2,429	2,064	2,429	2,271
18,650	18,700	2,436	2,071	2,436	2,279
18,700	18,750	2,444	2,079	2,444	2,286
18,750	18,800	2,451	2,086	2,451	2,294
18,800	18,850	2,459	2,094	2,459	2,301
18,850	18,900	2,466	2,101	2,466	2,309
18,900	18,950	2,474	2,109	2,474	2,316
18,950	19,000	2,481	2,116	2,481	2,324
19,000					
19,000	19,050	2,489	2,124	2,489	2,331
19,050	19,100	2,496	2,131	2,496	2,339
19,100	19,150	2,504	2,139	2,504	2,346
19,150	19,200	2,511	2,146	2,511	2,354
19,200	19,250	2,519	2,154	2,519	2,361
19,250	19,300	2,526	2,161	2,526	2,369
19,300	19,350	2,534	2,169	2,534	2,376
19,350	19,400	2,541	2,176	2,541	2,384
19,400	19,450	2,549	2,184	2,549	2,391
19,450	19,500	2,556	2,191	2,556	2,399
19,500	19,550	2,564	2,199	2,564	2,406
19,550	19,600	2,571	2,206	2,571	2,414
19,600	19,650	2,579	2,214	2,579	2,421
19,650	19,700	2,586	2,221	2,586	2,429
19,700	19,750	2,594	2,229	2,594	2,436
19,750	19,800	2,601	2,236	2,601	2,444
19,800	19,850	2,609	2,244	2,609	2,451
19,850	19,900	2,616	2,251	2,616	2,459
19,900	19,950	2,624	2,259	2,624	2,466
19,950	20,000	2,631	2,266	2,631	2,474

If line 43 (taxable income) is—		And you are—			
At least	But less than	Single	Married filing jointly *	Married filing separately	Head of a household
		Your tax is—			
20,000					
20,000	20,050	2,639	2,274	2,639	2,481
20,050	20,100	2,646	2,281	2,646	2,489
20,100	20,150	2,654	2,289	2,654	2,496
20,150	20,200	2,661	2,296	2,661	2,504
20,200	20,250	2,669	2,304	2,669	2,511
20,250	20,300	2,676	2,311	2,676	2,519
20,300	20,350	2,684	2,319	2,684	2,526
20,350	20,400	2,691	2,326	2,691	2,534
20,400	20,450	2,699	2,334	2,699	2,541
20,450	20,500	2,706	2,341	2,706	2,549
20,500	20,550	2,714	2,349	2,714	2,556
20,550	20,600	2,721	2,356	2,721	2,564
20,600	20,650	2,729	2,364	2,729	2,571
20,650	20,700	2,736	2,371	2,736	2,579
20,700	20,750	2,744	2,379	2,744	2,586
20,750	20,800	2,751	2,386	2,751	2,594
20,800	20,850	2,759	2,394	2,759	2,601
20,850	20,900	2,766	2,401	2,766	2,609
20,900	20,950	2,774	2,409	2,774	2,616
20,950	21,000	2,781	2,416	2,781	2,624
21,000					
21,000	21,050	2,789	2,424	2,789	2,631
21,050	21,100	2,796	2,431	2,796	2,639
21,100	21,150	2,804	2,439	2,804	2,646
21,150	21,200	2,811	2,446	2,811	2,654
21,200	21,250	2,819	2,454	2,819	2,661
21,250	21,300	2,826	2,461	2,826	2,669
21,300	21,350	2,834	2,469	2,834	2,676
21,350	21,400	2,841	2,476	2,841	2,684
21,400	21,450	2,849	2,484	2,849	2,691
21,450	21,500	2,856	2,491	2,856	2,699
21,500	21,550	2,864	2,499	2,864	2,706
21,550	21,600	2,871	2,506	2,871	2,714
21,600	21,650	2,879	2,514	2,879	2,721
21,650	21,700	2,886	2,521	2,886	2,729
21,700	21,750	2,894	2,529	2,894	2,736
21,750	21,800	2,901	2,536	2,901	2,744
21,800	21,850	2,909	2,544	2,909	2,751
21,850	21,900	2,916	2,551	2,916	2,759
21,900	21,950	2,924	2,559	2,924	2,766
21,950	22,000	2,931	2,566	2,931	2,774
22,000					
22,000	22,050	2,939	2,574	2,939	2,781
22,050	22,100	2,946	2,581	2,946	2,789
22,100	22,150	2,954	2,589	2,954	2,796
22,150	22,200	2,961	2,596	2,961	2,804
22,200	22,250	2,969	2,604	2,969	2,811
22,250	22,300	2,976	2,611	2,976	2,819
22,300	22,350	2,984	2,619	2,984	2,826
22,350	22,400	2,991	2,626	2,991	2,834
22,400	22,450	2,999	2,634	2,999	2,841
22,450	22,500	3,006	2,641	3,006	2,849
22,500	22,550	3,014	2,649	3,014	2,856
22,550	22,600	3,021	2,656	3,021	2,864
22,600	22,650	3,029	2,664	3,029	2,871
22,650	22,700	3,036	2,671	3,036	2,879
22,700	22,750	3,044	2,679	3,044	2,886
22,750	22,800	3,051	2,686	3,051	2,894
22,800	22,850	3,059	2,694	3,059	2,901
22,850	22,900	3,066	2,701	3,066	2,909
22,900	22,950	3,074	2,709	3,074	2,916
22,950	23,000	3,081	2,716	3,081	2,924

* This column must also be used by a qualifying widow(er).

(Continued on page 67)

23,000 – 25,000

At least	But less than	Single	Married filing jointly*	Married filing separately	Head of a household
23,000					
23,000	23,050	3,089	2,724	3,089	2,931
23,050	23,100	3,096	2,731	3,096	2,939
23,100	23,150	3,104	2,739	3,104	2,946
23,150	23,200	3,111	2,746	3,111	2,954
23,200	23,250	3,119	2,754	3,119	2,961
23,250	23,300	3,126	2,761	3,126	2,969
23,300	23,350	3,134	2,769	3,134	2,976
23,350	23,400	3,141	2,776	3,141	2,984
23,400	23,450	3,149	2,784	3,149	2,991
23,450	23,500	3,156	2,791	3,156	2,999
23,500	23,550	3,164	2,799	3,164	3,006
23,550	23,600	3,171	2,806	3,171	3,014
23,600	23,650	3,179	2,814	3,179	3,021
23,650	23,700	3,186	2,821	3,186	3,029
23,700	23,750	3,194	2,829	3,194	3,036
23,750	23,800	3,201	2,836	3,201	3,044
23,800	23,850	3,209	2,844	3,209	3,051
23,850	23,900	3,216	2,851	3,216	3,059
23,900	23,950	3,224	2,859	3,224	3,066
23,950	24,000	3,231	2,866	3,231	3,074
24,000					
24,000	24,050	3,239	2,874	3,239	3,081
24,050	24,100	3,246	2,881	3,246	3,089
24,100	24,150	3,254	2,889	3,254	3,096
24,150	24,200	3,261	2,896	3,261	3,104
24,200	24,250	3,269	2,904	3,269	3,111
24,250	24,300	3,276	2,911	3,276	3,119
24,300	24,350	3,284	2,919	3,284	3,126
24,350	24,400	3,291	2,926	3,291	3,134
24,400	24,450	3,299	2,934	3,299	3,141
24,450	24,500	3,306	2,941	3,306	3,149
24,500	24,550	3,314	2,949	3,314	3,156
24,550	24,600	3,321	2,956	3,321	3,164
24,600	24,650	3,329	2,964	3,329	3,171
24,650	24,700	3,336	2,971	3,336	3,179
24,700	24,750	3,344	2,979	3,344	3,186
24,750	24,800	3,351	2,986	3,351	3,194
24,800	24,850	3,359	2,994	3,359	3,201
24,850	24,900	3,366	3,001	3,366	3,209
24,900	24,950	3,374	3,009	3,374	3,216
24,950	25,000	3,381	3,016	3,381	3,224
25,000					
25,000	25,050	3,389	3,024	3,389	3,231
25,050	25,100	3,396	3,031	3,396	3,239
25,100	25,150	3,404	3,039	3,404	3,246
25,150	25,200	3,411	3,046	3,411	3,254
25,200	25,250	3,419	3,054	3,419	3,261
25,250	25,300	3,426	3,061	3,426	3,269
25,300	25,350	3,434	3,069	3,434	3,276
25,350	25,400	3,441	3,076	3,441	3,284
25,400	25,450	3,449	3,084	3,449	3,291
25,450	25,500	3,456	3,091	3,456	3,299
25,500	25,550	3,464	3,099	3,464	3,306
25,550	25,600	3,471	3,106	3,471	3,314
25,600	25,650	3,479	3,114	3,479	3,321
25,650	25,700	3,486	3,121	3,486	3,329
25,700	25,750	3,494	3,129	3,494	3,336
25,750	25,800	3,501	3,136	3,501	3,344
25,800	25,850	3,509	3,144	3,509	3,351
25,850	25,900	3,516	3,151	3,516	3,359
25,900	25,950	3,524	3,159	3,524	3,366
25,950	26,000	3,531	3,166	3,531	3,374

26,000 – 28,000

At least	But less than	Single	Married filing jointly*	Married filing separately	Head of a household
26,000					
26,000	26,050	3,539	3,174	3,539	3,381
26,050	26,100	3,546	3,181	3,546	3,389
26,100	26,150	3,554	3,189	3,554	3,396
26,150	26,200	3,561	3,196	3,561	3,404
26,200	26,250	3,569	3,204	3,569	3,411
26,250	26,300	3,576	3,211	3,576	3,419
26,300	26,350	3,584	3,219	3,584	3,426
26,350	26,400	3,591	3,226	3,591	3,434
26,400	26,450	3,599	3,234	3,599	3,441
26,450	26,500	3,606	3,241	3,606	3,449
26,500	26,550	3,614	3,249	3,614	3,456
26,550	26,600	3,621	3,256	3,621	3,464
26,600	26,650	3,629	3,264	3,629	3,471
26,650	26,700	3,636	3,271	3,636	3,479
26,700	26,750	3,644	3,279	3,644	3,486
26,750	26,800	3,651	3,286	3,651	3,494
26,800	26,850	3,659	3,294	3,659	3,501
26,850	26,900	3,666	3,301	3,666	3,509
26,900	26,950	3,674	3,309	3,674	3,516
26,950	27,000	3,681	3,316	3,681	3,524
27,000					
27,000	27,050	3,689	3,324	3,689	3,531
27,050	27,100	3,696	3,331	3,696	3,539
27,100	27,150	3,704	3,339	3,704	3,546
27,150	27,200	3,711	3,346	3,711	3,554
27,200	27,250	3,719	3,354	3,719	3,561
27,250	27,300	3,726	3,361	3,726	3,569
27,300	27,350	3,734	3,369	3,734	3,576
27,350	27,400	3,741	3,376	3,741	3,584
27,400	27,450	3,749	3,384	3,749	3,591
27,450	27,500	3,756	3,391	3,756	3,599
27,500	27,550	3,764	3,399	3,764	3,606
27,550	27,600	3,771	3,406	3,771	3,614
27,600	27,650	3,779	3,414	3,779	3,621
27,650	27,700	3,786	3,421	3,786	3,629
27,700	27,750	3,794	3,429	3,794	3,636
27,750	27,800	3,801	3,436	3,801	3,644
27,800	27,850	3,809	3,444	3,809	3,651
27,850	27,900	3,816	3,451	3,816	3,659
27,900	27,950	3,824	3,459	3,824	3,666
27,950	28,000	3,831	3,466	3,831	3,674
28,000					
28,000	28,050	3,839	3,474	3,839	3,681
28,050	28,100	3,846	3,481	3,846	3,689
28,100	28,150	3,854	3,489	3,854	3,696
28,150	28,200	3,861	3,496	3,861	3,704
28,200	28,250	3,869	3,504	3,869	3,711
28,250	28,300	3,876	3,511	3,876	3,719
28,300	28,350	3,884	3,519	3,884	3,726
28,350	28,400	3,891	3,526	3,891	3,734
28,400	28,450	3,899	3,534	3,899	3,741
28,450	28,500	3,906	3,541	3,906	3,749
28,500	28,550	3,914	3,549	3,914	3,756
28,550	28,600	3,921	3,556	3,921	3,764
28,600	28,650	3,929	3,564	3,929	3,771
28,650	28,700	3,936	3,571	3,936	3,779
28,700	28,750	3,944	3,579	3,944	3,786
28,750	28,800	3,951	3,586	3,951	3,794
28,800	28,850	3,959	3,594	3,959	3,801
28,850	28,900	3,966	3,601	3,966	3,809
28,900	28,950	3,974	3,609	3,974	3,816
28,950	29,000	3,981	3,616	3,981	3,824

29,000 – 31,000

At least	But less than	Single	Married filing jointly*	Married filing separately	Head of a household
29,000					
29,000	29,050	3,989	3,624	3,989	3,831
29,050	29,100	3,996	3,631	3,996	3,839
29,100	29,150	4,004	3,639	4,004	3,846
29,150	29,200	4,011	3,646	4,011	3,854
29,200	29,250	4,019	3,654	4,019	3,861
29,250	29,300	4,026	3,661	4,026	3,869
29,300	29,350	4,034	3,669	4,034	3,876
29,350	29,400	4,041	3,676	4,041	3,884
29,400	29,450	4,049	3,684	4,049	3,891
29,450	29,500	4,056	3,691	4,056	3,899
29,500	29,550	4,064	3,699	4,064	3,906
29,550	29,600	4,071	3,706	4,071	3,914
29,600	29,650	4,079	3,714	4,079	3,921
29,650	29,700	4,086	3,721	4,086	3,929
29,700	29,750	4,096	3,729	4,096	3,936
29,750	29,800	4,109	3,736	4,109	3,944
29,800	29,850	4,121	3,744	4,121	3,951
29,850	29,900	4,134	3,751	4,134	3,959
29,900	29,950	4,146	3,759	4,146	3,966
29,950	30,000	4,159	3,766	4,159	3,974
30,000					
30,000	30,050	4,171	3,774	4,171	3,981
30,050	30,100	4,184	3,781	4,184	3,989
30,100	30,150	4,196	3,789	4,196	3,996
30,150	30,200	4,209	3,796	4,209	4,004
30,200	30,250	4,221	3,804	4,221	4,011
30,250	30,300	4,234	3,811	4,234	4,019
30,300	30,350	4,246	3,819	4,246	4,026
30,350	30,400	4,259	3,826	4,259	4,034
30,400	30,450	4,271	3,834	4,271	4,041
30,450	30,500	4,284	3,841	4,284	4,049
30,500	30,550	4,296	3,849	4,296	4,056
30,550	30,600	4,309	3,856	4,309	4,064
30,600	30,650	4,321	3,864	4,321	4,071
30,650	30,700	4,334	3,871	4,334	4,079
30,700	30,750	4,346	3,879	4,346	4,086
30,750	30,800	4,359	3,886	4,359	4,094
30,800	30,850	4,371	3,894	4,371	4,101
30,850	30,900	4,384	3,901	4,384	4,109
30,900	30,950	4,396	3,909	4,396	4,116
30,950	31,000	4,409	3,916	4,409	4,124
31,000					
31,000	31,050	4,421	3,924	4,421	4,131
31,050	31,100	4,434	3,931	4,434	4,139
31,100	31,150	4,446	3,939	4,446	4,146
31,150	31,200	4,459	3,946	4,459	4,154
31,200	31,250	4,471	3,954	4,471	4,161
31,250	31,300	4,484	3,961	4,484	4,169
31,300	31,350	4,496	3,969	4,496	4,176
31,350	31,400	4,509	3,976	4,509	4,184
31,400	31,450	4,521	3,984	4,521	4,191
31,450	31,500	4,534	3,991	4,534	4,199
31,500	31,550	4,546	3,999	4,546	4,206
31,550	31,600	4,559	4,006	4,559	4,214
31,600	31,650	4,571	4,014	4,571	4,221
31,650	31,700	4,584	4,021	4,584	4,229
31,700	31,750	4,596	4,029	4,596	4,236
31,750	31,800	4,609	4,036	4,609	4,244
31,800	31,850	4,621	4,044	4,621	4,251
31,850	31,900	4,634	4,051	4,634	4,259
31,900	31,950	4,646	4,059	4,646	4,266
31,950	32,000	4,659	4,066	4,659	4,274

* This column must also be used by a qualifying widow(er).

(Continued on page 68)

2005 Tax Table—Continued

32,000 / 33,000 / 34,000

At least	But less than	Single	Married filing jointly *	Married filing separately	Head of a household
32,000					
32,000	32,050	4,671	4,074	4,671	4,281
32,050	32,100	4,684	4,081	4,684	4,289
32,100	32,150	4,696	4,089	4,696	4,296
32,150	32,200	4,709	4,096	4,709	4,304
32,200	32,250	4,721	4,104	4,721	4,311
32,250	32,300	4,734	4,111	4,734	4,319
32,300	32,350	4,746	4,119	4,746	4,326
32,350	32,400	4,759	4,126	4,759	4,334
32,400	32,450	4,771	4,134	4,771	4,341
32,450	32,500	4,784	4,141	4,784	4,349
32,500	32,550	4,796	4,149	4,796	4,356
32,550	32,600	4,809	4,156	4,809	4,364
32,600	32,650	4,821	4,164	4,821	4,371
32,650	32,700	4,834	4,171	4,834	4,379
32,700	32,750	4,846	4,179	4,846	4,386
32,750	32,800	4,859	4,186	4,859	4,394
32,800	32,850	4,871	4,194	4,871	4,401
32,850	32,900	4,884	4,201	4,884	4,409
32,900	32,950	4,896	4,209	4,896	4,416
32,950	33,000	4,909	4,216	4,909	4,424
33,000					
33,000	33,050	4,921	4,224	4,921	4,431
33,050	33,100	4,934	4,231	4,934	4,439
33,100	33,150	4,946	4,239	4,946	4,446
33,150	33,200	4,959	4,246	4,959	4,454
33,200	33,250	4,971	4,254	4,971	4,461
33,250	33,300	4,984	4,261	4,984	4,469
33,300	33,350	4,996	4,269	4,996	4,476
33,350	33,400	5,009	4,276	5,009	4,484
33,400	33,450	5,021	4,284	5,021	4,491
33,450	33,500	5,034	4,291	5,034	4,499
33,500	33,550	5,046	4,299	5,046	4,506
33,550	33,600	5,059	4,306	5,059	4,514
33,600	33,650	5,071	4,314	5,071	4,521
33,650	33,700	5,084	4,321	5,084	4,529
33,700	33,750	5,096	4,329	5,096	4,536
33,750	33,800	5,109	4,336	5,109	4,544
33,800	33,850	5,121	4,344	5,121	4,551
33,850	33,900	5,134	4,351	5,134	4,559
33,900	33,950	5,146	4,359	5,146	4,566
33,950	34,000	5,159	4,366	5,159	4,574
34,000					
34,000	34,050	5,171	4,374	5,171	4,581
34,050	34,100	5,184	4,381	5,184	4,589
34,100	34,150	5,196	4,389	5,196	4,596
34,150	34,200	5,209	4,396	5,209	4,604
34,200	34,250	5,221	4,404	5,221	4,611
34,250	34,300	5,234	4,411	5,234	4,619
34,300	34,350	5,246	4,419	5,246	4,626
34,350	34,400	5,259	4,426	5,259	4,634
34,400	34,450	5,271	4,434	5,271	4,641
34,450	34,500	5,284	4,441	5,284	4,649
34,500	34,550	5,296	4,449	5,296	4,656
34,550	34,600	5,309	4,456	5,309	4,664
34,600	34,650	5,321	4,464	5,321	4,671
34,650	34,700	5,334	4,471	5,334	4,679
34,700	34,750	5,346	4,479	5,346	4,686
34,750	34,800	5,359	4,486	5,359	4,694
34,800	34,850	5,371	4,494	5,371	4,701
34,850	34,900	5,384	4,501	5,384	4,709
34,900	34,950	5,396	4,509	5,396	4,716
34,950	35,000	5,409	4,516	5,409	4,724

35,000 / 36,000 / 37,000

At least	But less than	Single	Married filing jointly *	Married filing separately	Head of a household
35,000					
35,000	35,050	5,421	4,524	5,421	4,731
35,050	35,100	5,434	4,531	5,434	4,739
35,100	35,150	5,446	4,539	5,446	4,746
35,150	35,200	5,459	4,546	5,459	4,754
35,200	35,250	5,471	4,554	5,471	4,761
35,250	35,300	5,484	4,561	5,484	4,769
35,300	35,350	5,496	4,569	5,496	4,776
35,350	35,400	5,509	4,576	5,509	4,784
35,400	35,450	5,521	4,584	5,521	4,791
35,450	35,500	5,534	4,591	5,534	4,799
35,500	35,550	5,546	4,599	5,546	4,806
35,550	35,600	5,559	4,606	5,559	4,814
35,600	35,650	5,571	4,614	5,571	4,821
35,650	35,700	5,584	4,621	5,584	4,829
35,700	35,750	5,596	4,629	5,596	4,836
35,750	35,800	5,609	4,636	5,609	4,844
35,800	35,850	5,621	4,644	5,621	4,851
35,850	35,900	5,634	4,651	5,634	4,859
35,900	35,950	5,646	4,659	5,646	4,866
35,950	36,000	5,659	4,666	5,659	4,874
36,000					
36,000	36,050	5,671	4,674	5,671	4,881
36,050	36,100	5,684	4,681	5,684	4,889
36,100	36,150	5,696	4,689	5,696	4,896
36,150	36,200	5,709	4,696	5,709	4,904
36,200	36,250	5,721	4,704	5,721	4,911
36,250	36,300	5,734	4,711	5,734	4,919
36,300	36,350	5,746	4,719	5,746	4,926
36,350	36,400	5,759	4,726	5,759	4,934
36,400	36,450	5,771	4,734	5,771	4,941
36,450	36,500	5,784	4,741	5,784	4,949
36,500	36,550	5,796	4,749	5,796	4,956
36,550	36,600	5,809	4,756	5,809	4,964
36,600	36,650	5,821	4,764	5,821	4,971
36,650	36,700	5,834	4,771	5,834	4,979
36,700	36,750	5,846	4,779	5,846	4,986
36,750	36,800	5,859	4,786	5,859	4,994
36,800	36,850	5,871	4,794	5,871	5,001
36,850	36,900	5,884	4,801	5,884	5,009
36,900	36,950	5,896	4,809	5,896	5,016
36,950	37,000	5,909	4,816	5,909	5,024
37,000					
37,000	37,050	5,921	4,824	5,921	5,031
37,050	37,100	5,934	4,831	5,934	5,039
37,100	37,150	5,946	4,839	5,946	5,046
37,150	37,200	5,959	4,846	5,959	5,054
37,200	37,250	5,971	4,854	5,971	5,061
37,250	37,300	5,984	4,861	5,984	5,069
37,300	37,350	5,996	4,869	5,996	5,076
37,350	37,400	6,009	4,876	6,009	5,084
37,400	37,450	6,021	4,884	6,021	5,091
37,450	37,500	6,034	4,891	6,034	5,099
37,500	37,550	6,046	4,899	6,046	5,106
37,550	37,600	6,059	4,906	6,059	5,114
37,600	37,650	6,071	4,914	6,071	5,121
37,650	37,700	6,084	4,921	6,084	5,129
37,700	37,750	6,096	4,929	6,096	5,136
37,750	37,800	6,109	4,936	6,109	5,144
37,800	37,850	6,121	4,944	6,121	5,151
37,850	37,900	6,134	4,951	6,134	5,159
37,900	37,950	6,146	4,959	6,146	5,166
37,950	38,000	6,159	4,966	6,159	5,174

38,000 / 39,000 / 40,000

At least	But less than	Single	Married filing jointly *	Married filing separately	Head of a household
38,000					
38,000	38,050	6,171	4,974	6,171	5,181
38,050	38,100	6,184	4,981	6,184	5,189
38,100	38,150	6,196	4,989	6,196	5,196
38,150	38,200	6,209	4,996	6,209	5,204
38,200	38,250	6,221	5,004	6,221	5,211
38,250	38,300	6,234	5,011	6,234	5,219
38,300	38,350	6,246	5,019	6,246	5,226
38,350	38,400	6,259	5,026	6,259	5,234
38,400	38,450	6,271	5,034	6,271	5,241
38,450	38,500	6,284	5,041	6,284	5,249
38,500	38,550	6,296	5,049	6,296	5,256
38,550	38,600	6,309	5,056	6,309	5,264
38,600	38,650	6,321	5,064	6,321	5,271
38,650	38,700	6,334	5,071	6,334	5,279
38,700	38,750	6,346	5,079	6,346	5,286
38,750	38,800	6,359	5,086	6,359	5,294
38,800	38,850	6,371	5,094	6,371	5,301
38,850	38,900	6,384	5,101	6,384	5,309
38,900	38,950	6,396	5,109	6,396	5,316
38,950	39,000	6,409	5,116	6,409	5,324
39,000					
39,000	39,050	6,421	5,124	6,421	5,331
39,050	39,100	6,434	5,131	6,434	5,339
39,100	39,150	6,446	5,139	6,446	5,346
39,150	39,200	6,459	5,146	6,459	5,354
39,200	39,250	6,471	5,154	6,471	5,361
39,250	39,300	6,484	5,161	6,484	5,369
39,300	39,350	6,496	5,169	6,496	5,376
39,350	39,400	6,509	5,176	6,509	5,384
39,400	39,450	6,521	5,184	6,521	5,391
39,450	39,500	6,534	5,191	6,534	5,399
39,500	39,550	6,546	5,199	6,546	5,406
39,550	39,600	6,559	5,206	6,559	5,414
39,600	39,650	6,571	5,214	6,571	5,421
39,650	39,700	6,584	5,221	6,584	5,429
39,700	39,750	6,596	5,229	6,596	5,436
39,750	39,800	6,609	5,236	6,609	5,444
39,800	39,850	6,621	5,244	6,621	5,454
39,850	39,900	6,634	5,251	6,634	5,466
39,900	39,950	6,646	5,259	6,646	5,479
39,950	40,000	6,659	5,266	6,659	5,491
40,000					
40,000	40,050	6,671	5,274	6,671	5,504
40,050	40,100	6,684	5,281	6,684	5,516
40,100	40,150	6,696	5,289	6,696	5,529
40,150	40,200	6,709	5,296	6,709	5,541
40,200	40,250	6,721	5,304	6,721	5,554
40,250	40,300	6,734	5,311	6,734	5,566
40,300	40,350	6,746	5,319	6,746	5,579
40,350	40,400	6,759	5,326	6,759	5,591
40,400	40,450	6,771	5,334	6,771	5,604
40,450	40,500	6,784	5,341	6,784	5,616
40,500	40,550	6,796	5,349	6,796	5,629
40,550	40,600	6,809	5,356	6,809	5,641
40,600	40,650	6,821	5,364	6,821	5,654
40,650	40,700	6,834	5,371	6,834	5,666
40,700	40,750	6,846	5,379	6,846	5,679
40,750	40,800	6,859	5,386	6,859	5,691
40,800	40,850	6,871	5,394	6,871	5,704
40,850	40,900	6,884	5,401	6,884	5,716
40,900	40,950	6,896	5,409	6,896	5,729
40,950	41,000	6,909	5,416	6,909	5,741

* This column must also be used by a qualifying widow(er).

(Continued on page 69)

If line 43 (taxable income) is— / And you are—

Columns: Single | Married filing jointly* | Married filing separately | Head of a household — Your tax is—

* This column must also be used by a qualifying widow(er).

41,000

At least	But less than	Single	Married filing jointly*	Married filing separately	Head of a household
41,000	41,050	6,921	5,424	6,921	5,754
41,050	41,100	6,934	5,431	6,934	5,766
41,100	41,150	6,946	5,439	6,946	5,779
41,150	41,200	6,959	5,446	6,959	5,791
41,200	41,250	6,971	5,454	6,971	5,804
41,250	41,300	6,984	5,461	6,984	5,816
41,300	41,350	6,996	5,469	6,996	5,829
41,350	41,400	7,009	5,476	7,009	5,841
41,400	41,450	7,021	5,484	7,021	5,854
41,450	41,500	7,034	5,491	7,034	5,866
41,500	41,550	7,046	5,499	7,046	5,879
41,550	41,600	7,059	5,506	7,059	5,891
41,600	41,650	7,071	5,514	7,071	5,904
41,650	41,700	7,084	5,521	7,084	5,916
41,700	41,750	7,096	5,529	7,096	5,929
41,750	41,800	7,109	5,536	7,109	5,941
41,800	41,850	7,121	5,544	7,121	5,954
41,850	41,900	7,134	5,551	7,134	5,966
41,900	41,950	7,146	5,559	7,146	5,979
41,950	42,000	7,159	5,566	7,159	5,991

42,000

At least	But less than	Single	Married filing jointly*	Married filing separately	Head of a household
42,000	42,050	7,171	5,574	7,171	6,004
42,050	42,100	7,184	5,581	7,184	6,016
42,100	42,150	7,196	5,589	7,196	6,029
42,150	42,200	7,209	5,596	7,209	6,041
42,200	42,250	7,221	5,604	7,221	6,054
42,250	42,300	7,234	5,611	7,234	6,066
42,300	42,350	7,246	5,619	7,246	6,079
42,350	42,400	7,259	5,626	7,259	6,091
42,400	42,450	7,271	5,634	7,271	6,104
42,450	42,500	7,284	5,641	7,284	6,116
42,500	42,550	7,296	5,649	7,296	6,129
42,550	42,600	7,309	5,656	7,309	6,141
42,600	42,650	7,321	5,664	7,321	6,154
42,650	42,700	7,334	5,671	7,334	6,166
42,700	42,750	7,346	5,679	7,346	6,179
42,750	42,800	7,359	5,686	7,359	6,191
42,800	42,850	7,371	5,694	7,371	6,204
42,850	42,900	7,384	5,701	7,384	6,216
42,900	42,950	7,396	5,709	7,396	6,229
42,950	43,000	7,409	5,716	7,409	6,241

43,000

At least	But less than	Single	Married filing jointly*	Married filing separately	Head of a household
43,000	43,050	7,421	5,724	7,421	6,254
43,050	43,100	7,434	5,731	7,434	6,266
43,100	43,150	7,446	5,739	7,446	6,279
43,150	43,200	7,459	5,746	7,459	6,291
43,200	43,250	7,471	5,754	7,471	6,304
43,250	43,300	7,484	5,761	7,484	6,316
43,300	43,350	7,496	5,769	7,496	6,329
43,350	43,400	7,509	5,776	7,509	6,341
43,400	43,450	7,521	5,784	7,521	6,354
43,450	43,500	7,534	5,791	7,534	6,366
43,500	43,550	7,546	5,799	7,546	6,379
43,550	43,600	7,559	5,806	7,559	6,391
43,600	43,650	7,571	5,814	7,571	6,404
43,650	43,700	7,584	5,821	7,584	6,416
43,700	43,750	7,596	5,829	7,596	6,429
43,750	43,800	7,609	5,836	7,609	6,441
43,800	43,850	7,621	5,844	7,621	6,454
43,850	43,900	7,634	5,851	7,634	6,466
43,900	43,950	7,646	5,859	7,646	6,479
43,950	44,000	7,659	5,866	7,659	6,491

44,000

At least	But less than	Single	Married filing jointly*	Married filing separately	Head of a household
44,000	44,050	7,671	5,874	7,671	6,504
44,050	44,100	7,684	5,881	7,684	6,516
44,100	44,150	7,696	5,889	7,696	6,529
44,150	44,200	7,709	5,896	7,709	6,541
44,200	44,250	7,721	5,904	7,721	6,554
44,250	44,300	7,734	5,911	7,734	6,566
44,300	44,350	7,746	5,919	7,746	6,579
44,350	44,400	7,759	5,926	7,759	6,591
44,400	44,450	7,771	5,934	7,771	6,604
44,450	44,500	7,784	5,941	7,784	6,616
44,500	44,550	7,796	5,949	7,796	6,629
44,550	44,600	7,809	5,956	7,809	6,641
44,600	44,650	7,821	5,964	7,821	6,654
44,650	44,700	7,834	5,971	7,834	6,666
44,700	44,750	7,846	5,979	7,846	6,679
44,750	44,800	7,859	5,986	7,859	6,691
44,800	44,850	7,871	5,994	7,871	6,704
44,850	44,900	7,884	6,001	7,884	6,716
44,900	44,950	7,896	6,009	7,896	6,729
44,950	45,000	7,909	6,016	7,909	6,741

45,000

At least	But less than	Single	Married filing jointly*	Married filing separately	Head of a household
45,000	45,050	7,921	6,024	7,921	6,754
45,050	45,100	7,934	6,031	7,934	6,766
45,100	45,150	7,946	6,039	7,946	6,779
45,150	45,200	7,959	6,046	7,959	6,791
45,200	45,250	7,971	6,054	7,971	6,804
45,250	45,300	7,984	6,061	7,984	6,816
45,300	45,350	7,996	6,069	7,996	6,829
45,350	45,400	8,009	6,076	8,009	6,841
45,400	45,450	8,021	6,084	8,021	6,854
45,450	45,500	8,034	6,091	8,034	6,866
45,500	45,550	8,046	6,099	8,046	6,879
45,550	45,600	8,059	6,106	8,059	6,891
45,600	45,650	8,071	6,114	8,071	6,904
45,650	45,700	8,084	6,121	8,084	6,916
45,700	45,750	8,096	6,129	8,096	6,929
45,750	45,800	8,109	6,136	8,109	6,941
45,800	45,850	8,121	6,144	8,121	6,954
45,850	45,900	8,134	6,151	8,134	6,966
45,900	45,950	8,146	6,159	8,146	6,979
45,950	46,000	8,159	6,166	8,159	6,991

46,000

At least	But less than	Single	Married filing jointly*	Married filing separately	Head of a household
46,000	46,050	8,171	6,174	8,171	7,004
46,050	46,100	8,184	6,181	8,184	7,016
46,100	46,150	8,196	6,189	8,196	7,029
46,150	46,200	8,209	6,196	8,209	7,041
46,200	46,250	8,221	6,204	8,221	7,054
46,250	46,300	8,234	6,211	8,234	7,066
46,300	46,350	8,246	6,219	8,246	7,079
46,350	46,400	8,259	6,226	8,259	7,091
46,400	46,450	8,271	6,234	8,271	7,104
46,450	46,500	8,284	6,241	8,284	7,116
46,500	46,550	8,296	6,249	8,296	7,129
46,550	46,600	8,309	6,256	8,309	7,141
46,600	46,650	8,321	6,264	8,321	7,154
46,650	46,700	8,334	6,271	8,334	7,166
46,700	46,750	8,346	6,279	8,346	7,179
46,750	46,800	8,359	6,286	8,359	7,191
46,800	46,850	8,371	6,294	8,371	7,204
46,850	46,900	8,384	6,301	8,384	7,216
46,900	46,950	8,396	6,309	8,396	7,229
46,950	47,000	8,409	6,316	8,409	7,241

47,000

At least	But less than	Single	Married filing jointly*	Married filing separately	Head of a household
47,000	47,050	8,421	6,324	8,421	7,254
47,050	47,100	8,434	6,331	8,434	7,266
47,100	47,150	8,446	6,339	8,446	7,279
47,150	47,200	8,459	6,346	8,459	7,291
47,200	47,250	8,471	6,354	8,471	7,304
47,250	47,300	8,484	6,361	8,484	7,316
47,300	47,350	8,496	6,369	8,496	7,329
47,350	47,400	8,509	6,376	8,509	7,341
47,400	47,450	8,521	6,384	8,521	7,354
47,450	47,500	8,534	6,391	8,534	7,366
47,500	47,550	8,546	6,399	8,546	7,379
47,550	47,600	8,559	6,406	8,559	7,391
47,600	47,650	8,571	6,414	8,571	7,404
47,650	47,700	8,584	6,421	8,584	7,416
47,700	47,750	8,596	6,429	8,596	7,429
47,750	47,800	8,609	6,436	8,609	7,441
47,800	47,850	8,621	6,444	8,621	7,454
47,850	47,900	8,634	6,451	8,634	7,466
47,900	47,950	8,646	6,459	8,646	7,479
47,950	48,000	8,659	6,466	8,659	7,491

48,000

At least	But less than	Single	Married filing jointly*	Married filing separately	Head of a household
48,000	48,050	8,671	6,474	8,671	7,504
48,050	48,100	8,684	6,481	8,684	7,516
48,100	48,150	8,696	6,489	8,696	7,529
48,150	48,200	8,709	6,496	8,709	7,541
48,200	48,250	8,721	6,504	8,721	7,554
48,250	48,300	8,734	6,511	8,734	7,566
48,300	48,350	8,746	6,519	8,746	7,579
48,350	48,400	8,759	6,526	8,759	7,591
48,400	48,450	8,771	6,534	8,771	7,604
48,450	48,500	8,784	6,541	8,784	7,616
48,500	48,550	8,796	6,549	8,796	7,629
48,550	48,600	8,809	6,556	8,809	7,641
48,600	48,650	8,821	6,564	8,821	7,654
48,650	48,700	8,834	6,571	8,834	7,666
48,700	48,750	8,846	6,579	8,846	7,679
48,750	48,800	8,859	6,586	8,859	7,691
48,800	48,850	8,871	6,594	8,871	7,704
48,850	48,900	8,884	6,601	8,884	7,716
48,900	48,950	8,896	6,609	8,896	7,729
48,950	49,000	8,909	6,616	8,909	7,741

49,000

At least	But less than	Single	Married filing jointly*	Married filing separately	Head of a household
49,000	49,050	8,921	6,624	8,921	7,754
49,050	49,100	8,934	6,631	8,934	7,766
49,100	49,150	8,946	6,639	8,946	7,779
49,150	49,200	8,959	6,646	8,959	7,791
49,200	49,250	8,971	6,654	8,971	7,804
49,250	49,300	8,984	6,661	8,984	7,816
49,300	49,350	8,996	6,669	8,996	7,829
49,350	49,400	9,009	6,676	9,009	7,841
49,400	49,450	9,021	6,684	9,021	7,854
49,450	49,500	9,034	6,691	9,034	7,866
49,500	49,550	9,046	6,699	9,046	7,879
49,550	49,600	9,059	6,706	9,059	7,891
49,600	49,650	9,071	6,714	9,071	7,904
49,650	49,700	9,084	6,721	9,084	7,916
49,700	49,750	9,096	6,729	9,096	7,929
49,750	49,800	9,109	6,736	9,109	7,941
49,800	49,850	9,121	6,744	9,121	7,954
49,850	49,900	9,134	6,751	9,134	7,966
49,900	49,950	9,146	6,759	9,146	7,979
49,950	50,000	9,159	6,766	9,159	7,991

* This column must also be used by a qualifying widow(er).

(Continued on page 70)

2005 Tax Table—*Continued*

50,000

At least	But less than	Single	Married filing jointly*	Married filing separately	Head of a household
		Your tax is—			
50,000	50,050	9,171	6,774	9,171	8,004
50,050	50,100	9,184	6,781	9,184	8,016
50,100	50,150	9,196	6,789	9,196	8,029
50,150	50,200	9,209	6,796	9,209	8,041
50,200	50,250	9,221	6,804	9,221	8,054
50,250	50,300	9,234	6,811	9,234	8,066
50,300	50,350	9,246	6,819	9,246	8,079
50,350	50,400	9,259	6,826	9,259	8,091
50,400	50,450	9,271	6,834	9,271	8,104
50,450	50,500	9,284	6,841	9,284	8,116
50,500	50,550	9,296	6,849	9,296	8,129
50,550	50,600	9,309	6,856	9,309	8,141
50,600	50,650	9,321	6,864	9,321	8,154
50,650	50,700	9,334	6,871	9,334	8,166
50,700	50,750	9,346	6,879	9,346	8,179
50,750	50,800	9,359	6,886	9,359	8,191
50,800	50,850	9,371	6,894	9,371	8,204
50,850	50,900	9,384	6,901	9,384	8,216
50,900	50,950	9,396	6,909	9,396	8,229
50,950	51,000	9,409	6,916	9,409	8,241

51,000

At least	But less than	Single	Married filing jointly*	Married filing separately	Head of a household
51,000	51,050	9,421	6,924	9,421	8,254
51,050	51,100	9,434	6,931	9,434	8,266
51,100	51,150	9,446	6,939	9,446	8,279
51,150	51,200	9,459	6,946	9,459	8,291
51,200	51,250	9,471	6,954	9,471	8,304
51,250	51,300	9,484	6,961	9,484	8,316
51,300	51,350	9,496	6,969	9,496	8,329
51,350	51,400	9,509	6,976	9,509	8,341
51,400	51,450	9,521	6,984	9,521	8,354
51,450	51,500	9,534	6,991	9,534	8,366
51,500	51,550	9,546	6,999	9,546	8,379
51,550	51,600	9,559	7,006	9,559	8,391
51,600	51,650	9,571	7,014	9,571	8,404
51,650	51,700	9,584	7,021	9,584	8,416
51,700	51,750	9,596	7,029	9,596	8,429
51,750	51,800	9,609	7,036	9,609	8,441
51,800	51,850	9,621	7,044	9,621	8,454
51,850	51,900	9,634	7,051	9,634	8,466
51,900	51,950	9,646	7,059	9,646	8,479
51,950	52,000	9,659	7,066	9,659	8,491

52,000

At least	But less than	Single	Married filing jointly*	Married filing separately	Head of a household
52,000	52,050	9,671	7,074	9,671	8,504
52,050	52,100	9,684	7,081	9,684	8,516
52,100	52,150	9,696	7,089	9,696	8,529
52,150	52,200	9,709	7,096	9,709	8,541
52,200	52,250	9,721	7,104	9,721	8,554
52,250	52,300	9,734	7,111	9,734	8,566
52,300	52,350	9,746	7,119	9,746	8,579
52,350	52,400	9,759	7,126	9,759	8,591
52,400	52,450	9,771	7,134	9,771	8,604
52,450	52,500	9,784	7,141	9,784	8,616
52,500	52,550	9,796	7,149	9,796	8,629
52,550	52,600	9,809	7,156	9,809	8,641
52,600	52,650	9,821	7,164	9,821	8,654
52,650	52,700	9,834	7,171	9,834	8,666
52,700	52,750	9,846	7,179	9,846	8,679
52,750	52,800	9,859	7,186	9,859	8,691
52,800	52,850	9,871	7,194	9,871	8,704
52,850	52,900	9,884	7,201	9,884	8,716
52,900	52,950	9,896	7,209	9,896	8,729
52,950	53,000	9,909	7,216	9,909	8,741

53,000

At least	But less than	Single	Married filing jointly*	Married filing separately	Head of a household
53,000	53,050	9,921	7,224	9,921	8,754
53,050	53,100	9,934	7,231	9,934	8,766
53,100	53,150	9,946	7,239	9,946	8,779
53,150	53,200	9,959	7,246	9,959	8,791
53,200	53,250	9,971	7,254	9,971	8,804
53,250	53,300	9,984	7,261	9,984	8,816
53,300	53,350	9,996	7,269	9,996	8,829
53,350	53,400	10,009	7,276	10,009	8,841
53,400	53,450	10,021	7,284	10,021	8,854
53,450	53,500	10,034	7,291	10,034	8,866
53,500	53,550	10,046	7,299	10,046	8,879
53,550	53,600	10,059	7,306	10,059	8,891
53,600	53,650	10,071	7,314	10,071	8,904
53,650	53,700	10,084	7,321	10,084	8,916
53,700	53,750	10,096	7,329	10,096	8,929
53,750	53,800	10,109	7,336	10,109	8,941
53,800	53,850	10,121	7,344	10,121	8,954
53,850	53,900	10,134	7,351	10,134	8,966
53,900	53,950	10,146	7,359	10,146	8,979
53,950	54,000	10,159	7,366	10,159	8,991

54,000

At least	But less than	Single	Married filing jointly*	Married filing separately	Head of a household
54,000	54,050	10,171	7,374	10,171	9,004
54,050	54,100	10,184	7,381	10,184	9,016
54,100	54,150	10,196	7,389	10,196	9,029
54,150	54,200	10,209	7,396	10,209	9,041
54,200	54,250	10,221	7,404	10,221	9,054
54,250	54,300	10,234	7,411	10,234	9,066
54,300	54,350	10,246	7,419	10,246	9,079
54,350	54,400	10,259	7,426	10,259	9,091
54,400	54,450	10,271	7,434	10,271	9,104
54,450	54,500	10,284	7,441	10,284	9,116
54,500	54,550	10,296	7,449	10,296	9,129
54,550	54,600	10,309	7,456	10,309	9,141
54,600	54,650	10,321	7,464	10,321	9,154
54,650	54,700	10,334	7,471	10,334	9,166
54,700	54,750	10,346	7,479	10,346	9,179
54,750	54,800	10,359	7,486	10,359	9,191
54,800	54,850	10,371	7,494	10,371	9,204
54,850	54,900	10,384	7,501	10,384	9,216
54,900	54,950	10,396	7,509	10,396	9,229
54,950	55,000	10,409	7,516	10,409	9,241

55,000

At least	But less than	Single	Married filing jointly*	Married filing separately	Head of a household
55,000	55,050	10,421	7,524	10,421	9,254
55,050	55,100	10,434	7,531	10,434	9,266
55,100	55,150	10,446	7,539	10,446	9,279
55,150	55,200	10,459	7,546	10,459	9,291
55,200	55,250	10,471	7,554	10,471	9,304
55,250	55,300	10,484	7,561	10,484	9,316
55,300	55,350	10,496	7,569	10,496	9,329
55,350	55,400	10,509	7,576	10,509	9,341
55,400	55,450	10,521	7,584	10,521	9,354
55,450	55,500	10,534	7,591	10,534	9,366
55,500	55,550	10,546	7,599	10,546	9,379
55,550	55,600	10,559	7,606	10,559	9,391
55,600	55,650	10,571	7,614	10,571	9,404
55,650	55,700	10,584	7,621	10,584	9,416
55,700	55,750	10,596	7,629	10,596	9,429
55,750	55,800	10,609	7,636	10,609	9,441
55,800	55,850	10,621	7,644	10,621	9,454
55,850	55,900	10,634	7,651	10,634	9,466
55,900	55,950	10,646	7,659	10,646	9,479
55,950	56,000	10,659	7,666	10,659	9,491

56,000

At least	But less than	Single	Married filing jointly*	Married filing separately	Head of a household
56,000	56,050	10,671	7,674	10,671	9,504
56,050	56,100	10,684	7,681	10,684	9,516
56,100	56,150	10,696	7,689	10,696	9,529
56,150	56,200	10,709	7,696	10,709	9,541
56,200	56,250	10,721	7,704	10,721	9,554
56,250	56,300	10,734	7,711	10,734	9,566
56,300	56,350	10,746	7,719	10,746	9,579
56,350	56,400	10,759	7,726	10,759	9,591
56,400	56,450	10,771	7,734	10,771	9,604
56,450	56,500	10,784	7,741	10,784	9,616
56,500	56,550	10,796	7,749	10,796	9,629
56,550	56,600	10,809	7,756	10,809	9,641
56,600	56,650	10,821	7,764	10,821	9,654
56,650	56,700	10,834	7,771	10,834	9,666
56,700	56,750	10,846	7,779	10,846	9,679
56,750	56,800	10,859	7,786	10,859	9,691
56,800	56,850	10,871	7,794	10,871	9,704
56,850	56,900	10,884	7,801	10,884	9,716
56,900	56,950	10,896	7,809	10,896	9,729
56,950	57,000	10,909	7,816	10,909	9,741

57,000

At least	But less than	Single	Married filing jointly*	Married filing separately	Head of a household
57,000	57,050	10,921	7,824	10,921	9,754
57,050	57,100	10,934	7,831	10,934	9,766
57,100	57,150	10,946	7,839	10,946	9,779
57,150	57,200	10,959	7,846	10,959	9,791
57,200	57,250	10,971	7,854	10,971	9,804
57,250	57,300	10,984	7,861	10,984	9,816
57,300	57,350	10,996	7,869	10,996	9,829
57,350	57,400	11,009	7,876	11,009	9,841
57,400	57,450	11,021	7,884	11,021	9,854
57,450	57,500	11,034	7,891	11,034	9,866
57,500	57,550	11,046	7,899	11,046	9,879
57,550	57,600	11,059	7,906	11,059	9,891
57,600	57,650	11,071	7,914	11,071	9,904
57,650	57,700	11,084	7,921	11,084	9,916
57,700	57,750	11,096	7,929	11,096	9,929
57,750	57,800	11,109	7,936	11,109	9,941
57,800	57,850	11,121	7,944	11,121	9,954
57,850	57,900	11,134	7,951	11,134	9,966
57,900	57,950	11,146	7,959	11,146	9,979
57,950	58,000	11,159	7,966	11,159	9,991

58,000

At least	But less than	Single	Married filing jointly*	Married filing separately	Head of a household
58,000	58,050	11,171	7,974	11,171	10,004
58,050	58,100	11,184	7,981	11,184	10,016
58,100	58,150	11,196	7,989	11,196	10,029
58,150	58,200	11,209	7,996	11,209	10,041
58,200	58,250	11,221	8,004	11,221	10,054
58,250	58,300	11,234	8,011	11,234	10,066
58,300	58,350	11,246	8,019	11,246	10,079
58,350	58,400	11,259	8,026	11,259	10,091
58,400	58,450	11,271	8,034	11,271	10,104
58,450	58,500	11,284	8,041	11,284	10,116
58,500	58,550	11,296	8,049	11,296	10,129
58,550	58,600	11,309	8,056	11,309	10,141
58,600	58,650	11,321	8,064	11,321	10,154
58,650	58,700	11,334	8,071	11,334	10,166
58,700	58,750	11,346	8,079	11,346	10,179
58,750	58,800	11,359	8,086	11,359	10,191
58,800	58,850	11,371	8,094	11,371	10,204
58,850	58,900	11,384	8,101	11,384	10,216
58,900	58,950	11,396	8,109	11,396	10,229
58,950	59,000	11,409	8,116	11,409	10,241

* This column must also be used by a qualifying widow(er).

(Continued on page 71)

If line 43 (taxable income) is—		And you are—			
At least	But less than	Single	Married filing jointly *	Married filing separately	Head of a household
		Your tax is—			
59,000					
59,000	59,050	11,421	8,124	11,421	10,254
59,050	59,100	11,434	8,131	11,434	10,266
59,100	59,150	11,446	8,139	11,446	10,279
59,150	59,200	11,459	8,146	11,459	10,291
59,200	59,250	11,471	8,154	11,471	10,304
59,250	59,300	11,484	8,161	11,484	10,316
59,300	59,350	11,496	8,169	11,496	10,329
59,350	59,400	11,509	8,176	11,509	10,341
59,400	59,450	11,521	8,186	11,521	10,354
59,450	59,500	11,534	8,199	11,534	10,366
59,500	59,550	11,546	8,211	11,546	10,379
59,550	59,600	11,559	8,224	11,559	10,391
59,600	59,650	11,571	8,236	11,571	10,404
59,650	59,700	11,584	8,249	11,584	10,416
59,700	59,750	11,596	8,261	11,596	10,429
59,750	59,800	11,609	8,274	11,609	10,441
59,800	59,850	11,621	8,286	11,621	10,454
59,850	59,900	11,634	8,299	11,634	10,466
59,900	59,950	11,646	8,311	11,646	10,479
59,950	60,000	11,659	8,324	11,659	10,491
60,000					
60,000	60,050	11,671	8,336	11,673	10,504
60,050	60,100	11,684	8,349	11,687	10,516
60,100	60,150	11,696	8,361	11,701	10,529
60,150	60,200	11,709	8,374	11,715	10,541
60,200	60,250	11,721	8,386	11,729	10,554
60,250	60,300	11,734	8,399	11,743	10,566
60,300	60,350	11,746	8,411	11,757	10,579
60,350	60,400	11,759	8,424	11,771	10,591
60,400	60,450	11,771	8,436	11,785	10,604
60,450	60,500	11,784	8,449	11,799	10,616
60,500	60,550	11,796	8,461	11,813	10,629
60,550	60,600	11,809	8,474	11,827	10,641
60,600	60,650	11,821	8,486	11,841	10,654
60,650	60,700	11,834	8,499	11,855	10,666
60,700	60,750	11,846	8,511	11,869	10,679
60,750	60,800	11,859	8,524	11,883	10,691
60,800	60,850	11,871	8,536	11,897	10,704
60,850	60,900	11,884	8,549	11,911	10,716
60,900	60,950	11,896	8,561	11,925	10,729
60,950	61,000	11,909	8,574	11,939	10,741
61,000					
61,000	61,050	11,921	8,586	11,953	10,754
61,050	61,100	11,934	8,599	11,967	10,766
61,100	61,150	11,946	8,611	11,981	10,779
61,150	61,200	11,959	8,624	11,995	10,791
61,200	61,250	11,971	8,636	12,009	10,804
61,250	61,300	11,984	8,649	12,023	10,816
61,300	61,350	11,996	8,661	12,037	10,829
61,350	61,400	12,009	8,674	12,051	10,841
61,400	61,450	12,021	8,686	12,065	10,854
61,450	61,500	12,034	8,699	12,079	10,866
61,500	61,550	12,046	8,711	12,093	10,879
61,550	61,600	12,059	8,724	12,107	10,891
61,600	61,650	12,071	8,736	12,121	10,904
61,650	61,700	12,084	8,749	12,135	10,916
61,700	61,750	12,096	8,761	12,149	10,929
61,750	61,800	12,109	8,774	12,163	10,941
61,800	61,850	12,121	8,786	12,177	10,954
61,850	61,900	12,134	8,799	12,191	10,966
61,900	61,950	12,146	8,811	12,205	10,979
61,950	62,000	12,159	8,824	12,219	10,991

If line 43 (taxable income) is—		And you are—			
At least	But less than	Single	Married filing jointly *	Married filing separately	Head of a household
		Your tax is—			
62,000					
62,000	62,050	12,171	8,836	12,233	11,004
62,050	62,100	12,184	8,849	12,247	11,016
62,100	62,150	12,196	8,861	12,261	11,029
62,150	62,200	12,209	8,874	12,275	11,041
62,200	62,250	12,221	8,886	12,289	11,054
62,250	62,300	12,234	8,899	12,303	11,066
62,300	62,350	12,246	8,911	12,317	11,079
62,350	62,400	12,259	8,924	12,331	11,091
62,400	62,450	12,271	8,936	12,345	11,104
62,450	62,500	12,284	8,949	12,359	11,116
62,500	62,550	12,296	8,961	12,373	11,129
62,550	62,600	12,309	8,974	12,387	11,141
62,600	62,650	12,321	8,986	12,401	11,154
62,650	62,700	12,334	8,999	12,415	11,166
62,700	62,750	12,346	9,011	12,429	11,179
62,750	62,800	12,359	9,024	12,443	11,191
62,800	62,850	12,371	9,036	12,457	11,204
62,850	62,900	12,384	9,049	12,471	11,216
62,900	62,950	12,396	9,061	12,485	11,229
62,950	63,000	12,409	9,074	12,499	11,241
63,000					
63,000	63,050	12,421	9,086	12,513	11,254
63,050	63,100	12,434	9,099	12,527	11,266
63,100	63,150	12,446	9,111	12,541	11,279
63,150	63,200	12,459	9,124	12,555	11,291
63,200	63,250	12,471	9,136	12,569	11,304
63,250	63,300	12,484	9,149	12,583	11,316
63,300	63,350	12,496	9,161	12,597	11,329
63,350	63,400	12,509	9,174	12,611	11,341
63,400	63,450	12,521	9,186	12,625	11,354
63,450	63,500	12,534	9,199	12,639	11,366
63,500	63,550	12,546	9,211	12,653	11,379
63,550	63,600	12,559	9,224	12,667	11,391
63,600	63,650	12,571	9,236	12,681	11,404
63,650	63,700	12,584	9,249	12,695	11,416
63,700	63,750	12,596	9,261	12,709	11,429
63,750	63,800	12,609	9,274	12,723	11,441
63,800	63,850	12,621	9,286	12,737	11,454
63,850	63,900	12,634	9,299	12,751	11,466
63,900	63,950	12,646	9,311	12,765	11,479
63,950	64,000	12,659	9,324	12,779	11,491
64,000					
64,000	64,050	12,671	9,336	12,793	11,504
64,050	64,100	12,684	9,349	12,807	11,516
64,100	64,150	12,696	9,361	12,821	11,529
64,150	64,200	12,709	9,374	12,835	11,541
64,200	64,250	12,721	9,386	12,849	11,554
64,250	64,300	12,734	9,399	12,863	11,566
64,300	64,350	12,746	9,411	12,877	11,579
64,350	64,400	12,759	9,424	12,891	11,591
64,400	64,450	12,771	9,436	12,905	11,604
64,450	64,500	12,784	9,449	12,919	11,616
64,500	64,550	12,796	9,461	12,933	11,629
64,550	64,600	12,809	9,474	12,947	11,641
64,600	64,650	12,821	9,486	12,961	11,654
64,650	64,700	12,834	9,499	12,975	11,666
64,700	64,750	12,846	9,511	12,989	11,679
64,750	64,800	12,859	9,524	13,003	11,691
64,800	64,850	12,871	9,536	13,017	11,704
64,850	64,900	12,884	9,549	13,031	11,716
64,900	64,950	12,896	9,561	13,045	11,729
64,950	65,000	12,909	9,574	13,059	11,741

If line 43 (taxable income) is—		And you are—			
At least	But less than	Single	Married filing jointly *	Married filing separately	Head of a household
		Your tax is—			
65,000					
65,000	65,050	12,921	9,586	13,073	11,754
65,050	65,100	12,934	9,599	13,087	11,766
65,100	65,150	12,946	9,611	13,101	11,779
65,150	65,200	12,959	9,624	13,115	11,791
65,200	65,250	12,971	9,636	13,129	11,804
65,250	65,300	12,984	9,649	13,143	11,816
65,300	65,350	12,996	9,661	13,157	11,829
65,350	65,400	13,009	9,674	13,171	11,841
65,400	65,450	13,021	9,686	13,185	11,854
65,450	65,500	13,034	9,699	13,199	11,866
65,500	65,550	13,046	9,711	13,213	11,879
65,550	65,600	13,059	9,724	13,227	11,891
65,600	65,650	13,071	9,736	13,241	11,904
65,650	65,700	13,084	9,749	13,255	11,916
65,700	65,750	13,096	9,761	13,269	11,929
65,750	65,800	13,109	9,774	13,283	11,941
65,800	65,850	13,121	9,786	13,297	11,954
65,850	65,900	13,134	9,799	13,311	11,966
65,900	65,950	13,146	9,811	13,325	11,979
65,950	66,000	13,159	9,824	13,339	11,991
66,000					
66,000	66,050	13,171	9,836	13,353	12,004
66,050	66,100	13,184	9,849	13,367	12,016
66,100	66,150	13,196	9,861	13,381	12,029
66,150	66,200	13,209	9,874	13,395	12,041
66,200	66,250	13,221	9,886	13,409	12,054
66,250	66,300	13,234	9,899	13,423	12,066
66,300	66,350	13,246	9,911	13,437	12,079
66,350	66,400	13,259	9,924	13,451	12,091
66,400	66,450	13,271	9,936	13,465	12,104
66,450	66,500	13,284	9,949	13,479	12,116
66,500	66,550	13,296	9,961	13,493	12,129
66,550	66,600	13,309	9,974	13,507	12,141
66,600	66,650	13,321	9,986	13,521	12,154
66,650	66,700	13,334	9,999	13,535	12,166
66,700	66,750	13,346	10,011	13,549	12,179
66,750	66,800	13,359	10,024	13,563	12,191
66,800	66,850	13,371	10,036	13,577	12,204
66,850	66,900	13,384	10,049	13,591	12,216
66,900	66,950	13,396	10,061	13,605	12,229
66,950	67,000	13,409	10,074	13,619	12,241
67,000					
67,000	67,050	13,421	10,086	13,633	12,254
67,050	67,100	13,434	10,099	13,647	12,266
67,100	67,150	13,446	10,111	13,661	12,279
67,150	67,200	13,459	10,124	13,675	12,291
67,200	67,250	13,471	10,136	13,689	12,304
67,250	67,300	13,484	10,149	13,703	12,316
67,300	67,350	13,496	10,161	13,717	12,329
67,350	67,400	13,509	10,174	13,731	12,341
67,400	67,450	13,521	10,186	13,745	12,354
67,450	67,500	13,534	10,199	13,759	12,366
67,500	67,550	13,546	10,211	13,773	12,379
67,550	67,600	13,559	10,224	13,787	12,391
67,600	67,650	13,571	10,236	13,801	12,404
67,650	67,700	13,584	10,249	13,815	12,416
67,700	67,750	13,596	10,261	13,829	12,429
67,750	67,800	13,609	10,274	13,843	12,441
67,800	67,850	13,621	10,286	13,857	12,454
67,850	67,900	13,634	10,299	13,871	12,466
67,900	67,950	13,646	10,311	13,885	12,479
67,950	68,000	13,659	10,324	13,899	12,491

* This column must also be used by a qualifying widow(er).

(Continued on page 72)

2005 Tax Table—Continued

If line 43 (taxable income) is—		And you are—			
At least	But less than	Single	Married filing jointly *	Married filing separately	Head of a household
		Your tax is—			

68,000

At least	But less than	Single	MFJ *	MFS	HoH
68,000	68,050	13,671	10,336	13,913	12,504
68,050	68,100	13,684	10,349	13,927	12,516
68,100	68,150	13,696	10,361	13,941	12,529
68,150	68,200	13,709	10,374	13,955	12,541
68,200	68,250	13,721	10,386	13,969	12,554
68,250	68,300	13,734	10,399	13,983	12,566
68,300	68,350	13,746	10,411	13,997	12,579
68,350	68,400	13,759	10,424	14,011	12,591
68,400	68,450	13,771	10,436	14,025	12,604
68,450	68,500	13,784	10,449	14,039	12,616
68,500	68,550	13,796	10,461	14,053	12,629
68,550	68,600	13,809	10,474	14,067	12,641
68,600	68,650	13,821	10,486	14,081	12,654
68,650	68,700	13,834	10,499	14,095	12,666
68,700	68,750	13,846	10,511	14,109	12,679
68,750	68,800	13,859	10,524	14,123	12,691
68,800	68,850	13,871	10,536	14,137	12,704
68,850	68,900	13,884	10,549	14,151	12,716
68,900	68,950	13,896	10,561	14,165	12,729
68,950	69,000	13,909	10,574	14,179	12,741

69,000

At least	But less than	Single	MFJ *	MFS	HoH
69,000	69,050	13,921	10,586	14,193	12,754
69,050	69,100	13,934	10,599	14,207	12,766
69,100	69,150	13,946	10,611	14,221	12,779
69,150	69,200	13,959	10,624	14,235	12,791
69,200	69,250	13,971	10,636	14,249	12,804
69,250	69,300	13,984	10,649	14,263	12,816
69,300	69,350	13,996	10,661	14,277	12,829
69,350	69,400	14,009	10,674	14,291	12,841
69,400	69,450	14,021	10,686	14,305	12,854
69,450	69,500	14,034	10,699	14,319	12,866
69,500	69,550	14,046	10,711	14,333	12,879
69,550	69,600	14,059	10,724	14,347	12,891
69,600	69,650	14,071	10,736	14,361	12,904
69,650	69,700	14,084	10,749	14,375	12,916
69,700	69,750	14,096	10,761	14,389	12,929
69,750	69,800	14,109	10,774	14,403	12,941
69,800	69,850	14,121	10,786	14,417	12,954
69,850	69,900	14,134	10,799	14,431	12,966
69,900	69,950	14,146	10,811	14,445	12,979
69,950	70,000	14,159	10,824	14,459	12,991

70,000

At least	But less than	Single	MFJ *	MFS	HoH
70,000	70,050	14,171	10,836	14,473	13,004
70,050	70,100	14,184	10,849	14,487	13,016
70,100	70,150	14,196	10,861	14,501	13,029
70,150	70,200	14,209	10,874	14,515	13,041
70,200	70,250	14,221	10,886	14,529	13,054
70,250	70,300	14,234	10,899	14,543	13,066
70,300	70,350	14,246	10,911	14,557	13,079
70,350	70,400	14,259	10,924	14,571	13,091
70,400	70,450	14,271	10,936	14,585	13,104
70,450	70,500	14,284	10,949	14,599	13,116
70,500	70,550	14,296	10,961	14,613	13,129
70,550	70,600	14,309	10,974	14,627	13,141
70,600	70,650	14,321	10,986	14,641	13,154
70,650	70,700	14,334	10,999	14,655	13,166
70,700	70,750	14,346	11,011	14,669	13,179
70,750	70,800	14,359	11,024	14,683	13,191
70,800	70,850	14,371	11,036	14,697	13,204
70,850	70,900	14,384	11,049	14,711	13,216
70,900	70,950	14,396	11,061	14,725	13,229
70,950	71,000	14,409	11,074	14,739	13,241

71,000

At least	But less than	Single	MFJ *	MFS	HoH
71,000	71,050	14,421	11,086	14,753	13,254
71,050	71,100	14,434	11,099	14,767	13,266
71,100	71,150	14,446	11,111	14,781	13,279
71,150	71,200	14,459	11,124	14,795	13,291
71,200	71,250	14,471	11,136	14,809	13,304
71,250	71,300	14,484	11,149	14,823	13,316
71,300	71,350	14,496	11,161	14,837	13,329
71,350	71,400	14,509	11,174	14,851	13,341
71,400	71,450	14,521	11,186	14,865	13,354
71,450	71,500	14,534	11,199	14,879	13,366
71,500	71,550	14,546	11,211	14,893	13,379
71,550	71,600	14,559	11,224	14,907	13,391
71,600	71,650	14,571	11,236	14,921	13,404
71,650	71,700	14,584	11,249	14,935	13,416
71,700	71,750	14,596	11,261	14,949	13,429
71,750	71,800	14,609	11,274	14,963	13,441
71,800	71,850	14,621	11,286	14,977	13,454
71,850	71,900	14,634	11,299	14,991	13,466
71,900	71,950	14,646	11,311	15,005	13,479
71,950	72,000	14,660	11,324	15,019	13,491

72,000

At least	But less than	Single	MFJ *	MFS	HoH
72,000	72,050	14,674	11,336	15,033	13,504
72,050	72,100	14,688	11,349	15,047	13,516
72,100	72,150	14,702	11,361	15,061	13,529
72,150	72,200	14,716	11,374	15,075	13,541
72,200	72,250	14,730	11,386	15,089	13,554
72,250	72,300	14,744	11,399	15,103	13,566
72,300	72,350	14,758	11,411	15,117	13,579
72,350	72,400	14,772	11,424	15,131	13,591
72,400	72,450	14,786	11,436	15,145	13,604
72,450	72,500	14,800	11,449	15,159	13,616
72,500	72,550	14,814	11,461	15,173	13,629
72,550	72,600	14,828	11,474	15,187	13,641
72,600	72,650	14,842	11,486	15,201	13,654
72,650	72,700	14,856	11,499	15,215	13,666
72,700	72,750	14,870	11,511	15,229	13,679
72,750	72,800	14,884	11,524	15,243	13,691
72,800	72,850	14,898	11,536	15,257	13,704
72,850	72,900	14,912	11,549	15,271	13,716
72,900	72,950	14,926	11,561	15,285	13,729
72,950	73,000	14,940	11,574	15,299	13,741

73,000

At least	But less than	Single	MFJ *	MFS	HoH
73,000	73,050	14,954	11,586	15,313	13,754
73,050	73,100	14,968	11,599	15,327	13,766
73,100	73,150	14,982	11,611	15,341	13,779
73,150	73,200	14,996	11,624	15,355	13,791
73,200	73,250	15,010	11,636	15,369	13,804
73,250	73,300	15,024	11,649	15,383	13,816
73,300	73,350	15,038	11,661	15,397	13,829
73,350	73,400	15,052	11,674	15,411	13,841
73,400	73,450	15,066	11,686	15,425	13,854
73,450	73,500	15,080	11,699	15,439	13,866
73,500	73,550	15,094	11,711	15,453	13,879
73,550	73,600	15,108	11,724	15,467	13,891
73,600	73,650	15,122	11,736	15,481	13,904
73,650	73,700	15,136	11,749	15,495	13,916
73,700	73,750	15,150	11,761	15,509	13,929
73,750	73,800	15,164	11,774	15,523	13,941
73,800	73,850	15,178	11,786	15,537	13,954
73,850	73,900	15,192	11,799	15,551	13,966
73,900	73,950	15,206	11,811	15,565	13,979
73,950	74,000	15,220	11,824	15,579	13,991

74,000

At least	But less than	Single	MFJ *	MFS	HoH
74,000	74,050	15,234	11,836	15,593	14,004
74,050	74,100	15,248	11,849	15,607	14,016
74,100	74,150	15,262	11,861	15,621	14,029
74,150	74,200	15,276	11,874	15,635	14,041
74,200	74,250	15,290	11,886	15,649	14,054
74,250	74,300	15,304	11,899	15,663	14,066
74,300	74,350	15,318	11,911	15,677	14,079
74,350	74,400	15,332	11,924	15,691	14,091
74,400	74,450	15,346	11,936	15,705	14,104
74,450	74,500	15,360	11,949	15,719	14,116
74,500	74,550	15,374	11,961	15,733	14,129
74,550	74,600	15,388	11,974	15,747	14,141
74,600	74,650	15,402	11,986	15,761	14,154
74,650	74,700	15,416	11,999	15,775	14,166
74,700	74,750	15,430	12,011	15,789	14,179
74,750	74,800	15,444	12,024	15,803	14,191
74,800	74,850	15,458	12,036	15,817	14,204
74,850	74,900	15,472	12,049	15,831	14,216
74,900	74,950	15,486	12,061	15,845	14,229
74,950	75,000	15,500	12,074	15,859	14,241

75,000

At least	But less than	Single	MFJ *	MFS	HoH
75,000	75,050	15,514	12,086	15,873	14,254
75,050	75,100	15,528	12,099	15,887	14,266
75,100	75,150	15,542	12,111	15,901	14,279
75,150	75,200	15,556	12,124	15,915	14,291
75,200	75,250	15,570	12,136	15,929	14,304
75,250	75,300	15,584	12,149	15,943	14,316
75,300	75,350	15,598	12,161	15,957	14,329
75,350	75,400	15,612	12,174	15,971	14,341
75,400	75,450	15,626	12,186	15,985	14,354
75,450	75,500	15,640	12,199	15,999	14,366
75,500	75,550	15,654	12,211	16,013	14,379
75,550	75,600	15,668	12,224	16,027	14,391
75,600	75,650	15,682	12,236	16,041	14,404
75,650	75,700	15,696	12,249	16,055	14,416
75,700	75,750	15,710	12,261	16,069	14,429
75,750	75,800	15,724	12,274	16,083	14,441
75,800	75,850	15,738	12,286	16,097	14,454
75,850	75,900	15,752	12,299	16,111	14,466
75,900	75,950	15,766	12,311	16,125	14,479
75,950	76,000	15,780	12,324	16,139	14,491

76,000

At least	But less than	Single	MFJ *	MFS	HoH
76,000	76,050	15,794	12,336	16,153	14,504
76,050	76,100	15,808	12,349	16,167	14,516
76,100	76,150	15,822	12,361	16,181	14,529
76,150	76,200	15,836	12,374	16,195	14,541
76,200	76,250	15,850	12,386	16,209	14,554
76,250	76,300	15,864	12,399	16,223	14,566
76,300	76,350	15,878	12,411	16,237	14,579
76,350	76,400	15,892	12,424	16,251	14,591
76,400	76,450	15,906	12,436	16,265	14,604
76,450	76,500	15,920	12,449	16,279	14,616
76,500	76,550	15,934	12,461	16,293	14,629
76,550	76,600	15,948	12,474	16,307	14,641
76,600	76,650	15,962	12,486	16,321	14,654
76,650	76,700	15,976	12,499	16,335	14,666
76,700	76,750	15,990	12,511	16,349	14,679
76,750	76,800	16,004	12,524	16,363	14,691
76,800	76,850	16,018	12,536	16,377	14,704
76,850	76,900	16,032	12,549	16,391	14,716
76,900	76,950	16,046	12,561	16,405	14,729
76,950	77,000	16,060	12,574	16,419	14,741

* This column must also be used by a qualifying widow(er).

(Continued on page 73)

77,000

At least	But less than	Single	Married filing jointly *	Married filing separately	Head of a household
77,000	77,050	16,074	12,586	16,433	14,754
77,050	77,100	16,088	12,599	16,447	14,766
77,100	77,150	16,102	12,611	16,461	14,779
77,150	77,200	16,116	12,624	16,475	14,791
77,200	77,250	16,130	12,636	16,489	14,804
77,250	77,300	16,144	12,649	16,503	14,816
77,300	77,350	16,158	12,661	16,517	14,829
77,350	77,400	16,172	12,674	16,531	14,841
77,400	77,450	16,186	12,686	16,545	14,854
77,450	77,500	16,200	12,699	16,559	14,866
77,500	77,550	16,214	12,711	16,573	14,879
77,550	77,600	16,228	12,724	16,587	14,891
77,600	77,650	16,242	12,736	16,601	14,904
77,650	77,700	16,256	12,749	16,615	14,916
77,700	77,750	16,270	12,761	16,629	14,929
77,750	77,800	16,284	12,774	16,643	14,941
77,800	77,850	16,298	12,786	16,657	14,954
77,850	77,900	16,312	12,799	16,671	14,966
77,900	77,950	16,326	12,811	16,685	14,979
77,950	78,000	16,340	12,824	16,699	14,991

78,000

At least	But less than	Single	Married filing jointly *	Married filing separately	Head of a household
78,000	78,050	16,354	12,836	16,713	15,004
78,050	78,100	16,368	12,849	16,727	15,016
78,100	78,150	16,382	12,861	16,741	15,029
78,150	78,200	16,396	12,874	16,755	15,041
78,200	78,250	16,410	12,886	16,769	15,054
78,250	78,300	16,424	12,899	16,783	15,066
78,300	78,350	16,438	12,911	16,797	15,079
78,350	78,400	16,452	12,924	16,811	15,091
78,400	78,450	16,466	12,936	16,825	15,104
78,450	78,500	16,480	12,949	16,839	15,116
78,500	78,550	16,494	12,961	16,853	15,129
78,550	78,600	16,508	12,974	16,867	15,141
78,600	78,650	16,522	12,986	16,881	15,154
78,650	78,700	16,536	12,999	16,895	15,166
78,700	78,750	16,550	13,011	16,909	15,179
78,750	78,800	16,564	13,024	16,923	15,191
78,800	78,850	16,578	13,036	16,937	15,204
78,850	78,900	16,592	13,049	16,951	15,216
78,900	78,950	16,606	13,061	16,965	15,229
78,950	79,000	16,620	13,074	16,979	15,241

79,000

At least	But less than	Single	Married filing jointly *	Married filing separately	Head of a household
79,000	79,050	16,634	13,086	16,993	15,254
79,050	79,100	16,648	13,099	17,007	15,266
79,100	79,150	16,662	13,111	17,021	15,279
79,150	79,200	16,676	13,124	17,035	15,291
79,200	79,250	16,690	13,136	17,049	15,304
79,250	79,300	16,704	13,149	17,063	15,316
79,300	79,350	16,718	13,161	17,077	15,329
79,350	79,400	16,732	13,174	17,091	15,341
79,400	79,450	16,746	13,186	17,105	15,354
79,450	79,500	16,760	13,199	17,119	15,366
79,500	79,550	16,774	13,211	17,133	15,379
79,550	79,600	16,788	13,224	17,147	15,391
79,600	79,650	16,802	13,236	17,161	15,404
79,650	79,700	16,816	13,249	17,175	15,416
79,700	79,750	16,830	13,261	17,189	15,429
79,750	79,800	16,844	13,274	17,203	15,441
79,800	79,850	16,858	13,286	17,217	15,454
79,850	79,900	16,872	13,299	17,231	15,466
79,900	79,950	16,886	13,311	17,245	15,479
79,950	80,000	16,900	13,324	17,259	15,491

80,000

At least	But less than	Single	Married filing jointly *	Married filing separately	Head of a household
80,000	80,050	16,914	13,336	17,273	15,504
80,050	80,100	16,928	13,349	17,287	15,516
80,100	80,150	16,942	13,361	17,301	15,529
80,150	80,200	16,956	13,374	17,315	15,541
80,200	80,250	16,970	13,386	17,329	15,554
80,250	80,300	16,984	13,399	17,343	15,566
80,300	80,350	16,998	13,411	17,357	15,579
80,350	80,400	17,012	13,424	17,371	15,591
80,400	80,450	17,026	13,436	17,385	15,604
80,450	80,500	17,040	13,449	17,399	15,616
80,500	80,550	17,054	13,461	17,413	15,629
80,550	80,600	17,068	13,474	17,427	15,641
80,600	80,650	17,082	13,486	17,441	15,654
80,650	80,700	17,096	13,499	17,455	15,666
80,700	80,750	17,110	13,511	17,469	15,679
80,750	80,800	17,124	13,524	17,483	15,691
80,800	80,850	17,138	13,536	17,497	15,704
80,850	80,900	17,152	13,549	17,511	15,716
80,900	80,950	17,166	13,561	17,525	15,729
80,950	81,000	17,180	13,574	17,539	15,741

81,000

At least	But less than	Single	Married filing jointly *	Married filing separately	Head of a household
81,000	81,050	17,194	13,586	17,553	15,754
81,050	81,100	17,208	13,599	17,567	15,766
81,100	81,150	17,222	13,611	17,581	15,779
81,150	81,200	17,236	13,624	17,595	15,791
81,200	81,250	17,250	13,636	17,609	15,804
81,250	81,300	17,264	13,649	17,623	15,816
81,300	81,350	17,278	13,661	17,637	15,829
81,350	81,400	17,292	13,674	17,651	15,841
81,400	81,450	17,306	13,686	17,665	15,854
81,450	81,500	17,320	13,699	17,679	15,866
81,500	81,550	17,334	13,711	17,693	15,879
81,550	81,600	17,348	13,724	17,707	15,891
81,600	81,650	17,362	13,736	17,721	15,904
81,650	81,700	17,376	13,749	17,735	15,916
81,700	81,750	17,390	13,761	17,749	15,929
81,750	81,800	17,404	13,774	17,763	15,941
81,800	81,850	17,418	13,786	17,777	15,954
81,850	81,900	17,432	13,799	17,791	15,966
81,900	81,950	17,446	13,811	17,805	15,979
81,950	82,000	17,460	13,824	17,819	15,991

82,000

At least	But less than	Single	Married filing jointly *	Married filing separately	Head of a household
82,000	82,050	17,474	13,836	17,833	16,004
82,050	82,100	17,488	13,849	17,847	16,016
82,100	82,150	17,502	13,861	17,861	16,029
82,150	82,200	17,516	13,874	17,875	16,041
82,200	82,250	17,530	13,886	17,889	16,054
82,250	82,300	17,544	13,899	17,903	16,066
82,300	82,350	17,558	13,911	17,917	16,079
82,350	82,400	17,572	13,924	17,931	16,091
82,400	82,450	17,586	13,936	17,945	16,104
82,450	82,500	17,600	13,949	17,959	16,116
82,500	82,550	17,614	13,961	17,973	16,129
82,550	82,600	17,628	13,974	17,987	16,141
82,600	82,650	17,642	13,986	18,001	16,154
82,650	82,700	17,656	13,999	18,015	16,166
82,700	82,750	17,670	14,011	18,029	16,179
82,750	82,800	17,684	14,024	18,043	16,191
82,800	82,850	17,698	14,036	18,057	16,204
82,850	82,900	17,712	14,049	18,071	16,216
82,900	82,950	17,726	14,061	18,085	16,229
82,950	83,000	17,740	14,074	18,099	16,241

83,000

At least	But less than	Single	Married filing jointly *	Married filing separately	Head of a household
83,000	83,050	17,754	14,086	18,113	16,254
83,050	83,100	17,768	14,099	18,127	16,266
83,100	83,150	17,782	14,111	18,141	16,279
83,150	83,200	17,796	14,124	18,155	16,291
83,200	83,250	17,810	14,136	18,169	16,304
83,250	83,300	17,824	14,149	18,183	16,316
83,300	83,350	17,838	14,161	18,197	16,329
83,350	83,400	17,852	14,174	18,211	16,341
83,400	83,450	17,866	14,186	18,225	16,354
83,450	83,500	17,880	14,199	18,239	16,366
83,500	83,550	17,894	14,211	18,253	16,379
83,550	83,600	17,908	14,224	18,267	16,391
83,600	83,650	17,922	14,236	18,281	16,404
83,650	83,700	17,936	14,249	18,295	16,416
83,700	83,750	17,950	14,261	18,309	16,429
83,750	83,800	17,964	14,274	18,323	16,441
83,800	83,850	17,978	14,286	18,337	16,454
83,850	83,900	17,992	14,299	18,351	16,466
83,900	83,950	18,006	14,311	18,365	16,479
83,950	84,000	18,020	14,324	18,379	16,491

84,000

At least	But less than	Single	Married filing jointly *	Married filing separately	Head of a household
84,000	84,050	18,034	14,336	18,393	16,504
84,050	84,100	18,048	14,349	18,407	16,516
84,100	84,150	18,062	14,361	18,421	16,529
84,150	84,200	18,076	14,374	18,435	16,541
84,200	84,250	18,090	14,386	18,449	16,554
84,250	84,300	18,104	14,399	18,463	16,566
84,300	84,350	18,118	14,411	18,477	16,579
84,350	84,400	18,132	14,424	18,491	16,591
84,400	84,450	18,146	14,436	18,505	16,604
84,450	84,500	18,160	14,449	18,519	16,616
84,500	84,550	18,174	14,461	18,533	16,629
84,550	84,600	18,188	14,474	18,547	16,641
84,600	84,650	18,202	14,486	18,561	16,654
84,650	84,700	18,216	14,499	18,575	16,666
84,700	84,750	18,230	14,511	18,589	16,679
84,750	84,800	18,244	14,524	18,603	16,691
84,800	84,850	18,258	14,536	18,617	16,704
84,850	84,900	18,272	14,549	18,631	16,716
84,900	84,950	18,286	14,561	18,645	16,729
84,950	85,000	18,300	14,574	18,659	16,741

85,000

At least	But less than	Single	Married filing jointly *	Married filing separately	Head of a household
85,000	85,050	18,314	14,586	18,673	16,754
85,050	85,100	18,328	14,599	18,687	16,766
85,100	85,150	18,342	14,611	18,701	16,779
85,150	85,200	18,356	14,624	18,715	16,791
85,200	85,250	18,370	14,636	18,729	16,804
85,250	85,300	18,384	14,649	18,743	16,816
85,300	85,350	18,398	14,661	18,757	16,829
85,350	85,400	18,412	14,674	18,771	16,841
85,400	85,450	18,426	14,686	18,785	16,854
85,450	85,500	18,440	14,699	18,799	16,866
85,500	85,550	18,454	14,711	18,813	16,879
85,550	85,600	18,468	14,724	18,827	16,891
85,600	85,650	18,482	14,736	18,841	16,904
85,650	85,700	18,496	14,749	18,855	16,916
85,700	85,750	18,510	14,761	18,869	16,929
85,750	85,800	18,524	14,774	18,883	16,941
85,800	85,850	18,538	14,786	18,897	16,954
85,850	85,900	18,552	14,799	18,911	16,966
85,900	85,950	18,566	14,811	18,925	16,979
85,950	86,000	18,580	14,824	18,939	16,991

* This column must also be used by a qualifying widow(er).

(Continued on page 74)

T-10

86,000

At least	But less than	Single	Married filing jointly*	Married filing separately	Head of a household
86,000	86,050	18,594	14,836	18,953	17,004
86,050	86,100	18,608	14,849	18,967	17,016
86,100	86,150	18,622	14,861	18,981	17,029
86,150	86,200	18,636	14,874	18,995	17,041
86,200	86,250	18,650	14,886	19,009	17,054
86,250	86,300	18,664	14,899	19,023	17,066
86,300	86,350	18,678	14,911	19,037	17,079
86,350	86,400	18,692	14,924	19,051	17,091
86,400	86,450	18,706	14,936	19,065	17,104
86,450	86,500	18,720	14,949	19,079	17,116
86,500	86,550	18,734	14,961	19,093	17,129
86,550	86,600	18,748	14,974	19,107	17,141
86,600	86,650	18,762	14,986	19,121	17,154
86,650	86,700	18,776	14,999	19,135	17,166
86,700	86,750	18,790	15,011	19,149	17,179
86,750	86,800	18,804	15,024	19,163	17,191
86,800	86,850	18,818	15,036	19,177	17,204
86,850	86,900	18,832	15,049	19,191	17,216
86,900	86,950	18,846	15,061	19,205	17,229
86,950	87,000	18,860	15,074	19,219	17,241

87,000

At least	But less than	Single	Married filing jointly*	Married filing separately	Head of a household
87,000	87,050	18,874	15,086	19,233	17,254
87,050	87,100	18,888	15,099	19,247	17,266
87,100	87,150	18,902	15,111	19,261	17,279
87,150	87,200	18,916	15,124	19,275	17,291
87,200	87,250	18,930	15,136	19,289	17,304
87,250	87,300	18,944	15,149	19,303	17,316
87,300	87,350	18,958	15,161	19,317	17,329
87,350	87,400	18,972	15,174	19,331	17,341
87,400	87,450	18,986	15,186	19,345	17,354
87,450	87,500	19,000	15,199	19,359	17,366
87,500	87,550	19,014	15,211	19,373	17,379
87,550	87,600	19,028	15,224	19,387	17,391
87,600	87,650	19,042	15,236	19,401	17,404
87,650	87,700	19,056	15,249	19,415	17,416
87,700	87,750	19,070	15,261	19,429	17,429
87,750	87,800	19,084	15,274	19,443	17,441
87,800	87,850	19,098	15,286	19,457	17,454
87,850	87,900	19,112	15,299	19,471	17,466
87,900	87,950	19,126	15,311	19,485	17,479
87,950	88,000	19,140	15,324	19,499	17,491

88,000

At least	But less than	Single	Married filing jointly*	Married filing separately	Head of a household
88,000	88,050	19,154	15,336	19,513	17,504
88,050	88,100	19,168	15,349	19,527	17,516
88,100	88,150	19,182	15,361	19,541	17,529
88,150	88,200	19,196	15,374	19,555	17,541
88,200	88,250	19,210	15,386	19,569	17,554
88,250	88,300	19,224	15,399	19,583	17,566
88,300	88,350	19,238	15,411	19,597	17,579
88,350	88,400	19,252	15,424	19,611	17,591
88,400	88,450	19,266	15,436	19,625	17,604
88,450	88,500	19,280	15,449	19,639	17,616
88,500	88,550	19,294	15,461	19,653	17,629
88,550	88,600	19,308	15,474	19,667	17,641
88,600	88,650	19,322	15,486	19,681	17,654
88,650	88,700	19,336	15,499	19,695	17,666
88,700	88,750	19,350	15,511	19,709	17,679
88,750	88,800	19,364	15,524	19,723	17,691
88,800	88,850	19,378	15,536	19,737	17,704
88,850	88,900	19,392	15,549	19,751	17,716
88,900	88,950	19,406	15,561	19,765	17,729
88,950	89,000	19,420	15,574	19,779	17,741

89,000

At least	But less than	Single	Married filing jointly*	Married filing separately	Head of a household
89,000	89,050	19,434	15,586	19,793	17,754
89,050	89,100	19,448	15,599	19,807	17,766
89,100	89,150	19,462	15,611	19,821	17,779
89,150	89,200	19,476	15,624	19,835	17,791
89,200	89,250	19,490	15,636	19,849	17,804
89,250	89,300	19,504	15,649	19,863	17,816
89,300	89,350	19,518	15,661	19,877	17,829
89,350	89,400	19,532	15,674	19,891	17,841
89,400	89,450	19,546	15,686	19,905	17,854
89,450	89,500	19,560	15,699	19,919	17,866
89,500	89,550	19,574	15,711	19,933	17,879
89,550	89,600	19,588	15,724	19,947	17,891
89,600	89,650	19,602	15,736	19,961	17,904
89,650	89,700	19,616	15,749	19,975	17,916
89,700	89,750	19,630	15,761	19,989	17,929
89,750	89,800	19,644	15,774	20,003	17,941
89,800	89,850	19,658	15,786	20,017	17,954
89,850	89,900	19,672	15,799	20,031	17,966
89,900	89,950	19,686	15,811	20,045	17,979
89,950	90,000	19,700	15,824	20,059	17,991

90,000

At least	But less than	Single	Married filing jointly*	Married filing separately	Head of a household
90,000	90,050	19,714	15,836	20,073	18,004
90,050	90,100	19,728	15,849	20,087	18,016
90,100	90,150	19,742	15,861	20,101	18,029
90,150	90,200	19,756	15,874	20,115	18,041
90,200	90,250	19,770	15,886	20,129	18,054
90,250	90,300	19,784	15,899	20,143	18,066
90,300	90,350	19,798	15,911	20,157	18,079
90,350	90,400	19,812	15,924	20,171	18,091
90,400	90,450	19,826	15,936	20,185	18,104
90,450	90,500	19,840	15,949	20,199	18,116
90,500	90,550	19,854	15,961	20,213	18,129
90,550	90,600	19,868	15,974	20,227	18,141
90,600	90,650	19,882	15,986	20,241	18,154
90,650	90,700	19,896	15,999	20,255	18,166
90,700	90,750	19,910	16,011	20,269	18,179
90,750	90,800	19,924	16,024	20,283	18,191
90,800	90,850	19,938	16,036	20,297	18,204
90,850	90,900	19,952	16,049	20,311	18,216
90,900	90,950	19,966	16,061	20,325	18,229
90,950	91,000	19,980	16,074	20,339	18,241

91,000

At least	But less than	Single	Married filing jointly*	Married filing separately	Head of a household
91,000	91,050	19,994	16,086	20,353	18,254
91,050	91,100	20,008	16,099	20,367	18,266
91,100	91,150	20,022	16,111	20,381	18,279
91,150	91,200	20,036	16,124	20,395	18,291
91,200	91,250	20,050	16,136	20,409	18,304
91,250	91,300	20,064	16,149	20,423	18,316
91,300	91,350	20,078	16,161	20,437	18,329
91,350	91,400	20,092	16,174	20,451	18,341
91,400	91,450	20,106	16,186	20,466	18,354
91,450	91,500	20,120	16,199	20,483	18,366
91,500	91,550	20,134	16,211	20,499	18,379
91,550	91,600	20,148	16,224	20,516	18,391
91,600	91,650	20,162	16,236	20,532	18,404
91,650	91,700	20,176	16,249	20,549	18,416
91,700	91,750	20,190	16,261	20,565	18,429
91,750	91,800	20,204	16,274	20,582	18,441
91,800	91,850	20,218	16,286	20,598	18,454
91,850	91,900	20,232	16,299	20,615	18,466
91,900	91,950	20,246	16,311	20,631	18,479
91,950	92,000	20,260	16,324	20,648	18,491

92,000

At least	But less than	Single	Married filing jointly*	Married filing separately	Head of a household
92,000	92,050	20,274	16,336	20,664	18,504
92,050	92,100	20,288	16,349	20,681	18,516
92,100	92,150	20,302	16,361	20,697	18,529
92,150	92,200	20,316	16,374	20,714	18,541
92,200	92,250	20,330	16,386	20,730	18,554
92,250	92,300	20,344	16,399	20,747	18,566
92,300	92,350	20,358	16,411	20,763	18,579
92,350	92,400	20,372	16,424	20,780	18,591
92,400	92,450	20,386	16,436	20,796	18,604
92,450	92,500	20,400	16,449	20,813	18,616
92,500	92,550	20,414	16,461	20,829	18,629
92,550	92,600	20,428	16,474	20,846	18,641
92,600	92,650	20,442	16,486	20,862	18,654
92,650	92,700	20,456	16,499	20,879	18,666
92,700	92,750	20,470	16,511	20,895	18,679
92,750	92,800	20,484	16,524	20,912	18,691
92,800	92,850	20,498	16,536	20,928	18,704
92,850	92,900	20,512	16,549	20,945	18,716
92,900	92,950	20,526	16,561	20,961	18,729
92,950	93,000	20,540	16,574	20,978	18,741

93,000

At least	But less than	Single	Married filing jointly*	Married filing separately	Head of a household
93,000	93,050	20,554	16,586	20,994	18,754
93,050	93,100	20,568	16,599	21,011	18,766
93,100	93,150	20,582	16,611	21,027	18,779
93,150	93,200	20,596	16,624	21,044	18,791
93,200	93,250	20,610	16,636	21,060	18,804
93,250	93,300	20,624	16,649	21,077	18,816
93,300	93,350	20,638	16,661	21,093	18,829
93,350	93,400	20,652	16,674	21,110	18,841
93,400	93,450	20,666	16,686	21,126	18,854
93,450	93,500	20,680	16,699	21,143	18,866
93,500	93,550	20,694	16,711	21,159	18,879
93,550	93,600	20,708	16,724	21,176	18,891
93,600	93,650	20,722	16,736	21,192	18,904
93,650	93,700	20,736	16,749	21,209	18,916
93,700	93,750	20,750	16,761	21,225	18,929
93,750	93,800	20,764	16,774	21,242	18,941
93,800	93,850	20,778	16,786	21,258	18,954
93,850	93,900	20,792	16,799	21,275	18,966
93,900	93,950	20,806	16,811	21,291	18,979
93,950	94,000	20,820	16,824	21,308	18,991

94,000

At least	But less than	Single	Married filing jointly*	Married filing separately	Head of a household
94,000	94,050	20,834	16,836	21,324	19,004
94,050	94,100	20,848	16,849	21,341	19,016
94,100	94,150	20,862	16,861	21,357	19,029
94,150	94,200	20,876	16,874	21,374	19,041
94,200	94,250	20,890	16,886	21,390	19,054
94,250	94,300	20,904	16,899	21,407	19,066
94,300	94,350	20,918	16,911	21,423	19,079
94,350	94,400	20,932	16,924	21,440	19,091
94,400	94,450	20,946	16,936	21,456	19,104
94,450	94,500	20,960	16,949	21,473	19,116
94,500	94,550	20,974	16,961	21,489	19,129
94,550	94,600	20,988	16,974	21,506	19,141
94,600	94,650	21,002	16,986	21,522	19,154
94,650	94,700	21,016	16,999	21,539	19,166
94,700	94,750	21,030	17,011	21,555	19,179
94,750	94,800	21,044	17,024	21,572	19,191
94,800	94,850	21,058	17,036	21,588	19,204
94,850	94,900	21,072	17,049	21,605	19,216
94,900	94,950	21,086	17,061	21,621	19,229
94,950	95,000	21,100	17,074	21,638	19,241

* This column must also be used by a qualifying widow(er).

(Continued on page 75)

If line 43 (taxable income) is—		And you are—				If line 43 (taxable income) is—		And you are—			
At least	But less than	Single	Married filing jointly *	Married filing separately	Head of a household	At least	But less than	Single	Married filing jointly *	Married filing separately	Head of a household
		Your tax is—						Your tax is—			
95,000						**98,000**					
95,000	95,050	21,114	17,086	21,654	19,254	98,000	98,050	21,954	17,836	22,644	20,004
95,050	95,100	21,128	17,099	21,671	19,266	98,050	98,100	21,968	17,849	22,661	20,016
95,100	95,150	21,142	17,111	21,687	19,279	98,100	98,150	21,982	17,861	22,677	20,029
95,150	95,200	21,156	17,124	21,704	19,291	98,150	98,200	21,996	17,874	22,694	20,041
95,200	95,250	21,170	17,136	21,720	19,304	98,200	98,250	22,010	17,886	22,710	20,054
95,250	95,300	21,184	17,149	21,737	19,316	98,250	98,300	22,024	17,899	22,727	20,066
95,300	95,350	21,198	17,161	21,753	19,329	98,300	98,350	22,038	17,911	22,743	20,079
95,350	95,400	21,212	17,174	21,770	19,341	98,350	98,400	22,052	17,924	22,760	20,091
95,400	95,450	21,226	17,186	21,786	19,354	98,400	98,450	22,066	17,936	22,776	20,104
95,450	95,500	21,240	17,199	21,803	19,366	98,450	98,500	22,080	17,949	22,793	20,116
95,500	95,550	21,254	17,211	21,819	19,379	98,500	98,550	22,094	17,961	22,809	20,129
95,550	95,600	21,268	17,224	21,836	19,391	98,550	98,600	22,108	17,974	22,826	20,141
95,600	95,650	21,282	17,236	21,852	19,404	98,600	98,650	22,122	17,986	22,842	20,154
95,650	95,700	21,296	17,249	21,869	19,416	98,650	98,700	22,136	17,999	22,859	20,166
95,700	95,750	21,310	17,261	21,885	19,429	98,700	98,750	22,150	18,011	22,875	20,179
95,750	95,800	21,324	17,274	21,902	19,441	98,750	98,800	22,164	18,024	22,892	20,191
95,800	95,850	21,338	17,286	21,918	19,454	98,800	98,850	22,178	18,036	22,908	20,204
95,850	95,900	21,352	17,299	21,935	19,466	98,850	98,900	22,192	18,049	22,925	20,216
95,900	95,950	21,366	17,311	21,951	19,479	98,900	98,950	22,206	18,061	22,941	20,229
95,950	96,000	21,380	17,324	21,968	19,491	98,950	99,000	22,220	18,074	22,958	20,241
96,000						**99,000**					
96,000	96,050	21,394	17,336	21,984	19,504	99,000	99,050	22,234	18,086	22,974	20,254
96,050	96,100	21,408	17,349	22,001	19,516	99,050	99,100	22,248	18,099	22,991	20,266
96,100	96,150	21,422	17,361	22,017	19,529	99,100	99,150	22,262	18,111	23,007	20,279
96,150	96,200	21,436	17,374	22,034	19,541	99,150	99,200	22,276	18,124	23,024	20,291
96,200	96,250	21,450	17,386	22,050	19,554	99,200	99,250	22,290	18,136	23,040	20,304
96,250	96,300	21,464	17,399	22,067	19,566	99,250	99,300	22,304	18,149	23,057	20,316
96,300	96,350	21,478	17,411	22,083	19,579	99,300	99,350	22,318	18,161	23,073	20,329
96,350	96,400	21,492	17,424	22,100	19,591	99,350	99,400	22,332	18,174	23,090	20,341
96,400	96,450	21,506	17,436	22,116	19,604	99,400	99,450	22,346	18,186	23,106	20,354
96,450	96,500	21,520	17,449	22,133	19,616	99,450	99,500	22,360	18,199	23,123	20,366
96,500	96,550	21,534	17,461	22,149	19,629	99,500	99,550	22,374	18,211	23,139	20,379
96,550	96,600	21,548	17,474	22,166	19,641	99,550	99,600	22,388	18,224	23,156	20,391
96,600	96,650	21,562	17,486	22,182	19,654	99,600	99,650	22,402	18,236	23,172	20,404
96,650	96,700	21,576	17,499	22,199	19,666	99,650	99,700	22,416	18,249	23,189	20,416
96,700	96,750	21,590	17,511	22,215	19,679	99,700	99,750	22,430	18,261	23,205	20,429
96,750	96,800	21,604	17,524	22,232	19,691	99,750	99,800	22,444	18,274	23,222	20,441
96,800	96,850	21,618	17,536	22,248	19,704	99,800	99,850	22,458	18,286	23,238	20,454
96,850	96,900	21,632	17,549	22,265	19,716	99,850	99,900	22,472	18,299	23,255	20,466
96,900	96,950	21,646	17,561	22,281	19,729	99,900	99,950	22,486	18,311	23,271	20,479
96,950	97,000	21,660	17,574	22,298	19,741	99,950	100,000	22,500	18,324	23,288	20,491
97,000											
97,000	97,050	21,674	17,586	22,314	19,754						
97,050	97,100	21,688	17,599	22,331	19,766						
97,100	97,150	21,702	17,611	22,347	19,779						
97,150	97,200	21,716	17,624	22,364	19,791						
97,200	97,250	21,730	17,636	22,380	19,804						
97,250	97,300	21,744	17,649	22,397	19,816						
97,300	97,350	21,758	17,661	22,413	19,829						
97,350	97,400	21,772	17,674	22,430	19,841						
97,400	97,450	21,786	17,686	22,446	19,854						
97,450	97,500	21,800	17,699	22,463	19,866						
97,500	97,550	21,814	17,711	22,479	19,879						
97,550	97,600	21,828	17,724	22,496	19,891						
97,600	97,650	21,842	17,736	22,512	19,904						
97,650	97,700	21,856	17,749	22,529	19,916						
97,700	97,750	21,870	17,761	22,545	19,929						
97,750	97,800	21,884	17,774	22,562	19,941						
97,800	97,850	21,898	17,786	22,578	19,954						
97,850	97,900	21,912	17,799	22,595	19,966						
97,900	97,950	21,926	17,811	22,611	19,979						
97,950	98,000	21,940	17,824	22,628	19,991						

$100,000 or over — use the Tax Computation Worksheet on page 72

* This column must also be used by a qualifying widow(er).

- 76 -

T-12

Earned Income Credit Tables

2005 Earned Income Credit (EIC) Table
Caution. This is **not** a tax table.

1. To find your credit, read down the "At least – But less than" columns and find the line that includes the amount you were told to look up from your EIC Worksheet.

2. Then, go to the column that includes your filing status and the number of qualifying children you have. Enter the credit from that column on your EIC Worksheet.

Example. If your filing status is single, you have one qualifying child, and the amount you are looking up from your EIC Worksheet is $2,455, you would enter $842.

If the amount you are looking up from the worksheet is—		And your filing status is—		
		Single, head of household, or qualifying widow(er) and you have—		
At least	But less than	No children	One child	Two children
		Your credit is—		
2,400	2,450	186	825	970
2,450	2,500	189	842	990

If the amount you are looking up from the worksheet is—		And your filing status is—					
		Single, head of household, or qualifying widow(er) and you have—			Married filing jointly and you have—		
At least	But less than	No children	One child	Two children	No children	One child	Two children
		Your credit is—			Your credit is—		
$1	$50	$2	$9	$10	$2	$9	$10
50	100	6	26	30	6	26	30
100	150	10	43	50	10	43	50
150	200	13	60	70	13	60	70
200	250	17	77	90	17	77	90
250	300	21	94	110	21	94	110
300	350	25	111	130	25	111	130
350	400	29	128	150	29	128	150
400	450	33	145	170	33	145	170
450	500	36	162	190	36	162	190
500	550	40	179	210	40	179	210
550	600	44	196	230	44	196	230
600	650	48	213	250	48	213	250
650	700	52	230	270	52	230	270
700	750	55	247	290	55	247	290
750	800	59	264	310	59	264	310
800	850	63	281	330	63	281	330
850	900	67	298	350	67	298	350
900	950	71	315	370	71	315	370
950	1,000	75	332	390	75	332	390
1,000	1,050	78	349	410	78	349	410
1,050	1,100	82	366	430	82	366	430
1,100	1,150	86	383	450	86	383	450
1,150	1,200	90	400	470	90	400	470
1,200	1,250	94	417	490	94	417	490
1,250	1,300	98	434	510	98	434	510
1,300	1,350	101	451	530	101	451	530
1,350	1,400	105	468	550	105	468	550
1,400	1,450	109	485	570	109	485	570
1,450	1,500	113	502	590	113	502	590
1,500	1,550	117	519	610	117	519	610
1,550	1,600	120	536	630	120	536	630
1,600	1,650	124	553	650	124	553	650
1,650	1,700	128	570	670	128	570	670
1,700	1,750	132	587	690	132	587	690
1,750	1,800	136	604	710	136	604	710
1,800	1,850	140	621	730	140	621	730
1,850	1,900	143	638	750	143	638	750
1,900	1,950	147	655	770	147	655	770
1,950	2,000	151	672	790	151	672	790
2,000	2,050	155	689	810	155	689	810
2,050	2,100	159	706	830	159	706	830
2,100	2,150	163	723	850	163	723	850
2,150	2,200	166	740	870	166	740	870
2,200	2,250	170	757	890	170	757	890
2,250	2,300	174	774	910	174	774	910
2,300	2,350	178	791	930	178	791	930
2,350	2,400	182	808	950	182	808	950
2,400	2,450	186	825	970	186	825	970
2,450	2,500	189	842	990	189	842	990
2,500	2,550	193	859	1,010	193	859	1,010
2,550	2,600	197	876	1,030	197	876	1,030
2,600	2,650	201	893	1,050	201	893	1,050
2,650	2,700	205	910	1,070	205	910	1,070
2,700	2,750	208	927	1,090	208	927	1,090

If the amount you are looking up from the worksheet is—		And your filing status is—					
		Single, head of household, or qualifying widow(er) and you have—			Married filing jointly and you have—		
At least	But less than	No children	One child	Two children	No children	One child	Two children
		Your credit is—			Your credit is—		
2,750	2,800	212	944	1,110	212	944	1,110
2,800	2,850	216	961	1,130	216	961	1,130
2,850	2,900	220	978	1,150	220	978	1,150
2,900	2,950	224	995	1,170	224	995	1,170
2,950	3,000	228	1,012	1,190	228	1,012	1,190
3,000	3,050	231	1,029	1,210	231	1,029	1,210
3,050	3,100	235	1,046	1,230	235	1,046	1,230
3,100	3,150	239	1,063	1,250	239	1,063	1,250
3,150	3,200	243	1,080	1,270	243	1,080	1,270
3,200	3,250	247	1,097	1,290	247	1,097	1,290
3,250	3,300	251	1,114	1,310	251	1,114	1,310
3,300	3,350	254	1,131	1,330	254	1,131	1,330
3,350	3,400	258	1,148	1,350	258	1,148	1,350
3,400	3,450	262	1,165	1,370	262	1,165	1,370
3,450	3,500	266	1,182	1,390	266	1,182	1,390
3,500	3,550	270	1,199	1,410	270	1,199	1,410
3,550	3,600	273	1,216	1,430	273	1,216	1,430
3,600	3,650	277	1,233	1,450	277	1,233	1,450
3,650	3,700	281	1,250	1,470	281	1,250	1,470
3,700	3,750	285	1,267	1,490	285	1,267	1,490
3,750	3,800	289	1,284	1,510	289	1,284	1,510
3,800	3,850	293	1,301	1,530	293	1,301	1,530
3,850	3,900	296	1,318	1,550	296	1,318	1,550
3,900	3,950	300	1,335	1,570	300	1,335	1,570
3,950	4,000	304	1,352	1,590	304	1,352	1,590
4,000	4,050	308	1,369	1,610	308	1,369	1,610
4,050	4,100	312	1,386	1,630	312	1,386	1,630
4,100	4,150	316	1,403	1,650	316	1,403	1,650
4,150	4,200	319	1,420	1,670	319	1,420	1,670
4,200	4,250	323	1,437	1,690	323	1,437	1,690
4,250	4,300	327	1,454	1,710	327	1,454	1,710
4,300	4,350	331	1,471	1,730	331	1,471	1,730
4,350	4,400	335	1,488	1,750	335	1,488	1,750
4,400	4,450	339	1,505	1,770	339	1,505	1,770
4,450	4,500	342	1,522	1,790	342	1,522	1,790
4,500	4,550	346	1,539	1,810	346	1,539	1,810
4,550	4,600	350	1,556	1,830	350	1,556	1,830
4,600	4,650	354	1,573	1,850	354	1,573	1,850
4,650	4,700	358	1,590	1,870	358	1,590	1,870
4,700	4,750	361	1,607	1,890	361	1,607	1,890
4,750	4,800	365	1,624	1,910	365	1,624	1,910
4,800	4,850	369	1,641	1,930	369	1,641	1,930
4,850	4,900	373	1,658	1,950	373	1,658	1,950
4,900	4,950	377	1,675	1,970	377	1,675	1,970
4,950	5,000	381	1,692	1,990	381	1,692	1,990
5,000	5,050	384	1,709	2,010	384	1,709	2,010
5,050	5,100	388	1,726	2,030	388	1,726	2,030
5,100	5,150	392	1,743	2,050	392	1,743	2,050
5,150	5,200	396	1,760	2,070	396	1,760	2,070
5,200	5,250	399	1,777	2,090	399	1,777	2,090
5,250	5,300	399	1,794	2,110	399	1,794	2,110
5,300	5,350	399	1,811	2,130	399	1,811	2,130
5,350	5,400	399	1,828	2,150	399	1,828	2,150
5,400	5,450	399	1,845	2,170	399	1,845	2,170
5,450	5,500	399	1,862	2,190	399	1,862	2,190

(Continued on page 53)

2005 Earned Income Credit (EIC) Table—Continued (Caution. This is **not** a tax table.)

If the amount you are looking up from the worksheet is—		Single, head of household, or qualifying widow(er) and you have—			Married filing jointly and you have—		
At least	But less than	No children	One child	Two children	No children	One child	Two children
		Your credit is—			Your credit is—		
5,500	5,550	399	1,879	2,210	399	1,879	2,210
5,550	5,600	399	1,896	2,230	399	1,896	2,230
5,600	5,650	399	1,913	2,250	399	1,913	2,250
5,650	5,700	399	1,930	2,270	399	1,930	2,270
5,700	5,750	399	1,947	2,290	399	1,947	2,290
5,750	5,800	399	1,964	2,310	399	1,964	2,310
5,800	5,850	399	1,981	2,330	399	1,981	2,330
5,850	5,900	399	1,998	2,350	399	1,998	2,350
5,900	5,950	399	2,015	2,370	399	2,015	2,370
5,950	6,000	399	2,032	2,390	399	2,032	2,390
6,000	6,050	399	2,049	2,410	399	2,049	2,410
6,050	6,100	399	2,066	2,430	399	2,066	2,430
6,100	6,150	399	2,083	2,450	399	2,083	2,450
6,150	6,200	399	2,100	2,470	399	2,100	2,470
6,200	6,250	399	2,117	2,490	399	2,117	2,490
6,250	6,300	399	2,134	2,510	399	2,134	2,510
6,300	6,350	399	2,151	2,530	399	2,151	2,530
6,350	6,400	399	2,168	2,550	399	2,168	2,550
6,400	6,450	399	2,185	2,570	399	2,185	2,570
6,450	6,500	399	2,202	2,590	399	2,202	2,590
6,500	6,550	399	2,219	2,610	399	2,219	2,610
6,550	6,600	396	2,236	2,630	399	2,236	2,630
6,600	6,650	392	2,253	2,650	399	2,253	2,650
6,650	6,700	388	2,270	2,670	399	2,270	2,670
6,700	6,750	384	2,287	2,690	399	2,287	2,690
6,750	6,800	381	2,304	2,710	399	2,304	2,710
6,800	6,850	377	2,321	2,730	399	2,321	2,730
6,850	6,900	373	2,338	2,750	399	2,338	2,750
6,900	6,950	369	2,355	2,770	399	2,355	2,770
6,950	7,000	365	2,372	2,790	399	2,372	2,790
7,000	7,050	361	2,389	2,810	399	2,389	2,810
7,050	7,100	358	2,406	2,830	399	2,406	2,830
7,100	7,150	354	2,423	2,850	399	2,423	2,850
7,150	7,200	350	2,440	2,870	399	2,440	2,870
7,200	7,250	346	2,457	2,890	399	2,457	2,890
7,250	7,300	342	2,474	2,910	399	2,474	2,910
7,300	7,350	339	2,491	2,930	399	2,491	2,930
7,350	7,400	335	2,508	2,950	399	2,508	2,950
7,400	7,450	331	2,525	2,970	399	2,525	2,970
7,450	7,500	327	2,542	2,990	399	2,542	2,990
7,500	7,550	323	2,559	3,010	399	2,559	3,010
7,550	7,600	319	2,576	3,030	399	2,576	3,030
7,600	7,650	316	2,593	3,050	399	2,593	3,050
7,650	7,700	312	2,610	3,070	399	2,610	3,070
7,700	7,750	308	2,627	3,090	399	2,627	3,090
7,750	7,800	304	2,644	3,110	399	2,644	3,110
7,800	7,850	300	2,662	3,130	399	2,662	3,130
7,850	7,900	296	2,662	3,150	399	2,662	3,150
7,900	7,950	293	2,662	3,170	399	2,662	3,170
7,950	8,000	289	2,662	3,190	399	2,662	3,190
8,000	8,050	285	2,662	3,210	399	2,662	3,210
8,050	8,100	281	2,662	3,230	399	2,662	3,230
8,100	8,150	277	2,662	3,250	399	2,662	3,250
8,150	8,200	273	2,662	3,270	399	2,662	3,270
8,200	8,250	270	2,662	3,290	399	2,662	3,290
8,250	8,300	266	2,662	3,310	399	2,662	3,310
8,300	8,350	262	2,662	3,330	399	2,662	3,330
8,350	8,400	258	2,662	3,350	399	2,662	3,350
8,400	8,450	254	2,662	3,370	399	2,662	3,370
8,450	8,500	251	2,662	3,390	399	2,662	3,390

If the amount you are looking up from the worksheet is—		Single, head of household, or qualifying widow(er) and you have—			Married filing jointly and you have—		
At least	But less than	No children	One child	Two children	No children	One child	Two children
		Your credit is—			Your credit is—		
8,500	8,550	247	2,662	3,410	399	2,662	3,410
8,550	8,600	243	2,662	3,430	396	2,662	3,430
8,600	8,650	239	2,662	3,450	392	2,662	3,450
8,650	8,700	235	2,662	3,470	388	2,662	3,470
8,700	8,750	231	2,662	3,490	384	2,662	3,490
8,750	8,800	228	2,662	3,510	381	2,662	3,510
8,800	8,850	224	2,662	3,530	377	2,662	3,530
8,850	8,900	220	2,662	3,550	373	2,662	3,550
8,900	8,950	216	2,662	3,570	369	2,662	3,570
8,950	9,000	212	2,662	3,590	365	2,662	3,590
9,000	9,050	208	2,662	3,610	361	2,662	3,610
9,050	9,100	205	2,662	3,630	358	2,662	3,630
9,100	9,150	201	2,662	3,650	354	2,662	3,650
9,150	9,200	197	2,662	3,670	350	2,662	3,670
9,200	9,250	193	2,662	3,690	346	2,662	3,690
9,250	9,300	189	2,662	3,710	342	2,662	3,710
9,300	9,350	186	2,662	3,730	339	2,662	3,730
9,350	9,400	182	2,662	3,750	335	2,662	3,750
9,400	9,450	178	2,662	3,770	331	2,662	3,770
9,450	9,500	174	2,662	3,790	327	2,662	3,790
9,500	9,550	170	2,662	3,810	323	2,662	3,810
9,550	9,600	166	2,662	3,830	319	2,662	3,830
9,600	9,650	163	2,662	3,850	316	2,662	3,850
9,650	9,700	159	2,662	3,870	312	2,662	3,870
9,700	9,750	155	2,662	3,890	308	2,662	3,890
9,750	9,800	151	2,662	3,910	304	2,662	3,910
9,800	9,850	147	2,662	3,930	300	2,662	3,930
9,850	9,900	143	2,662	3,950	296	2,662	3,950
9,900	9,950	140	2,662	3,970	293	2,662	3,970
9,950	10,000	136	2,662	3,990	289	2,662	3,990
10,000	10,050	132	2,662	4,010	285	2,662	4,010
10,050	10,100	128	2,662	4,030	281	2,662	4,030
10,100	10,150	124	2,662	4,050	277	2,662	4,050
10,150	10,200	120	2,662	4,070	273	2,662	4,070
10,200	10,250	117	2,662	4,090	270	2,662	4,090
10,250	10,300	113	2,662	4,110	266	2,662	4,110
10,300	10,350	109	2,662	4,130	262	2,662	4,130
10,350	10,400	105	2,662	4,150	258	2,662	4,150
10,400	10,450	101	2,662	4,170	254	2,662	4,170
10,450	10,500	98	2,662	4,190	251	2,662	4,190
10,500	10,550	94	2,662	4,210	247	2,662	4,210
10,550	10,600	90	2,662	4,230	243	2,662	4,230
10,600	10,650	86	2,662	4,250	239	2,662	4,250
10,650	10,700	82	2,662	4,270	235	2,662	4,270
10,700	10,750	78	2,662	4,290	231	2,662	4,290
10,750	10,800	75	2,662	4,310	228	2,662	4,310
10,800	10,850	71	2,662	4,330	224	2,662	4,330
10,850	10,900	67	2,662	4,350	220	2,662	4,350
10,900	10,950	63	2,662	4,370	216	2,662	4,370
10,950	11,000	59	2,662	4,390	212	2,662	4,390
11,000	11,050	55	2,662	4,400	208	2,662	4,400
11,050	11,100	52	2,662	4,400	205	2,662	4,400
11,100	11,150	48	2,662	4,400	201	2,662	4,400
11,150	11,200	44	2,662	4,400	197	2,662	4,400
11,200	11,250	40	2,662	4,400	193	2,662	4,400
11,250	11,300	36	2,662	4,400	189	2,662	4,400
11,300	11,350	33	2,662	4,400	186	2,662	4,400
11,350	11,400	29	2,662	4,400	182	2,662	4,400
11,400	11,450	25	2,662	4,400	178	2,662	4,400
11,450	11,500	21	2,662	4,400	174	2,662	4,400

(Continued on page 54)

Need more information or forms? See page 7.

E-2

2005 Earned Income Credit (EIC) Table—*Continued*   (**Caution.** This is **not** a tax table.)

If the amount you are looking up from the worksheet is—		Single, head of household, or qualifying widow(er) and you have—			Married filing jointly and you have—		
At least	But less than	No children	One child	Two children	No children	One child	Two children
		Your credit is—			Your credit is—		
11,500	11,550	17	2,662	4,400	170	2,662	4,400
11,550	11,600	13	2,662	4,400	166	2,662	4,400
11,600	11,650	10	2,662	4,400	163	2,662	4,400
11,650	11,700	6	2,662	4,400	159	2,662	4,400
11,700	11,750	2	2,662	4,400	155	2,662	4,400
11,750	11,800	0	2,662	4,400	151	2,662	4,400
11,800	11,850	0	2,662	4,400	147	2,662	4,400
11,850	11,900	0	2,662	4,400	143	2,662	4,400
11,900	11,950	0	2,662	4,400	140	2,662	4,400
11,950	12,000	0	2,662	4,400	136	2,662	4,400
12,000	12,050	0	2,662	4,400	132	2,662	4,400
12,050	12,100	0	2,662	4,400	128	2,662	4,400
12,100	12,150	0	2,662	4,400	124	2,662	4,400
12,150	12,200	0	2,662	4,400	120	2,662	4,400
12,200	12,250	0	2,662	4,400	117	2,662	4,400
12,250	12,300	0	2,662	4,400	113	2,662	4,400
12,300	12,350	0	2,662	4,400	109	2,662	4,400
12,350	12,400	0	2,662	4,400	105	2,662	4,400
12,400	12,450	0	2,662	4,400	101	2,662	4,400
12,450	12,500	0	2,662	4,400	98	2,662	4,400
12,500	12,550	0	2,662	4,400	94	2,662	4,400
12,550	12,600	0	2,662	4,400	90	2,662	4,400
12,600	12,650	0	2,662	4,400	86	2,662	4,400
12,650	12,700	0	2,662	4,400	82	2,662	4,400
12,700	12,750	0	2,662	4,400	78	2,662	4,400
12,750	12,800	0	2,662	4,400	75	2,662	4,400
12,800	12,850	0	2,662	4,400	71	2,662	4,400
12,850	12,900	0	2,662	4,400	67	2,662	4,400
12,900	12,950	0	2,662	4,400	63	2,662	4,400
12,950	13,000	0	2,662	4,400	59	2,662	4,400
13,000	13,050	0	2,662	4,400	55	2,662	4,400
13,050	13,100	0	2,662	4,400	52	2,662	4,400
13,100	13,150	0	2,662	4,400	48	2,662	4,400
13,150	13,200	0	2,662	4,400	44	2,662	4,400
13,200	13,250	0	2,662	4,400	40	2,662	4,400
13,250	13,300	0	2,662	4,400	36	2,662	4,400
13,300	13,350	0	2,662	4,400	33	2,662	4,400
13,350	13,400	0	2,662	4,400	29	2,662	4,400
13,400	13,450	0	2,662	4,400	25	2,662	4,400
13,450	13,500	0	2,662	4,400	21	2,662	4,400
13,500	13,550	0	2,662	4,400	17	2,662	4,400
13,550	13,600	0	2,662	4,400	13	2,662	4,400
13,600	13,650	0	2,662	4,400	10	2,662	4,400
13,650	13,700	0	2,662	4,400	6	2,662	4,400
13,700	13,750	0	2,662	4,400	2	2,662	4,400
13,750	14,400	0	2,662	4,400	0	2,662	4,400
14,400	14,450	0	2,653	4,388	0	2,662	4,400
14,450	14,500	0	2,645	4,378	0	2,662	4,400
14,500	14,550	0	2,637	4,367	0	2,662	4,400
14,550	14,600	0	2,629	4,357	0	2,662	4,400
14,600	14,650	0	2,621	4,346	0	2,662	4,400
14,650	14,700	0	2,613	4,336	0	2,662	4,400
14,700	14,750	0	2,605	4,325	0	2,662	4,400
14,750	14,800	0	2,597	4,315	0	2,662	4,400
14,800	14,850	0	2,589	4,304	0	2,662	4,400
14,850	14,900	0	2,582	4,294	0	2,662	4,400
14,900	14,950	0	2,574	4,283	0	2,662	4,400
14,950	15,000	0	2,566	4,273	0	2,662	4,400
15,000	15,050	0	2,558	4,262	0	2,662	4,400
15,050	15,100	0	2,550	4,252	0	2,662	4,400

If the amount you are looking up from the worksheet is—		Single, head of household, or qualifying widow(er) and you have—			Married filing jointly and you have—		
At least	But less than	No children	One child	Two children	No children	One child	Two children
		Your credit is—			Your credit is—		
15,100	15,150	0	2,542	4,241	0	2,662	4,400
15,150	15,200	0	2,534	4,230	0	2,662	4,400
15,200	15,250	0	2,526	4,220	0	2,662	4,400
15,250	15,300	0	2,518	4,209	0	2,662	4,400
15,300	15,350	0	2,510	4,199	0	2,662	4,400
15,350	15,400	0	2,502	4,188	0	2,662	4,400
15,400	15,450	0	2,494	4,178	0	2,662	4,400
15,450	15,500	0	2,486	4,167	0	2,662	4,400
15,500	15,550	0	2,478	4,157	0	2,662	4,400
15,550	15,600	0	2,470	4,146	0	2,662	4,400
15,600	15,650	0	2,462	4,136	0	2,662	4,400
15,650	15,700	0	2,454	4,125	0	2,662	4,400
15,700	15,750	0	2,446	4,115	0	2,662	4,400
15,750	15,800	0	2,438	4,104	0	2,662	4,400
15,800	15,850	0	2,430	4,094	0	2,662	4,400
15,850	15,900	0	2,422	4,083	0	2,662	4,400
15,900	15,950	0	2,414	4,073	0	2,662	4,400
15,950	16,000	0	2,406	4,062	0	2,662	4,400
16,000	16,050	0	2,398	4,051	0	2,662	4,400
16,050	16,100	0	2,390	4,041	0	2,662	4,400
16,100	16,150	0	2,382	4,030	0	2,662	4,400
16,150	16,200	0	2,374	4,020	0	2,662	4,400
16,200	16,250	0	2,366	4,009	0	2,662	4,400
16,250	16,300	0	2,358	3,999	0	2,662	4,400
16,300	16,350	0	2,350	3,988	0	2,662	4,400
16,350	16,400	0	2,342	3,978	0	2,662	4,400
16,400	16,450	0	2,334	3,967	0	2,653	4,388
16,450	16,500	0	2,326	3,957	0	2,645	4,378
16,500	16,550	0	2,318	3,946	0	2,637	4,367
16,550	16,600	0	2,310	3,936	0	2,629	4,357
16,600	16,650	0	2,302	3,925	0	2,621	4,346
16,650	16,700	0	2,294	3,915	0	2,613	4,336
16,700	16,750	0	2,286	3,904	0	2,605	4,325
16,750	16,800	0	2,278	3,894	0	2,597	4,315
16,800	16,850	0	2,270	3,883	0	2,589	4,304
16,850	16,900	0	2,262	3,872	0	2,582	4,294
16,900	16,950	0	2,254	3,862	0	2,574	4,283
16,950	17,000	0	2,246	3,851	0	2,566	4,273
17,000	17,050	0	2,238	3,841	0	2,558	4,262
17,050	17,100	0	2,230	3,830	0	2,550	4,252
17,100	17,150	0	2,222	3,820	0	2,542	4,241
17,150	17,200	0	2,214	3,809	0	2,534	4,230
17,200	17,250	0	2,206	3,799	0	2,526	4,220
17,250	17,300	0	2,198	3,788	0	2,518	4,209
17,300	17,350	0	2,190	3,778	0	2,510	4,199
17,350	17,400	0	2,182	3,767	0	2,502	4,188
17,400	17,450	0	2,174	3,757	0	2,494	4,178
17,450	17,500	0	2,166	3,746	0	2,486	4,167
17,500	17,550	0	2,158	3,736	0	2,478	4,157
17,550	17,600	0	2,150	3,725	0	2,470	4,146
17,600	17,650	0	2,142	3,714	0	2,462	4,136
17,650	17,700	0	2,134	3,704	0	2,454	4,125
17,700	17,750	0	2,126	3,693	0	2,446	4,115
17,750	17,800	0	2,118	3,683	0	2,438	4,104
17,800	17,850	0	2,110	3,672	0	2,430	4,094
17,850	17,900	0	2,102	3,662	0	2,422	4,083
17,900	17,950	0	2,094	3,651	0	2,414	4,073
17,950	18,000	0	2,086	3,641	0	2,406	4,062
18,000	18,050	0	2,078	3,630	0	2,398	4,051
18,050	18,100	0	2,070	3,620	0	2,390	4,041

(Continued on page 55)

Need more information or forms? See page 7.   - 54 -

E-3

2005 Earned Income Credit (EIC) Table—*Continued* (**Caution.** This is **not** a tax table.)

If the amount you are looking up from the worksheet is—		And your filing status is—					
		Single, head of household, or qualifying widow(er) and you have—			Married filing jointly and you have—		
At least	But less than	No children	One child	Two children	No children	One child	Two children
		Your credit is—			Your credit is—		
18,100	18,150	0	2,062	3,609	0	2,382	4,030
18,150	18,200	0	2,054	3,599	0	2,374	4,020
18,200	18,250	0	2,046	3,588	0	2,366	4,009
18,250	18,300	0	2,038	3,578	0	2,358	3,999
18,300	18,350	0	2,030	3,567	0	2,350	3,988
18,350	18,400	0	2,022	3,557	0	2,342	3,978
18,400	18,450	0	2,014	3,546	0	2,334	3,967
18,450	18,500	0	2,006	3,535	0	2,326	3,957
18,500	18,550	0	1,998	3,525	0	2,318	3,946
18,550	18,600	0	1,990	3,514	0	2,310	3,936
18,600	18,650	0	1,982	3,504	0	2,302	3,925
18,650	18,700	0	1,974	3,493	0	2,294	3,915
18,700	18,750	0	1,966	3,483	0	2,286	3,904
18,750	18,800	0	1,958	3,472	0	2,278	3,894
18,800	18,850	0	1,950	3,462	0	2,270	3,883
18,850	18,900	0	1,942	3,451	0	2,262	3,872
18,900	18,950	0	1,934	3,441	0	2,254	3,862
18,950	19,000	0	1,926	3,430	0	2,246	3,851
19,000	19,050	0	1,918	3,420	0	2,238	3,841
19,050	19,100	0	1,910	3,409	0	2,230	3,830
19,100	19,150	0	1,902	3,399	0	2,222	3,820
19,150	19,200	0	1,894	3,388	0	2,214	3,809
19,200	19,250	0	1,886	3,378	0	2,206	3,799
19,250	19,300	0	1,878	3,367	0	2,198	3,788
19,300	19,350	0	1,870	3,356	0	2,190	3,778
19,350	19,400	0	1,862	3,346	0	2,182	3,767
19,400	19,450	0	1,854	3,335	0	2,174	3,757
19,450	19,500	0	1,846	3,325	0	2,166	3,746
19,500	19,550	0	1,838	3,314	0	2,158	3,736
19,550	19,600	0	1,830	3,304	0	2,150	3,725
19,600	19,650	0	1,822	3,293	0	2,142	3,714
19,650	19,700	0	1,814	3,283	0	2,134	3,704
19,700	19,750	0	1,806	3,272	0	2,126	3,693
19,750	19,800	0	1,798	3,262	0	2,118	3,683
19,800	19,850	0	1,790	3,251	0	2,110	3,672
19,850	19,900	0	1,783	3,241	0	2,102	3,662
19,900	19,950	0	1,775	3,230	0	2,094	3,651
19,950	20,000	0	1,767	3,220	0	2,086	3,641
20,000	20,050	0	1,759	3,209	0	2,078	3,630
20,050	20,100	0	1,751	3,199	0	2,070	3,620
20,100	20,150	0	1,743	3,188	0	2,062	3,609
20,150	20,200	0	1,735	3,177	0	2,054	3,599
20,200	20,250	0	1,727	3,167	0	2,046	3,588
20,250	20,300	0	1,719	3,156	0	2,038	3,578
20,300	20,350	0	1,711	3,146	0	2,030	3,567
20,350	20,400	0	1,703	3,135	0	2,022	3,557
20,400	20,450	0	1,695	3,125	0	2,014	3,546
20,450	20,500	0	1,687	3,114	0	2,006	3,535
20,500	20,550	0	1,679	3,104	0	1,998	3,525
20,550	20,600	0	1,671	3,093	0	1,990	3,514
20,600	20,650	0	1,663	3,083	0	1,982	3,504
20,650	20,700	0	1,655	3,072	0	1,974	3,493
20,700	20,750	0	1,647	3,062	0	1,966	3,483
20,750	20,800	0	1,639	3,051	0	1,958	3,472
20,800	20,850	0	1,631	3,041	0	1,950	3,462
20,850	20,900	0	1,623	3,030	0	1,942	3,451
20,900	20,950	0	1,615	3,020	0	1,934	3,441
20,950	21,000	0	1,607	3,009	0	1,926	3,430
21,000	21,050	0	1,599	2,998	0	1,918	3,420
21,050	21,100	0	1,591	2,988	0	1,910	3,409
21,100	21,150	0	1,583	2,977	0	1,902	3,399
21,150	21,200	0	1,575	2,967	0	1,894	3,388
21,200	21,250	0	1,567	2,956	0	1,886	3,378
21,250	21,300	0	1,559	2,946	0	1,878	3,367
21,300	21,350	0	1,551	2,935	0	1,870	3,356
21,350	21,400	0	1,543	2,925	0	1,862	3,346
21,400	21,450	0	1,535	2,914	0	1,854	3,335
21,450	21,500	0	1,527	2,904	0	1,846	3,325
21,500	21,550	0	1,519	2,893	0	1,838	3,314
21,550	21,600	0	1,511	2,883	0	1,830	3,304
21,600	21,650	0	1,503	2,872	0	1,822	3,293
21,650	21,700	0	1,495	2,862	0	1,814	3,283
21,700	21,750	0	1,487	2,851	0	1,806	3,272
21,750	21,800	0	1,479	2,841	0	1,798	3,262
21,800	21,850	0	1,471	2,830	0	1,790	3,251
21,850	21,900	0	1,463	2,819	0	1,783	3,241
21,900	21,950	0	1,455	2,809	0	1,775	3,230
21,950	22,000	0	1,447	2,798	0	1,767	3,220
22,000	22,050	0	1,439	2,788	0	1,759	3,209
22,050	22,100	0	1,431	2,777	0	1,751	3,199
22,100	22,150	0	1,423	2,767	0	1,743	3,188
22,150	22,200	0	1,415	2,756	0	1,735	3,177
22,200	22,250	0	1,407	2,746	0	1,727	3,167
22,250	22,300	0	1,399	2,735	0	1,719	3,156
22,300	22,350	0	1,391	2,725	0	1,711	3,146
22,350	22,400	0	1,383	2,714	0	1,703	3,135
22,400	22,450	0	1,375	2,704	0	1,695	3,125
22,450	22,500	0	1,367	2,693	0	1,687	3,114
22,500	22,550	0	1,359	2,683	0	1,679	3,104
22,550	22,600	0	1,351	2,672	0	1,671	3,093
22,600	22,650	0	1,343	2,661	0	1,663	3,083
22,650	22,700	0	1,335	2,651	0	1,655	3,072
22,700	22,750	0	1,327	2,640	0	1,647	3,062
22,750	22,800	0	1,319	2,630	0	1,639	3,051
22,800	22,850	0	1,311	2,619	0	1,631	3,041
22,850	22,900	0	1,303	2,609	0	1,623	3,030
22,900	22,950	0	1,295	2,598	0	1,615	3,020
22,950	23,000	0	1,287	2,588	0	1,607	3,009
23,000	23,050	0	1,279	2,577	0	1,599	2,998
23,050	23,100	0	1,271	2,567	0	1,591	2,988
23,100	23,150	0	1,263	2,556	0	1,583	2,977
23,150	23,200	0	1,255	2,546	0	1,575	2,967
23,200	23,250	0	1,247	2,535	0	1,567	2,956
23,250	23,300	0	1,239	2,525	0	1,559	2,946
23,300	23,350	0	1,231	2,514	0	1,551	2,935
23,350	23,400	0	1,223	2,504	0	1,543	2,925
23,400	23,450	0	1,215	2,493	0	1,535	2,914
23,450	23,500	0	1,207	2,482	0	1,527	2,904
23,500	23,550	0	1,199	2,472	0	1,519	2,893
23,550	23,600	0	1,191	2,461	0	1,511	2,883
23,600	23,650	0	1,183	2,451	0	1,503	2,872
23,650	23,700	0	1,175	2,440	0	1,495	2,862
23,700	23,750	0	1,167	2,430	0	1,487	2,851
23,750	23,800	0	1,159	2,419	0	1,479	2,841
23,800	23,850	0	1,151	2,409	0	1,471	2,830
23,850	23,900	0	1,143	2,398	0	1,463	2,819
23,900	23,950	0	1,135	2,388	0	1,455	2,809
23,950	24,000	0	1,127	2,377	0	1,447	2,798
24,000	24,050	0	1,119	2,367	0	1,439	2,788
24,050	24,100	0	1,111	2,356	0	1,431	2,777

(Continued on page 56)

- 55 -   *Need more information or forms? See page 7.*

E-4

2005 Earned Income Credit (EIC) Table—Continued   (Caution. This is **not** a tax table.)

If the amount you are looking up from the worksheet is—		Single, head of household, or qualifying widow(er) and you have—			Married filing jointly and you have—			If the amount you are looking up from the worksheet is—		Single, head of household, or qualifying widow(er) and you have—			Married filing jointly and you have—		
At least	But less than	No children	One child	Two children	No children	One child	Two children	At least	But less than	No children	One child	Two children	No children	One child	Two children
24,100	24,150	0	1,103	2,346	0	1,423	2,767	27,100	27,150	0	624	1,714	0	944	2,135
24,150	24,200	0	1,095	2,335	0	1,415	2,756	27,150	27,200	0	616	1,703	0	936	2,124
24,200	24,250	0	1,087	2,325	0	1,407	2,746	27,200	27,250	0	608	1,693	0	928	2,114
24,250	24,300	0	1,079	2,314	0	1,399	2,735	27,250	27,300	0	600	1,682	0	920	2,103
24,300	24,350	0	1,071	2,303	0	1,391	2,725	27,300	27,350	0	592	1,672	0	912	2,093
24,350	24,400	0	1,063	2,293	0	1,383	2,714	27,350	27,400	0	584	1,661	0	904	2,082
24,400	24,450	0	1,055	2,282	0	1,375	2,704	27,400	27,450	0	576	1,651	0	896	2,072
24,450	24,500	0	1,047	2,272	0	1,367	2,693	27,450	27,500	0	568	1,640	0	888	2,061
24,500	24,550	0	1,039	2,261	0	1,359	2,683	27,500	27,550	0	560	1,630	0	880	2,051
24,550	24,600	0	1,031	2,251	0	1,351	2,672	27,550	27,600	0	552	1,619	0	872	2,040
24,600	24,650	0	1,023	2,240	0	1,343	2,661	27,600	27,650	0	544	1,608	0	864	2,030
24,650	24,700	0	1,015	2,230	0	1,335	2,651	27,650	27,700	0	536	1,598	0	856	2,019
24,700	24,750	0	1,007	2,219	0	1,327	2,640	27,700	27,750	0	528	1,587	0	848	2,009
24,750	24,800	0	999	2,209	0	1,319	2,630	27,750	27,800	0	520	1,577	0	840	1,998
24,800	24,850	0	991	2,198	0	1,311	2,619	27,800	27,850	0	512	1,566	0	832	1,988
24,850	24,900	0	984	2,188	0	1,303	2,609	27,850	27,900	0	504	1,556	0	824	1,977
24,900	24,950	0	976	2,177	0	1,295	2,598	27,900	27,950	0	496	1,545	0	816	1,967
24,950	25,000	0	968	2,167	0	1,287	2,588	27,950	28,000	0	488	1,535	0	808	1,956
25,000	25,050	0	960	2,156	0	1,279	2,577	28,000	28,050	0	480	1,524	0	800	1,945
25,050	25,100	0	952	2,146	0	1,271	2,567	28,050	28,100	0	472	1,514	0	792	1,935
25,100	25,150	0	944	2,135	0	1,263	2,556	28,100	28,150	0	464	1,503	0	784	1,924
25,150	25,200	0	936	2,124	0	1,255	2,546	28,150	28,200	0	456	1,493	0	776	1,914
25,200	25,250	0	928	2,114	0	1,247	2,535	28,200	28,250	0	448	1,482	0	768	1,903
25,250	25,300	0	920	2,103	0	1,239	2,525	28,250	28,300	0	440	1,472	0	760	1,893
25,300	25,350	0	912	2,093	0	1,231	2,514	28,300	28,350	0	432	1,461	0	752	1,882
25,350	25,400	0	904	2,082	0	1,223	2,504	28,350	28,400	0	424	1,451	0	744	1,872
25,400	25,450	0	896	2,072	0	1,215	2,493	28,400	28,450	0	416	1,440	0	736	1,861
25,450	25,500	0	888	2,061	0	1,207	2,482	28,450	28,500	0	408	1,429	0	728	1,851
25,500	25,550	0	880	2,051	0	1,199	2,472	28,500	28,550	0	400	1,419	0	720	1,840
25,550	25,600	0	872	2,040	0	1,191	2,461	28,550	28,600	0	392	1,408	0	712	1,830
25,600	25,650	0	864	2,030	0	1,183	2,451	28,600	28,650	0	384	1,398	0	704	1,819
25,650	25,700	0	856	2,019	0	1,175	2,440	28,650	28,700	0	376	1,387	0	696	1,809
25,700	25,750	0	848	2,009	0	1,167	2,430	28,700	28,750	0	368	1,377	0	688	1,798
25,750	25,800	0	840	1,998	0	1,159	2,419	28,750	28,800	0	360	1,366	0	680	1,788
25,800	25,850	0	832	1,988	0	1,151	2,409	28,800	28,850	0	352	1,356	0	672	1,777
25,850	25,900	0	824	1,977	0	1,143	2,398	28,850	28,900	0	344	1,345	0	664	1,766
25,900	25,950	0	816	1,967	0	1,135	2,388	28,900	28,950	0	336	1,335	0	656	1,756
25,950	26,000	0	808	1,956	0	1,127	2,377	28,950	29,000	0	328	1,324	0	648	1,745
26,000	26,050	0	800	1,945	0	1,119	2,367	29,000	29,050	0	320	1,314	0	640	1,735
26,050	26,100	0	792	1,935	0	1,111	2,356	29,050	29,100	0	312	1,303	0	632	1,724
26,100	26,150	0	784	1,924	0	1,103	2,346	29,100	29,150	0	304	1,293	0	624	1,714
26,150	26,200	0	776	1,914	0	1,095	2,335	29,150	29,200	0	296	1,282	0	616	1,703
26,200	26,250	0	768	1,903	0	1,087	2,325	29,200	29,250	0	288	1,272	0	608	1,693
26,250	26,300	0	760	1,893	0	1,079	2,314	29,250	29,300	0	280	1,261	0	600	1,682
26,300	26,350	0	752	1,882	0	1,071	2,303	29,300	29,350	0	272	1,250	0	592	1,672
26,350	26,400	0	744	1,872	0	1,063	2,293	29,350	29,400	0	264	1,240	0	584	1,661
26,400	26,450	0	736	1,861	0	1,055	2,282	29,400	29,450	0	256	1,229	0	576	1,651
26,450	26,500	0	728	1,851	0	1,047	2,272	29,450	29,500	0	248	1,219	0	568	1,640
26,500	26,550	0	720	1,840	0	1,039	2,261	29,500	29,550	0	240	1,208	0	560	1,630
26,550	26,600	0	712	1,830	0	1,031	2,251	29,550	29,600	0	232	1,198	0	552	1,619
26,600	26,650	0	704	1,819	0	1,023	2,240	29,600	29,650	0	224	1,187	0	544	1,608
26,650	26,700	0	696	1,809	0	1,015	2,230	29,650	29,700	0	216	1,177	0	536	1,598
26,700	26,750	0	688	1,798	0	1,007	2,219	29,700	29,750	0	208	1,166	0	528	1,587
26,750	26,800	0	680	1,788	0	999	2,209	29,750	29,800	0	200	1,156	0	520	1,577
26,800	26,850	0	672	1,777	0	991	2,198	29,800	29,850	0	192	1,145	0	512	1,566
26,850	26,900	0	664	1,766	0	984	2,188	29,850	29,900	0	185	1,135	0	504	1,556
26,900	26,950	0	656	1,756	0	976	2,177	29,900	29,950	0	177	1,124	0	496	1,545
26,950	27,000	0	648	1,745	0	968	2,167	29,950	30,000	0	169	1,114	0	488	1,535
27,000	27,050	0	640	1,735	0	960	2,156	30,000	30,050	0	161	1,103	0	480	1,524
27,050	27,100	0	632	1,724	0	952	2,146	30,050	30,100	0	153	1,093	0	472	1,514

(Continued on page 57)

Need more information or forms? See page 7.

E-5

2005 Earned Income Credit (EIC) Table—Continued (Caution. This is **not** a tax table.)

If the amount you are looking up from the worksheet is—		Single, head of household, or qualifying widow(er) and you have—			Married filing jointly and you have—		
At least	But less than	No children	One child	Two children	No children	One child	Two children
		Your credit is—			Your credit is—		
30,100	30,150	0	145	1,082	0	464	1,503
30,150	30,200	0	137	1,071	0	456	1,493
30,200	30,250	0	129	1,061	0	448	1,482
30,250	30,300	0	121	1,050	0	440	1,472
30,300	30,350	0	113	1,040	0	432	1,461
30,350	30,400	0	105	1,029	0	424	1,451
30,400	30,450	0	97	1,019	0	416	1,440
30,450	30,500	0	89	1,008	0	408	1,429
30,500	30,550	0	81	998	0	400	1,419
30,550	30,600	0	73	987	0	392	1,408
30,600	30,650	0	65	977	0	384	1,398
30,650	30,700	0	57	966	0	376	1,387
30,700	30,750	0	49	956	0	368	1,377
30,750	30,800	0	41	945	0	360	1,366
30,800	30,850	0	33	935	0	352	1,356
30,850	30,900	0	25	924	0	344	1,345
30,900	30,950	0	17	914	0	336	1,335
30,950	31,000	0	9	903	0	328	1,324
31,000	31,050	0	*	892	0	320	1,314
31,050	31,100	0	0	882	0	312	1,303
31,100	31,150	0	0	871	0	304	1,293
31,150	31,200	0	0	861	0	296	1,282
31,200	31,250	0	0	850	0	288	1,272
31,250	31,300	0	0	840	0	280	1,261
31,300	31,350	0	0	829	0	272	1,250
31,350	31,400	0	0	819	0	264	1,240
31,400	31,450	0	0	808	0	256	1,229
31,450	31,500	0	0	798	0	248	1,219
31,500	31,550	0	0	787	0	240	1,208
31,550	31,600	0	0	777	0	232	1,198
31,600	31,650	0	0	766	0	224	1,187
31,650	31,700	0	0	756	0	216	1,177
31,700	31,750	0	0	745	0	208	1,166
31,750	31,800	0	0	735	0	200	1,156
31,800	31,850	0	0	724	0	192	1,145
31,850	31,900	0	0	713	0	185	1,135
31,900	31,950	0	0	703	0	177	1,124
31,950	32,000	0	0	692	0	169	1,114
32,000	32,050	0	0	682	0	161	1,103
32,050	32,100	0	0	671	0	153	1,093
32,100	32,150	0	0	661	0	145	1,082
32,150	32,200	0	0	650	0	137	1,071
32,200	32,250	0	0	640	0	129	1,061
32,250	32,300	0	0	629	0	121	1,050
32,300	32,350	0	0	619	0	113	1,040
32,350	32,400	0	0	608	0	105	1,029
32,400	32,450	0	0	598	0	97	1,019
32,450	32,500	0	0	587	0	89	1,008
32,500	32,550	0	0	577	0	81	998
32,550	32,600	0	0	566	0	73	987
32,600	32,650	0	0	555	0	65	977
32,650	32,700	0	0	545	0	57	966
32,700	32,750	0	0	534	0	49	956
32,750	32,800	0	0	524	0	41	945
32,800	32,850	0	0	513	0	33	935
32,850	32,900	0	0	503	0	25	924
32,900	32,950	0	0	492	0	17	914
32,950	33,000	0	0	482	0	9	903
33,000	33,050	0	0	471	0	*	892
33,050	33,100	0	0	461	0	0	882
33,100	33,150	0	0	450	0	0	871
33,150	33,200	0	0	440	0	0	861
33,200	33,250	0	0	429	0	0	850
33,250	33,300	0	0	419	0	0	840
33,300	33,350	0	0	408	0	0	829
33,350	33,400	0	0	398	0	0	819
33,400	33,450	0	0	387	0	0	808
33,450	33,500	0	0	376	0	0	798
33,500	33,550	0	0	366	0	0	787
33,550	33,600	0	0	355	0	0	777
33,600	33,650	0	0	345	0	0	766
33,650	33,700	0	0	334	0	0	756
33,700	33,750	0	0	324	0	0	745
33,750	33,800	0	0	313	0	0	735
33,800	33,850	0	0	303	0	0	724
33,850	33,900	0	0	292	0	0	713
33,900	33,950	0	0	282	0	0	703
33,950	34,000	0	0	271	0	0	692
34,000	34,050	0	0	261	0	0	682
34,050	34,100	0	0	250	0	0	671
34,100	34,150	0	0	240	0	0	661
34,150	34,200	0	0	229	0	0	650
34,200	34,250	0	0	219	0	0	640
34,250	34,300	0	0	208	0	0	629
34,300	34,350	0	0	197	0	0	619
34,350	34,400	0	0	187	0	0	608
34,400	34,450	0	0	176	0	0	598
34,450	34,500	0	0	166	0	0	587
34,500	34,550	0	0	155	0	0	577
34,550	34,600	0	0	145	0	0	566
34,600	34,650	0	0	134	0	0	555
34,650	34,700	0	0	124	0	0	545
34,700	34,750	0	0	113	0	0	534
34,750	34,800	0	0	103	0	0	524
34,800	34,850	0	0	92	0	0	513
34,850	34,900	0	0	82	0	0	503
34,900	34,950	0	0	71	0	0	492
34,950	35,000	0	0	61	0	0	482
35,000	35,050	0	0	50	0	0	471
35,050	35,100	0	0	40	0	0	461
35,100	35,150	0	0	29	0	0	450
35,150	35,200	0	0	18	0	0	440
35,200	35,250	0	0	8	0	0	429
35,250	35,300	0	0	**	0	0	419
35,300	35,350	0	0	0	0	0	408
35,350	35,400	0	0	0	0	0	398
35,400	35,450	0	0	0	0	0	387
35,450	35,500	0	0	0	0	0	376
35,500	35,550	0	0	0	0	0	366
35,550	35,600	0	0	0	0	0	355
35,600	35,650	0	0	0	0	0	345
35,650	35,700	0	0	0	0	0	334
35,700	35,750	0	0	0	0	0	324
35,750	35,800	0	0	0	0	0	313
35,800	35,850	0	0	0	0	0	303
35,850	35,900	0	0	0	0	0	292
35,900	35,950	0	0	0	0	0	282
35,950	36,000	0	0	0	0	0	271
36,000	36,050	0	0	0	0	0	261
36,050	36,100	0	0	0	0	0	250

*If the amount you are looking up from the worksheet is at least $31,000 ($33,000 if married filing jointly) but less than $31,030 ($33,030 if married filing jointly), your credit is $2. Otherwise, you cannot take the credit.

**If the amount you are looking up from the worksheet is at least $35,250 but less than $35,263, your credit is $1. Otherwise, you cannot take the credit.

(Continued on page 58)

Need more information or forms? See page 7.

E-6

2005 Earned Income Credit (EIC) Table—*Continued* (**Caution.** This is **not** a tax table.)

If the amount you are looking up from the worksheet is—		Single, head of household, or qualifying widow(er) and you have—			Married filing jointly and you have—			If the amount you are looking up from the worksheet is—		Single, head of household, or qualifying widow(er) and you have—			Married filing jointly and you have—		
At least	But less than	No children	One child	Two children	No children	One child	Two children	At least	But less than	No children	One child	Two children	No children	One child	Two children
		Your credit is—			Your credit is—					Your credit is—			Your credit is—		
36,100	36,150	0	0	0	0	0	240	36,850	36,900	0	0	0	0	0	82
36,150	36,200	0	0	0	0	0	229	36,900	36,950	0	0	0	0	0	71
36,200	36,250	0	0	0	0	0	219	36,950	37,000	0	0	0	0	0	61
36,250	36,300	0	0	0	0	0	208	37,000	37,050	0	0	0	0	0	50
36,300	36,350	0	0	0	0	0	197	37,050	37,100	0	0	0	0	0	40
36,350	36,400	0	0	0	0	0	187	37,100	37,150	0	0	0	0	0	29
36,400	36,450	0	0	0	0	0	176	37,150	37,200	0	0	0	0	0	18
36,450	36,500	0	0	0	0	0	166	37,200	37,250	0	0	0	0	0	8
36,500	36,550	0	0	0	0	0	155	37,250	37,263	0	0	0	0	0	1
36,550	36,600	0	0	0	0	0	145	37,263 or more		0	0	0	0	0	0
36,600	36,650	0	0	0	0	0	134								
36,650	36,700	0	0	0	0	0	124								
36,700	36,750	0	0	0	0	0	113								
36,750	36,800	0	0	0	0	0	103								
36,800	36,850	0	0	0	0	0	92								

Need more information or forms? See page 7.

E-7

Appendix A
Accessing and Downloading IRS Tax Forms and Publications

In order to view IRS tax forms and publications, you must have Adobe (Acrobat Reader) installed on your computer. If you do not have Adobe Acrobat Reader on your computer, you can download a copy free from the Adobe web site:

http://www.adobe.com/products/acrobat/main.html

- To access and download forms and publications, you must first go to the IRS website: www.irs.gov
- This will take you to the IRS web page, entitled **"Internal Revenue Service IRS.gov."** On this page you will see a number of different links to various tax sites. Click on the link for <u>Forms and Publications</u> on the left side of the screen. This will lead you to a page titled, **"Forms and Publications."**

    1. If you know the form number, the title, or keywords from the tax form or publication, enter the keywords in the box provided under Search for... and then click on Go. This will bring up a list of the versions of the form or publication that contain your keyword. Click on the link to the Form or Publication you are interested in viewing. Depending on your browser, either the material you selected will be opened in Acrobat Reader or you will receive additional instructions on how to open the material. If you are using either Internet Explorer or Netscape as your browser and are having difficulty opening the material, you can right click on the link and select the option that allows you to save the link to your computer. In Netscape, this option is called, "<u>S</u>ave Link As. . . ." In Internet Explorer, this option is called, "Save Target <u>A</u>s . . ." Once you have saved the .pdf file on your computer, you can then open it up directly from Acrobat Reader.

    2. To browse for a particular form, from the "Forms and Publications" page select the link for <u>Form and Instruction number</u>. As you scroll down the list of forms, click on the desired form to highlight (select) it. More than one form can be selected at a time by holding the **Ctrl** button down when you click on additional forms. To

view the selected forms, click on the gray **Review Selected Files** button. This will bring up a screen with a list of your selections. To select a particular form, click in the link. Depending on your browser, either the selected material will be opened in Acrobat Reader or you will receive additional instructions on how to open the material. See 1. above for instructions on how to save the file by right clicking on the link.

3. To browse for a particular publication, from the "Forms and Publications" page select the link for <u>Publications number</u>. As you scroll down the list of publications, click on the desired publication to highlight (select) it. More than one publication can be selected at a time by holding the **Ctrl** button down when you click on additional publications. To view the selected publications, click on the gray **Retrieve Selected Files** button. This will bring up a screen with a list of your selections. To select a particular publication, click in the link. Depending on your browser, either the selected material will be opened in Acrobat Reader or you will receive additional instructions on how to open the material. See 1. above for instructions on how to save the file by right clicking on the link.

4. **Fill-in Forms:** For each tax form and schedule, information can be typed in using the computer. This is not a computer software package, so the individual must still do the work and calculations. However, please note that not all information can be typed in when using Fill-in Forms. Some items will have to be added by hand on the final printout (for example, occupation, signature, date, etc.). Once the information has been entered on to the form, the form can be saved as a .pdf file and accessed at a later time. Use the instructions in 1. and 2. above to locate the form or schedule that you want to use.

Index

A

Abandoned spouses qualifying as heads of household, 1-21

Accelerated cost recovery system (ACRS), 8-2

Accountable reimbursement plans, 6-2–6-3, 7-14–7-15
requirements for, 6-3

Accounting methods for businesses, 7-2–7-4, 14-24

Accrual method of accounting, 7-3–7-4, 14-24

Accrued interest on bonds, 3-13–3-14

Accumulated adjustments account (AAA) for S corporation income and losses, 14-19–14-20

Accumulated earnings and profits (AEP)
carried over from C to S corporations, 14-13
dividends paid from, 10-11

Accumulated earnings tax (AET), corporations subject to, 14-27

Acquisition indebtedness as an itemized deduction, 5-12

Active income defined, 9-12

Active participants, special $25,000 deduction for, 9-13–9-14

Active participation distinguished from material participation, 9-13

Actual method to compute car and truck expenses
used by employees, 6-5–6-6

used by self-employed individuals, 7-10–7-11

Additional exemption
for individuals providing rent-free housing to Hurricane Katrina displaced persons, 1-11

Additional standard deductions for age and blindness, 1-7–1-8

Additional taxes, statutory limit for assessing, 1-25

Adjusted basis of property
defined, 10-3
formula for calculating, 10-3
increased by capital additions, 10-3
reduced by capital recoveries, 10-3–10-4
reduced by depreciation allowed or allowable, 8-3

Adjusted gross income (AGI)
deductions for, 1-6
deductions from, 1-6

Adjustments to income. *See* Gross income adjustments

Adoption assistance
as a fringe benefit, 4-6
reported on Form W-2, amounts received from, 13-11

Adoption costs, nondeductible, 6-17

Adoption credit, 2-20, 2-22

Advertising expenses of self-employed individuals, 7-10

Alimony
deduction of payment of, 4-24

inclusion in gross income of receipt of, 3-7–3-8
recapture of, 3-8, 4-24
rules for, 3-7–3-8

Alternative depreciation system (ADS), 8-9–8-10, 8-18–8-19, 9-3, 12-5, 14-29
optional recovery periods used to depreciate real property, 8-18–8-19
optional recovery periods used to depreciate tangible personal property, 8-9–8-10

Alternative minimum tax (AMT)
calculating, 12-7–12-10
corporations subject to, 14-27
minimum tax credit for, 12-7
tax rate for calculating, 12-7

Alternative minimum taxable income (AMTI), 12-4–12-10
exemption allowed in calculating, 12-7
itemized deductions allowed in calculating, 12-6–12-7
preferences and adjustments in calculating, 12-4–12-6
recovery of costs as a preference item in calculating, 12-4–12-5

Ambulance costs as a medical deduction, 5-8

Amended tax return, 12-21–12-24

Amortization
of corporate organizational costs, 14-26